Paris

SO-AUZ-593

5th Edition

Christopher McIntosh and Eileen Townsend Jones

Prentice Hall Travel

New York • London • Toronto • Sydney • Tokyo • Singapore

THE AMERICAN EXPRESS ® TRAVEL GUIDES

Published in the United States by
Prentice Hall General Reference
A division of Simon & Schuster, Inc.
15 Columbus Circle
New York, NY 10023

First published 1983 in the United
Kingdom by Mitchell Beazley
International Ltd, Michelin House
81 Fulham Road, London SW3 6RB as
*The American Express Pocket Guide
to Paris,* reprinted 1985. Second
edition 1986. Third edition 1989.
Fourth edition 1991. This edition,
revised and updated, published 1993.

Edited, designed and produced by
Castle House Press, Llantrisant
Mid Glamorgan CF7 8EU, Wales

Library of Congress Catalog Card
Number 92-082892
ISBN 0-671-84751-1

The editors thank Neil Hanson and Alex
Taylor of Lovell Johns, David Haslam,
Sharon Charity, Sally Darlington, Melanie
Gould, Anna Holmes and Andrea
Thomas for their assistance during the
preparation of this edition.

Thanks to Jonathan Cape Ltd (UK) and
Charles Scribner's Sons (USA) for
permission to print the extract from *A
Moveable Feast* by Ernest Hemingway;
to Andre Deutsch Ltd (UK) and Harper
and Row Publishers Inc. (USA) for the
extract from *Quartet* by Jean Rhys; and
to Doubleday (UK) for the extract from
A Vision of Britain © The Prince of
Wales 1989.

FOR THE SERIES:
Series Editor:
 David Townsend Jones
Map Editor: David Haslam
Indexer: Hilary Bird
Gazetteer: Anne Evans
Cover design: Roger Walton Studio

FOR THIS EDITION:
Edited on desktop by:
 Eileen Townsend Jones
Art editors: Castle House Press
Illustrators: Jeremy Ford (David
 Lewis Artists), Illustra Design Ltd.,
 Rodney Paull, Karen Cochrane,
 Sylvia Hughes-Williams, David Evans
Cover photo: Joe Cornish

FOR MITCHELL BEAZLEY:
Art Director: Tim Foster
Managing Editor: Alison Starling
Production: Matthew Batchelor

PRODUCTION CREDITS:
Maps by Lovell Johns, Oxford,
 England
Paris Métro map
 by TCS, Aldershot, England
Typeset in Garamond and
 News Gothic
Desktop layout in Ventura
 Publisher
Linotronic output by
 Tradespools Limited, Frome,
 England

Contents

How to use this book   6
Key to symbols; Information for readers   7
About the authors   8

Introduction: Paris — living past, living future   11

Culture, history and background

Landmarks in the history of Paris   15
Who's who   20
The architecture of Paris   26
The cultural heritage   33
Suggestions for further reading   36

Basic information

Before you go
>**37:** Documents; Insurance. **38:** Money; Customs. **39:** Getting
>there. **40:** Climate; Clothes. **41:** General Delivery; French
>Government Tourist Offices overseas.

Getting around
>**41:** Airports to city. **42:** Public transport; Métro; RER. **43:** Buses;
>Taxis; Driving. **44:** Car rental; Walking. **45:** Railways; Air travel;
>Cycling; River travel. **46:** Paris Héliport.

On-the-spot information
>**46:** Public holidays; Time zones; Banks and currency exchange;
>Shopping hours. **47:** Rush hours; Postal services; Telephones.
>**48:** Public lavatories. **49:** Electricity; Laws and regulations;
>Etiquette; Tipping; Disabled travelers. **50:** Publications;
>English-language bookstores.

Useful numbers and addresses
>**51:** Tourist information; Telephone services; Post offices; Tour
>operators; Guides and interpreters. **52:** River/canal trips; Airlines;
>Places of worship. **53:** Libraries; Embassies and consulates;
>Youth organizations.

Emergency information
>**54:** Emergency services; Hospitals; Medical/dental emergencies;
>Pharmacies; Help lines; Car accidents. **55:** Car breakdowns;
>Lost passports/travelers checks/property; Emergency phrases.

Planning your visit

When to go   56
Events in the Paris calendar   56
Organizing your time — five days in Paris   59

The districts of Paris

Arrondissements and *quartiers*   62
The *quartiers* A to Z   66

Sightseeing

Paris on foot   86
The open spaces of Paris   90
Parks and open spaces A to Z   91
Sights classified by type   100
Sights and places of interest   102
A to Z of Paris sights   103

Where to stay

Making your choice   192
  Reservations; Tipping; Meals   192
  Location; Prices and paying; Vocabulary   193
  Price categories; Hotels listed by *arrondissement* 194
A to Z of Paris hotels   195
Accommodation alternatives   205

Eating and drinking

Dining out in Paris   206
  Choosing a place to eat; Fast food   207
  Using the menu   208
  Choosing and ordering wine   209
  Styles of cuisine   210
  Price categories; Restaurants listed by *arrondissement* 212
A to Z of Paris restaurants   213
Cafés   226

Entertainments *by Virginie Duverger*

Paris after dark   230
Performing arts   232
Nightlife   238

Shopping

A seductive city for shopping   242

Recreation

Paris for children   263
Activities and sports   267

Excursions

Environs of Paris   273
Short trips   273
Cathedrals and châteaux   278
    278: Chartres. **279:** Fontainebleau. **281:** Reims.
    284: Rouen. **287:** Versailles.
EuroDisney   291

Words and phrases

A guide to French   295
Food and drink (with menu guide)   302

Index   309
List of street names   323
International conversion formulae   at back of book
Clothing sizes chart   at back of book

Maps

Orientation map of Paris   64-65
Latin Quarter   72
Le Marais   74
Montmartre   77
Opéra Quarter   81
St-Germain   83
Area: the Seine — Grand Palais to Notre Dame   87
Area: Montparnasse and St-Germain   89
Bois de Boulogne   92
Bois de Vincennes   99
Northern France   274
Versailles   288
Key to main map pages   327
Paris city guide   Maps **1-16**
Paris environs   Maps **17-18**
Paris Métro   at back of book

How to use this book

Few guidelines are needed to understand how this book works:

- For the general organization of the book, see CONTENTS on the pages preceding this one.
- Wherever appropriate, chapters and sections are arranged alphabetically, with headings appearing in **CAPITALS.**
- Often these headings are followed by location and practical information printed in *italics*.
- As you turn the pages, you will find subject headers, similar to those used in telephone directories, printed in CAPITALS in the top corner of each page.
- If you still cannot find what you need, check in the comprehensive and exhaustively cross-referenced INDEX at the back of the book.
- Following the index, a LIST OF STREET NAMES provides map references for all roads and streets mentioned in the book that are located within the areas covered by the main city maps.

CROSS-REFERENCES
These are printed in SMALL CAPITALS, referring you to other sections or alphabetical entries in the book. Care has been taken to ensure that such cross-references are self-explanatory. Often, page references are also given, although their excessive use would be intrusive and ugly.

FLOORS
We use the European convention in this book: "ground floor" means the floor at ground level (called by Americans the "first floor").

AUTHOR'S ACKNOWLEDGMENTS
Eileen Townsend Jones would like to thank: Nicolle Roques and her staff at the Bureau de Tourisme in Paris, for their endeavors to help, particularly with obscure points; Virginie Duverger and Marie Guibert, for their supreme efforts on ENTERTAINMENTS and SHOPPING; Marijke Naber at the Grand Louvre, for helping me through a minefield; Jean-Pierre and Wendy Richard, for moral support; Sharon Charity, Andrea Thomas and Matthew Batchelor, for helping with the logjam; Simon Hoggart, for kind permission to quote from a piece written for *The Guardian;* Barbara Rowe, without whom the book would not have happened; and David and Robin, without whom . . .

Key to symbols

☎ Telephone
Ⓕⓧ Facsimile (fax)
★ Recommended sight
𝒊 Tourist information
⚓ Parking
🏛 Building of architectural interest
▣ Free entrance
▧ Entrance fee payable
📷̶ Photography forbidden
𝑿 Guided tour
▆ Cafeteria
✚ Special interest for children
⌘ Hotel
▲ Simple hotel
🏨 Luxury hotel
✿ Good value (in its class)
▢ Cheap
◫ Inexpensive
◫ Moderately priced
◫ Expensive
◫ Very expensive
▦ Air conditioning

▭ Secure garage
⌂ Quiet hotel
✈ Elevator
♿ Facilities for disabled people
▢ TV in each room
☎ Telephone in each room
🐕̶ Dogs not allowed
⚘ Garden
❦ Good view
≋ Swimming pool
Ⴚ Gym/fitness facilities
⟋ Sauna
Ⴘ Bar
▣ Mini-bar
👥 Conference facilities
⌨ Business center
🍽 Restaurant
🍲 Simple restaurant
△ Luxury restaurant
☰ Good wines
🍴 Open-air dining
♫ Live music

About the authors

Christopher McIntosh, who wrote the original *American Express Pocket Guide to Paris* (1983), is the author of many books and articles ranging from travel to biography. They include *The Swan King,* a biography of Ludwig II of Bavaria, and the original *American Express Washington, DC* (1987; now in its third edition). Contributors to the first edition of *Paris* were **Susan Heller Anderson**, **Robert Barton-Clegg**, **Peter Graham** and **William Green**.

This fifth edition in the series' new, larger format was extensively revised, updated and expanded by **Eileen Townsend Jones**, a freelance writer and senior editor for the *American Express Travel Guides.*

For this edition, **Virginie Duverger** contributed ENTERTAINMENTS, **Marie Guibert** was a major contributor to SHOPPING, and **Jean Gattégno** acted as consultant for EATING AND DRINKING.

A message from the series editor

Months of concentrated work have gone into ensuring that this edition is as accurate and up to date as possible as it goes to press. But time and change are forever the enemies, and in between editions we very much appreciate our readers writing to advise us of any changes that they discover.

Please do so — but please also be aware that we have no control over restaurants, or whatever, that take it into their heads, after we publish, to move, or change their telephone number, or, worse still, close down. Our authors and editors aim to exclude trendy ephemera and to recommend places that give every appearance of being stable and durable. Their judgment is rarely wrong. Changes in telephone numbers are something else. We apologise for the world's telephone authorities, who seem to change their numbers like you and I change shirts.

My serious point is that we are striving to tailor the series to the very distinctive tastes and requirements of our discerning international readership, and your feedback is therefore extremely valuable. I particularly wish to thank the readers who wrote to me during the preparation of this edition. Time prevents us from responding to most such letters, but they are all welcomed and frequently contribute to the process of preparing the next edition.

Please write to me at **Mitchell Beazley**, Michelin House, 81 Fulham Road, London SW3 6RB; or, in the US, c/o American Express Travel Guides, **Prentice Hall Travel**, 15 Columbus Circle, New York, NY 10023.

David Townsend Jones, Series Editor, American Express Travel Guides

Paris

Paris — living past, living future

To go to Paris is not just to experience a beautiful city (some would say the most beautiful of all); it is to feel the pulse of a civilization that has held the admiration of the world for centuries — the civilization of France. The Parisian regards Paris not only as the capital of a great nation, but as the capital of all true culture.

He can be forgiven if he feels he has no need to travel. Why should he go to the Himalayas when he can look at the Île de la Cité reflected in the waters of the Seine? Why should he learn other languages when his own is so perfect?

All Parisians are absolutely conscious of their heritage. They may seem arrogant — but they have much to be arrogant about. Think of the countless songs that have been written about Paris; the books that have been inspired by it; the millions of pilgrims that have beaten a path to the city over the centuries.

"Paris," wrote Henry James, "is the greatest temple ever built to material joys and the lust of the eyes." His words are as apt today as when they were written in the 1870s. Paris is indeed a temple, the doors of which are always open to anyone who is receptive to beauty, civilized values and the delights of the senses. As a result, the visitor is almost inevitably transformed in some way by the experience.

But it is not enough just to walk in and passively wait for the magic to work. You must become a little bit Parisian in the way you look at things and the way you react, understand something of the spirit of Paris and the history and traditions that have shaped it. And you must avoid rigid preconceptions and expectations. Allow for the unexpected and elusive moments of pleasure that Paris so often gives.

The clearness of the air, the glittering sunshine,
and the cool shadows add to the enchantment of the scene.
In bright day, it dazzles the eye like a steel mirror . . . .
Paris is a splendid vision,
a fabric dug out of the earth and hanging over it.
(William Hazlitt, Notes of *A Journey Through France and Italy,*
1826)

People come here from all over the world and for a variety of reasons: to see the Paris of the travel brochures (the Tour Eiffel, Notre-Dame and Montmartre); to explore the great museums; to enjoy the famous quality of Parisian food and wine; or to test Paris' reputation as the city of Eros. If you come for the last reason you may not find exactly what you had expected. Paris is not a particularly wicked city compared with many others in Europe, despite its red-light districts and the scarlet reputation that was established almost a century ago. What it does have is a subtle sensuality that bubbles over into the whole environment, giving zest to the very air of the city. You can see it in the easy flow of intimacy between the lovers strolling by the Seine or idling on the café terraces. It is impossible not to be affected by it, however imperceptibly.

As for the inhabitants of Paris themselves, they can seem somewhat abrupt, even abrasive to the outsider, but this is usually a surface impression. Underneath you will find a good-humored courtesy and friendliness that does them eternal credit.

THE METROPOLIS
Remember that Paris is not just a vast museum for tourists. It is also a busy, thriving metropolis, and one that copes superbly well with the problems that face all modern cities. While other capitals might crumble under the strain, Paris remains one of the smoothest-running urban machines in the world.

What might be called "Greater Paris," that is the whole metropolitan area, covers 479 square kilometers (185 square miles) and has a population of just over 9 million. But with only a few exceptions, including the inevitable EuroDisney, this guide focuses on the city proper.

Cut in two by the Seine, and surrounded by the beltway, or ring road, known as the Périphérique, the city of Paris covers only 106 square kilometers (41 square miles) and has just over 2 million inhabitants. Although these inhabitants are very tightly crammed into a small area, somehow, by a miraculous sleight of hand, Paris gives an impression of spaciousness.

The Métro carries 4 million passengers a day — and does the job with the minimum of fuss, and with subsidized fares at a very low cost. For the entertainment of its citizens and visitors, the city has a superabundance of restaurants, cafés and nightclubs. There are dozens of municipal libraries, concert halls and café-theaters, hundreds of cinemas, theaters and art galleries.

The administration of the city is handled by a city council of 109 members who are elected for a 6-year term and meet in the palatial Hôtel de Ville. The council is headed by a mayor, who also sits for a 6-year term. For more than a century, the city had no mayor, and was controlled by the national government through a Prefect of Paris.

This arrangement proved unsatisfactory because, as a result, the people of Paris had no direct influence over the running of their city. It was partly this state of affairs that allowed what are now thought to have been grave planning errors of judgment. The building of the Tour Montparnasse, and the construction of a highway along part of the riverside footpath, during President Pompidou's era, are now regarded as two such mistakes.

In 1977, Paris was once again given a mayor in the person of the energetic Jacques Chirac, also twice prime minister, who has done much, since that time, to improve the city's quality of life and environment.

STARTING TO CHANGE
Those who knew Paris more than 30 years ago, in the days before President De Gaulle came to power, remember a city that seemed to be a symphony in shades of gray — the prevailing atmosphere one of picture-postcard scruffiness and exquisitely faded charm. The water was hazardous, plumbing was often antediluvian, and the franc was a precarious currency.

Today all this has changed. Paris, along with the whole of France, has become much more buoyant. The *Mairie,* or town hall, has taken the townscape firmly in hand. Buildings are being cleaned and restored; monuments have been re-gilded. Planning controls have prevented unwarranted demolitions and inappropriate developments. The avenue des Champs-Élysées has been pulled up by its bootstraps to restore its position as a first-class shopping and touristic thoroughfare. Street-cleaning operations have been impressively, and quite visibly, streamlined — smart, green-uniformed workers push smart, green brooms, and look cheerful the while.

In a city crowded with buildings, improvements to the open spaces have also benefitted the environment. A number of small parks and squares exist, many dating from the 19th century. As well as ancient trees and pretty, often witty statues, some old, some new, all now offer play facilities for children, benches or seats upon which to pass the time, and well-tended flower beds. And more are to be created. Parisians are apartment-dwellers and courtyard-tenders — their need for green space within their external environment has been recognized.

But throughout the 1980s, this prospering, confident Paris was also seized by an urge to build on a vast and grandiose scale. The government of François Mitterrand, determined to put France and the French capital at the cutting edge of urban renewal, financed numerous costly, ambitious, architecturally challenging projects: the Opéra Bastille, the Cité des Sciences at La Villette, the Grande Arche at La Défense surrounded by a huge, gleaming "Manhattan-sur-Seine" complex of skyscrapers. Most breathtaking in its scope and daring was the transformation of the Musée du Louvre, symbolized by I.M. Pei's glass pyramid thrusting through the Cour Napoléon.

And the work continues, and projects planned five years earlier are about to come to fruition: the transformed Jardins du Carrousel and Palais de la Mode, the TGB-Bibliothèque de France and the International Conference Center. Private money, following the lead set by the government and its *grands travaux,* or major works, has provided a number of other major schemes, including the Grand Écran Gaumont, now the largest cinema screen in Paris, and the American Center at Bercy.

THE SOBER '90s

The city's population has decreased annually for the last ten years by about 20,000, with more people seeking life in the suburbs as a way of cutting costs. This has been partially stemmed by attractive housing subsidies. There have also been attempts to create jobs by inviting light industry back into the city. Not surprisingly, the 1980s phenomenon of abject poverty has begun to show itself in Paris as elsewhere. The cardboard-box-dwellers are present in many central areas and there are beggars, many tragically young, to be encountered, particularly in the métro stations.

Around the turn of the decade, the sense that the French people and their government were heading broadly in the same direction was visibly fading. Among other manifestations of growing divisions in French society, loudly voiced doubts were aired that questioned the ultimate point and benefit of such enormously costly projects as the Grand Louvre.

A telling exchange was recently overheard between a French couple from the provinces and a site manager overseeing the external renovation of the Richelieu wing of the Louvre, where a sizeable army of stone masons were patiently, lovingly restoring weatherworn sculptures and elaborate carved pediments to their original glory. "For the cost of all this," said the couple, gesturing incredulously at the vast open space of the Cour Carrée, "we could have had a new autoroute, or thousands of jobs for the unemployed."

Will it soon come down to this hard choice, this questioning of the most cherished aspirations to French greatness? Will an increasingly divided French electorate continue to assent to ambitious public works?

For a decade and more, most American and, in particular, British visitors to Paris can only have wondered at the vision and energy of France's political leaders in investing heavily in the country's future prosperity. The politicians' message seemed to be that France and its capital were in the first rank and were determined to stay there: an unexceptional message, to be sure, but one that unavoidably means investing public — in other words, taxpayers' — money on a lavish scale, with an eye to the medium, not the short, term.

If this vision of France as a great economic and cultural power is to survive into the 21st century, its fast-changing yet timeless capital must continue its drive to reinvent itself. Paris vibrantly embodies and epitomizes that vision. Witness the city in the midst of its current adventure while you can, lest forces prevail that stem the flow.

Paris is a veritable ocean. Throw in the plumb line
and you will never know the depth of it . . . .
(Honoré de Balzac, *Le Père Goriot* 1834)

Culture, history and background

Landmarks in the history of Paris

THE GALLIC ORIGINS
3rdC BC: The Parisii, a Gallic tribe, made the Île de la Cité their fortified capital. They prospered from the river trade and from fishing, hunting and gathering.

THE ROMAN ERA
52BC-c.AD486: In **52BC** Julius Caesar's Roman legions conquered the island, which they called Lutetia, and in due course it became an important Roman center, with the governor's palace erected on the island, and the forum and arena on the Left Bank.

As early as the **2nd or 3rd decade AD**, a society of mercantile watermen had established itself in Paris, and these boatmen were to play an important role in the history of the city. The symbol of Paris is a ship, and her motto is *fluctuat nec murgitur* (she is tossed but does not sink).

In **AD250** St-Denis came to Paris, introducing Christianity and becoming the city's first bishop. But Rome was still officially pagan, and St-Denis was decapitated by an angry mob.

Several Roman emperors stayed at Lutetia, notably Constantius Chlorus, who made it his headquarters in AD292. His son, Constantine the Great (**c.274-337**), who made Christianity the official religion of the empire, also stayed there for a time, as did Julian the Apostate, who became Emperor of Rome in **360**. In that year Lutetia was named Paris.

EARLY MIDDLE AGES
5thC AD: In the vacuum left by the departure of the Romans, Paris stood in danger of being engulfed by barbarians, but the morale of the city was restored by a religious young woman from Nanterre, named Geneviève, who, in **451**, correctly assured the Parisians that Attila the Hun and his hordes would not attack the city. Ten years later, when the city was besieged by the Franks, she helped relieve the famine. She later became patron saint of Paris.

THE MEROVINGIANS
508-752: In **508** the Christianized King Clovis of the Frankish Merovingian line made Paris his capital, and it remained in Merovingian hands until **752**, when the last of the dynasty, Childeric, was finally ousted by Pepin the Short, father of Charlemagne.

THE CAROLINGIANS
752-987: This was an uneasy period for Paris, with frequent raids by Norman pirates. These culminated in a great siege in **885-86** which ended in defeat of the Normans by Count Eudes, who was elected King of France in **887**.

THE CAPETIANS
987-996: Hugues Capet elected King of France at Senlis; his territories were not extensive, however. His descendants reigned from father to son until 1328, establishing the principle of monarchy in France. Paris re-established as capital.

    996-1108: The reigns of Robert the Pious, Henri I and Philippe I. The building of Notre-Dame cathedral was begun in Philippe's reign. **1108-37**: Reign of Louis VI the Fat.

    1137-80: Louis VII the Young, husband of Eleanor of Aquitaine. Having been divorced by Louis, in **1152** Eleanor married Henri Plantagenet, subsequently Henry II of England, who ruled both NW France and Aquitaine, far more land than the French king. **1163**: laying of foundation stone at Notre-Dame.

    1180-1223. Philippe Auguste erected the fortress of the Louvre and constructed a great defensive wall around the city: the Philippe-Auguste girdle. His reign also laid the foundation of the University of Paris.

    1223-85: The reigns of Louis VIII, Louis IX, who was canonized, and Philippe III. The Sorbonne was established in the reign of Louis IX. Pierre de Montreuil built La Sainte-Chapelle to house relics of the true cross, which Louis IX had bought for a vast sum, and he worked on the St-Denis basilica, prototype of the Gothic style.

    1285-1314: Philippe IV the Fair. Fair only in looks, Philippe was a cruel and vicious king who crushed the Templars, persecuted the Jews and caused misery and poverty among the Parisians, through high taxation, forced labor and debasement of the currency. It was he who built the Conciergerie. **1302**: French parliament moved to Paris.

    1314-28: The reigns of Louis X the Quarrelsome, Jean I (a few months only), Philippe V the Tall, and Charles IV the Fair, the last of the Capetians.

THE VALOIS
1328-50: Philippe VI, first of the Valois kings, whose reign marked the start of a chaotic period for France; the country was weakened by the Hundred Years' War with England, which broke out in **1337**.

    1350-64: Reign of Jean II. In **1358**, death of Étienne Marcel, provost of the merchants and mayor of the city, who led a popular uprising.

    1364-80: Charles V the Wise, who restored order to France, built the Bastille and erected a wall on the Right Bank beyond the Philippe-Auguste wall.

    1380-1422: Charles VI the Well-Beloved. A weak king, under whose reign the English invaders, and with them chaos, returned. In **1420** Paris was captured by Henry V of England.

    1422-61: Charles VII the Victorious. In **1429** Joan of Arc relieved Orléans, but tried in vain to recapture Paris, which remained in English hands until **1436**, when Charles VII recaptured it. In **1431** Henry VI of England had himself crowned in Paris at Notre-Dame. In **1453** (at the end of the Hundred Years' War) the English withdrew from all of France except Calais.

1461-83: Louis XI. A cunning, authoritarian, but enlightened king. Under his reign Paris prospered. The city's first school of medicine was opened and its first printing press was set up, at the Sorbonne.

1483-1515: The reigns of Charles VIII and Louis XII, each of whom married Anne of Brittany; her lands were ceded to France after her death in **1514**.

1515-47: François I, great patron of the arts, who was with Leonardo da Vinci when he died near Amboise. François helped to introduce the Italian Renaissance to France and acquired the first masterpieces for the Louvre. He began the reconstruction of the Louvre, and under his rule many magnificent buildings grew up in Paris.

1547-59: Henry II was killed in a jousting accident. His wife, Catherine de Medici, began the Tuileries palace.

1559-89: The reigns of Henry II and Catherine de Medici's three sons, François II, Charles IX and Henry III. During this period Paris was the scene of many bloody conflicts between the Catholics and the Protestants, culminating in the St-Bartholomew's Day massacre in **1572**, when 3,000 Huguenots were murdered in Paris. Henry III was then forced to flee Paris when the Catholic league turned against him in **1588**. He was murdered at St-Cloud while laying siege to Paris in **1589**. During his reign the construction of the Pont-Neuf was begun.

THE BOURBONS

1589-1610: Henry IV *(Le Vert Galant)* allayed for a time the religious uprisings by converting from Protestantism to Catholicism, and issuing the Edict of Nantes, allowing Protestants some freedom of worship. In Paris, he extended the Louvre and the Tuileries, created the place des Vosges and completed the Pont-Neuf. He was assassinated by a fanatic named Ravaillac.

1610-43: Louis XIII. The 17thC was known as "Le Grand Siècle." Paris was now growing more magnificent as each year passed. The Île St-Louis was developed, Marie de Medicis built the palais du Luxembourg, and Cardinal Richelieu, first minister and far more powerful than the young king, built the Palais-Royal and founded the Académie Française. The arts flourished, but brutality was also much in evidence, and gruesome public executions were frequent. In **1622** Paris became a bishopric.

1643-1715: Louis XIV the "Sun King," under whom France reached its zenith of power and prestige. Versailles was built and became the royal court, and the capital acquired many splendid new buildings and institutions: Les Invalides, the Salpêtrière, Gobelins, the Louvre colonnade and the Comédie Française.

In **1648**, when Louis XIV was still too young to rule, Paris had been convulsed by the Fronde uprising, a bloody protest against the centralized power of the monarchy. When Louis XIV took the reins of power in **1661**, he tightened the grip, abolishing the municipal institutions and

ce of mayor, so that Paris was ruled by the state. This was to remain
ase until the Revolution. In **1685** the king ordered the Revocation
the Edict of Nantes, causing thousands of Protestants to flee.

1715-74: Louis XV's reign saw financial crisis, disastrous wars with
England over Québec and West Indian colonies and the growing un-
popularity of the crown. But Paris was further enriched architecturally by
the Panthéon, the Palais-Bourbon and the place de la Concorde. Another
encircling wall, known as the Farmers General Wall, was erected as a
customs barrier, and further added to popular discontent.

1774-92: Louis XVI. The government was now financially, politically
and morally bankrupt. Discontent among all classes was rife. Louis XVI,
an ineffectual king, was unable to stem the tide of revolution.

THE REVOLUTION

1789-99: One of the great turning points in the history of France, and
of the world. The Revolution began symbolically with the storming of
the Bastille on **July 14, 1789**. In October of that year, a mob invaded
Versailles and the king returned to Paris. At first he remained on the
throne while various reforms were carried out, but by **1792** he was
deposed and imprisoned, and the following year he and his queen,
Marie-Antoinette, were executed. Extremists, including Danton, Marat
and de Robespierre, instituted the Reign of Terror, in which 2,800
people in Paris alone were executed, and another 14,000 in the rest of
the country.

The Reign of Terror finally ended with the fall and execution of de
Robespierre in **1794**. The Revolution itself could be said to have ended
when, in **1799**, Napoleon appointed himself First Consul — in effect,
dictator of France.

THE CONSULATE AND FIRST EMPIRE

1799-1815: After a period of stagnation, Paris began, under Napoleon,
to enjoy a new period of expansion and prosperity. The Farmers
General Wall was done away with, the office of Prefect of the Seine
was created, and many of the exiled nobles returned. The foundations
of large-scale industry were laid, and the arts flourished once more. On
the negative side, the city was terrorized by Napoleon's police under
the ruthless first Prefect of Police, Joseph Fouché.

In **1804** Napoleon had himself crowned Emperor in Notre-Dame.
Under Napoleon, France was master of Europe until **1814**, when Paris
fell to the invading allied armies. Napoleon abdicated at Fontainebleau
and was exiled to the island of Elba. In **1815** he escaped from Elba and
returned to France for his final campaign, which ended, in **June 1815**,
at Waterloo. He was sent again into exile, this time to St Helena, where
he died in **1821**.

THE RESTORATION

1815-48: After Napoleon's defeat, the Bourbon monarchy was restored
and Louis XVIII crowned king. He was succeeded in **1824** by Charles
X, who was himself ousted during the short-lived July Revolution in

Paris in favor of Louis-Philippe of the Orléans line.

These were years of modernization for Paris. Between **1812-15** the Ourcq, St-Denis and St-Martin canals were built, and **1837** saw the opening of the first French railway line, from Paris to St-Germain-en-Laye. Pleasure steamers plied the Seine; gas lighting was installed; and a new wall, the Thiers fortifications, was erected around the city in **1841-45.** Although this has vanished, its line is marked by the present boulevard Périphérique. In **1832**, 19,000 Parisians perished in a cholera epidemic.

THE SECOND REPUBLIC AND SECOND EMPIRE

1848-70: Louis-Philippe was ousted in the "Year of Revolutions" which swept through Europe in **1848**; a Second Republic was declared, only to give way to a Second Empire under Napoleon III (Emperor **1852-70**). This was a key period in the development of Paris. Baron Haussmann, Prefect of the Seine, drove his great boulevards through the city, which was divided into the present 20 *arrondissements.* Haussmann's idea behind the building of the boulevards was partly to create streets too wide for barricading in the event of further street fighting and revolution.

Among other new buildings, the Opéra and Les Halles sprang up, as well as the main stations, the sewers *(égouts)* and the Bois de Boulogne and Vincennes. In **1855** and **1867** spectacular international exhibitions were held in the capital. This lively period was ended by the Franco-Prussian War.

THE THIRD REPUBLIC

1870-1945: The Third Republic was declared in **1870**. Napoleon III surrendered at Sedan. Paris was besieged by the Prussians and fell to them in early **1871**. St-Cloud château was burned down, and Napoleon III fled to England. Paris was taken over by the revolutionary government, the Commune, between **March and May 1871**. Although this was finally suppressed, the city suffered terrible damage.

After Paris had recovered, a new period of expansion and prosperity set in, symbolized by the World Exhibition of **1889** and the building of the Eiffel Tower. The year **1900** saw the opening of the first Métro line in Paris, and the city then played host to another World Exhibition.

During World War I, Paris sustained little physical damage, and comparatively little during World War II, with only a few brief bombing raids. The fall of France brought German occupation to Paris, which lasted from **1940** until the city was liberated in **1944**. General De Gaulle led the new provisional government, which held power for just over a year.

SINCE WORLD WAR II

1946: The inauguration of the Fourth Republic. A new constitution. Government by coalition of Socialists, Communists, Radicals and Catholic Democrats.

1958: French army takes power in Algeria. Fourth Republic falls and De Gaulle forms the Fifth Republic. **1959**: EEC (European Economic

Community, or Common Market) founded, with France included among the six members.

1962: Algeria granted independence.

1968: Student riots and demonstrations in the streets of Paris, reaching a peak in May.

1969: Electoral defeat of De Gaulle. Election of Georges Pompidou as President. Les Halles market transferred to Rungis, in the suburbs.

1970: De Gaulle's death. **1973**: Tour Montparnasse and the boulevard Périphérique are completed. **1974**: Pompidou's death. Election of Valéry Giscard d'Estaing as President.

1977: Election of Jacques Chirac as the first mayor of Paris since 1871. Opening of the Centre Georges Pompidou. **1981**: Electoral defeat of Giscard d'Estaing. A socialist government elected, under the leadership of François Mitterrand.

1986: Appointment of a conservative prime minister, Jacques Chirac, under the continued presidency of Mitterrand. Opening of the Musée d'Orsay and the Cité des Sciences at La Villette. **1988**: Re-election of Mitterrand and appointment of a socialist prime minister, Michel Rocard. Renovations to the Les Halles district completed.

1989: Bicentenary of the French Revolution. Opening of the Louvre pyramid. **1990** Opening of the new Opéra Bastille and the Grande Arche at La Défense. **1991-92**: Arrival — and departure — of Edith Cresson, first woman Prime Minister, and a socialist. Her replacement is Pierre Bérégovoy.

1992: Paris, and the rest of France, votes "yes" (but by an overall majority of only 1 percent) to ratify the controversial Maastricht Treaty, considered to be the cornerstone of future European integration.

1993: Projected opening of the Richelieu phase of Le Grand Louvre and the Palais de la Mode below the Jardins du Carrousel.

Who's who

The following selection pays particular attention to those artists and architects, writers, performers and politicians whose names are likely to be encountered by the visitor to Paris.

Baltard, Victor *(1805-74)*   Architect of Les Halles and the church of St-Augustin. Pioneer of iron construction methods.

de Balzac, Honoré *(1799-1850)*   Author of the great series of novels and stories called *La Comédie Humaine.* Many of these portray intimately the life of Paris, its inhabitants and their social mores.

Barrault, Jean-Louis *(born 1910)*   Author, outstanding mime artist and theater director, who reached international fame with his performance in Marcel Carne's celebrated film *Les Enfants du Paradis* (1944).

Bartholdi, Frédéric Auguste *(1834-1904)*   Sculptor of the Statue of Liberty.

Brancusi, Constantin *(1876-1957)*   Romanian sculptor, active mainly in Paris. Also worked in co-operation with Modigliani.

Braque, Georges *(1882-1963)* Painter, linked initially with the Fauves but best known as the co-founder, with Picasso, of Cubism.

Bruant, Libéral *(1635-97)* Architect of Salpêtrière chapel (1670) and the Hôtel des Invalides (1670-77).

Chagall, Marc *(1887-1985)* Russian painter and stained glass designer; member of the Paris School. Although he was mainly active in France, Chagall's lyrical paintings remained firmly rooted to his Jewish and Russian background.

Chevalier, Maurice *(1888-1972)* Actor, dancer and singer, who often appeared in English-speaking movies as the embodiment of urbane Parisian charm.

Clemenceau, Georges *(1841-1929)* Politician and journalist. Known as "the tiger" because of his tough belligerence. Clemenceau was Premier in 1906-09 and 1917-20.

Cocteau, Jean *(1889-1963)* A flamboyant genius who achieved fame as an artist, novelist *(Les Enfants Terribles)*, screenwriter and film director *(La Belle et la Bête)*, and playwright *(Orphée)*.

Colbert, Jean-Baptiste *(1619-83)* Most effective of Louis XIV's ministers. His wise financial policies greatly enriched the state.

Colette *(1873-1954)* Author of vividly sensual and perceptive novels, such as *Chéri* and *La Chatte*.

Corot, Jean-Baptiste-Camille *(1796-1875)* Landscape painter, whose lyrical, Italianate pictures won him great praise at the Salon. His earlier, naturalistic style influenced later artists.

Courbet, Gustave *(1819-77)* Painter and founder of the Realist movement. Courbet painted landscapes, portraits and scenes of modern life, but much of his work had a political content. He was imprisoned for his part in the destruction of the Vendôme Column.

De Gaulle, Charles *(1890-1970)* Soldier and statesman. After leading the Free French during World War II, he headed a provisional government from 1944-46. In 1958 he came out of retirement to lead France again, and drew up a new constitution. He resigned in 1969.

Degas, Edgar *(1834-1917)* Impressionist painter, draftsman and sculptor. Best known for his depictions of horse-racing and ballet scenes.

Delacroix, Eugène *(1798-1863)* Leading Romantic painter, noted for his dashing use of color. Painted many Arab scenes following North African travels.

Delorme, Philibert *(1515-70)* Architect to Henri II and Diane de Poitiers. Little work now remains, but the tomb of François I at St-Denis survives and part of the lovely rood screen at St-Étienne du Mont is attributed to him.

Derain, André *(1880-1954)* Leading Fauvist painter; also influenced by Cézanne and primitive African art. Like Braque, he produced designs for the Ballet Russe.

Dreyfus, Alfred *(1859-1935)* Jewish army officer imprisoned in 1894 on a false charge of treason. The subsequent attempts by Zola and others to exonerate him split France into bitterly opposed factions and exposed an ugly streak of anti-Semitism.

Dufy, Raoul *(1877-1953)* Painter, graphic artist, textile designer. Lively colorist, heavily under the influence of Matisse. Best known for his seascapes and beach scenes.

Eiffel, Gustave *(1832-1923)* Engineer, initially known for work on bridges and viaducts. Tour Eiffel constructed for World Exhibition of 1889. Collaborated on Bon Marché department store.

Epstein, Sir Jacob *(1880-1959)* American-born sculptor, active mainly in England. Studied in Paris 1902-5 and mixed with the School of Paris circle. His tomb of Oscar Wilde can be seen at Père Lachaise cemetery.

Fantin-Latour, Henri *(1836-1904)* Painter and lithographer, best known for elaborate flower pictures.

Foujita, Tsuguharu (or Léonard) *(1886-1968)* Japanese painter and draftsman; settled in Paris in 1913.

Gambetta, Léon Michel *(1838-82)* French leader during Franco-Prussian War of 1870-71. Famous for his daring escape from Paris by balloon when the city was under siege.

Garnier, Charles *(1825-98)* Second Empire architect, principally known for the majestic Opéra, built between 1862 and 1875.

Gauguin, Paul *(1848-1903)* Painter and graphic artist, a leading figure in the Post-Impressionist and Symbolist movements. His early Impressionist work was overtaken by his taste for primitivism, which stemmed from his lengthy stays in Tahiti.

Geneviève, Sainte *(c.422-512)* Patron saint of Paris. She calmed the Parisians by correctly predicting that Attila the Hun would not attack the city in AD451. Ten years later, she smuggled in food when Paris was besieged by the Franks.

Géricault, Théodore *(1791-1824)* Romantic painter, best known for horse-racing pictures, portraits of mental patients, and treatment of macabre subjects.

Giscard d'Estaing, Valéry *(born 1926)* Finance minister under De Gaulle. Leader of Independent Republican Party from 1967. President of France 1974-81.

Goujon, Jean *(1510-68)* Architect and sculptor, active in Rouen and Paris. His remaining works include sculptural decoration at the Louvre and reliefs at Hôtel Carnavalet.

Guimard, Hector *(1867-1942)* Architect and designer; a leading exponent of Art Nouveau. Remembered for his Métro station entrances.

Hardouin-Mansart, Jules *(1646-1708)* Great-nephew of François Mansart. Appointed chief architect to Louis XIV in 1675. Carried out extensions at Versailles (The Grand Trianon), the Dôme church at Les Invalides (1680-91), and Place Vendôme (1685).

Haussmann, Georges Eugène *(1809-91)* As Prefect of the Seine under Napoleon III, Haussmann reshaped large areas of Paris, creating an infrastructure of boulevards, squares, parks and bridges. His grand, triumphal style is still an integral part of the city's personality.

Hugo, Victor *(1802-85)* A towering figure in French literature and the leader of the Romantic movement in France. Author of *Notre-Dame de Paris* (The Hunchback of Notre-Dame) and *Les Misérables,* he was also a member of parliament. As writer and politician he was a fierce champion of liberty and justice.

Ingres, Jean-Auguste-Dominique *(1780-1867)* Painter and draftsman, working in a graceful Neoclassical style. Talented portraitist; also painted historical scenes and exotic harem pictures. Delacroix's chief rival in the Salon.

Lafayette, Marquis de *(1757-1834)* A dashing and glamorous figure who fought against Britain in the American War of Independence, commanded the Paris National Guard after the fall of the Bastille, and was the main author of the Declaration of Rights.

Le Brun, Charles *(1619-90)* Painter, draftsman and decorative artist. First director of Gobelins Tapestry factory in 1663.

Le Lorrain, Robert *(1666-1743)* Sculptor, famous for his *Horses of Apollo* high relief at the Hôtel de Rohan stables.

Le Nôtre, André *(1613-1700)* Creator of French landscape gardening; royal gardener, 1637. Created gardens at Versailles, St-Cloud, Tuileries and Fontainebleau.

Le Vau, Louis *(1612-70)* Major Baroque architect. Converted Versailles from a hunting lodge into a royal palace; carried out notable work at the Louvre.

Malraux, André *(1901-76)* Novelist, art historian, revolutionary fighter, resistance hero and De Gaulle's Minister of Culture from 1958-69.

Manet, Edouard *(1832-83)* Painter who came to prominence with his scandalous *Le déjeuner sur l'herbe*. Later in life came under the influence of the Impressionists, for whom he was a father figure.

Mansart, François *(1598-1668)* Architect who created the Classical style in French architecture, (e.g., the Hôtel Carnavalet), and gave his name to the steeply pitched Mansard roof.

Matisse, Henri *(1869-1954)* Painter, sculptor, draftsman and designer. Leader of the Fauvist group. Noted for works that used luminous areas of primary color.

Mazarin, Jules *(1602-61)* Cardinal and statesman. Chief Minister of France during the regency of Anne of Austria, mother of Louis VII.

Mitterrand, François *(born 1916)* Leader of the Socialist Party and President of the Republic since 1981.

Monet, Claude Oscar *(1840-1926)* Foremost Impressionist painter. His *Impression: soleil levant* gave the movement its name. He adhered to his liking of open-air painting, often producing several pictures of the same subject under different light conditions. In later life, he concentrated on the portrayal of his garden at Giverny.

Montreuil, Pierre de *(died 1267)* Master mason. Work at the cathedrals of Notre-Dame and St-Denis is ascribed to him.

Moreau, Gustave *(1826-98)* Leading Symbolist painter, with a taste for depicting mysterious and exotic mythologies. Private means freed him from the need to sell his paintings. The bulk of his work is preserved at the Musée Gustave Moreau.

Nanteuil, Robert *(1623-78)* Engraver of portraits. Appointed royal draftsman in 1658. Executed fine pastel portraits of Louis XIV and his circle.

Piaf, Edith *(1915-63)*   Singer, actress and cabaret performer, whose small size and lively personality won her the nickname *"La Môme"* (the sparrow), and whose inspired rendition of such songs as *La vie en rose, Milord* and *Je ne regrette rien* seemed to epitomize the real spirit of postwar Paris.

Picasso, Pablo *(1881-1973)*   Spanish painter, draftsman, designer and innovator; the most influential artist of the 20thC and, with Braque, a founder of the Cubist movement. Leading figure in the School of Paris. His "Blue Period" 1901-4; his "Rose Period" 1904-6. Close links with the Surrealists. Lived in Occupied Paris; later moved to the South of France.

Pigalle, Jean-Baptiste *(1714-85)*   Versatile sculptor whose work ranged from portraits to tomb sculpture. His nude study of Voltaire is especially notable.

Pilon, Germain *(1527-90)*   Sculptor of tomb effigies, medals and portrait busts. Influenced by the School of Fontainebleau. Remarkable tomb sculpture at St-Denis.

de Pompadour, Marquise *(1721-64)*   Mistress of Louis XV and a ruthless political intriguer. For 20 years she unofficially controlled the French government. A lavish patron of the arts, she also helped to lead France into financial, political and military disaster.

Pompidou, Georges *(1911-74)*   De Gaulle's successor as president, he remained in office until his death. Many of the less well-considered new building developments in Paris resulted from his campaign to "modernize" the city.

Poussin, Nicolas *(1593/4-1665)*   Influential painter, draftsman and decorative artist in the French classical tradition. Painted mythologies, landscapes and religious pictures.

Pradier, Jean Jacques *(1790-1852)*   Swiss Neoclassical sculptor, active in France. Carved symbolic Victory figures for tomb of Napoleon at Les Invalides.

Proust, Marcel *(1871-1922)*   One of the most influential novelists of all time. His fame rests on a seven-part work, *À la Recherche du Temps Perdu* (Remembrance of Things Past), a minutely detailed and searching autobiographical work. Proust was born in Paris and lived there for most of his life.

Puvis de Chavannes, Pierre *(1824-1919)*   Symbolist painter. Murals in the Sorbonne, the Panthéon, and at the Hôtel de Ville.

de Richelieu, Armand-Jean du Plessis *(1585-1642)*   Cardinal and effective ruler of France under Louis XIII, he greatly increased the power of France and of the crown. He was an energetic patron of literature and founded the Académie Française.

de Robespierre, Maximilien *(1758-94)*   Revolutionary leader and architect of the Reign of Terror, executed, in his turn, on the guillotine.

Rodin, Auguste *(1840-1917)*   Greatest sculptor of his period, whose works are now housed in the Hôtel Biron.

Rousseau, Henri Julien "Le Douanier" *(1844-1910)*   Celebrated naive painter. Nickname derived from his job with the Paris customs office. Best known for exotic jungle scenes, which were actually inspired by local botanical gardens. Admired by the Surrealists.

Rude, François *(1784-1855)* Romantic sculptor and fervent supporter of Napoleon. Stirring heroic reliefs on the Arc de Triomphe.

Sartre, Jean-Paul *(1886-1980)* Novelist, playwright, existentialist philosopher, left-wing polemicist and doyen of the Left Bank intelligentsia, with his lifetime companion Simone de Beauvoir. He expounded his ideas in philosophical works such as *L'Être et le Néant* (Being and Nothingness) and in novels such as *Les Chemins de la Liberté* (Roads to Freedom).

Seurat, Georges *(1859-91)* Founder of the Neo-Impressionist movement; developed the style known as pointillism.

Soufflot, Jacques-Germain *(1713-80)* Neoclassical architect, famed for his domed Panthéon, the striking result of his Italian studies.

Toulouse-Lautrec, Henri de *(1864-1901)* Painter and graphic artist from Albi, in the south. He settled in Montmartre, where his lifestyle gave him the source material for his famed scenes of music-halls, cafés and Parisian low-life.

Utrillo, Maurice *(1883-1955)* A self-taught painter who became known for his atmospheric Montmartre street scenes.

Van Gogh, Vincent *(1853-90)* Dutch-born painter and draftsman, working mainly in France. Links with Gauguin. His emotionally-charged pictures, with vibrant and expressive coloring, were widely influential. His career was cut short by mental breakdown and eventual suicide.

Viollet-le-Duc, Eugène-Emmanuel *(1814-79)* Architect and indefatigable instigator of the 19thC Gothic revival. Responsible for the restoration of many medieval buildings, including Sainte-Chapelle and St-Denis basilica.

Watteau, Jean-Antoine *(1684-1721)* The most important French painter of his period, Watteau specialized in lyrical scenes of costumed figures in pastoral settings.

Zola, Émile *(1840-1902)* Prolific novelist, member of the Naturalist School. His great series of 20 volumes, *Les Rougon-Macquart,* are all connected by the appearance of members of the same family.

No one wept; this was a family funeral when the old head of the family has died — a time for dignity rather than tears. But then the people of Paris love this kind of occasion. Most of all they love to demonstrate how unmoved they are by great events.
"You see that old Charlot's died," said a barman near the Bibliothèque Nationale . . . . A student . . . explained: "The French needed De Gaulle for their national pride, but they never loved him. People admired him because he was so arrogant on their behalf . . . " I found one man prepared to admit outright that he was a Gaullist, a taxi driver. Was he sorry the General had died? With the Gallic shrug which is still the most common gesture here, he took his hands off the wheel and as the cab swerved smoothly toward an overtaking bus, he said "Non."
As we missed the bus by about a foot he added gently,
"Perhaps my wife will be sorry."
(Simon Hoggart, *The Guardian,* November 11, 1972)

The architecture of Paris

Perhaps the most striking element of Paris as a whole is its visual harmony. Although there are samples of many different periods and styles, each blends with the other in such a way as to create an environment that is both diverse and unified. Only in the past thirty years have any really disruptive elements been introduced, and even these have not destroyed the overall sense of unity. Just about every great architectural style is represented in Paris, from Roman to the most contemporary flights of fancy.

Roman *(1st to 4thC AD)*
The only examples of the Roman era still visible are the Thermal Baths in the **Thermes de Cluny** (pictured left) and the restored **Arènes de Lutèce**. Both provide evidence of the heavy, grandiose and colossal elements typical of Roman concrete and brick architecture, with massive walls, barrel vaults and big rounded arches. France has comparatively few Gallo-Roman remains, although some traces are evident in the foundations of the **St-Denis basilica** in Paris.

Romanesque *(11th and 12thC)*
Skillful use was made of vaulting and pillars to create a striking sense of space. The style is characterized by rounded arches and monumental simplicity, the columns smooth except perhaps for a flourish of carving at the top. There are few examples of the Romanesque in Paris, but those that are include the bell tower and small chancel columns of **St-Germain-des-Prés**, the capitals in **St-Pierre, Montmartre**, the belfry abutting the apse in **St-Germain l'Auxerrois** and part of the crypt of the **St-Denis** basilica (pictured below).

Early Gothic *(12th and 13thC)*
In place of the rounded arches and plainness of the Romanesque style, the Gothic builders used pointed arches and made great play with stained glass, sculptural decoration and vertical emphasis.

It was pre-eminently an ecclesiastical style, with the ideal of liberating much space, to create a sense of void over solid and, using verticals rather than horizontals, of bringing a soaring, aspiring quality.

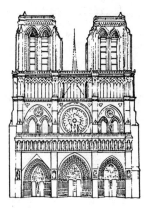

The forerunner of Gothic architecture in Europe was the **St-Denis** basilica, designed by architect Abbot Suger, on the outskirts of Paris. In the Early Gothic churches, windows were small and decoration comparatively restrained.

But the outstanding example to be seen in Paris is the magnificent cathedral of **Notre-Dame** (pictured right), the construction of which began in 1163 and was completed in 1330.

Mid-Gothic *(13th and 14thC)*
As the Gothic builders became more skillful at distributing weight through the use of buttresses, they were able to liberate larger areas of wall for stained-glass windows. The **Sainte-Chapelle** is one of the finest examples of this period to be found anywhere. The chapel, designed by Pierre de Montreuil, is on two stories, with the walls of the upper story completely filled by stained-glass windows. The cathedral of **Notre-Dame at Chartres** is one of the most renowned examples of the High Gothic architectural style, and served as the experiment that opened the way for later, even more spectacular architectural developments.

Late or Flamboyant Gothic *(15thC)*
In the late phase of the Gothic period, builders abandoned themselves to exuberant decoration, characterized by Flamboyant (literally "flame-like") window tracery and columns rising into elaborate fan-vaulting.

The best examples are to be seen in the ambulatory of **St-Séverin** and the outstanding facade at **St-Germain l'Auxerrois**. Other Parisian buildings that illustrate this exotic style are the **Hôtel de Sens** (now the Bibliothèque Forney, pictured left), with its highly decorated turrets and battlements, the **Hôtel de Cluny** (now the Musée National du Moyen Âge), the **Tour St-Jacques** and the little cloister at the **Temple des Billettes**, in the Marais.

The church of **St-Maclou at Rouen** is another quite outstanding example.

Renaissance *(16thC)*

Military campaigns in Italy led the French to a gradual understanding of the Renaissance. In architecture it was marked by a return to Greek and Roman forms and motifs: allegorical sculptures, Classical columns, balustrades, pediments and rounded arches. François I (1515-47) was a patron of the arts who did much to introduce Renaissance architecture to France. One of its leading exponents was Pierre Lescot, who designed part of the **Cour Carrée** at the Louvre. Other examples are the courtyard of the **Hôtel Carnavalet** (pictured left), the **Porte Dorée** (golden gate) at Fontainebleau, built by Gilles Le Breton, the **Fontaine des Innocents** near the Forum des Halles and, in interior decoration, the beautiful rood-screen at **St-Étienne-du-Mont**.

French Baroque and Renaissance Classicism *(17thC)*

In essence, the Baroque style is a more ornate version of Renaissance Classicism. **Versailles** is a striking example; another is the E wing of the **Louvre**. In ecclesiastical architecture, Baroque includes the so-called "Jesuit" style (based on the church of Gésu in Rome).

Paris has many churches of this kind: the **Sorbonne church** (by Jacques Lemercier), **Val-de-Grâce**, **St-Paul-St-Louis**, all showing the Baroque liking for domes.

One of the outstanding architects of this period was François Mansart, who also gave his name to the high-pitched Mansard roof, seen, for example, on the **Val-de-Grâce** cloister. His great-nephew, Jules Hardouin-Mansart, merged Baroque with the simple lines of Classicism in many superb secular buildings, notably the mansions in **place Vendôme**, and at the **Dôme church** (right) at Les Invalides.

Rococo *(18thC)*

After the death of Louis XIV, and with a child king on the throne, a new, lighter style made its appearance, which was characterized by elaborate but graceful ornamentation. This was Rococo *(Rocaille)*; it was more restrained than elsewhere and was mainly used as a feature of interior decoration — for example,

Germain Boffrand's Oval Salon of the **Hôtel de Soubise**. The **Hôtel Biron** (now the Musée Rodin) is an example of the refined elegance of the Rococo age.

The 18thC Classical, monumental architecture reached its peak in Paris with such structures as the **Louvre colonnade**, the **École Militaire** and **place de la Concorde**.

Neoclassicism *(late 18th to early 19thC)*

Between the 1780s and 1830s there was a revival of interest in Classical antiquity, in marked contrast to the ornate Rococo style. Once again, order, balance and clarity became the keynotes. **La Madeleine** illustrates the style, and Paris has the supreme examples of Neoclassicism in the **Panthéon** and the chapel at **Versailles**.

Consulate, Empire and Restoration *(early 19thC)*

Buildings of this period are less imaginative, a heavier version of the Classical style, as in the **Arc de Triomphe** and **La Madeleine**.

Second Empire/early Third Republic *(mid-19th to early 20thC)*

Uniformity went by the board and was replaced by a great mixture of styles, drawing on many periods. Advanced engineering, exemplified by the **Tour Eiffel**, was often combined with great extravagance of decoration, at least partly because the structural problems solved by the use of iron allowed great decorative freedom. A typical Second-Empire building is Charles Garnier's spectacular **Opéra** (right) which opened in 1875 and is one of the largest theaters in the world.

This extravagant architectural rhetoric was carried into the Third Republic period with such edifices as the **Sacré-Coeur**, the **Grand Palais** and **Petit Palais**, and **Pont Alexandre III**. The Grand Palais interior illustrates particularly well the combination of practicality and decorativeness, and its use of stylized natural forms can be seen as a precursor of the architectural experiments that characterize Art Nouveau.

Art Nouveau *(late 19th to early 20thC)*

Here the mood changes markedly. Art Nouveau decorations on buildings are fluid in appearance, characterized by many elongated loops and an almost Baroque elaborateness of form. It is most obvious in the flowing and sinuous cast-iron entrances to some **Métro stations**, designed by Hector Guimard between 1898-1904.

Guimard was an important architect in the Art Nouveau style in Paris, and had been much influenced by the leading Northern European exponent of Art Nouveau, the Belgian architect Victor Horta.

Art Nouveau forms can be seen readily around Paris, particularly in restaurants; there are a number of superb examples, including **Julien**, with its murals by Alphonse Mucha, and **La Fermette Marbeuf 1900**.

Interwar *(1918-39)*

Modernity and functionalism were the keynotes, as elsewhere, during this period, but echoes of tradition were sometimes retained. The combination is seen in the vast **Palais de Chaillot** (below). A full-blown example of Art Deco is the **Palais de Tokyo**, where good use was made of reinforced stone and concrete to achieve the clean, straight building lines. Both owe their existence to the Paris Exhibition of 1937.

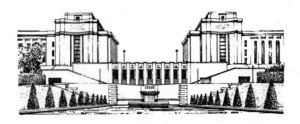

A fine example of slightly more human proportions is the building at place St-Augustin occupied by the **Cercle National des Armées de Terre, de Mer et de l'Air**. Its linear facade is filled with the stylized military imagery that was so successfully interpreted by the architects of the prewar period.

Thinking was dangerously radical during this period, with some old buildings that would today have been held in high esteem demolished to "make way for the twentieth century." The historic parts of the city to the east of the Louvre were fortunately spared from Le Corbusier's *Plan Voisin* (1925), which projected total demolition of the *quartier* as far as the **Hôtel de Ville**, and replacing it with eighteen gigantic skyscrapers.

Postwar *(from 1945)*

The 1950s were relatively stagnant, as the nation recovered from World War II. Some bleak expanses of glass, steel and concrete arose in the 1960s, particularly the **Tour Montparnasse** and the **Palais des Congrès** at Porte-Maillot.

The **Forum des Halles**, a shopping, leisure and entertainment complex completed in 1979, had the disadvantage of having replaced Baltard's 19th century market hall, which was much regretted once lost forever. But its uplifting rooflines and conscious emulation of those old, metallic shapes, its lively use of garden landscaping, make it a success from the outside, even if its shopping malls feel much the same as shopping malls the world over.

Both praised and criticized for its innovative design in its heyday,

Rogers and Piano's **Centre Pompidou** has stood the test of time less well and its exterior is seen by many as waywardly ugly, with its massive bulk and its primary colors.

> While in Paris last year, I was much impressed
> by a visit I made to a formerly rundown area of the city
> in Montparnasse. An agreed framework had led
> to the retention of traditional street patterns on a narrower,
> more intimate scale, which opened out, at various points,
> into small squares or piazzas.
> The height of the buildings was limited and so the retention
> of human scale was ensured. And it contrasted
> spectacularly with the vast, impersonal 1960s monoliths,
> seemingly about to trample, Gulliver-like,
> on their miniature neighbours.
> (HRH The Prince of Wales, *A Vision of Britain*, 1989)

New Paris *(1975-present)*

But planning policies for Paris changed with the arrival of mayor Jacques Chirac in the mid-1970s. Skyscraper developments were no longer permitted, and the city committed itself once more to retaining its glorious and much-admired unity while allowing a growing dialogue with the world's leading architects.

The product of this policy has been two-pronged. A massive restoration and cleaning program has transformed buildings in many parts of the city, and the boulevards and squares now shine with a fresh gleam — an impression enhanced still further with the re-gilding of statues and monuments for the 1989 French Revolution bicentenary celebrations.

Old buildings, both major monuments and much less significant structures such as office and apartment blocks are being restored, district by district, aided by grants from the city and subject to tight planning laws. Proud of its historic streets and buildings, Paris is now showing them off to best advantage.

The wealth of significant new and newly-converted buildings seems never-ending, each project more impressive than the last. Italian architect Gae Aulenti converted the disused Gare d'Orsay into a thrilling exhibition space, while Ieoh Ming Pei's glass-and-steel pyramid has merged the late

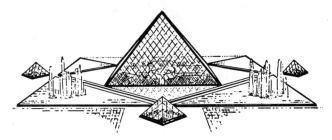

20thC with the stately buildings of the **Louvre** in a way that must surely still take the breath away in the years to come.

Another landmark has been added onto the precise axes laid out 200 years earlier, with the completion in 1989 of the marble-cladded **Grande Arche** at La Défense, by von Spreckelsen. Jean Nouvel's innovative **Institut du Monde Arabe**, with its light-sensitive window apertures, has enlivened spirits since it opened in 1987, although Carlos Ott's new Opéra Bastille has met with a more muted response despite its transformation of the place de la Bastille.

The public debate on architectural projects is a lively one, and a surprisingly large number of citizens express informed opinions. The fashion for building underground, exemplified below the pyramid at the **Grand Louvre**, has been followed across the street in the Jardins du Carrousel, where a subterranean **Palais de la Mode** will house the spring and autumn fashion collections from fall 1993. Less enthusiastically greeted so far, is Dominique Perrault's **TGB-Bibliothèque de France** already underway at Tolbiac, where four glass towers, L-shaped like open volumes, belie a vast underground complex of reading rooms and archives. Objections seem to lie less with the design itself than with its suitability for the storage of the precious books from the National Archive.

Frank Gehry, prolific Californian architect, has suddenly emerged as a contributor to the Paris skyline. His brilliantly colorful townscape at **Festival Disney** at Marne-La-Vallée has caused less excitement than his lively and more populist new **American Center** in the developing district of Bercy.

Gehry's **American Center** at Bercy

The cultural heritage

It is hard to pinpoint the beginning of Paris' greatness as a center of culture and the arts. Its cultural roots can be traced back as far as the Gallo-Roman period, but in more recent times a point of origin can be seen in François Villon (born 1431), who is widely considered to be France's (and Paris') first great poet, and who combined the writing of brilliant verse with living as a thief among the maze of tiny streets and taverns of the Latin Quarter.

Villon was a forerunner of the great cultural outburst that came when Italian Renaissance art and architecture reached France under the influence of François I. François also stimulated a new interest in music, particularly songs accompanied by the lute, which were often heard in his court, and brought important Italian masterpieces — among them the *Mona Lisa* — to Paris. Literature also flourished, and it was at this time that François Rabelais (c.1494-c.1553) wrote his roistering and satirical stories of *Gargantua* and *Pantagruel.* The same period saw the emergence of the *Pléiade,* a group of seven poets who broke with medieval traditions, introduced Italian Renaissance forms and established the alexandrine (line of 12 syllables) as the basic meter of French verse. One member of the group was Jean Antoine de Baïf, who in 1571 established an Academy of Music and Poetry in Paris.

The 17thC, known as "Le Grand Siècle," was culturally even richer. Drama was dominated by the tragedians Corneille (1606-84) and Racine (1639-99), and by Molière (1622-73), an actor and writer of sparkling comedies. The fondness at this time for strict rules of form in literature and drama found its most extreme expression in the Académie Française, founded by Cardinal Richelieu in 1635.

More stimulating and less conservative as a milieu for writers and thinkers were the *salons,* which began to flourish at about the same time, and provided a forum for philosophers and literati to exchange ideas and sharpen their wits on one another.

When Louis XIV began to reign in 1661, he proved to be the greatest patron of the arts since François I. He founded the Comédie Française, the Royal Academy of Painting and Sculpture, which was later reborn as the École des Beaux-Arts, and the Royal Academy of Music, appointing as its operatic director the versatile composer Jean-Baptiste Lully. The literary arts also reached a new peak in the trenchant compositions of Madame de Sévigné, and in Madame de Lafayette's novel *La Princesse de Clèves,* and Pascal's anonymously published *Lettres Provinciales.*

While France declined politically under Louis XV and XVI, the nation's artistic and literary life remained vigorous. Painting was dominated by Jean-Antoine Watteau, who was one of the greatest Rococo artists, then later Jean-Honoré Fragonard with his delicate eroticism, and the court painter François Boucher, who became famous for his portraits of Louis XV's mistress, Madame de Pompadour.

In music, operas were composed by Rameau and the German, Gluck, who had his greatest successes in Paris. And the world of letters resounded to the philosophy and wit of Voltaire, Rousseau, Montesquieu,

Diderot and d'Alembert. In such company, the *salons* enjoyed their heyday under the patronage of some of the most fashionable hostesses, among them Madame de Lambert, Madame de Deffand, Madame Geoffrin and Madame de Pompadour herself. Despite revolution and war, the early half of the 19thC saw the flowering of great artists in all fields: Eugène Delacroix in painting, Hector Berlioz in music, Honoré de Balzac and Victor Hugo in literature.

Under the Second Empire, Parisian life once again became a glorious party, dancing to the tunes of Offenbach and captured in the caricatures of Daumier. But it was in the late 19thC, after Paris had recovered from the Franco-Prussian war, that the period of greatest cultural efflorescence began.

The artistic world felt itself alienated from bourgeois society and had carved out its own territory, "Bohemia," the world so vividly portrayed by Henri Murger in his novel *Scènes de la Vie de Bohème.* In the Second Empire, one of the favorite hostelries had been the Brasserie des Martyrs in rue des Martyrs, where Murger rubbed shoulders with the poet Baudelaire and the painter Gustave Courbet. Later the scene shifted to other cafés such as the Guerbois and the Nouvelle Athènes, where could be found a remarkable mixture of artistic rebels, drop-outs and failures, and a handful who became famous, among them writers such as Zola and "Impressionist" painters: Monet, Pissarro, Renoir and Degas.

The late 19th to early 20thC, and most particularly the Belle Époque (1900-14), brought forth many schools in the various branches of the arts. On the stage, Sarah Bernhardt was the toast of Paris. There were the "Symbolist" poets and painters, with their interest in the strange, the surreal, the mythological: Gustave Moreau in painting, Villiers de l'Isle Adam in literature; and there was Marcel Proust with his odyssey, *À la Recherche du Temps Perdu,* which shows that even in the early decades of the 20thC the tradition of the *salon* was still alive.

At the same time, the foundations of modern art were being laid. Picasso, for example, was already at work in Paris in 1901. He lived and worked in a remarkable artists' and writers' lodging house in Montmartre called the Bateau-Lavoir, in the company of other avant-garde painters such as Van Dongen, Braque and Juan Gris, and writers such as Max Jacob and Guillaume Apollinaire.

Montmartre continued to be an artistic center until well into the 20th century — Utrillo, for example, lived there, and its streets appear in many of his paintings. But between World Wars I and II, most of the artists and writers preferred Montparnasse, and it was here that James Joyce, Henry Miller, Ernest Hemingway, F. Scott Fitzgerald and Gertrude Stein sought inspiration. Miller's *Tropic of Cancer* and Hemingway's *A Moveable Feast* both vividly describe the Paris they knew.

In the interwar period, Paris gave birth to Surrealism, one of the most influential artistic and literary movements of modern times. Its founder was a poet, André Breton, but its best-known exponents were painters: René Magritte, André Masson, Salvador Dalí and Max Ernst. Literature also flourished in Paris in the interwar and postwar years in the hands of many celebrated writers producing works in a variety of genres — among them André Gide, Colette, Jean Cocteau, Georges Simenon, Albert Camus, Jean-Paul Sartre and Simone de Beauvoir.

After 1945 the focus of intellectual life moved once again, this time to the St-Germain-des-Prés quarter, where the cafés were frequented by Sartre and his circle. The postwar years are also strongly associated with the cabaret singer, Edith Piaf, whose compelling voice and passionate life-style made her a legend both in her lifetime and beyond her untimely death in 1963.

Today the attitude of the French toward their culture remains impressive. The new building program of the past ten years, when viewed along with the enormous number of renovations of existing facilities, has produced a scenario for the world of letters, the performing and the visual arts that is healthy on every front. The energetic and expansive approach of Jack Lang, the Minister for Culture for a number of years, has had a positive impact on every sphere of cultural interest.

The new Opéra Bastille has provided another major performance venue and has allowed the expansion and concentration of both contemporary dance and ballet at the Opéra Garnier. The Orchestre National de l'Opéra de Paris, based at Opéra Bastille, is under the musical direction of international star Myung-Whun Chung. Theater presentations are more daringly avant-garde than they once were, with the Théâtre Jean-Louis Barrault no longer the lone voice in a busy performance scene.

Performance art reaching out to the people is now an almost everyday occurrence, and there are artists, street poets, musicians and mime-artists who perform with verve and imagination at a number of busy spots including the Centre Pompidou, the Musée d'Orsay, the Forum des Halles and on boulevard St-Germain.

The movie industry is still alive and well. Audience numbers may have diminished a little in the past ten years, but the French are still keen movie-goers and this public appreciation has meant that there are funds available to give the industry support.

As a nation, the French show no sign of losing their appreciation of the arts. It is immediately noticeable that the book trade is still thriving and that works of art, both ancient and contemporary, are viewed with pride. Colorful posters advertising art exhibitions are commonly found in the windows of even the lowliest of cafés, and are put there with no fear of alienating the clientele. Unlike in some other countries that we could mention . . . .

Suggestions for further reading

The following titles, among many others, have been invaluable to the author in the updating of this guide. All should be obtainable from one of the English-language bookstores in Paris (see page 50 for details).

Fireside browsing
Paris — Architecture, History, Art by Ian Littlewood, with photographs by John Heseltine *(George Philip, London 1992)*. Sensitive analysis of the Paris neighborhoods, with first class photographs.

Les Plus Beaux Restaurants de Paris by Roger Gain *(Gallimard, Paris 1989)*. Detailed descriptions of 52 exquisite restaurants, with lavish photographs.

Guide de Paris Mystérieux (Tchou, Paris 1989). Fat compilation of quaint, often obscure historical facts about every corner of Paris; many line illustrations.

Paris, A Literary Companion by Ian Littlewood *(John Murray)*. Extracts from many literary sources.

Le Nouveau Paris by Harald A. Jahn *(L'Iconothèque, Paris 1991)*. Intelligent analysis of the new architectural projects.

Works of literature
A Sentimental Education by Gustave Flaubert *(Paris 1869)*
A Moveable Feast by Ernest Hemingway *(London 1964)*
Tropic of Cancer by Henry Miller *(Paris 1934)*
Down and Out in Paris and London by George Orwell *(London 1933)*
Quartet by Jean Rhys *(London 1928)*
L'Assommoir by Émile Zola *(Paris 1877)*
Nana by Émile Zola *(Paris 1880)*
Les Misérables by Victor Hugo *(Paris 1862)*

Books to use on the ground
Paris Up Close by Vivienne Menkes-Ivry *(Passport Books, Chicago 1992)*, published *(Duncan Petersen, 1992)* in the UK as *3D City Guides — Paris*. Detailed walks around much of the city; using fascinating isometric maps.

Paris Humeurs by Danièle Laufer and Andrée Fortin *(Nathan, Paris 1990)*. Explores Paris by themes: Japanese, Jewish, for poets, for fishermen, by bicycle etc.

Slow Walks in Paris by Michael Leitch *(Hodder & Stoughton, London 1989)*. Leisurely, detailed strolls for those with lots of time.

The Guide to the Architecture of Paris by Norval White *(Scribner's, New York, 1991)*. Extraordinarily detailed analysis of every building worth looking at, purely from an architect's viewpoint. Broken up into walks.

For business
Paris Anglophone edited by David Applefield *(Frank Books, Vincennes, published annually)*. Useful reference work, with every conceivable address and telephone number.

Basic information

Before you go

DOCUMENTS REQUIRED

Visitors to France, if they are US or Canadian citizens or Japanese nationals, or are resident in the European Community (EC), do not need a visa — a **passport or identity card** is sufficient.

For stays of longer than 3 months, you will need to apply for a *carte de séjour*, from the French Embassy in Washington, DC, or from the nearest French consulate. There are eight French consulates in the US: in Boston, Chicago, Detroit, Houston, Los Angeles, New Orleans, New York and San Francisco. For British citizens the same applies. Contact the visa section of the French Consulate *(6A Conway Place, South Kensington, London SW7 2EW ☎ 071-581-5292)*.

If you wish to drive while in France, you need a valid full **driver's license** and you must be aged 18 or over. An international driver's license is not needed. If you are bringing a car into the country, you will also need the **vehicle registration certificate**, a **national identity plate** or sticker displayed at the rear of the vehicle, and a **certificate of insurance** or **international green card** proving that you have third-party insurance.

TRAVEL AND MEDICAL INSURANCE

Before setting out, it is advisable to take out an insurance policy that covers loss of deposits paid to airlines, hotels, tour operators, etc., and the cost of dealing with emergency requirements, such as special tickets home and extra nights in a hotel, as well as cover against theft, and a medical insurance policy. Contact your local travel agent or insurance broker well before departure.

There is a reciprocal agreement between EC countries whereby visitors entitled to full UK benefits can obtain emergency medical and dental treatment for the same cost as the nationals themselves. To benefit from this you must have form **E111**, which can now be obtained from any Post Office and will be authorized at the counter while you wait. Accompanying the E111 is a leaflet, *Health Care For Visitors to EC Countries,* which gives details on how to claim.

Keep your E111 when you return: it has no expiry date. Study also their booklet *The Traveller's Guide to Health,* which gives comprehensive information on vaccinations and diseases and provides useful health checklists.

In France you are only entitled to a refund of approximately 75 percent of the medical services expenses that you pay, and about 70 percent of the cost of medicines, so it is still wise to take out private insurance.

A useful organization is **IAMAT** (International Association for Medical Assistance to Travelers), which has a list of English-speaking doctors who will call, for a fee. IAMAT has member hospitals and clinics throughout Europe, including a number in France, although their representation in Paris itself is slight. Membership of IAMAT is free. For further information, and a directory of doctors and hospitals, write to **IAMAT** *(in the US at 417, Center St., Lewiston, NY 14092 or, in Europe at 37 Voirets, 1212 Grand-Lancy, Genève, Switzerland).*

The **American Hospital** *(63 blvd. Victor-Hugo, Neuilly-sur-Seine* ☎ *46-41-25-25, map17C3),* accepts Blue Cross and Blue Shield medical insurance. There is also a **British Hospital** *(Hôpital Franco-Britannique, 3 rue Barbès, 92300 Levallois-Perret* ☎ *47-58-13-12, map17C3).*

MONEY

The unit of currency is the franc (f), which consists of 100 centimes (c). There are coins for 5c, 10c, 20c and 50c, 1f, 2f, 5f and 10f, and notes for the following amounts: 20f, 50f, 100f, 200f and 500f. There is no limit to the amount of currency you can bring into France, but you can take out no more than 50,000f when you leave, unless large sums are declared on entry. On days preceding public holidays, banks are open only in the morning, although exchange bureaux are open longer.

Travelers checks issued by American Express, Thomas Cook, Barclays and Citibank are widely recognized; make sure you read the instructions included with your travelers checks. It is important to note separately the serial numbers of your checks and the telephone number to call in case of loss. Specialist travelers check companies such as American Express provide extensive local refund facilities for lost checks through their own offices or agents.

Major international **charge/credit cards** such as American Express, Diners Club, Eurocard (MasterCard) and Carte Bleue (Visa) are widely accepted, the two latter cards being nowadays almost universal. In this book, acceptance of Mastercard and Visa cards is not shown, because most establishments accept most cards; establishments that accept American Express (AE) and Diners Club (CB) cards are marked thus; and if cards are not accepted, the words "no cards" appear.

American Express also has a **MoneyGram**® money transfer service that makes it possible to wire money worldwide in just minutes, from any American Express Travel Service Office. This service is available to all customers and is not limited to American Express Card members. For address see page 51.

CUSTOMS

Following a special agreement reached in 1991, travelers within the European Community will continue to be eligible to make duty-free purchases until the end of June 1999. After that date, duty- and tax-free shopping will be restricted to travelers arriving in and leaving the EC.

An EC agreement has increased personal allowances of duty-free drinks and tobacco. With effect from January 1, 1993, everyone aged over 17 years will be entitled to import 60 liters of champagne or 90 liters of table wine, 110 liters of beer, 10 liters of spirits or 20 liters of fortified wine, plus 800 cigarettes or one kilo of rolling tobacco into another EC member country, provided they are for **personal use** only.

The duty-free limits for people entering France from a non-EC country such as the US are far lower: 2 liters of table wine and one liter of spirits, or two liters of sparkling wine; 200 cigarettes or 250 grams of rolling tobacco; 50 grams of perfume.

At the time of writing, the duty-free import allowance for all other goods (perfume, electrical goods and gifts bought tax-free) was still ECU (European Currency Unit) 45 (about £32 or $55) in all EC countries, although there is pressure from industry to increase this amount.

Remember, import restrictions are different outside the EC. Find out from your local Customs and Excise office before you leave, or, when in Paris, from the **Office du Tourisme et des Congrès** *(127 av. des Champs-Élysées, 8ᵉ* ☎ *47-23-61-72, map 5 F3. Métro: George-V).*

You are entitled to bring, free of duty and tax, any item clearly intended for personal or professional use and which you intend to take with you when you leave. Make sure that you are carrying dated receipts for more valuable items such as electrical goods, computers, luxury clothing, cameras and watches, or you may be charged duty.

Prohibited and restricted goods include narcotics, gold and weapons. A more detailed list can be obtained from the **French Government Tourist Office** in your own country. For addresses see page 41.

Visitors are exempt from paying Value Added Tax (**TVA**) on purchases above a certain amount, on completion of a simple form (the *détaxe* form) and presentation of a passport at the time of purchase. However, to validate the refund, which will be made to you at your home address or through a charge/credit card repayment, you must present the paperwork and goods at a customs checkpoint before going through the passport control on leaving the country. Leave enough time to do this — it can take a few minutes.

For fuller details, see the section on VAT refunds in SHOPPING.

GETTING THERE
By air   There are daily flights to Paris from many parts of the world, including many US cities. Direct, regular nonstop flights to France's capital leave from Boston, Chicago, Houston, Miami, New York and Washington, DC. Flying time from the East Coast is approximately $6\frac{1}{2}$ hours by subsonic jet or $3\frac{1}{2}$ hours by Concorde. There are daily flights from Toronto and Montréal.

From the UK the journey takes about an hour. There is an almost hourly shuttle service from London (Heathrow), run by British Airways and Air France, which both also fly from Gatwick. Stansted airport near London has flights to Paris run by Air France and Air UK, and London City Airport in London's Docklands is served by Brymon Airways/Air France and London City Airways.

Other cities also offer regular flights, including Aberdeen, Belfast, Birmingham, Bristol, Cardiff, Edinburgh, Glasgow, Manchester, Newcastle and Southampton. Dublin is served by Aer Lingus and Air France.

Paris has two passenger airports, and both are within easy reach of the city: **Roissy/Charles de Gaulle** to the N and **Orly** to the s.

By train　There is a regular train-and-boat service from London's Victoria Station, and a slightly more expensive but faster train-and-hovercraft service from Charing Cross and Victoria (most frequent in summer). The fastest, via Dover to Calais and on to Paris (Gare du Nord), takes about 7 hours.

The French high-speed train known as the TGV *(train grande vitesse)* is due to be ready to carry passengers from the Channel Tunnel to Lille and Paris by 1994.

By road, ferry or hovercraft　There are several routes across the Channel for both motorists and foot passengers. The major British ports with frequent ferry services are Dover, Portsmouth and Newhaven. From these ports you can sail direct to Dunkerque, Calais, Boulogne, Dieppe or Le Havre.

Until the much-delayed Channel Tunnel finally connects Dover with Calais some time in late 1993, the hovercraft is the quickest way of crossing the Channel — 35mins from Dover to Calais in good weather — for those with or without cars. Hovercrafts operate between Dover and Calais or Boulogne. There are crossings several times a day throughout the year, these being more frequent in summer. The A26/A1 between Calais and Paris is a fast and direct route linking the capital to one of the Channel ports, so head for Calais if you are in a hurry.

By bus　Traveling by bus is the cheapest means of getting to Paris from England. From Victoria Coach Station in London, you can travel with **Eurolines UK** *(☎(071) 730-0202)*, which has two daily departures *(noon and 9pm)* throughout the year with an extra morning departure in high summer only, or with **Hoverspeed** *(☎(0304) 240241)*, which operates a daytime service at least twice daily all year round. Both have a journey time of about 9hrs. It is wise to reserve ahead, especially if you plan to travel during the summer.

CLIMATE

In August many Parisians evacuate the city, as Paris can be unpleasantly and surprisingly hot — temperatures average 23˚C (75˚F), and you might think you were much farther south. Fall is often warm; spring brings clear blue skies, but can be cool. Winter can be uncomfortably cold and damp.

CLOTHES

The famous Parisian *chic* is evident wherever you go; both men and women are beautifully turned out, rarely casually or scruffily dressed. Yet the French are tolerant of informality: you don't normally need to wear a tie to a smart restaurant, and women can feel free to wear trousers on virtually any occasion. Pack one warm garment even for spring, a light raincoat, and an umbrella.

GENERAL DELIVERY (POSTE RESTANTE)
The central post office in Paris *(52 rue du Louvre, 75001 Paris* ☎*40-28-20-00, map 9 G9),* will keep all correspondence marked *poste restante* unless it is specifically addressed to another Parisian post office. Ensure that the name of the addressee is written clearly on the envelope.

You will need identification when you collect your mail and you may be charged a small fee. If the letter is addressed to two people, e.g., Mr and Mrs, addressees must collect the letter together. Travel companies such as American Express will also hold mail.

TOURIST INFORMATION
Useful free information on visiting Paris or France can be obtained from the **French Government Tourist Office**.
- **London**   178, Piccadilly, London W1V OAL ☎(071) 491-7622.
- **New York**   610 Fifth Avenue, New York NY 10020
  ☎1-900-990 0040 (50¢ per minute).
- **Toronto**   30 St Patrick St., Suite 700, Toronto, Ontario M5T 3A3.
- **Montréal**   1981 Avenue McGill College, Suite 490, Montréal, Québec H3A 2W9.
- In the United States, there are other branches in Beverly Hills, Chicago and Dallas.

Getting around

FROM THE AIRPORTS TO THE CITY
Trains run every 15 minutes between 5.30am-11.30pm to the Gare du Nord from **Roissy/Charles de Gaulle**; the journey takes 35 minutes. Air France buses *(* ☎*42-99-20-18; recorded message in French and English)* take 25 minutes when traffic is clear, but up to an hour at rush hours. They leave every 15-20 minutes, between 5.40am-11pm, to deposit passengers at the Porte Maillot *(map 5 E1)* and place Charles De Gaulle *(1 av. Carnot, map 5 E3)* terminals.

From **Orly** Airport, to the s of Paris, trains take about 40 minutes and leave every 15 minutes for the Gare d'Austerlitz or Gare St-Michel. Air France buses *(* ☎*43-23-97-10; recorded message in French and English)* leave every 12-15 minutes between 5.40am-11pm; the journey takes about 40 minutes.

The **Orlybus** service operates to and from Denfert-Rochereau, opposite the RER station. The bus leaves Orly-Sud from Gate H and Orly-Ouest from Gate D. There are four buses an hour and the journey takes about 25 minutes.

There are **taxis** at each airport, but a taxi ride to your destination will certainly be expensive and will not necessarily be any quicker. From Roissy/Charles de Gaulle Airport allow at least 30 minutes, or more in rush hour. Orly Airport is a cheaper, shorter journey, and should take only 20 minutes.

PUBLIC TRANSPORT

Paris has one of the best public transport systems in the world, run by the **RATP** (Réseau Autonome du Transport Parisien). Bus, Métro and inner RER systems use the same tickets, which are much cheaper if you buy a book *(carnet)* of ten, obtainable from bus or Métro stations, *tabacs* and, increasingly, from slot machines in the street. *Billets de tourisme* (tourist tickets) are also obtainable. New, money-saving schemes seem to be brought in each year, usually priced according to the number of days and the travel zones to be covered, and it will be best to ask what is currently on offer.

The **RATP information number** (☎ *43-46-14-14 for all inquiries)* has a few English-speaking operators if you call between 9am and 6pm. Or you can visit in person: **RATP Information Centers** are centrally situated at place de la Madeleine, 8ᵉ (☎ *40-06-71-45)* and at 53ter quai des Grands-Augustins, 6ᵉ (☎ *40-46-43-60).*

No ticket on any of the systems is valid until it has been punched *(composter)* or otherwise validated by passing through a machine usually positioned at the platform entrance. Be sure to do this, as bands of mobile ticket inspectors frequently impose on-the-spot fines on anyone traveling without the correct ticket.

MÉTRO

Unlike some subway systems, the Paris Métro is very clean, efficient and quite easy to understand. Each line is designated by a number, as well as by the names of the end stations. Once you know your direction of travel, simply follow the signs for the name and number you need. On platforms, the other directions are marked with orange *correspondance* signs. Smoking is prohibited.

Inside Paris, one ticket is valid no matter how far you go or how many changes you make, and you should retain your ticket until you reach your destination, as you may occasionally come across a ticket-operated barrier when you leave. The Métro runs from 5.30am-1.15am — these times are from the termini.

Métro stations are a popular haunt for musicians of all kinds; the larger, busier stations also have a number of vendors on the concourses selling fruit, jewelry, luggage etc. As in many great cities, you will also come across beggars, some of whom have taken to addressing a half-full carriage with an apology for their need to ask for money before doing the rounds. The public response, these days, is not necessarily unfavorable. Pickpockets exist, here as everywhere.

RER (RÉSEAU EXPRESS RÉGIONAL)

This is a fast suburban service which consists of three lines. **Line A** goes from St-Germain-en-Laye, Poissy or Cergy, in the w, to Boissy-St-Léger and Marne-La-Vallée (for EuroDisney) in the e. **Line B** goes from Robinson and St-Rémy-les-Chevreuses, in the s, to Roissy and Mitry-Claye in the n. **Line C** connects Versailles and St-Quentin-en-Yvelines in the sw to Dourdan, Rungis and Orly Airport in the se.

Within the Métro area, the Métro/Bus/RER standard ticket can be used.

For traveling into the suburbs, you will need a supplementary ticket; the cost varies with the distance. The service runs from 5.30am to 12.30am.

BUSES
On the buses, one ticket is valid for up to two *sections* (fare stages or zones) and two tickets are valid for three stages or more within the city boundary. When you enter the bus you have to punch your ticket by inserting it into the machine behind the driver (but do *not* punch any special discount tickets). Tickets can also be bought from the driver, but they are more expensive. Buses run from 7am-8.30pm, except to main-line rail stations, where the service operates until 12.30am.

Night buses (**Noctambus**) leave the Châtelet *(av. Victoria or rue St-Martin, map 9I9)* hourly from 1.30-5.30am, serving ten suburban destinations and returning again on the hour from 2-5am. Look for stops with a black and yellow owl symbol.

For **bus information** ☎43-46-14-14. You may find an English-speaking operator between 9am and 6pm.

RATP also runs 50-minute sightseeing bus tours on Sundays and public holidays from the last week in April to the end of September. Look out for information on the **Balabus** scheme.

TAXIS
At the last count there were 14,000 taxis in the city. They can be ordered by telephone *(☎49-36-10-10; you will be asked which area you are in),* picked up at a cabstand or, if you are lucky, hailed in the street. For taxis equipped for handicapped people (&) call the same number. Some drivers will accept an American Express card, but ask when calling the cab.

Whenever possible, go to a **cabstand** rather than telephoning for a cab, as the meter starts to run once the taxi leaves its base. Cabstands *(stations de taxi)* can be found at stations, and at regular intervals on main streets, usually near intersections.

Cabs have a light on the roof: if the white light is on, the cab is free; a smaller orange light means the cab is occupied; no light means the driver is off-duty. All registered cabs are equipped with meters and the metered time and distance will be charged according to the time of day and the zones of travel. You will also pay a **supplement** for each item of baggage, for a fourth person, or if you are picked up at a station. But the supplement is not large enough to warrant the nuisance of finding your own cab once you're away from the station.

Under normal circumstances give the driver a **tip** of 12-15 percent.

Beware of **pirate drivers** at stations who offer to take you for a "first-class" fare, which will be about five times the normal one. These characters still exist, but you will not encounter them at cabstands.

GETTING AROUND BY CAR
If you value your fender it is wise to avoid driving in Paris — the Parisian drives as if he were on the dodgems at a fairground, and parks as though he were shoving a book into a tight shelf. The **parking**

problem is severe, and meters are ubiquitous — they run from 9am-7pm and are watched over by blue-uniformed ladies sometimes known as *pervanches* (periwinkles). There are also a number of underground garages. In *zones bleues* (streets where blue parking signs are displayed), a *disque de contrôle* (parking disc) must be shown. These are obtainable from hotels, garages and tourist offices.

You should be aware of the following **laws**:

- **Speed limits** are 60kph (37mph) in the city and in built-up areas, 80kph (50mph) on the Périphérique, 90kph (56mph) on country roads, 130kph (80mph) on toll autoroutes and 110kph (68mph) on free autoroutes and four-lane highways/dual-carriageways.
- Cars coming from the right sometimes have priority. Look for the signs *priorité à droite* (warning that cars on the right take priority over you) or *vous avez priorité* (you have right of way). You will see signs saying simply *rappel* (reminder). This is a reminder that a previous command, such as priority, still applies. All you have to do is remember which . . . .
- **Seat-belts** are compulsory.
- **Children under ten** must not travel in the front seat.
- The use of **car telephones** while driving is prohibited.

Information on autoroute traveling, including free maps and a hotel reservation service, can be obtained from **Renseignements d'Autoroutes** *(3 rue Edmond Valentin, 75007 Paris* ☎ *47-05-90-01, map 6 H4, open Mon-Fri 9am-noon, 2-6pm)*. It is worth knowing that you can pay autoroute tolls by charge/credit card.

RENTING A CAR

It is worth renting a car for trips out to the suburbs or out of the city, although within the central area rentals are expensive and garages are scarce.

Most international car rental companies have offices in Paris, and there are also many reliable and often cheaper Parisian firms. Payment by charge/credit card avoids the need for a large cash deposit. A current driver's license is required, and the minimum age is usually 21, although some companies have raised it to 25. Make sure the car is fully insured, even if it means making separate arrangements for insurance against damage to other vehicles and injury to your passengers.

Various companies are represented at the airports, and you can make fly-drive arrangements before you leave your home country.

GETTING AROUND ON FOOT

Paris is a city built on a human scale and is therefore easy and pleasant to walk in. If you are not in a hurry, this is the most enjoyable way of getting about. A combination of walking and use of the excellent public transportation system is ideal for exploring Paris. Getting across busy roads, however, can be hazardous, even at crosswalks, where drivers are supposed to yield but often don't. The motto in Paris is *walk with confidence,* so follow their example. The only people dithering on the boulevards are the foreign visitors.

RAILWAY SERVICES

France's rail services are run by the **SNCF** (Société Nationale de Chemins de Fer). When traveling by train, as with the Métro, RER and buses, you must validate any ticket purchased in France at the machine at the platform entrance. If you fail to do this, you will be treated as if you are traveling without a ticket and will have to pay an on-the-spot fine or a surcharge.

The rail stations for travel beyond Paris are: **Gare d'Austerlitz** (southwest), **Gare de L'Est** (east), **Gare de Lyon** (southeast), **Gare Montparnasse** (west), **Gare du Nord** (north), **Gare St-Lazare** (northwest).

For general information and times of trains ☎45-82-50-50.

DOMESTIC AIRLINES

Air Inter is France's major internal airline. The central office is located at 49 av. des Champs-Élysées, 8ᵉ ☎42-89-38-88. Map **6F4**.

USING A BICYCLE

If you are prepared to brave the traffic, cycling in Paris can be an excellent way of exploring the city. The SNCF *Train Plus Vélo* scheme is popular. It allows you to make a train journey and then have the use of a waiting bicycle on arrival, from one of a number of centers including those as far afield as Fontainebleau and Rambouillet.

Bicycles can be rented from the following:
* **Bicyclub** 8 place de la Porte-de-Champerret, 17ᵉ ☎47-66-55-92. Map **17C3**. This telephone number connects to a recorded message giving details of 7 locations in the Île de France: Bois de Boulogne, Bois de Vincennes, Canal de l'Ourcq, Vallée de Chevreuse, St-Germain-en-Laye, Fontainebleau and Rambouillet. Each center has its own telephone number where reservations can be made. Open Sat, Sun, hols 9am-7pm; closed winter (Bois de Boulogne and Fontainebleau daily). Rentals by the hour, the day or the week.
* **Paris By Cycle** 99 rue de la Jonquière, 17ᵉ ☎42-63-36-63 and 78 rue de l'Ouest, 14ᵉ ☎40-47-08-04. Both open every day, all year round. Also at Bois de Boulogne, Carrefour des Cascades, Porte de Passy, 16ᵉ, weekends only. All types of bicycle including tandems.
* **Paris-Vélo** (Rent-A-Bike) 2 rue du Fer-à-Moulin, 5ᵉ ☎43-37-59-22. Map **15L10**.
* **La Maison du Vélo** 8 rue de Belzunce, 10ᵉ ☎42-81-24-72, map **4E10**, is open Tues-Sat. They do not rent bikes, but they have English-speaking staff and offer repairs and very friendly advice, as well as sales.

BY RIVER

Apart from the many trips to be taken on the Seine, the Marne and the canals, which are purely for pleasure, there's **Batobus**, a river bus service that stops at 5 points along the Seine: **Port de la Bourdonnais** at the Trocadéro near the Tour Eiffel, **Port de Solférino** near the Musée d'Orsay, **Quai Malaquais**, near the Pont des Arts outside the Institut de France, **Quai de Montebello** opposite Notre-Dame, and

Quai de l'Hôtel de Ville *(departures approx. every half hour from any stop, 10am-7.45pm* ☎*44-11-33-44)*. This is a quick, inexpensive and slightly unusual way to get around from one sight to another.

PARIS HÉLIPORT
The main heliport is situated in the 15e *(4 av. de la Porte de Sèvres, map 17D3. Business or pleasure inquiries* ☎*45-54-04-44)*. See also HELICOPTER FLIGHTS in ACTIVITIES AND SPORTS.

On-the-spot information

PUBLIC HOLIDAYS
New Year's Day, January 1; Easter Monday; Labor Day, May 1; VE Day, May 8; Ascension Day (sixth Thursday after Easter); Whit Monday (second Monday after Ascension); Bastille Day, July 14; Assumption, August 15; All Saints' Day, November 1; Remembrance Day, November 11; December 25. Most museums close on these days, but some stores and restaurants remain open.

TIME ZONES
Paris is 6 hours ahead of Eastern Standard Time, and 7-9 hours ahead of the other US time zones.

It is 1 hour ahead of Greenwich Mean Time (British time) in the winter and 2 hours ahead in summer, i.e., 1 hour ahead of Great Britain most of the year.

BANKS AND CURRENCY EXCHANGE
In general, banks are open Monday to Friday 9am-4.30pm, but there are no standardized banking hours. They all close on the afternoon before a public holiday. Foreign exchanges at airports and in most stations stay open late and are often open on weekends.

The **American Express Travel Service** office *(11 rue Scribe, 9^e* ☎*47-77-77-07, map 7F7)* is open Monday to Friday 9am-5pm.

Money can also be changed in larger hotels, but the exchange rate will be less good than in banks. It is advisable to ask about exchange rates and commission, as these can vary considerably. Remember that you need your passport when changing money.

Eurocheques can be cashed up to a value of about £100, at all banks displaying the Eurocard sign. The Eurocard will also give a similar amount through cash-dispensing machines, but note that on-street machines are much less common than in the UK.

SHOPPING HOURS
Department stores usually remain open from 9.30am-6.30pm without interruption from Monday to Saturday, and some are open later one night each week. Smaller boutiques generally open from 10am-7pm Monday to Saturday, although they often close for an hour at lunch.

While neighborhood shops still often observe the traditional Monday closing, stores in main shopping areas stay open. And, while August was once the universal vacation month, most of the larger stores now stay open all summer. See also SHOPPING.

RUSH HOURS

Between 7.30-9am and 5-7pm, the Métro is packed with workers going to and from their offices. On Friday evenings the weekend traffic out of Paris is very heavy. Try very hard to avoid leaving Paris on the first and last days of July or August, when the entire population of Paris is either leaving for or returning from vacation. If you are traveling to either airport during the rush hours, allow plenty of extra time.

POSTAL SERVICES

Street corner signs on major intersections direct you toward the neighborhood post office with the words *Bureau des Postes,* usually followed by the address. Post office buildings are marked by a sign with a blue swallow on a white disc or by the letters **PTT**.

Normal opening hours are Monday to Friday 8am-7pm, Saturday 8am-noon. The main post offices are at 48-52 rue du Louvre, 1er *(map 8 G9, open 24hrs* ☎ *40-28-20-00)* and at 71 av. des Champs-Élysées, 8e *(*☎*44-13-66-00, map 6 F4; open 7 days 8am-10pm, but after 7pm service is restricted to simple postal and telephone transactions).*

Stamps *(timbres)* can be bought in tobacconists *(tabacs),* hotels and newsdealers, and in yellow vending machines. Mailboxes are also yellow and are marked *boîte aux lettres.* Allow 7-10 days for mail to reach France, and for your letters to reach the US. Letters normally travel between Paris and the UK in 3-4 days.

Addresses in Paris must all include the **postal zip code**, which combines **750-** with the numbers of the *arrondissements.* Thus the zip code in the 1er is 75001, and so on up to the 20^{e}, where the zip code is 75020. Usefully, the zip code thus shows at once the *arrondissement* in which any address is to be found.

TELEPHONE SERVICES

Almost all telephones now accept cards, not cash, and it can be quite difficult to find coin-operated telephones in stations and at airports. When you find one, it will take 50c, 1f, 2f and 5f coins. In bars, cafés and restaurants, you will still find coin-operated phones. Public telephones are also found in post offices and cafés as well as in the street.

Phonecards *(télécartes)* These can be bought at post offices, and at shops displaying the sign *Télécarte en vente ici* (phonecards sold here), but note that 40f is the cheapest available.

Dialing For **international calls**, look in the telephone directory for the direct dialing code for your country.

- **19** gives an international connection, then wait for another tone.
- Make a **1** for the United States or Canada, **44** for the United Kingdom, **353** for Ireland.
- Then the area code (leaving off any initial 0) and then the number.

Ringing tone   This is a shrill, intermittent tone preceded by about a dozen fast pips. The busy or engaged tone is less shrill and more rapid.
Collect calls   Known in France as an *appel pcv,* a collect/reverse charge call is made by keying **19**, then wait for the tone, then key **33** for the international operator.
Home Direct   France Telecom also offers the Home Direct service if you wish to call abroad. Key the Home Direct number for your country and you will be connected (toll free) with a local operator. Then you agree the method of payment (charge/credit card, AT&T card, collect call etc) and the call is made for you.
- **ATT USA Direct**   ☎19-00-11
- **MCI US Direct**   ☎19-00-19
- **Sprint US Direct**   ☎19-00-87
- **Canada Direct**   ☎19-00-16
- **UK Direct**   ☎19-00-44
- **Ireland Direct**   ☎19-00-353

International directory inquiries   ☎19-33-12, then the dialing code for the country required. This type of inquiry works out rather expensive (7f).
Directory inquiries   ☎**12** for numbers within France.
Making calls within France   Throughout France, telephone numbers consist of 8 digits. For Paris and the surrounding area, the number is preceded by **1** if dialing from outside the area. (Regional numbers used to be prefixed by 16, but this has been discontinued.)
To call Paris from outside France   Simply key in your international dialing code, then **33** for France, **1** for Paris, then the 8-figure number.
Charges   The cost of telephone calls in France is not terribly expensive. Nevertheless, if you want to call home, the cheapest time is after 10.30pm and on Sundays and holidays.
Telephone directories   It's useful, and reassuring to know that there are several pages explaining the telephone system in English, at the front of the first telephone directory (the one that starts with A). If you are looking for a number in the business directory, you will need to know which arrondissement to look under.
Telegrams   These can be sent from any post office or by telephone. To send a telegram abroad ☎05-33-44-11, a toll-free number.

PUBLIC LAVATORIES (REST ROOMS)

Those who knew Paris before modernization will remember the abundance of quaint, perforated-iron kiosks known as *vespasiennes.* Now almost none remain, and the French-style hole-in-the-floor has almost disappeared too.

Modern lavatories of the self-cleaning kind *(sanisettes)* are to be found in abundance and are clean and well looked after.

You will find lavatories in many Métro stations and public parks, and you can use the facilities of nearly every café. Often you will find a lady presiding, who will expect a nominal sum (1 or 2f); in cafés leave a similar small tip in the saucer at the bar, if you have not bought a drink.

ELECTRIC CURRENT

The electric current is 220V (50 cycles AC). Plugs *(prise de courant)* are standard European, with two round prongs. Adaptors *(transformateurs)* can be bought at any good electrical store or department store in Paris, or before you leave home, and, usually, in airport departure lounge shops.

LAWS AND REGULATIONS

- **Smoking** is now banned in all public places, except in specially designated areas. This new law, introduced late in 1992, has met with some derision, for the French as a nation are still comparatively heavy smokers. How the enforcement is carried out remains to be seen. The expectation is that smoking will indeed be outlawed on public transport and in public buildings, theaters etc., that designated areas will be created in restaurants, and that nightclubs will ignore the ban altogether.
- Laws against **drug abuse** are as strongly enforced as elsewhere, with greater penalties for the buying and selling of drugs.
- **Hitch-hiking** is forbidden on autoroutes, although it is tolerated on other roads.

CUSTOMS AND ETIQUETTE

The French are among the most manner-conscious of all nations, and observe a rather rigid code of behavior in personal relationships, which is, however, beginning to be broken down by the younger generation. This consciousness is exemplified by the *vous* and *tu* forms of address; the former applies to everyone except relations, close friends and children.

Hand-shaking is common when greeting or saying goodbye among friends, as well as between acquaintances and strangers, and close friends kiss each other energetically on alternate cheeks at least twice and often three times. It is customary, when addressing someone, to say *Madame* or *Monsieur* without using a surname.

TIPPING

Tipping is less widely practiced in France today, as bars, restaurants and hotels all include 15 percent service and taxes in their prices *(service compris,* which can also be seen as *s.c.)*. If the service has been particularly good, you can show your appreciation by leaving a small extra tip for the waiter.

Small tips of only a few francs should be given to cloakroom attendants, tour guides, doormen, hairdressers and cinema usherettes. Airport and railway porters have a fixed charge per item, while taxi drivers will expect 12-15 percent.

DISABLED TRAVELERS

Special facilities for the disabled are becoming more and more commonplace in France. The **Comité National Français de Liaison pour la Réadaptation des Handicapés** *(38 blvd. Raspail, 75007*

Paris ☎ *45-48-90-13, map 13J7)* offers bilingual information for the handicapped visitor to Paris. They prefer requests in writing.

For further information on travel in Europe, and details of tour operators specializing in tours for handicapped people, write to the **Travel Information Service** *(Moss Rehabilitation Hospital, 12th St. and Tabor Rd., Philadelphia, Pa. 19141),* or to **Mobility International USA** *(PO Box 3551, Eugene, Or. 97403).*

In the UK, contact **RADAR** *(25 Mortimer St., London W1N 8AB* ☎ *(071) 637-5400),* who can provide a factsheet on travel to France. They also publish *Holidays and Travel Abroad.*

A guidebook *Access in Paris* is published by **Access Project** (PHSP) *(39, Bradley Gardens, London W13 8HE).* Researched by disabled visitors, it gives a comprehensive guide to the city. The 100-page book is free of charge *(send £6 to cover printing, postage and packing).*

These organizations can recommend travel agents specializing in holidays for the handicapped, wheelchair and hand-controlled-car rental.

The Paris **Office du Tourisme** (see opposite for address) publishes comprehensive lists of hotels and sights that give full details of wheelchair accessibility.

A brief guide (in English) to facilities for disabled travelers at Roissy/Charles de Gaulle and Orly airports can be obtained, free of charge, from **Aéroports de Paris** *(291 blvd. Raspail, 75675 Paris* ☎ *43-35-70-00, map 13M7).* More than 300 rail stations have wheelchairs and mobile steps.

LOCAL PUBLICATIONS
Useful publications giving full details of current events, theaters and movie theaters, shows, sports, etc., are the weekly *Pariscope* and *l'Officiel des Spectacles.* They can be bought at most newsstands; their week runs from Wednesday to Tuesday.

MAJOR ENGLISH BOOKSTORES
Probably because of the large British and American community in Paris, there are some truly excellent, sizeable bookstores that specialize in English-language publications.

- **Abbey Bookshop**   29 rue de la Parcheminerie, 5e, map 9J9.
- **Attica**   64 rue de la Folie Méricourt, 11e, map **10**G12. Language books only.
- **Attica**   23 rue Jean-de-Beauvais, 5e, map **14**J9. Literature only.
- **Brentano's**   37 av. de l'Opéra, 2e, map **7**F7; an American accent.
- **Galignani**   224 rue de Rivoli, 1er, map **7**G7.
- **Gibert Jeune**   5 pl. St-Michel, 6e, map **8**I9.
- **Le Nouveau Quartier Latin**   78 blvd. St-Michel, 6e, map **14**K8.
- **Shakespeare and Co**.   37 rue de la Bûcherie, 5e, map **14**J9; also has regular poetry readings.
- **W.H. Smith**   248 rue de Rivoli, 1er, map **7**G7.
- **The Village Voice**   6 rue Princesse, 6e, map **14**J8; not just a bookstore — also a snug little café, where occasional readings take place.

Useful numbers and addresses

TOURIST INFORMATION

- The **Office du Tourisme et des Congrès** (convention and visitors bureau) *(127 av. des Champs-Élysées, 8ᵉ ☎ 47-23-61-72, map **5**F3. Métro: George-V)* is open all year round, 9am-8pm, but is closed on December 25 and January 1. The staff speak a number of languages and offer all kinds of information, including a hotel reservation service.

- There are branches at **Gare de Lyon**, **Gare de Montparnasse** and **Gare de l'Est** *(all open Mon-Sat 8am-9pm in summer, close at 8pm in low season)*. The **Gare du Nord** branch opens as above, but is also open Sunday 1-8pm in the summer.

  At the **Gare d'Austerlitz**, the office is open from Monday to Saturday 8am-3pm. There is an office at the **Eiffel Tower**, open daily from May to September 11am-6pm.

- **American Express Travel Service** *(11 rue Scribe, 9ᵉ ☎ 47-77-77-07, map **7**F7. Métro: Opéra)* is a valuable source of information for any traveler in need of help, advice or emergency services. A bilingual toll-free tourist advice and information service is available *(Mar-Oct Mon-Sat 8.30am-8pm ☎ 05-201-202)*.

TELEPHONE SERVICES

Tourist events (in English) ☎47-20-88-98
Speaking clock ☎36-99
Traffic report ☎48-94-33-33, if you want to speak to a person and not a recorded message
Weather ☎36-65-02-75 (Paris), 36-65-01-01 (France). Weather calls are charged at a 5-unit minimum.

MAIN POST OFFICES

For full details, see POSTAL SERVICES on page 47.
52 rue du Louvre, 1ᵉʳ ☎40-28-20-00, map **8**G9
71 av. des Champs-Élysées, 8ᵉ ☎44-13-66-00, map **6**F4

TOUR OPERATORS

The following companies run bus tours around Paris. Reservations are advised in all cases.

- **American Express**   11 rue Scribe, 9ᵉ ☎47-77-77-07, map **7**F7
- **Cityrama**   4 place des Pyramides, 1ᵉʳ ☎42-60-30-14, map **7**G7
- **Paris-Vision (France-Tourisme)**   214 rue de Rivoli, 1ᵉʳ ☎42-60-31-25, map **7**G7

GUIDES AND INTERPRETERS

- **Contact Paris**   ☎43-22-42-27.
- **Espaces et contacts**   ☎42-65-63-16.
- **Association des Guides-Interprètes et Conférenciers**   This association of guide-interpreters and speakers coordinates guides in various languages ☎47-82-24-91.

- **Club National des Guides et Couriers**   The national guides and messengers club has couriers who speak a number of foreign languages ☎42-80-01-27.

RIVER AND CANAL TRIPS

Some companies offer just the excursion, others include dinner and music. You can simply travel along the Seine or venture up the canals, and many permutations are on offer. Sightseeing by riverboat is a pleasant way to glimpse some of Paris' more unusual viewpoints.

- **Bateaux-Mouches**   Pont de l' Alma, 8ᵉ ☎42-25-96-10, map 6G4
- **Bateaux Vedettes de Paris-Île-de-France**   Port de Suffren, 7ᵉ ☎47-05-71-29, map 11I2
- **Bateaux Vedettes Parisiens Tour Eiffel**   Port de la Bourdonnais, 7ᵉ ☎47-05-50-00, map 11H3
- **Bateaux Vedettes Pont-Neuf**   Sq. du Vert-Galant, 1ᵉʳ ☎46-33-98-38, map 8I8
- **Canauxrama Canal St-Martin**   Port de l'Arsenal, 12ᵉ, to La Villette, 19ᵉ ☎42-39-15-00, map 16K12
- **Paris Canal**   Seine and Canal St-Martin: from quai Anatole France, 7ᵉ, to La Villette, 19ᵉ ☎42-40-96-97, map 7H6

AIRLINES

- **Aer Lingus**   47 av. de l'Opéra, 2ᵉ ☎47-42-12-50, map 8G8
- **Air Canada**   31 rue Falguière, 15ᵉ ☎43-20-12-00, map 13K5
- **Air France**   119 av. des Champs-Élysées, 8ᵉ ☎45-35-61-61, map 5F3
- **Air Inter**   49 av. des Champs-Élysées, 1ᵉʳ ☎42-89-38-88, map 6F4
- **British Airways**   12 rue de Castiglione, 1ᵉʳ ☎47-78-14-14, map 7G7
- **Continental**   92 av. des Champs-Élysées, 1ᵉʳ ☎42-25-31-81, map 6F4
- **Delta**   4 rue Scribe, 9ᵉ ☎47-68-92-92, map 7F7
- **TWA**   101 av. des Champs-Élysées, 8ᵉ ☎47-20-62-11, map 5F3
- **United Airlines**   34 av. de l'Opéra, 2ᵉ ☎48-97-82-82

PLACES OF WORSHIP

For information on all denominations of churches in the Paris area, contact the **Centre d'informations et documentations religieuses** located at Notre-Dame cathedral (☎ 46-33-01-01, open Mon-Fri 9am-noon, 2-6pm).

- **American Cathedral in Paris**   23 av. George-V, 8ᵉ ☎47-20-17-92, map 6G4
- **American Church in Paris**   65 quai d'Orsay, 7ᵉ ☎47-05-07-99, map 6H4
- **St George's** (Anglican)   7 rue Auguste-Vacquerie, 16ᵉ ☎47-20-22-51, map 5F3

- **St Joseph's English-speaking Catholic Church**   50 av. Hoche, 8ᵉ ☎42-27-28-56, map **5E3**
- **St Michael's English Church** (Anglican)   5 rue d'Aguesseau, 8ᵉ ☎47-42-70-88, map **7F6**
- **Scots Kirk**   17 rue Bayard, 8ᵉ ☎48-78-47-94, map **6G4**
- **Synagogue**   44 rue de la Victoire, 9ᵉ ☎45-26-95-36, map **3E8**
- **Union Liberale Israelite de France Synagogue** (English Rabbi)   24 rue Copernic, 16ᵉ ☎47-04-37-27, map **5F2**

MAJOR LIBRARIES
- **American Library in Paris**   10 rue du Général-Camou, 7ᵉ ☎45-51-46-82, map **5H3**
- **Bibliothèque Publique d'Informations**   Centre National d'Art et de Culture Georges-Pompidou, Plateau Beaubourg, 4ᵉ ☎49-55-12-33, map **9H10**
- **Bibliothèque Nationale**   4 rue Vivienne, 2ᵉ ☎47-03-81-26, map **8G8**
- **British Council Library**   11 rue Constantine, 7ᵉ ☎49-55-73-00, map **12H5**

EMBASSIES AND CONSULATES
Always contact the consulate on general matters. The embassy will deal with higher-profile, diplomatic affairs only. Unless stated, embassy and consulate are at the same address.
- **Australia**   4 rue Jean-Rey, 15ᵉ ☎40-59-33-00, map **11I2**
- **Canada**   35 av. Montaigne, 8ᵉ ☎47-23-01-01, map **6G4**
- **Ireland**   4 rue Rude, 16ᵉ ☎45-00-20-87, map **5E2**
- **Japan**   7 av. Hoche, 8ᵉ ☎47-66-02-22, map **6E4**
- **New Zealand**   7ter rue Léonard-de-Vinci, 16ᵉ ☎45-00-24-11, map **5F2**
- **United Kingdom** (embassy)   35 rue du Faubourg-St-Honoré, 8ᵉ ☎42-66-91-42, map **7F6**
- **United Kingdom** (consulate)   9 av. Hoche, 8ᵉ ☎42-66-38-10, map **6E4**
- **United States of America** (embassy)   2 av. Gabriel, 8ᵉ ☎42-96-12-02, map **7G6**
- **United States of America** (consulate)   2 rue St-Florentin, 1ᵉʳ ☎as embassy, map **7G6**. Recorded information, in English ☎40-39-84-11.

YOUTH ORGANIZATIONS
L'Acceuil des Jeunes en France *(12 rue des Barres, 4ᵉ ☎42-72-72-09, map 9I10)* looks after hostel reservations for young visitors, and can provide useful general information. It has other branches around Paris *(Gare du Nord, map 4D10; 119 rue St-Martin, 4ᵉ, map 9H10; 139 blvd. St-Michel, 5ᵉ, map 14L8)*.

Emergency information

EMERGENCY SERVICES
- **Police**   ☎17
- **Fire** *(Sapeurs pompiers)*   ☎18
- **Ambulance**   ☎15 or 43-78-26-26 (SAMU)

There is no unified ambulance service — the operator will offer you the numbers of several companies.

HOSPITALS
For information on Assistance Publique (National Health) hospitals, including tracing patients ☎40-27-30-00, 9am-5.30pm. Addresses of English-speaking hospitals are given on page 38.

MEDICAL AND DENTAL EMERGENCIES
- **Medical service**   ☎45-67-50-50 (24 hours)
- **Dental emergencies**   ☎47-07-33-68 (9am-midnight; in the 13e)

PHARMACIES
It is always possible to find out the nearest late-night pharmacy by telephoning the local *mairie* or town hall. These numbers can be found in the front pages of all telephone directories.
Late-night pharmacies *(pharmacies de garde)*
- 84 av. des Champs-Élysées, 8e ☎45-62-02-41 (24 hours), map **5F3**
- 9 pl. Pigalle, 9e ☎48-78-38-12 (9am-1am), map **3D8**

English-speaking pharmacies
- **British and American Pharmacy**   1 rue Auber, 9e, map **7F7** ☎47-42-49-40
- **Swann Pharmacy**   6 rue Castiglione, 1er ☎42-60-72-96, map **7G7**

HELP LINES
- **Samaritans** (called **SOS Help**: English-speaking) ☎47-23-80-80 *(3-11pm, all year round)*

AUTOMOBILE ACCIDENTS
- Do not admit liability or incriminate yourself.
- Ask any witness(es) to stay and give a statement.
- Contact the police.
- Exchange names, addresses, car details and insurance company details with any other drivers involved.
- In serious accidents, ask the police to contact the sheriff's clerk *(huissier)* to make out a legally acceptable account of the incident. In a dispute his report will be considered to be authoritative.

CAR BREAKDOWNS
- Put on flashing hazard warning lights and place a warning triangle 50m (55 yards) behind the car.
- If in a rented car, ring the number you have been given.

LOST PASSPORT
Contact the local *commissariat de police* and your consulate (see page 53) immediately. Commissariat numbers are listed in the front pages of any telephone directory.

LOST TRAVELERS CHECKS
Notify the local police immediately, then follow the instructions provided with your travelers checks, or contact the issuing company. Contact your consulate (see page 53) or American Express (see page 51) if you are stranded with no money.

LOST PROPERTY
If you have lost something on the street or on public transportation, go to the **Bureau des Objets Trouvés** *(36 rue des Morillons, 15ᵉ. Open Mon-Fri 9am-6pm. No information given by telephone. Métro: Convention).* Report all losses to the police.

EMERGENCY PHRASES
Help! *Au secours!*
There has been an accident. *Il y a eu un accident.*
Where is the nearest telephone? *Où se trouve le téléphone?*
Call a doctor/ambulance! *Appelez un médecin/une ambulance!*
Call the police! *Appelez la police!*

Planning your visit

When to go

The city of Paris is at its most hectic and crowded during the months of April and May and then once again during September and October. However, Paris in the spring — a cliché as old as the hills and therefore undoubtedly true — is a delight that is worth the extra hassle. The air is fresh and warm, and the light of the spring sun on the tall buildings brings their often austere beauty into sharp focus.

> When spring comes to Paris the humblest mortal alive
> must feel that he dwells in paradise.
> (Henry Miller, *Tropic Of Cancer*, 1934)

August is still the quietest month of the year, but no longer dead as it used to be when most Parisians went on their annual vacation and half the city closed down. Nowadays August is a relaxing and pleasant time to visit Paris, and very few of the museums are closed, although the choice of restaurants can be a little more restricted.

Events in the Paris calendar

It is worth considering the annual events that take place in any city, before planning your trip. You may wish to capitalize on events such as the twice-yearly round of fashion shows, or you may find it useful to avoid the period at all costs. Such events as those listed below may not always take place at exactly the same day each year, so specific details are not given. Consult the months either side of your chosen month, for events that vary their annual dates.

The **Office du Tourisme et des Congrès** (☎ *47-20-60-20)* will give further details, and have English-speaking staff. For sporting events, call **Allô Sports** (☎ *42-76-54-54).*

See also ACTIVITIES AND SPORTS for details of sporting fixtures, and PUBLIC HOLIDAYS on page 46.

JANUARY
• **Fashion shows** (summer collections): see HAUTE COUTURE in SHOPPING for addresses. • End January: **Prix d'Amérique** at Vincennes racecourse.

FEBRUARY

• End February to early March: **Five Nations Trophy** Rugby International at Parc des Princes, 16e.

MARCH

• End March or early April: **Prix du Président de la République** at Auteuil racecourse, Bois de Boulogne. • Palm Sunday to May: **Throne Fair**, Vincennes. • Mid-March to mid-May: **Spring flower shows** at the Bagatelle and Floral gardens, Bois de Boulogne. • March or April: **Les 25km de Paris**: walkathon starting at place d'Italie, 13e. • Easter week: **Foire aux Pains d'Épice** (Gingerbread Fair) in place de la Nation.

APRIL

• End April to early May: **Paris Fair** (commercial leisure exhibition) at Parc des Expositions, 15e. • April to end October: **Son et Lumière** at Hôtel des Invalides (separate versions in English and French). • April or May: **Paris international marathon**, from avenue des Champs-Élysées, 8e to avenue Foch, 16e.

MAY

• Early May to end June: **Paris Festival**, featuring opera, concerts, dance performances. • May to September (Sunday only): **Grandes Eaux Musicales**, a display of illuminated fountains at Versailles. • **Course des Garçons de Café**, a waiters' race, complete with balanced trays. Ask Office du Tourisme for details. • **La Transparisienne** themed group rally/ramble (Beaux-Arts/Nature etc) across Paris. • Mid-May to end June: **Versailles music and drama festival**. • **Festival de St-Denis** — recitals and sacred music at the basilica of St-Denis.

• May or June: **French Rugby Championship final** at Parc des Princes, 16^e. • End May to early June: **French Open Tennis Championships** at Stade Roland-Garros, 16^e. • **Boulogne-Billancourt Jazz Festival**. • End May to September: **Rose flower show** at the Bagatelle gardens, Bois de Boulogne. • May or June: **Soccer Cup Final** at Parc des Princes, 16^e.

JUNE

• Early June (odd years only): **Paris Air Show**, a display of old and new planes, at Le Bourget Airport. • Early June to mid-July: **Marais festival** with music, plays and exhibitions. • Early June to end September: **rose display** at L'Häy-les-Roses. • Mid-June: **Grand Steeplechase de Paris** at Auteuil racecourse, Bois de Boulogne.

• June 24: **Nuits de la St-Jean** in Montmartre; giant firework display in the gardens of Sacré-Coeur. • End June: **Grand Prix de Paris** at Longchamp racecourse, Bois de Boulogne. • One day in last week June: **Paris-Villages** — popular neighborhood events and processions. • End June: **National Music Day**; live events all over Paris.

JULY

• **Fashion shows** (winter collections): see *Haute couture* in SHOPPING for addresses. • Early July to end August: **Festival Musique en l'Île** — orchestral chamber music at the church of St-Louis en l'Île. • July 14: **Bastille Day**, a national holiday, celebrated with dancing, and a huge military parade along avenue des Champs-Élysées, and in the evening, a firework spectacle at Trocadéro in the 16ᵉ. • Mid to end-July: the **Tour de France** cycle race finishes in avenue des Champs-Élysées. • Mid-July to September: **Festival Estival de Paris**. Classical music concerts and recitals in all parts of the city. • Several evening dates in July and again in September: **Grande Fête de Nuit** firework spectacular at Versailles (see VERSAILLES).

SEPTEMBER

• **Festival de Montmartre**. • Early September: start of the **Tour de France des Grands-mères Automobiles** (cars built between 1905 and 1932) at place de la Concorde (tour ends there also, mid-September). • Several evening dates in September (and July): **Grande Fête de Nuit** firework spectacular at Versailles (see VERSAILLES). • Mid-September to end December: **Festival d'Automne** — concerts, plays, dance and exhibitions, all over Paris.

OCTOBER

• First Sunday: **Prix de l'Arc de Triomphe** at Longchamp race-course, Bois de Boulogne. • Early October: **Montmartre wine festival**. • Early October (even years only): **Paris auto show** at Parc des Expositions. • Early October: **Rallye Paris-Deauville**, a long-distance walking marathon, leaving from Trocadéro fountains, 16ᵉ. • October to December: **Festival d'Art Sacré** — concerts in churches; various parts of town. • End October to early November: **Paris Jazz Festival** in various concert halls and other venues. • End October-early November, leading up to All Saints' Day: **Paris Tennis Open** at Bercy, 12ᵉ. • October 1993: **Fashion collections** shown in new PALAIS DE LA MODE.

NOVEMBER

• November 11: national public holiday and **Armistice Day ceremony** held at Arc de Triomphe. • Mid-November: **Paris International Dance Festival** — classical and contemporary dance competitions. • Mid-November to Mid-December: **Paris Guitar Festival**.

DECEMBER

• During December: **Christmas decorations and illuminations** especially in and around the GRANDS BOULEVARDS, OPÉRA QUARTER, avenue Montaigne, rue Royale, avenue des Champs-Elysées, rue du Faubourg St-Honoré and Champ-de-Mars. • **Crêche de Noël** at place de l'Hôtel de Ville. • New Year's Eve: **street celebrations**, particularly in the Latin Quarter.

Organizing your time — 5 days in Paris

If your stay in Paris is only to be a short one, the way to avoid frustration and cultural indigestion is to accept that you must be selective. You cannot see Paris in two days, and our aim is to let you see enough to entice you straight back on the next boat or plane. How and what you select will inevitably be your own choice, but you will find here some suggested full-day programs for a five-day visit, for you to adapt to suit your taste and timetable. Consult the lists on pages 100-101, which detail the full range of sights. If you have enough energy for more than just a good meal at the end of the day, turn to the chapter on ENTERTAINMENTS for some ideas.

If you have more time, the programs below will give you the basis for more detailed explorations of each area. The CLASSIFIED LIST OF SIGHTS groups all the sights into themes — helpful if you want to explore a favorite topic in depth. Unmissable sights are coded ★

There are also various suggested WALKS (see page 86-90), and whole-day EXCURSIONS to a number of places including VERSAILLES and EURODISNEY near the end of the book.

DAY ONE — an overview; a taste of Paris ancient and modern

- Morning: head E to the ancient quarter of the MARAIS, passing through PLACE DES VOSGES to the GRAND CARNAVALET museum, which gives a splendid overview of the history of Paris. Then walk W, to see the gigantic, over-modern POMPIDOU CENTER. Have lunch either in this area or continue toward the FORUM DES HALLES, which merits time for exploration. There are shops and museums, to be sure, but stand back and see the Forum for what it is — a late 20thC reinterpretation of a model of 19thC engineering.
- Afternoon: cross the SEINE via the PONT-NEUF, Paris' oldest bridge, and turn onto the ÎLE DE LA CITÉ. You walk past the PALAIS DE JUSTICE, the SAINTE-CHAPELLE and the gloomy CONCIERGERIE. Stop and visit one, if you have time, or head straight on for NOTRE-DAME, which deserves a full visit including an envigorating trip up the tower and the CRYPTE ARCHÉOLOGIQUE.
- Evening: if you can take any more, the LATIN QUARTER is just across the river. Here you can find a wide choice of places to dine, perhaps on the BOULEVARD ST-GERMAIN.

DAY TWO — a day of views

- Morning: start at a point of your choosing on the AVENUE DES CHAMPS-ÉLYSÉES and ascend the ARC DE TRIOMPHE for a view down the grandest axis in the city. Then take the métro from Charles-de-Gaulle-Étoile to Champ-de-Mars and go up the TOUR EIFFEL, perhaps having lunch in one of its restaurants.
- Afternoon: awaiting you, a direct choice: a leisurely boat trip up the SEINE or a further walk through the stately CHAMP-DE-MARS toward the HÔTEL DES INVALIDES where you might visit the MUSÉE DE L'ARMÉE, the DÔME church and Napoleon's tomb. The MUSÉE RODIN is also close by.

• Evening: many restaurants are to be found around the rue du Bac/boulevard St-Germain area.

DAY THREE — another overview . . . and Montmartre

• Whole day: start early and take in PARISTORIC off boulevard des Batignolles. This charming but not over-long cinematic presentation will fill you with images of Paris that you may want to pursue, as it traces the history of Paris through a series of dazzling scenes. Head then for nearby MONTMARTRE, where the whole day can be spent exploring the many streets, squares, museums, cafés, and of course, the basilica of SACRÉ-COEUR. A number of sensations await you, including the short trip up the *Butte* on the funicular railway, the little tourist train around the *quartier* and the view from the top of the basilica. Add this view to your collection.

DAY FOUR — the Left Bank

• Morning: begin at PLACE DE LA CONCORDE and take a stroll through the TUILERIES gardens. Cross the SEINE at the little Pont Solférino and spend the morning in the MUSÉE D'ORSAY — a chance to experience the world of 19thC art in a gloriously converted railway station. Have lunch at the museum.
• Afternoon: take off along the boulevard St-Germain, to explore the ST-GERMAIN QUARTER. Browse around the antique stores in rue Jacob, visit the church of ST-GERMAIN-DES-PRÉS, take coffee in Les Deux Magots on the boulevard, or head back toward rue de Seine to look at the many art galleries there.
• Evening: stay for dinner. The choice of restaurants is almost endless.

DAY FIVE — saving the best till last

• Morning: a visit to the LOUVRE has to be started early. Plan to spend at least half a day, but don't expect to see more than a few highlights. Even if you don't go inside, spend a few minutes in the courtyard around the extraordinary new glass-and-steel pyramid, for an insight into the dynamism of the new French approach to architecture. Eat lunch at the museum.
• Afternoon: leave via the PALAIS-ROYAL and walk up avenue de l'Opéra toward the thrilling OPÉRA GARNIER, the former opera house that is now dedicated to dance. Try to find time to take a guided tour, for a glorious glimpse of the 19thC opulence within. Spend some time shopping in the OPÉRA QUARTER, or head E toward the GRANDS BOULE-VARDS along boulevard des Italiens. In boulevard Haussmann are the city's two major department stores, **Au Printemps** and **Galeries Lafayette**, as well as many other opportunities to take home some gifts or souvenirs.

Alternatively, head another 5 minutes farther E, to reach Passage Jouffroy and Passage des Panoramas on boulevard Montmartre. Here you will find a quaint collection of small shops selling every-thing from antiquarian books to fine walking sticks. If you have an hour to spare, visit the MUSÉE GRÉVIN, a splendid, high-class waxwork museum full of characters from France's past and the world's present. (Will Michael Jackson still be there in 1994? And what about George Bush?) Its *Belle Époque* decor is dazzling.

- Evening: eat dinner somewhere truly special on your last night in town, remembering to reserve ahead. Consult our restaurant recommendations in WHERE TO EAT, making your choice according to the location of your hotel. Consider having a romantic meal on one of the boats on the Seine (but reserve ahead for this).

WHAT ELSE?

- Much of "new" Paris is tremendously exciting. Only the Louvre pyramid is mentioned above because much of New Paris is spread out in places that do not fit conveniently into concentrated "day" visits. See NEW PARIS on page 31 to choose which elements you can find a way to see.

The last time I see Paris will be on the day I die.
The city was inexhaustible, and so is its memory.
(Elliot Paul, *The Last Time I Saw Paris,* 1942)

The districts of Paris

Arrondissements and quartiers

Paris is a compact city bounded by a ring road (beltway), the Périphérique, and divided into 20 administrative districts *(arrondissements)*. Each *arrondissement* has its own style and character — say the word *"seizième"* to a Parisian, and he will conjure up an image of a certain urban ambience and life-style; he will even hear a special accent. Within the *arrondissements,* and often overlapping them, are *quartiers* (quarters), such as MONTMARTRE, MONTPARNASSE and the LATIN QUARTER. This seeming inconsistency stems from the arranging of the *arrondissement* boundaries by Napoleon III, whose intention was to split existing villages to lessen their revolutionary tendencies.

The SEINE divides the city into **Rive Droite** (Right Bank) and **Rive Gauche** (Left Bank) with the two islands, ÎLE DE LA CITÉ and ÎLE ST-LOUIS, in the middle. The Right Bank is conspicuous by its affluence and smartness and its high concentration of imposing buildings, large shops, museums and theaters. The districts of bright lights (and red ones) are also mostly concentrated on the Right Bank. The Left Bank has its share of fine buildings and some dazzle, but on the whole its charm is more subtle, romantic and Bohemian.

From a visitor's point of view, the districts of greatest interest are the 1er to the 9e, with a few pockets in outlying places. Much of this central area is superb walking territory. The districts on the outskirts beyond the *Périphérique* do not belong to Paris proper, except for the BOIS DE BOULOGNE and BOIS DE VINCENNES, but there are places of interest, such as LA DÉFENSE, the FLEA MARKET at Clignancourt, and ST-DENIS basilica.

IDENTIFYING THE ARRONDISSEMENTS; POSTAL CODES

On maps and in common usage, the twenty *arrondissements* are shown by a numeral followed by the superior letter ^{er} or ^{e} representing *premier, deuxième, troisième* etc. The 1er is in the center, and the numbers are allocated in a spiral that works outward in a clockwise direction. See the ORIENTATION MAP on the following pages.

Postal codes are easy to decipher. In postal addresses, the number of the *arrondissement* is preceded by the Paris code **750**, giving a 5-figure postal code — for example the 9e is 75009, the 18e is 75018. The postal code precedes the word **Paris** and is generally written "75009 – Paris."

The following list describes briefly the most significant *quartiers,* with their corresponding, often overlapping *arrondissements*

OPÉRA QUARTER *(part of 1ᵉʳ, 2ᵉ and 9ᵉ; maps 7 & 8)*. An area of grand architecture, smart shops and highbrow culture. Glossy and expensive, but somewhat fraying at the edges.

LES GRANDS BOULEVARDS *(part of 9ᵉ and 10ᵉ; maps 3, 7 & 8)*. Just E of the smart Opéra quarter; strong magnet for shoppers, with a good range of restaurants, hotels and cafés. The big cinemas are on the boundary of the 9ᶜ and 10ᶜ.

LES HALLES *(part of 1ᵉʳ; map 9)*. An exhilaratingly revitalized area following massive redevelopment; shops, restaurants, sights cultural and otherwise, and the FORUM itself.

LE MARAIS *(3ᵉ and part of 4ᵉ; maps 9 & 10)*. An old, gracious district, now very fashionable. Blessed with many fine 17thC mansions *(hôtels)*, museums, narrow rambling streets, and a strong flavor of the past.

ÎLE DE LA CITÉ AND ÎLE ST-LOUIS *(part of 1ᵉʳ and 4ᵉ; maps 9 & 10)*. The first is the historic heart of Paris containing the CONCIERGERIE, PALAIS DE JUSTICE, SAINTE CHAPELLE and NOTRE-DAME. Busy and touristic. The Île St-Louis, by contrast, is charming, quiet and residential.

LATIN QUARTER *(5ᵉ; map 14)*. This area, originally known as the Université, has remained the learned quarter of Paris. Youthful, cosmopolitan, colorful, Bohemian, with a large student population.

ST-GERMAIN *(6ᵉ and part of 7ᵉ; maps 7 & 8 and 13 & 14)*. A quarter with a wide boulevard, tiny side streets, old buildings, and a thriving café life. Intellectual, artistic and elegant.

MONTPARNASSE *(straddling 14ᵉ and 15ᵉ; map 13)*. Cosmopolitan, former Bohemian colony, torn apart by redevelopment, but retaining some of its old character.

EIFFEL TOWER, LES INVALIDES AND ENVIRONS *(remainder of 7ᵉ; maps 11 & 12)*. Quiet, mainly residential area dominated by the axes of the CHAMP-DE-MARS and HÔTEL DES INVALIDES complex.

PALAIS DE CHAILLOT AND ENVIRONS *(16ᵉ; map 11)*. Cluster of museums set in an opulent residential *arrondissement*.

AVENUE DES CHAMPS-ÉLYSÉES AND RUE DU FAUBOURG-ST-HONORÉ *(8ᵉ; maps 5 & 6)*. Busy with tourists, businesspeople, professional workers; expensive, classy stores; embassies.

PARC DE MONCEAU AND ENVIRONS *(straddles 8ᵉ and 17ᵉ; map 1)*. Stolid and residential.

MONTMARTRE *(18ᵉ; map 3)*. Often referred to as the "Butte;" location of the SACRÉ-COEUR basilica. Rambling, picture-postcard quaintness, side by side with neon-lit but shabby razzle-dazzle.

BELLEVILLE/MÉNILMONTANT *(straddling 19ᵉ and 20ᵉ)*. Its former dilapidated charm now largely eroded by redevelopment. Strong North African flavor. Notable mainly for PÈRE LACHAISE cemetery.

BASTILLE/BERCY *(12ᵉ; map 16)*. Both areas transformed by redevelopment. The Opéra Bastille now complete; the works at Bercy will add the Cité du Vin et d'Alimentaire and the American Center to the recent Palais Omnisports and the Ministère des Finances.

TOLBIAC *(13ᵉ; map 16)*. An area of little distinction until now has suddenly become the focus of attention, as the swathe of land below the Gare d'Austerlitz reemerges to house the TGB (Bibliothèque de France).

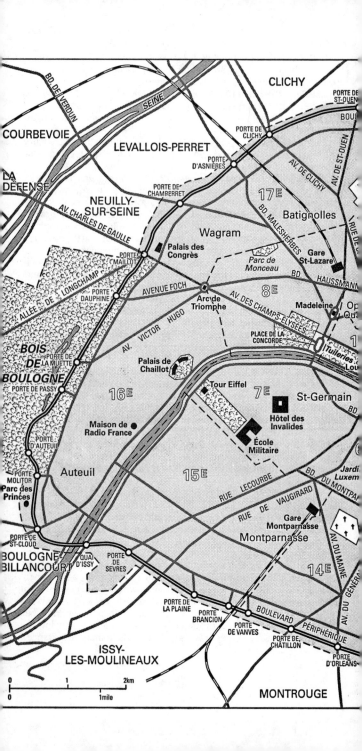

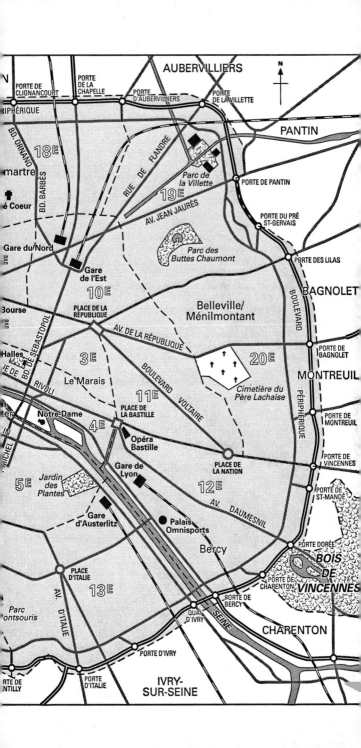

The *quartiers*

Not all of Paris falls conveniently under a well-known area name and by no means all the important sights are to be found within these areas. Nevertheless, the *quartiers* described below are those that deserve to be visited in their own right. The spirit of each of these places — their past, their present or their future — will provide as much satisfaction as can be gained by entering a particular building.

BERCY
In the 12ᵉ, to the E of the Bastille and the Gare de Lyon, on the Right Bank. Map 16M13. Métro: Bercy
This formerly run-down docklands quarter has been undergoing major surgery since 1989, following a government plan to revitalize the E of the city as it had in the W at LA DÉFENSE. The first improvement to this part of Paris was the OPÉRA BASTILLE, completed in 1990. In the second phase, the new **Parc de Bercy** will extend SE from the **Palais Omnisports**, covering what was once an area of old wine warehouses. By 1993-4, the transformation of the old ENTREPÔTS DE BERCY into a center of French wines and gastronomy *(Cité du Vin et d'Alimentaire)* will be complete.

The AMERICAN CENTER, a cultural center serving the American community and all Americanophiles, will be open by midsummer 1993, in an interesting new building designed by American architect Frank Gehry (see picture on page 32), next door to the Palais Omnisports. It currently runs its program of events and classes from temporary premises nearby.

The **Pavillons de Bercy**, warehouses that have been designated as listed buildings, will accommodate major exhibitions, a conference center and a **museum of wines and gastronomy**, using an architectural style that remains in keeping with the original ideas of the architect LHeureux in 1897. The area will also incorporate two hotels, a number of brasseries, restaurants and wine-bars, a cinema, and a park with lakes and mini-vineyards.

Another of the new developments in Bercy was the Ministry of Finance, which relocated in 1989 from its offices in a wing of the LOUVRE to a bold and often-criticized new building that straddles the road and has its feet in the water. The new **TGB-Bibliothèque de France**, due for completion in 1995, will be located at Tolbiac on the opposite bank of the Seine.

A new bridge across the Seine will eventually be constructed at this point, as well as two new Métro stations.

LA DÉFENSE
To the NW of Paris. Map 17C3. RER: La Défense.
This vast commercial and residential complex, lying beyond the river to the NW of Paris, has been nicknamed "Manhattan-sur-Seine." Certainly it has the brutality but arguably less style than "Manhattan-sur-Hudson." Begun in the 1960s, it dominates the western horizon of the city with its growing cluster of skyscrapers.

The monolithic marble-covered cube of the GRANDE ARCHE at 90m (295ft) high draws all eyes on the western end of La Défense. Through the two verticals of the arch, as wide across as the avenue des Champs-Élysées, the dramatic W-E alignment of La Défense with the ARC DE TRIOMPHE and the LOUVRE comes into sharp focus.

The main zone of La Défense focuses on a 1.2km-long ($\frac{3}{4}$ mile) podium running approximately W-E and descending toward the Seine in a series of terraces laid out with trees. On the S side, the prospect contains a brutal Joan Miró sculpture, *Les Deux Personnages,* which is painted in primary colors. Opposite stands Calder's giant red mobile.

The forest of glass, steel and concrete surrounding the podium includes such buildings as the spectacular **CNIT**, a vast three-cornered hall that forms a flamboyant showcase for new technologies and includes the **World Trade Center**, and **Les Quatre Temps**, the largest shopping center in Europe with a floor space twice the area of all the shops in avenue des Champs-Élysées. Soaring skyscrapers rise on every side, many of them the headquarters of French multinational companies.

From the western end of the podium there is a view of the outlying town of **Nanterre** and its bizarre apartment buildings painted in splotches of gray, blue, brown and green as though camouflaged.

La Défense is a symbol of the aggressive prosperity that has overtaken France in the past 25 years. Despite its multitude of amenities, many find it a place that dwarfs and crushes the spirit, although others are inspired by its vast scale and commercial drama. Crucially, in Paris, modern man's desire to build such structures has been concentrated into one area well away from the center.

GRANDS BOULEVARDS

To the E of the Opéra quarter, in the 9ᵉ and 10ᵉ. Map 7F7-10G11. Métro: Opéra, Madeleine, Rue Montmartre, Bonne-Nouvelle, Strasbourg-St-Denis, République.

Les Grands Boulevards is the name given to the string of boulevards extending from the churches of ST-AUGUSTIN and LA MADELEINE in the W to place de la République in the E — namely the boulevards Haussmann, Capucines, Italiens, Montmartre, Poissonnière, Bonne-Nouvelle, St-Denis and St-Martin.

They were constructed under Louis XIV to replace an obsolete line of fortifications, and soon became known just as "the Boulevards." In the mid-18thC, the boulevards became elegant and fashionable places to live, but the main stretch from boulevard Montmartre to place de la République has long since become rather tawdry, made interesting only by the rather incongruous presence of the PORTES ST-DENIS and ST-MARTIN, two glorious triumphal arches erected in the 1670s to commemorate the military victories of Louis XIV.

> It is a pleasant thing to walk along the boulevards and see
> how men live in Paris. One man has live snakes crawling
> about him and sells soap and essences. Another sells books
> which lie upon the ground. Another under my window all day
> offers a gold chain. Half a dozen walk up and down

with some dozen walking sticks under the arm. A little further,
one sells cane tassels at 5 sous. Here sits Boots
brandishing his brush at every dirty shoe. Then you pass
several tubs of gold fish. Then a man sitting at his table
cleaning gold and silver spoons with emery
and haranguing the passengers on its virtues.
Then a person who cuts profiles with scissors —
'Shall be happy to cut yours, Sir'.
Then a table of card puppets which are made to crawl
then a hand organ . . . then a flower merchant.
Then a bird shop with 20 parrots, 4 swans, hawks and nightingales.
All of these are the mere boutiques on the sidewalk, moved about
from place to place as the sun or rain or the crowd may lead them.
(Ralph Waldo Emerson, *Journals,* July 1833)

The presence of Paris' major department stores, **Galeries Lafayette**
and **Au Printemps**, has made the triangle bounded by boulevard Haussmann in the N a focal point for stores offering quality goods, and it is to
this part of town that you should make one intensive shopping foray.

If you find yourself in need of a rest while shopping, head for the
tranquil square around the CHAPELLE EXPIATOIRE, to the W of the *Grands
Magasins* in the direction of ST-AUGUSTIN. Or visit one of the excellent
cafés within the big stores.

Boulevards Montmartre and Poissonnière have shifted their emphasis
away from shopping toward entertainment. In this part of town there are
a number of large movie theaters showing new film releases, including
the **Grand Rex**, a rightly famous pile built along classic Art Deco lines.
There are also several notable theaters along this stretch of the boulevard,
the **Théâtre des Variétés**, the **Théâtre des Nouveautés** and the
Théâtre du Gymnase. (See PERFORMING ARTS.)

LES HALLES

*In the center, to the NE of the Louvre, in the 1er. Map 9H9. Métro: Les Halles,
Châtelet-Les-Halles.*

This area of the city is bounded roughly by rue Étienne-Marcel and RUE
DE RIVOLI to the N and S, with the BOURSE DU COMMERCE and the POMPIDOU
CENTER marking the W and E boundaries. The FORUM DES HALLES is in the
natural center.

During the 12thC the area became a bustling food market (Zola called
it "the belly of Paris") and it remained so until 1979, when the traders all
moved to a huge new site at Rungis, near the airport at Orly, taking the
atmosphere with them and leaving the city of Paris with the problem of
deciding what to do with the area.

The following years saw a total transformation. The graceful old
glass-and-iron market hall, built under Napoleon III, was torn down and
the ensuing hole in the ground was replaced by a commercial complex,
the FORUM DES HALLES. These were radical changes, but the *quartier*
adjusted to a new role as a center of entertainment, shopping and culture.

Some of the old buildings have been renovated; the 16thC **Fontaine**

des Innocents *(pl. Joachim du Bellay)* has been restored, and much of the area has been pedestrianized. The old market has mostly disappeared and the renovation or rebuilding genie has swept through. There remain a few food merchants, and a number of characterful bars and restaurants, including PHARAMOND (see WHERE TO EAT), a glory of Art Nouveau decorative tiles and AU PIED DE COCHON (the haven for lovers of shellfish and pigs' feet) on the one hand, and CAFÉ COSTES (see CAFÉS), flagship of Postmodern designer Philippe Starck, on the other.

ÎLE DE LA CITÉ AND ÎLE ST-LOUIS ★
1er and 4e. Maps 9 & 10. Métro: Cité, Pont Marie.

The Île de la Cité floats in the Seine like a graceful galleon carrying more than 2,000 years of history as its cargo, for it was here that Paris began, when the tribe known as the Parisii settled on the island, in the 3rdC. Trailing behind it is the smaller and less heavily laden Île St-Louis.

Île de la Cité

A visit to the CRYPTE ARCHÉOLOGIQUE in the square in front of NOTRE-DAME takes the visitor back to the Île de la Cité's earliest times, and the different stages of settlement can be seen in layers. Another good place to begin is the little garden on a spit of land at the N end of the Îles approached by a stairway from the PONT-NEUF.

On the other side of the bridge, where the island begins to widen out, is a charming little triangular square, **place Dauphine**, which André Breton describes in his novel Nadja as "one of the most profoundly secluded places I know." Farther on, straddling the width of the island and bounded by boulevard du Palais, is the vast historic complex containing the PALAIS DE JUSTICE, the SAINTE CHAPELLE and the CONCIERGERIE. Across the boulevard is the rather forbidding **Préfecture de Police**, headquarters of the immortal Inspector Clouseau, offset by the **flower market** in place Louis Lépine, which becomes, on Sunday, a colorful **bird market**.

The focal point of the island is the **place du Parvis-Notre-Dame**, crowned by NOTRE-DAME cathedral and bounded on the N side by the **Hôtel-Dieu** hospital, the foundations of which date from the 7thC. A riverside walk leads round the S side of the cathedral to the garden of **square de l'Île de France**, at the E tip of the island. At the very end is the **Mémorial de la Déportation**, an underground vault commemorating the French victims of the concentration camps. Its stark simplicity conveys solemnity, dignity and compassion.

Immediately to the N of the cathedral lies a cluster of streets, including **rue Chanoinesse**. The name of this street derives from the canons of Notre-Dame whose houses used to line the street. Only two of these, #22 and #24, remain — they date from the 16thC, but there are many fine facades belonging to later periods.

Off rue Chanoinesse is **rue de la Colombe**, where the line of the old Gallo-Roman wall is traced in the cobblestones. Continue N to **quai aux**

Fleurs; there are no flowers here, but of interest are two stone heads over the doorways of #9 and #11. These represent the ill-fated lovers Abelard and Héloïse, who lived in a house on the spot in the 12thC. The quai aux Fleurs leads E from here to the **pont St-Louis**, linking the two islands. From the bridge there is a fine view of the lacework of flying buttresses and spires at the eastern end of Notre-Dame.

Île St-Louis

The Île St-Louis, named after Louis IX of France, has a different and quieter atmosphere from its neighbor, being more private and picturesque. Many of the fine houses have remained intact. Two of the finest are the **Hôtel de Lausun** *(17 quai d'Anjou)* — admire the magnificent drainpipes — and the **Hôtel Lambert** *(1-3 quai d'Anjou)*, both designed by Louis XIV's architect Le Vau. The former can be visited by application to the Town Hall (☎ 42-77-40-40).

The island is an architectural feast and also the town's first real-estate development, built as a unit in the 17thC. All along the river-front are houses with stately porticos and interesting stone carving, many of them also bearing plaques commemorating the distinguished men who lived there — aristocrats, politicians, artists, poets. The poet Baudelaire lived at #22 quai de Béthune. The scientist Marie Curie lived at #36 quai d'Orléans from 1912 until her death in 1934.

In the 19thC, the house at #6 quai d'Orléans was a meeting place for expatriate Polish artists and writers and today is the **Adam Mickiewicz Museum** (☎ 43-54-35-61 ▣ *Open Thurs 3-6pm or by appointment; closed hols)*, named after the man who is considered to be the Polish Dante. It contains the mementoes of his life and of other famous Poles such as Chopin. There is also a library and a fine collection of pictures by French as well as Polish artists.

The spine of the island is **rue St-Louis-en-l'Île**, with its **church** of the same name, built between 1664-1725 and marked by a curious pierced spire and an ornate wrought-iron clock. The street is full of little shops and restaurants, many with old and interesting frontages. At #35 is the tiny bookstore **Librairie Ulysse**, which specializes in rare second-hand as well as new travel books. Two doors away, at #31, is **Berthillon**, one of the best ice cream shops in Europe, with a constant line of customers outside to prove it. (A newer branch, **La Flore en L'Île** *(2 rue Jean du Bellay)*, is at the western tip opposite the pont St-Louis.)

For those who prefer a cup of tea, there is the **Salon de Thé St-Louis** at #81, where no fewer than 54 varieties are served. Devotees of beer might be interested in the **Brasserie de l'Île St-Louis**, beside the pont St-Louis. Much frequented by rugby-playing types, especially Englishmen, it has the boisterously convivial atmosphere of an Alsatian beer hall.

But the Île St-Louis is mostly a peaceful place, with its quiet streets, and a tree-lined riverside walk runs around most of the island. Its little park, **sq. Barye**, at the E end, has a tiny play area for small children where parents can sit and read peacefully.

The **quays** that line the banks of the Seine on either side of the Île de la Cité and Île St-Louis afford some superb views (◀≦) of the islands and of Notre-Dame. Particularly magnificent are the riverscape views from pont des Arts, sq. René Viviani, pont de l'Archevêché, pont de la Tournelle and pont de Sully on the Left Bank, and quai de la Mégisserie and quai des Célestins on the Right Bank.

The parapets of the quays are lined with stalls (the famous *bouquinistes*), selling second-hand books, especially along the Left Bank (see SHOPPING).

LATIN QUARTER ★
On the Left Bank, between Île de la Cité and the Jardin du Luxembourg, in the 5ᵉ.
Map 14. Métro: St-Michel, Cluny-La-Sorbonne, Maubert-Mutualité, Cardinal-Lemoine.
The name *Quartier Latin* carries with it the image of a way of life: colorful, vibrant, rebellious, Bohemian and, above all, cosmopolitan. The Latin Quarter lies at the heart of the Left Bank and comprises most of the 5ᵉ and a sliver of the 6ᵉ districts, taking in the streets immediately to the W of the **boulevard St-Michel**.

Its name derives from the presence of the SORBONNE university and other colleges in the district, the scholars of which formerly spoke Latin. The area is still full of students, not only from the Sorbonne but also from the neighboring COLLÈGE DE FRANCE, the university of Jussieu a little farther to the E and the École Normale Supérieure to the S.

The term Latin Quarter is doubly appropriate, for the area now called the **Montagne Ste-Geneviève**, around the PANTHÉON, was once the focal point of the Roman colony. Although the governor had his palace on the ÎLE DE LA CITÉ, it was *here* that the forum, temple and baths were built. Virtually the only Roman remains to be seen in Paris are the great thermal baths at the THERMES DE CLUNY museum and in the ARÈNES DE LUTÈCE.

The main artery of the Latin Quarter is boulevard St-Michel, or **Boul'Mich** as it is known by all. This busy tree-lined thoroughfare, full of bookstores and cafés, rises at the S end of the JARDINS DU LUXEMBOURG gardens and descends S toward the Seine into place St-Michel, which is dominated by the huge St-Michel fountain.

The Boul'Mich is intersected by the other great artery of the Left Bank, **boulevard St-Germain**. At their junction is the MUSÉE NATIONAL DU MOYEN ÂGE/THERMES DE CLUNY, in the Flamboyant Gothic Hôtel de Cluny, one of many architectural riches in the district. Here, too, is the refurbished Métro station of Cluny-La-Sorbonne, which at track level boasts the signatures of literary giants from across the centuries, spread across its vast mosaic-and-ceramic ceiling.

Turn up rue Soufflot and you will be confronted by the massive facade of the repository of France's greatest men, the PANTHÉON, standing on the Montagne Ste-Geneviève. Behind it to the left is the exquisite church of ST-ETIENNE-DU-MONT and to the left, the **Ste-Geneviève library**, built in the mid-19thC on the site of the medieval Montaigu college. Behind it in rue Clotilde is the **Lycée Henri IV**, the buildings of which incorporate the refectory and belfry of the old abbey of Ste-Geneviève.

There are three other important churches in the area: ST-SÉVERIN, ST-JULIEN-LE-PAUVRE and **St-Nicolas-du-Chardonnet**; the latter is the stronghold of traditional Catholics, and still holds Mass in Latin.

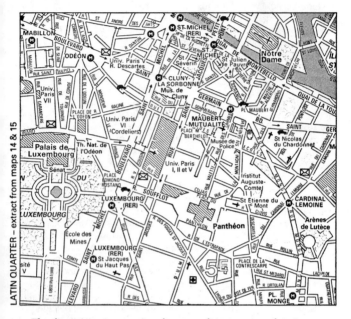

The district's main attraction, however, lies not so much in its monuments as in the tortuous streets that twist around each other along the riverbank. The strongest impression of the cosmopolitan Bohemian life comes from the streets around St-Séverin and St-Julien-le-Pauvre. Here are restaurants of many nationalities, small bookstores, intimate little cafés, nightclubs and experimental cinemas.

The pedestrian zone of **rue de la Huchette** and its tributaries is particularly full of color and atmosphere. Leading off rue de la Huchette is the amusingly named **rue du Chat-qui-Pêche** (Street of the Fishing Cat), said to be the smallest street in Paris.

A stone's throw to the E *(37 rue de la Bûcherie)* is one of the most enticing bookstores in the city, **Shakespeare and Co**, which specializes in English-language material, both new and second-hand. Between the wars, Sylvia Beach owned the original Shakespeare and Co at 12 rue de l'Odéon, which was the meeting place of expatriate literati such as James Joyce, Ezra Pound, Henry Miller and Ernest Hemingway. Eventually it was reincarnated in its present location by a genial American, George Whitman, who still runs the place with great verve, and from time to time accommodates penniless writers in rooms above the shop.

In the Latin Quarter one senses fewer barriers than in many other districts; the area seems to offer an invitation to anyone that goes there, to participate in its life. No doubt this is because of the presence of so many nationalities and so many students.

LE MARAIS ★

3ᵉ and 4ᵉ. Maps **9** & **10**. *Métro: Hôtel-de-Ville, St-Paul, Chemin-Vert, Temple, St-Sébastien-Froissart, Filles-du-Calvaire, Arts-et-Métiers, Rambuteau.*

This fascinating district has a grave beauty that is haunting, powerful and peculiarly un-Parisian. The stamp of the Middle Ages is still firmly imprinted on the narrow, huddled streets, lined by venerable houses built in the 16th-18thC.

The name means "marshland," and this is what the area was, until in the 12thC it was drained by the Knights Templar. It became the site of many other religious communities that have since disappeared but bequeathed their names to certain streets: rue des Blancs-Manteaux, rue des Filles-du-Calvaire, rue Ste-Croix-de-la-Bretonnerie. The Knights' fortress, the Temple, became a prison during the Revolution, and it was here that the royal family was held. Today nothing remains of the building. The site, lying at the N of the Marais, is now a charming and secluded little park, the **sq. du Temple**.

In the 15thC, the Marais had begun to be a fashionable residential district for the aristocracy, and by the 17thC it had reached its heyday, abounding in gracious mansions of the kind that became the model for the traditional French *hôtel,* with a courtyard at the front and a formal garden at the back. There are more mansions remaining in the Marais than in any other district of Paris. By the early 18thC, the nobility began to move W to the Faubourg-St-Germain. The Marais became less favored and thereby began a gradual decline, which lasted until De Gaulle's Minister of Culture, André Malraux, made it a conservation area in 1962, just in time to save it from wholesale redevelopment. Since that time, a restoration program has uncovered many treasures.

Not surprisingly, the Marais possesses what is claimed to be the oldest house in Paris, **3 rue Volta**, built in about 1300, and also the second oldest, **51 rue de Montmorency**, built in 1407 as a charitable lodging house. The house is now a restaurant. Near rue Volta is the **Quartier du Temple**, which includes the MUSÉE NATIONAL DES TECHNIQUES (Technological Museum) and the church of ST-NICOLAS-DES-CHAMPS.

This northern part of the Marais also boasts, to the W, the ARCHIVES NATIONALES and MUSÉE DE L'HISTOIRE DE FRANCE, housed in the outstanding **Hôtel de Soubise** and **Hôtel de Rohan**, and, to the E, the GRAND CARNAVALET museum, which occupies two adjoining mansions, the **Hôtel de Carnavalet** and the **Hôtel Le Peletier St-Fargeau**. Just to the N of the Archives Nationales, in rue des Archives, is another notable feature, the **Hôtel de Guénégaud des Brosses**, now housing the MUSÉE DE LA CHASSE, a quietly harmonious Mansart building.

Around the GRAND CARNAVALET is a wealth of beautiful *hôtels*. Best known are the **Hôtel Libéral-Bruand** in rue de la Perle, and the **Hôtel Salé** in rue de Thorigny, which is the home of the MUSÉE PICASSO.

Also worth a detour in nearby rue de Turenne are the **Hôtel de Montrésor**, now a school, and the **Hôtel du Grand-Veneur**, former home of the master of the royal hunt. The facade is adorned with a boar's head and other symbols of hunting; inside, the impressive staircase is decorated with trophies *(ask the caretaker, if you wish to visit)*. Farther

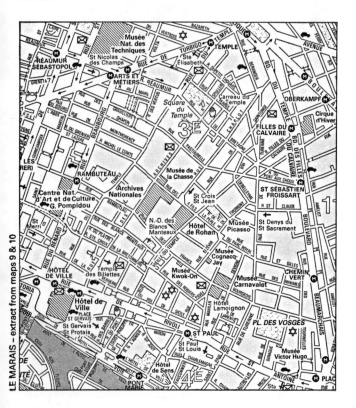

along the street is **St-Denys-du-Sacrement**, built in 1835 in the Roman style, which contains a *Deposition* by Delacroix.

An itinerary

Beginning at the Seine, a short itinerary takes in some of the southern part of the Marais' most interesting features. Just E of the HÔTEL DE VILLE is the church of **St-Gervais-St-Protais**. A Gothic building with a superb Classical facade, it contains some fine works of art, including lovely stained glass, and, in the N transept, a Flemish *Passion* painted on wood. Walk down to the river and along to the HÔTEL DES AR-CHEVÊQUES DE SENS, one of the oldest mansions in the city and now in use by the City of Paris as the **Bibliothèque Forney** *(open Tues-Fri 1.30-8.30pm, Sat 10am-8.30pm)*. Continue E for a short distance, then turn N up rue des Jardins-St-Paul, off which an archway to the right leads into the **Village St-Paul** *(closed Tues, Wed)*, a huddle of tiny craft studios and *bric-a-brac*-style antique stores.

Twisting N, turn left at rue St-Antoine to visit the church of **St-Paul-St-**

Louis, built in the Jesuit style in the 17thC. Return down rue St-Antoine to the 17thC **Hôtel de Sully** *(#62),* which is now the headquarters of the administration of national monuments and where temporary exhibitions on architecture and conservation are held. There is a particularly fine inner courtyard, and the interior contains paneling and painted ceilings *(interior open Sat-Sun* 🎦 *ⵌ).* Turn up rue de Birague into the graceful red-brick expanse of PLACE DES VOSGES. Leave it by the NW corner and walk W down **rue des Francs-Bourgeois** to the corner of rue Pavée (on the left) and the **Hôtel de Lamoignon,** now the Paris Historical Library *(open Mon-Sat 9.30am-6pm),* with its curious little corner tower jutting out over the sidewalk. The courtyard and building are of majestic proportions, the facade divided by tall Corinthian pilasters.

Opposite is the CARNAVALET museum and beyond it, up rue Payenne, is **sq. Georges-Cain,** a magical little oasis of a garden, full of intriguing fragments of sculpture. In the same street are two interesting buildings, the **Hôtel de Chatillon,** at #13, and the **Hôtel de Polastron-Polignac,** next door. At #8 rue Elzévir (the next street along, which runs parallel with rue Payenne) is the COGNACQ-JAY museum.

Retrace your steps to the Hôtel de Lamoignon, walk S down rue Pavée and immediately right into the area which for centuries has been a **Jewish quarter.** In this street, rue des Rosiers, and in rue des Écouffes (the second street on the left) and nearby streets, synagogues, kosher food stores and Hebrew booksellers abound.

At the end of rue des Rosiers, turn right into rue Vieille-du-Temple. At #47 is the **Hôtel des Ambassadeurs de Hollande** *(not open to the public),* one of the finest mansions in the Marais and once the home of Beaumarchais, who wrote the *Marriage of Figaro* there. Next left, on the street of the same name, is the graceful little church of **Notre-Dame-des-Blancs-Manteaux,** with its ornate Flemish wooden pulpit. Opposite the church is the attractive **rue Aubriot,** dating from the Middle Ages.

Continue past the church to the next intersection and turn left down the rue des Archives. Glimpse, down the first street on the right (the rue du Plâtre), the brilliant primary colors of the Pompidou Center. The rue des Archives has the curious nickname of "the street where God was boiled." The name dates from 1290, when a moneylender was said to have cut up a host (communion bread) with a knife. To his surprise the host began to bleed, whereupon he threw it into boiling water, which immediately turned red. The unfortunate man was apprehended and burned at the stake, and soon afterward a church was built on the site of his house to commemorate the miracle.

Around this church the monastery of Carmes-Billettes grew up in the 14thC. The **Temple des Billettes,** on the left after the next intersection, was rebuilt in the 18thC and is now Lutheran. The charming little **cloister** survives, the only complete medieval cloister in Paris, with a Gothic vaulted ceiling. It is usually open to wander around: look for the doorway to the left of the main church door, next to an old-fashioned English shoemaker.

Continue a little farther along rue des Archives and take the next turn right along rue de la Verrerie to reach another interesting church, that of

St-Merri, completed in 1612, but anachronistically built in the Flamboy-ant Gothic style. It has a richly decorated W front, and the oldest bell in Paris, made in 1331.

A block to the N of this church, up rue St-Martin, lies the POMPIDOU CENTER, taking the visitor with a jolt from some of the oldest architecture in Paris to a building that proclaims itself firmly in the 20thC. Alternatively, head in the opposite direction to reach the HÔTEL DE VILLE: turn left when you reach the rue de Rivoli, from where there is a good view of the TOUR ST-JACQUES.

MONTMARTRE ★

To the N of the city, in the 18ᵉ. Map 3. Métro: Abbesses, Pigalle, Blanche, Anvers, Barbès-Rochechouart, Château-Rouge, Marcadet-Poissonniers, Jules-Joffrin, Lamarck-Caulaincourt.

In AD250 the martyred St-Denis is said to have picked up his severed head and walked up and over a hill to the N of the city. Since then millions of people have made the journey in more conventional style up through the winding streets of what is now called Montmartre or simply the **Butte** (hillock). Montmartre is a district full of contrasts. By turn quiet, raucous, quaint, sordid and hauntingly beautiful, it is a must on the itinerary of anyone wishing to absorb the spirit of Paris.

> The lights winking up at a pallid moon,
> the slender painted ladies, the wings of the Moulin Rouge,
> the smell of petrol and perfume and cooking . . . .
> The place Blanche, Paris, Life itself . . . .
> (Jean Rhys, *Quartet,* 1928)

For centuries Montmartre was a country village, bristling with wind-mills that supplied flour to the city below. Then in the 19thC it became part of Paris, and its picturesque charm and atmosphere and low rents attracted painters, sculptors, writers and musicians. The late 19thC was the heyday of Bohemian Montmartre, when Toulouse-Lautrec drew the cancan girls at the **Moulin Rouge** in place Blanche, when Picasso, Braque and others created Cubism at the **Bateau-Lavoir** studios (burned down in 1970 but since rebuilt) in place Émile-Goudeau, and when artists' models hung about place Pigalle looking for work. By 1914, most of the artists had migrated to the Left Bank, and the great tourist influx had already begun.

Today Montmartre has a number of different faces. The garish nightlife that Toulouse-Lautrec loved to portray has now spread all along boule-vard de Clichy and the surrounding streets. Pigalle today has become decidedly sleazy, the artists' models now replaced by numerous members of an older profession. This is the Montmartre of neon lights, strip clubs and cheap glitter. Farther up the hill in the area around the SACRÉ-COEUR, the ghost of the old Montmartre still lingers, but strictly for the tourists' benefit. Yet behind the facade of fake Bohemianism, Montmartre is still a village, an ordinary community endowed with a strong sense of its own history. This aspect is most evident on the N side, an area of quiet residential streets.

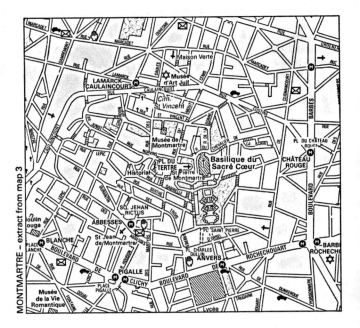

MONTMARTRE – extract from map 3

There are several ways to begin a visit to Montmartre — probably the easiest is to take the Métro to Lamarck-Caulaincourt. Climb the stairs heading s and cross rue Caulaincourt. Look at once for a sign directing you along **rue St-Vincent** toward the **Cimetière St-Vincent**, final resting place of Utrillo, and the **Musée de Montmartre**. At the pretty, countrified intersection with **rue des Saules** is the café **Lapin Agile**, a famous meeting place in the Bohemian days. A pretty cottage on a rather dull street, it was saved, almost 100 years ago, from demolition by speculative builders when it was bought by cabaret singer Aristide Bruant. On the slope to the right is a little **vineyard**, the last survivor within the Parisian boundaries. Every year, on the first Saturday in October, the vintage is celebrated by festivities and a procession.

Head up rue des Saules and turn left into the pretty **rue Cortot**. Here is the entrance to the **Musée de Montmartre** (☎ *46-06-61-11. Map3 C8* ▨ *☛ Open 11am-5.30pm, closed Mon and some bols).* A house with a terraced garden, inhabited by many artists in the past, it contains interesting mementoes of the district.

Within a short walk is the Butte's most prominent feature, the magnificent church of the SACRÉ-COEUR. Beside this landmark is the church of **St-Pierre de Montmartre**, a remnant of the great medieval abbey of Montmartre. Downhill to the w lies **place du Tertre** with its cafés and cobbled, leafy square. The artists are still there, selling their pictures, although perhaps their numbers have declined in favor of the charcoal portrait artists and their ilk. Just off place du Tertre is the **Espace Montmartre** (*11 rue Poulbot* ☎ *42-64-40-10. Map 3 C8* 🔲 *Open summer 10am-10pm, winter 10am-7pm*). This building houses the ESPACE SALVADOR DALÍ, a humorous and spectacular tribute to the master of the surreal, and the **Historial de Montmartre**, which has a wax museum with historical tableaux featuring Utrillo, Steinlen, Toulouse-Lautrec, Van Gogh, Victor Hugo and Chopin, among others.

Some of these people are buried in the Butte's two cemeteries, the small **Cimetière St-Vincent** and the much larger **Cimetière de Montmartre**. Beyond the smaller cemetery, to the N of rue Caulaincourt, is a museum of Jewish art, the **Musée d'Art Juif** (*42 rue des Saules* ☎ *42-57-84-15. Map 3 C8* 🔲 ✗ *Open Sun-Thurs 3-6pm, closed Fri, Sat, Aug, Jewish hols*).

Other ways up

An alternative route up the Butte is to leave the métro at Place Pigalle and make your way up on foot through the winding streets — or at Place Blanche. Here, opposite the **Moulin-Rouge**, you can take a little tourist train (*daily every half hour 10am-7pm, or till midnight on weekends and in summer* 🔲) that will bump and bounce you all the way to the top, with a running commentary in French and English. It takes away the pain of walking, but of course removes most of the pleasure of experiencing Montmartre, as progress, while slow, is not slow enough for anything much to stay in the memory. Let the train take the strain, but only if you're in a terrible hurry or not that good on your feet.

The well-loved funicular that carried thousands up the S slope of the Butte is no more. A brand new system (🔲) now operates the gleaming, spacious carriages as on an escalator, and each of the two tracks can operate independently of the other, carrying an estimated total of 4,500 visitors per hour. The trip, which lasts little more than a minute, costs more than a single métro ticket, but the experience is sweetened by the smooth ride and the removal of the need to walk up all those steps to reach Sacré Coeur.

✿ Children brought up the hill to satisfy the curiosity of adults will enjoy the view out over Paris, but this may last for only a minute or two. If their attention palls, whisk them away to a quiet and attractive playground in **Parc de la Turlure** (*just behind Sacré Coeur to the right*) or **square Suzanne Buisson** (*off avenue Junot*).

MONTPARNASSE

*To the S of the city, in the 14ᵉ. Map **13**. Métro: Montparnasse-Bienvenüe.*
Montparnasse, or "Mount Parnassus," was in Greek legend the mountain sacred to Apollo and the Muses. This was the nickname given to a grassy mound, formed from the debris of old quarries, which in the 17thC became a favorite haunt with student versifiers, who would gather to recite their poems. In the 18thC, the mound was leveled off, but the name stuck, and so did the carefree, pleasure-loving image. By the time of the Revolution, cafés and pleasure gardens had sprung up in Montparnasse, and it was here that the cancan was first performed.

In many ways Montparnasse is to the Left Bank what Montmartre is to the Right. Both are situated on hills; both, in their heyday, have been haunts of artists and literati, and both have since undergone a change of image. Montmartre now thrives on its picture-postcard quaintness, whereas Montparnasse became the victim of an uncharacteristically hard-nosed policy of redevelopment, exemplified by the TOUR MONTPAR-NASSE and a crop of mostly indifferent new buildings surrounding the redeveloped railway station: an exception is the elegantly modern **Meridien Montparnasse** hotel (see WHERE TO STAY). The once charming **rue de la Gaîté**, home of a number of lively little theaters in days gone by, has seen some of those theaters run to seed and the area become swamped by ever more shops selling "marital aids" and girlie magazines.

Do not scorn the TOUR MONTPARNASSE (◀€) just because it is ugly. The view from the top is breathtaking — perhaps one of the best to be had anywhere in Paris, and there is no need to wait in line for the privilege.

There are still glimpses of the old Montparnasse, as it struggles valiantly to survive, along boulevard du Montparnasse, which was once the center of flourishing artistic endeavor. Among those drawn to the boulevard and its surrounding streets were artists Rousseau, Van Dongen, Modigliani, Chagall and Whistler, writers Rilke, Apollinaire, Max Jacob and Cocteau, musicians Satie and Stravinsky, and political exiles including Lenin and Trotsky. Between the wars, the district was popular with American expatriates, most notably Ernest Hemingway.

The crowd of artists and intellectuals thronged the new cafés of the boulevard: La Coupole, Le Sélect, Le Dôme, La Rotonde and La Closerie des Lilas, which was one of Hemingway's favorite retreats. In *A Moveable Feast* the author recalls seeing the English occultist, Aleister Crowley, at the café, "a rather gaunt man wearing a cape." Crowley was another of the colorful characters who frequented the district, and he appears pseudonymously as Oliver Haddo, the villain of Somerset Maugham's novel *The Magician,* in which a Montparnasse café scene is vividly described.

Those were the days when Montparnasse was one mad, continuous party, a period that is vividly described by Georges-Michel in his novel *Les Montparnos* (1924). It was this writer who coined the word "Montparno" to refer to an inhabitant of the district.

Today the sparkling café life of Montparnasse has declined. Only La Coupole, Le Sélect and La Closerie des Lilas (see WHERE TO EAT) keep alive something of the atmosphere. The writers have dispersed, although there are still many artists' studios in the area.

Montparnasse enjoyed a brief moment of glory during the Liberation of Paris in 1944, when the **Gare Montparnasse** was used as the headquarters of General Leclerc. It was here that the German military governor signed his surrender. In 1967 it was demolished to make way for the present station complex, which incorporates huge blocks of offices and apartments. A new wave of modernization began again in the late 1980s, bringing the station into the age of the high-speed TGV train.

The station is the point of arrival from Brittany, so Montparnasse is traditionally a Breton area, especially rue Montparnasse, where there are still excellent restaurants serving *crêpes* and Breton cider.

The streets to the NW of the station are relatively unspoiled. Here you will find the MUSÉE DE LA POSTE in boulevard de Vaugirard and the MUSÉE BOURDELLE in the street named after the sculptor Antoine Bourdelle.

The sculptor is buried in the tranquil **Cimetière de Montparnasse** *(open 8am-5.30pm, Sat 8.30am, Sun 9pm)*, which also contains the graves of writers such as Baudelaire and Maupassant, de Beauvoir and Sartre, composers César Franck and Saint-Saëns, and other distinguished figures. The more recent *provocateur* Serge Gainsbourg also lies here. One of the graves has a bronze effigy of a couple sitting up in bed — no doubt very daring for its time. Another is decorated with Brancusi's sculpture, *The Kiss*, a tender and moving piece. A map of the cemetery is obtainable from the gate house.

One other attraction brings visitors to Montparnasse these days — a visit to the CATACOMBS, where, at place Denfert-Rochereau, you can penetrate the peace of thousands of ex-Parisians who have rested here for around 200 years. Unlike the cemetery, this is a less-than-uplifting place, but much visited nevertheless.

OPÉRA QUARTER

In the center, to the N of the Louvre, in the 9e and 2e. Maps 7 & 8. Métro: Opéra, Madeleine, Havre-Caumartin, Chaussée d'Antin Lafayette, Richelieu-Drouot, Quatre-Septembre, Pyramides, Tuileries, Palais-Royal Musée du Louvre.

This distinctive area surrounding the magnificent old OPÉRA building falls roughly between boulevard Haussmann and RUE DE RIVOLI to the N and S, and rue de Richelieu and the MADELEINE to the E and W. More than any other district of Paris, it bears the stamp of Baron Haussmann, Napoleon III's energetic Prefect of the Seine, who replanned much of central Paris in the years 1853-70 and whose signature was the wide boulevard and spacious townscape. It was he who carved out **place de l'Opéra**, which many considered unnecessarily large at the time, as well as **avenue de l'Opéra**, rue Auber and rue Halévy, which clasp the ornate Opéra buildings as in a forked stick.

Boulevard des Italiens and its extensions were already a fashionable area for rich pleasure-seekers, but with Haussmann's developments and the Gare St-Lazare near at hand, the quarter also became a thriving commercial and financial center. This transformation was accelerated by the building of the Métro at the beginning of the century.

The district today preserves both of these aspects. Everywhere you look there seem to be palatial banks, such as the frothy pile of the Crédit Lyonnais in **boulevard des Italiens**, and huge shops — the renovated Trois Quartiers in **boulevard de la Madeleine**, Au Printemps and Galeries Lafayette in **boulevard Haussmann**. There are also many smaller but often more expensive shops, some bearing anglophile names like "Old England," others inimitably French, like the couturiers in the elegant **rue St-Honoré**, which becomes the even more elegant RUE DU FAUBOURG-ST-HONORÉ.

The most luxurious street of all, however, is **rue de la Paix**, leading from the Opéra to PLACE VENDÔME and lined with sumptuous couturiers and jewelers, including **Cartier**.

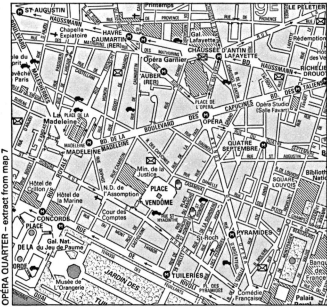

OPÉRA QUARTER – extract from map 7

So step by step, you reach the place de l'Opéra. It is here
that Paris makes one of its grandest impressions.
You have before you the façade of the *Théâtre,* enormous and bold,
resplendent with colossal lamps between the elegant columns,
before which open rue Auber and rue Halévy; to the right,
the great furnace of the Boulevard des Italiens; to the left,
the flaming Boulevard des Capucines, which stretches out
between the two burning walls of the Boulevard Madeleine,
and turning around, you see the three great diverging streets
which dazzle you like so many luminous abysses;
rue de la Paix, all gleaming with gold and jewels,
at the end of which the Colonne Vendôme rises
against the starry sky; Avenue de l'Opéra inundated with electric light;
rue du Quatre Septembre shining with its thousand gas jets,
and seven continuous lines of carriages issuing
from the two Boulevards and five streets, crossing each other rapidly
on the square, and a crowd coming and going under a shower
of rosy and whitest light diffused from the great ground-glass globes,
which produce the effect of wreaths and garlands of full moons,
colouring the trees, high buildings and the multitude
with the weird and mysterious reflections
of the final scene in a fairy ballet.
(Edmondo de Amicus, *Studies of Paris,* 1879)

Theaters in the district, apart from the Opéra itself, include the **Olympia** auditorium in boulevard des Capucines, but its future is currently uncertain; the highly-regarded **Salle Favart** (Opéra Comique) and the COMÉDIE FRANÇAISE, the seat of Classical French drama. One of the Comédie's greatest (and funniest) dramatists, Molière (1622-73), is commemorated by the **Molière fountain**, near the site of his house in rue de Richelieu. The fountain is a grand affair with a bronze statue of the playwright sitting on a pedestal supported by two languid female figures — a somewhat solemn monument for so humorous a writer.

Another appealing fountain lies a short distance farther up rue de Richelieu in **sq. Louvois**, a small park beside the BIBLIOTHÈQUE NATIONALE. Pudgy cherubs on dolphins support a great bowl decorated with the signs of the zodiac, surmounted by four buxom women representing France's great rivers, the Seine, Saône, Loire and Garonne. The park, with its chestnut trees, is one of the few intimate little retreats in the district.

In the search for imposing architectural riches, you need only cross the road to the BIBLIOTHÈQUE NATIONALE or go W to PLACE VENDÔME and the MADELEINE, or S to the PALAIS-ROYAL or the church of ST-ROCH. One rather curious monument lies on the N fringes of the quarter. This is the CHAPELLE EXPIATOIRE, built by order of Louis XVIII to the memory of his brother and sister-in-law, Louis XVI and Marie-Antoinette. It stands in **sq. Louis XVI**, now another tranquil little garden off boulevard Haussmann, but formerly a cemetery where lie victims of the guillotine. Louis XVI and Marie-Antoinette were also buried here, until Louis XVIII had their bodies removed to ST-DENIS. Inside, the chapel is a Classical mausoleum, like a miniature Panthéon, with statues of the unfortunate couple, and a gloomy crypt.

At #5 rue Daunou is the famous American watering-hole, **Harry's New York Bar**. On the night before a US presidential election, a mock poll is held among the clientele. More often than not it predicts the winner.

ST-GERMAIN QUARTER
*On the Left Bank, in the 6ᵉ and 7ᵉ. Maps **7** & **8**, **13** & **14**. Métro: Mabillon, Odéon, St-Germain-des-Prés, Rue-du-Bac, Solférino.*

The St-Germain district is really made up of two adjacent quarters: **St-Germain-des-Prés**, consisting roughly of the northern half of the 6ᵉ; and the Faubourg-St-Germain, comprising the NE section of the 7ᵉ. These two areas have their own distinct personalities, complementing each other well.

The former community first grew up around the great medieval monastery and church of ST-GERMAIN-DES-PRÉS, but for centuries it lay outside the Paris boundaries and remained cut off from the life of the city. Its only link with the Right Bank was a ferry *(bac)*, which was reached by rue du Bac. This remained the case until the 17thC, when Louis XIV began to extend the LOUVRE, for which purpose stone had to be brought from the quarries at Denfert-Rochereau in the S. The ferry was too slow a means of bringing it across the river, and so the **pont-Royal** was built, ending the isolation of St-Germain.

It was also Louis XIV who established the ÉCOLE DES BEAUX-ARTS, across

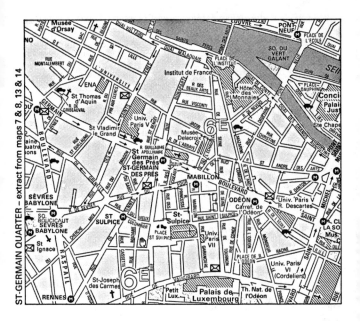

the river from the Louvre. Later, after the Louvre had become a museum, the narrow footbridge known as the Passerelle des Arts (now **pont des Arts**) was built, to allow the students to cross the river to look at the works of art. The construction of the pont-Royal turned St-Germain-des-Prés into a thriving community, and it soon became a favorite haunt of writers and intellectuals.

The Faubourg-(suburb) St-Germain is, as the name implies, of more recent origin. During the reign of Louis XIV, the aristocracy had been concentrated around the court at Versailles, but under the more relaxed regime of Louis XV they felt able to take up residence in Paris again and chose the plain to the E of the HÔTEL DES INVALIDES as the place to build their homes.

The result can be seen today in the gracious houses that line such streets as rue de Lille, rue de l'Université, rue de Grenelle and rue de Varenne. In recent years the majority of the larger ones have become government buildings or embassies. The **Hôtel de Matignon** *(57 rue de Varenne)* is now the residence of the Prime Minister, while the **Hôtel de Courteilles** *(110 rue de Grenelle)* has become the Ministry of Education. Rue de Grenelle is also the site of the lovely QUATRE-SAISONS fountain. A few well-heeled families still live in the area, and the atmosphere retains the privileged, inward-looking quality that it has always possessed, whether dominated by aristocrats or civil servants.

The buildings belong to a felicitous period when French architecture had thrown off the Italian influence and blossomed into a light but restrained elegance. This was typified by the **Hôtel Biron** (★) at the western end of rue de Varenne. Now the MUSÉE RODIN, this is one of the few houses in the area that you can enter easily.

> I love that *quartier!* [the Faubourg St-Germain] If ever I go
> to Paris again I shall reside there . . . . *There,* indeed, you are
> among the French, the fossilized remains of the old régime —
> the very houses have an air of desolate, yet venerable grandeur.
> You cross one of the numerous bridges,
> and you enter another time — you are inhaling
> the atmosphere of a past century; no flaunting *boutique,*
> French in its trumpery, English in its prices,
> stares you in the face . . . . Vast hotels, with their gloomy frontals
> and magnificent contempt for comfort; shops, such as shops
> might have been in the aristocratic days of Louis Quatorze . . .
> all strike on the mind with a vague
> and nameless impression of antiquity;
> a something solemn even in gaiety, and faded in pomp,
> appears to linger over all you behold.
> (Edward Bulwer-Lytton, *Pelham,* circa 1840)

The link between these two areas is boulevard St-Germain, a great bow-shaped thoroughfare that touches the Seine at each end. Begin a stroll down the boulevard perhaps somewhere near the secluded little church of **St-Thomas d'Aquin**, which lies just off the route to the N. This is still the Faubourg-St-Germain, but, approaching the church of ST-GER-MAIN-DES-PRÉS itself, everything becomes busier, more colorful and more cosmopolitan. Turn right opposite the church into **rue des Ciseaux**, a little Italian enclave with many pizzerias. This spills over into the **rue des Canettes** (Duckling St.), which runs up to ST-SULPICE — see the little ducklings over the doorway of #18.

Farther E, **rue Grégoire de Tours** is full of Greek restaurants. This street leads into **rue de Buci**. Here and in the neighboring **rue de Seine** is one of the best outdoor food markets in the city of Paris.

The church of ST-GERMAIN-DES-PRÉS dominates the intersection of boulevard St-Germain, rue de Rennes and rue Bonaparte. This is the heart of the district that has come to be known as the "*Capitale des Lettres*" (Literary Capital), a role that it began to take on in the 17thC when the Comédie Française played in what is now rue de l'Ancienne Comédie. **Le Procope** (see WHERE TO EAT), at #**13**, was the haunt of Molière, Corneille, Racine and, in later centuries, Voltaire, Balzac, Verlaine and Anatole France.

Between the wars, the quarter was fueled by an influx of writers from Montmartre and Montparnasse, who met habitually in the three great cafés in front of St-Germain-des-Prés: **Flore, Lipp** and **Les Deux Magots** (see WHERE TO EAT and CAFÉS). Publishers, booksellers, painters and art dealers also set up shop there in increasing numbers.

After World War II, St-Germain became the headquarters of a new generation of intelligentsia, revolving around Jean-Paul Sartre and the

Existentialists. In those days they crowded into jazz cellars such as the Tabou in rue Dauphine, and small bars such as the Bar Vert in rue Jacob. The atmosphere of the district has inevitably changed since then, but the "*Germanopratins*," as the inhabitants are called, are friendly and bubbling, and there is always a lively atmosphere, especially around place St-Germain-des-Prés by the church, where most evenings you will find street performers at work.

A gentler atmosphere of festivity is often to be found nearby in the quaint little tree-lined **rue de Furstemberg**, where the glow of the old-fashioned street lamps attracts singers, guitarists and harpists. The great 19thC artist Delacroix had his studio here (it is now the MUSÉE DELACROIX) and the Romantic spirit is still strongly felt, especially at night.

Apart from the Delacroix, there are few museums in this part of Paris. As well as the MUSÉE D'ORSAY and the RODIN, there is the MUSÉE DE LA MONNAIE and the LÉGION D'HONNEUR. However, the district makes up for this deficiency in the density of its small art galleries (mostly around rue de Seine and rue Mazarine) and its second-hand bookstores. If you like to drink coffee while you browse, you can try the bookstore-café **Un Moment . . . en Plus** *(1 rue de Varenne, 7ᵉ ☎ 42-22-23-45).*

There are many little pockets in St-Germain where history can be found. One of them is **cour du Commerce-St-André**, an ancient alley off rue St-André-des-Arts. If you look through the windows of #**4** you will see part of one of the towers of the medieval city wall. At #**9** was the site of the workshop of a German carpenter called Schmidt, who built the first guillotine and tested it out on unfortunate sheep.

Much of the attraction of St-Germain lies in unexpected moments of visual delight: an old shop front, a flourish of carved stonework above a well-proportioned doorway, the glimpse of a cobbled courtyard through an arch. See the area at leisure if you want to be sure not to miss its subtle pleasures as well as its more obvious attractions. Better still, make St-Germain your hotel base for several days.

Sightseeing

Paris on foot

Paris is a wonderful city for walking. It is small enough to walk across in a couple of hours, and there is so much to see per square kilometer that even the shortest stroll provides a confirmation of the diversity of Paris. While it is essential to spend some time actually visiting the sights, try to take the chance to appreciate the fine texture of the urban landscape by going there on foot.

The first of the three mapped walks that follow is designed to give a first glimpse of the important sights. The second takes you along the banks of the Seine, while the third delves into the literary Left Bank. Other detailed itineraries and guides are included within the entries in THE QUARTIERS OF PARIS (pages 66-85).

WALK 1: GETTING TO KNOW PARIS
*Walks 1 and 2 can be traced on the map opposite. See also maps **7**, **8** & **9**.*
Allow at least half a day. Métro: Opéra, Louvre-Rivoli.
This walk is designed as an introduction to Paris, taking a broad spiral route round its heart. It encompasses many well-known landmarks, and contrasts great boulevards with rambling side streets, the Right Bank and the Left.

Begin at place de l'Opéra, dominated by the ornate OPÉRA GARNIER itself and forming one of the main intersections of the city. This is the heart of the Paris of Haussmann, creator of grand townscapes, and the area is full of smart shops. Walk SW down boulevard des Capucines and boulevard de la Madeleine, which ends at the Neoclassical church of the MADELEINE itself, looking, as it is meant to, like a stray building from the ancient civilization of Rome.

From here, go straight ahead, down rue Royale to PLACE DE LA CONCORDE, passing between two splendid matching buildings of the Louis XV period, the one on your right housing the famous HÔTEL DE CRILLON (see WHERE TO STAY). Cross the river by the Pont de la Concorde, opposite the ASSEMBLÉE NATIONALE, and turn left to walk down the great artery of the Left Bank, boulevard St-Germain, perhaps pausing for coffee at one of its host of famous cafés (see CAFÉS).

Just beyond the church of ST-GERMAIN-DES-PRÉS, turn left into rue de Buci, to browse in the charming maze of old streets between the boulevard and the Seine, with their many little book and antique stores, art galleries and food stalls. Rue de Buci becomes rue St-André-des-Arts;

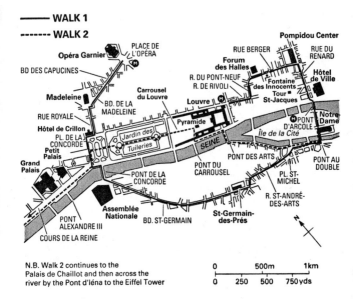

——— WALK 1

------ WALK 2

N.B. Walk 2 continues to the
Palais de Chaillot and then across the
river by the Pont d'Iéna to the Eiffel Tower

follow this E to place St-Michel, the focal point of the LATIN QUARTER. Stop somewhere along the boulevard for lunch. This presents no problems, as the area is full of good restaurants.

Continue across by the Pont au Double to the ÎLE DE LA CITÉ and NOTRE-DAME cathedral and return to the Right Bank by the Pont d'Arcole, walking N with the HÔTEL DE VILLE on the right and the Gothic eminence of the TOUR ST-JACQUES to the left. Rue du Renard leads straight on to reach the E side of the POMPIDOU CENTER, a lively cultural complex in a futuristic building. To reach the main entrance, cut left across the bottom (S) edge of the building through the lively piazza. If time allows, ride the escalator ( ) up to the top floor for a superb view.

Having seen the center, turn W along rue Berger, past the exquisite but often overcrowded Fontaine des Innocents. This route soon brings you to the FORUM DES HALLES. This vast shopping complex has risen from the ashes of the old food market. It houses several visitor attractions too, including a branch of the MUSÉE GRÉVIN which has a series of Belle Époque scenarios, and the PARC OCÉANIQUE JACQUES COUSTEAU, although time will probably not allow you to visit.

Now turn left down rue du Pont-Neuf, where you will soon intersect the elegant RUE DE RIVOLI, with its colonnade and luxurious shops. Turn right, walking toward the GRAND LOUVRE. You will probably not have time to enter, today, but make ten minutes to approach the building from its front (W) side, in order to see the new glass-and-steel pyramids and fountains. Set off for home from the Louvre-Rivoli Métro, which, with its low reliefs and statues, is Paris' most attractive Métro station.

WALK 2: A RIVERSIDE WALK

Allow 3hrs. Maps 8, 7, 6 & 5 and walk map on previous page. Métro: Cité, Champ-de-Mars Tour Eiffel.

Most of the great capitals of Europe have their equivalents of the Seine, but few have as intimate a relationship with their rivers as Paris does. History and romance flow thickly in its waters, and Parisians love it tenderly. This walk, beginning and ending at Paris' two greatest landmarks, does not stay on the river banks all the time, since major roads run along much of them, but the Seine, with its ever-changing vistas, will never be far away.

The beginning is where Paris itself began: on the ÎLE DE LA CITÉ. And what could be a more appropriate starting point than the brass compass marker set into the ground by the W door of NOTRE-DAME, from which all distances from the capital are measured? Walk across the Pont au Double, then turn W along the Left Bank, passing some of the *bouquinistes,* the booksellers with their rows of enticing little hutches full of books. Continue along the Left Bank, from where there are magnificent views across the river, until you draw level with the LOUVRE.

Cross the Pont des Arts footbridge, and turn left along the river bank, walking alongside the Louvre. For a glimpse of the marvelously adventurous glass pyramid entrance to the museum, take the first turning on the right. Remember that if you wish to visit the museum, it is unwise to allow less than half a day.

Then cross the road into the gardens of the CARROUSEL DU LOUVRE. Massive excavations have been taking place here for several years, but 1993 sees the completion of another underground project, for the expanse of garden in front of the ARC DE TRIOMPHE DU CARROUSEL now has below it the new PALAIS DE LA MODE.

Go W through the TUILERIES gardens and cross PLACE DE LA CONCORDE.

Now return to the river by walking along the cours la Reine, staying on the upper level long enough to see the sumptuous PONT ALEXANDRE III and the two exhibition buildings, GRAND PALAIS and PETIT PALAIS. Then descend to the lower footpath and follow it past the departure quay for the Bateaux-Mouches near Pont de l'Alma. The lower walkway is not continuous from here, so return at certain points to the road above. Continue in this way until you reach the gardens of the PALAIS DE CHAILLOT. Cross the river by the Pont d'Iéna to arrive at the foot of the EIFFEL TOWER, one of the great symbols of Paris and a suitable place to end the walk. To reach the nearest Métro station, Champ-de-Mars Tour Eiffel, turn right along quai Branly.

WALK 3: THE LITERARY LEFT BANK

Allow 3hrs. Maps 13, 14, 7 & 8 and walk map opposite. Métro: Raspail, St-Michel.

Almost any walk in Paris would be a "literary" walk, since there is hardly a corner that does not have some link with a writer or poet; but this one is particularly rich in literary associations.

Start at MONTPARNASSE cemetery, which contains the graves of many literary figures including Maupassant, Huysmans and Baudelaire. Walk to the intersection of boulevard du Montparnasse and boulevard Raspail.

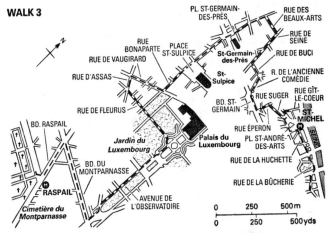

WALK 3

Close by are the Dôme, Coupole, Select and Rotonde, cafés that were the haunts of Hemingway, Fitzgerald, Miller and other expatriate writers of the interwar years. By the Rotonde on boulevard Raspail stands a cast of Rodin's famous *Balzac*.

Turn right along boulevard du Montparnasse. At the corner with avenue de l'Observatoire is LA CLOSERIE DES LILAS, another old haunt of the American literary set, and still much favored by the Parisian *literati*.

Walk down the avenue de l'Observatoire into the JARDINS DU LUXEM-BOURG, where you will find memorials to many writers, including (on the E side) Murger (author of *La Bohème*), Flaubert, Stendhal, George Sand and Lecomte de L'Isle. On the W side is a particularly striking tribute to the poet Paul Verlaine. Leave the gardens on the W side by rue de Fleurus), passing #27, where Gertrude Stein lived.

Turn right into rue d'Assas. Now follow for a while the walk taken one night by d'Artagnan, in Dumas' *Three Musketeers*, while dreaming of his beloved, as he was "passing along a lane on the spot where rue d'Assas is now situated." Turning into what must have been rue de Vaugirard, d'Artagnan made for the house of his fellow musketeer Aramis, "situated between rue Cassette and rue Servandoni" (still in existence). "The hero passed rue Cassette and caught sight of the door of his friend's house, shaded by a mass of sycamore and clematis, which formed a vast arch above it." This must have been somewhere near where rue Bonaparte begins. Walk down this street, which is full of antiquarian bookstores, to place St-Sulpice.

> St-Sulpice! The fat belfries, the garish posters over the door,
>   the candles flaming inside. The Square so beloved
> of Anatole France with that drone and buzz from the altar,
>   the splash of the fountain, the pigeons cooing . . . .
>   (Henry Miller, *Tropic of Cancer*, 1934)

Continue down rue Bonaparte to reach place St-Germain-des-Prés. Here is the heart of ST-GERMAIN, once known as the "Capitale des Lettres" thanks to the presence of such poets as Apollinaire (who lived at 202 boulevard St-Germain) and later of Jean-Paul Sartre, Simone de Beauvoir, Raymond Queneau and Albert Camus. It was in the cafés here — Les Deux Magots, for example — that the Existentialist philosophy was nurtured.

Continue N on rue Bonaparte, then turn right into rue des Beaux-Arts. "I am dying beyond my means," declared Oscar Wilde, who died at #13 in 1900. Even so, he would not recognize the contemporary luxury of the HÔTEL GUY LOUIS DUBOUCHERON, as it is now known (see WHERE TO STAY).

Turn right into rue de Seine, where at #21 there is the house once inhabited by George Sand. Turn left into rue de Buci, right into rue de l'Ancienne-Comédie, and walk S to Le Procope *(#13),* which has been a literary haunt since it was founded in 1686 (see WHERE TO EAT). Molière and Racine came here when the *Comédie Française* was at #14 in the same street. Later it was patronized by Balzac, Hugo, Verlaine *et al.*

Back on boulevard St-Germain, continue your journey E past the Carrefour de l'Odéon and then turn left down rue Éperon and right into rue Suger, where J.K. Huysmans was born at #11 in 1848. This road leads to place St-André-des-Arts, where there is a café called Gentilhomme, described by Jack Kerouac in his *Satori in Paris.* Just around the corner in rue Gît-le-Coeur is the Hôtel Vieux Paris where he, Allen Ginsberg and others of the "Beat Generation" used to stay when they were in town.

From here turn left into boulevard St-Michel, and before the Seine turn right along rue de la Huchette and on into rue de la Bûcherie, to find the famous bookstore, Shakespeare and Co., at #37. The shop is as full of atmosphere as it is of books, and continues the splendid literary tradition of this part of Paris in the lively poetry readings attended by young literati.

The open spaces of Paris

The lungs of Paris — the BOIS DE BOULOGNE and the BOIS DE VINCENNES are clearly visible on a map that is otherwise heavily built up. And the streets themselves are built "up," too, in the form of stately apartment blocks, often four or five stories high, that give to the most modest streets a feeling of solidity and cool elegance.

Parisians have solved their need for open space in two ways. In private, behind the cover of the massive entrance gates, lie the verdant courtyards. An occasional glimpse of a mysterious, romantic, shady haven of greenness is all that most tourists ever get, unless they happen to choose a hotel that is thus equipped. In public, they have provided themselves with a vast number of little, formal parks, or *squares.* What is more, they use them. Whenever the weather allows, the parks and squares are full of people — they read alone, they romance in pairs, they chat in gaggles, their children play on the swings, their elderly feed the ducks, they admire their statues, both old and new.

Their approach is a strict one. In the main, these gardens are formally laid out, with lawns, planted beds, ornamental ponds and lakes. And they do not sit on the grass. They do not walk on the grass. And they respect these basic rules of society. In some countries, this would be the end of it — there would be nowhere to sit. In the larger Paris parks, there are portable chairs, in their hundreds. In the smaller parks, there are benches, in their dozens. The parks are full of people, and they are all sitting comfortably.

The carefully positioned statues commemorate everything from giggling turn-of-the-century working girls *(square de Montholon, 9^e, N of rue Lafayette)* to soldiers who sacrificed all for their country *(square Marcel Pagnol, 8^e, near the church of ST-AUGUSTIN)*. When you see a *square*, stop and go in. They are invariably havens of peace in the busiest of streets, and to sit in one for a short while will make you feel positively Parisian.

Parks and open spaces A to Z

ARÈNES DE LUTÈCE
Entrances in rue Monge (next door to Hôtel des Arènes) and rue de Navarre, 5e. Map 15K10. Open dawn to dusk &. Métro: Place Monge, Jussieu, Cardinal-Lemoine.

Turning off the street into what you might expect to be an ordinary Parisian park, you walk down a stone corridor and suddenly emerge into a Gallo-Roman amphitheater with terraces for spectators. All but demolished by barbarian invasions in the 3rdC, the arena was rediscovered quite by chance in 1869 during construction work on rue Monge, and was restored 50 years later.

Now it is enjoying a second and quieter lease on life surrounded by greenery, and it makes an ideal place for watching a game of *boules* or for simply sitting and imagining life in *Lutetia* — as Paris was known in the Roman era.

BOULOGNE, BOIS DE
To the w edge of Paris, beyond the Périphérique and in the crook of the Seine. Located on map 17C3-D3; detailed map on following page.

"I will not describe the Bois de Boulogne. It is simply a beautiful, cultivated, endless, wonderful wilderness." This was Mark Twain's reaction in *The Innocents Abroad* to the 900ha (2,224 acre) park on the western outskirts of Paris, which was once a royal hunting forest. Today, the Bois could no longer be described as a wilderness — there are too many roads. Furthermore, it is, in places, rather monotonous, and much of it is haunted by libidinous characters, especially at night.

However, there are many spots of great beauty, and you must be prepared to seek these out. The most delightful of all must surely be the **Bagatelle** *(█ open daily)*— a relatively small park-within-a-park where in the 18thC the Count of Artois, the future King Charles X, built himself an enchanting little villa (constructed in less than 70 days on a bet with

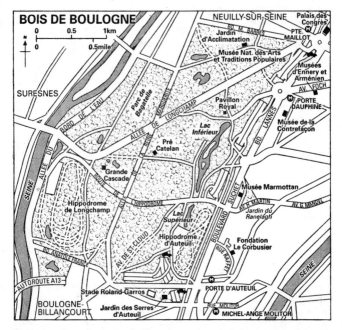

Marie-Antoinette) surrounded by a romantic and picturesque garden with artificial waterfalls, grottoes, Gothic ruins and other follies. Later, a second building, the Trianon, was added near the villa. Today the Bagatelle (the word means trifle) is a place of potent magic, with a renowned flower garden.

The **château de la Bagatelle** is now open for tours *(on weekend afternoons Mid-Mar to end Oct ☎ 40-71-75-23 for information)*. There is also an elegant restaurant, **La Roseraie de la Bagatelle**, where you can sip afternoon tea languidly and dream.

Another appealing oasis in the Bois is the **Pré Catelan** ( ) also a self-contained park. Its attractions include a majestic copper beech with a wider span of branches than any other tree in Paris. In addition, the Pré has a **Shakespeare Garden** ( ) containing plants mentioned in the master's works. The **Théâtre de la Verdure** (open-air theater) holds performances here June-Sept *(☎ 42-76-47-72 for program details)*. A first-class restaurant of the same name (LE PRÉ CATELAN, see WHERE TO EAT) also nestles here.

If you have children with you, the spot to head for is the **Jardin d'Acclimatation** ( ), children's paradise on the N side of the Bois *(open daily)*. A little train runs there from Porte-Maillot. Here you will find a zoo, a go-kart track, merry-go-rounds, a miniature golf course and a café, **La Ferme du Golf**, one of the few places where youngsters can sit in a farmyard and eat an ice cream or pizza, while goats, sheep and ducks mill around their tables.

Within the Jardin d'Acclimatation is the **Musée en Herbe** (☎ 40-67-97-66 ▨ ⅋ ✻ *open Sun-Fri 10am-6pm, Sat 2-6pm)*, which lets children discover art while having fun. Lively temporary exhibitions are mounted, and there is a supervised studio in which children can paint or draw impressions of what they have seen. The MUSÉE DES ARTS ET TRADITIONS POPULAIRES is also nearby.

Other attractions in the Bois include lakes (the **Lac Inférieur** has boating facilities), two racecourses (**Auteuil** and **Longchamp**) and Paris' municipal floral garden, the **Jardin des Serres d'Auteuil**.

Perhaps one of the best and most enjoyable methods of traveling about in the Bois is on two wheels. However, you may prefer, like the Englishman who broke the bank at Monte Carlo, to "walk along the Bois de Boulogne with an independent air."

BUTTES CHAUMONT, PARC DES
Rue Manin, 19ᵉ. Map 18C5 ⇚ ▣ ✻ *Open daily. Métro: Buttes-Chaumont.*
This park is totally unlike any other in Paris and has a strongly romantic appeal. Brilliantly landscaped by Haussmann on a disused quarry site, it has steeply undulating wooded contours and a lake with a rocky island rising dramatically from the center, spanned by two high bridges. On the island, one path leads up a flight of steps through a grotto-like tunnel to the summit, which is crowned by a small Classical temple with an open colonnade. From here there is a superb view over the city to the N, E and W, with MONTMARTRE and the SACRÉ-COEUR standing out against the horizon.

This is one of the few Parisian parks where you can actually sit on the grass. For children, there are rides in a donkey cart, and a boating lake, and, for adults, on the W side, there is an inviting restaurant, the **Pavillon du Lac** (☎ 42-02-08-97, *open daily noon-2.30pm only)* with tables overlooking the lake.

CANAL ST-MARTIN
19ᵉ and 10ᵉ. Map 4. Métro: Louis Blanc, J. Bonsergent, Goncourt.
Built in the early 19thC, the Canal St-Martin links the Seine with the Canal St-Denis and the Canal de l'Ourcq. It is a working canal, running through a tunnel for some of its length, but it has its picturesque moments too.

A major improvement has been the construction of a new boating marina (Port de Plaisance) in the Bassin de l'Arsenal, S of place de la Bastille. The canal heads N from there through an eerily-lit tunnel that runs below the place de la Bastille, although the shafts of light that pierce the half-darkness have a certain beauty. Once out in the light of day, the next stretch is more romantic, with its chestnut-tree-lined banks, quaint locks and hump-backed bridges.

Beyond this point, the canal enters into the Bassin de La Villette, which was a major port at the turn of the century. The first glimpse of the high-tech CITÉ DES SCIENCES ET DE L'INDUSTRIE at the former abattoir district of La Villette is a huge dragon children's slide and the gleaming sides of the **Géode**, a spherical cinema made of reflective steel.

Not far ahead, past the Crimea swing-bridge, is the crossroads where the Canal St-Denis swings off to the left to rejoin the Seine. Straight ahead is the Canal de l'Ourcq, constructed originally to bring clean water to Paris, which narrows down at the start of its 108km (67 miles) stretch to the river Ourcq.

You can take a very pleasant boat trip up the canal, during the warmer months, from the Bassin de l'Arsenal, or from various other starting points, some as far W as the quai d'Orsay. Tour operators are listed on page 52.

CHAMP-DE-MARS
7ᵉ. Map 11I3. Métro: Champ de Mars, École-Militaire.
The Champ-de-Mars is the back garden of the TOUR EIFFEL. It was originally laid out in the 1760s as a parade ground for the ÉCOLE MILITAIRE, hence its name, after Mars, the god of war. These days it is anything but martial — just a typically tranquil Parisian park with a symmetrical pattern of tree-lined avenues and numerous pleasant and secluded little corners in which to sit and read or contemplate the wonders of Eiffel's engineering.

A fine new series of statues was erected here in 1989. The composition, created by sculptor Yvan Theimer, commissioned for the bicentenary of the French Revolution, depicts the bronze figures of man, woman and child, in his *Monument to the Rights of Man*.

If you have children in tow, it is worth making a short detour away from the river to the S, where there are excellent playgrounds, pony rides and an old-fashioned merry-go-round.

LUXEMBOURG, JARDINS DU ▥
Map 14J8 ▣ ⚥ ✗ Guides walks once a month, Apr-Oct. Métro: Luxembourg, Port-Royal.
The **Palais du Luxembourg**, which houses the French Senate, was built between 1612-24 by Marie de Medicis, the widow of Henry IV. Finding the Louvre boring as a place of residence, she bought the house and grounds of the Duc de Piney-Luxembourg, then standing in a semirural position on the S edge of the city.

Beside the duke's house (now known as the **Petit Luxembourg**) she built a grandiose mansion designed by Salomon de Brosse in the style of the Pitti Palace in Florence, but keeping the traditional French layout around a grand courtyard. However, her stay was short-lived, for in 1630, only five years after she had moved in, she was banished for life to Cologne.

During the Reign of Terror (1793-4) the palace became a prison, but after 1795 it housed the higher parliamentary assemblies, and the building underwent a series of alterations and enlargements. The Petit Luxembourg next door is now the residence of the Senate's president.

The **gardens**, like the palace, are French, with Italian touches such as the Baroque **Medici fountain**, which stands at the end of a long pool filled with goldfish and flanked by shaded walkways. The focal point of the gardens is a large octagonal pool, surrounded by formal terraces and *parterres* and usually filled with a fleet of toy sailboats. The rest is an engaging mixture of formality and intimacy, with plenty of little secret corners as well as broad, straight avenues.

> I threw myself on a bench and began to wonder if there was anything better in the world worth doing than to sit in an alley of clipped limes smoking, thinking of Paris and of myself.
> (George Augustus Moore, *Memoirs,* 1906)

One of the great delights of this park is its statues. Here you will find, among others, Delacroix, Verlaine, George Sand, Stendhal and Flaubert. You may guess the importance to the French of the various literary names, by comparing the size and complexity of their public tributes. In **avenue de l'Observatoire**, which forms an extension to the gardens, is an exuberant fountain with an armillary sphere held up by female figures representing the four quarters of the globe.

The gardens also have tennis courts, an elegant circular pond where you (or your child) can rent boats, donkey rides, a large marionette theater, the **Théâtre du Luxembourg** (☎ *43-26-46-47, afternoon shows),* a school of bee-keeping and arboriculture, and an open-air café under the trees — reminiscent of a painting by Renoir.

MONCEAU, PARC DE
Entrance in blvd. de Courcelles, 8ᵉ. Map 6E4-5. Métro: Monceau, Villiers.
This is an unusual, rather poetic place. The entrance, through a gateway in a tall railing along boulevard de Courcelles, reveals a picturesque garden in the English style.

Beside a little lake there is a semicircular Roman colonnade, and dotted about among the chestnuts, acacias and plane trees are curious objects: a pyramid, a stone archway, some Classical columns. These are all follies remaining from the garden designed for the Duke of Orléans by the writer and painter Carmontel in the late 18thC.

A delightful spot for a shady picnic lunch on warm days, it is characteristically used to full advantage by Parisians.

MONTSOURIS, PARC DE
Blvd. Jourdan, 14ᵉ. Map 18D4 ☛ Métro: Cité-Universitaire.
The most striking feature of this appealing park, with its hills, lake and rambling paths, is a Moorish-looking building with onion domes, a replica of the Bey of Tunis' palace, given by the Bey for the Paris Exhibition of 1867.

The nearby Cité Universitaire, a student residential complex, set in grounds just s of the park, is interesting because the buildings date from the 1920s, each building representing the traditional architecture of a different country. The Brazilian and Swiss pavilions were designed by Le Corbusier.

The park also contains the Paris meteorological observatory and a tower marking the s bearing of the former Paris meridian.

PÈRE LACHAISE, CIMETIÈRE DU

20ᵉ. Map 18D5. Open daily. Métro: Père-Lachaise.

Like many old cemeteries, this one, the largest in Paris, has a power-fully romantic appeal. Named after Louis XIV's confessor, this cemetery was originally the site of a Jesuit house of retreat, and its hilly ground was laid out in 1804. The closely huddled graves encompass a wide variety of sepulchral art.

It is easy to lose your way among the twisting, tree-lined lanes, but in return for a small tip, the custodian will provide a map that marks the graves of the many celebrities buried here. These include Molière, Balzac, de Musset, Chopin, Rossini, Colette, Edith Piaf, Oscar Wilde, Modigliani and Jim Morrison. The monument to Wilde is a massive block by Jacob Epstein, adorned with a winged Egyptian figure. The tomb of Abelard and Héloïse, erected in 1779, has been thoroughly restored.

One of the most visited graves is that of the spiritualist Allan Kardec, whose followers can sometimes be seen communing with his spirit by passing their hands over his statue.

LA SEINE

Lovers, painters and songwriters have for so long made the Seine their own that it is easy to forget the vital role played by the river in Paris' history, as an artery of trade and a strategic route since Roman times. In fact, without the Seine there would be no Paris. It is not for nothing that the badge of Paris depicts a boat, for the men who operated the river trade were for centuries the leading citizens of the town, and it was their corporation that formed the municipal administration in the Middle Ages.

The river winds its way for seven miles through Greater Paris, and is crossed by bridges at 31 different points. The oldest bridge is the PONT-NEUF (meaning new bridge), completed in 1607.

Parisians often measure the level of the water by looking at the statue of the *Zouave* (an Algerian soldier of the Second Empire), which stands at the E side of the Pont de l'Alma. When the *Zouave* has his feet in the water it is a sign that the river is getting dangerously high. In the notorious floods of 1910, the water reached his chin.

It comes as a surprise to some Americans to find the Statue of Liberty in Paris. But there she stands — midstream, near the pont de Grenelle, which you will probably only see if you have reason to go to the MAISON DE RADIO FRANCE.

The Seine provides some of the most beautiful riverscapes in the world. To get to know the river at close hand, walk along the riverside path (see WALK 2 on page 88), or take a trip on one of the many riverboats that ply its waters.

TUILERIES, JARDIN DES

1ᵉʳ. Map 7H7 ☎ Métro: Tuileries.

French formal gardening at its most elegant is exemplified in the Jardin des Tuileries. Laid out by Le Nôtre, gardener to Louis XIV, the gardens occupy a splendid site bounded by the GRAND LOUVRE, PLACE DE LA

CONCORDE and RUE DE RIVOLI, with the twin JEU DE PAUME and ORANGERIE pavilions on raised terraces at the W end. The central avenue, with its two ponds, is dramatically aligned with AVENUE DES CHAMPS-ÉLYSÉES and the Louvre.

There seem to be almost as many statues in the gardens as there are trees: ancient gods and goddesses, allegorical figures of rivers and the seasons, and, near the Concorde entrance, a bust of Le Nôtre himself. There are many modern sculptures, forming a sort of extension of the reorganized Louvre.

Although it is quite plainly popular with Parisians, the peacefulness of the Tuileries, given its location smack in the middle of the city, is striking. Birdsong stills the roar of traffic, which is muffled by massed trees. Children can pass the time happily in their own special play areas, and there is a pond where toy wooden sailboats can be rented.

There has not been peace everywhere, though. A massive excavation project between the ARC DE TRIOMPHE DU CARROUSEL and the LOUVRE has disrupted the area for three years. By fall 1993, this, the latest of the *grands travaux,* will result in a new fashion center (see PALAIS DE LA MODE). The gardens will be reinstated and the subterranean complex will be almost invisible from above, apart from a sweeping granite staircase on the rue de Castiglione/Pont Solférino axis and an inverted pyramid illuminating the 9,000 sq.m (95,000sq.ft) main gallery below.

However, contrasted with the gaiety of the gardens and the dust of the excavations, is the tragic specter of the vanished Tuileries palace, which once ran N-S between the two projecting western pavilions of the Louvre, with the ARC DE TRIOMPHE DU CARROUSEL forming the entrance to its courtyard.

Queen Catherine de Medicis built the palace in the 16thC but never lived there because her astrologer warned her against it, and subsequently an evil spell seemed to afflict the building. It witnessed violent and dramatic events, such as the escape of Louis XVI and his family across the gardens in 1792, the massacre of the Swiss Guards at the same date, and the riots that led to the departure of Charles X in 1830 and of Louis-Philippe in 1848. Finally, the palace was sacked and burned by the *Communards* in 1871.

LA VILLETTE, PARC DE
At the intersection of the Canal de l'Ourcq and the Canal St-Denis, at the extreme NE corner of Paris, this area, including the Bassin de la Villette, is in the final stages of a vast redevelopment program from which has emerged a futuristic park and museum complex. See entry in A TO Z OF PARIS SIGHTS.

VINCENNES, BOIS DE
To the E edge of Paris, beyond the Périphérique. Located on map 18D5; detailed map on page 99.
This great open space of woodland lies to the SE of Paris at the opposite pole to the BOIS DE BOULOGNE. It is a little larger (995ha.) and a little less fashionable than its counterpart and yet in no way inferior.

Château de Vincennes

Av. de Paris, 94300 Vincennes ☎*43-28-15-48* ▨ ✗ *compulsory for both keep and chapel. Open Oct-Mar 10am-4.30pm, Apr-Sept 10am-6pm. Métro: Château-de-Vincennes. RER: Vincennes.*

The Château de Vincennes is made up of a series of buildings of different periods, parts of which have served at various times as royal residence, prison, porcelain factory and arsenal. The main entrance is approached across a vast moat, and the whole place has a rather forbidding aspect that mirrors its grim history. Henry V of England died in the keep in 1422, and in 1944 the Germans executed 26 members of the Resistance, who had blown up part of the castle and set fire to one of the pavilions. The **keep** *(donjon)* — the only medieval example near Paris — houses a small **museum** of the castle's history.

Opposite the keep is a Gothic chapel, the **Sainte-Chapelle**, which was founded by Charles V in 1379, and modeled on the one of the same name on the ÎLE DE LA CITÉ. It has some fine stonework and magnificent **stained-glass windows**. Both chapel and keep can only be seen with a guide. To the s of the keep and chapel are two 17thC **pavilions** facing each other across a courtyard. Louis XIV spent his honeymoon in one of these buildings in 1660.

The restoration of the château was begun on the order of Napoleon III and continued spasmodically for a century. It is now complete.

Bois de Vincennes ★
☲ ✤

Enclosed by Philippe Auguste in the 12thC as a royal hunting ground, the Bois de Vincennes was made into a park for the citizens of Paris by Louis XV and was given to the city by Napoleon III in 1860. Since then, many inroads have been made into it, and much of the greenery has been lost. In recent years, however, the city of Paris has started to reclaim some of the lost parkland; thousands of trees have been planted and new avenues laid out.

Starting at the château and traveling clockwise, you come first to an attractive floral garden, the **parc floral** *(Esplanade du Château de Vincennes* ☎*43-43-92-95; open daily from 9.30am, closes Apr-Sept 8pm, Oct and Mar 6pm, Nov-Feb 5pm).* An important visitor attraction these days, this garden, as well as being planted with an interesting variety of flora, has a lake, an excellent children's play area, a butterfly farm, a restaurant and riding stables. Flower shows are held regularly, and there is a busy program of entertainments for children (clowns, puppets, magic) and adults (jazz, choral singers, popular events).

Beyond the theater to the E is the **Lac des Minimes**, which has three islands, a restaurant and boating facilities, and the garden of the **School of Tropical Agronomy**, with its Oriental touches and its **temple** commemorating the Indo-Chinese killed in World War I.

Turning s you come to the **École du Breuil** (a school of horticulture), with more lovely gardens and an arboretum. Close by is the **Hippodrome de Vincennes**, a racecourse where you are more likely to find trotting races than the flat-racing and steeplechases of the Bois de Boulogne.

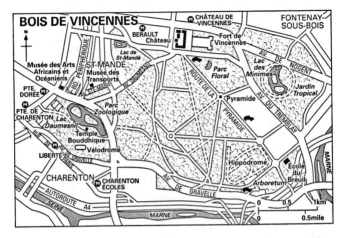

A walk E through the woods will bring you to Lac **Daumesnil**, a popular boating place with a plush café-restaurant on one of its two islands. On the s bank is the **Temple Bouddhique** (Buddhist temple), which contains the largest effigy of Buddha in Europe, made of glass fiber and covered with gold leaf.

On the N side of the lake is the largest of the Paris zoos, the **Parc Zoologique de Paris**, *(53 av. St-Maurice ☎ 43-43-84-95. Open 9am-5.30pm 🎞 ✿ 🕊 Métro: Porte Dorée, St-Mandé-de-Tourelles).* Here you can see elephants, bison, kangaroos, peacocks, and many other animals and birds roaming in natural-looking surroundings. There are two cafés and a huge artificial rock from the top of which you have an excellent view over the Bois to the E and Paris to the W.

See also the ARTS AFRICAINS ET OCÉANIENS museum, which is close by and may merit a diversion.

Sights classified by type (1)

Entries listed below will be found either in the A TO Z OF PARIS SIGHTS or in the preceding chapters, THE QUARTIERS OF PARIS and PARKS AND OPEN SPACES.

Look for the ★ symbol against the most important sights and 🏛 for buildings of great architectural interest. Good views are indicated using the ◁≡ symbol, and there is a special list, called VIEWPOINTS, which gives the low-down on the high places. Look out for ✱ indicating special interest for children.

CHURCHES (all 🏛)
Chapelle Expiatoire
Dôme ★
Madeleine ★
Notre-Dame de Paris
  ★ ◁≡
Sacré-Coeur, Basilique
  du ★ ◁≡
St-Augustin
Sainte-Chapelle ★
St-Denis, Basilique
St-Étienne-du-Mont
St-Eustache
St-Germain l'Auxerrois
St-Germain-des-Prés
St-Joseph-des-Carmes
St-Julien-le-Pauvre
St-Louis-Les-Invalides
St-Nicolas-des-Champs
St-Roch
St-Séverin
St-Sulpice
Val-de-Grâce

STREETS, SQUARES, QUARTIERS
Bastille, pl. de la
Bercy
Champs-Élysées, av.
  des ★
Charles-de-Gaulle, place
Cité Universitaire
Concorde, place de
  la ★
La Défense 🏛 ◁≡
Rue du Faubourg-St-
  Honoré
Grands Boulevards
Les Halles
Île de la Cité ★
Latin Quarter ★
Marais ★
Montmartre ★
Montparnasse
Rue Mouffetard
Opéra Quarter
Rue de Paradis
"Passages"

Pont Alexandre III
Pont-Neuf
Rue de Rivoli
St-Germain Quarter
Place Vendôme 🏛 ★
La Villette
Place des Vosges 🏛

FAMOUS HOMES
Balzac, Maison de
Bourdelle, Musée
  Antoine
Camondo, Musée
  Nissim de
Le Corbusier, Fondation
Delacroix, Musée
  Eugène
d'Ennery, Musée
Hugo, Maison Victor 🏛
Moreau, Musée Gustave
Pasteur, Musée
Piaf, Musée Édith,
Vie Romantique, Musée
  de la (Maison Renan-
  Scheffer)
Zadkine, Musée

GENERAL INTEREST
Air et de l'Espace,
  Musée de l'
Automobile, Centre
  International de l' ✱
Canal St-Martin
Catacombes
Cité de la Musique
Cousteau, Parc
  Océanique Jacques
  ✱
Cristalleries, Musée des
Égouts (Sewers)
Entrepôts de Bercy
Flea Market
Gobelins
Grévin, Musée ✱
Historial de Montmartre
Hôtel des Ventes
Marché aux Puces
Les Martyrs de Paris

Napoleon's Tomb
Opéra Bastille
Opéra Garnier
Palais des Congrès
Palais de la Mode
Paristoric
Pavillon de l'Arsenal
Père Lachaise, Cimetière
Publicité, Musée de la
Radio-France, Maison
  de 🏛
Rock'n'Roll Hall of Fame

HISTORIC BUILDINGS (all 🏛)
Archevêques de Sens,
  Hôtel des
Assemblée Nationale
Beaux-Arts, École des
Bibliothèque Nationale
Bourse du Commerce
Bourse des Valeurs
Collège de France
Comédie Française
Conciergerie ★
École Militaire
Hôtel de Ville
Institut de France
Hôtel des Invalides ★
Luxembourg Palais du
Observatoire de Paris
Opéra Garnier ★
Palais de Chaillot
Palais de l'Élysée
Palais de Justice
Palais-Royal
Palais de Tokyo
Panthéon ★ ◁≡
Salpêtrière
Sorbonne
Vincennes, Château de

SCIENCE AND TECHNOLOGY
Cité des Sciences et de
  l'Industrie ★ ✱
Techniques, Musée
  des ✱

A to Z of Paris sights

AIR ET DE L'ESPACE, MUSÉE DE (Air and Space Museum)

Aéroport du Bourget, Le Bourget ☎ *48-35-99-99, map 18B5. Open May-Oct 10am-6pm, Nov-Apr 10am-5pm; closed Mon. Bus 152 from Porte de La Villette, bus 350 from Gare de l'Est, Gare du Nord or Porte de la Chapelle.*

This was the first aeronautical museum in the world, when it opened its doors in 1919. Housed at Le Bourget airport since 1975, the museum has expanded considerably, and in the mid 1980s added a large gallery with a fine collection of the earliest flying machines up to 1918.

150 planes from all parts of the world, spanning from 1919 to the conquest of space, are housed in six other exhibition halls, and 20 Concorde and Mirage 2000 prototypes are to be found in an outside display area.

ARC DE TRIOMPHE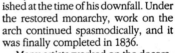

Pl. Charles-de-Gaulle, 8ᵉ ☎ *43-80-31-31. Map 5F3* 🔲 ◁€ *Open Apr 1-Sept 30 10am-5.30pm, winter 10am-4.30pm. Closed public holidays. Métro: Charles-de-Gaulle-Étoile.*

As much a symbol of Paris as the TOUR EIFFEL or NOTRE-DAME, the Arc de Triomphe is the largest structure of its kind in the world — 50m (164 feet) high and 45m (148 feet) wide — and its massive bulk dominates the PLACE CHARLES-DE-GAULLE, formerly the place de l'Étoile, from which the twelve broad avenues radiate to create the star shape.

The quickest — and safest way to reach it, positioned as it is at the center of the immense traffic circle, is by a tunnel that leads from the N side of the avenue des Champs-Élysées.

The ponderous and imposing arch is clean and shining right now, having received a thorough clean-up at the time of the bicentenary celebrations in 1989. In a way, it is surely one of the biggest "white elephants" ever created. The term is curiously appropriate, for an earlier plan for the site was to erect a vast stone elephant containing an amphitheater, banqueting hall and other apartments.

The present arch was begun in 1806, on the orders of Napoleon, who wanted a monument to French military victories, but it remained unfin-

ished at the time of his downfall. Under the restored monarchy, work on the arch continued spasmodically, and it was finally completed in 1836.

Many artists worked on the decoration of the exterior, which includes four huge relief sculptures at the bases of the pillars: *The Triumph of 1810* by Cortot; *Resistance* and *Peace* by Etex; and *The Departure of the Volunteers* (commonly known, for obvious reasons, by the name of *La Marseillaise*) by Francois Rude, which is generally considered to be the best of the four.

Higher up are reliefs of battles and a crowded frieze, and engraved around the top are the names of major victories won during the Revolutionary and Napoleonic periods. On the inside walls appear the names of lesser victories and of 558 generals.

Set into the ground under the arch is the **Tomb of the Unknown Soldier**, commemorating the dead of World Wars I and II, whose memory is kept alight by an eternal flame — a few years ago, an irreverent person cooked an omelet over it. The arch seems to invite such disrespectful gestures: in 1919 the aviator Godefroy flew under it in an airplane, defying a police ban.

Inside is a **museum of the arch's history**, which runs a continuous audiovisual program in French and English recounting the monument's great moments. But this little collection is no substitute for the real thing, and you must mount to the viewing platform for what is one of the best views in Paris. To the NE is the GRANDE ARCHE at LA DÉFENSE, constructed on an axis with the Arc de Triomphe that continues on through PLACE DE LA CONCORDE and the gardens of the TUILERIES as far as the GRAND LOUVRE with its pyramid.

Like many other disproportionately large and grandiose monuments in Paris, the arch has merged comfortably into the townscape, settling down to an almost comfortable existence like a retired general. But no trip to Paris would be complete without a visit.

ARC DE TRIOMPHE DU CARROUSEL
Pl. du Carrousel, 1ᵉʳ. Map 8H8. Métro: Tuileries, Palais-Royal Musée du Louvre.

This graceful arch, with its rose-colored marble columns, is linked with the greater ARC DE TRIOMPHE by the splendid axis formed by the CHAMPS-ÉLYSÉES and the TUILERIES, culminating now at LA DÉFENSE in the NE outskirts of Paris.

Completed in 1809, it commemorates Napoleon's victories in 1805 (including Austerlitz and Ulm), which are depicted on six marble low reliefs. It was formerly surmounted by the four gilded bronze horses from St Mark's in Venice. When these were returned to Italy in 1815 they were replaced by a bronze group, representing the Restoration, riding in a chariot drawn by four horses. The arch once formed the gateway to the Tuileries Palace, which burned down in 1871, and for many years it floated in the gardens between the great jaws of the LOUVRE like a dainty morsel about to be swallowed by a whale.

Massive excavation and rebuilding works have disrupted its peace for the past 4 years. By the summer of 1993, the ground below its feet will have been reinstated and newly laid out formal gardens will begin to re-establish. Paris' latest major project, the creation of an underground PALAIS DE LA MODE will be complete.

ARCHIVES NATIONALES: MUSÉE DE L'HISTOIRE DE FRANCE (National
Archives: Museum of French History) 🏛
Hôtel de Soubise, 60 rue des Francs-Bourgeois, 3ᵉ; Hôtel de Rohan, 87 rue Vieille-du-Temple, 3ᵉ ☎40-27-60-00. Map 10H11 🔳 ✖ Open 2-5pm. Closed Tues. Métro: Rambuteau, Hôtel-de-Ville.

How many tumultuous events have started with an innocent-looking document? The Revocation of the Edict of Nantes by Louis XIV removed freedom of worship, and drove thousands of Protestants out of France. The Revocation and the original Edict are both in the Historical Museum of France, and form part of a collection of documents belonging to the National Archives and housed in one of the great mansions of the MARAIS district, the **Hôtel de Soubise**.

Here also are the wills of Louis XIV and Napoleon, the Concordat of 1802 between Napoleon and the Holy See, the Declaration of the Rights of Man, letters by Joan of Arc and by Voltaire — snippets of history skillfully displayed and carefully illustrated with the use of maps, photographs and captions to create an intriguing scrapbook of the French nation.

The National Archives themselves, which take up 280km (175 miles) of shelving, have been housed in the Hôtel de Soubise since 1808 and in the adjacent **Hôtel de Rohan** since 1927.

There is more to see than just the documents. The Hôtel de Soubise itself, with its elegant, colonnaded **courtyard**, is worth visiting on its own account. It was built in 1705-8 for the Princesse de Soubise, on the site of a medieval mansion, of which one tower remains, overlooking rue des Archives. It was sumptuously decorated by some of the greatest artists and craftsmen of the era, including Boucher, van Loo and Lemoyne.

Leaving the main room of the museum on the first floor, formerly the guardroom, one passes through a series of **private apartments**. Particularly worth seeing are the Princess' Oval Salon, with its eight paintings of the loves of Psyche by Charles Natoire, and also her small bedroom, which now houses a permanent exhibition on the French Revolution. There are also temporary exhibitions in the apartments.

The **Hôtel de Rohan** (officially called the Hôtel de Strasbourg) is around the corner in rue Vieille-du-Temple. As well as being part of the National Archives, is now frequently used for temporary exhibitions. It was lived in by four successive cardinals of Strasbourg who decorated their **apartments** with rich extravagance. One of the rooms, the **Monkey Cabinet**, retains its original panels, decorated with animals by Christophe Huet in 1745.

The remainder of the interior is the result of skillful restoration. The courtyard has a fine relief by Robert le Lorrain, *The Horses of Apollo*.

ARÈNES DE LUTÈCE

A Gallo-Roman amphitheater with terraces for spectators, tucked away off rue Monge in the 5ᵉ. See PARKS AND OPEN SPACES on page 91.

ARMÉE, MUSÉE DE L'   See HÔTEL DES INVALIDES.

ARMÉNIEN, MUSÉE (Armenian Museum)

*59 av. Foch, 16ᵉ ☎45-56-15-88. Off map **5F1** and see BOIS DE BOULOGNE map on page 92 ⊡ Open Thurs, Sun 2-6pm. Closed Aug. Métro: Victor Hugo, Porte Dauphine.*

This small museum of works of art, documents and domestic objects provides an intriguing view of 3,000 years of Armenian history and culture. It is in the same building as the MUSÉE D'ENNERY, which houses the private collection of 19thC dramatist and librettist Adolphe d'Ennery and his wife.

ART MODERNE, MUSÉE NATIONAL D'   See POMPIDOU CENTER.

ART MODERNE DE LA VILLE DE PARIS, MUSÉE D' (Museum of Modern Art of the City of Paris) 🏛

Palais de Tokyo, 11 av. du Président-Wilson, Paris 16ᵉ ☎47-23-61-27. Map *11G3* 🚉 ⟵ 💺 ✿ *Open 10am-5.30pm (Wed until 8.30pm). Closed Mon. Métro: Iéna, Alma-Marceau.*

A lively museum, housed in the w wing of the PALAIS DE TOKYO. This stately building is a typical example of 1930s style, which once seemed so aggressively modern and yet now bears the hallmarks of another time. Something of the same feeling is also evoked as you enter the museum, and it is helpful to see the paintings in the context of their periods: for example, Raoul Dufy's huge canvas *La Fée Électricité* (The Good Fairy Electricity).

Other items in this very fine collection include Cubist paintings by Picasso and Braque, canvases of the Fauve school (Matisse, Derain) and works by artists of the Paris school (Modigliani, Soutine, Pascin). There are also temporary exhibitions.

On the top floor is **ARC** *(Animation, Recherche, Confrontation),* an area devoted to offbeat contemporary exhibitions and to concerts, lectures and other cultural events. Down on the lowest level is the **Musée des Enfants** *(entrance at 14 av. de New York),* where children are able to take part in various taught creative activities, from painting to dancing.

ARTS AFRICAINS ET OCÉANIENS, MUSÉE NATIONAL DES (Museum of African and Oceanic Arts)

293 av. Daumesnil, 12ᵉ ☎44-74-84-80. Map *18D5* and see BOIS DE VINCENNES *map on page 99* 🚉 ✗ *by prior arrangement* ✿ ⟵ *Open Mon, Wed-Fri 10am-noon, 1.30-5.30pm; Sat, Sun 12.30-6pm (aquarium 10am-6pm). Closed Tues. Métro: Porte-Dorée.*

This museum, housed in a building put up for the Colonial Exhibition of 1931, contains a superb collection of ethnic art: Benin bronzes, masks from New Guinea, Aboriginal bark paintings and a particularly fine display of North African Islamic art. Down in the basement is one of the best tropical aquariums in Europe, complete with crocodiles, where admission is free for under-18s.

ARTS ASIATIQUES GUIMET, MUSÉE NATIONAL DES

6 pl. d'Iéna, 16ᵉ ☎47-23-61-65. Map *5G3* 🚉 ✗ *Open 9.45am-5pm. Closed Tues. Métro Iéna.*

If the East holds any appeal for you, then this treasure house of Asian art is a must. Its nucleus is a collection formed by the 19thC industrialist Émile Guimet, whose intention was to gather together objects illustrating the civilizations and religions of the Orient.

Since the museum became a national one, it has been greatly enriched by the addition of other Oriental collections, and now houses a splendid, wide-ranging array of works of art from Afghanistan, Pakistan, India, Vietnaml Laos, Kampuchea, China, Korea, Japan, Thailand, Tibet and Nepal. The museum is justly renowned for its Kampuchean sculptures, as well as for its magnificent Tibetan *tangkas* (devotional paintings used for meditation), and ritual instruments reflecting the richly colorful and highly symbolic world of Tantric Buddhism.

Scholars are welcome to visit the museum's research and study center, which houses a library, a photographic archive and an auditorium.

ARTS DÉCORATIFS, MUSÉE DES (Museum of Decorative Arts) 🏛

107 rue de Rivoli, 1er ☎42-60-32-14. Map 7H7🔲 Joint admission if required, with Musée des Arts de la Mode et du Textile and Musée de la Publicité ♿ ✗ Open 12.30-6pm, Sun noon-6pm. Closed Mon, Tues, public holidays. Métro: Tuileries, Palais-Royal Musée du Louvre.

Founded in the 1870s as part of an attempt to combat mediocrity in the applied arts, this museum presents a panorama of decorative art from the Middle Ages to the 20thC. Housed in the **Pavilion Marsan** of the GRAND LOUVRE, up to 130,000 exhibits are set out in a series of rooms furnished and decorated in the style of different eras.

Here you can see medieval carvings, chests and tapestry work, Renaissance stained glass, elaborate inlaid 17thC furniture, 18thC Vincennes porcelain and 20thC Art Nouveau paneling. One of the most striking rooms is a complete Second Empire **Italianate salon** with richly painted and gilded wood paneling.

A further series of impressive displays show furniture and household objects from more recent years, and the Art Nouveau and Art Deco rooms are a wonder to behold. The museum also houses a large and important **toy collection (**👶**)**.

In the same building is the MUSÉE DES ARTS DE LA MODE ET DU TEXTILE, which deals with women's fashions from the Middle Ages onward, and the MUSÉE DE LA PUBLICITÉ, which exhibits themed shows displaying printed publicity material through the ages. The three museums are run by the Union des Arts Décoratifs, together with the MUSÉE NISSIM DE CAMONDO.

There is also an extensive library dedicated to the decorative arts *(open Tues-Sat 10am-5.30pm, Mon 1.45-5.30pm, closed Sun).*

ARTS DE LA MODE ET DU TEXTILE, MUSÉE DES

109 rue de Rivoli, 1er ☎42-60-32-14. Map 7H7🔲 Joint admission if required, with Musée des Arts Décoratifs and Musée de la Publicité ♿ 👶 Open 12.30-6pm, Sun 11am-6pm. Closed Mon, Tues, public holidays. Métro: Tuileries, Palais-Royal Musée-du-Louvre.

Not to be confused with the MUSÉE DE LA MODE, this museum is more specifically oriented to the fashion industry and its history, providing a record by preserving examples of important collections and items of clothing, and illustrating the development of style.

It will be complemented, by fall 1993, by the nearby presence of the PALAIS DE LA MODE, the new focal point for the world of fashion based around the Paris fashion houses, below the JARDINS DES TUILERIES.

ARTS ET TRADITIONS POPULAIRES, MUSÉE DES (Museum of Popular Arts and Traditions)

6 av.du Mahatma Gandhi, Bois de Boulogne, 16ᵉ ☎*44-17-60-00. Map **17**C3 and see* BOIS DE BOULOGNE *map on page 92* ▣ ᕗ *✗ by prior arrangement* ✿ *Open 10am-5.15pm. Closed Tues. Métro: Les Sablons.*

A cock from a church steeple, models of fishing boats, Breton peasant costumes, a blacksmith's forge, a clairvoyant's consulting room complete with crystal ball and tarot cards — these and many more curiosities are to be found in this colorful museum dealing with French folk art and culture from the beginning of the Iron Age to the 20thC.

A visit adds another dimension to a pleasant excursion to the BOIS DE BOULOGNE.

ASSEMBLÉE NATIONALE (National Assembly) ▥

33 quai d'Orsay, 7ᵉ ☎*40-63-60-00. Map **7**H6 ▣ ▰ ✗ compulsory. In session: open Sat 9-11am, 2-4pm. Out of session: open Mon-Sat 9-11am, 2-5pm (Sat 4pm). Métro: Assemblée Nationale, Invalides.*

The French lower house of parliament (called the Assemblée Nationale or Chambre des Députés) meets in the Palais-Bourbon, a mansion originally built by the Duchess of Bourbon, a daughter of Louis XIV, and later acquired by the State and extensively altered. Only the great courtyard facing s preserves most of its original features. The facade looking onto the Seine, with its heavy Greek-style portico, was constructed in the time of Napoleon.

The National Assembly jealously guards its independence from the Government and the State. No minister can be a *député* as well, and the president cannot enter the building, although he can be received in the adjacent house of the president of the Assembly, the **Hôtel de Lassay**.

The 577 deputies meet in an ornate, semicircular chamber of red, white and gold. The marble speaker's tribune was originally adorned with a Napoleonic eagle (tactfully changed into a cock when republicanism finally triumphed), but the room retains an aspect of imperial splendor.

During sessions you can watch from a public gallery, but seats are limited. The first ten people in the line on any given day are admitted on showing a passport or identity card.

Other parts of the building to which visitors are given access include the **library**, a discreetly grand room with a Delacroix ceiling depicting a history of civilization.

AUTOMOBILE, CENTRE INTERNATIONAL DE L'

25 rue d'Estienne d'Orves, Pantin ☎*48-43-79-14. Map **18**C5 ▣ ᕗ ▰ ✿ Open 10.30am-6.30pm (Tues 10pm). Métro: Hoche.*

Anyone who has ever wanted to see below the hood of a Bugatti, or daydream over cars that have seen the Daytona track, should head for this center dedicated to the glory of the automobile, from the early days of its conception to first glimpses of things to come.

Different makes of car are on show, from many countries of origin, and the program of exhibits changes every 3-4 months. Children are welcome at the center, and there are organized activities for over-3s, audiovisual road-safety instruction, and, for older children, driving-simulation games.

The traditional base of the French automobile industry is to the w of Paris. This center provides an eastern counterbalance at Pantin, and has revitalized the former Motobécane works.

BALZAC, MAISON DE
47 rue Raynouard, 16ᵉ ☎*42-24-56-38. Off map 11I1* 🚃 *ƙ Open 10am-5.40pm. Closed Mon, public holidays. Métro: Passy, La Muette.*

This house is the only survivor of the several Paris homes lived in by Honoré de Balzac (1799-1850), the author of the great series of novels entitled *La Comédie Humaine*. It would no doubt appeal to Balzac's sense of irony to find it being used as a museum to his memory, for he considered it somewhat degradingn He fled there from his creditors in 1840, renting it in the name of his housekeeper in order to avoid their attentions, and remained there for seven years. It was here that he wrote some of his last novels, including *La Rabouilleuse, Une Ténébreuse Affaire* and *La Cousine Bette.*

Whatever reservations Balzac may have had about it, to the modern visitor, his house appears an idyllic place that still possesses the flavor of his era and the stamp of his personality. It is approached from a terrace lying below the level of rue Raynouard. Passing through a gate that seems to lead nowhere, one suddenly descends some steps into the hidden garden of a charming, rustic-looking building with pale turquoise shutters. It appears to be a single-story cottage but is, in fact, the top floor of a large house, which has another entrance on a lower street.

The house is full of fascinating mementoes of Balzac, including a series of tradesmen's invoices. One of them is from a glove-maker, and the caption reveals that Balzac once bought 60 pairs of gloves in a month. Personal effects on display include his coffee pot — he often drank 30 cups a day to sustain his prodigious output. There is also a library of books by and about Balzac.

BASTILLE, PLACE DE LA
4ᵉ. Map 16J12. Métro: Bastille.

Built between 1370-82, the Bastille served for four centuries as a fortress and prison — mainly for powerful people who had fallen foul of the king. On July 14, 1789 it was stormed by a Revolutionary mob and afterwards demolished, an event still annually celebrated with gusto in France. Now all that remains of the Bastille is a line of cobblestones at the w side of the square, marking out the ground plan of the once formidable building with its projecting towers. There are pictures of the Bastille before — and during — its storming and demolition, to be seen at the GRAND CARNAVALET museum.

Today, place de la Bastille is a huge, bustling intersection, bounded on the s side by the Arsenal Basin. This contains a boating marina, the **Port de Plaisance de l'Arsenal**, and is surrounded by movie theaters, cafés and shops. It is dominated by the **Colonne de Juillet** (July column), a massive memorial surmounted by the gilded, allegorical

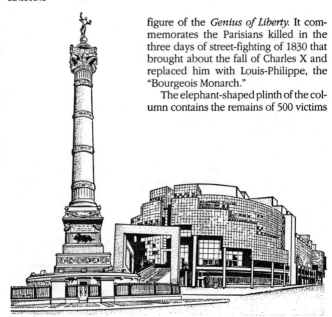

figure of the *Genius of Liberty.* It commemorates the Parisians killed in the three days of street-fighting of 1830 that brought about the fall of Charles X and replaced him with Louis-Philippe, the "Bourgeois Monarch."

The elephant-shaped plinth of the column contains the remains of 500 victims of the fighting, as well as another 196 who died in the 1848 uprising against Louis-Philippe. Curiously, an Egyptian mummy is also housed there. Their marble-lined crypt can be entered through a door in the plinth.

The completion in 1990 of the new opera house, the OPÉRA BASTILLE, came as a welcome relief not only to lovers of opera but to the inhabitants of the area, for it lifted the blight caused by the years of continuing building work.

BEAUBOURG
Familiar name for the POMPIDOU CENTER.

BEAUX-ARTS, ÉCOLE NATIONALE SUPÉRIEURE
(School of Fine Arts) 𝔪
Exhibition entrance at 17 quai Malaquais, 6ᵉ ☎*46-60-34-57. Map 8I8. Open 8am-8pm (library 1-6pm); closed Sat, Sun, Aug, public holidays. Métro: St-Germain-des-Prés.*

In his *Paris Sketch Book,* 150 years ago, the English novelist William Makepeace Thackeray wrote of this building: "With its light and elegant fabric, its pretty fountain, its archway of the Renaissance, and fragments of sculpture, you can hardly see, on a fine day, a place more *riant* and pleasing." His words apply equally well today.

The former Couvent (convent) des Petits Augustins has housed the School of Fine Arts since 1817. Although the main buildings date from the 19thC, the chapel and cloisters are much earlier. There is no permanent exhibition gallery, but exhibitions of painting and sculpture are held here several times a year. But it is a pleasure simply to wander through the courtyards and mingle with the students.

BERCY   See THE QUARTIERS OF PARIS.

BIBLIOTHÈQUE NATIONALE (National Library) 𝗺
58 rue de Richelieu, 2ᵉ ☎47-03-81-26. Map 8G8 ⬛ Medallions and Antiques Gallery open noon-6pm. Mansart and Mazarine Galleries open noon-6pm. Photography Gallery (in the Rotonde Colbert, entered from 2 rue Vivienne) open noon-6pm. All closed Sun, public holidays. Métro: Bourse, Palais-Royal Musée-du-Louvre.

As befits one of the world's greatest collections of books, manuscripts, prints, maps, medallions and other treasures, the Bibliothèque is housed in a splendid mansion, the main entrance of which is in rue de Richelieu, reached via a fine courtyard. The building was created by Cardinal Mazarin in the 17thC out of two adjacent houses, the Hôtel Tubeuf and the Hôtel Chivry, and the resulting complex covers an entire block. After Mazarin's death, the mansion was split between different owners.

Part of it, which had come into the hands of the crown, became the repository of the royal library, later the National Library, which ultimately took over the whole of Mazarin's mansion. Since 1537, a copy of every French book published has, by law, been kept there.

Accredited scholars have access to the library's service departments, and members of the public can view the **medallion collection** on the first floor, the temporary exhibitions in the ground floor **Mansart Gallery** and the superb **Mazarin Gallery** at the top of the imposing stairway, and those in the **Rotonde Colbert** photographic gallery. Through a glass door, the magnificent Second Empire reading room, with its domed ceiling and cast-iron columns, gives the impression of a Byzantine cathedral.

The national library has announced its relocation to Tolbiac *(127-141 quai de la Gare, 13ᵉ, map 16M13)*, to the E of Paris, near the Gare d'Austerlitz and immediately across the river from the ambitious developments at Bercy. Work began in 1990 on a still controversial scheme for the **TGB** (short for *Très Grande Bibliothèque*) or **Bibliothèque de France** by a young French architect, Dominique Perrault.

It echoes yet again a trend toward building underground. The reading rooms will be lit from the side, via a 12,000sq.m (130,000 sq.ft) garden punched through the piazza from above, and four L-shaped glass-and-steel towers will stand one at each corner of the piazza, in the shape of open books.

Present opinions estimate completion by 1995, but time alone will tell. The future use of the beautiful but cramped building in the rue de Richelieu has yet to be decided.

BOIS DE BOULOGNE

This 900ha (2,224 acre) park on the western outskirts of Paris contains within its boundaries the racecourses of Longchamp and Auteuil, the Jardin d'Acclimatation and the Pré Catelan, with its Shakespeare Garden. See PARKS AND OPEN SPACES on page 91.

BOURDELLE, MUSÉE ANTOINE

16 rue Antoine-Bourdelle, 15ᵉ ☎45-48-67-27. Map 13K6 ⛝ ▣ on Sun ⅋.
✗ Tues 2.30pm only. Open 10am-5.30pm. Closed Mon, public holidays. Métro: Falguière, Montparnasse-Bienvenüe.

This charming oasis in MONTPARNASSE was for 45 years the home and studio of Antoine Bourdelle (1861-1929), a sculptor of genius who, along with his friend Rodin, helped to give sculpture a new lease on life. Where Rodin's work has the fluidity of emotion, Bourdelle's is characterized by the thrusting harnessed power of the will, seen in such creations as his *Héracles Archer* and *Tête d'Apollon*. These and Bourdelle's paintings, including portraits, landscapes and still-lifes, are displayed in a series of light, spacious rooms and leafy courtyards.

Part of the museum is used for temporary exhibitions by other sculptors. The museum has been undergoing extension and renovation work is due for completion early in 1993.

BOURSE DES VALEURS (Stock Exchange) ⛿

4 pl. de la Bourse (entrance through railings in rue Vivienne), 2ᵉ ☎42-33-99-83.
Map 8F8 ⛝ ✗ᵒ ✗ compulsory, every half hour from 11am-1pm; identification essential. Closed Sat, Sun, hols. Métro: Bourse.

Outwardly a serene, 19thC Classical building surrounded by Corinthian columns, inwardly a scene of high-level stress, as international money transactions are conducted at the speed of lightning. Gone are the days of wild gesticulations and yelling "*Je prends!*" for computers and telephones have made the process more efficient for the brokers, and quieter into the bargain.

To enable visitors to make sense of the spectacle of the dealing room floor, which they will witness from a gallery at the end of the tour, they are first given a series of film shows and lectures on the workings of the Bourse and the stock market. The whole tour lasts for an hour and a half, and is not geared toward foreign visitors with a less-than-good grasp of French. If you have an interest in money matters at this level, and your French can stand the pace, it is a fascinating show. Remember to take your passport.

BOURSE DU COMMERCE (Commodities Exchange)

2 rue de Viarmes, 1ᵉʳ. Map 9H9. Métro: Châtelet-Les-Halles, Les Halles.

Victor Hugo compared this drum-shaped building to a jockey's cap without the peak. Built in the 18thC and modified in the 19th, it once served as a corn exchange. Now the majestic domed hall at the western boundary of the FORUM DES HALLES is the scene of a busy commodity market for such products as sugar, coffee, cocoa and grain.

The building's site has had a varied history. Louis XII had a mansion there which he lost at a game of cribbage with his chamberlain, who proceeded to convert it into a convent for repentant girls — postulants had to prove that they had lived a life of prostitution. In 1572 Catherine de Medicis dislodged the girls to make way for a magnificent palace, the Hôtel de Soissons, constructed for her by Philibert Delorme and Bullant. All that remains today is the curious column on the S side of the present building, said to have been used as an observatory by the queen's astrologerl Cosimo Ruggieri.

BUTTES CHAUMONT, PARC DES

This landscaped park in the NE in the 10ᵉ has a strongly romantic appeal, with its wooded contours and lake. See PARKS AND OPEN SPACES on page 93.

CAMONDO, MUSÉE NISSIM DE 🏛

63 rue de Monceau, 8ᵉ ☎ 45-63-26-32. Map 1E5 🔲 *𝒳 Open 10am-noon, 2-5pm. Closed Mon, Tues. Métro: Villiers, Monceau.*

Like the nearby CERNUSCHI museum, this is a private house and contents which have been bequeathed to the nation. Its creator, Count Moïse de Camondo, was a rich collector with a passion for 18thC decorative art. In 1910 he built a house in the style of the Petit Trianon at VERSAILLES, where he set out to re-create the atmosphere of an 18thC interior. Thanks to his discrimination and finely tuned visual sense, the effect is one of harmony combined with the highest quality. The furniture is by such master cabinet-makers as Jacob, Riesener and Saunier, and the tapestries come from the great workshops of GOBELINS, Beauvais and Aubusson — one particularly fine set depicts the famous fables of La Fontaine.

The museum is sumptuous, although it is hard to imagine such objects ever being approached other than on tiptoe.

A school of bookbinding *(Centre des Arts du Livre ☎ 45-63-37-39, closed Sat, Sun)* has been set up close by. All aspects of binding, gilding and decoration are covered here, and anyone connected with books — librarians, typographers, illustrators or printers — are welcome. Plans are afoot to stage exhibitions open to the general public.

CANAL ST-MARTIN

The Canal St-Martin links the Seine with the Canal de l'Ourcq, in the 19ᵉ and 10ᵉ in the NE of the city. See PARKS AND OPEN SPACES on page 93.

CARNAVALET, MUSÉE   Now called the GRAND CARNAVALET.

CATACOMBES (Catacombs)

1 pl. Denfert-Rochereau, 14ᵉ ☎ 43-22-47-63. Map 13M7 🔲 *𝒳 (extra* 🔲*). Open Tues-Fri 2-4pm, Sat, Sun 9-11am, 2-4pm. Closed Mon, public holidays. Métro: Denfert-Rochereau.*

Here is a creepy experience: a walk of three-quarters of an hour through a subterranean necropolis. These are not ancient catacombs like the ones in Rome, but former stone quarries that were filled with the bones cleared from many Parisian cemeteries during the 18th and 19thC. They have been open to the public since 1874 but the visitor sees only a small part of the 300km (187 miles) of tunnels.

The tunnels leading to the ossuary pass a representation of a fort, carved out of the rock by an 18thC tunnel worker in his leisure time. Then a chamber with black and white painted pillars leads off to a doorway over which are the words: *"Arrête! C'est ici l'empire de la mort."* ("Stop! This is the empire of death.") Beyond it stretches tunnel after tunnel, lined on each side with neatly-piled bones interspersed with rows of grinning skulls and enlivened by plaques bearing inscriptions of death.

There are 5 to 6 million skeletons here. The whole place is a *memento mori* of the most dramatic kind.

CERNUSCHI, MUSÉE

7 av. Velasquez, 8ᵉ ☎45-63-50-75. Map 1E5 ▨ ▣ on Sun ᕀ Open 10am-5.40pm. Closed Mon, public holidays. Métro: Villiers, Monceau.

Paris possesses this interesting museum of Chinese art, situated in a fine house just near the E gate of the PARC DE MONCEAU, thanks to a colorful Milanese financier named Cernuschi. A disciple of Garibaldi, Cernuschi was once condemned to death for his Revolutionary activities, but was reprieved by Napoleon III and later became a French citizen. Before his death in 1896 he bequeathed his house and magnificent collection of Chinese objects to the city of Paris.

Smaller and less impressive than the collection in the MUSÉE GUIMET, this exhibition nevertheless gives a very informative picture of the development of Chinese art from prehistoric times. It includes a selection of paintings by modern Chinese artists, but perhaps the most evocative picture is a 13thC ink-and-brush drawing of a bird on a twig, which combines humor and simplicity with sophistication (it is the one on the left as you face into the museum).

A treasured recent acquisition is a 7thC Tang-epoch wooden funerary statue from NW China. An imposing Buddha dominates the central hall.

CHAMP-DE-MARS

The Champ-de-Mars, an 18thC military parade ground and now a formal park, extends below the TOUR EIFFEL. See PARKS AND OPEN SPACES on page 94.

CHAMPS-ÉLYSÉES, AVENUE DES ★

8ᵉ. Maps 5-7. Métro: Charles-de-Gaulle-Étoile, George-V, Franklin-D-Roosevelt, Champs-Élysées-Clemenceau, Concorde.

If there is one Parisian street that is known throughout the world it is this one. It forms a great triumphal tree-lined sweep from PLACE DE LA CONCORDE to the ARC DE TRIOMPHE. At its lower end, as far as the intersection known as the **Rond-Point**, it is bounded by strips of park. Then, along the stretch that climbs in a shallow ramp toward the Arc de Triomphe, it is lined by imposing buildings: offices, smart shops, movie theaters, airline offices, restaurants and sidewalk cafés.

The tone of this part of the avenue has been deteriorating in the past ten years, and this problem is now being taken in hand. Mayor Chirac's 5-year 200-million-franc refurbishment plan, with the planting of a second row of trees, clampdowns on parking, street signs etc. should be completed by 1995.

The lower part of the avenue was laid out by Louis XIV's gardener, Le Nôtre, in 1670, and the upper part some 40 years later. However, the road remained a muddy and unsalubrious thoroughfare until it acquired an element of fashion and style in the 18thC with the building of the grand houses in RUE DU FAUBOURG-ST-HONORÉ. From very early in its history it was frequented by ladies of pleasure. In 1778, for example, a Swiss guard apprehended a priest there, in the company of a young black woman to whom he claimed to be giving religious instruction. Half a century later, Balzac wrote of the "dark-eyed houris" who frequented the avenue. Their successors are still operating here today.

The street is an obvious route for processions. It was down the Champs-Élysées that the victorious German troops marched in 1940, and four years later, the same street witnessed the triumphant return of De Gaulle. Walk down it and you will feel a swell of exultation, but curiously, despite its many cafés, it is not the most inviting place to linger. The ghosts of all those marchers seem to hurry you on.

CHAPELLE EXPIATOIRE
Square Louis XVI, 29 rue Pasquier, 8ᵉ ☎ *42-65-35-80. Map 7F6. Open summer 10am-1pm, 2-5pm; winter closes 4pm; spring/autumn closes 5pm. Closed hols.*
This solidly built chapel, in a little square off boulevard Haussmann, was erected by Louis XVIII, in memory of Louis XVI and Marie Antoinettel on the site of a graveyard where 3,000 victims of the Revolution, including the royal couple, were buried. Within the chapel there are monuments dedicated to them.

The two-story chapel is surrounded on all sides by a temple-like portico and arcade, and overlooks a peaceful little square which offers a pleasant place to sit down, as a respite from shopping on the GRANDS BOULEVARDS.

CHARLES-DE-GAULLE, PLACE (Place de l'Étoile)
8ᵉ. Map 5F3. Métro: Charles-de-Gaulle-Étoile.
The great intersection encircling the ARC DE TRIOMPHE was given its present name after De Gaulle's death in 1970, but most Parisians still call it by its apt former name, the place de l'Étoile (star). The ARC DE TRIOMPHE, at the center of the star shape, was built between 1806-36, but it was not until 1854 that Haussmann was commissioned by Napoleon III to create the grand townscape that we see there today.

Twelve great avenues radiate from l'Étoile. They include **Avenue des Champs-Élysées**, which plunges down to PLACE DE LA CONCORDE, gracious, park-lined **Avenue Foch** with its luxurious buildings stretching toward the BOIS DE BOULOGNE, and **Avenue de la Grand Armée**, which points to Neuilly and LA DÉFENSE.

Place Charles-de-Gaulle is one of the most photographed parts of Paris — especially from the air, where its layout looks particularly dramatic.

CHASSE ET DE LA NATURE, MUSÉE DE LA (Museum of Hunting and Nature) 🏛

60 rue des Archives, 3ᵉ ☎*42-72-86-43. Map 10H11* 🖾 *𝄭 ♣ Open 10am-12.30pm, 1.30-5.30pm. Closed Tues, hols. Métro: Rambuteau, Hôtel-de-Ville.*

Everything you ever needed to know about hunting is assembled in an attractive old MARAIS mansion: hunting weapons of all kinds, stuffed animals, paintings of famous hunters and huntresses such as *Diana* by Breughel and Rubens, and *St-Eustache,* by Cranach.

The building, the **Hôtel de Guénégaud des Brosses,** with its well-mannered courtyard and dignified design, was built by François Mansart between 1648-51 and was in a dilapidated condition when François Sommer took it over in the early 1960s. His own big-game trophies are among those on display. Now the building stands beautifully restored, to delight architectural as well as hunting enthusiasts.

CINÉMA HENRI-LANGLOIS, MUSÉE DU 🏛

Palais de Chaillot, pl. du Trocadéro, 16ᵉ ☎*45-53-74-39. Map 11H2* 🖾 *🕮 ▬ ♣ 𝄭 (compulsory, at 10am, 11am, 2pm, 3pm, 4pm). Closed Tues, public holidays. Métro: Trocadéro.*

The modest entrance to this museum (allied to the CINÉMATHÈQUE FRAN-ÇAISE) at the bottom of a flight of steps in the PALAIS DE CHAILLOT does not prepare the visitor for the riches within. The museum staff take visitors first through the early technology of cinematography, dating back to 1895, then through a series of galleries full of the trappings that have enabled movie-makers to create a world of make-believe.

There are sets from famous movies such as *The Cabinet of Doctor Caligari,* costumes such as the tunic worn by Rudolph Valentino in *The Sheik,* Garbo's robes, papier-mâché monsters, a robot from Fritz Lang's *Metropolis . . .* and much more. The conducted visit takes about an hour and a quarter.

CINÉMATHÈQUE FRANÇAISE

Palais de Chaillot, Jardin du Trocadéro, av. Albert-de-Mun, 16ᵉ ☎*47-04-24-24. Map 11H2* 🖾 *Métro: Trocadéro.*

The film library in the PALAIS DE CHAILLOT is a national institution for the screening of distinguished films from all periods of cinema history. See also THE PERFORMING ARTS.

CITÉ DE LA MUSIQUE
CITÉ DES SCIENCES ET DE L'INDUSTRIE (City of Science and Industry)

Both to the NE of Paris in the developing PARC DE LA VILLETTE.

CITÉ DU VIN ET D'ALIMENTAIRE   See ENTREPÔTS DE BERCY.

CITÉ UNIVERSITAIRE

Blvd. Jourdan, 14ᵉ. Map 18D4. Métro: Cité-Universitaire.

This sprawling student community on the s perimeter of Paris, inaugurated in 1925, with its pavilions for different nations, is an excellent place to study contrasting styles of architecture. Each building reflects some aspect of its country's architecture: the Greek pavilion is a Hellenic temple, and the Indo-Chinese building resembles a pagoda.

Admirers of Le Corbusier will be interested in the Swiss and Brazilian halls which he designed.

CLEMENCEAU, MUSÉE

8 rue Franklin, 16ᵉ ☎*45-20-53-41. Map **11H2** 🖼 ✗ Open Tues, Thurs, Sat, Sun 2-5pm. Métro: Passy.*
The apartment where the statesman Georges Clemenceau lived from 1895 until his death in 1929 is preserved exactly as he left it, down to the quill pen with which he wrote. The environment has the stamp of an exceptionally powerful and many-faceted personality.

CLUNY, THERMES DE/MUSÉE NATIONAL DU MOYEN ÂGE 🏛

6 pl. Paul-Painlevé, 5ᵉ ☎*43-25-62-00. Map **9J9** 🖼 Open 9.30am-5.15pm. Closed Tues, public holidays ✗ (Museum) Wed 3.15pm ✗ (Thermal Baths) daily. Métro: Cluny-La-Sorbonne.*
This outstanding museum in the LATIN QUARTER is a remarkable archeological site housing a great collection of ancient and medieval objects.

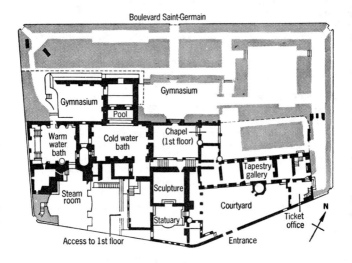

It comprises two buildings: the remains of the Gallo-Roman baths or **Thermes de Lutèce** (circa AD200) and the exquisite Flamboyant Gothic **Hôtel de Cluny**. One of only four such buildings now remaining in Paris, the hôtel was constructed at the end of the 15thC as a Parisian residence for the abbot of Cluny, in Burgundy. The U-shaped building incorporated the ruins of the thermal baths and enclosed an inner courtyard. The internal layout has remained remarkably intact; the chapel, on the first floor, has an exquisite vaulted Flamboyant Gothic ceiling.

The Gallo-Roman Baths would have consisted of three large rooms, the hot steam bath, the tepid bath and the *frigidarium* or cold bath. This 15m-high (50ft) cold-water bath has survived, and is the oldest vaulted room in France. The foundations of the other spaces are still clearly visible, together with the drains and hot-air ducts.

The museum contains one of the richest medieval collections in the world, yet the entire collection can be viewed comfortably in half a day. Many treasures, both ecclesiastical and domestic objects, are arranged to present a picture of everyday life. There is a complete panorama of monumental sculpture, and the recently rediscovered 21 heads of the Kings of Judah, from the cathedral of Notre-Dame, can now be seen. The museum contains a large array of ecclesiastical and votive items such as reliquary boxes, patens, chalices and candle holders, a dazzling display of dozens of pieces of stained glass work spanning the centuries, as well as textiles and tapestries, furniture, metalwork and paintings.

This is an opportunity to see one of the finest collections of medieval tapestry work in existence. The museum's most famous exhibit, in a special first-floor hall, is the set of six late 15thC tapestries known as the *Lady with the Unicorn* (★), woven in lively detail, in beautiful, muted colors. Five of the tapestries symbolically illustrate the five senses, and the sixth is thought to illustrate mastery of them. A card explaining what is happening in each tapestry can be found in a box near the door. Look for the little smile on the face of the unicorn as he catches sight of himself in the mirror.

COGNACQ-JAY, MUSÉE

8 rue Elzévir, 3ᵉ ☎40-27-07-21. Map **10**I11 ▨ ▣ on Sun ✗ Open 10am-5.40pm. Closed Mon, hols. Métro: St-Paul, Chemin Vert.

Ernest Cognacq, creator of the Samaritaine chain of shops, and his wife, Louise Jay, opened to the public their collection of 18thC art in the 1920s. Paradoxically, Cognacq was no art-lover — he boasted that he had never entered the Louvre — and he became a collector purely for status reasons. However, with expert advice he succeeded in acquiring many works of the highest rank, such as Boucher's *Le Retour de Chasse de Diane,* Tiepolo's *Le Festin de Cléopatre* and Reynolds' portrait of Lord Northington. Watteau, Fragonard, Rembrandt and Gainsborough are among other artists represented.

There is also a remarkable collection of porcelain ornaments, gold and silver boxes and other small *objets d'art.* Formerly in the Opéra quarter, the museum has relocated to the **Hôtel Donon** in the MARAIS.

COLLÈGE DE FRANCE

Rue des Écoles, 5ᵉ. Map **14**J9. Métro: Maubert-Mutualité.

This great institute of learning in the LATIN QUARTER was founded in 1529 by Francois I at the instigation of the scholar Guillaume Budé, whose statue now stands in the w courtyard. The college was founded to counteract the hidebound dogmatism of the neighboring SORBONNE and was for a time known as the "Three-Language College" because Hebrew, Greek and Latin were taught there. Subsequently, its syllabus expanded to include many other academic disciplines from Arabic to physics, and today it maintains a high reputation, as well as a liberal admissions policy.

Smaller and less bombastic in architecture than the Sorbonne, it has something of the intimate atmosphere of a small Oxford or Cambridge college.

LA COMÉDIE FRANÇAISE 🏛

2 rue de Richelieu, 1ᵉʳ ☎ 44-58-14-00. Map 8H8 ☒ ✗ on first Sun of month at 10am (call Mon-Fri to reserve ahead). Métro: Palais-Royal Musée-du-Louvre, Pyramides.

After it was founded in 1680 by Louis XIV, this famous company of actors moved house several times and finally settled on the present site at the end of the 18thC. The theater, which has evolved over the years into the grand colonnaded building that it occupies today, is set in a prime position next to the PALAIS-ROYAL.

Despite its name, the company does not necessarily perform comedies. Traditionally the repertoire has emphasized classical French dramatists such as Molière, Corneille and Racine, but lately it has been widened to include modern and foreign playwrights.

LA CONCIERGERIE

1 quai de l'Horloge, Île de la Cité, 4ᵉ ☎ 43-54-30-06. Map 9I9 ☒ Reduced joint ticket with Sainte-Chapelle ✗ Open June-Aug 9.30am-6.30pm, Sept, Apr, May 9.30am-6pm, Oct-Mar 10am-4.30pm. Closed hols. Métro: Cité, Châtelet St-Michel.

The Conciergerie has a gloomy atmosphere that matches its gloomy history as a place of imprisonment, death and torture. Part of the great palace built on the N side of the ÎLE DE LA CITÉ by King Philippe the Fair (1284-1314), it is now incorporated into the PALAIS DE JUSTICE complex. The name is derived from the title of the royal officer called the Concierge ("*Comte des Cierges*" or Count of the Candles). He was superintendent of the palace and was empowered to administer justice in its environs. Increasingly the Conciergerie took on the functions of a prison, especially after the building became for a time the seat of parliament, which was also the country's supreme court.

It was here that such malefactors as Ravaillac, assassin of Henry IV, and Damiens, who attempted to kill Louis XV, were brought and hideously tortured before being executed. However, it was during the Revolution that the Conciergerie received its real baptism of blood. Its most famous prisoner was Marie-Antoinette, who was kept here before being taken to the guillotine. Her cell is now a chapel to her memory, but her name is only one of a list of many who passed through on their way to execution. The Revolutionary leader Danton condemned 22 Girondins, de Robespierre condemned Danton, the Thermidor Convention condemned de Robespierre . . . . In all, nearly 2,600 prisoners were sent for execution from the Conciergerie between the winter of 1793 and summer of 1794. You can still see the grim little room where they were shaved and relieved of their possessions before being taken to the tumbrils. In 1792, 288 prisoners were murdered in the prison itself.

Despite the unpleasant vibrations created by this history, the building does, in fact, possess some beautiful features: the **Salle des Gardes**, the first room you enter, with its elegant vaulting and carved bosses; the magnificent **Salle des Gens d'Armes**, 69m (226 feet) long and 27m (88 feet) wide, with three rows of eight pillars, which is sometimes used as a setting for concerts; and the **kitchen**, with its four fireplaces, each big enough to roast an ox, which, in the 14thC, provided food for 5,000.

The chapel, which housed the 22 condemned Girondin deputies, now contains a depressing but intriguing little collection of mementoes, including a guillotine blade, Marie-Antoinette's crucifix and two portraits of her from life.

CONCORDE, PLACE DE LA ★

8ᵉ. Map 7G6. Métro: Concorde.

The largest square in Paris is also arguably the most striking and beautiful townscape in the world, but to appreciate the square fully, you must brave the whirling blizzard of traffic and cross the road to the center. It is advisable to use the two official crossings.

This vantage point provides stately vistas in all directions: W up AVENUE DES CHAMPS-ÉLYSÉES to the ARC DE TRIOMPHE, with the GRANDE ARCHE at LA DÉFENSE just visible through it; E through the TUILERIES gardens to the LOUVRE, with the JEU DE PAUME and the ORANGERIE on either side; S across the **Pont de la Concorde** to the ASSEMBLÉE NATIONALE and N up **rue Royale** to LA MADELEINE between the matching colonnaded facades of the **Hôtel de Crillon** (see WHERE TO STAY) on the left and the **Hôtel de la Marine** on the right.

There once stood in the middle an equestrian statue of Louis XV, in whose reign the square was laid out. This was removed during the Revolution and replaced briefly by an allegorical statue of Liberty. Now the site is occupied by the 3,300yr-old **obelisk of Luxor**, given to King Louis-Philippe by Mohammed Ali, Viceroy of Egypt, and erected in 1836.

A few meters from this spot stood the guillotine which, during the Revolution, claimed over a thousand victims including Louis XVI and Marie-Antoinette. Two **fountains** resplendent with water nymphs and sea-gods stand to the N and S of the obelisk.

Marking the octagonal perimeter of the original square are eight **statues** allegorically representing the towns of Lyon, Marseille, Bordeaux, Nantes, Lille, Strasbourg, Rouen and Brest. The curious pavilions on which they rest were once let out as tiny dwelling houses with just two rooms, one above the other. Other statues of note are the **Marly horses**, sculpted by Guillaume Coustou in the 1740s, which flank the E end of avenue des Champs-Élysées, and the **statues** of Fame and Mercury on winged horses by Coysevox, which stand on either side of the entrance to the Tuileries.

I never cross the Place de la Concorde without thinking
of the contrast between its spacious exhilarating gaiety
and its tragic history. The noble simplicity of its proportions,
the dignity of the tall old mansions of the rue de Rivoli
that frame it on the north side, and the aerial sweep of its vistas
across the river to the dome of the Invalides, and along
the leafy avenue of the Bois de Boulogne
to the Arc de Triomphe,
make a spectacle of light and air
irresistibly gladdening.
(Richard Le Gallienne, *From a Paris Garret,* 1943)

Place de la Concorde is the magnificent pulsating heart of Paris, as breathtaking by day as it is by night, when floodlights transform its buildings, obelisks, fountains and statues into a stunning *tableau vivant.*

CONSERVATOIRE NATIONAL DE MUSIQUE   See LA VILLETTE, PARC DE.

LE CORBUSIER, FONDATION

Villa La Roche, 10 sq. du Docteur-Blanche, 16ᵉ ☎42-88-41-53. Map 17D3 and see map on page 92 ☒ Open 10am-12.30pm, 1.30-6pm (Fri 5pm); closed Sat, Sun, Aug, public holidays. Métro: Jasmin, Ranelagh, Porte d'Auteuil.

The name Le Corbusier is synonymous with modern French architecture. This foundation, the purpose of which is to present Le Corbusier's work to the public, occupies two villas designed by the master himself in 1923. It encompasses a library, a photographic archive and a collection of paintings and sculptures by the architect. Temporary exhibitions are also held on various aspects of his work.

COUSTEAU, PARC OCÉANIQUE JACQUES

Forum des Halles, Level 3, Grande Galerie, 1ᵉʳ. Enter through the Porte du Louvre, near the Bourse du Commerce ☎40-26-13-78. Map 9H9 ☒ �& ✳ Open 10am-7pm (Tues and Thurs 5.30pm). Closed Mon. School holidays except summer, open daily 10am-7pm. Métro: Les Halles, Châtelet-Les Halles, Louvre-Rivoli.

The sea has come to the heart of Paris. If the idea of a stroll through the belly of a blue whale appeals to you, then so will all the other revelations of the mysteries of the deep, explored with dedication and enthusiasm by Jacques-Yves and Jean-Michel Cousteau and assembled into an experience that covers every aspect of life under the sea. Visitors can explore shipwrecks, come face-to-face with a giant squid, and steer well clear of the sharks, as well as learning about modern diving and filming techniques.

Intrigued? Then bowl along, for this is a stunning show. Five-thousand square meters of caverns were carved out on several levels deep beneath the Forum des Halles, to make room for a sequence of dynamic experiences. They include a fascinating introductory video account of Jacques-Yves Cousteau's life and work (he is now a sprightly octogenarian); a ride up into space which then plunges into the ocean depths; a sort of cinematic immersion among a chorus line of whales, almost too beautiful to bear; the aforesaid stroll through a life-sized blue whale, 30m long (that's just under 100 feet!), past organs recognizably very similar to our own; a video'd question-and-answer session with Jacques-Yves Cousteau (you question; he answers); and truly eye-opening displays of how animals adapted to the sea, from the polar bear through to the whale, how the Cousteaus invented and developed the revolutionary turbosail, and much, much more.

Two things impress particularly. One is that all this is done without the presence anywhere of a single live creature, which would be anathema to Cousteau. The other is the sheer conviction of the place: there is a fierce, inspiring dedication here to the natural environment and to fellowship with the wild. Jacques-Yves Cousteau himself is clearly adored by those among the staff who have met him.

Allow $1\frac{1}{2}$ hours minimum, and be prepared to go round the entire circuit again if you feel like it (they won't mind). Certainly, bring the children — there's masses for them to see, including an excellent interactive section aimed primarily at young visitors.

CRYPTE ARCHÉOLOGIQUE   See NOTRE-DAME.

DALÍ, ESPACE SALVADOR

Espace Montmartre, 11 rue Poulbot, 18ᵉ ☎ *42-64-40-10. Map 3C8* ⬛ *Open summer 10am-10pm, winter 10am-7pm. Métro: Anvers, Abbesses, Blanche, Pigalle.*

L'Univers Fantasmagorique de Dalí (the Crazy World of Dalí) is a re-creation in the 1990s of the life and work of Salvador Dalí (1904-89), the larger-than-life Surrealist artist whose popularity in the 20thC has been surpassed only by that of Picasso. Dalí lived and worked in Montmartre in the late 1920s, when he first dabbled with Surrealism — a style of interpretation that was to influence him for the remainder of his life.

Some 330 of Dalí's works have been gathered together to make a spectacle that uses all the senses — special, surreal sound effects and visual tricks set off the extraordinary collection of work.

DELACROIX, MUSÉE NATIONAL EUGÈNE

6 rue de Furstemberg, 6ᵉ ☎ *43-54-04-87. Map 8I8* ⬛ ✗ *Open Mon, Wed-Fri 9.45am-12.30pm, 2-5.15pm; Sat, Sun 9.45am-5.15pm. Closed Tues. Métro: St-Germain-des-Prés, Mabillon.*

Eugène Delacroix (1798-1863) was one of the great romantic painters of the 19thC, a Wagner among artists. His vivid canvases of battle scenes, lion hunts and other stirring subjects have a controlled fire to them, like Delacroix himself, whom the poet Baudelaire described as "a volcanic crater artistically concealed beneath bouquets of flowers."

In his last years, Delacroix lived a life of almost monastic seclusion, in a charming Left Bank apartment with a studio overlooking a little garden. This apartment is now preserved as a museum, and is full of photographs, letters, portraits and other mementoes of the artist.

DÔME CHURCH   See HÔTEL DES INVALIDES.

ÉCOLE MILITAIRE
Pl. Joffre, 7ᵉ. Map 12J4. Not open to public except by special arrangement.
Write to: La Direction Générale, École Militaire, 1 pl. Joffre, 75007-Paris. Métro:
École-Militaire.

Where its neighbor, the HÔTEL DES INVALIDES, is an officer in ceremonial
dress, the École Militaire is a sergeant major bawling out across the
CHAMP-DE-MARS to the TOUR EIFFEL. The long Classical facade has a great
central-domed portico, and the vast courtyard facing place de Fontenoy is imposing. It still serves as a military academy, for which purpose
it was built by Gabriel in the reign of Louis XV. Napoleon was sent
there at age 15 in 1784 — when he passed out he was told he could go
far, given the right circumstances!

ÉGOUTS (Sewers)
Entrance at corner of quai d'Orsay and pl. de la Résistance, 7ᵉ ☎47-05-10-29.
Map 12H4 ▨ ✗ obligatory. Open 11am-5pm; last admission 4pm winter, 5pm
summer. Closed Thurs, Fri, also last 3 wks in Jan. Métro: Alma-Marceau.

"Below Paris," wrote Victor Hugo in *Les Misérables,* "is another city."
He was referring to the sewer network, the existence of which is vital
to the gracious city above. Created by the engineer Eugène Belgrand in
1850, the sewers have been in need of massive maintenance for some
years. A 5-year renovation program began in 1991. Laid end-to-end, its
tunnels would stretch from Paris to Istanbul, and a small section of this
labyrinth just a few steps from the TOUR EIFFEL has been equipped for
public viewing.

Visitors are shown an exhibition of documents on the history of the
sewers, followed by an audiovisual display about the workings of the
system. A guided tour takes visitors through dripping tunnels, past
waste-collection pits and along the edge of a murky gray river. Instructive
but smelly. Once you know the odor of the sewers, you will occasionally
catch whiffs of it from gratings as you walk through the city.

ENNERY, MUSÉE NATIONAL D'
59 av. Foch, 16ᵉ ☎45-53-57-96. Off map 5F1 and see map on page 92 ▣ ✗
Open Thurs, Sun 2-5pm. Closed Mon-Wed, Fri, Sat, Aug. Métro: Dauphine.

Ming vases, *netsuke,* images of Buddha, porcelain dogs, Chinese furniture — these and other Oriental objects collected by the 19thC dramatist Adolphe d'Ennery and his wife are displayed in part of their opulent
house. He bought indiscriminately, and perhaps one in ten of the
objects have any real value. However, the museum has a curious,
musty charm. The house is shared with the MUSÉE ARMÉNIEN.

ENTREPÔTS DE BERCY (Cité du Vin et d'Alimentaire)
Quai de Bercy, 12ᵉ. Map 16M13. Métro: Bercy.

By 1993-4, the transformation will be complete of the run-down dock-
land area to the E of the **Palais Omnisports** and the AMERICAN CENTER
by the water's edge at Bercy. The Pavillons de Bercy, warehouses that

are now listed buildings, will accommodate a center of wines and gastronomy, including a **museum**, major exhibitions and a conference center. There will also be two hotels, a number of brasseries, restaurants and wine-bars, and a park with lakes and mini-vineyards.

See also BERCY on page 66.

L'ÉTOILE, PLACE DE   See CHARLES-DE-GAULLE, PLACE.

FAUBOURG-ST-HONORÉ, RUE DU
*8ᵉ. Maps **5-8**. Métro: Ternes, St-Philippe-du-Roule, Madeleine.*
The Parisian equivalent of Fifth Avenue or Knightsbridge, or the Via Tornabuoni, this glossy shopping thoroughfare runs parallel to AVENUE DES CHAMPS-ÉLYSÉES. It is full of gracious houses that were built by the aristocracy when the district took over from the MARAIS as the fashionable place to live.

Today, few people, apart from the president (see PALAIS DE L'ÉLYSÉE), actually live here, and the old mansions have found new uses. **#35** houses the **British Embassy** and **#96** (opposite the Palais de l'Elysée), the **Ministry of the Interior**. Another mansion, at **#112**, disappeared in the 1920s to make way for the discreetly opulent **Hôtel Bristol** (see WHERE TO STAY). For the rest, the street is mostly occupied by smart shops with such famous names as Heim, Hermès, Lanvin, Yves-St-Laurent, Courrèges and Helena Rubinstein. Beside the window of the Hermès store spurts a fine jet of perfume at passers-by, filling the air with the aroma of high living.

FLEA MARKET   See MARCHÉ AUX PUCES and SHOPPING.

FORUM DES HALLES
*1ᵉʳ. Map **9**H9. Métro: Les Halles; RER: Châtelet-Les-Halles.*
Opened in the mid 1980s, the Forum des Halles is the end result of the redevelopment of the old vegetable market, Les Halles. Conceived not long after the still controversial POMPIDOU CENTER, and with fears still fresh in people's minds of further modern horrors within their city, this commercial and entertainments center plummeted down where the other thrust boldly up.

Built on four descending levels, the Forum's glass-and-aluminum walls lead the eye down to a sunken courtyard; the four levels are connected by any number of walkways. The overall design has a spare, crisp elegance and avoids the use of harsh colors, favoring instead the muted tones of ocher and white marble. Architect Paul Chemetov, who also designed the stark new Ministry of Finance building that straddles the road in BERCY, has been praised for the boldness of his work.

And the consensus of opinion is that in design terms it has succeeded where the Pompidou Center failed. The Forum still feels bang up to date and has retained its air of dignity.

There are around 200 shops (including fashion boutiques, jewelers, booksellers and furniture stores), movie theaters and many restaurants.

Acting as it does as a magnet for visitors and shoppers in considerable numbers, the Forum has become host to a range of visitor attractions that vary in their tone from the vibrant educational and conservationist tones of the PARC OCÉANIQUE JACQUES COUSTEAU to the tacky shock-horrors of LES MARTYRS DE PARIS.

There is a branch of the excellent GRÉVIN waxworks museum *(Grand Balcon, Forum des Halles, 1er, map 9 H9* ☎ *42-26-28-50, open Mon-Sat 10.30am-6.45pm, Sun, bols 1-8pm* 🚇 ♿ *)*, which is devoted to the Paris of the Belle Époque and contains an imaginary reconstruction of a Parisian street of 1885.

The Forum is also home to the **Vidéothèque de Paris** *(2 Grande Galerie, porte St-Eustache, 1er* ☎ *40-26-34-30, open Sun, Tues-Fri 12.30-8.30pm, Sat 10am-8.30pm, closed Mon* 🚇 💻 *)*, an archive of film material of all eras relating to Paris. The Vidéothèque has three projection rooms where films from a collection of 4,500 titles are shown, with a different theme each week. There are facilities for individual viewing.

There is also the **Musée de l'Holographie** *(Level 1, 15 Grand Balcon, Forum des Halles* ☎ *40-39-96-83, open Mon-Sat 10am-7pm, Sun, bols 1-7pm* 🚇 🏃 *)* and the ROCK'N'ROLL HALL OF FAME, where teenagers throng to see waxen images of their favorite stars.

At the N side of the Forum is the **Pavillon des Arts** *(101 rue Rambuteau, 1er* ☎ *42-33-82-50, open 12.45-7.30pm, closed Mon, bols)*, a striking steel-and-glass building for temporary exhibitions.

At the W end of the Forum there is a highly imaginative facility for children, the **Jardin d'Enfants aux Halles**. It has tunnels and mountains as well as slides, in the area in front of the church of ST-EUSTACHE *(one-hour sessions for 7-11s, on the hour; closed Fri and Sun morning, plus Mon* 🚇 *reserve on site)*. Staff speak English. Also near the FONTAINE DES INNOCENTS is an old-fashioned merry-go-round. A splendid and contrasting feast of color.

From the lowest level there is access to the Métro and RER, and there are two large underground garages. Adult Parisians avoid the Forum on weekends, when swarms of young people invade.

The one neutral aspect of the Forum is the gardens above ground. Faced with the challenge of replacing the elegant lines of the architect Baltard's old cast-iron-and-glass market buildings, Chemetov moved underground, leaving the older buildings immediately next to the site (the BOURSE DU COMMERCE and the ÉGLISE ST-EUSTACHE) standing proudly above the rooflines of the new Forum. The gardens that provide the lid to this enormous, cavernous space have tried to echo what was lost through ornamental wood- and ironwork suggestive of the earlier style. The gardens are pleasant enough, but are nothing to write home about.

GOBELINS, MANUFACTURE NATIONALE DES (Tapestry Factories)
42 av. des Gobelins, 13e ☎ *43-37-12-60. Map **15**M10* 🚇 *Open Tues, Wed, Thurs* 🏃 *compulsory, lasting 75mins starts 2pm and 3pm. Métro: Gobelins, Place d'Italie.*

If you have ever struggled with a home tapestry kit and found that it tried your patience, you should visit the Gobelins factory to find out what patience really means. Here, skilled weavers, carefully chosen and trained from the age of 16, work their way millimeter by millimeter across huge upright looms at the rate of as little as one square meter a year. Thus it can take 3-4 years to complete a single tapestry with two or three people working on it full time.

The techniques used are essentially the same as when the Gobelins was founded as a royal factory under Louis XIV, but the tapestries are now worked in a far wider range of colors (14,920 altogether), and the subjects are no longer scenes of royal occasions and the like, but copies of modern paintings or designs.

The Gobelins is a state enterprise, and its products are never sold. They are either made use of by the government or given as gifts. The atmosphere of the factory complex in the SE of Paris is rather like an old university college, with a cobbled quadrangle, garden, and apartments for the employees.

A guided tour of the factory is given, which incorporates the two other state workshops of **Savonnerie** (carpets) and **Beauvais** (tapestries made on a horizontal loom). In an era of mass-production, here is craftsmanship of the highest standard.

GRAND CARNAVALET, MUSÉE HISTORIQUE DE LA VILLE DE PARIS 🏛 ★
23 rue de Sévigné, 3ᵉ ☎42-72-21-13. Map 10/11 🖼 (📷 on Sun) ♿ ✗ Open 10am-5.40pm. Closed Mon, hols. Métro: St-Paul, Chemin-Vert.

Newly renamed the Grand Carnavalet, this important museum is still often referred to simply as the Musée Carnavalet. For a thorough exploration of this important museum, it is advisable to buy the English-language *General Guide*, obtainable at the bookstore at the main entrance. This illustrated book, while a little more expensive than the price of an admission ticket (unless you go on a Sunday, when admission is free), will guide you efficiently around the many rooms, giving good, brief explanations of the major exhibits.

If you visited no other building in Paris but this one, you would still come away with a good understanding of the spirit of the city. Every phase of Parisian history, from prehistoric times to the present day, is illustrated, in painting, sculpture, models, furniture and decoration — all on view in a series of splendid rooms in two exquisite mansions of the MARAIS, the Hôtel Carnavalet and the Hôtel Le Peletier de Saint-Fargeau.

The Hôtel Carnavalet played its own part in the history of the city. Built in the 1540s and later modified by Mansart, it possesses a gracious entrance courtyard with allegorical reliefs of the four seasons, and a contemporary statue of Louis XIV by Coysevox, anachronistically dressed as a Roman general wearing a wig. From 1677-96 the house was occupied by Mme de Sévigné, who immortalized herself by a series of lively and witty letters, and who played hostess to distinguished writers and thinkers of her time. Her apartments are on view, and she still seems to cast her benign spell over the building.

HÔTEL CARNAVALET: Its rooms cover the period from **Prehistory to 1789**. Prehistoric, Bronze and Iron Age exhibits, relics of the Gallo-Roman settlement of Lutetia, the Merovingian and Carolingian periods and the Paris of the Middle Ages are all laid out, room after fascinating room. Roman finds including coffins, leather shoes, domestic implements . . . a room full of old tradesmen's signs, as well as the entire front of a druggist's shop . . . the contents are absorbing but, importantly, the number of exhibits always seems manageable. By being selective, it is perfectly possible to move through each room and taken it in without it taking up the entire day.

Many are the insights into domestic life, but one of the highlights of the museum are the many models, most of them old models rather than pieces commissioned by the management, showing parts of the city. A model of the Île de La Cité in 1527, made at the beginning of the 20thC using an old engraving, shows houses and other buildings right up close to the front of Notre-Dame. Throughout the centuries, there are dozens of paintings and drawings of the townscape. In some instances, remarkably little has changed.

HÔTEL LE PELETIER DE SAINT-FARGEAU: This now contains all the material from the **Revolution to the present day**. There is a vast section dedicated to the Revolution, and here you will find models of the guillotines, portraits of Revolutionary leaders, placards, paintings of the royal family in captivity, and even being executed. Other rooms contain relics from the First and Second Empires, including many memorabilia of the Emperor Napoleon. There are numerous busts and paintings of politicians and society beauties, including François Gérard's famous portrait of Madame Récamier.

The 20thC is represented by paintings and in a number of dazzling room settings. Two valuable examples of Art Nouveau are to be seen in the private room designed for the Café de Paris in 1899 by Henri Sauvage, and the interior of Fouquet's jewelry shop, which was totally designed by Alphonse Mucha. The opulent decor of the ballroom of the Hôtel de Wendel, created in 1924, is the climax to the visit.

The Hôtel Le Peletier de Saint-Fargeau was built around 1690 for Michel Le Peletier, a State Councillor and financial administrator. Its style is more sober, as befitted the house of a magistrate, and the main staircase and gilt-paneled room on the first floor are the only original items of interior decoration. The two buildings have been ingeniously linked together and access is possible between the two at either ground or first floor level.

LE GRAND LOUVRE ▥ ★

Palais du Louvre, 1ᵉʳ. NB: telephone numbers will all change from November 1993. Recorded message ☎40-20-51-51; reception desk ☎40-20-53-17; Minitel ☎3615-Louvre. Map 8H8 ▨ ✗ General, for individuals (extra ▨), in English 3-6 times daily according to season, except Tues; register 15mins early. Groups must reserve up to 2mths in advance ☎40-20-51-77 for groups using a museum guide or ☎40-20-57-60 for groups coming with their own guide ▬ ═ Museum open 9am-6pm, evening opening until 10pm on Mon (partial) and Wed; Hall Napoléon (below pyramid: galleries of the history of the Louvre, and the Medieval Louvre moats, and all facilities) open 9am-10pm; bookstore open 9.30am; Hall Napoléon (temporary exhibitions) open 10am onward. All closed Tues. Métro: Palais-Royal Musée du Louvre.

"I never knew what a palace was until I had a glimpse of the Louvre," wrote the 19thC American author Nathaniel Hawthorne. Today he would be surprised to find the main courtyard, the cour Napoléon, dominated by a crisp glass-walled pyramid, flanked by three smaller pyramids and seven stretches of water, two with fountains, which mark the new entrance to the museum. The work of the Chinese-American architect I.M. Pei, this pyramid is only one feature of a vast new development, begun in 1981 on the initiative of President Mitterrand, and which will be completed by 1997 at a cost of 5.7 billion francs.

It involved massive underground excavations to create new galleries, a centralized public reception area, and all the facilities that a museum handling 5 million visitors each year could need. The three wings of the vast palace now have a much-needed central focal point, and distances between the many galleries have been considerably shortened. The next major phase of the development happens in November 1993, the bicentenary of the Louvre first being opened to the public; the conversion of the Richelieu (N) wing. The *Grand Louvre* will soon emerge in all its glory.

In the process of excavating the cour Napoléon and the cour Carrée, some 20,000 artifacts were found, the relics of a *quartier* that was demolished in 1852. More exciting still was the discovery of the foundations of the original 12thC fortress, built by Philippe Auguste, renovated by Charles V as a residence and then demolished by François I in the 16thC in order to create a palace that was expanded piecemeal by every major French monarch up to Napoleon III.

Above these foundations is the **cour Carrée** (★), which was designed by Pierre Lescot for François I in the Renaissance style. In the 17thC Louis XIII commissioned Lemercier to extend the w facade of the Cour Carrée in the same style, and the remainder was built by Louis XIV. Particularly noteworthy is the majestic **colonnade** (★) of 52 Corinthian columns along the outside of the court. This was the work of Claude Perrault, and is one of the outstanding examples of the Classical style in Paris. From the cour Carrée, the Louvre grew haphazardly westward in two gigantic wings as successive monarchs added pavilion after pavilion until it finally linked up with the now vanished Tuileries palace. Today the Louvre is so vast that it can only be encompassed in a single sweep of the eye by observing it from the air or from a high vantage point.

The art collection grew in a similarly piecemeal way. Begun by François I, it was built up by his successors and continued to expand after the building was opened to the public in 1793. The greatest leaders were the greatest collectors: François himself, then later Louis XIV and Napoleon. As the collection grew, more and more of the palace was opened up to accommodate it.

There are so many exhibits that if you were to spend half a minute in front of each one, it would take three months, night and day, to see the whole collection. So, clearly, anyone visiting the Louvre must ration their time carefully. If possible, try to make more than one visit. A good idea for the first-time visitor is to take one of the general guided tours. Then, having obtained a bird's-eye view of the museum, return later to explore individual parts in greater detail.

What follows is a brief guide to the main sections and their highlights. Bear in mind that the locations of many exhibits will change, since the museum will continue its expansion and development program over a number of years, taking best advantage of the increase in space given by the acquisition of the Richelieu wing.

It is not possible to give a detailed floor plan in this edition, as **80 percent of the total collection will be relocated between 1993-1997**. However, the public information offered by the museum's management could not be better. A simple color- and number-coding system (see illustration overleaf) is now in operation, and a free orientation guide is available, in English and other languages.

November 1993 will be the next time of major upheaval, when the **Richelieu wing is opened**. We have attempted, here, to give an accurate picture of what you can expect to see until that time. From December 1993 onward, there will be a new means of signposting, new telephone numbers, exhibits in different rooms, or out of sight for months. This is all beyond the remit of a time-sensitive guidebook, but will be handled with expertise by the museum's management team.

In the **Hall Napoléon**, a bank of video screens offers day-by-day information on all changeable elements; eight reception staff are on call to answer any specific questions about the museum or its exhibits; and a computer database is there to help them in their task. There are free programs — even themed visits are offered, on such subjects as the birth of Christian art, and these encompass a number of different disciplines in various departments of the museum.

The exterior

Large-scale repairs and renovations have been taking place both inside and out, and by 1996, the restoration of the stonework and facades of the Louvre will be completed, after a period of 12 years. By the end of 1993, the roofs, facades and statues of the cour Napoléon will have been overhauled. The effects of weathering, and, more seriously, of pollution, have taken a serious toll on the 86 statues of great men who line the cour Napoléon at first-floor level, and each imperfect piece of stone has been replaced and reworked on site, to a high standard of perfection. A small number, including the statues of Poussin, Rabelais and Colbert, have been totally remade.

The third phase, from 1993-96, will involve the N and S facades on the Jardins du Carrousel, extending as far as the Pavillon de Flore and the Pavillon de Marsan at the W edges, as well as the facades facing N toward RUE DE RIVOLI, S toward the river, and E toward ST-GERMAIN L'AUXERROIS.

Reception area and underground galleries

The main entrance to the museum is through the pyramid. From the spacious underground reception area, the **Hall Napoléon**, there are striking views of the palace through the glass walls of the pyramid. Here are two restaurants, one cafeteria and two cafés, a museum shop and bookstore, a post office and an auditorium. This is also the gathering point for anyone wishing to take a guided tour. A display of chalco-

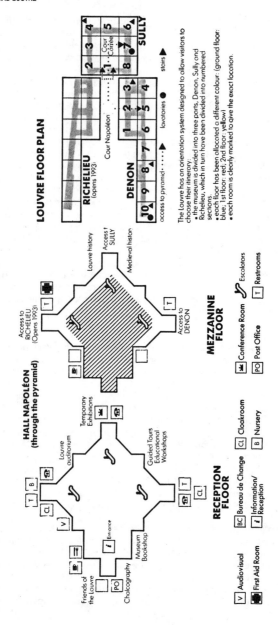

LOUVRE FLOOR PLAN

RICHELIEU
(opens 1993)

Cour Napoléon

SULLY

Cour Carrée

DENON

▲ stairs   ● lavatories

access to pyramid · · · · ▲

The Louvre has an orientation system designed to allow visitors to choose their itinerary:
• the museum is divided into three parts, Denon, Sully and Richelieu, which in turn have been divided into numbered sections.
• each floor has been allocated a different colour: (ground floor: blue; 1st floor: red; 2nd floor: yellow)
• each room is clearly marked to give the exact location.

HALL NAPOLÉON
(through the pyramid)

Access to RICHELIEU
(Opens 1993)

Louvre history

Medieval history

Access to SULLY

Access to DENON

Louvre auditorium

Temporary Exhibitions

Guided Tours
Educational Workshops

MEZZANINE FLOOR

🎤 Conference Room   ⤴ Escalators
PO Post Office   T Restrooms

RECEPTION FLOOR

Entrance

Friends of the Louvre

Choicography

Museum Bookshop

BC Bureau de Change   CL Cloakroom
i Information/Reception   B Nursery

V Audiovisual   ✚ First Aid Room

130

graphy (copper and brass engravings) is also here, along with temporary exhibition spaces that are well signposted. The huge crypt under the cour Carrée contains the massive, cyclopean remains of the ramparts and keep of the 12thC fortress. Continue via the Gothic **Crypt of St-Louis**; this area also boasts a display of the wealth of objects found during the excavation. For a startling time-warp effect, go straight from here into the Egyptian galleries, where you will come face to face with an enormous sphinx.

The museum above ground has seven departments: Greek, Etruscan and Roman Antiquities, Oriental Antiquities, Egyptian Antiquities, *Objets d'Art,* Graphic Arts, Paintings and Sculptures.

Greek, Etruscan and Roman antiquities

This heading encompasses every chapter in the history of Classical art, from early Hellenic times to the end of the Roman Empire. The department occupies ground- and first-floor galleries in the Denon wing as well as part of the Sully wing, which includes the 16thC **Salle des Caryatides**. This was once used as a ballroom, with its row of caryatids looking curiously like some of the exhibits.

The armless *Venus de Milo* (★) was found in 1820 by a peasant on the Greek island of Milos and is one of the most prized items. Dating from the 3rd-2ndC BC, she embodies all the idealized beauty and dignity invested by the Greeks in their portrayals of the human form. Her face is rather masculine, a reminder that the Greeks of that time particularly exalted male physical beauty.

Another famous exhibit in this section is the headless *Winged Victory of Samothrace* (★ c.200BC). She dominates a grand staircase, which was rebuilt in the 1930s especially for her display. Remade from pieces found in 1863, the left wing entirely remade using the right wing as a model, the statue commemorates a naval victory and was created in the style of a ship's figurehead, symbolizing victory with far more impact than any triumphal arch.

Belonging to a much earlier period (6thC BC) is the *Hera of Samos.* In this work and the other statues nearby, you can see the stiffness and frontal emphasis often found in ancient Egyptian statues — so different from the *Venus de Milo. Hera,* in her enclosed roundness, recalls statuary made from tree-trunks. Look out, too, for the *Rampin Horseman.* He has an archaic smile, and his beard and hair are stylized, geometrical approximations of reality. The bronze *Apollo of Piombino* (5thC BC) has superb copper inlay.

Oriental antiquities

This section is closed until November 1993. After that time, it will be possible to see artefacts drawn mainly from the civilizations of Mesopotamia, the Far Eastern section of the collection being in the MUSÉE NATIONAL D'ARTS ASIATIQUES. Among the most impressive items here are the black basalt stele bearing the *Code of Law of King Hammurabi of Babylon* (1792-50BC), the *Stele of the Vultures* and the *Stele of Naram-Sim.*

Egyptian antiquities

This section will be in reorganization from 1993-95. This is one of the finest Egyptian collections in the world, thanks to long-standing French prominence in this field. Founded in 1826, its first curator was the great Egyptologist Champollion, decipherer of the Rosetta stone, which is now in the British Museum in London. Situated in ground-and first-floor galleries in Sully wing, the collection contains such masterpieces as the great sandstone **bust of Amenophis IV** (Akhenaton), which was presented to France by Egypt in 1972. Look, too, for the superb **Gebel-el-Arak knife,** dating from about 3400BC, the **jewels of Rameses II** and the statue of Queen Karomama.

Sculptures

Housed on the ground floor of Denon wing, but moving in 1993 to the new Richelieu wing (ground floor), this section encompasses the whole history of French sculpture, from its origins to the 19thC, and includes works by foreign sculptors, such as Michelangelo's *Captives* and Benvenuto Cellini's bronze relief of the *Nymph of Fontainebleau.* The French sculptures range from austere medieval religious images, through Renaissance works such as German Pilon's *Three Graces.*

The section showing Italian and Nordic sculptures *(formerly in the basement of Denon wing, which is now closed)* will be on view in *Denon wing first floor and basement from early 1994.*

Objets d'art and furniture

Currently located on the N and E sides of Sully wing, the collection of *Objets d'art will be located from November 1993 onward both here and in the Richelieu wing first floor.* The **Galerie d'Apollon** was luxuriously decorated in 1661; its murals by Le Brun feature a Sun God Apollo, symbolizing the Sun King, Louis XIV. The central ceiling was painted by Delacroix in 1848. This is an appropriate setting for the **Crown Jewels** — gorgeous crowns and regalia used at the coronation of the French kings, as well as priceless jewels such as the 137-carat diamond known as the **Regent,** purchased from England in 1717.

The other galleries on the first floor of the Sully wing, known as the **Colonnade Galleries,** have beautiful ceilings and paneling, and present a wide panorama of decorative art and craftsmanship from the Middle Ages to the time of Napoleon. *These galleries will be closed in November 1993, and when they reopen, will house Egyptian Antiquities.*

Paintings

This department is the museum's greatest pride, and constitutes one of the most comprehensive collections of paintings in the world. *By 1993, hardly a single painting will be found in its former place,* and a further 2,000 will have been added to the 4,000 that were already on view. From the vast Salle Sully, you can catch a marvelous view along one of Paris' great axes: from the pyramid and the ARC DE TRIOMPHE DU CARROUSEL through to L'ÉTOILE and LA DÉFENSE.

The collection was begun by Francois I, who acquired the Louvre's most famous exhibit, Leonardo da Vinci's *Mona Lisa* (★), along with other Italian masterpieces. Also called *La Gioconda,* thanks to the most mysterious of smiles, she is now displayed behind bullet-proof glass, and is the subject of major security precautions.

The Louvre undoubtedly has the richest collection of Leonardos possessed by any museum in the world, as it also includes *Bacchus,* a *John the Baptist,* the *Virgin of the Rocks,* a small portrait of a lady, *La Belle Ferronnière,* and the *Virgin and Child with Ste-Anne.* In each of Leonardo's paintings you will see how he has suppressed two-dimensional line in favor of mass and tone value, creating three-dimensional illusion. This technique is called *chiaroscuro,* Italian for "light-shadow." Further, by use of very thin coats of glaze, hard outlines are obscured, giving the subject a hazy look. This technique is called *sfumato,* Italian for haze. Leonardo also strove to reveal the intention of the soul through gestures. In the *Virgin of the Rocks* (★), the group is held together by various significant gestures: pointing, praying, blessing and protecting. In the *Virgin and the Child with Ste-Anne* (★), Mary is shown sitting on the lap of her mother Ste-Anne and reaching out toward the baby Jesus, who, in turn, reaches toward his future sacrifice for mankind, which is symbolized by a lamb. The *Mona Lisa* is not the only one smiling. That mysterious smile can be found elsewhere, for instance in the *John the Baptist.*

In addition to the Leonardos, there is a wealth of paintings by Titian, Raphael, Veronese, and other artists of the Italian Renaissance, as well as earlier and later Italian works.

A small but distinguished Spanish collection includes such masterpieces as El Greco's *Christ Crucified* and Murillo's *The Young Beggar,* as well as works by Goya and Velázquez. English works are also not numerous, but include portraits by Gainsborough and Reynolds.

The Flemish, Dutch and German masters are well represented, and there is a series of Rembrandts. *These will all be in Richelieu wing from November 1993.*

French paintings form the bulk of the collection, and range from the 14th-19thC. In Sully wing, around the cour Carrée, there are 45 newly-opened halls where the great collection of French painters is now on view. You will find Poussin's limpid canvases of mythological and allegorical subjects, La Tour's religious paintings with their striking effects of light and shadow, and Watteau's delicate scenes of gaiety touched with a nuance of melancholy.

New spaces in the Richelieu wing are to be dedicated to the Northern Schools and Early French paintings from the 14th-17thC. If it is size and splendor you want, then move round into the 19thC rooms in Denon wing, where you will find David's vast painting *The Coronation of Napoleon* and works by other 19thC painters such as Delacroix and Corot.

Graphic arts

In the past, the graphic arts (drawings, engravings, pastels) were never on permanent display. *From December 1992 to 1995,* the museum will open various rooms in all three wings, where the graphic arts will be on permanent view. These works will be exhibited on a rotating basis, being completely replaced about four times a year.

1997 will mark the end of a period of enormous upheaval for this great museum. Every museum-goer in the civilized world should offer congratulations on so fine a transformation — and be thankful when it is at last possible to view the collections in an uninterrupted way.

GRAND ORIENT DE FRANCE, MUSÉE DU (Freemasonry Museum)

16 rue Cadet, 9ᵉ ☎*45-23-20-92. Map 3E9* 🖸 💱 ✗ *Open 2-6pm. Closed Sun, public holidays. Métro: Cadet.*

What did Lafayette, Garibaldi and Franklin D. Roosevelt have in common? Answer: they were all Freemasons, as you will discover from this intriguing museum of Masonic documents, mementoes and regalia, related to European Freemasonry. L'Hôtel Cadet is the headquarters of Freemasonry in France, located in a plain modern building in a modest street near the Folies Bergère.

GRAND PALAIS, GALERIES NATIONALES DU 🏛

Av. du Général Eisenhower, 8ᵉ ☎*43-13-17-17. Map 6G5* 🔁 💻 *Open 10am-8pm, Wed 10am-10pm. Closed Tues. Métro: Champs-Élysées-Clemenceau.*

The Grand Palais and the PETIT PALAIS, built for the Universal Exhibition of 1900, echo each other like two thunderous fanfares across av. Winston-Churchill, which runs from AV. DES CHAMPS-ÉLYSÉES to the PONT ALEXANDRE III. Some people would call them fussy and pompous, but it would be fairer to call them joyous and exuberant pieces of architectural rhetoric, although the Grand Palais oversteps the mark perhaps with its gargantuan porticoes, its frescoes and its mass of *cartouches* and swags of carved stonework.

The western part of the building is now given over to the PALAIS DE LA DÉCOUVERTE, a science museum. The rest of the Grand Palais is used for temporary art exhibitions and other large-scale trade shows and exhibitions. The interior is as imposing as the exterior, particularly the main hall, with its lavish mosaic frieze and central spiral staircase. The building is dominated by a huge 43m dome (141ft) and unmistakeable glass-and-iron vaulted roof.

The N section of the building, fronted by a pleasing little garden with a fountain, contains a good little restaurant.

LES GRANDS BOULEVARDS

This is the name given to the string of boulevards in the 9ᵉ and 10ᵉ extending roughly from the MADELEINE to place de la République — bds. Capucines, Italiens, Montmartre, Poissonnière, Bonne-Nouvelle, St-Denis and St-Martin. See THE QUARTIERS OF PARIS on page 67.

GRANDE ARCHE DE LA DÉFENSE 🏛

Take the Grande Arche exit from RER ☎*49-07-27-57* ◀ ⬆ *to roof* 🔲 *Open Mon-Sat 9am-6pm, Sun, hols 9am-8pm. Last admission 1hr earlier.*

The newest great arch in a city of arches, the awesome, monolithic Grande Arche focuses all eyes on the western end of LA DÉFENSE. The Danish architect J.O. von Spreckelsen described his winning design as

J.O. von Spreckelsen's **Grande Arche**

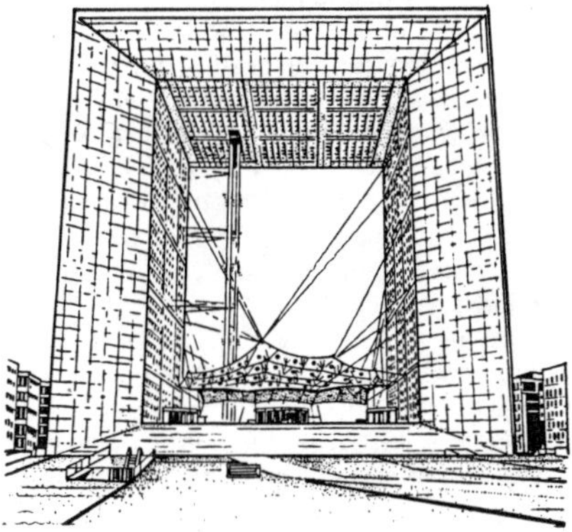

"an open cube — a window on the world." It is certainly that.

From the cavernous space beneath it — as wide as the avenue des Champs-Élysées — can be seen the dramatic W-E alignment of the arch with the ARC DE TRIOMPHE, the obelisk at PLACE DE LA CONCORDE, the ARC DE TRIOMPHE DU CARROUSEL and the GRAND LOUVRE. Above soars the vast marble-covered cube of the arch, 90m (295ft) high and lined with office windows: a void large enough to shelter Notre-Dame.

Two monumental staircases ascend from the concourse to the vault of the arch, which is overhung with "clouds" that billow like the sails of a clipper ship 20m (60ft) above the heads of visitors.

Panoramic elevators rise and fall, carrying visitors into the roof. From here, another startling alignment is revealed: that with the TOUR EIFFEL and the TOUR MONTPARNASSE. The immense roof also houses an exhibition gallery, a bookstore and a conference center.

Below the Grande Arche is **La Cité de l'Automobile**, a conference, exhibition and sales center geared toward the automobile industry. It also has a marvelous 180° IMAX cinematic dome.

The arch, interestingly, houses more than 4,500 workers within its walls. More than a million visitors have passed through since its opening in 1989, and the revenue from this has amply repaid the investment. What is more, the cost to the State has been minimal.

GRÉVIN, MUSÉE

10 blvd. Montmartre, 9e ☎42-46-13-26. Map ***8F9*** *Open 365 days, 1-7pm, longer during school vacations. Métro: Richelieu-Drouot, Rue Montmartre.*

Cabinet fantastique is the claim of the words over the entrance, and fantasy is certainly what you experience here. This is the original Musée Grévin, founded in 1882 by designer Alfred Grévin. The involvement of the financier Gabriel Thomas ensured the financial backing, and the building developed as the *Belle Époque* became more *belle*.

In 1900, he built the lovely first-floor theater, with the assistance of sculptor Antoine Bourdelle, who contributed the sculptures. The stage curtain bears an original painting by Jules Cheret. The whimsical Palais des Mirages was bought after the 1900 World Exposition, and has been operational within the Grévin since 1904.

As you enter, a grotto with distorting mirrors takes you one step away from reality. Then, suddenly, you have arrived in a glorious, domed hall where it is hard to know whether to look up at the gilding or around you at the various witty juxtapositions of famous characters. Some of the waxworks are of contemporary French personalities, but the vast majority are international figures — François Mitterrand . . . Woody Allen . . . Michael Jackson . . . .

Even more alluring are the historical tableaux — Napoleon and Josephine surrounded by an entourage, and in a lavish drawing room that is actually furnished with original pieces from the period. There are the inevitable scenes from the French Revolution, including Louis XVI and Marie Antoinette in prison, and Marat, seen slumped in the actual wooden bath in which he died. The figures are so well made that you never doubt they'll all move the second you look away.

A trip to the movies is also part of the fare — a series of movie sets takes you through the age of Gable and Lombard, Hitchcock, Monroe (complete with skirt swirling in the updraft), Chaplin, Liza Minelli. Even Sylvester Stallone is there. And the Invisible Man.

Upstairs, in a lovely and very nostalgic *spectacle d'illusion* in the *palais des mirages,* visitors are miraculously transported, inside a blacked-out spherical mirrored hall, into a variety of exotic environments, including a jungle.

Don't miss the performances of magic and conjuring that take place each afternoon in the lovely first-floor theater, where many of today's stars of the world of magic have made their début over the years.

There is another Grévin in Paris at the FORUM DES HALLES *(Grand Balcon, Level 1, Forum des Halles, rue Pierre Lescot, 1ᵉʳ 9 H9* ☎ *42-26-28-50, open Mon-Sat 10.30am-6.45pm, Sun, hols 1-7pm* 🔳 ♿ *),* where the Paris of the Belle Époque is re-created in 21 scenes, including an imaginary reconstruction of a Parisian street of 1885 and a *son et lumière* of Paris in 1900. The likes of Toulouse-Lautrec, Jules Verne, Émile Zola and Auguste Renoir appear in settings with their contemporaries, and most amusingly, a lovely turn-of-the-century theater has such performers on its stage as Brigitte Bardot, Sophia Loren and Édith Piaf.

GUIMET, MUSÉE   See ARTS ASIATIQUES, MUSÉE NATIONAL DES

LES HALLES
This area of the city — a bustling food market from the 12thC until 1979 — is bounded roughly by rue Étienne-Marcel and RUE DE RIVOLI to the N and S, with the BOURSE DU COMMERCE and the POMPIDOU CENTER marking the W and E boundaries. See THE QUARTIERS OF PARIS on page 68.

HÉBERT, MUSÉE NATIONAL ERNEST 🏛
85 rue du Cherche-Midi, 6ᵉ ☎ *42-22-23-82. Map **13**K6* 🔳 🚻 *Open 12.30-6pm, Sat, Sun 2-6pm; closed Tues. Métro: St-Placide, Falguière, Sèvres-Babylone.*

Housed in the Hôtel de Montmorency, a small and gracious 18thC mansion on the Left Bank, this museum is devoted mainly to temporary exhibitions of the works of society painter Ernest Hébert (1817-1908) and his contemporaries.

HENNER, MUSÉE NATIONAL JEAN-JACQUES
43 av. de Villiers, 17ᵉ ☎47-63-42-73. Map 1D4 ▨ ✗ Open 10am-noon, 2-5pm. Closed Mon. Métro: Malesherbes, Wagram.
This collection contains about 700 paintings, drawings and sketches by the Alsatian artist Jean-Jacques Henner (1829-1905), who was one of the great individualists among painters. Following no school, but inspired by the old masters, he created canvases of a delicate luminosity and haunting grace.

EN HERBE, MUSÉE   See BOIS DE BOULOGNE on page 93.

HISTOIRE DE FRANCE, MUSÉE DE L'   See ARCHIVES NATIONALES.

HISTOIRE NATURELLE, MUSÉUM NATIONAL D'   See JARDIN DES PLANTES.

HISTORIQUE DE LA VILLE DE PARIS, MUSÉE   See GRAND CARNAVALET.

HOMME, MUSÉE DE L' (Museum of Mankind)
Palais de Chaillot, pl. du Trocadéro 16ᵉ ☎45-05-72-72. Map 11H2 ▨ ✗ ☰ Open 9.45am-5.15pm. Closed Tues, public holidays. Métro: Trocadéro.
Occupying the w wing of the PALAIS DE CHAILLOT, this museum contains one of the world's most important collections devoted to anthropology, ethnology and prehistory. The objects are, for the most part, arranged according to geographical region, and include all manner of intriguing objects, from a Navajo sand-painting to Japanese costumes. The excellent South American section includes a shriveled Inca mummy in a fetal position, which inspired Munch's painting *The Scream*.

There is an area devoted to the arts and technologies of different world regions, and another to anthropology, dealing with the biological and physical characteristics of man.

There is a fine restaurant with superb views of the TOUR EIFFEL.

HÔTEL DE ROHAN
18thC Marais mansion built for the bishops of Strasbourg. See ARCHIVES NATIONALES.

HÔTEL DES ARCHEVÊQUES DE SENS 🏛
1 rue du Figuier, 4ᵉ ☎42-78-14-60. Map 10I11. Forney Library open Tues-Fri 1.30-8.30pm, Sat 10am-8.30pm. Closed Sun, Mon. Métro: Pont-Marie, St-Paul.
This mansion at the s edge of the MARAIS is such a perfect specimen of medieval architecture, with its pepper-pot turrets and pointed arches, that if you came upon it without prior knowledge you might think it was 19thC imitation Gothic, or perhaps a stray building from a Hollywood movie set in the Middle Ages (see the illustration on page 27).

In fact it is one of the oldest houses in Paris and was built by Tristan de Salazar, Archbishop of Sens, between 1475 and 1507. It was an anachronism even in its day, since the archbishop, who came from a military family, could not resist adding a few touches to create the illusion of a fortified castle — a dungeon, watch-tower and watchwalk. The building was a late burst of Gothic feudalism at the dawn of the French Renaissance.

It is now owned by the City of Paris and houses the **Forney Library**, a library of science, technology, arts and crafts. Make a point of seeing the jewel-like formal garden fronting the building, and wander in to inspect the fine courtyard.

HÔTEL DE SOUBISE

18thC Marais mansion with a superb courtyard. See ARCHIVES NATIONALES.

HÔTEL DES VENTES (Auction rooms)

Hôtel Drouot-Richelieu, 9 rue Drouot, 9ᵉ ☎48-00-20-20. Map **3**F8 ▣ Open Mon-Sat 11am-6pm. Closed Sun, Aug. Métro: Richelieu-Drouot. *Hôtel Drouot-Montaigne*, 15 av. Montaigne, 8e ☎48-00-20-80. Map **6**G4 ▣ Hours as above. Métro: Alma-Marceau.

The Parisian equivalent of Christie's, or Sotheby's or Parke Bernet, the Hôtel des Ventes has, like auction rooms everywhere, an atmosphere of glamor and excitement. In France, auctioneering is a more strictly regulated business than in most countries, and is controlled by the Compagnie des Commissaires Priseurs, the auctioneers' professional body, whose members can display a gold plaque outside their door.

The old Hôtel des Ventes, which stood on the site of the Hôtel Drouot-Richelieu, was demolished in the 1970s. However, in 1980 the new Hôtel Drouot was completed — a stylish building of steel, dark-tinted glass and concrete, with traditional touches such as a steep, vaulted roof and dormer windows.

In recent years, operations have diversified and the most prestigious sales now take place in the well-heeled av. Montaigne showroom. Both auction houses have various rooms, where all kinds of objects — French tapestries, Italian drawings, autographed letters, Chinese vases — change hands under the eye of a *commissaire priseur* perched behind a high desk. A fascinating place to visit even if you are not bidding.

HÔTEL DE VILLE (Town Hall) ▥

Pl. de l'Hôtel-de-Ville, 4ᵉ ☎42-76-40-40. Map **9**I10. Building open Mon-Fri 9am-6.30pm, Sat 9am-6pm ✗ to salons, Mon only 10.30am (▣). Métro: Hôtel-de-Ville.

There has been a town hall on this site since 1357, when one of the earliest mayors of Paris, Étienne Marcel, moved the city council there. His equestrian statue now stands facing toward the Seine by the s side of the building.

The first town hall was replaced by a more imposing one in Renaissance style, which was burned down by the *Communards* in 1871. The present edifice (1874-82) is a fairly convincing copy of its predecessor, but has a ponderous 19thC touch to the ornate facade, because of its numerous statues of Parisian dignitaries ensconced in niches.

Before 1830, the **place de l'Hôtel-de-Ville** formed part of the riverside and was called place de Grève. The *grève,* meaning strand or foreshore, was a meeting place for a number of unemployed Parisians, who became known as *grévistes.* Today, the term *faire la grève* (to go on strike) has connotations of another variation on a theme of unemployment. The place de Grève was also the scene of numerous executions over the centuries.

For many years Paris had no mayor and was governed by a prefect of the city. But in 1977 the office of mayor was re-established, and the Hôtel de Ville is his HQ. The 109 councilors meet in a spacious, wood-paneled chamber, which can be viewed during sessions, from a public gallery. Other rooms can be visited by conducted tour on Monday mornings.

A feast of visual extravagance, these rooms must have kept an army of artists and craftsmen employed. For those interested in *fin-de-siècle* decor and painting, there is plenty of reason to visit.

The City of Paris has its public relations department at the Hôtel de Ville *(entrance at 29 rue de Rivoli).* Here you can find exhibitions on Paris as well as other information relating to the municipality.

HUGO, MAISON DE VICTOR 🏛
6 pl. des Vosges, 4ᵉ ☎42-72-16-65. Map 10l12 ▨ (▣ on Sun) ✗ Open 10am-5.40pm. Closed Mon. Métro: St-Paul, Chemin-Vert, Bastille.

This is the house where Victor Hugo, author of *Notre-Dame de Paris* (The Hunchback of Notre-Dame), lived from 1832-48. By the time of his death in 1885, Hugo had attained the status of national hero. He was given a spectacular public funeral attended by mourners in their thousands, and was buried with the high and mighty few great men, in the PANTHÉON.

Many people do not realize that Hugo, as well as being a great writer and distinguished public figure, was also an artist of genius, and the house is full of hundreds his drawings, paintings and lithographs — mostly dream-like or surrealistic works depicting eerie landscapes with curious vegetation and somber castles. There are also many portraits, documents and other mementoes of his public and private life.

Hugo was also an accomplished interior decorator, and the mansion contains several replicas of rooms in other houses that he lived in. One room is devoted to illustrations of *Notre-Dame de Paris* by various artists and also contains Rodin's powerful bust of Hugo.

ÎLE DE LA CITÉ AND ÎLE ST-LOUIS
The SEINE divides the city into **Rive Droite** (Right Bank) and **Rive Gauche** (Left Bank) with the two islands, ÎLE DE LA CITÉ and ÎLE ST-LOUIS, in the middle. See THE QUARTIERS OF PARIS on page 69.

INSTITUT DE FRANCE
21-25 quai de Conti, 6ᵉ. Map 8l8. Not open to public except cultural groups by arrangement. Métro: Pont-Neuf, Mabillon.

> There is no venerable forest, no mountain road,
> no prairie or plain where the sun sets so triumphally
> as behind the dome of the Institut. This is Paris
> going to sleep in her glory.
> (Émile Zola, *L'Oeuvre*, 1886)

The institute is indeed a majestic building, with a concave semicircular facade facing the Seine. It was founded as a college and library with money bequeathed by Cardinal Mazarin, and was built by the prolific architect Le Vau in 1663-4 on the site of the Nêsle gate and tower, which had formed part of the medieval city wall.

The college was suppressed after the Revolution, and in 1805 the building became the seat of the recently created Institut de France, which it remains to this day. Of the five learned academies that make up the institute, the best known is the **Académie Française**. This comprises 40 distinguished literary figures, approved by the head of state, whose main task is to protect the interests of the French language.

Zola, even though he wrote with such reverence of the building, was one of many famous Frenchmen, including Balzac, Maupassant, Proust and Molière, who were refused admission to the Académie Française. Most of its honored members have attained total obscurity.

INVALIDES, HÔTEL NATIONAL DES 🏛

Esplanade des Invalides, 7ᵉ ☎ *45-55-92-30. Map 12I5. Métro: Invalides, Latour-Maubourg, Varenne.*

When Louis XIV's architects designed this building in the 1670s as a military hospital and rest home for his wounded, elderly or infirm soldiers *(invalides)*, they poured into it all the architectural rhetoric of the Sun King's era.

Most of the building, whose foundations were finally laid in 1671, is the work of Libéral Bruant, with the esplanade by Robert de Cotte. The 196m-long **facade** (645ft) overlooks a wide **esplanade** that sweeps down to the Seine; the great portico is guarded by statues of Mars and Minerva; the dormer windows in the roof are framed by huge suits of armor crafted in stone; the **courtyard**, with its double colonnade, is particularly fine; Jules Hardouin-Mansart's **Dôme church**, which seems to be part of the facade but is, in fact, set well back, dominates the whole edifice, especially now with its regilded roof.

In its heyday, this building housed nearly 6,000 old soldiers. Now the number has dwindled to a handful, and the Hôtel des Invalides has a new but related role as the home of four museums and as the resting place of Napoleon Bonaparte.

Musée de l'Armée (Army Museum)

☎ *45-55-37-70* 🎟 *Tickets valid for two consecutive days; also valid for Napoleon's tomb. Open Apr-Sept 10am-6pm, Oct-Mar 10am-5pm.*

This collection of militaria, one of the largest in the world, is divided into two sections, housed on the E and W sides of the courtyard. The E side tells the story of the French Army, illustrated by pictures, models and military mementoes of all kinds.

Two large rooms on the ground floor, the **Salle Turenne** and the **Salle Vauban**, were once refectories for the inmates of the building. Now the former contains a fine collection of flags and standards, including those from World War I, while the latter is devoted mainly to exhibits relating to the cavalry, among them a row of life-sized dummies of dashing uniformed men on horseback.

Upstairs, a series of rooms covers different periods of French military history, dealing, commendably, with defeat as well as victory. Predictably, Napoleon I features prominently. His death mask is here, as is a reconstruction of the room at Longwood House, St Helena, where he died in 1821.

On the third floor, where there were once craft workshops manned by the *invalides*, there are now exhibits relating to the Second Empire and the Franco-Prussian War.

On the w side of the courtyard are two more former refectories, the **Salle François I** and the **Salle Henri IV**, which look back to the days when soldiers went into battle clad in armor.

Two rooms at the rear are filled with 15th-17thC weapons, and there are also displays of prehistoric and Oriental weaponry. Upstairs, the exhibits are from World Wars I and II. There is also a room filled with model artillery guns; look out of the window into the **cour de la Victoire** and you will see an impressive collection of the real thing.

Musée des Plans-Reliefs (Museum of Relief Maps and Plans)
☎45-51-95-05 ▨ *Joint ticket (see* MUSÉE DE L'ARMÉE *above). Open Apr-Sept 10am-5.45pm; Oct-Mar 10am-4.45pm.*

Housed on the fourth floor, this museum owes its origin to Louvois, Louis XIV's Secretary of State for War, who suggested to the king that scale-models be made of French fortified frontier and maritime towns. This was done, and the practice was continued by subsequent regimes up to the end of the 19thC. Here are finely-detailed miniature versions of many towns, including Mont Saint-Michel, Metz and Strasbourg.

If your interest lies in seeing Paris in *plan-relief,* make time to visit the GRAND CARNAVALET museum, where there are many such models, some more than 200 years old.

The museum has a small collection of posters, documents and relics from World Wars I and II, and holds temporary exhibitions on related subjects. The entrance to this little **Musée des Deux Guerres Mondiales** is in the NW corner of the **cour d'Honneur**.

Another small outpost is the **Musée de l'Histoire Contemporaine** (☎45-51-93-02, *closed Jan-Feb, July-Sept),* which mounts several temporary exhibitions each year on war-related topics.

Musée de l'Ordre de la Libération (Museum of the Order of Liberation)
51bis blvd. de La Tour-Maubourg ☎47-05-35-15 ▨ *Open 2-5pm. Closed Sun.*

The Order of Liberation was created by Général De Gaulle to honor those who gave outstanding service in the liberation of France. The museum, not linked with the Musée de l'Armée, has photographs, documents and mementoes of the Free French, the Resistance, the Deportation and the Liberation.

St-Louis-des-Invalides

This church, with its cool, light, barrel-vaulted interior, was where soldiers of the Hôtel des Invalides worshiped. Its main entrance faces the cour d'Honneur. When the Dôme church was added, the two opened into one another and shared a common altar. A barrier in the form of a glass screen now separates them. Berlioz's *Requiem* received its first public performance here in 1837, on the superb 17thC organ.

Dôme church and tomb of Napoleon ▥ ★

▨ *Joint ticket (see MUSÉE DE L'ARMÉE above).*

When the rest of Hôtel des Invalides had been completed, Louis XIV decided that it needed an added touch of splendor — and he commissioned Hardouin-Mansart to add the Dôme church to the s side of the building. It was begun in 1677 and completed by Robert de Cotte after Mansart's death in 1708.

With its high, slender, gilded **dome** and its **portico** with two rows of columns (Doric below, Corinthian above), it is considered one of the great masterpieces of its era. The dome itself, regilded in 1989 for the Bicentennial, gleams in a most self-congratulatory way from just about every vantage point in Paris.

However, the church is less visited for its architecture than for the fact that it contains one of the most prestigious graves in the world, the **tombeau de Napoléon 1er**, whose body was brought to Paris from St Helena in 1840, already 19 years after his death. The elaborate crypt and tomb, designed by Visconti, was not ready for a further 21 years, and the emperor was finally entombed amid lavish funeral celebrations in 1861.

A moving *son et lumière* performance, entitled *Le Retour des Cendres*, takes place in the courtyard on summer evenings. *Les cendres*, or, literally, the remains (rather than the ashes, for Napoleon had been buried conventionally), had been parted with by the British most reluctantly, and their return was greeted as a national triumph by the French, despite the intervention of the years.

The Emperor now lies encased in six coffins, one inside the other, which in turn are enclosed within a movingly beautiful red porphyry sarcophagus on its pedestal of green granite. This rests in an open circular **crypt** surrounded by a gallery in which are reliefs commemorating his achievements.

Napoleon's son, the King of Rome, who died in 1832 at the age of 21, also lies here. This was not the young man's original resting place. His remains were brought to Paris in 1940, on the centenary of the return of the emperor's remains. The instigator of this was A. Hitler Esq.

Pause to appreciate the rest of the interior: the altar with its elaborate *baldachin* supported on twisted columns; the **cupola** with its vivid paintings by La Fosse; and the side chapels containing the tombs of Maréchal Foch and other military heroes.

> I wish my remains to repose on the banks of the Seine among the people of France whom I have loved so much.

Napoleon would have been pleased with his final resting place.

JACQUEMART-ANDRÉ, MUSÉE

158 blvd. Haussmann, 8ᵉ ☎45-62-39-94. *Map 6E5* ▨ 🚉 𝒦 *Open 1-6pm. Closed Mon, Tues, Aug. Métro: St-Philippe-du-Roule, Miromesnil.*

The opulent interior of what was once a private house forms a pleasing setting for the 18thC and Italian Renaissance works that were collected voraciously yet discerningly by the Banker Edouard André and his wife, the portraitist Nélie Jacquemart. She continued to add to the collection after André's death in 1881, eventually bequeathing it to the INSTITUT DE FRANCE, along with the grand Neoclassical house that her husband had built in 1875.

Among the collection you will find sculptures by Donatello, paintings by Botticelli, Titian and Uccello, including the magnificent *St George Slaying the Dragon.* There are French 18thC painters galore — Watteau, Fragonard, Greuze and Boucher — and foreign schools by Rembrandt, Reynolds, Murillo and others. There are frescoes by Tiepolo, a Savonnerie carpet, four GOBELINS tapestries depicting the seasons, and a wealth of furniture and *objets d'art.* The Boucicault *Book of Hours,* which once belonged to Diane de Poitiers, is also there to be seen.

JARDIN DES PLANTES/MUSÉUM NATIONAL D'HISTOIRE NATURELLE

(Botanical Gardens/National Museum of Natural History)
57 rue Cuvier, 5ᵉ ☎40-79-30-00. *Map 15K10-11. Gardens* ▨ *Zoo and museum galleries* ▨ 𝒦 ▣ ✦ *Gardens and zoo open daily 7.15am (summer) or 8.15am (winter) to dusk. Gallery of Entomology open daily 2-5pm; closed Tues. Other galleries open Mon, Wed-Fri 10am-5pm; Sat-Sun 11am-6pm; closed Tues and public holidays. Métro: Jussieu.*

"This morning," wrote Henry Miller in *Tropic of Cancer,* "having nothing better to do, I visited the Jardin des Plantes. Marvelous pelicans here from Chapultepec and peacocks with studded fans that look at you with silly eyes." He might have added that there are llamas, pink flamingos, orang-outans, South American eagles, a round animal house built under Napoleon in the shape of a Legion of Honor cross, a reptile house, an open-air café, excellent playing facilities for children, and much more.

The Jardin des Plantes has many facets. It is a park and botanical garden, zoo and museum of natural history rolled into one. The easiest way to understand its quite complex layout is to pick up an English-language leaflet with map from the information office, located in a well-signed building near the NW *(rue Cuvier)* entrance to the garden.

The **menagerie** is the oldest public zoo in the country and dates back to the Revolution. Despite some rather antiquated installations (some of which are being improved), it is very popular, particularly with children, who seem to enjoy its small scale.

Look out for the new **micro-zoo,** where 6,000 of the planet's tiniest creatures can be viewed through microscopes. In the **vivarium,** which houses snakes and reptiles, try to spot the Surinam toad *(pipa pipa),* so apparently past its sell-by date as to require a permanent notice reading, "Non. Je ne suis pas mort." (It *has,* once or twice, been seen to twitch energetically.)

Near the zoo, the **botanical garden**, established in the 17thC as a medicinal herb garden, contains a wide variety of European and tropical plants. Some of the specialized areas, such as the **alpine garden**, are open for shorter hours than the main gardens. Tunnel-like avenues of plane trees lead down to the Seine.

Along the SE side of the garden are buildings that house departments of the Natural History Museum. They include the following galleries:

Paleontology: Skeletons, bones and pickled organs, both human and animal, and casts of prehistoric monsters.

Paleobotany: A small collection of plant fossils, petrified tree trunks and other such recondite objects that will be of interest mainly to specialists.

Mineralogy: Fossils, crystalline growths and precious stones.

There is also a gallery for interesting temporary exhibitions. Giant indeed is the cross-section of a giant redwood, a gift in 1927 from the American Legion Department of California.

Entomology: Just beyond these buildings, outside the perimeter of the garden proper, is the Gallery of Entomology, which claims to display "the most beautiful insects of the world."

Evolution: An ambitious program of renovation of the long-closed Gallery of Zoology, at the W end of the garden, will transform it into the **Gallery of Evolution**, which, by fall 1993, will become the centerpiece of the museum's permanent exhibitions.

✗   Ornithological walks take place each Wed at 9.15am throughout the year, if you want to make better acquaintance with the dozens of bird species that live in the gardens. Free themed walks also happen monthly *(Sept-June)* — details from the ticket office.

JEU DE PAUME, GALERIE NATIONALE DU ⌐

Place de la Concorde, 1ᵉʳ (entrance off rue de Rivoli) ☎ 47-03-12-50. Map **7**G6
🚻 ♨ *Open Wed-Fri noon-7pm, Sat, Sun noon-9.30pm; closed Mon. Métro: Concorde, Tuileries.*

This Second-Empire pavilion matches its twin, the ORANGERIE DES TUILERIES, in a corresponding position straight across the TUILERIES gardens. Originally the tennis court *(jeu de paume)* of Napoleon III, the building was widely known for many years as the home of one of the world's greatest collections of Impressionist paintings. This entire collection was rehoused in 1986, in the MUSÉE D'ORSAY.

The almost inevitable substantial refurbishment took place, and the Jeu de Paume has now reopened as a major gallery for contemporary art. Architect Antoine Stinco's stark scheme has stripped the building within bare of all decoration, leaving the large spaces created by the restoration work to speak for themselves when displaying very large and unusual works of art. The grand, clean Classical lines of the exterior have remained unaltered.

There is no permanent collection, but a program of exhibitions focusing on little-known contemporary artists, a video screening room, a good bookstore and an excellent little designer-café, selling designer-snacks at surprisingly un-designer prices.

LATIN QUARTER

This area, at the very heart of the Left Bank, comprises most of the 5ᵉ and a sliver of the 6ᵉ. The home of THE SORBONNE and the traditional student quarter, the *Quartier Latin* is the streets around the intersection of boulevard St-Michel and boulevard St-Germain. See THE QUARTIERS OF PARIS on page 71.

LÉGION D'HONNEUR, MUSÉE NATIONAL DE LA ☷

2 rue de Bellechasse, 7ᵉ ☎*45-55-95-16. Map 7H6* ▨ ✗ *by prior arrangement. Open 2-5pm. Closed Mon, public holidays. Métro: Musée d'Orsay, Solférino.*

The museum is housed in the Hôtel de Salm, a fine 18thC mansion, built in Palladian style and resembling the White House in Washington, DC. Former occupants have included the writer Mme de Staël, and Napoleon Bonaparte. The house was acquired by the Grand Chancellery of the Legion of Honor, soon after the Order's creation by Napoleon in 1802. It was burned down during the *Commune* in 1871 and almost immediately rebuilt in 1878.

The museum's function is devotion to the history of chivalric orders and other awards for distinction. Many such awards from foreign countries are featured, and examples of Britain's Victoria Cross and Order of the Bath are to be seen, as well as a rich selection of French insignia, regalia and documents.

The section on the Legion of Honor itself reveals that Rodin, Utrillo and Colette were among the recipients.

LOUVRE, MUSÉE DU   See GRAND LOUVRE on page 127.

LUXEMBOURG, PALAIS DU   See JARDINS DU LUXEMBOURG on page 94.

LA MADELEINE ☷

Pl. de la Madeleine, 8ᵉ ☎*42-65-52-17. Map 7F6* ✗ *Open 7.30am-7pm, Sun 7.30am-1.30pm, 3.30-7pm. Métro: Madeleine.*

Built to look like a Roman temple, this grand edifice, with its simple lines and colonnade of soaring Corinthian columns, stands at the hub of one of the most prosperous districts of Paris, confident of its own architectural splendor, yet apparently still uncertain of its role as a Christian church.

Begun as a church in 1764, during the reign of Louis XV (it was designed by Constant d'Ivry as a small-scale version of St-Louis-des-Invalides), it never seems to have quite thrown off the image of the bank that it nearly became in the early 19thC — other ideas included a theater, a banqueting hall, a Temple of Glory to Napoleon's army, and a railway station. After much debate and many changes of design, it was finally consecrated as a church in 1842.

Contrasting with the rather austere exterior, the sensual beauty of the interior comes as something of a surprise — a feast of softly colored marble, gilt Corinthian columns, rich murals, and some fine sculpture, including Rude's *Baptism of Christ* and the *Ascension of the Magdalen* by Marochetti, which dominates the high altar.

The church possesses a superb organ, and concerts are held here several times a week, including free Sunday afternoon concerts during the academic year. The building is closed during concerts.

The building is currently undergoing a major program of refurbishments, especially to the roof, the basement rooms, and the statues.

LE MARAIS

This ancient and dignified *quartier* contains the finest mansion houses in the capital. Built on the site of marshland *(marais)* drained in the 12thC, it extends across the 3e and 4e, to the E of the HÔTEL DE VILLE. See THE QUARTIERS OF PARIS on page 73.

MARCHÉ AUX PUCES (Flea Market)

Rue des Rosiers, St-Ouen. Map 18C4. Open Sat, Sun, Mon. Métro: Porte-de-Clignancourt.
There were once spectacular bargains to be had at this sprawling bazaar lying in an otherwise uninteresting area to the N of the boulevard Périphérique. Alas, this is no longer the case, and virtually the only cheap stalls are the ones selling tawdry modern goods.

The market, now more than 2,000 stalls extending about 4 miles, consists of a maze of alleys lined with booths, or more often, small shops, selling an intriguing variety of antiques and bric-à-brac, furniture and second-hand clothes. There is an official guide, listing stallholders by type, published in English and Japanese, as well as French (☎ 40-12-93-21).

For prospective buyers the extent of the market may be frustrating, but it can be fun just to stroll and observe, and there are plenty of cafés. See also MARKETS in SHOPPING.

MARINE, MUSÉE DE LA (Maritime Museum) 🏛

Palais de Chaillot, pl. du Trocadéro, 16e ☎45-53-31-70. Map 11H2 📼 ✳ Open 10am-6pm. Closed Tues. Métro: Trocadéro.
The symbol of Paris is a ship, so it is appropriate that the city should possess a fine maritime museum. There is hardly anything relating to the French Navy and to seafaring in general that you will not find here, from old ship's cannons and figureheads to the bridge of a modern warship, from astrolabes to radar equipment.

The museum is proud of its collection of model ships from the 17thC to the present day. The earliest dates from the creation of the French navy by Colbert in 1678, and includes warships, merchantmen, fishing craft and pleasure boats. The mysteries of 18th and 19thC shipbuilding are explained, as well as underwater exploration, navigation instruments, the development of the steamship, the great French explorers and engineers such as de Lesseps and La Pérouse.

A series of paintings on naval themes includes Vernet's series of 13 images of the ports of France. Another prized possession is a sumptuous barge that was commissioned to be made for Napoleon, in cream, green and gold, propelled by 28 oars.

Workshop activities for 8-11s are held from time to time.

MARMOTTAN, MUSÉE 🏛

2 rue Louis-Boilly, 16ᵉ ☎ *42-24-07-02. See map on page 92* 🎨 📷 ✗ *Open 10am-5.30pm. Closed Mon. Métro: La Muette, Ranelagh.*

This collection was begun by the 19thC industrialist Jules Marmottan and enlarged by his son Paul, who left it, along with his imposing house, to the Académie des Beaux-Arts, which now administers it as a museum. Its appeal lies not so much in the value of the individual works as in the wayward charm of a private collection, comprising paintings, furniture and ornaments, displayed in a series of beautiful rooms.

Although there are works of many periods, there are three periods that deserve special mention: a very fine collection of works of art and Empire-style furniture from the Napoleonic era; a superb little group of medieval (13thC) miniatures (the Wildenstein Bequest); and enough works by Monet and his contemporaries to make this museum second only to the MUSÉE D'ORSAY for works by the Impressionists. Paintings include Monet's *Impression, Soleil Levant,* from which the term Impressionist is derived, and also many of his paintings of water lilies.

The proximity of the Musée Marmottan to the BOIS DE BOULOGNE suggests a day-long visit, taking in also some of the other museums in the immediate area: ARTS ET TRADITIONS POPULAIRES, ENNERY, ARMÉNIEN, FONDATION LE CORBUSIER, CONTREFAÇON.

LES MARTYRS DE PARIS

Porte du Louvre, Forum des Halles, 1ᵉʳ ☎ *40-28-08-13. Map 9H9* 🎨 *Open 10.30am-6.30pm. Closed at Christmas. Métro: Châtelet-Les Halles.*

Les plus horribles histoires de l'histoire, says the literature, and that's about the size of it. This is an opportunity to see just how unpleasant people really were to one another in times gone by, all brought vividly to life in an endless stream of eerily-lit scenarios each more nasty than the last. From the team that brought you **The London Dungeon**. Need we describe the sort of thing? Well, put it this way — if you thought the thumbscrews and the rack sounded bad, how would you feel about being suspended in a cage over a fire, with only a wild cat for company?

Two floors of gory detail, covering tortures (general and specific) and uncomfortable historical situations (such as the ultra-pious lady who chose a life of contemplation totally walled up inside something the size of a small tool shed, fed occasionally by generous members of the public. She lived there for 48 years . . . . Or Louis XVI, who lost his head for his country).

Teenagers will probably love this, but the management will accept no responsibility for subsequent nightmares. Adults should stick to the MUSÉE GRÉVIN unless they are after real vicarious thrills.

MODE ET DU COSTUME, MUSÉE DE LA (Fashion Museum) 🏛

Palais Galliéra, 10 av. Pierre 1ᵉʳ-de-Serbie, 16ᵉ ☎ *47-20-85-23. Map 5G3* 🎨 ✗ *Open (when temporary exhibitions are on view) 10am-5.40pm. Closed Mon. Métro: Iéna, Alma-Marceau.*

To many people, Paris and fashion are synonymous. Visit this stylish museum and you are sure to learn something new about the art of dressing. The museum has no permanent collection but plays host to an intermittent series of well-mounted temporary exhibitions on various aspects of clothing and its history.

Even if fashion does not interest you, it is worth taking a look at the building. The **Palais Galliéra** was built in a striking Neoclassical style by the Duchesse de Galliéra in the decade 1878-88. The s front gives onto a charming public garden with a truly Italian feel, where the sun splashes down onto the colonnaded facade and over the park with its fountains, statues and shaded benches.

MONCEAU, PARC DE

Along boulevard de Courcelles, in the 8e, this is a picturesque English-style garden. See PARKS AND OPEN SPACES on page 95.

MONDE ARABE, L'INSTITUT DU (known as IMA) 🏛

Rue des Fossés-St-Bernard, 5e ☎40-51-38-38. Map 15J10 🚇 ᗌ ⟋ ⥲ ◁
Open 10am-6pm. Closed Mon. Métro: Jussieu, Cardinal-Lemoine, Sully-Morland.
Islamic architecture for the space age might be an apt description of architect Jean Nouvel's building, which houses this important institute. The s side of the building, for example, is shielded from the sun by windows fitted with metal screens based on Islamic patterns. Light-sensitive apertures are designed to open and close like the lens of a camera.

The overall effect of the building can seem rather harsh and inhospitable, with its razor-sharp edges, dull gray tones and windswept plaza. Don't be put off, for the design, as hi-tech within as it is without, provides a cool, shady, peaceful environment in which the Arab civilizations are celebrated and explained. Steel, glass, light and shade are the basic materials not only of the entire building, but of the inspired modes of display of the museum's treasured artworks and artifacts. A real high point is a gallery of modern Arab art, containing a permanent display of work as interesting and adventurous as any to be seen in Paris.

To the Anglo-Saxon eye, Arab culture both secular and religious can seem acutely exotic, even remote. But it sits naturally here at the heart of the French capital, which until a generation ago ruled an empire in North Africa. Even now France retains many active political and cultural ties with North Africa, and 2 million Arabs live in metropolitan France, forming the largest Arab community outside the Middle East. The institute is the result of a collaboration between France and 19 Arab countries.

Other facilities include a library, an audiovisual center, an excellent shop and a top-floor restaurant (see WHERE TO EAT) with a terrace commanding a fine view over Notre-Dame, the Îles de la Cité and St-Louis, and the Right Bank.

LE MONDE DE L'ART

18 rue de Paradis, 10e ☎42-46-43-44. Map 4E10. Open 1-8pm. Closed Sun, Mon 🔲

Housed in what was once the exquisite premises of the Hyppolyte Boulanger ceramic tile manufacturer, is a bold, bold, bold gallery of contemporary art. What is most interesting about the place is the contrast between the old, which has been lovingly preserved in all its turn-of-the-century splendor, and the art work itself, which is upbeat, modern and mostly rather experimental.

The leading light behind the organization is Raphaël Doueb, who sees the center developing as an international forum for all the arts.

Rue de Paradis is rather off the beaten track for most tourists, but you may be in this part of town to see the MUSÉE GRÉVIN, the PORTES ST-DENIS AND ST-MARTIN or the **Musée des Cristalleries** at the House of Baccarat just along the street.

As admission is free, it is worth calling in to look at the building whether or not the exhibits are to your taste. If you like both, then this is an exhilarating 30 minutes.

MONNAIE, MUSÉE DE LA

11 quai de Conti, 6ᵉ ☎ 40-46-55-26. Map 8I8 ▨ ▨ ✗ by appointment. Open 1-6pm, (Wed 1-9pm). Closed Mon, public holidays. Visits to workshops Tues, Fri at 2.15pm. Métro: Pont-Neuf, Odéon, St-Michel.

This simple but dignified mansion, which overlooks the Seine, across from the GRAND LOUVRE, was once the home of the Princess de Conti, but was taken over by Louis XV in the 18thC and remodeled by Jacques Denis Antoine to serve as the Royal Mint.

There is a permanent **museum of coins and medals** and the equipment for making them; the museum brings to life the objects that we take almost for granted, explaining how they are produced and used. There are often small exhibitions on related subjects.

As the making of coins has been transferred elsewhere, the workshops in the building now concentrate on the manufacture of medallions of all kinds. There is a sales gallery in the building *(accessible from 2 rue Guénégaud)* where a selection of medallions are available.

They are not necessarily solemn objects — one has the cancan as its theme and shows a high-kicking leg. The Mint will even create your own medallion — if you can afford it.

MONTAGNE STE-GENEVIÈVE   See LATIN QUARTER on page 71.

MONTMARTRE

The hill of Montmartre, with the brilliant white spires of SACRÉ-COEUR dominating the northern skyline, is still the metropolitan village of Paris. See THE QUARTIERS OF PARIS on page 76.

MONTPARNASSE

To the s of the JARDIN DU LUXEMBOURG, Montparnasse is visited for the views offered from the top of the TOUR MONTPARNASSE. The area has never regained its erstwhile atmosphere of bohemian intellectualism, which seeped away during the redevelopment of the 1970s. See THE QUARTIERS OF PARIS on page 78.

MONTSOURIS, PARC DE   See PARKS AND OPEN SPACES on page 95.

MONUMENTS FRANÇAIS, MUSÉE NATIONAL DES ▥
Palais de Chaillot, pl. du Trocadéro, 16ᵉ ☎44-05-39-10. Map 11H2 ▨ ✗ ໔
Open 9am-6pm. Closed Tues. Métro: Trocadéro.

Try to imagine part of the facade of Chartres cathedral standing right next door to a tympanum from Reims, a pair of gargoyles from Nantes and some sculptures from Notre-Dame, and you will get some idea of what to expect when you enter this museum.

You might well wonder whether you had stumbled into the CINÉMA museum, also housed in the PALAIS DE CHAILLOT, and were looking at relics of a Hollywood movie studio's props department — except that the replicas here are better made than on any movie . . . so well made, in fact, that, even close up, it is hard to tell that these are not stone- or wood-carvings but plaster copies. The same skill is seen in the department devoted to mural painting, where you may suddenly find yourself apparently inside a 12thC Romanesque church, painted with biblical scenes in flat ochers, browns and reds.

The original idea behind the museum was to restore French sculpture to its rightful place among the arts by showing casts of distinguished works. Formerly called the Museum of Comparative Sculpture, it was given its present title in 1937 and widened to include mural paintings and a small amount of stained glass. For the student of sculpture it is a treasure house; for the lay visitor, an enjoyable feast of make-believe.

MOREAU, MUSÉE GUSTAVE
14 rue de La Rochefoucauld, 9ᵉ ☎48-74-38-50. Map 3E8 ▨ ✗ Open Thurs-Mon 10am-12.45pm, 2-5.15pm; Wed 11am-5.15pm. Closed Tues. Métro: Trinité, St Georges.

> His sad and scholarly works breathed a strange magic,
> an incantatory charm which stirred you
> to the depths of your being.
> (J.K.Huysmans, *Art Moderne*, 1882)

The house and studio of the symbolist painter Gustave Moreau (1826-98), located on the edge of MONTMARTRE, where he lived a reclusive life, now hold a collection of the strange, dream-like works that are filled with mysterious symbolism. Many of these are large canvases, and the studio is all the more charming for having been adapted by the artist himself to the needs of his work.

Moreau left an enormous body of work to the nation; only Picasso and Turner have ever left larger bequests.

MOUFFETARD, RUE
5ᵉ. Map 15K9-L10. Métro: Place Monge.

This narrow, crowded market street, heart of one of the few authentic Parisian "villages" that survive and flourish, begins at **place de la Contrescarpe**, one of those little leafy village squares that bring a feeling of rusticity to parts of Paris. From here, rue Mouffetard descends s in a haphazard fashion. It is lined with charming old houses and shopfronts with interesting signs, such as at **#122**, which reads "At the Sign of the Clear Spring" and has a well carved on the facade, and **#134** with its swirling pattern of birds, foliage and wild boar. At **#101** and **104** are the entrances to two tiny, quaint *passages,* **passage des Patriarches** and **passage des Postes.**

The street itself remains a bustling shopping area, the food stores bursting with ripe cheeses, fruit and delicacies.

At its lower end is the little church of **St-Médard**. In the 1720s there grew here up a curious cult; groups of people assembled in the charnel house and took part in orgies of convulsion, hysteria and self-mortification in the hope of attaining miraculous cures or visions. These meetings of *convulsionnaires* were stopped by a royal order in 1732.

MOYEN ÂGE, MUSÉE NATIONAL DU   See CLUNY, THERMES DE

NOTRE-DAME DE PARIS, CATHÉDRALE DE 🏛 ★
Pl. du Parvis-Notre-Dame 4ᵉ ☎ *43-26-07-39. Map* **9**J10. *Church* 🔲 ✗ ◀€ *Open 8am-7pm; for museum and towers see below. Métro: Cité, St Michel.*

One of the world's great architectural masterpieces, the cathedral of Notre-Dame dominates the skyline of central Paris with its lacy facade and its two solid rectangular towers. It has fascinated artists and writers over the centuries, and was the setting for Victor Hugo's famous novel *Notre-Dame de Paris* (The Hunchback of Notre-Dame), whose hero, the bell-ringer Quasimodo, has become a figure of legend. "A vast symphony in stone" is how the novelist described it.

For 800 years the history of Paris has unraveled around the cathedral. Its towers have looked down upon wars, revolutions, executions, pilgrimages and, today, a virtually unceasing stream of tourists. It is one of the symbols not only of Paris but of France itself, and appropriately, set into the ground just in front of the main doorway, is a brass plaque marking the zero point from which all distances from Paris are measured.

The site of Notre-Dame has been a place of worship since pagan times, when a temple to Jupiter stood there. Later came two adjacent Christian churches, one to the Virgin Mary and the other to St Stephen. These were removed in the 12thC, when the building of Notre-Dame began — a process that was to take nearly 200 years. By 1330 the cathedral stood complete in its essential form, although in the 17th and 18thC sweeping internal alterations were carried out. During the Revolution, most of the statues of the portals and choir chapels were destroyed, the bells were melted down, the treasures were plundered, and the cathedral became a Temple of Reason.

In the mid-19thC, a magnificent restoration was carried out by the architect and restorer of ancient buildings Viollet-le-Duc, who replaced hundreds of destroyed carvings, as well as building a new spire and creating new vaults and walls. He aspired not only to restoring the existing building but to help it to be what he felt it should have been — Gothic above all things. During the *Commune* of 1871 the whole cathedral very nearly perished when the *Communards* made a bonfire of chairs in the choir. Luckily the building was saved by the lack of air and the dampness of the walls. A spot of "cleaning" was also carried out in the early 1960s, under the De Gaulle administration.

More — and major — renovations are in progress today. In 1991, a 10-year program of works began, and sections of the structure are likely to be shrouded or enveloped in scaffolding for some time. Many of the cathedral's current structural problems are caused by wear and tear and atmospheric pollution. The Île de la Cité has always suffered badly from exhaust emission from the cars of tourists who gather in the vicinity, often keeping the engine running to maintain their air conditioning. Before the restoration program started, a ban on cars parking in front of the cathedral was imposed.

Eleven million people visit Notre-Dame each year. It is a wonder that it does not feel more like a railway station.

As you enter

An unusual feature of the cathedral is that its floor is absolutely level with the street, so that it seems to welcome passers-by to enter without formality.

Before going into the building, spend a while taking in the abundant sculptures on the **facade** (★), remembering that most are skillful copies or restorations done under the direction of Viollet-le-Duc. It was he who instigated the carving of the 28 kings of Israel who stand in a row known as the **King's Gallery**, across the facade. The heads of the originals of these are now in the MUSÉE DU MOYEN ÂGE (CLUNY) museum.

The three doorways are known as the **portals of the Virgin Mary**, of **the Last Judgment** and of **Ste Anne**, and the stonework is richly carved with appropriate figures, such as Christ sitting in judgment (over the central doorway) flanked by the Virgin Mary and St John as intercessors. Look for some of the smaller carvings, such as the zodiacal signs on the left-hand portal, and the curious medallions on the central one, representing virtues and vices: purity is a salamander, and pride is a man being thrown from a horse (these have also been given an alchemical interpretation).

The other facades also have some fine carving; the most famous sculpture of all is that of the **Virgin**, by the door of the N transept, carved in the 13thC and unscathed in the Revolution, except for the loss of the Child.

Inside the cathedral

Once you are inside the cathedral, before looking at the individual features, take in the majestic construction of the building; its walls rise in the traditional Gothic manner, through three tiers of arches to a ribbed, vaulted ceiling that seems infinitely far away. Stand in the cen-

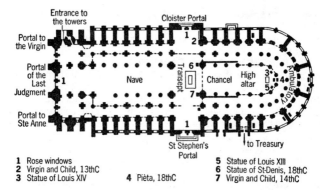

1 Rose windows
2 Virgin and Child, 13thC
3 Statue of Louis XIV

4 Pièta, 18thC

5 Statue of Louis XIII
6 Statue of St-Denis, 18thC
7 Virgin and Child, 14thC

ter of the transept and you will feel the full impact of the architecture. From here you will also get a good view of the **rose windows** — three great shimmering pools of light and color to the N, S and W. Only the N rose, made in 1270, retains most of its original glass. The S window was extensively restored in the 18thC and the W window in the 19thC. It is partly hidden by the largest organ in France, which has been refurbished as part of the current overall scheme.

Features of the transept that are worth seeing include the lovely 14thC statue of the *Virgin and the Child* against the S pillar flanking the entrance to the chancel, and the 18thC statue of *St-Denis* against the opposite pillar.

Around the **nave** is a series of **chapels** containing many fine sculptures and paintings, mostly from the 17thC. In the **St Peter chapel** on the S side there is some beautiful 14thC woodwork, carved with representations of saints. In the **ambulatory** there are more chapels, filled with the mausoleums of various bishops of Paris.

The **high altar** in the chancel was made in the 19thC to a design by Viollet-le-Duc. Behind it is an 18thC *Piéta*, to the right a statue of Louis XIII, who in 1638 consecrated his kingdom to the Virgin. To the left is a statue of Louis XIV.

On the S side of the ambulatory, a door leads to the **treasury** (▨ *open 9.30am-6pm, closed Sun),* where a collection of plate and other treasures, including a reliquary said to contain a fragment of the Cross, can be inspected.

No visit to Notre-Dame would be complete without climbing the **towers** (☎ *43-54-22-63* ▨ ◁€ *open Apr-Sept 10am-6pm, Oct-Mar 10am- 5pm, closed Sun; check according to season and weather).* You ascend 387 steps via the N tower, then cross over to the S one, passing a series of splendid gargoyles and carved monsters, including the **striga** (a kind of vampire), who gazes, chin resting on his hands, over the city. In the S tower you can visit, with a guide, the belfry containing the great 13-ton bell that is rung only on special occasions.

The S tower can be climbed to the top, and on the descent you pass a room containing a **museum of the cathedral's history**. For a more detailed presentation of the building's history, cross the street to the

cathedral museum *(☎43-25-42-92 ▨ open Wed, Sat, Sun 2.30-6pm)*, which houses a worthwhile and fascinating collection of objects, pictures and documents that illustrate the cathedral's history.

NOTRE-DAME DE PARIS: CRYPTE ARCHÉOLOGIQUE
Pl. du Parvis-Notre-Dame, 4ᵉ ☎43-29-83-51. Map 9I9 ▨ Open 10am-6pm Apr-Sept, 10am-5pm Oct-Mar. Closed public holidays. Métro: Cité, St Michel.

This museum resulted from the discovery of an important archeological site in front of NOTRE-DAME, and it was roofed over after the excavation finished. The resulting vault is the largest structure of its kind in the world.

Descending a stairway from the square, one literally steps down into the Paris of an earlier age, finding an underground chamber where Gallo-Roman ramparts jostle the cellars of medieval houses. The remains are superbly presented, with information on the early history of Paris, illustrated by detailed models of the city at various stages.

OBSERVATOIRE DE PARIS ▥
61 av. de l'Observatoire, 14ᵉ. Map 14M8 ▣ ✗ compulsory. Open first Sat in month only, by arrangement: apply in writing to Secretariat at above address. RER: Port-Royal.

This chaste building, with its two-domed octagonal towers, was built between 1667-72. No iron was used in the construction because it might have affected the instruments, and wood was also avoided for fear of fire. The s wall of the building marks the latitude of Paris.

Today, the Observatory remains a major research center for astronomy and related services. In theory the building and its small museum can be visited by guided tour on the first Saturday of every month, but there is usually a waiting list, sometimes of 2-3 months. However, the charming **garden** behind the Observatory, entered from blvd. Arago, is open to all, free of charge.

OPÉRA BASTILLE
120 rue de Lyon, 12ᵉ ☎40-01-17-89. Map 16J12 ▣ Open 11am-6.30pm. Closed Sun ☲ ▣ ⚂ Métro: Bastille.

Despite its splendor, the much-loved OPÉRA GARNIER had been declared technically inadequate some years earlier, when the decision was taken in 1982 to build a new opera house on the site of the Bastille. No facilities to store large-scale scenery meant no repertoire of works; a limited seating capacity meant high ticket prices and an unquenchable demand. Poor rehearsal and studio space did not allow the Opéra to work as it should.

Architect Carlos Ott won the commission, in the face of competition from 750 contenders, and work began in 1985. The new opera house (pictured on page 110), its multifaceted glass frontage dominating place de la Bastille, was inaugurated during the Bicentenary celebrations in 1989, was formally opened in 1990, and finally opened in 1991, to reveal to the world a large prestigious opera house in its finished form. The modern glass ceiling echoes the lusters and decorated ceilings of the opera houses of an earlier age, reflecting the gray-blue granite of the walls and the oak block floor, as well as the giddying tiers of balconies that sweep up toward the roof.

As well as the main auditorium (2,700 seats), the Opéra Bastille houses a 500-seat amphitheater and a small studio (see also PERFORMING ARTS). Acoustic and other technical problems bedeviled the scheme even after it opened, and perhaps a year elapsed before the difficulties were solved. Programming of the Opéras Bastille and Garnier is done jointly, under the global promotional title of **Opéra de Paris**, and while the full-scale operatic performances now happen exclusively at the Opéra Bastille, the glorious Opéra Garnier now serves as a major venue for both ballet and contemporary dance.

The vast building welcomes visitors throughout the day, with bookstalls, a restaurant and cafeteria, and permanent and temporary exhibitions. Some say that the period of its conception and birth was troubled. Others are not kind about the building's design. Yet London's Barbican Centre overcame similar problems and achieved international credibility very quickly. No doubt the Opéra Bastille is set to do the same.

See also PLACE DE LA BASTILLE on page 109.

OPÉRA GARNIER 🏛

Pl. de l'Opéra, 9ᵉ ☎47-42-53-71. Map 7F7 ✗ 11am-5pm ▨ (☎40-01-17-89 for program details). Closed Sun, Aug. Métro: Opéra.

When Charles Garnier, architect of the Opéra, was asked by the Empress Eugénie whether the building was to be in the Greek or Roman style, he replied indignantly, "It is neither Greek nor Roman. It is in the Napoleon III style, Madame!"

In fact, no building epitomizes more strikingly the heavy opulence of that era. During its construction between 1862-75 the builders encountered an underground lake, which now lies beneath the cellars of the building, and where the "Phantom of the Opéra" had his dwelling. Above, however, all is brightness and gaiety.

The ornate facade, with its multitude of columns, friezes, winged figures and busts of famous composers, is the architectural equivalent of Offenbach's music: lighthearted and irresistible. Inside the building the tone changes. The richly colored marble staircase, where caryatids hold elaborate candelabra, evokes the setting for Belshazzar's Feast.

> If the world were ever reduced
> to the dominion of a single gorgeous potentate,
> the foyer [of the Opéra] would do very well
> for his throne room.
> (Henry James, *Parisian Sketches,* 1875-76)

As for the auditorium, it has all the right ingredients: red velvet, gold leaf and an abundance of plaster nymphs and cherubs. The only discordant element is the domed ceiling painted by Chagall — exquisite but out of place.

During the day you can walk around the building in return for a small fee, but really the only way to see the Opéra is to attend a performance there. The removal of the major operatic performances to the OPÉRA BASTILLE in 1990 has permitted the Opéra Garnier to establish a fine, varied program of international ballet and contemporary dance. See also PERFORMING ARTS.

OPÉRA QUARTER

The area surrounding the magnificent OPÉRA GARNIER extends roughly from boulevard Haussmann and RUE DE RIVOLI to the N and S, and rue de Richelieu and the MADELEINE to the E and W. It contains many exclusive shops, as well as the major department stores on the GRANDS BOULEVARDS. See THE QUARTIERS OF PARIS on page 80.

ORANGERIE DES TUILERIES, MUSÉE DE L' 🏛

Pl. de la Concorde, Jardin des Tuileries, 1ᵉʳ ☎42-97-48-16. Map 7G6. Open 9.45am-5.15pm. Closed Tues. Métro: Concorde.
Across the Tuileries from the JEU DE PAUME is this matching pavilion housing the Walter-Guillaume collection of paintings. Exhibits cover the period from the end of the Impressionist era to 1930, and include works by Renoir, Cézanne, Matisse, Derain, Soutine and Picasso.

The gallery's other major possession is a collection of eight huge *Grandes Nymphéas* (Waterlilies) canvases by Claude Monet, painted at Giverny between 1915 and the artist's death in 1926. These complement the collection on view in the MUSÉE MARMOTTAN.

ORSAY, MUSÉE D' 🏛 ★

1 rue de Bellechasse, 7ᵉ ☎40-49-48-14. General recorded information ☎45-49-11-11. Map 7H7 ▦ ✗ Open Tues, Wed, Fri, Sat 10am-6pm, Thurs 10am-9.45pm, Sun 9am-6pm (June 20-Sept 20 opens daily 9am). Closed Mon ♿ ▰
▣ Métro: Solférino. RER: Musée d'Orsay.
What better place for a major museum of the 19thC than the former Gare d'Orsay, a splendid example of *fin-de-siècle* grandeur, which has been beautifully restored and skillfully converted for museum use?

The building

The site of the former Palais d'Orsay, occupied only by the strangely romantic ruins of the cour des Comptes since the razing of the palace in the *Commune* of 1871, was bought by the Paris-Orléans railway company, which felt itself to be disadvantaged by the remoteness of its Gare d'Austerlitz. This became the location of a monumental yet modern new station, designed by Victor Laloux, which opened 2 months after the World Fair, in July 1900. Built around metal structures, the edifice was meant to be decorative as well as functional. In response to criticisms of the construction of such a large metal structure just across the river from the TUILERIES, Laloux masked it with a stone facade along the quay and the front of the hotel on rue de Bellechasse.

With its single hall, 32m (105 feet) in height, 16 underground railway tracks and vast reception areas, the station was, for close on 40 years, the terminus of the main line to the SW with about 200 departures each day.

But from being a symbol of progress, the station became the victim of progress. The electrification of the railroad network produced the need for longer trains, and without the space to extend its platforms, the station ended its long-distance service in 1939 and activities were restricted to suburban lines. Deprived of a large part of its lifeblood, the station quickly became too large.

Its uses varied from a center for the dispatch of packages destined for prisoners of war, to a reception center for those same returning prisoners, from the platform for De Gaulle's 1958 announcement of his plans to return to power to a movie location for Orson Welles' production of Kafka's *The Trial* (1962) and Bertolucci's *Le Conformiste* (1970).

In 1961, the SNCF placed the building on the market. Many projects were proposed; all projected the disappearance of the station, and the inclusion of a large modern hotel in the plans. This was the way of things in the years before Paris learned to recognize the value of its historic buildings (see ARCHITECTURE). Yet the demolition of Laloux's work was prevented by the Minister for Cultural Affairs, Jacques Duhamel, in 1971, and it became a listed Historic Building in 1973. By 1978, the idea of a major national museum that would concentrate on the arts of the period 1848-1914 was formally agreed, architects were briefed, and work finally began in 1980.

The challenge of turning a space that had been designed for people to pass through into one where people would be encouraged to linger, of mastering the immense volume of space without breaking or enclosing it, was met in a concise and imaginative way by the Italian lady architect Gae Aulenti. The existing glass panes, metal structures and decorative moldings might have provoked imitation — yet the reshaping was done through contrast and simplicity, concentrating uniquely on the solid medium of stone.

Unlike in many vast buildings that have been adapted for museum use, a visitor to the d'Orsay can "see" the entire layout from the point of entry. The 1st- and 2nd-floor exhibits are arranged in hanging galleries, with the floor-to-ceiling drop always visible at the heart of the building.

Galleries showing the permanent collection are kept apart from temporary exhibition areas, themed displays and information areas, and it is the museum's policy is to allow each work to speak for itself, in a neutral environment, rather than being suggestively shown in a setting of a particular period.

The collections

The entire collection now comprises 2,500 paintings and 250 pastel drawings, 1,500 sculptures, 1,100 *objets d'art* and 13,000 photographs, and is constantly being added to. Works have been gathered together from various collections, including those formerly housed in the JEU DE PAUME museum, the PALAIS DE TOKYO, the LOUVRE, the ARTS DÉCORATIFS museum, the châteaux of VERSAILLES and FONTAINEBLEAU, as well as a number of private collections.

PAINTING: The museum covers two important phases: first, **from the late 1840s to the early 1870s**, marked by the birth of Impressionist painting; and second, **from Impressionism to the birth of Modern Art, around 1905**. While each of these phases had numerous influences, each has nevertheless two distinguishable and principal movements.

In the **first phase**, these are: the movement arising from the heritage of the great **Neo-Classicists** (Ingres and co.), and from the **Romanticists** (late works of Delacroix), which influenced such artists as Gustave Moreau, Puvis de Chavannes, and the first Degas; and the **Realists**, from Daumier and the Barbizon painters to the early **Impressionists**, by way of Millet, Courbet and Manet.

In the **second phase**, from **1870-1907/10**, the two major movements are: the main **Impressionist** wave that began in 1870, and the **Post-Impressionists** that responded to the stimulus of Impressionism, namely Cézanne, Van Gogh, Lautrec, Redon and Seurat, and the **Neo-Impressionists**, Gauguin and the Pont-Aven school.

Secondly, the diverse forms of painting that emerged from the *salons*, the official eclecticism of the Third Republic, which ranged from the **Second-Empire** Bourguereau to the **naturalists** Cormon and Bastien-Lepage, the brilliant end-of-century **portrait artists**, Boldini, Besnard and Blanche, **foreign influences** such as the American Homer and the Spaniard Sorolla, the *Bande Noire* painters such as Cottet, and, finally, the **symbolists**.

The museum also offers a perspective on **20thC art**, with works by Dufy, Klimt, Matisse, Munch, Rousseau and Van Dongen.

SCULPTURES: In the 60 years of constant evolution and change in painting, the art of **sculpture** had remained closed to esthetic innovations. With Rodin's *L'Age d'Airain* (1877), sculpture entered a grand new adventure, which would lead toward modernity. Exceptions in this field were perhaps, the small number of **painter/sculptors**, Daumier, Degas, Gauguin and Renoir, who were pioneers of the new paths that were opening up.

FURNITURE AND OBJETS D'ART: The creation of *objets d'art* and **furniture** was deeply influenced by the introduction of new manufacturing techniques. The English "**Arts and Crafts**" movement pioneered by the Englishman William Morris, Rossetti and Burne-Jones was echoed in France by Viollet-le-Duc, who brought contemporary detail to works of architecture.

Art Nouveau forms finally allowed the architect to take his contribution beyond that of structure, and examples can be seen of the urban furniture of Guimard and the furnishings of Frank Lloyd Wright and Van de Velde.

PHOTOGRAPHY: The newborn art of **photography** was, meanwhile, exploring many different perspectives. Photographic journalism, social observation, fictional photography and "living paintings," landscape and aerial photography, all produced leading exponents over the period of 60 years.

ARCHITECTURE The period covered by the museum spans Haussmann's urban planning, Garnier's OPÉRA, the construction of the TOUR EIFFEL, the classic styles of Duban and Viollet-le-Duc and the Baroque styles of Lefuel and Garnier. These led to the Art Nouveau explosion, which became the source of 20thC inspiration. The Musée d'Orsay's rich storehouse has gathered together entire collections of the graphic work of some architects, including Eiffel and Garnier.

An itinerary

No floor plan need be given here — the Musée d'Orsay is laid out in such a way that the visitor can follow the clear signs, and gauge the scale of the exhibition areas so easily that a diagram would be superfluous. In any case, most museums, especially new ones, change the use of their spaces from time to time.

GROUND FLOOR: Begin by passing through the **Second Empire** collection. Here is the cool, formal Classicism of Ingres, the fluid, romantic canvases from Delacroix's later period, the calm, pastoral scenes of Millet and Corot, and the early work of the **Impressionists-to-be**: Manet, Monet and Renoir. There are also some striking sculptures in the center aisle, as well as a broad-ranging architecture section and a large area devoted to the OPÉRA GARNIER, with a model of the OPÉRA QUARTER under a glass floor and a cut-away model of the Opéra building itself.

TOP FLOOR: If you follow the recommended route, you then go straight to the upper level, where you find the great **Impressionist** collection, shown to best advantage in the natural light. Here you will see classics such as Monet's *Rouen Cathedral,* Van Gogh's *Self-Portrait,* Renoir's joyful *Moulin de la Galette,* and many more. Other works on this floor include the eerie scenes of "Douanier" Rousseau and the paintings of the Pont-Aven school: Gauguin, Bernard and Sérusier.

While on the top floor, you might wish to visit the café located behind the face of the enormous station clock — you can watch the hands moving as you sip your coffee.

MIDDLE FLOOR: Finally, descend to the middle level, to the glass-domed rooms overlooking the Seine. Among the paintings exhibited here are the uncanny visions of the **Symbolists** and, as a total contrast, the vivid canvases of Bonnard. The **decorative arts** are well represented on this floor. There is a series of rooms with superb **Art Nouveau** objects gathered from France and beyond (Charles Rennie Mackintosh, William Morris and Frank Lloyd Wright are to be found in company with Hector Guimard and René Lalique), and a section devoted to the **decorative arts of the Third Republic** is appropriately housed in one of the ornate public rooms of the old station hotel.

===   The elegant former restaurant of the hotel has sprung to life again as the **Restaurant du Musée d'Orsay** *(entrance at 62bis rue de Lille ☎ 45-49-42-33, closed Sun eve, Mon ← ▥ to ▥ AE ◉)*, a large, bright room, all white and gold, with chandeliers and an exquisitely painted ceiling — a dining ambience wholly in keeping with the spirit of the museum.

PALAIS-BOURBON   See ASSEMBLÉE NATIONALE.

PALAIS DE CHAILLOT 血
Pl. du Trocadéro, 16ᵉ. Map 11H2. Métro: Trocadéro.

The commanding height on the Right Bank of the Seine, known as the Chaillot, has been occupied by a series of buildings. It began as a country house built by Catherine de Medicis in the 1580s.

After the Restoration, Charles X wanted to build a monument to commemorate the French capture of the Trocadéro fort near Cadiz in Spain. This was never built, but the name stuck and was given to an elaborate palace created there for the Paris Exhibition of 1878. Its successor, built for the Exhibition of 1937, was called the Palais de Chaillot, and the name Trocadéro was kept for the square onto which the N side of the building faces. The whole complex is aligned with the TOUR EIFFEL and the CHAMP-DE-MARS across the river, creating a dramatic townscape.

With its simple lines, Neoclassical colonnades and heroic sculptures, the palace is reminiscent of the monumental Fascist and Soviet architecture of the period. But it has aged well, and its sandstone facade has a crisp elegance.

From a spacious piazza with a magnificent view of the Eiffel Tower, two curving wings reach out, embracing a garden that slopes down toward the Seine, the central axis of which is laid out in a descending series of fountains and pools.

The Palais de Chaillot now houses the following museums: DU CINÉMA, DE L'HOMME, DE LA MARINE and DES MONUMENTS FRANÇAIS. Also housed here are the film library of the CINÉMATHÈQUE FRANÇAISE and the **Théâtre National de Chaillot**, with its two auditoriums.

PALAIS DES CONGRÈS: CENTRE INTERNATIONAL DE PARIS

*Pl. de la Porte-Maillot, 17ᵉ. Map **5**D1-E1. Métro: Porte-Maillot.*

A streamlined, multipurpose building, opened in 1974, dominates the chaotic spaghetti intersection by the NE corner of the BOIS DE BOULOGNE. It comprises the Palais des Congrès and a vast hotel. The palais itself is a low-rise block, housing exhibition halls, shops, restaurants, movie theaters, conference rooms, a discotheque, an air terminal and the huge and impressive **Main Conference Hall**, home of the Paris Symphony Orchestra and also used for conferences *(no admittance unless attending a performance)*.

Beside this is the high-rise Hôtel Concorde-LaFayette, with 1,000 rooms. The complex, known as the **Centre International de Paris** (CIP), is a planners' dream, with every facility — except, some feel, charm.

PALAIS DE LA DÉCOUVERTE (Palace of Discovery) ▥

*Av. Franklin-D-Roosevelt, 8ᵉ ☎40-74-80-00; ☎43-59-18-21 (recorded message). Map **6**G5 ▨ ▣ in Grand Palais. Open Tues-Sat 9.30am-6pm, Sun, hols 10am-7pm. Closed Mon. Planetarium lectures 4 or 5 times a day. Métro: Champs-Élysées-Clemenceau, Franklin-D-Roosevelt.*

The imposing W wing of the Grand Palais, with its huge domed entrance hall, is a place in which to wonder at the properties of the symbol Pi, the structure of the atom, the nature of laser beams or the fundamentals of genetics. These and many other branches of discovery are imaginatively presented and kept up to date. What makes the Palais de la Découverte attractive is that attendants are present in every room to explain and demonstrate the exhibits.

The museum has a **planetarium** where different aspects of the universe are projected onto a hemispherical dome. There are regular temporary exhibitions, film shows and lectures.

PALAIS DE L'ÉLYSÉE
55 rue du Faubourg-St-Honoré, 8ᵉ. Map 6F5. Métro: St-Philippe-du-Roule, Champs-Élysées-Clemenceau, Miromesnil.
Built in 1718 for the Comte d'Evreux and later lived in by Madame de Pompadour and Napoleons I and III (Napoleon I signed his abdication here), this palace, with its extensive garden, has since 1873 been the official residence of the French president and the meeting place of the Council of Ministers. The public is not allowed in, but you can glimpse the elegant facade and courtyard beyond a heavily guarded gateway.

PALAIS GALLIÉRA   See MODE ET DU COSTUME, MUSÉE DE LA.

PALAIS DE JUSTICE DE PARIS (Law Courts)
2 blvd. du Palais, 1ᵉʳ ☎43-29-12-55. Map 9I9 ⊡✿ Open Mon-Fri 9am-5pm. Closed Sat, Sun, hols. Métro: Cité, St-Michel; RER: Châtelet-les-Halles.
Together with SAINTE-CHAPELLE and the CONCIERGERIE, the Palais de Justice forms a vast complex of buildings running the whole width of the ÎLE DE LA CITÉ, with an imposing courtyard and entrance on boulevard du Palais. There was a palace here in Roman times, and later the site was occupied by a magnificent royal residence, which in the 14thC became the seat of parliament.

It was here that Louis XIV proclaimed to parliament *"L'État, c'est moi!"* Since the Revolution, the buildings have been occupied by civil and criminal law courts.

The most impressive room in the complex of courts and galleries is the **Lobby** *(Salle de Pas-Perdus)*, formerly the great hall of the palace, which was twice destroyed by fire, the second time during the *Commune* of 1871. It was rebuilt in its present form in the 1870s.

The royal courtiers are now replaced by lawyers and litigants scurrying about the "cathedral of chicanery," as Balzac called it. If you want to see them in action, you can visit any except the juvenile court.

PALAIS DE LA MODE
Jardins du Carrousel, 1ᵉʳ. Map 7H7. Métro: Tuileries.
The transformation of the JARDINS DU CARROUSEL will, by fall 1993, be completed. Massive excavation works have disrupted the area for several years, the aim being to provide a major new focus for the world of Paris fashion. The completion of the new underground Palais de la Mode will be a feather in the cap of architect Gérard Grandval. His subterranean complex will be almost invisible from above, apart from a splendid sweeping granite staircase on the rue de Castiglione/Pont Solférino axis and the inverted pyramid that allows light to enter the 9,000 sq.m (95,000 sq.ft) gallery below.

Design work needed to be amended as the excavation work progressed, with the emergence of parts of the massive city wall built by Charles V. They have been turned into a feature in the large hall.

This much-needed new venue for the twice-yearly Paris fashion shows will contain four halls, the largest seating 1,500, as well as all the facilities that such an enterprise could conceivably need: press rooms, changing facilities, exhibition spaces, restaurants and so on. The first fashion shows are scheduled for October 1993.

The JARDINS DES TUILERIES above are being reinstated, and within a year or two, the unsuspecting eye might hardly know what lies below the ground.

PALAIS-ROYAL 🏛

Pl. du Palais-Royal, 1ᵉʳ. Map 8H8. Métro: Palais-Royal Musée-du-Louvre.

Few buildings in Paris have played as many different roles as the Palais-Royal. Built by Cardinal Richelieu in the 17thC as his private palace, it later came into the hands of the Orléans family, one of whom was the dissolute regent Philippe II of Orléans, who turned the palace into a scene of frenzied orgies.

His descendant, the so-called "Philippe Égalité," needing to raise money, built matching terraces of apartment houses around the garden, with an arcade at ground level in which there were premises for trades-men. These buildings form the splendid quadrangle, the **cour d'Honneur**, that one can enter to the N of the palace.

This much prized courtyard has been the subject of government expenditure during 1992, and a reworking has taken shape, under the guidance of an American landscape architect resident in France, Mark Rudkin. Statues in need of repair have been taken away for surgery and others have taken their place. He has met the challenge of navigating around the much-criticized sculpture, which consists of a series of black-and-white columns of unequal height, created by the artist Buren. More pleasing are two great bowls of water upon which oscillate large stainless-steel spheres. An interesting planting scheme will keep the garden all of a single color — one year red, the next blue, and so on.

In the heated period before the Revolution, this quadrangle was the scene of rallies and demonstrations — the "nucleus of the Revolution," Marat called it. Then, after the execution of Philippe Égalité, the palace, its gardens and cafés, became a center of gambling and prostitution.

Returned to the Orléans family at the Restoration, the palace was sacked during the Revolution of 1848 and set on fire by the mob during the *Commune* of 1871.

Now the office of the Council of State and closed to the public, the Palais-Royal seems content after its hectic past.

PALAIS DE TOKYO

Palais de Tokyo, 11 av. du Président-Wilson, Paris 16ᵉ ☎47-23-61-27. Map 11G3 ▨ ♿ ▣ Open 10am-5.30pm (Wed until 8.30pm). Closed Mon. Subject to change once building conversion begins. Métro: Iéna, Alma-Marceau.

This elegant building is a typical example of the Art Deco architecture of the 1930s. It has housed several museums, including the MUSÉE D'ART MODERNE DE LA VILLE DE PARIS.

The transformation of the Palais de Tokyo into the Palais des Arts de l'Image is due to take place between 1993 and 1995. The Palace will be equipped with every piece of new technology to enable it to become the focal point of cinematic and photographic knowledge. The halls and monumental staircases are to be sensitively refurbished and the building will be given a general *grands travaux* treatment.

Its reopening is planned for the end of 1994, doubly appropriate because 1995 sees the entry of the cinema industry into its second century. A team headed by French director Michel Piccoli is in charge of programming the celebratory events.

PANTHÉON 🏛 ★

Pl. du Panthéon, 5ᵉ ☎ *43-54-34-51. Map **14**K9* 🖼 *admission to crypt and dome* ✗ ⚐ *in crypt. Open Apr-Sept 10am-6pm, Oct-Mar 10am-5.30pm. Closed hols* ⇔ *Métro: Cardinal-Lemoine. R.E.R: Luxembourg.*

For half of its life this building has led a schizophrenic existence. It was initiated by Louis XV in thanksgiving for his recovery from an illness, and was intended as a more magnificent shrine to Paris' patroness Ste-Geneviève than the old abbey church of that name that stood on the site. Situated in a commanding position on the Montagne Ste-Geneviève, this *panthéon* was built in the form of a Greek cross, with a **dome** at the intersection and a massive **portico** with Corinthian columns.

The history

Hardly had it been completed than the new Revolutionary government decided to change it from a church into a mausoleum for the remains of great Frenchmen.
For this purpose, many of the windows were removed and blocked up, hence its rather bald and forbidding appearance. Twice it was to revert to its role as a church and then be changed back again to a secular mausoleum. The last occasion was in 1885 when it was finally secularized to provide a suitable resting place for Victor Hugo. Across the pediment overlooking the square are emblazoned in gold letters the words *Aux Grands Hommes La Patrie Reconnaissante* (the people give thanks to their Great Men).

The present

The former church is closed to the public on the ground floor. It has been closed for some time, and predictions are that it will not reopen until perhaps 1998. The sad truth is that the building, its dome an architectural *tour-de-force,* is suffering from a combination of structural problems, made worse by the northern European climate. The weight of the dome has begun to cause undue pressure on the columns that support it, while the windows, which were constructed without expansion gaps, have begun to buckle and fracture, a problem caused by changes of temperature and lack of heating.

Furthermore, the stonework covering the vaulting is cracking apart, because the iron framework beneath is now exhibiting the same discomfort as the windows. And, to cap it all, the lack of heating, which has always been a problem, causes condensation, which is helping to rot the concealed iron structure and is ruining the priceless paintings both on the ceilings and the walls.

The recent discovery of Soufflot's first building plans are making the task of restoration much easier, for much of the iron structure was undetectable. All this is no reason not to visit. Trips into the dome and the crypt might be like seeing heaven and hell on the same day. It is all a question of which you visit first.

The dome

For the uplifting part, make the trip up to the dome. It gives access to one of the most rewarding views, and is one of the easiest of Paris' tall buildings to climb. There are 250 steps, but after only 100, you reach the main gallery, where it is impossible not to stop and look down into the main body of the former church. Curiously devoid of all ecclesiastical trappings and with a great empty expanse of floor, it still feels like a church despite its many years of deconsecration. The famous canvases by Puvis de Chavannes (on the ground floor) are no longer visible, but being in the gallery allows you to see at close quarters into the triple cupolas of the dome, with its frescoes depicting *Justice* and *Glory*.

Another stair leads to a higher vantage point within the cupola. Then, after a thrilling (but safely enclosed) walk out across the roof, you reach the circular colonnaded viewing platform, from where, because of its wide construction, you feel supported rather than threatened by the height. A panorama of 360° can be viewed, and there are useful boards indicating the many buildings to be seen — a facility encountered still quite rarely at the tops of tall buildings.

The crypt

In a series of vaulted corridors beneath the building lie the remains of a number of illustrious Frenchmen. The tombs are housed four to a gloomy little room, and there is very little difference between one tomb and the next. Voltaire and Rousseau take pride of place; their tombs are much larger and grander than any others, and they effectively greet visitors upon arrival. Rousseau's tomb seems to reflect his continual search for truth — for through a door, at one end of the plinth, reaches a hand holding a torch. Hugo shares his compartment with Zola — a curious pair of cell-mates, each probably outscribbling the other to this day. Others buried here include the building's architect, Soufflot, the chemist Berthelot and the wartime Resistance leader Jean Moulin.

But there is here no joy in the celebration of death. The mausoleum is fascinating, but chilling, and a return to the daylight is most welcome.

PARADIS, RUE DE

10°. Map 3E9-4E10. Métro: Château-d'Eau, Poissonnière.

An unexpected jewel in the hinterland between the GRANDS BOULEVARDS and the Gare du Nord, this street is monopolized by retailers and wholesalers of glass and ceramic tableware. The goods displayed in these shops range from the breathtakingly vulgar to the stunningly beautiful, although fortunately the latter predominates. At #30bis can be found the glassware museum, the **Musée des Cristalleries** or **Musée Baccarat** (☎*47-70-64-30* 🔄 *open Mon-Fri 9am-6pm, Sat 10am-noon, 2-5pm; closed Sun, public holidays),* run by the firm of Baccarat and containing a dazzling collection of glass objects dating from the early 19thC to the present day.

Another interesting stopover point is LE MONDE DE L'ART at #18. This is a gallery of contemporary art, housed in what was once the premises of a ceramic tile manufacturer. It has a superb tiled entrance, and some portions of the interior also have a turn-of-the-century feel, although most of the building has been adapted for its current use in a most imaginative way. Admission is free.

PARISTORIC

Espace Hébertot, 78bis blvd. des Batignolles, 17e ☎*42-93-93-46* 🔄 *Open daily (all year round) 9am-6pm hourly; Sat, Sun open until 9pm. Métro: Rome, Villiers.*
A 40-minute cinematic experience that brings the city of Paris to life in a devastatingly beautiful sweep through the 2,000 years of her history from Roman Lutèce to the Grande Arche. Image pours into image on the giant screen, as each era of history is unfolded, through its personalities, its buildings and its monuments.

There is a fine soundtrack, and simultaneous translation is available in 7 languages. Recommended as an introduction to Paris or as a quick refresher for nostalgic visitors at the end of their stay.

"PASSAGES"

Maps **8** & **9**.
Of interest as much for their architectural qualities as for the shopping opportunities, Paris' many arcades *(passages)* merit exploration.

Long before pedestrian zones came into vogue, Paris had many arcades, covered walkways and colonnades where the elegant *flâneur* could stroll or window-shop, unhampered by traffic and sheltered from the rain. At the beginning of the 19thC there were about 140 arcades in Paris. The depredations of Haussmann and later developers have reduced the number to a couple of dozen, and some are now rather down-at-heel, although they are gradually acquiring a new lease on life with the increase in pedestrianization schemes around the city.

The first and second *arrondissements* are particularly rich in arcades and passages, and to link them up creates a charming, offbeat walk.
• Begin at the PALAIS-ROYAL by entering at the SE end of the garden and going counterclockwise round the colonnade, with its stamp and medal dealers, booksellers, and pipe store (pipe stores are a notable feature of the arcades). Then double back down rue de Montpensier, exploring the four covered passages (**de Richelieu, Potier, Hulot** and **de Beaujolais**), which link this street with rue de Richelieu. Then turn right along rue de Beaujolais and go through **passage des Deux Pavillons.**

Across rue des Petits-Champs are the entrances to the beautiful **Galerie Colbert** and **Galerie Vivienne**. Return to rue des Petits-Champs and turn right, walking past rue Ste-Anne, and turning right up **passage Choiseul**, full of smart boutiques, leading to rue St-Augustin.

• Another little foray into the arcades will take you N along rue de Choiseul to boulevard des Italiens. Turn toward boulevard Montmartre and continue traveling E past rue Vivienne to the point, next to the MUSÉE GRÉVIN, where the two arcades lead off the boulevard. To the N, passage Jouffroy extends into passage Verdeau.

To the s, passage des Panoramas links up with a small rabbit warren of arcades, with a curious mixture of shops and restaurants. Here you are no longer in the land of the very wealthy. These pretty arcades retain their 150-year-old feel, but their shops sell everything from walking canes and antiques and second-hand books, to imported artifacts from the Third World, sarees, and silk stationery.

• One gallery that is apart from the others still merits a visit if you are near the FORUM DES HALLES. Emerge into rue Montmartre and skirt round LES HALLES by ST-EUSTACHE. Walk through the colonnade surrounding the BOURSE DU COMMERCE, then cross rue du Louvre and turn left down rue Jean-Jacques Rousseau to the lovely **Galerie Véro-Dodat**. This arcade, with its gracefully proportioned shop fronts and carved mahogany paneling, is bathed in a gentle, warm, brown light.

It provokes a general feeling that to walk too fast will disturb the dust of decades, yet there are thriving shops here, and an attractive restaurant and café.

PASTEUR, MUSÉE

25 rue du Dr-Roux, 15ᵉ ☎45-68-82-82. Map 12L5 ▨ ✿ ⚔ by prior arrangement. Open 2-5.30pm. Closed Sat, Sun, Aug, public holidays. Métro: Pasteur.

The name of Louis Pasteur (1822-95) has been immortalized in the word "pasteurization." His development of immunization and other disease-controlling methods has become legendary, and has saved innumerable lives. Pasteur's house, now surrounded by the buildings of the Pasteur Institute, is a museum affording an interesting glimpse of both the scientific and private life of this great man. His remains rest in a magnificent tomb in the basement, built in the form of a small Byzantine chapel, with rich mosaics illustrating different aspects of his work.

PAVILLON DE L'ARSENAL

21 blvd. Morland, 4ᵉ ☎42-76-33-97. Map 10J11 ▨ Open Tues-Sat 10.30am-6.30pm, Sun 11am-7pm; Closed Mon. Métro: Sully-Morland.

An initiative taken by the City administration to keep the public aware of its city both old and new, this fine building houses all manner of information and exhibitions relating to the City of Paris itself.

Plans and models of projected redevelopments can be inspected here, and the building serves as a venue for information on all kinds of schemes for public debate.

PÈRE LACHAISE, CIMETIÈRE DU

This is the largest cemetery in Paris and has a strong romantic appeal, due to the celebrity of some of its occupants. See PARKS AND OPEN SPACES on page 96.

166

PETIT PALAIS, MUSÉE DU ▥

Av. Winston-Churchill, 8ᵉ ☎42-65-12-73. *Map* **6G5** ▦ ✘ *by prior arrangement. Open 10am-5.40pm (hours of temporary exhibitions vary). Closed Mon, holidays. Métro: Champs-Élysées-Clemenceau.*

Completed in 1900 along with the neighboring GRAND PALAIS, in time for the World Exhibition, the Petit Palais has rather more harmonious proportions and a less obtrusive personality than the other. Lying a stone's throw from the AVENUE DES CHAMPS-ÉLYSÉES, it houses the **Musée des Beaux-Arts de la Ville de Paris**, whose galleries divide into two groups.

In the galleries facing the outside of the building, you will pass from ancient Egyptian and Classical sculptures, through medieval and Renaissance art, to paintings, furniture and porcelain of the 18thC. The inner galleries are devoted to French art of the 19th and early 20thC. This is a wonderfully rich collection including works by Delacroix, Courbet, Corot, Manet, Monet, Cézanne, Pissarro, Sisley, Redon and Bonnard. Among famous individual works are Courbet's painting of two sleeping women, *Le Sommeil*, and Bonnard's vibrant *Nu dans le Bain*. Bonnard's palette is here on display as well — a riot of color like his paintings. The museum also offers a program of changing exhibitions.

The galleries are surrounded by a courtyard, which, with its Roman-style colonnade, pool and garden, is a charming place for a short break.

PIAF, MUSÉE ÉDITH

5 rue Crespin du Gast, 11ᵉ ☎43-55-52-72. *Open 1-6pm, by appointment only. Closed Fri-Sun, Sept, holidays. Métro: Ménilmontant.*

Piaf — one of the very few names that rings out the word "Paris," whenever it is spoken. Her generation, and her time, are long gone, yet her memory lives on in the heart of every Frenchman, and her songs — *Non, je ne regrette rien; La Vie en Rose; Milord,* are unforgettable far beyond the boundaries of France.

The daughter of an acrobat, she started her career in music hall, where she acquired the name *Piaf* (Parisian *argot* for little sparrow). This perfectly suited the waif-like little woman and the "street-life" subject matter of her songs.

Her unhappy life revolved around marred marital relationships, sex, drugs, illness and personal tragedy, and her resonant voice overflowed with the emotions of her circumstances.

This small, privately-run museum of memorabilia is dedicated to her. Note that visits are by appointment only.

PICASSO, MUSÉE

Hôtel Salé, 5 rue de Thorigny, 3ᵉ ☎42-71-25-21. *Map* **10H11** ▦ ✘ ㏿ ▣ *Open 9.15am-5.15pm (10pm Wed). Closed Tues. Métro: Chemin-Vert, St-Paul.*

Picasso was rare among major artists in that all his life he kept a significant proportion of his own paintings and sculpture for his personal collection. Much of this collection passed to the French government in lieu of tax after Picasso's death, and it was decided to create a new museum to house it. The Hôtel Salé, a gracious 17thC MARAIS mansion, both emphasizes and complements the modernity of Picasso's work.

Although many of his famous paintings are already in other museums, this collection gives a unique personal view of the whole span of Picasso's long, creative life. The works range from his astonishing childhood creations such as *Girl with Bare Feet*, painted when he was only 14, through his blue, rose and Cubist periods, to the inimitable style of his later years. The joy, anguish and turbulence of his private life are brought out in these works, for Picasso was an extraordinarily self-revelatory artist.

The museum contains works by other artists from Picasso's collection, including paintings by Cézanne, Renoir, Matisse and Rousseau.

It is also worth noting that its modern cafeteria is excellent.

POMPIDOU CENTER (Centre National d'Art et de Culture Georges-Pompidou) 🏛

Plateau Beaubourg, 4ᵉ ☎44-78-12-33. *Map* **9H10** 🚊 ➡ ♣ 🗺 *for museums*
🗺 *on Sun. Day passes available* ✗ *daily at 3.30pm with English-speaking guides*
◀ *Open Mon, Wed, Thurs, Fri noon-10pm; Sat, Sun, holidays 10am-10pm.*
Closed Tues. Métro: Hôtel-de-Ville, Rambuteau, Châtelet.

Like the Eiffel Tower nearly a century ago, the Centre Georges-Pompidou (or **Centre Beaubourg** as it is informally known) has aroused both shock and admiration. It is now one of the major attractions of the city, with eight million visitors a year, and a place that pulsates with energy. Shaped like a giant matchbox on its side, brightly painted as though in a child's coloring book, and enveloped in a cat's cradle of gleaming steel girders, it looks like a crazy oil refinery. Even if you are a die-hard opponent of modern architecture, it will take your breath away, especially at night.

It is one of the most revolutionary buildings of its age. Built on the initiative of President Georges Pompidou as part of the redevelopment of Les Halles and opened in 1977, it was designed by the British architect Richard Rogers and the Italian Renzo Piano. The building is turned "inside-out," with its intestines — pipes, shafts, escalators, etc. — festooned around the outside, thus liberating large areas of space within. The main escalator runs in a transparent tube up the front

of the building, so that the visitor can see a changing panorama of the city while ascending the five stories for the superb view at the top.

The Beaubourg radiates a sense of celebration that spills over into the surrounding area. A never-ending succession of street entertainers, everything from poets to jugglers and fire-eaters, can be encountered on the vast, sloping piazza.

Beaubourg's function is to provide a multimedia center where modern art and culture are excitingly accessible. It has four main departments.

Musée National d'Art Moderne
Opening hours as given above, for center.

Housed on the third and fourth floors, this is the largest museum of its kind in the world, and one of the most stimulating, housing every form of the plastic arts of the 20thC. The third floor is devoted to frequently changing exhibitions of contemporary works, that is from about 1965 to the present. The fourth floor houses a permanent exhibition of works from 1905 onward, starting with **Fauvism** (from the French *fauve,* meaning wild beast) and progressing through **Cubism**, **Abstract Expressionism**, **Dadaism**, **Surrealism**, and other movements right up to the present day.

Under Cubism, for example, you will find a number of painters who, in their different ways, shared the same tendencies: an interest in elementary forms, such as the cube and the cylinder, and a renunciation of color in favor of light and shape. The works represented include Georges Braque's *Young Girl with a Guitar,* Picasso's *Seated Woman* and Fernand Léger's *La Noce,* which also anticipates Futurism in its suggestion of movement through repetition of shapes in a sequence. In a similar way, Surrealism is represented by artists as diverse as Salvador Dalí, Max Ernst and Joan Miró, all of whom developed in very different directions.

Progressing through the galleries, you will find that certain artists reappear as they pass through different phases. Picasso crops up at intervals as his style and subject matter change. We see him pass through a period of interest in Classical Antiquity, exemplified by his *Minotaur,* then his work becomes increasingly abstract. Other painters — Kandinsky, Matisse, Braque, Léger — also manifest changing styles. Thus one perceives the dynamic way in which 20thC art has developed, with schools merging, overlapping and breaking away.

The works also include many sculptures, such as Constantin Brancusi's deliciously simple *Seal* in gray-and-white marble, and Raoul Haussmann's Dadaist work *The Spirit of our Times,* showing a dummy-like head with a purse, watch and other oddments stuck to the skull.

For a proper understanding of this museum and the way the paintings are presented, it is worth joining a guided tour (details above) with one of the center's lively *animateurs.* Alternatively there is an excellent audio guide to the collection.

Bibliothèque Publique d'Information (Public Information Library)
This is essentially a library (🗔) of the 20thC; it has some half a million books, and plans to reach a million.

Centre de Création Industrielle (Industrial Design Center)
A gallery on the ground floor presents exhibitions on all aspects of our planned environment.

Institut de Recherches Contemporaines Acoustiques Musicales (Institute for Contemporary Acoustic and Musical Research, known as IRCAM)
The underground studios are closed to the public, but lectures and demonstrations are held here. On the top floor there is a large gallery for temporary exhibitions.

Other features of the Beaubourg include a **library** and supervised **play center** for children, a reconstruction of the **studio of the sculptor Brancusi**, a lively cinema (the **Salle Garance**), an **auditorium** for lectures, concerts and theatrical performances, and a top-floor serve-yourself **restaurant**, with a superb view over Paris.

PONT ALEXANDRE III
7ᵉ and 8ᵉ. Map 6H5-G5. Métro: Champs-Élysées-Clemenceau, Invalides.
The broadest bridge in Paris and also one of the most beautiful, it forms part of a great triumphal way leading down avenue Winston-Churchill, past the GRAND PALAIS and PETIT PALAIS, across the Seine and down the esplanade to HÔTEL DES INVALIDES. Built for the 1900 World Exhibition, it was named after Czar Alexander III of Russia (1845-94).

The bridge is flanked by two massive pillars at each end, whose recently regilded decorations represent, on the Right Bank, medieval and modern France, and, on the Left, Renaissance France and the era of Louis XIV. All along the bridge are cast-iron lamp standards with the ornate, prosperous look that characterized the Belle Époque.

PONT-NEUF
1ᵉʳ. Map 8I8-9. Métro: Pont-Neuf.

> Of all the bridges which were ever built,
> the whole world who have passed over the Pont-Neuf
> must own that it is the noblest, the finest, the grandest,
> the lightest, the longest, the broadest that ever
> conjoined land and land together
> upon the face of the terraqueous globe.

Thus wrote the 18thC English novelist Laurence Sterne of the bridge that spans the SEINE in two sections, divided by the W spike of the ÎLE DE LA CITÉ. He might have added that, despite its name, it is also the oldest. Work started in 1578 on what was the first bridge to have no houses or shops on it.

Completed in 1607 under Henry IV, whose equestrian statue stands at the center, it has 12 arches, all of slightly different sizes. The bridge, the two halves of which are not quite in line, was designed by Androuet du Cerceau. The cornices overlooking the river are carved with a row of amusing faces caricaturing Henry IV's ministers and courtiers, and there are comic carvings of stall-holders, pickpockets and tooth-drawers. The semicircular niches along its length would have served the array of stallholders who plied their trade there despite the ban on shops.

> It must have been a joyous hurly-burly of humanity,
> that old Pont Neuf. Even now one feels, or imagines,
> that something of that old warm, noisy life still clings about it,
> and, at all events, among bridges it seems companionable
> compared to the others, perhaps because they are cold-blooded
> steel, and it still preserves its warm old stone.
> (Richard Le Gallienne, *From A Paris Garret*, 1943)

PORTE ST-DENIS AND PORTE ST-MARTIN
*Blvd. de Bonne Nouvelle and blvd. St-Martin, 10ᵉ. Map **9**F10. Métro: Strasbourg-St-Denis.*

These two triumphal arches, situated close to one another on the GRANDS BOULEVARDS, were built in the 1670s to commemorate Louis XIV's military victories. They replaced two fortified gates that had disappeared along with the old perimeter wall. Both bear reliefs glorifying the Sun King, but the porte St-Denis is the grander and more elaborate of the two.

The immediate area holds little interest, and the presence of these two fine arches is uplifting. This stretch of the GRANDS BOULEVARDS is beyond the area of interest for quality stores. Its main attractions are the big cinemas, particularly the Art Deco **Grand Rex**, the RUE DE PARADIS with its crystal and glassware emporia, the little theaters on the boulevards, and the MUSÉE GRÉVIN.

POSTE, MUSÉE DE LA
*34 blvd. de Vaugirard, 15ᵉ ☎42-79-23-45. Map **13**L5-6 ☒ ✗ on request. Open 10am-6pm. Closed Sun, public holidays. Métro: Montparnasse-Bienvenüe, Pasteur, Falguière.*

Did you know that in 1870, during the Siege of Paris, microfilm messages were carried out of the city by pigeons whose wings were stamped with a postmark? This is one of many snippets of information to be gleaned here, in four floors of imaginative displays on philately and the history of worldwide postal communication — everything relating to the subject, from postmen's uniforms and mailboxes to modern sorting machines and stamp-making equipment.

There are stamps galore and a ground-floor gallery showing postage-stamp art.

PRÉFECTURE DE POLICE, MUSÉE DES COLLECTIONS HISTORIQUES DE LA
*4 rue de la Montagne-Ste-Geneviève, 5ᵉ ☎43-29-21-57, ext (poste) 336. Map **9**J9 ☒ Open Mon-Fri 9am-5pm, Sat 10am-5pm. Métro: Maubert-Mutualité, St-Michel.*

A sober but fascinating collection of documents and objects is housed in this little museum in the heart of the LATIN QUARTER. It presents a panorama of police and criminal activity in Paris from the *ancien régime* to the 20thC.

It includes a frightening display of criminal tools and weapons, and documents such as the orders for the arrest of such prominent figures as Danton and Marat's assassin Charlotte Corday.

PUBLICITÉ, MUSÉE DE LA
*107 rue de Rivoli, 1ᵉʳ ☎42-60-32-14. Map **7**H7 ☒ Joint admission if required, with Musée des Arts Décoratifs and Musée des Arts de la Mode et du Textile ☒ ௵ Open 12.30-6pm, Sun 11am-6pm. Closed Mon, Tues, public holidays. Métro: Tuileries, Palais-Royal Musée-du-Louvre.*

Posters and other forms of publicity material from France and beyond are organized into first-rate temporary themed exhibitions in this new museum, which relocated from cramped quarters in rue de Paradis only recently. Exhibits are drawn from an archive of more than 120,000 items, some dating as far back as the end of the 18thC.

There is also a video and reference library.

QUATRE-SAISONS, FONTAINE DES (Four Seasons Fountain)
57-59 rue de Grenelle, 7ᵉ. Map 7l6. Métro: Rue-du-Bac.

When this fountain was built by Bouchardon in the 1730s, to supply water to the district, Voltaire complained that such a splendid monument should not have been erected in so narrow a street.

He had a point, for the two-tiered facade cannot be seen to best effect unless you are standing immediately in front of it. A central portico with a seated figure representing Paris is flanked by elegant reclining personifications of the Seine and Marne; and on either side are curved walls adorned with statues of the four seasons.

RADIO-FRANCE, MUSÉE DE 🏛
116 av. du Président Kennedy, 16ᵉ ☎42-30-21-80 📷 ₲ 🖼 (in museum)
✗ (compulsory) at 10.30am, 11.30am, 2.30pm, 3.30pm, 4.30pm. Closed Sun, public holidays. Métro: Mirabeau.

This huge glass-and-aluminum edifice, shaped like a giant cylinder, is the nerve center of French radio. Built between 1953-63, it is a statistician's delight — 500m (800 yards) in circumference, with 3,500 personnel, 58 studios and 1,000 offices.

Architecturally, though, it may leave the visitor cold. Its main attractions are the extensive **museum of the history of radio and television** and the concerts and shows held there on a regular basis.

Immediately outside, midstream and keeping company with the pont de Grenelle, is a surprising replica of the Statue of Liberty.

RENAN-SCHEFFER MAISON   See VIE ROMANTIQUE, MUSÉE DE LA.

RIVOLI, RUE DE
1ᵉʳ and 4ᵉ. Map 7G6-10l11. Métro: Hôtel-de-Ville, Châtelet, Louvre-Rivoli, Palais-Royal Musée-du-Louvre, Tuileries, Concorde.

Like so many long Parisian thoroughfares, rue de Rivoli begins with one personality and ends with another. It starts at PLACE DE LA CONCORDE and runs down beside the TUILERIES and the GRAND LOUVRE in a long, uniform colonnade, with many smart shops and an elegant café or two — a place for promenading in style. This section was laid out between 1800-35.

> At Paris I took an upper apartment for a few days
> in one of the hotels on the rue de Rivoli;
> my front windows looking into the garden of the Tuileries
> (where the principal difference between nursemaids and the
> flowers seemed to be that the former were locomotive
> and the latter not).
> (Charles Dickens, *The Uncommercial Traveller,* 1861)

Beyond the Louvre, the street becomes progressively less formal as it wends its way past the HÔTEL DE VILLE and on through the MARAIS to end at PLACE DE LA BASTILLE. It ends, however, not with a whimper but with a bang, with the marvelous facade of the church of **St-Paul-St-Louis**.

ROCK'N'ROLL HALL OF FAME

*Porte du Louvre, Forum des Halles, 1ᵉʳ ☎40-28-08-13. Map **9**H9. Open 10.30am-6.30pm. Closed at Christmas ▨ Métro: Châtelet-les-Halles.*

Live on stage . . . Elvis Presley, Jimi Hendrix. In rehearsal . . . Sting. In concert . . . Bob Geldof, Eric Clapton. Thrilling . . . Michael Jackson. In The Cavern . . . John, Paul, George and Ringo. Doin' what comes nat'rally . . . Madonna. Rockin'an'a'rollin' . . . Little Richard.

Loud music, bright lights, stars till they come out of your ears. The only trouble with figures of people you know and love like your own kids, is that they never look as realistic. The music might make up for it, however. Go if you're under 25. If you're older, live with your memories.

RODIN, MUSÉE ▨ ★

*Hôtel Biron, 77 rue de Varenne, 7ᵉ ☎47-05-01-34. Map **12**I5 ▨ ♿ ✗ ▣ Open 10am-5.45pm (4.45pm in winter). Closed Mon. Métro: Varenne.*

Auguste Rodin (1840-1917) is widely considered to be the greatest sculptor of the 19thC. You will see why when you visit this museum, housed in a splendid 18thC mansion near LES INVALIDES. It is impossible not to marvel at the way in which Rodin magically transformed stone, clay or bronze into the living tissue of human emotion and experience. Take, for example, his famous work, *Le Baiser* (The Kiss), which powerfully evokes in white marble the tenderness of love between man and woman; or his *Homme qui Marche* (Walking Man), which embodies all the urgency and thrust of human aspiration; or *La Cathédrale,* where a pair of hands speaks of piety and contemplation.

The delightful garden surrounding the museum makes an ideal setting for many of Rodin's works. Here we find, among others, casts of his *Balzac, Le Penseur* (The Thinker), *La Porte de l'Enfer* (The Gates of Hell) and *Les Bourgeois de Calais* (The Burghers of Calais). Temporary exhibitions of work by other artists are held in a building near the entrance.

The lovely **Hôtel Biron** was built by Gabriel The Elder for a rich wig-maker in 1728, and was subsequently lived in by, among others, Marshal Biron, who was beheaded in 1793. Later the building became a convent, and much of the painted and gilt paneling was ripped out, although some has been restored.

At the beginning of this century the building was bought by the State

and was made available for artists. Rodin himself occupied a ground-floor studio from 1907 until his death. A massive development of the museum is taking place from 1991-94, allowing more of the collection to be displayed, together with the work of other sculptors. Plans submitted by architect Henri Gaudin include the relocation of the reception area and administrative offices into the old chapel, and the creation of an underground viewing gallery, linked to the basement of the existing building.

SACRÉ-COEUR, BASILIQUE DU 🏛 ★

Pl. du Parvis-du-Sacré-Coeur, 18ᵉ ☎42-51-17-02. Map 3C9. Church 📷 ₺ Open 6.45am-11pm. Dome and crypt 📷 ◁€ Open Apr-Sept 9am-7pm; Oct-Mar 9am-6pm. Métro: Abbesses, Anvers, Château-Rouge, Lamarck-Caulaincourt.

Subject of countless travel posters and paintings, the Sacré-Coeur has acquired the status of a visual cliché. However, seen afresh, in its superb setting on Montmartre's hill, the Butte, it has stunning impact and beauty, whether glimpsed from a train as it draws into one of the northern stations, or revealed suddenly as you turn a corner on one of the old streets nearby. (See also MONTMARTRE on page 76.)

The church rose, phoenix-like, from the ashes of the Franco-Prussian War of 1870. As a reaction to the despair aroused by France's defeat, parliament vowed, in 1873, to erect a church in Paris as a symbol of contrition and a manifestation of hope. A competition was held and there were 78 entries. The winner was an architect named Abadie, with a Romano-Byzantine design. The first stone was laid in 1875 and the cathedral was completed by 1914, but World War I delayed its consecration until 1919. Since 1885, worshipers have kept up perpetual adoration before the high altar, continuing even through the German occupation.

The material used for the church was Château-Landon stone, which hardens and whitens with age — you can see how much grayer the stonework of the interior is, compared with the gleaming exterior. The design is not to everyone's taste, but many find the outline of its five beehive-like domes pleasing.

Approach the church by the long flight of steps from the s (or you can go part of the way by funicular, or the whole way up, from Place Blanche, on the little tourist train). This way you get the full impact of the main facade, with its great portico surmounted on each side by equestrian statues of St-Louis and Joan of Arc. The bell tower to the N, which is higher than the rest of the church, contains one of the largest bells in the world, weighing nearly 17 tons.

The **interior** is light and elegantly proportioned. The eye follows the great rounded arching sweeps of stonework, up to the cupola with its clerestory and its two encircling balconies and down again to the nave, coming to rest on the natural focal point, the great mosaic in the alcove above the high altar. This **mosaic**, one of the largest in the world, depicts Christ with outstretched arms, exposing a golden heart. Grouped around him are worshipers, including the Virgin, St Michael and Joan of Arc.

The **crypt**, entered by a stairway from the w aisle, is somewhat gloomy and severe. It contains the church treasury and a number of chapels, the central one possessing a *Pièta* on the altar.

> I then came out and surveyed Paris from the front.
> I could distinguish most of the landmarks —
> Notre Dame, Panthéon, Invalides,
> Gare d'Orléans, St Sulpice, and Louvre.
> Never before had I such a just idea of the immense size
> of the Louvre. I could also see the Opéra (that centre of
> *Paris qui s'amuse*), with its green roof . . . .
> (Arnold Bennett, *Journal,* October 4, 1903)

By the same stairway one ascends a narrow and twisting staircase to the **dome**. The 360° panorama is breathtaking, but the views out over Paris are vertiginous.

ST-AUGUSTIN

*46 blvd. Malesherbes, 8e Open daily. Map **2E6**. Open daily. Métro: St-Augustin.*

Surprisingly little fuss is made of this Second Empire church on the intersection of boulevards Haussmann and Malesherbes, considering that its architect was Victor Baltard, architect of Les Halles. It has the distinction of being the first truly large building in which a cast-iron frame and supporting pillars were used, for Baltard was a past master at new construction techniques.

A member of the Reformed Church, like Haussmann, Baltard aimed to make the church the expression of his Christian faith allied with his technical skill. He chose Roman and Byzantine forms for his inspiration.

The constraint on him was the site itself — a narrow space between two great avenues. When you look at the building from the vast place St-Augustin, the frontage does indeed seem small — almost weighed down by the weight of the dome. His only option for the building to make its presence felt was to go for height. The church measures almost 100m in length and the dome is some 80m high, and spreads out, from 22m at the portals to 40m at the transept.

Yet the individual features of the facade are pleasing. The rose window measures some 8m across. The main doors are of oak covered with figured bronze bearing some lovely low-reliefs by Mathurin Moreau.

All in all, St-Augustin undoubtedly represented just what was wanted by the bourgeoisie of the boulevards in the 1870s.

SAINTE-CHAPELLE ⅲ ★

4 blvd. du Palais, 1ᵉʳ ☎*43-54-30-09. Map* **9**I**9** ■■■ *Reduced joint ticket with* CONCIERGERIE ✗ *Open Apr-Sept 9.30am-6.30pm, Oct-Mar 10am-5pm. Closed hols. Métro: Châtelet, St-Michel, Cité.*

It is hard to describe the beauty of this church without hyperbole; its interior is one of the most thrilling visual experiences that Paris affords. Formerly adjacent to a palace of the medieval kings, it now stands hidden away in a side courtyard of the PALAIS DE JUSTICE on the ÎLE DE LA CITÉ. It was built by Louis IX (St-Louis) in the 1240s, to house relics believed to be the Crown of Thorns and a portion of the True Cross (which cost the king more than the church itself). They were kept in a tabernacle on a platform over the high altar, and on feast days, the king would take out the Crown of Thorns and hold it up before his courtiers and the public. The relics are now kept in NOTRE-DAME.

When the Revolution came, the church suffered the indignity of being turned into a flour shop, then a club and finally a storage place for archives. Under the *Commune* in 1871 it narrowly escaped destruction by fire.

The building has an unusual "double-decker" construction with two chapels, one above the other. The upper one, dedicated to the Holy Crown and the Holy Cross, was intended only for the king and his retinue.

The lower one, dedicated to the Virgin Mary, was for the staff of the chapel and certain officials of the court.

Entering by the rather dark **lower chapel**, you will see the low ceiling supported by columns painted in the 19thC. From here, mount a spiral staircase to the **upper chapel** (★) and emerge into a soaring chamber to be dazzled by the jeweled light that pours through the enormous **stained-glass windows** (★) on every side. The remarkable effect of lightness was achieved by what was then the revolutionary technique of supporting the roof on buttresses.

The **window** to the left of the entrance depicts scenes from Genesis.

The remainder, taken clockwise, show more Old Testament events, as well as the story of Christ. The next-to-last window is devoted to Ste-Hélène and the True Cross, together with St-Louis and the relics of the Crucifixion. The **rose window** to the W shows scenes from the Apocalypse.

The Sainte-Chapelle and its neighbor, the CONCIERGERIE, present a striking contrast. The latter represents the baseness and cruelty of the Middle Ages; the former embodies all that was God-seeking in the medieval world.

ST-DENIS, BASILIQUE

*Pl. de l'Hôtel-de-Ville, St-Denis. Map **18**B4 Open Apr-Sept Mon-Sat 10am-7pm, Sun 1-7pm; Oct-Mar Mon-Sat 10am-5pm, Sun 1pm-5pm. Métro: St-Denis-Basilique.*

Visitors on their way to Paris from Roissy/Charles-De-Gaulle Airport are often surprised to see an imposing cathedral rising out of grim industrial surroundings. It is the Basilique St-Denis, necropolis of the kings of France and precursor of the Gothic style of architecture that swept over Europe.

It was in the 12thC that the learned Abbot Suger, friend of Louis VII, decided to rebuild his church dedicated to the Apostle of France, St-Denis. Having been beheaded in Montmartre by the ungrateful Gallo-Romans for trying to show them Christianity, St-Denis walked northward with his head tucked under his arm until he fell down, on the spot where his church was later founded. The prestige of being buried near the relics of a saint made the church a natural choice for a royal necropolis for all but a handful of French kings and their queens, starting with Dagobert in the 7thC.

The **tombs and statuary** of the kings are as good a reason for visiting St-Denis as the church itself. The tombs are empty, however. During the Revolution, 800 royal bodies were pitched into a communal grave in the crypt under the N transept. Luckily the tombs were saved from destruction, the archeologist Lenoir having had the foresight to remove them to safety some time earlier.

In the late 13thC, Louis IX (St-Louis) ordered purely symbolic effigies of all his ancestors back to the 7thC, but, from the death of Philippe The Bold in 1285, likenesses were taken from real portraits. Particularly notable are the **Renaissance mausoleums** of François I and Henry II. Unfortunately, all the tombs are chained off, and close inspection is difficult.

The beginnings of lightness, harmony and rational disposition of the elements in the church itself, proclaim the spirit of a new age and the close of the Dark Ages. Elements that had been developed separately were now combined for the first time: the Latin cross plan with radiating pilgrimage chapels, the pointed arch, the ribbed groin vault. You can see these facets of Suger's original plan in the ambulatory, apse and facade. The latter has an air of dissymmetry, with its pointed Gothic and rounded Romanesque arches and its missing N tower. The facade boasts the first-ever **rose window**, a feature that was soon to become standard.

Within the church, a further progress toward lightness was made in the next century, when the architect Pierre de Montreuil gave the nave, side aisles and chancel an architectural lift that recalls his masterwork, the SAINTE-CHAPELLE.

ST-ÉTIENNE-DU-MONT 血 ★

Pl. Ste-Geneviève, 5ᵉ. Map 14K9. Open daily. Métro: Cardinal-Lemoine.

Built between 1492-1626, the church is a mixture of styles that defy all the rules of architectural purity. The result is rather like a crazy composite photograph, amalgamating elements from contrasting buildings.

Take the main **facade**, with its three pediments piled one on top of the other, combining Classical motifs with a Gothic rose window stuck in the middle. The **belfry** is similarly eclectic, begun in the Medieval style and topped with a little Renaissance dome. Nevertheless, the whole effect is pleasing.

The interior, which preserves greater consistency of style, has some remarkable features, notably the 16thC **rood screen**, with its delicately pierced stonework and its two flanking spiral stairways. This is the only surviving rood screen in Paris and is worth going a long way to see. The interior of the church is exquisitely light and airy, and the sight of it comes as a welcome relief if your spirit is subdued after visiting the PANTHÉON nearby.

There is also the Flamboyant **vaulting** over the transept, the 5.5m (18 feet) hanging **keystone**, the splendidly ornate **organ loft** (1630) and the richly carved wooden **pulpit** (1650). At the w end of the nave is a slab indicating where the Archbishop of Paris was assassinated by an unfrocked priest in 1857. Those buried in the church include the writers Pascal and Racine, both commemorated by plaques on either side of the entrance to the Lady Chapel.

There is also a **chapel to Ste-Geneviève**, created in 1803 and containing the stone on which her body had rested in the former abbey church of Ste-Geneviève before her remains were destroyed during the Revolution. All that is left of her body is a bone or two, now preserved in an elaborate reliquary.

Although the church was badly plundered and damaged during the Revolution, it was later skillfully restored and today contains some valuable works of art. A medium-term restoration program to the facade is expected to be completed by the end of 1993.

The **cloister of the two charnel houses**, at the far end of the church, is easily missed, yet it contains a series of **stained glass panels** that is considered to be second only to the windows at the SAINTE-CHAPELLE. The cloister once looked out over a small charnel house, which in turn opened out onto a larger cemetery, hence its name. Its main interest lies in the 12 stained glass panels, put together in 1734 from the remains of 22 original windows. These panels infill the arches of the cloister, so the brilliantly colored glass can be seen at eye level. Like all domestic glass of the time, the colors were embedded into the glass with enamel. An inexpensive booklet is available, which explains the content of each panel of glass, as well as the history of the church.

ST-EUSTACHE ⅏

2 rue du Jour, 1ᵉʳ. Map 9H9. Open daily. Métro: Les Halles.

This lovely church, the largest in Paris after NOTRE-DAME, deserves to be better known than it is. For centuries it has stood at the focal point of Parisian history and, until recently, was the local church of Les Halles market. Now it surveys the FORUM DES HALLES with the solid equanimity of the Middle Ages confronting the transience of the present day.

The site was originally occupied by a small 13thC chapel to Ste-Agnes, later rededicated to St-Eustache, the 2ndC Roman who, like St-Hubert later on, is said to have seen a vision of the Cross between the antlers of a stag. The building with its elegant flying buttresses, took shape between 1532-1640. It is a curious mixture, the form being Gothic, the details Classical.

Many famous names crop up in the history of the church. Cardinal Richelieu, Mme de Pompadour and Molière were baptized in it, and Louis XIV celebrated his first communion here. During the Revolution, the church was pillaged, then made a Temple of Agriculture. In 1844 it suffered a worse fate, when it was devastated by a fire. It was completely restored by Baltard, the architect of Les Halles market, and today stands as one of the finest of Paris' architectural monuments.

The interior is thrilling, with its exhilarating vertical emphasis. Everything thrusts upward to the ceiling with its delicate network of **ribbed vaulting** and elaborately **carved bosses**. The **stained glass** is luxurious, and there are some important **works of art** here, including an early Rubens, *Pilgrims at Emmaus,* and Pigalle's sculpture of the Virgin, on the altar of the Lady Chapel.

One of the church's proudest possessions is its **organ**. This is one of the finest in the city, after a thorough restoration. Concerts are held here periodically, carrying on a well-established musical tradition. It was here in 1855 that Berlioz conducted the first performance of his *Te Deum.*

ST-GERMAIN L'AUXERROIS ⅏

2 pl. du Louvre, 1ᵉʳ. Map 8H8. Open daily. Métro: Louvre Rivoli, Pont-Neuf.

Opposite the E end of the GRAND LOUVRE stands a church that embodies a fascinating resumé of medieval architecture. There has been a church on this site since the 6thC, when an oratory dedicated to St-Germanus was built. The present building is the fourth on the spot and is a combination of 500 years of architectural design.

- **12thC**: the oldest part of the building is the Romanesque **belfry** behind the transept crossing. It played a somber role during the Wars of Religion when, in 1572, Catherine de Medicis ordered the bells to ring out to signal the start of the Massacre of St-Bartholomew. Three thousand Huguenots, in town to celebrate the marriage of Henri de Navarre to his cousin Marguerite de Valois, were slaughtered in their beds and thrown from the windows.
- **13thC**: the Gothic **ambulatory** and **chancel**, the **Lady Chapel** on the right and the **central portal** were all added.
- **14thC**: St-Germain l'Auxerrois became the royal parish church when Charles V transformed the Louvre from fortress to medieval palace. The **nave** dates from this century.
- **15thC**: the unusual and Flamboyant Gothic **porch** was built, with its lovely multi-ribbed vaulting.
- **16thC**: the Renaissance came, leaving its mark on the **doorway** N of the choir. The late Gothic **transept portals** were added.
- In the **17thC**, Versailles was built, the court abandoned the Louvre to the court artists, who made their studios there, and St-Germain became their parish church. Many artists, sculptors and poets are buried here. Even today artists and show people come here on Ash Wednesday to celebrate a special mass. Royalists have not been forgotten: every year on January 21, the anniversary of his execution in 1793, a Mass is said for Louis XVI.

ST-GERMAIN-DES-PRÉS 𝖎𝖎𝖎

Pl. St-Germain-des-Prés, 6ᵉ. Map 8I8. Open daily. Métro: St-Germain-des-Prés, Mabillon.

The oldest church in Paris stands passively at the hub of the lively ST-GERMAIN QUARTER. Its origin dates back to AD542, when the Merovingian King Childebert I, son of Clovis, brought back from Spain the tunic of St-Vincent, and a golden cross said to have been made by Solomon. To receive these relics he built a monastery and church which was at first called the Basilica of St-Vincent and St-Croix but later came to be named after St-Germanus, the Bishop of Paris, who consecrated the church in AD558 and was buried there.

As the burial place of the Merovingian kings and a seat of the great Benedictine order, it became virtually a miniature state in its own right, possessing 17,000 hectares (42,000 acres) of land, its buildings fortified by towers and a moat fed from the Seine. For centuries it stood in meadows called the Pré aux Clercs (a curious thought, this, as you survey the contemporary city-center scene).

The church was destroyed twice by the Normans, and its present form dates from the 11thC. During the Revolution, the abbey was dissolved and the property subjected to an orgy of vandalism in which the royal tombs and most of the buildings were destroyed, the church itself being turned into a saltpeter factory. Of the once-splendid complex, only the church, minus its transepts, and the abbot's palace on the NE side remain.

Except for a few capitals and columns, nothing that can be seen in the church is earlier than 11thC. The interior is an interesting mixture of different periods, with its **Romanesque arches**, Gothic **vaulting** and polychrome **wall painting** by the 19thC artist Hippolyte Flandrin. The **works of art** in the church include a 14thC Virgin and Child known as *Notre-Dame de Consolation*, and a number of fine **tombs**, including that of John Casimir, a 17thC Polish king who became abbot of St-Germain. There are also tombs of two Scottish noblemen, William and James Douglas, courtiers of Henry IV and Louis XIII respectively.

Beside the church, facing s, a little garden shaded by chestnut trees is a tranquil and secluded refuge from the busy blvd. St-Germain.

ST-GERMAIN QUARTER
The area that really constitutes the "Left Bank," known as St-Germain, is made up of two adjacent quarters: **St-Germain-des-Prés**, in the northern half of the 6ᵉ; and the **Faubourg-St-Germain** in the NE section of the 7ᵉ. See THE QUARTIERS OF PARIS on page 82.

ST-JOSEPH-DES-CARMES ⅲ
70 rue de Vaugirard, 6ᵉ. Map 13J7. Métro: Rennes, St-Placide.
This elegant little church forms part of the **Institut Catholique de Paris** complex, which stands on the site once occupied by a great Carmelite monastery with vast gardens, many treasures and a priceless library.

During the Revolution, the monastery was closed, its treasures confiscated and the buildings turned into a prison where, in September 1792, 115 priests and three bishops were massacred. Their bones are buried in the crypt of the church, which today possesses a gloomy atmosphere despite its fine works of art. These include, to the left of the transept, a marble *Virgin and Child* after a model by Bernini.

ST-JULIEN-LE-PAUVRE ⅲ
1 rue St-Julien-le-Pauvre, 5ᵉ. Map 14J9. Open daily. Métro: St-Michel, Maubert Mutualité.
This enchanting little building, set in a charming garden, **sq. René Viviani**, facing NOTRE-DAME from the Left Bank, is the oldest complete church in Paris, built between 1170-1240. Only parts of ST-GERMAIN-DES-PRÉS are older. The beauty of the interior, with its elegantly foliated **capitals**, is all the more potent for its modesty. The **wooden screen** (iconostasis) across the choir is a reminder that this is now a church of the Melchite (Greek Catholic) rite. From the square there is also an attractive view across rue St-Jacques to ST-SÉVERIN.

ST-MICHEL, BOULEVARD
Called the *Boul 'Mich,* this is the main artery of the Left Bank. See LATIN QUARTER on page 71.

ST-NICOLAS-DES-CHAMPS ⅲ
254 rue St-Martin, 3ᵉ. Map 9G10. Open daily. Métro: Arts-et-Métiers, Réaumur-Sébastopol.
Begun in the 12thC, this church boasts distinguished features from different periods: a Flamboyant Gothic **facade** and **belfry**, a fine Re-

naissance **doorway** on the S side and many paintings from the 17th-19thC. In the St-Michel chapel, a pudgy archangel steps daintily on a pitiful bald-headed devil.

The high altar is curiously like a stone bath complete with lion's feet. In short, the church is a mixture of beauty and bathos.

ST-ROCH ▥

296 rue St-Honoré, 1er. Map 7G7. Open daily. Métro: Pyramides, Tuileries.

As Paris grew westward in the 17thC, the need arose for a new parish church in the vicinity of the PALAIS-ROYAL. St-Roch was created, and the author of the *Grand Siècle,* Louis XIV himself, laid the first stone in 1635. The interior is marked by some of the great creative personalities that make the 17thC alive to us today.

There is the tomb of André Le Nôtre, a kind old man, friend to Louis XIV and the first gardener to make history, with the park of Versailles. He also created the nearby TUILERIES. Other **tombs** include those of the playwright Corneille and the philosopher Diderot.

The church itself was designed by some of the most important architects of the 17thC, notably Jacques Lemercier, and work was prolonged into the 18thC, making for a combination of Classical and Baroque elements, with a Jesuit-style facade designed by de Cotte in 1736.

Unlike the Gothic churches of Paris, the church is not oriented E-W but N-S because of the terrain. It is also unusually long, with one chapel following another, beyond the chancel.

In the **nave,** one can admire the vaulting, which has penetrating arches. This part of the building was financed in 1719 by John Law, the Scottish wheeler-dealer of the Mississippi Bubble. The **pulpit** is in the highly theatrical Baroque style by Challe (1755).

The round-domed room beyond the chancel, the **Lady Chapel,** was designed by Jules Hardouin-Mansart. Its ceiling portrays the cloudscape of the *Triumph of the Virgin* by J.B. Pierre (1750); and above the altar, with its nativity group, is a mass of clouds in gilded stucco. Behind the Lady Chapel is the small Holy Communion Chapel, and behind this a Calvary Chapel. The church has three organs and excellent acoustics, making it a fine musical auditorium, and concerts take place regularly.

As you leave, pause by the bullet-riddled **facade.** These marks are a reminder of a terrible battle that took place in front of the church in 1795. The Republican Convention was under attack by royalists and anarchists, but thanks to the technical skill of the leader of the Republican forces, the Revolution was saved. The leader: a 27-year-old general, Napoleon Bonaparte.

ST-SÉVERIN ▥

Rue des Prêtres St-Séverin, 5e. Map 14J9. Open daily. Métro: St-Michel, Cluny-La-Sorbonne.

Tucked away among the labyrinth of narrow streets in the LATIN QUARTER to the E of boulevard St-Michel, St-Séverin is one of the most cherished medieval churches in the city, possessing a quiet magic all of its own. The church is named after two saints named Séverin: a hermit who once lived on the site in an oratory dedicated to St-Martin, and a namesake of the same era who was Abbot of Agaune.

The present building was begun in the early 13thC and was much altered and enlarged in the 15thC, when it was stamped with the so-called Flamboyant (or flame-like) style to be seen in the shape of the stonework in the **stained-glass windows**. The double **ambulatory**, with its forest of columns, one of them with twisted veins, is particularly fine.

What the church lacks in size it makes up for in the perfection of its proportions and the delicacy of its decoration. Every arch, column, piece of ribbed vaulting and lozenge of stained glass sings out in joyful harmony. Perhaps this is why it is such a wonderful place for listening to music — don't miss a concert here if you get the chance. The only discordant note is the ungainly Baroque touch given to the chancel in the 18thC when part of the arcade was rounded and faced with false marble — the effect is comparable to that of a nun wearing an ostrich-feather hat.

Adjoining the church to the s is a little garden shaded by trees and bordered on two sides by the arcades of the former charnel house. Standing in the garden (possible during concerts), you may feel yourself to be in a time-warp, for beyond the cloistered calm stands the neon-lit front of a restaurant.

ST-SULPICE ▥

*Pl. St-Sulpice, 6ᵉ. Map **14**J8. Open Mon-Sat. Closed Sun, except services. Métro: St-Sulpice, Mabillon.*

Unlike many of the other great churches of Paris, this one does not form part of an imposing townscape. It looms unexpectedly out of the maze of narrow streets to the N of the PALAIS DE LUXEMBOURG.

Starting life as a modest medieval church dedicated to St Sulpicius, the 16thC Archbishop of Bourges, it was reconstructed in a piecemeal fashion between the years 1655-1788 by six different architects, the essential Classical form being the work of the Florentine Giovanni Servandoni. The result is not the hodgepodge that one might expect, but a grand and harmonious whole, apart from the nonmatching towers over the portico with its two tiers of columns.

During the Revolutionary period the church became a Temple of Reason, then of Victory. In November 1799, it was the scene of a sumptuous banquet in honor of Napoleon Bonaparte.

The interior houses vast recesses of space, and the stillness seems trapped beneath a great weight of stone. There are many interesting objects in the church, including two enormous shells serving as **holy-water stoups**, with rock-like bases sculpted by Pigalle.

Another feature worth noticing is the bronze **meridian line** running from a plaque set into the floor of the s transept to a marble obelisk in the N transept. The sunlight, passing through a window in the s transept, strikes the line at different points to mark the equinoxes and solstices.

The **Lady Chapel**, at the E end of the church, is heavily ornate, with Pigalle's *Virgin and Child* floating above a cascade of plaster clouds. Don't miss the Delacroix **murals** in the side chapel immediately to the right of the main door. The one depicting Jacob struggling with the Angel is particularly compelling. The splendid **organ**, with its 6,588 pipes, is one of the largest in the world, and organ recitals are given here frequently.

SALPÊTRIÈRE, HÔPITAL
Bd. de l'Hôpital, 13ᵉ. Map **15L11-16L12***. Métro: St-Marcel.*
The Hôtel des Invalides with a gentler voice could be the description of this sprawling hospital in SE Paris. It stands on the site of a former gunpowder factory, and its name derives from the 75-percent saltpeter content of that substance. Built by Louis XIV as a refuge for beggars, to a design by Le Vau, it became a hospital, an asylum for the insane, a house of correction for prostitutes, and a prison.

The inmates were often treated brutally, but toward the end of the 18thC, the Salpêtrière pioneered a more humane treatment of the insane, and today it has a justifiably distinguished reputation in the field of neurology and neuro-psychiatry, as well as a general hospital. The main **facade**, with its central domed **St-Louis chapel** designed by Libéral Bruand, is one of the most majestic in Paris.

SCIENCES ET DE L'INDUSTRIE, CITÉ DES (City of Science and Industry)
See LA VILLETTE, PARC DE.

SCULPTURE DE PLEIN AIR DE LA VILLE DE PARIS, MUSÉE DE LA (Open Air Sculpture Museum)
Quai St-Bernard, 5ᵉ ☎*43-26-91-90. Map* **15J11-K11** 🔲 *Always open. Métro: Jussieu, Gare d'Austerlitz.*
Only a city as basically civilized as Paris would dedicate 500 meters of prime riverside (between the ÎLE ST-LOUIS and the JARDIN DES PLANTES) for use as an open-air park for postwar sculpture. Established in 1980, beautifully planted with mature bushes and shrubs, with terraces, elevated plazas and cul-de-sacs, it makes a spectacular environment for a medium whose profile in the late 20thC remains curiously bland.

Not many of the several dozen pieces on show here raise the spirit (Ossip Zadkine's prehensile *Naissance des Formes* stands out), but the location and ambience of this 24-hour vantage point are something else. Watch the riverboats and pleasure boats U-turn at this point, around the Île St-Louis.

LA SEINE   See PARKS AND OPEN SPACES on page 96.

SEWERS   See ÉGOUTS.

LA SORBONNE
Rue de la Sorbonne, 5ᵉ. Map **14J9***. Métro: Cluny-La Sorbonne, Maubert-Mutualité, Luxembourg.*
The imposing buildings of the Sorbonne, which dominate the center of the LATIN QUARTER, testify to the long and distinguished history of this world-famous university. Founded in 1253 by Robert de Sorbon, con-

fessor to Louis IX, it began life as a college for 16 poor theological students, but grew rapidly into a powerful body which had its own government, laws and jurisdiction — virtually a state-within-a-state.

In the 17thC, its chancellor, Cardinal Richelieu, commissioned the architect Jacques Lemercier to reconstruct the college buildings and added the magnificent domed Jesuit-style **church**, the interior of which can, unfortunately, be seen only during temporary exhibitions.

The university was closed during the Revolution, then reopened by Napoleon as the premier university of France. Alas, it no longer exists as a university in its own right. After the student riots of 1968, in which it played a key role, the Sorbonne became merely part of the University of Paris, with its multitude of buildings scattered across the city.

However, the glory of the past still clings to the buildings: the great courtyard with its superb **sundial**, surmounted by a relief of Apollo in his chariot; the Baroque **library** possessing more than 1.5 million volumes; and the ornate **lecture rooms**, with their numerous murals.

It is amusing to walk around and rub shoulders with the students. They no longer talk Latin, as they did in the days when the name "Latin Quarter" was born; but they are heirs to an illustrious tradition.

TECHNIQUES, MUSÉE NATIONAL DES (formerly Conservatoire des Arts et Métiers) 🏛

292 rue St-Martin, Paris 3e ☎40-27-20-00. Map ***9G10*** *Open 10am-5.30pm. Closed Mon, public holidays. Métro: Réaumur-Sébastopol, Arts-et-Métiers.*

This large technical museum, and a college of technology, are housed in the former priory of **St-Martin-des-Champs** in the NW corner of the MARAIS. The two most distinguished elements that remain from the medieval priory are the beautifully proportioned and vaulted **refectory**, now a library *(visits by prior arrangement only),* and the church of **St-Martin-des-Champs**, which is now part of the museum. The collection of more than 80,000 items, of which not more than one tenth is on display, records developments in the engineering sciences over the last half-millennium.

If archeologists of the future ever discover this chapel and its contents, they might think that they have stumbled upon a bizarre temple of the 20thC dedicated to the worship of machinery. In the Gothic ambulatory, where the shrines of saints should be, there are engine components, car and airplane motors and similar objects, some of them placed in glass cases like holy relics, suggesting perhaps the cult of "Our Ford" in Huxley's Brave New World.

For the technically minded, the museum is fascinating. Here you can see models and displays demonstrating the technical progress of water power, the automobile, photography, television, musical instruments, printing, clockmaking, railways and aviation — and more — all examples of man's inventiveness and skill.

TOMBEAU DE NAPOLÉON 1er (Napoleon's Tomb)

The Emperor lies in state in the DÔME CHURCH. See HÔTEL NATIONAL DES INVALIDES.

TOUR EIFFEL (Eiffel Tower) 🏛

Champ-de-Mars, 7ᵉ ☎45-50-34-56. Map **11H3** 🔲 ϰ *for groups* ⭕ ⬅ ◄⊱
*Open 9.30am-11pm (July, Aug, hols, open till midnight). Métro: Bir-Hakeim,
Champ-de-Mars Tour-Eiffel, École-Militaire.*

The controversy that once raged over this world-famous tower has
long since died down, and it has become universally accepted as the
unofficial symbol of Paris. The reason for its construction in 1889 has
been almost forgotten: to commemorate the centenary of the French
Revolution. Those who think that Gustave Eiffel's design is bad enough
should remember that it was one of 700 submitted for a competition in
which rival proposals included a gigantic lighthouse capable of illuminating the entire city, and a tower shaped like a guillotine to honor the
victims of the Reign of Terror. Fortunately Gustave Eiffel's design was
unanimously accepted, and the iron tower was completed in time for
the centenary and the World Exhibition. It rose 300m (984 feet) and
was a miracle of engineering, comprising 9,547 tons of material. Today
its height, including aerials, is 320.75m (1,052 feet).

> A peculiar sensation, rather like taking a header into space, the
> sensation of coming down those open-work steps in the
> darkness, plunging every now and then into an infinite void,
> and one feels like an ant coming down the rigging of a
> man-of-war, rigging which has turned to iron.
> (Edmond de Goncourt, *Journal,* 2 July 1889)

At first is was widely reviled. The writer J.K. Huysmans scornfully
called it a "hollow candlestick," and a group of distinguished Parisians

published a manifesto declaring it a "disho-
nor to Paris." Many advocated its demolition,
but it was saved by World War I, when it
became an important military center for radio
and telegraphic transmission. In 1964 it was
classified as a national monument.

The journey to the summit is made in three
stages. The first and second platforms of the
tower, which can be reached by elevator or
stairs, support restaurants and souvenir
shops. The first-class restaurant, the **Jules
Verne** (see WHERE TO EAT) offers *nouvelle
cuisine* and panoramic dining, but is heavily
reserved. The third and top platforms, which
can be reached only by elevator, have a bar,
souvenir shops and the office, now restored,
in which Eiffel worked. The superb **panorama** (◄⊱ ★) over the city can be viewed
from behind glass or from a balcony. On a
clear day, you can see up to 70km (44 miles)
in any direction.

The tower has witnessed some strange
scenes in its history. One man died trying to

fly from it with artificial wings; in 1923 a daredevil journalist succeeded in riding a bicycle down from the first floor; and in 1954 it was scaled by a mountaineer. However, most people climb it for the view, or simply to be able to say that they have been to the top of the famous Eiffel Tower.

TOUR MONTPARNASSE (Montparnasse Tower)
Rue de l'Arrivée, 15ᵉ ☎45-38-52-56. Map 13L6 ▨ ◁€ ⇌ ⬛ ⏑ Open Apr-Sept 9.30am-11.30pm, Oct-Mar 10am-10pm (Fri, Sat 11pm). Métro: Montparnasse-Bienvenüe.

Opened in 1973, this 200m/656-foot-high tower, with its adjacent shopping center, dominates the whole quarter. Many regard it as one of the worst atrocities ever inflicted on Paris, a sad relic of Georges Pompidou's misguided attempts to "modernize" the French capital. It rises, like a vast black tombstone, from the center of MONTPARNASSE, dominating the skyline from almost every part of the city and introducing a discordant element into the otherwise human scale of central Paris. This trend has since been halted.

It must be admitted, however, that the view from the top of the tower is spectacular, and interestingly different from the one afforded by the TOUR EIFFEL. The 56th floor has a viewing gallery with a bar and a good restaurant (▥). You can also go right up onto the 59th-floor flat roof of the building via a very plain staircase.

The adjacent **Maine-Montparnasse** shopping center is a multilevel complex containing shops, restaurants and squash courts. It is linked to the tower by a vast podium which makes a good place for roller-skaters.

TOUR ST-JACQUES
Sq. de la Tour St-Jacques, 4ᵉ. Map 9I9. Métro: Châtelet.

This curiously haunting edifice, rising out of a little park off RUE DE RIVOLI, is all that remains of the medieval church of St-Jacques-la-Boucherie, which was once a starting point for pilgrims setting out for the shrine of St James of Compostella in Spain. The church was demolished in 1802, but the bell tower was spared, to be used for dropping globules of molten lead in the manufacture of shot. It was later bought and restored by the City of Paris, and now serves as a meteorological station.

At the base sits a statue of Blaise Pascal who, in 1647, carried out the first meteorological experiment with a barometer at the summit.

TRANSPORTS URBAINS, MUSÉE DES (Urban Transport Museum)
The former Urban Transport Museum at St-Mandé near Vincennes has closed its doors. It is expected to reopen in 1995, but in a different location yet to be decided. *(Contact M. Assa, 94 blvd. de Champigny, 94219-St Maur.)*

TUILERIES
Showing the art of French formal gardening at its most elegant, the Tuileries gardens extend W from the GRAND LOUVRE, along the right bank of the Seine. See PARKS AND OPEN SPACES on page 96.

UNESCO ⋔

7 place de Fontenoy, 7ᵉ ☎45-68-10-00. Map 12J4 ⊡ for exhibitions ▩ for performances ✘ for groups, by prior arrangement. Open 9.30am-12.30pm, 2-6pm. Closed Sat, Sun, hols ⬤ Métro: Ségur, Cambronne.

This Y-shaped structure must have seemed daringly modern when it was opened in 1958, but nowadays it has a rather old-fashioned look. In the grounds, the black metal Alexander Calder mobile and Henry Moore's *Figure in Repose* add to the period flavor, as does the Picasso mural in the interior.

They are security-conscious here, so one cannot just walk in and look without making prior arrangements, but there are regular exhibitions that the public can attend, and the main assembly chamber is used for spectacles ranging from circuses to piano recitals. The atmosphere is lively and international.

VAL-DE-GRÂCE ⋔

1 pl. Alphonse-Laveran, 5ᵉ. Map 14L9. Open daily. Métro: Port-Royal.

One of the great architectural treasures of Paris, the Val-de-Grâce hides its light under a bushel, tucked away as it is down rue St-Jacques. In 1622, Anne of Austria, wife of Louis XIII, installed a Benedictine convent here, for use as a retreat. The buildings still remain, including the superbly proportioned **cloister**. Later she added the church, in thanksgiving for the birth of a son (the future Louis XIV) in 1638, after 23 childless years of marriage; the young king himself laid the first stone of the building in 1645.

The church, in the Jesuit style, has many beautiful features including a **cupola**, painted with frescoes by Mignand, an unusual six-columned **baldachin** over the altar, and an attractive sculpted ceiling, whose pattern is reproduced in the floor tiles.

During the Revolution, the convent was turned into a military hospital, which it remains to this day. It houses a museum relating to the history of military medicine, but this is closed for alterations and is due to reopen in summer 1993. The Val-de-Grâce stands in an area devoted to medicine, with its large hospital and various medical institutions.

VENDÔME, PLACE ⋔ ★

1ᵉʳ. Map 7G7. Métro: Tuileries, Madeleine.

Few squares in the world convey such an impression of effortless opulence and wealth as this one. Built under Louis XIV to a design by Jules Hardouin-Mansart (1645-1708), it presents a uniform facade of the utmost beauty of proportion: an arcade at ground level, then Corinthian pilasters rising through two stories, topped by a roof with dormer windows. The keystones of the arches are carved with Bacchanalian faces, each with a different expression, like a ring of revelers at some expensive feast. This jolly throng has witnessed many dramatic events in the square. The statue of Louis XIV, which stood in the center, was destroyed during the Revolution and later replaced by a bronze column constructed by Denon, Gondouin and Lepère from 1806-10, commemorating Napoleon's victories in Germany and modeled on Trajan's column in Rome. This monument was pulled down during the *Commune* but later re-erected. It is surmounted by a statue of Napoleon.

> April 18, 1871 . . . . The scaffolding has been put up
> in readiness for the demolition of the Column.
> The square is the center of a fantastic tumult
> and a medley of amazing uniforms . . . . From all I hear,
> the employees of the Louvre are extremely worried.
> The *Venus de Milo* is hidden — guess where — at the Préfecture
> de Police . . . the silly employees fear the worst
> if the fanatical modernist [Courbet] lays his hands
> on a classical masterpiece.
> (Brothers Goncourt, *Goncourt Journals*, 1888-96)

Besides numerous financiers and aristocrats, the square housed such colorful characters as the Austrian F.A. Mesmer, inventor of mesmerism, who held sessions of "animal magnetism" at **#16**, and Chopin, who died at **#12**.

Today the square is occupied mainly by offices and expensive shops. The **Ministry of Justice** is at **#11** and **13**, and the luxurious **Ritz** (see WHERE TO STAY) is next door. You will also find here banks, jewelers and art dealers. Like a beautiful woman grown used to riches, place Vendôme has an aloofness that does not invite closer acquaintance — unless you happen to be very well-heeled.

VERSAILLES   See EXCURSIONS.

VIE ROMANTIQUE, MUSÉE DE LA (Maison Renan-Scheffer)
16 rue Chaptal, 9ᵉ ☎*48-74-95-38. Map 3D8* ✉ ✗ *Open 10am-5.30pm. Closed Mon, public holidays. Métro: St-Georges, Blanche, Pigalle.*
From 1830 this secluded house in Montmartre was the home of the painter Ary Scheffer and the scene of Friday-evening salons attended by such celebrities as Delacroix, Liszt, George Sand and Chopin. Another guest was the writer Ernest Renan, who married Scheffer's niece. Their daughter later took over the house and continued to hold salons there.

The ground floor houses a permanent exhibition of portraits and memorabilia connected with George Sand. Scheffer's studio has also been reconstructed, and the exhibit relates to many aspects of the literary and artistic life of the 19thC.

LA VILLETTE, PARC DE ★
19ᵉ. Map 18C5 ═ ✫ ✽ *Métro: Porte-de-la-Villette, Corentin-Cariou.*
This is one of Paris's most exciting recent developments. La Villette is a former cattle market and abattoir district at the intersection of the Canal de l'Ourcq and the Canal St-Denis, at the extreme NE corner of Paris. The area, including the Villette Basin, has undergone a vast redevelopment program and has now emerged as a futuristic park and museum complex covering 55 hectares (136 acres). The steel-and-glass frontage of the *cité* is three times the size of the POMPIDOU CENTER. The **Cité des**

189

Sciences et de l'Industrie, established in the late 1980s, has been followed by the **Cité de la Musique** (City of Music) *(211 av. Jean-Jaurès ☎ 42-40-27-28)*, which was inaugurated in 1990 and which will reach completion by 1994. It now also includes the **Conservatoire National de Musique**, which relocated here from cramped surroundings in the 8ᵉ, and its **museum**, with its impressive collection of instruments, including some exquisite harpsichords and spinets.

Elsewhere in the park is **Le Zénith**, a pop and rock music auditorium; a gallery devoted to electronic games; the **Maison de la Villette**, a center for the study of local history; and the **Théâtre Paris-Villette**.

Between these buildings, and flanking the canals, is a large area of attractively landscaped park with plenty of trees and grassy areas. There are also restaurants, bars and shops, as well as an excellent free play area for younger children. For scientifically minded adults and children, La Villette is an absorbing place for a day's outing.

Cité des Sciences et de l'Industrie (City of Science and Industry)

30 av. Corentin-Cariou, 19ᵉ ☎ 46-42-13-13 ▦ ⚹ ✿ Open 10am-6pm. Closed Mon. Self-guided audio tours available in English.

The Cité is already one of the largest and most imaginative scientific and technical centers in the world. Its permanent series of displays, called **Explora**, cover such themes as the nature of the earth and the universe, organic life, scientific laws, and language and communication. A brilliantly conceived series of installations, hands-on computers, videos, lasers and mathematical games enthralls even the nontechnically-minded.

Explora audio tours are available from the ticket office.

Elsewhere in the Cité is the **Médiathèque** resource and documentation center, offering free consultation of books, periodicals and educational computer programs, and the **planétarium**, an amphitheater where visitors can be whisked off into the universe thanks to an astronomical simulator and multisource projector. **L'Inventorium** takes child-

ren aged 3-6 and 6-12 into scientific explanations of today's world, through specially constructed fun and games. **La Géode**, a gleaming sphere of stainless steel, houses a panoramic cinema with a 1,000-square-meter (10,700-square-foot) hemispherical screen, multidirectional sound and OMNIMAX projection system, all of which gives spectators the impression of being enveloped in the image. Close to the Géode is the retired surveillance submarine **Argonaut**.

VINCENNES, BOIS AND CHÂTEAU DE See PARKS AND OPEN SPACES on page 97.

VOSGES, PLACE DES ▥ ★
*4ᵉ. Map **10**l11. Métro: St-Paul, Chemin-Vert.*

The oldest square in Paris is also arguably the most beautiful. It was built on the orders of Henry IV, who wished to create a square suitable for *fêtes* and ceremonial occasions, but it was not finished until 1612, two years after his death. Planned as a single unit of matching facades, it was begun with the **King's Pavilion** on the s side, which is counter-balanced to the N by the **Queen's Pavilion**. The buildings are constructed of red brick and pale gold stone, with an arcade at ground level in which are a number of shops and cafés — try **Ma Bourgogne** *(#19)* at the NW corner.

In its solid, quiet elegance, place des Vosges, like the rest of the MARAIS in which it is situated, is rather uncharacteristic of the city of Paris. The poet Gérard de Nerval left behind him a vivid description of the houses in the square at sunset:

> When you see their high windows and brick facades,
> interspersed and framed with stone, at the moment
> when they are lit up by the splendid rays of the setting sun,
> you feel the same veneration as you do
> before a parliamentary court, assembled in red robes
> trimmed with ermine.

The square had many distinguished residents. Mme de Sévigné was born at **#1bis**, Richelieu lived at **#21**, and Victor Hugo at **#6**, now a museum (see HUGO, MUSÉE VICTOR).

In the garden enclosed by the square, where summer *fêtes* and duels once took place, children now play and lovers stroll. Fashionable Paris has long since moved westward, but place des Vosges retains an aristocratic patina.

ZADKINE, MUSÉE
*100bis rue d'Assas, 6ᵉ ☎43-26-91-90. Map **14**K8 ▨ ✗ Tues 2.30pm. Open 10am-5.40pm. Closed Mon, hols. Métro: Port-Royal, Vavin, Notre-Dame-des-Champs.*

Here is a collection of works by the Russian-born painter Ossip Zadkine, assembled in the home where he lived and worked from 1928 until his death in 1967. The house, studio and garden are all crammed with Zadkine's creations, which display a remarkable range of styles, from his early primitive and Cubist sculptures to the monumental work of later years.

> If you are lucky enough to have lived in Paris as a young man,
> then whenever you go for the rest of your life,
> it stays with you,
> for Paris is a moveable feast.
> (Ernest Hemingway to a friend, 1950)

Where to stay

Making your choice

Hotel life in Paris can be a mixed delight: like any other city it has its hazards, but on the whole it is full of pleasant surprises. Few cities have such a rich and varied choice of hotels, and many of them preserve an old-fashioned style of management that is rapidly dying out elsewhere: as well as cleanliness, they offer courtesy, a high ratio of staff to guests, and often a quintessentially French atmosphere. On the debit side, however, Paris has its share of downmarket hotels, and smallness of rooms is a common characteristic, so it is wise to choose carefully and reserve well in advance.

RESERVATIONS
Although Paris boasts some 1,400 hotels from the French grade of one star and up, there can be problems getting a room on short notice: it is best to reserve at least a month in advance. Many reception staff speak some English, so you should not have a problem if you telephone. (If you prefer to write, see the SAMPLE RESERVATION LETTER on page 297). If reserving at the last minute is unavoidable, use the services of the tourist offices at Orly and Roissy/Charles-De-Gaulle airports, the Gare du Nord, Gare d'Austerlitz, Gare de Montparnasse, Gare de Lyon, Gare de l'Est and at the TOUR EIFFEL (details on page 51), or the main **Bureau de Tourisme** *(127 av. des Champs-Élysées, 8ᵉ, map 5 F3).*

July and August are two of the least heavily reserved months.

TIPPING
Hotel prices now always include all service and taxes. If you are particularly pleased with the service you can always slip a few more francs to the chambermaid and/or receptionist.

MEALS
French hotel breakfasts, except in the very best hotels (where you pay for the privilege), are the one blot on the nation's gastronomic copybook: too often, unexciting croissants or *baguette* and individually packed portions of butter and jam are served up.

A breakfast is not usually included in the price of the room, and unless you give priority to breakfasting in bed, you may find a better value round the corner from the hotel at a nearby café or *salon de thé.* Expect room service at breakfast time only in hotels with 3 or more stars.

CHOOSING YOUR LOCATION

Apart from price, a convenient location is usually the most important factor in choosing a hotel, so it is best to decide first on where you want to stay and then to pick the most suitable hotel in that area (see list following). You can deduce the *arrondissement* in which the hotel is located from the last two numbers of the zip code.

The two most popular areas for hotels are ST-GERMAIN (the 6ᵉ) and the AV. DES CHAMPS-ÉLYSÉES/rue St-Honoré district (8ᵉ). Both are central, and the former is one of the liveliest yet most historic parts of the city, whereas the latter is the most sophisticated and business-oriented. Becoming increasingly popular is the MARAIS (3ᵉ), where the lovely old town houses make ideal small hotels. MONTPARNASSE (14ᵉ), once Bohemian, has attracted giant luxury hotels such as the **Meridien Montparnasse**.

If you are reserving at the last minute through the Tourist Office's reservation service, do not be too put off if all you are offered is hotels in one of the less central of the 20 *arrondissements*. The capital is small and compact (it can be easily walked across in about two hours), and has an excellent Métro and bus system.

For a reminder of where the *arrondissements* are, refer to the ORIENTATION MAP on pages 64-65.

OUR RECOMMENDATIONS

The selection in this book has been made not only to give a wide choice of price and area, but also with other factors in mind: atmosphere, relative quiet and space. Addresses, telephone and fax numbers and nearest Métro stations are given, as well as symbols showing which hotels are particularly luxurious (▥) or simple (▰), and which represent a good value (♣). Other symbols show price categories, and give a resumé of the facilities that are available. See page 7 for the full list of symbols.

PRICES

In Paris you will find some of the best hotels in the world, but you can stay comfortably with just civilized bare essentials, where cleanliness and general atmosphere are what count. Prices in between will depend on the lavishness of the fittings and amenities, the size of the room and the quality and quantity of the service. All the hotels listed here have the standard amenities of toilet and bath and/or shower.

Major international **charge/credit cards** such as American Express, Diners Club, Eurocard (Mastercard), and Carte Bleue (Visa) are widely accepted, the two latter cards being almost universal. Throughout this book, **acceptance of Mastercard and Visa cards is not shown**, because most establishments accept most cards. Establishments that accept **American Express** (▤) and **Diners** (▣) are marked thus; and if cards are not accepted, the words "**no cards**" appear.

VOCABULARY

Words and phrases to be used when reserving ahead or when staying in a hotel can be found in WORDS AND PHRASES near the end of the book.

The prices corresponding to our price symbols are based on average charges for two people staying in a double room with bathroom/shower, inclusive of breakfast and Value-Added Tax (TVA in French). In practice, charges for one person are not much cheaper.

Although actual prices will inevitably increase, our relative price categories are likely to remain the same.

Symbol	Category	Current price
▥	very expensive	more than 1,400f
▤	expensive	800-1,400f
▧	moderate	550-800f
▨	inexpensive	300-550f
▭	cheap	under 300f

HOTELS LISTED BY ARRONDISSEMENT

1er
Ducs d'Anjou ▧
France et Choiseul ▤
Inter-Continental ▥ ♛
Lotti ▤ ♛
Meurice ▥ ♛
Montana-Tuileries ▧ ♣
Ritz ▤ ♛
des Tuileries ▤

4^e
de la Bretonnerie ▧
des Deux Îles ▧
Fauconnier ▭ ➤ ♣
Fourcy ▭ ➤ ♣
Maubuisson ▭ ➤ ♣
du Vieux Marais ▧ to ▤

5^e
Le Jardin des Plantes ▧ ♣

6^e
L'Abbaye St-Germain ▧ to ▤
L'Hôtel Guy Louis Duboucheron
  ▤ to ▥ ♛
des Marronniers ▧ ♣
Perreyve ▧
Relais Christine ▤
de Seine ▧ ♣
La Villa ▧ to ▤

7^e
Bac St-Germain ▧ to ▤
Duc de St-Simon ▤
Lenox ▧ ♣
Quai Voltaire ▧ ♣
Solférino ▧ to ▤
de Suède ▤

8^e
Université ▧ to ▤
Bradford ▧ to ▤
le Bristol ▥ ♛
de Crillon ▥ ♛
George-V ▥ ♛
Plaza-Athénée ▥ ♛
Résidence Lord Byron ▧ to ▤
Royal Monceau ▥ ♛

9^e
des Arts ▧
Chopin ▨
Grand Hôtel Inter-Continental ▤ ♛
Mondial ▧
Opéra Cadet ▧
William's ▧ to ▤

10^e
Terminus Nord ▧ ♣

12^e
Nouvel Hôtel ▧ to ▤ ♣

14^e
Lenox ▧ ♣
Meridien Montparnasse ▤ to ▥

15^e
Hilton International Paris ▤ ♛
Nikko de Paris ▤ ♛

16^e
Raphael ▥ ♛
Résidence Foch ▧ to ▤

17^e
Étoile ▤
Regent's Garden ▧ ♣

18^e
Terrass ▤

A to Z of Paris hotels

L'ABBAYE ST-GERMAIN
10 rue Cassette, 75006 Paris ☎*45-44-38-11* ⅂*45-48-07-86. Map* **13***J7* ▥ *to* ▥ *42 rms and 4 suites. No cards* ⌂ ♣ ▨ ✿ ♨ ☐ ☒ *Métro: St-Sulpice, Rennes.*
Location: In a short, quiet street close to St-Germain and the Luxembourg Gardens. This magnificent and extraordinary converted 17thC convent shows just what results can be obtained when the ancient and modern are skillfully combined. Contemporary sofas complement 18thC antiques in the newly renovated downstairs lobby, while the rooms themselves, some with original beams and alcoves, are tastefully decorated, with successfully unusual color schemes and fabrics. The courtesy and helpfulness of the staff are exemplary. With so much to recommend it, however, it can be extremely difficult to find a room here in peak periods. Reserve ahead.

DES ARTS ♨
7 Cité Bergère, 75009 Paris ☎*42-46-73-30* ⅂*48-00-94-42. Map* **3***F9* ▥ *26 rms* ⎙ ☐ ⌂ ♣ ☐ ▨ ☒ *Métro: Rue Montmartre.*
Location: In a surprisingly quiet little street just off the busy rue du Faubourg-Montmartre, near the Folies Bergère. A pretty and jolly little hotel with a nice family atmosphere. A profusion of flower-filled window boxes decorates the front of the hotel. Inside the doors, the light and airy, mirror-filled breakfast room has a very special permanent resident — Babar, a 30-year-old gray parrot with a nice line in conversation.

BAC ST-GERMAIN
66 rue du Bac, 75007 Paris ☎*42-22-20-03* ⅂*45-48-52-30. Map* **7***I6* ▥ *to* ▥ *21 rooms* ⎙ ☐ ♣ ☐ ▨
Location: At the intersection of rue du Bac with boulevard St-Germain. An ideal situation for being at the hub of St-Germain and close to the Musée d'Orsay. This little hotel was extensively modernized in 1989 and is discreetly modern. The rooms are

comfortable, although not large, and have safe, alarm clock, hairdryer, as well as cable TV. The big plus here is the breakfast — taken on the 7th-floor terrace with its panoramic view; they serve more than you can eat: fruits, cheeses and yogurts, all served by the very personable *patron*.

BRADFORD
10 rue St-Philippe-du-Roule, 75008 Paris ☎*43-59-24-20* ⅂*45-63-20-07. Map* **6***F4* ▥ *to* ▥ *46 rms and 2 suites* ⎙ ☐ ⌂ ♣ ☐ ▨ ✿ *Métro: St-Philippe-du-Roule, Franklin-D-Roosevelt.*
Location: Near rue du Faubourg-St-Honoré and av. des Champs-Élysées. Friendliness is one of the best features of this unassuming hotel, now part of the Best Western group. The rooms are large and pleasantly furnished and the authentic 1920s decoration is charming. Rooms are equipped with safes, and there is an ironing and babysitting service. The rooms whose numbers end with a 6 or 7 are the largest, as well as those on the 6th floor. Most welcome, in an area blighted by heavy traffic, is the almost total quiet and seclusion of the street.

DE LA BRETONNERIE
22 rue Ste-Croix-de-la-Bretonnerie, 75004 Paris ☎*48-87-77-63* ⅂*42-77-26-78. Map* **9***I10* ▥ *30 rms and 1 suite. Closed for part of Aug* ⌂ ♣ ☐ ▨ ☐ ✿ *Métro: Hôtel-de-Ville.*
Location: In the fascinating Marais district. This quiet hotel, housed in a tall 17thC building, has a cozy atmosphere. It combines modern comfort with good use of the building's distinctive traditional features, such as rough stone walls and exposed wooden beams. Furnishings and decoration harmonize well. Bedrooms are mostly spacious, and are equipped with safe and minibar.

LE BRISTOL ▦
112 rue du Faubourg-St-Honoré, 75008 Paris ☎*42-66-91-45* ⅂*42-66-68-68. Map*

6F5 ▥ 155 rms and 45 suites ▤ ▨ ⊑
🅰 ◉ ✳ ☐ 🖼 ✿ ≋ ⛟ 🏌 ⛵ ♈ ⚓
Métro: Champs-Élysées-Clemenceau, Miromesnil.

Location: In one of Paris' most exclusive and expensive streets. Heads of government and high-flying diplomats who have an appointment with the President at the Élysée Palace generally like to stay at the Bristol, which is conveniently located nearby. It is also one of Paris' finest hotels. Both traditional and luxurious, it is richly decorated with original oil paintings, antiques and Oriental carpets. Bathrooms are sumptuous, with several in Art Deco style. There is a hairdressing salon and massage parlor, conference room, and an excellent restaurant. The private garage and swimming pool are marks of distinction shared with few Paris hotels. For the luxury that you get, the prices are very reasonable.

CHOPIN
46 Passage Jouffroy, 75009 Paris ☎47-70-58-10 🖸42-47-00-70. Map **8F9** ▥ 36 rms ⌂ ✳ ☐ 🖼 *Métro: Rue Montmartre.*

Location: In one of Paris' distinctive arcades, close to the Opéra Quarter. One of the hotel's strongest selling points is its quiet aspect. In the center of one of the pretty arcades that branch unobtrusively off the noisy Grands Boulevards, this would be an ideally traffic-free place to stay in Paris. The charming mid-19thC Hôtel Chopin stands proudly in the passage Jouffroy, right next to the Musée Grévin and the antiquarian bookstores. It is excellently positioned for trips to the Grands Boulevards, the Opéra Quarter and the Folies Bergère, and offers guaranteed peace for the night's sleep. Most of the rooms are quite small but unobtrusively decorated, making much use of art gallery posters.

DE CRILLON ⚓
10 pl. de la Concorde, 75008 Paris ☎44-71-15-00 🖸44-71-15-02. Map **7G6** ▥ 163 rms ⊑ ⊑ 🅰 ◉ ✳ ▨ ☐ 🖼 ◁ 🏌 ♈ ⚓ *Métro: Concorde.*

Location: Overlooking one of the most famous townscapes in the world, at the hub of the Right Bank. The Hôtel de Crillon has long been established as one of the great classic hotels of the world. Its air of quiet excellence is symbolized by the fact that it displays no ostentatious signs, only its name in discreet letters over the entrance to its magnificent 18thC premises. In one of the best positions of any hotel in Paris, and formerly an aristocrat's mansion, it became a hotel in 1907, and the sumptuous decor and formal inner courtyard were preserved. Its wood-paneled, stately reception rooms are now deservedly classified on the list of national treasures. Here you will most certainly discover the last word in elegance and controlled good taste, along with an excellent gastronomic restaurant, **Les Ambassadeurs** (▥) and a famous bar.

DES DEUX ÎLES
59 rue St-Louis-en-l'Île, 75004 Paris ☎43-26-13-35 🖸43-29-60-25. Map **9J10** ▥ 17 rms. No cards ⊑ ⌂ ✳ ♿ ☐ 🖼 ♈ ≋ 🏌 *Métro: Pont-Marie.*

Location: On the Île St-Louis, the smaller and quieter of the Seine's two islands. The Hôtel des Deux Îles occupies a 17thC building in the quiet street that runs the length of the Île St-Louis. The decor brings a distinctly Indian Colonial feel throughout the hotel. The rooms here are not large, but they are delightfully decorated, with much of the furniture in cane and bamboo, and the tiled bathrooms are attractive; the bar in the vaulted cellar has an open fire in winter.

DUCS D'ANJOU
1 rue Ste-Opportune, 75001 Paris ☎42-36-92-24 🖸42-36-92-24. Map **9H9** ▥ 38 rms 🅰 ◉ ⌂ ✳ ☐ 🖼 🏌 *Métro: Châtelet-Les-Halles.*

Location: In the Halles/Beaubourg area, on the very pretty place Ste-Opportune. This hotel is a pleasant base from which to explore Paris; the métro intersection at Châtelet-Les-Halles gives easy access to just about every part of the city. Discreet modernization took place a couple of years ago, and all the bathrooms were refurbished in 1992. The reception area and bedrooms of this old hotel resound with primary colors and muted shades, and there is an abundance of art on the walls. The rooms in back are quieter, in summer, as place Ste-Opportune fills with young people visiting the Forum des Halles and the Beaubourg.

DUC DE ST-SIMON

14 rue de St-Simon, 75007 Paris ☎*45-48-35-66* ✆*45-48-68-25. Map 7I6* ▥ *34 rms. No cards* ▱ *‡* □ ▱ ✍ � *Métro: Rue-du-Bac.*

Location: In a calm street just off blvd. St-Germain. Quiet, cozy, intimate, welcoming and discreet are all descriptions that apply to this 19thC hotel. The Duc de St-Simon is remarkable for its period furnishings, as well as its flower arrangements. New pieces of antique furniture have been gradually added to the rooms, making it a delightful and consequently extremely popular hotel. More refurbishment work is due to be carried out in 1993.

ÉTOILE

3 rue de l'Étoile, 75017 Paris ☎*43-80-36-94* ✆*44-40-49-19. Map 5E3* ▥ *25 rms* ▰ ▱ ▨ ▣ *‡* □ ▱ ☟ ☢ *Métro: Ternes, Charles-De-Gaulle-Étoile.*

Location: Close to the Arc de Triomphe. A small, intimate hotel with sparkling, modern decor. Rooms have cable TV, mini-bar, marble bathrooms with hairdryer and magnifying mirror. There's a bar and mini-library in the lobby. Well suited to the businessman on a budget, as well as anyone who appreciates a family atmosphere.

FRANCE ET CHOISEUL

239 rue St-Honoré, 75001 Paris ☎*42-61-54-60* ✆*40-20-96-32. Map 7G7* ▥ *120 rms* ▨ ▣ *‡* □ ▱ ☟ ☢ *Métro: Concorde, Tuileries.*

Location: In the smart, fashionable area of rue St-Honoré and place Vendôme. An unhurried, timeless air and a courtly, old-fashioned style of management mark out this traditional Paris hotel with its upright Louis XV-style furniture. The rooms are small, but have been carefully modernized, each with its own up-to-date bathroom. There's a pretty patio at the rear.

GEORGE-V ▩

31 av. George-V, 75008 Paris ☎*47-23-54-00* ✆*47-20-40-00. Map 6F4* ▥ *301 rms* ▤ ▰ ▱ ▨ ▣ *‡* ☐ □ ▱ ☟ ☢ *Métro: George-V.*

Location: Just off avenue des Champs-Élysées, in the city's principal business area. The George-V is grand and unashamedly lavish. Flemish tapestries, sculptures, ormolu clocks and original paintings (including Renoir's *Le Vase des Roses*) complement the gracious 18thC-style furniture — all part of the package with a hotel from the Forte-Exclusive group.

The hotel has a delightful bar and a lovely inner courtyard, where in summer, meals are served amid red umbrellas and masses of potted plants as part of the excellent restaurant, **Les Princes** (▥), which serves traditional cuisine. There is also a deluxe brasserie, **Le Grill** (▥).

GRAND HÔTEL INTER-CONTINENTAL ▩

2 rue Scribe, 75009 Paris ☎*40-07-32-32* ✆*42-66-12-51. Map 7F7* ▥ *514 rms* ▤ ▱ ▨ ▣ *‡* □ ▱ ☟ ☢ ⚏ *Métro: Opéra.*

Location: On place de l'Opéra. Paris' largest old hotel was designed by Charles Garnier, architect of the Opéra, which dominates the view from the front windows. It now aims (although not exclusively) at the upper end of the business market. There are 17 daylit air-conditioned conference rooms. Air conditioning and soundproof double-glazing are now universal, and the rooms have received a luxury treatment, in a delightful range of pastel colors. A glass atrium covers the winter garden, which opens onto a statue-lined courtyard. The restoration of the public areas to their original splendor has now also been carried out. Guests can also make use of a sauna, sun lounge and gymnasium. The restaurant **L'Opéra** *(3 pl. de l'Opéra ☎40-07-30-10 ▥)* offers *haute brasserie* fare, and business lunches are to be had in the patio garden. **La Verrière** *(12 blvd. des Capucines ☎40-07-31-00)* offers *haute gastronomie.*

HILTON INTERNATIONAL PARIS 🏨

18 av. de Suffren, 75015 Paris ☎42-73-92-00 ▣*47-83-62-66. Map 11I3* ▥ *455 rms and 28 suites* ▤ ▬ ▨ ⇆ ▦ ▣ ▭ ⌂ ⇕ ♿ ▢ ⌸ � ✶ ⚓ Métro: Bir-Hakeim, Champ-de-Mars.*

Location: Close to the Seine and the Eiffel Tower. The Hilton International is considerably more luxurious and expensive than many others in the Hilton chain, and was the first modern hotel built in Paris after the war. Several excellent conference suites, including **Le Toit de Paris**, provide full secretarial services; it looks out toward the Eiffel Tower. One restaurant, **Le Western**, provides all-American far-west catering, the other, **La Terrasse**, offers traditional French fare. Indeed, in general, no expense is spared to provide home comforts for Americans in Paris.

L'HÔTEL GUY LOUIS DUBOUCHERON 🏨

13 rue des Beaux-Arts, 75006 Paris ☎43-25-27-22 ▣*43-25-64-81. Map 8I8* ▥ *to* ▥ *25 rms and 3 suites* ▤ ▨ ⇆ ▦ ▣ ⌂ ⇕ ▢ ⌸ ☼ ✶ ⚓ Métro: St-Germain-des-Prés.*

Location: In the heart of the St-Germain quarter. The style can only be described as ornate — antiques everywhere, pink Venetian marble in the bathrooms, and velvet on virtually every surface, from the elevator to the uniforms. You may be given the room containing Mistinguett's own Art Deco furniture, the bedroom that Oscar Wilde died in, or one of the two top-floor suites with flower-decked balconies and a view over the church of St-Germain-des-Prés. You might rub shoulders with any number of personalities (both real and aspiring) from showbiz, fashion or advertising. The facilities include a winter garden with restaurant **Le Bélier** (▥), and an intimate cellar bar. This extravaganza is the brainchild of Guy Louis Duboucheron, who converted it, 25 years ago, from the cheap, sleazy Hôtel d'Alsace that Oscar Wilde knew. For many years, it has been called, simply, L'Hôtel. Now its name has expanded to accommodate its owner. Quite rightly dubbed *Le Ritz du rive gauche*, this is a very small hotel that prides itself in offering a superb — but above all discreet — service.

INTER-CONTINENTAL 🏨

3 rue de Castiglione, 75001 Paris ☎44-77-11-11 ▣*44-77-14-60. Map 7G7* ▥ *450 rms* ▤ ▨ ⇆ ▦ ▣ ⌂ ⇕ ▢ ⌸ ⇇ ⚓ ☼ Métro: Concorde, Tuileries.*

Location: Close to place Vendôme. The hotel was built in 1878 by Charles Garnier, architect of the Paris Opéra, and also of the **Grand Hôtel**. Several of its amazingly ornate salons are now listed as historic monuments. Completely and intelligently renovated while keeping its original atmosphere almost intact, the hotel has all the trappings of a modern luxury hotel: 24-hour room service, a bar and discotheque, as well as a number of conference rooms, complete with secretaries, interpreters, and audiovisual facilities. The hotel also has a beautiful covered terrace, and its all-year restaurant, **La Terrasse Fleurie** *(▥ to ▥ ☎44-77-10-44)*, is a fashionable place to dine. The top-floor rooms afford a majestic view over the Tuileries Gardens.

LE JARDIN DES PLANTES ♣

5 rue Linné, 75005 Paris ☎47-07-06-20 ▣*47-07-62-74. Map 15K10* ▥ *33 rms* ⇆ ▦ ▣ ⌂ ⇕ ⚓ ♿ ▢ ☼ ▨ ▤ Métro: Jussieu, Place Monge.*

Location: Opposite the tranquil Jardin des Plantes, a 5min walk from the Sorbonne and the student quarter. Comfortable, clean and colorful, this charming hotel appeals to individual travelers. Americans particularly love the freedom to jog in the Jardin opposite. The well-appointed rooms are appropriately decorated, using floral themes, and art exhibitions enliven the vaulted basement lounge. There is a small sauna and a guests' ironing room. A delightful option is breakfast on the roof terrace, which has a fragrant rose garden.

LENOX ✿
9 rue de l'Université, 75007 Paris ☎42-96-10-95 ⊠42-61-52-83. Map **7**/**7** ▥ 34 rms ⁅ⁿ ⊕ ⇟ � ▢ ⌂ ⅄ *Métro: Rue-du-Bac.*

Location: Three minutes' walk from boulevard St-Germain and the Seine. One of those rare hotels that stands out, not only in its class, but by any standards, because of a special thoroughbred quality. Decor and furniture throughout have been done with excellent taste, and the place has an atmosphere of warm elegance. What's more, the staff is extremely friendly, and the service is willing. Its sister hotel in Montparnasse *(15 rue Delambre, 14*ᵉ ☎43-35-35-50, map13L7)* gives the same excellent value.

LOTTI ▦
7 rue de Castiglione, 75001 Paris ☎42-60-37-34 ⊠40-15-93-56. Map **7**G7 ▥ *133 rms* ⁅ⁿ ▱ ⇒ ⁅ⁿ ⊕ ⌂ ⇟ ᴧ ▢ ⌂ ▱ ✹ ⽬ *Métro: Tuileries.*

Location: Close to place Vendôme and the prestigious shops of rue St-Honoré. A luxury hotel of manageable proportions with a subdued but regal air, the Lotti, now part of the Jolly Hotels group, caters to the high society of many countries, but particularly Britain, Italy and France. Recently refurbished, the decor remains opulently traditional and tasteful, with no two bedrooms the same. There is a pleasant restaurant, Le Lotti (▥). The service throughout is quick, efficient and unobtrusive, and an air of calm and sophistication pervades the whole establishment.

DES MARRONNIERS ✿
21 rue Jacob, 75006 Paris ☎43-25-30-60 ⊠40-46-83-56. Map **8**/8 ▥ *37 rms. No cards* ⇟ ⌂ ✹ ⽫ ⅄ *Métro: St-Germain-des-Prés.*

Location: In the heart of St-Germain. Mother Nature has a strong hold on this tall hotel, from the profusion of leaves, flowers and birds on the wallpaper and carpets, the fruit on the crockery, and the flower-filled vases, to the delightful little garden at the back, with its veranda, white garden furniture, and chestnut trees (which give the hotel its name). There are two cozy lounges in the ancient vaulted cellars. Regarded by all critics as a delightful place — a real find.

MERIDIEN MONTPARNASSE
19 rue du Cdt René-Mouchotte, 75014 Paris ☎44-36-44-36 ⊠44-36-49-00. Map **13**L6 ▥ to ▥ *953 rms incl 35 suites* ▤ ⟵ ⌂ ⇒ ⁅ⁿ ⊕ ⇟ ᴧ ▢ ⌂ ⽬ ⅄ ⽱ *Métro: Montparnasse-Bienvenüe, Gaîté.*

Location: In the center of Montparnasse. This hotel was built as part of the Montparnasse redevelopment scheme. The building itself, by Pierre Dufau, who also designed part of La Défense, is an elegant white giant, rising 35 stories and contrasting strongly with its unlovely surroundings.

With Gare Montparnasse and Métro right outside, the hotel caters with renowned efficiency to its guests, which include tour groups and business executives. They appreciate the many facilities, which include a business suite with conference rooms, and three restaurants, including Le Montparnasse 25 (▥), which serves a decent enough *cuisine classique*, and buffet restaurant Justine (▥).

MEURICE ▦
228 rue de Rivoli, 75001 Paris ☎42-60-38-60 ⊠49-27-98-06. Map **7**G7 ▥ *179 rms incl 39 suites* ▤ ⇒ ⁅ⁿ ⊕ ⇟ ᴧ ▢ ⌂ ⽱ ⅄ ⽱ *Métro: Tuileries,Concorde.*

Location: Opposite the Tuileries Gardens and within walking distance to just about everywhere. Opened in 1816, the Meurice used to receive almost all the crowned heads of Europe. More recently the hotel has been patronized by members of the international set. It is now part of the Italian CIGA hotel group.

The splendid salons, with their gilded paneling, tapestries and huge chandeliers, have been added to the list of historical monuments. It has a gastronomic restaurant **Le Meurice**. Like many of the best hotels, the Meurice now has an excellent Business Center *(open Mon-Fri 9am-6pm)*, with conference rooms and secretarial services.

MONDIAL
5 rue Cité Bergère, 75009 Paris
☎47-70-55-56 📠48-01-03-62. Map **3**F9
▥ 70 rms 🍴 🚗 AE 💳 🖃 ☐ 🖾 🕭
Métro: Rue Montmartre.

Location: In a quiet back street just N of Bd. Poissonnière, handy for the Grands Boulevards or the Folies Bergère. Nothing fancy, but this is a clean, colorful, unpretentious and reasonably priced hotel laid out on six floors, in a bustling commercial district of Paris. A large, light lobby leads into spacious breakfast rooms, and pleasant WCs even in the public areas are a delight.

MONTANA-TUILERIES ♥
12 rue St-Roch, 75001 Paris ☎42-60-35-10 📠42-61-12-28. Map **7**G7 ▥ 25 rms 💳 🖃 ☐ ✚ 🕭 ☐ 🖾 🌠 ♈ Métro: Pyramides.

Location: Just off rue de Rivoli and rue St-Honoré. If you feel like giving yourself a treat but can't afford the luxury hotels that line rue de Rivoli, take a few steps down a side street and try this small but spacious hotel. The Montana-Tuileries has almost all the facilities of its more illustrious neighbors, but it won't cost the earth. Rooms are elegantly decorated, in a number of themes ranging from flowered prints to traditional styles. Following renovations, there are now several rooms in the ▥ price category.

NIKKO DE PARIS 🏩
61 quai de Grenelle, 75015 Paris ☎40-58-20-00 📠45-75-42-35. Map **11**J1 ▥ 779 rms 🍴 🚗 ⇌ AE 💳 ✚ 🕭 ☐ 🖾 📺 🕭
🍴 ♈ Métro: Bir-Hakeim.

Location: On the quais overlooking the Seine, opposite Maison de Radio-France. With admirable efficiency, the Japanese moved into the Paris hotel scene and in no time, the Nikko's res-

taurant, **Les Célébrités** (▥), won accolades. There are all the amenities of a smoothly run international hotel, from streamlined accommodations (with Japanese or Western decor) to a clutch of bars, a sauna, a swimming pool and a good Japanese restaurant, the **Benkay** (▥).

NOUVEL HÔTEL ♥
24 av. du Bel-Air, 75012 Paris ☎43-43-01-81 📠43-44-64-13 ▥ to ▥ 28 rms
AE 💳 🖃 ☐ 🖾 🕭 Métro: Nation.

Location: Not much more than a stone's throw from place de la Nation. The tranquility of this little hotel is astonishing. About the only thing that will wake you is the sound of the birds in the hotel's ivy-filled garden, where you can take breakfast on fine mornings. The rooms are prettily decorated, each with an individual touch. The service is cheerful and courteous. There is paying parking nearby, and the proximity of the Nouvel Hôtel to major roads makes it a good bet for those passing through Paris. Perhaps its old-world charm is what makes it so popular with American and British visitors.

OPÉRA CADET
24 rue Cadet, 75009 Paris ☎48-24-05-26 📠42-46-68-09 ▥ 91 rms AE 💳 🕭 ✚
☐ 🖾 🍴 ♈ 🖃 Métro: Cadet.

Location: Just off rue LaFayette, in a market-filled pedestrian street near the Grands Boulevards. A brand new, crisp and ultramodern designer feel makes this hotel just right for the visiting businessman or for anyone not looking for floral wallpaper. The rooms are generously sized; they are invitingly cool and are equipped with hairdryer and minibar, as well as a TV that receives foreign stations. Take breakfast in your room or in the delightful breakfast room overlooking the courtyard.

PERREYVE
63 rue Madame, 75006 Paris ☎45-48-35-01 📠42-84-03-30. Map **13**J7 ☐ 30 rms AE 💳 🖃 ✚ ☐ 🖾 Métro: Rennes, St-Sulpice.

Location: A quiet street near the Luxem-

bourg Gardens. The Jardin du Luxembourg, a pocket of relaxing greenery amid the hurly-burly of the Left Bank, is just round the corner from this charming hotel. The decor is in the best of taste, the rooms are comfortable, and the bathrooms, although small, are sparkling clean.

PLAZA-ATHÉNÉE ⬛

25 av. Montaigne, 75008 Paris ☎ *47-23-78-33* ⬛ *47-20-20-70. Map 6G4* ⬛ *210 rms, incl 41 suites* ⬛ ⬛ ⬛ ⬛ ⬛ ⬛ ⬛ ⬛ ⬛ ⬛ ⬛ ⬛ ⬛ *Métro: Alma Marceau, Franklin-D-Roosevelt.*

Location: Near the Seine and av. des Champs-Élysées, but away from the noise and bustle. This is possibly the most glamorous and elegant hotel of all in Paris, attracting a galaxy of stars, and a particular favorite of wealthy South Americans and Greeks. Afternoon tea can be taken in the elegant long gallery, and there is a beautiful inner patio. Its hallmarks are gorgeous period-style suites and attractive bedrooms, superb service, two celebrity-studded bars, an excellent classic gastronomic restaurant, the **Régence** (⬛), and a grill, the **Relais-Plaza** (⬛). A Trusthouse Forte Exclusive hotel.

QUAI VOLTAIRE ✿

19 quai Voltaire, 75007 Paris ☎ *42-61-50-91* ⬛ *42-61-62-26. Map 7H7* ⬛ *33 rms, 29 with bath* ⬛ ⬛ ⬛ ⬛ *on demand* ⬛ ⬛ ⬛ ⬛ *Métro: Solférino, Musée d'Orsay.*

Location: On the Left Bank overlooking the Seine, opposite the Tuileries Gardens. Most rooms in this light, bright little hotel afford a superb view over the Seine — a view enhanced by the tall French windows. The front rooms can unfortunately be rather noisy, so ask for rooms out back. The establishment has a cultural and literary past. Pissarro painted *Le Pont Royal* from the window of his room and the hotel was patronized by Charles Baudelaire and Oscar Wilde, as well as Sibelius and Wagner. It has a small, unostentatious bar — a choice meeting place for the lions of modern French literature.

RAPHAEL ⬛

17 av. Kléber, 75016 Paris ☎ *44-28-00-28* ⬛ *45-01-21-50. Map 5F2* ⬛ *89 rms* ⬛ ⬛ ⬛ ⬛ ⬛ ⬛ ⬛ ⬛ ⬛ ⬛ ⬛ ⬛ ⬛ *Métro: Kléber.*

Location: Near place Charles-de-Gaulle and the Arc de Triomphe. The smallest of the Parisian *palaces* (luxury hotels), the Raphael has a curious atmosphere that is heightened by dark wood-paneling, heavy tapestries, thick carpets, and a huge seascape by Turner. This, and its discreet location, may be what appeals to the movie stars and producers who stay here regularly. Strong business appeal, too, and a good range of meeting and conference facilities.

REGENT'S GARDEN ✿

6 rue Pierre-Demours, 75017 Paris ☎ *45-74-07-30* ⬛ *40-55-01-42. Map 5D3* ⬛ *41 rms incl 2 apartments* ⬛ ⬛ ⬛ ⬛ ⬛ ⬛ ⬛ ⬛ *Métro: Charles-de-Gaulle-Étoile.*

Location: A quiet street in a residential area not far from place Charles-De-Gaulle. The Regent's Garden lives up to its name by possessing a real garden (as opposed to a courtyard) complete with statues and fountains and where you can breakfast on spring and summer mornings. The building itself is typical of the showy *grand bourgeois* architecture of the mid-19thC. Its lofty rooms, whose ceilings sport decorative moldings, are furnished in appropriate style, with bedsteads, large mirrors and period furniture. Part of the Best-Western group, the hotel is a few minutes' stroll from the Arc de Triomphe.

RELAIS CHRISTINE

3 rue Christine, 75006 Paris ☎ *43-26-71-80* ⬛ *43-26-89-38. Map 8I8* ⬛ *51 rms* ⬛ ⬛ ⬛ ⬛ ⬛ ⬛ ⬛ ⬛ ⬛ ⬛ ⬛ *Métro: Mabillon, Odéon.*

Location: A quiet backwater in the heart of the Latin Quarter, close to place St-Michel. Rue Christine boasts one of the area's most distinguished hotels. This 16thC building, once a monastery, became many other things, including a publisher's book depot, before transformation into a hotel in 1979. Its comfortable, spacious and tastefully decorated rooms, several of which are split-level apartments, are individually furnished with period pieces. Those on the lower floors are rather dim, although one ground-floor room has a stone wall and a fine carved door. Private parking is available in the tranquil hotel courtyard.

RÉSIDENCE FOCH

10 rue Marbeau, 75016 Paris ☎*45-00-46-50* ⊠*45-01-98-68.* ▥ *to* ▥ *25 rms* ⁂⊙⌂♣□⊿✙ ⅌ *Métro: Porte-Maillot.*

*Location: In the expensive residential area of the 16*ᵉ. This small and exclusive luxury hotel is tucked away in the secluded calm of a tiny street near Paris' millionaires' row, av. Foch, a minute or two's stroll from the Bois de Boulogne, and very near the excellent **Le Petit Bedon** restaurant. Résidence Foch is furnished with pleasant antiques, has an intimate bar, and includes, among its attractive rooms, a large and brightly lit split-level suite on the top floor.

RÉSIDENCE LORD BYRON

5 rue de Châteaubriand, 75008 Paris ☎*43-59-89-98* ⊠*42-89-46-04. Map* **6F4** ▥ *to* ▥ *31 rms* ⌂♣□⊿✙✚ *Métro: Charles-de-Gaulle-Étoile, George-V.*

Location: Close to the Arc de Triomphe and av. des Champs-Élysées. One of the quietest and most pleasant places to stay, within a minute's walk from avenue des Champs-Élysées, and a must for anyone shunning the sometimes over-fussy service of the area's bigger hotels in the same high class. The furniture and decor are discreet and relaxing. Many rooms overlook an attractive inner courtyard with intricate trelliswork.

RITZ ▥

15 pl. Vendôme, 75001 Paris ☎*42-60-38-30* ⊠*42-60-23-71. Map* **7G7** ▥ *187 rms* ▤━⇥⁂⊙⌂♣⅋□⊿✚ ⅌⇜⅌ *Métro: Pyramides, Madeleine.*

Location: In the exclusive and beautiful place Vendôme. Arguably the most famous hotel in the world, the Ritz lives up to its reputation, exuding luxury, attentiveness and just the right amount of old-fashioned charm. It has not rested on its laurels like many other long-famous hotels, but has been sensitively renovated over a period of years. They kept the huge and splendid original baths whereas the telephones became computerized.

The benefits of staying at the Ritz are many: kind and unobtrusive service, beautiful period furnishings, a lovely inner garden, several chic bars, and a good restaurant, **L'Espadon**.

New facilities include the Ritz Health Club, which offers a spa, swimming pool and beauty center, the Ritz-Escoffier School of Gastronomy, and a private supper club, the **Ritz Club**.

ROYAL MONCEAU ▥

37 av. Hoche, 75008 Paris ☎*45-61-98-00* ⊠*45-63-28-93. Map* **6E4** ▥ *219 rms, incl 40 suites* ▤━⇥⁂⊙⌂♣□⊿ ✚⅌⚏⇜⅌ *Métro: Charles-de-Gaulle-Étoile, Courcelles.*

Location: Between the Arc de Triomphe and the attractive Parc Monceau. This is a favorite with international business clients, but all who can afford the Monceau would most certainly enjoy its serene, pastel charm and excellent features. In addition to its lovely, very "un-hotel-like" rooms and attentive staff, the Monceau also boasts two *haute cuisine* restaurants, both are favorites with many Parisians. Offering Italian fare, there is the well-known **Il Carpaccio** (▥), situated in the hotel's main building. In the courtyard is **Le Jardin** (▥), in a rotunda, offering imaginatively prepared gourmet fare and white-gloved service. In addition, there are two elegant cocktail bars. The hotel also features **Les Thermes**, an exclusive fitness club, which includes a swimming pool, a sauna and gym, massage, hydrotherapy, and its own separate health-conscious restaurant.

The Royal Monceau is also well equipped to cater to the corporate traveler, and has several fine rooms that are especially suitable for conference or banqueting functions, and a fully-equipped business center.

DE SEINE ♥
52 rue de Seine, 75006 Paris ☎*46-34-22-80* ⊠*46-34-04-74. Map 8I8* ▥ *30 rms* AE ⊚ ⌂ ≢ ⊡ ☐ ‰ *Métro: St-Germain-des-Prés, Mabillon.*
Location: In the heart of the bustling St-Germain quarter. The Hôtel de Seine is one of Paris's best-kept secrets. Run by the multilingual Monsieur Edouard with friendliness and great efficiency, the hotel itself is not fancy, but is, however, well-maintained and secure. It is excellent value for money. An easy walk from the *quai*, the hotel is a fine base from which to explore the Latin Quarter or for that other favorite French pastime, eating and café-hopping, with a remarkable choice virtually outside your door. Rue de Seine, known for its art galleries, also has a superb open-air food market.

As one might expect with all these advantages, the hotel is usually heavily reserved.

SOLFÉRINO
91 rue de Lille, 75007 Paris ☎*47-05-85-54* ⊠*45-55-51-16. Map 7H6* ▥ *to* ▥ *33 rms* ≢ ⊡ *Closed Christmas. Métro: Solférino, Assemblée Nationale.*
Location: In St-Germain, tucked between the Seine and blvd. St-Germain. The Solférino is a charming, old-fashioned and modest hotel with prettily and tastefully decorated, high-ceilinged bedrooms, a delightful little *salon* and a breakfast veranda with dainty cane furniture. Television is available on request. The faithful, mainly English and American, clientele are especially appreciative of the warm welcome extended by the Solférino's friendly staff.

DE SUÈDE
31 rue Vaneau, 75007 Paris ☎*47-05-00-08* ⊠*47-05-69-27. Map 13J6* ▥ *to* ▥ *41 rms* AE ⌂ ≢ ⅄ ☐ ⊡ ⇌ ‰ *Métro: Sèvres-Babylone, Vaneau.*
Location: In a plush area near the Hôtel Matignon. Cool elegance distinguishes this hotel, and that is just as it should be, since it backs onto the gardens of the Prime Minister's official residence, the Hôtel Matignon. If you want to try to glimpse the man, or simply admire the towering plane trees that grow here, ask for a room on the second or third floor. The hotel also has a large, gently-lit lounge in the Directoire style, and a pretty little inner courtyard where morning or afternoon refreshment may be taken.

TERMINUS NORD ♥
12 blvd. de Denain, 75010 Paris ☎*42-80-20-00* ⊠*42-80-63-89. Map 4E10* ▥ *220 rms* AE ⊚ ≢ ⅄ ☐ ⊡ ‰ ☝ ⅄ *Métro: Gare du Nord.*
Location: Opposite the Gare du Nord. Situated in an extremely convenient location for anyone in transit to or from the capital via the Gare du Nord, this hotel underwent its transformation a decade ago and is now firmly settled in the lower-middle range of respectable hotels that serve their purpose. Rooms facing the street are well insulated against street noise.

TERRASS
12 rue Joseph-de-Maistre, 75018 Paris ☎*46-06-72-85* ⊠*42-52-29-11. Map 3C8* ▥ *101 rms* ⇌ AE ⊚ ≢ ☐ ⊡ ⇇ ☝ ⅄ ⚓ *Métro: Blanche, Place Clichy.*
Location: On the edge of Montmartre. This first-class establishment, perched on an outcrop of the Butte de Montmartre, offers just about the best views of any hotel in Paris. You can see the Panthéon, the Opéra, Les Invalides, the Arc de Triomphe, the Eiffel Tower, and even La Défense from its restaurant terrace and from some of the rooms. Built in 1912 but modernized several times since then, the Terrass is the only 4-star hotel in Montmartre. Many of the rooms are light and sunny, and all the standard services are there. What's more, the prices are a little lower than for something comparable elsewhere.

DES TUILERIES
10 rue St-Hyacinthe, 75001 Paris ☎*42-61-04-17* ⊠*49-27-91-56. Map 7G7* ▥ *26 rms and 4 suites* ⊞ ⇌ ⌂ AE ⊚ ⌂ ≢ ☐ ⊡ ☝ ⅄ *Métro: Pyramides, Tuileries.*
Location: Close to place Vendôme and within easy reach of av. de l'Opéra and

the Tuileries Gardens. You won't find a much quieter street in the center of Paris than the tiny rue St-Hyacinthe. The Hôtel des Tuileries occupies a late 18thC building with a superb carved wooden front door. Modernization has been carried out onobtrusively, and each room has a different decor — now Japanese-style, now modern, now flowery, but always decorated with inspiration. All have marble-clad bathrooms Plenty of warm, old-fashioned velvet still abounds.

UNIVERSITÉ
22 rue de l'Université, 75007 Paris
☎42-61-09-39 ⓕ42-60-40-84. Map 7/7 ▥ to ▥ 28 rms. No cards ✿ □ ⌁ ✹ ☙ Métro: Rue-du-Bac.
Location: Between boulevard St-Germain and the Seine. This hotel is reserved well ahead by people who want to stay in style at the antique-dealing and publishing end of the St-Germain quarter. The establishment, which occupies a 17thC *hôtel particulier* (private house), has been completely refurbished, and is filled with antiques and tapestries. The rooms are decorated with individual style and the breakfast lounge, hall, and tiny courtyard are charming.

DU VIEUX MARAIS ♣
8 rue du Plâtre, 75004 Paris ☎42-78-47-22 ⓕ42-78-34-32. Map 9H10 ▥ to ▥ 30 rms ⌂ ✿ □ ⌁ ✹ ☙ Métro: Rambuteau, Hôtel de Ville.
Location: In the Marais. This charming quarter was a virtual slum a quarter of a century ago. Now almost completely renovated, it contains some of the priciest property in town, but perhaps still does not have its fair share of hotels. The Hôtel du Vieux Marais dates back to the 16thC, and every part of the 5-floor building is simply but brightly decorated. The rooms overlooking the courtyard are particularly attractive.

LA VILLA
29 rue Jacob, 75006 Paris ☎43-26-60-00 ⓕ46-34-63-63. Map 8/8 ▥ to ▥ 35 rms and 4 suites ▤ ⒶⒺ ✿ □ ⌁ ☙ ▤ ♪ ᠘ Métro: Mabillon, St-Germain-des-Prés.
Location: In the heart of St-Germain, between boulevard St-Germain and the Seine. In his search to create an *avant-garde* mood with the ultimate in designer chic, owner Vincent Darnaud took the gamble of entrusting his new hotel's entire design to the young but highly-regarded Marie-Christine Dorner. The result, startling in its simplicity, is a seductively balanced design that blends anthracite-colored marble, burnished metal, plane wood, leather, and sanded and engraved glass, with a thrilling sense of color throughout. Halogen-spotlit door-numbers pinpoint each superbly-appointed room. A split-level bar/jazz-cellar and roof terrace add further spice. Reserve well ahead: La Villa is *très à la mode* among architects and design folk.

WILLIAM'S
3 rue Mayran, 75009 Paris ☎48-78-68-35 ⓕ45-26-08-70. Map 3E9 ▥ to ▥ 30 rms ⒶⒺ ⊙ ⌂ ✿ □ ⌁ Métro: Cadet, RER Gare du Nord.
Location: Convenient for the Grands Boulevards; off rue LaFayette. An inexpensive and quite unusual little hotel, with every room facing out over the tranquil square Montholon. Many of the rooms are irregularly shaped, and quite small, but the decor is tastefully modern and the color-schemes quite striking, with an accent on red and purple. Extras include room service, room safe deposit box, hairdryer, alarm clock.

Other alternatives

APARTMENTS: You may prefer to rent your own apartment for a week or so. There are advantages, if you want to entertain friends, or if you would enjoy doing some cooking while you have access to all those lovely French ingredients, or if your stay will be longer than a normal vacation and you want to save on the hotel and restaurant bill.

Speak to **Rothray** *(10 rue Nicolas Flamel, 75004 Paris* ☎ *48-87-13-37* Fx *42-78-17-72).* Ray Lampard, a business executive who has himself lived in a number of capital cities, knows the difficulties of foreign travel. His company offers a friendly, efficient, reasonably priced and very flexible service (7 days' minimum stay, but you name the period, which can be infinitely variable) and there are various apartments, some small and some large, in the MARAIS/HALLES/POMPIDOU CENTER areas.

The small touches are nice, too. You can expect to find chilled wine and snacks awaiting you, and enough tea and coffee to see you through beyond arrival. And you can pay in your own currency, by personal check, if you prefer.

HOTEL-HOSTELS: At the other end of the range, you may find that good, clean, friendly hostel accommodation is all that you need. There are a number of hostels run by **MIJE** (Maisons Internationales de la Jeunesse et des Étudiants), which has three good hotel-hostels within the MARAIS.

The rooms have anything from two to six beds in them. These hotel-hostels are, in theory, for young people. In practice, anyone willing to share a room with one or more strangers of the same sex is welcome. All the buildings are superb 17thC former private houses in quiet locations. They have exposed beams, original floor tiles, stone flagging and antique furniture.

All are inexpensive (▢) and quiet (▱); and they all offer good value (♣). They have a central inquiries and reservations number (☎ *42-74-23-45).*

- **FAUCONNIER**   11 rue du Fauconnier, 75004 Paris. Map **10**I11. 100 beds 🏃 Métro: St-Paul-le-Marais. Location: In a small street by the Seine, opposite the Île St-Louis.
- **FOURCY**   6 rue de Fourcy, 75004 Paris. Map **10**I11. 219 beds. Métro: St-Paul-le-Marais. Location: Behind the Hôtel de Sens/Bibliothèque Forney.
- **MAUBUISSON**   12 rue des Barres, 75004 Paris. Map **9**I10. 90 beds. Métro: Hôtel-de-Ville. Location: Behind St-Gervais-St-Protais church near the Hôtel-de-Ville.

Eating and drinking

Dining out in Paris

French cuisine is renowned as the finest in the world; the superb standard of cooking in the average French household is matched by the unequaled quality of France's restaurants. Whereas provincial restaurants reflect local produce and traditions, those in Paris act as a focus for the rest of the country, bringing together the individual and varied regional cuisines. They seem continually interested in change and innovation, and are constantly striving for new limits of perfection. In Paris, with a little judicious choosing, you can quite simply have the gastronomic experience of a lifetime, whether it is a perfectly smoked Auvergne ham in a crowded wine bar, or a 5-course extravaganza in one of the city's revered establishments.

Cooking in France is regarded not as a necessity but as an art, and its leading exponents, such as Paul Bocuse, Michel Guérard, Joël Robuchon and Alain Senderens, are held in god-like esteem. They are the modern-day successors of the immortalized 19th and early 20thC chefs Carême and Escoffier, masters of *grande* or *haute cuisine;* but whereas Escoffier, for all his technical brilliance, put many strictures on French cuisine, many of today's great chefs have broken free from his rules and sought entirely new directions.

This style of cooking, pioneered in France since World War II by such chefs as Alexandre Dumaine, André Pic and Fernand Point, is termed just that: *nouvelle cuisine.* (The term *nouvelle cuisine* had in fact been used previously in the 1740s during a similar culinary seachange.) In keeping with the modern trend away from rich, heavy food, and with the emphasis on absolute freshness, *nouvelle cuisine* at its best is lighter and tastier than traditional French cuisine, and is often characterized by unusual combinations of high-quality ingredients, and carefully presented, smaller and more manageable portions. *Nouvelle cuisine* is not a total culinary revolution, because although the ideas are different, the methods remain the same, but it is a far-reaching adaptation of classic French cooking to the requirements of the late 20th century.

It must not be thought, however, that *nouvelle cuisine* has entirely swept traditional French cookery aside. On the contrary, the classic dishes will always remain, as will the excellent and ever popular *cuisine bourgeoise* that is the root of all French cooking. Regional cookery still flourishes, as a visit to Normandy or Nice, Alsace or the Auvergne or to many regionally-inspired restaurants in Paris will tell you.

We have concentrated, in our selection of restaurants, almost exclusively on French *cuisine*. But there are many other *cuisines* on offer, some at the highest standards. Some parts of Paris have a highly ethnic flavor, such as the Marais (4^e), which is packed with Jewish restaurants.

CHOOSING A PLACE TO EAT
There is little doubt that in Paris you can satisfy practically any mood or gastronomic whim. Apart from the restaurants proper, there are many other types of eating houses providing snacks and lighter meals. Since few people can even eat, let alone enjoy, two full-blooded French meals a day, it is a good idea to try a place of this kind for lunch, then to visit a restaurant in the evening, or vice versa.

If you can be persuaded to eat your main meal at midday, you stand a good chance of sampling the best food at the better establishments, with less risk of all the tables being taken, and at a lower cost. In France, lunch, like dinner, can last as long as you like, so try it, if you can spare part of an afternoon from the sightseeing or shopping timetable.

Brasseries are restaurants-cum-cafés, often with a long bar, which serve both large and light meals, and some of the best are included in the selection that follows. Choosing somewhere for a pleasant snack is unlikely to prove problematic or disappointing, but taking potluck with restaurants is more hazardous, although it can just as easily turn out to be a real find as a disaster. Look carefully at the menu in the window of the restaurant. If the chef takes any trouble, there will be a few *plats du jour, specialités* or unusual dishes; a drab list of easy-to-cook steaks and microwaveable stews bodes ill.

A packed restaurant is always a good sign, but this is no golden rule, as some good and less expensive restaurants are half-empty in the evening, while fashionable establishments do not fill up until 9pm. It is always worth making a reservation, particularly if the restaurant you have chosen is a well-established one.

FOR THOSE IN A HURRY . . .
If you do not have an hour and twenty minutes to spare (which might be the reasonable minimum time to allow to eat in a restaurant), here are some perfectly good alternatives.
To take out
Ask at the baker's for *un sandwich mixte,* to get one of those huge pieces of *baguette* that come stuffed with salad and cheese, ham, egg or tuna. People eat these quite happily on the street, too, and many street vendors sell nothing else.

Crêpes, to take out or eat in, come with dozens of different sweet or savory stuffings, and the modest *gauffre* (waffle) is a cheap and tasty way to keep the pangs of hunger at bay while you are streetside.

Hamburger chains and fast food outlets are surprisingly common, and **McDonald's**, and its clones, are everywhere. If you must have this kind of food, well, it doesn't cost a fortune. And the coffee to take out costs about five times less than a *café crème* in a decent café. But it isn't exactly Paris, so save it for when you get home.

To eat in

The **Drugstores**, which bear very little resemblance to their American namesakes, are popular too, serving simple brasserie-style fare and snacks, with continuous service throughout the day.

The ordinary **café**, always close at hand on just about every street corner, is a good place for a snack, and you can get anything from a *croque-monsieur* (ham-and-cheese sandwich fried in egg batter) to a midday *plat du jour*. The menus are often chalked on a board or displayed in the window. With the new ban on smoking in public places, introduced in fall 1992, it will be interesting to see if the traditional cafés lose anything of their old flavor.

The more prestigious *salons de thé* and their recent offshoots, sometimes called *tarteries*, specialize in quiches, pizzas and tarts. The **Tarte Julie** chain is reliable for quality. Another chain, **Pomme de Pain**, offers good bread-based meals and snacks.

Hamburger chains and fast food outlets are firmly established in Paris, and the ubiquitous **McDonald's** might prove a good bargain for family meals if the kids are feeling unadventurous, although the experience is hardly a French one.

Perhaps the very best place for a gourmet snack, however, is one of the cafés that serve a very wide range of excellent wines by the glass, with sandwiches of equally high quality. The **L'Écluse** group are worth looking out for, as well as an ever-increasing number of wine bars, such as **Willi's**. This type of food is not a particularly inexpensive option, but well worth treating oneself to, at least once.

THE RESTAURANT MENU

At first sight, a French menu can be a mystifying document. But, particularly if you are trying to estimate the likely cost, there are some things to look out for. Does the set menu *(menu à prix fixe* or *menu conseillé),* if available, include drink *(boisson comprise* or *b.c., vin compris* or *v.c.),* and is it free of *suppléments* on the dishes you want? If not, you may find yourself paying substantially more than the basic price.

Fortunately the service charge now has to be included, by law, in the quoted price. The days of uncertainty about percentages, and of deciding just how much of a tip the service actually merited, are a thing of the past.

The set menu is often very good value at more expensive restaurants. The choice of dishes may be rather limited, but the difference in price compared with the same fare *à la carte* is often considerable, even if portions are occasionally smaller.

The menu at a restaurant that offers only *à la carte* fare needs careful scrutiny too, because sometimes normally inexpensive dishes such as salads may be offered at a disproportionately high price.

Restaurants that offer both set-price *(prix fixe)* and *à la carte* menus often keep the former on a separate card, and you may find you have to ask specifically for this.

A full 5-course meal in France begins with hors-d'oeuvre, then continues with an *entrée* (often a fish dish), main course (often a *plat du jour)* and sometimes salad, before cheese, then a dessert and finally a black coffee. A true feast, but if all that sounds too much for your palate to cope with, you can order a main course with either a starter or dessert from the *à la carte* menu. To help you understand the menu, turn to the MENU GUIDE near the end of the book.

As you are handed the menu, you will probably be asked if you want an aperitif. The French prefer not to knock out their taste buds with a whiskey or dry Martini (the properly mixed version of which is unknown outside a few deluxe hotel bars). Instead they might order a *kir* (blackcurrant liqueur *(cassis)* with white wine), or a *kir royal,* (with champagne).

CHOOSING AND ORDERING WINE

The wine you choose when eating out depends very much on your choice of restaurant, and in Paris you can find the richest variety in the world. Among these you will also find differing degrees of seriousness about wine, ranging from the establishments that push the wine with the highest profit margin, to some, such as **L'Écluse,** whose primary interest is in featuring a dozen or so Bordeaux and offering light meals to match.

Although there is much talk about asking the advice of a wine-waiter *(sommelier),* in fact there are hardly two dozen Paris restaurants that have one who is properly qualified.

A restaurant need not have a *sommelier* to keep a good wine list, however. Try asking advice from the owner, who is not infrequently the person who greets and seats the customers, and is probably also the one who buys the wines.

Before asking for advice is the time to look at the wine list, so that you understand the price range and qualities offered. There are invariably some bargains, but they are not always easy to find. On average the mark-up is about three times higher than the price you will pay in a wine store.

French wines are classified into *Appellation Contrôlée, VDQS (Vin Délimité de Qualité Supérieure), Vin de Pays* or *Vin de Table,* but none of these titles bring a guarantee of quality. They simply mean that each category must conform to certain criteria of origin, vinification and grape variety. The criteria are more strict for *Appellation Contrôlée* than *VDQS,* and so on down the scale, and prices reflect this. Good value, however, can be found in each category.

Vin de Pays, literally "country wine," offers the best value in many restaurants. These wines are from lesser regions, but are made according to strict rules. Often they are labeled by their grape variety — Cabernet Sauvignon, Chardonnay etc. — which is not usually the case with *Appellation Contrôlée* wines.

The reputation of the grower, château or *négociant* (wine merchant) is another extremely important factor, particularly with Burgundies. If a name is not familiar, it is often wiser to choose according to the year, because a good vintage *VDQS* can often be better quality, and value, than a mediocre vintage of an *Appellation Contrôlée.* Most wine in the lower categories is blended by the shippers and does not carry vintage dates.

STYLES OF CUISINE
The following are the types of cuisine that you can expect to find in Paris restaurants.

Grande cuisine (haute cuisine)
Although the simpler classic dishes will survive no matter what, *grande cuisine* (also known as *haute cuisine*) on a grand scale has gone into irreversible decline, as labor costs have risen and people have become fussier about their digestions and waistlines. The cooking may necessitate 50 or more scullions in the kitchen, preparing rich and complicated dishes. Definitely food for a treat rather than for every day.

Nouvelle cuisine
The four main tenets of France's most recent school of cookery are that produce should be: fresh and of the highest quality; under-rather than over-cooked whenever possible; undisguised by rich, indigestible sauces; and often imaginatively combined with other ingredients. However, you still have to beware of chefs who exploit the idea of *nouvelle cuisine* by serving badly thought-out and often outlandish combinations of ingredients in amounts so tiny that they do not even cover the centers of the basketweave-patterned crockery that in such places seems to be *de rigueur*. Less unscrupulous and more dedicated chefs tend to reinterpret the well-established favorites of *cuisine bourgeoise* while retaining the better elements of *nouvelle cuisine*.

VDQS is being slowly phased out, leaving *AC* and *Vin de Pays* as the two categories. Whatever you choose, try to avoid the so-called *Réserve du Patron;* in most places, it is simply not worth the risk.

If you want only a half-bottle *(demie bouteille),* your choice is likely to be restricted to perhaps five wines across the whole list. *Vin de Table* is commonly served in carafes or jugs called *pichets*.

It is now rare to find old wines on restaurant lists. Perhaps it is a recognition that connoisseurs of fine wines will happily drink the *very* best at home, where the cost is merely expensive, rather than in a restaurant, where the cost may nearly double the bill.

WINE AND FOOD
Choosing wine to go with food is primarily a matter of common sense. A meal is a progression of tastes, and for this reason a dry wine is often chosen at the beginning of a meal to accompany the more simple-tasting first course. This progression may also be a cause of difficulties with cheese: some are too fatty or strong-tasting for the delicate old red that was drunk with the main course. Ordering a white or young red would be an anticlimax and, consequently, it is rare that a wine is specifically ordered to go with the cheese.

But you can always be adventurous and try following the guidance of your palate. It is interesting that the Lyonnais sometimes drink a light,

Cuisine bourgeoise
This can be classical, traditional or mainstream cooking, often with a regional flavor. It is the alchemy that turns a tough old bird or gristly cut of meat into a dish that melts in your mouth. *Cuisine bourgeoise* has never been more popular. An increasing number of Paris restaurants that once served nothing but *grande cuisine*, then tried pure *nouvelle cuisine*, now offer lighter versions of such stalwarts as *coq au vin, blanquette de veau, civet de lièvre*, and so on.

Regional cookery
The keynote of many French regional dishes lies in their extraordinary variety and in the ingenious use of mundane ingredients. Languedoc's *cassoulet* is an example, being made from white haricot beans, sausages, pork and preserved goose. Regional cookery lends an added dimension to some of Paris' best restaurants.

Ethnic cookery
Chinese (usually Vietnamese in disguise), unashamed Vietnamese, Italian, Russian and Jewish are the main non-French cuisines to be found in Paris, as well as North African food, from the former French colonies of Morocco, Tunisia and Algeria.

chilled Beaujolais with oysters; and one of Paris' best wine waiters dispels the myth than no wine goes with salad vinaigrette, suggesting that a young Chinon or Beaujolais agree perfectly well.

When eating regional food, it pays to pick a wine from the same area. Some partnerships are enshrined in gastronomic legend: red Bordeaux with lamb, Muscadet with shellfish. Others are less obvious but equally enjoyable: in the Loire Valley they enjoy salmon with a light red, such as Chinon or Saumur Champigny. Dishes from Provence, with their emphasis on strong olive oil, tomato and herb flavors, are well matched by Provençal and Rhône wines. The cuisine of the Lot and Dordogne, built around rich foods such as preserved duck, goose and truffles, is complemented by the red wines of Bergerac, Cahors and Duras.

HOW TO USE THIS CHAPTER
Our selection of restaurants has been made not only to give a good choice of price and area, but also with atmosphere, and style of cuisine in mind. Nearest **Métro stations** are given, as well as symbols showing particularly **luxurious** (⬠) or **simple** (⬤) restaurants, and those that represent a **good value** (♣) in their own class.

Open-air dining is indicated (⬤) as well as nearby **parking** (⬤). The **price band** symbols are explained below.

Major international **charge/credit cards** such as American Express, Diners Club, Eurocard (MasterCard) and Carte Bleue (Visa) are widely accepted, the two last cards being nowadays almost universal. Throughout this **book, acceptance of MasterCard and Visa cards is not shown,** because most establishments accept most cards; establishments that accept American Express ($\boxed{AE}$) and Diners Club ($\boxed{\bullet}$) are marked thus; if cards are not accepted, the words **"no cards"** appear.

Restaurants are listed alphabetically, for speed of reference. They are also listed by *arrondissement* below and on the following page. There is a 7-page **food and drink vocabulary and menu guide** in WORDS AND PHRASES near the end of the book.

The prices corresponding to our price symbols are based on the average price of a meal for one person, with house wine, service and tax included. Although actual prices will inevitably increase after publication, our relative price categories are likely to remain the same.

Symbol	Category	Current price
▥	very expensive	over 500 francs
▥	expensive	300-500 francs
▥	moderate	200-300 francs
▯	inexpensive	120-200 francs
▭	cheap	under 120 francs

RESTAURANTS LISTED BY ARRONDISSEMENT

1er
Bistro de la Gare-I ▯
Le Châtelet Gourmand ▯ to ▥ ♣
L'Écluse ▯
Gérard Besson ▥ to ▥
Le Grand Véfour ▥ △
Pharamond ▥ to ▥
Au Pied de Cochon ▥
La Terasse Fleurie ▥ ♣
Willi's ▯

2^{e}
Le Vaudeville ▥ to ▥

3^{e}
L'Ambassade d'Auvergne ▥
La Taverne des Templiers ▥

4^{e}
L'Ambroisie ▥ △
Miravile ▥
La Taverne du Sergent Recruteur ▥

5^{e}
L'Atelier de Maître Albert ▥ ♣
Le Balzar ▥
Bistrot de la Nouvelle Mairie ▯ ●
Dodin Bouffant ▥ ♣
Institut du Monde Arabe ▥ to ▥
Au Pactole ▥ to ▥
Toutoune ▥ ♣

6^{e}
L'Assiette au Boeuf-I ▭ to ▯
Bistro de la Gare-II ▯
Le Chat Grippé ▥

Le Cherche Midi ▯ to ▥
La Closerie des Lilas ▥
L'Écaille de PCB ▥
L'Écluse ▯
La Hulotte ▯ ♣
Lapérouse ▥
Lipp ▥
La Méditerranée ▥
Le Muniche ▥
Le Petit Zinc ▥
Polidor ▯ ● ♣
Le Procope ▥ to ▥

7^{e}
Bistrot de Paris ▥ to ▥
Chez Ribe ▯ ♣
Aux Fins Gourmets ▥
Jules Verne ▥
La Petite Chaise ▯
Le Sancerrois ▯ ●
Le Télégraphe ▥ to ▥
Thoumieux ▯

8^{e}
Bateaux-Mouches ▥ ♣
Baumann-Marbeuf ▥
Baumann-Napoléon ▥
Bistro de la Gare III ▥
Boulangerie St-Philippe ▥ to ▥ ●
La Boutique à Sandwichs ▭ to ▯ ● ♣
Le Bristol ▥ △
Chez Edgard ▥

Daru ▭ to ▭
L'Écluse ▭
La Fermette Marbeuf ▭
Laurent ▥ ⌂
Le Lord Gourmand
　　▭ to ▭
La Marcande ▥
Maxim's ▥ ⌂
Au Petit Montmorency ▥
Régence ▥ ⌂
Taillevent ▥ ⌂
Au Vieux Berlin ▭ to ▭

9e
Bistro de la Gare-IV ▭
Chartier ▭ 🍽 ♣
L'Écluse ▭
Le Grand Café ▭
Au Petit Riche ▭

10e
Brasserie Flo ▭
Julien ▥
Terminus Nord ▥

11e
Les Amognes ▭ to ▭
Chardenoux ▥ to ▥

12e
Le Trou Gascon ▭ to ▥

14e
L'Auberge de l'Argoat ▭ ♣
La Coupole ▭
Pavillon Montsouris ▭ to ▥ ♣

15e
Morot-Gaudry ▥
Pierre Vedel ▭ ♣

16e
Au Clocher du Village ▭ to ▥
Jamin (Robuchon) ▥
Le Pré Catelan ▥ ⌂
Le Vivarois ▥ ⌂

17e
Chez Fred ▥

18e
A. Beauvilliers ▥ ⌂
Le Maquis ▭ to ▥

A to Z of Paris restaurants

L'AMBASSADE D'AUVERGNE
22 rue du Grenier-St-Lazare, 3e
☎ *42-72-31-22. Map* **9**H10 ▭ AE ━
Métro: Rambuteau. RER: Les Halles.
Many Parisian café-owners hail from the Auvergne. When they have something to celebrate, they will, as often as not, head for this invitingly rustic "embassy" of Auvergnat tradition to savor the dishes of their childhood — such specialties as *mourtayrol* and *estofinado*. The Auvergnat cheeses are superb, as is the welcome, the family atmosphere . . . and the food.

L'AMBROISIE ⌂
9 pl. des Vosges, 4e ☎ *42-78-51-45. Map* **10**I11 ▥ AE ▣ ━ *Closed Sun, Mon.*
Métro: Bastille.
Master chef Bernard Pacaud's L'Ambroisie has a Michelin 3-star rating. Built toward the end of the 16thC, this fine house was refashioned by top gastronome decorator François-Joseph Graf, who brought to its high-ceilinged dining room a Venetian elegance. An immense tapestry dominates the tranquil, flower-decorated space. Pacaud's cooking is imaginatively *nouvelle*. A

relatively short menu seems the model of sobriety, yet every dish has wondrous subtleties. Book at least 2 weeks ahead.

LES AMOGNES
243 rue du Faubourg St-Antoine, 11e
☎ *43-72-73-05. Off map* **16**J14. *Closed Sun, Mon* ▭ *to* ▥ *Métro: Reuilly Diderot.*
This little restaurant, run by a pupil of Alain Senderens, serves excellent food with a southern flavor. It is original without being totally *nouvelle*.

L'ATELIER DE MAÎTRE ALBERT ♣
1-5 rue Maître-Albert, 5e ☎ *46-33-13-78.*
Map **15**J10 ▭ *Last orders midnight.*
Closed for lunch and Sun. Métro:
Maubert-Mutualité, St-Michel.
When a formula works, it's a good idea to stick to it, and that's how things are at this maze-like, low-lit restaurant. For years, contented Left Bankers have flocked back for the very reasonably-priced set dinner (no lunch). The cuisine tends toward the *nouvelle* and portions are generous. In winter the superb old stone fireplace springs to life with a blaze of logs, and the place feels positively medieval.

L'AUBERGE DE L'ARGOAT ♣

27 av. Reille, 14ᵉ ☎45-89-17-05. ▥ ▣
🍺 *Closed Sat, Sun. Métro: Cité
Universitaire, Porte-d'Orléans.*
A warm atmosphere prevails in this
little-known restaurant. The traditional
pride of place is given to fish, married
with unusual combinations of herbs
and vegetables. This little family restaurant goes from strength to strength,
with a fixed-price menu only. Good
value.

LE BALZAR

49 rue des Écoles, 5ᵉ ☎43-54-13-67. *Map
14J9* ▥ ▣ *Last orders 12.30am. Closed
Aug. Métro: Cluny-La-Sorbonne.*
Solid, traditional fare (grilled pigs' feet,
fillet of beef) is served in this old-fashioned Latin Quarter brasserie by dash-
ingly expert waiters in waistcoats and
long aprons. The clientele to be found
eating here (or having a drink in the
small café section) includes academics
and members of the literary and publishing world. Perennially popular;
reserve.

BATEAUX-MOUCHES ♣

Pont de l'Alma, 8ᵉ ☎42-25-96-10. *Map
6G4* ▥ *children* ▥ 🍺 ➤ ▣ 🅱 *Times
vary according to time of year. Call to
inquire. Métro: Alma-Marceau.*
Eating on a Bateaux-Mouches cruiser as
it chugs up and down the River Seine is
a romantic and remarkably neat way to
combine traffic-free sightseeing with
good classical food. Two options available — a moderately priced lunch trip
and a more lavish dinner outing (jacket
and tie required) — are both very good
value, considering that they include the
price of the river trip. You could even
take tea on board (one-week reservation).

BAUMANN-MARBEUF

15 rue Marbeuf, 8ᵉ ☎47-20-11-11. *Map
6G4* ▥ 🍺 ▣ 🅱 *Last orders 1am.
Métro: Franklin-D-Roosevelt.*
Climb one of the loveliest staircases in
Paris to arrive at one of the best brasseries around — complete with a
butcher who cuts his meat from a vant-

age point in the middle of the room.
They offer a wide choice of red meats,
and the house specialties are oysters
and *choucroute,* for which Baumann is
justly famed. Good wines, too, and all-
round cheerful service, which make this
a very popular place. Extraordinary
Louis XV chandeliers and mirrors everywhere give a Hollywood feel.

BAUMANN-NAPOLÉON

38 av. de Friedland, 8ᵉ ☎42-27-99-50.
Map 6E4 ▥ ▣ 🅱 *Closed Sat, Sun.
Métro: Charles-de-Gaulle-Étoile.*
This restaurant, and the **Marbeuf**
(above), are owned by Guy-Pierre Baumann, and serve a cuisine that is pre-
dominantly Alsatian. These days, the
Napoléon is exclusively a fish restaurant, and strikes a balance between
nouvelle and *classique cuisine.* Many
types of sauerkraut are featured, plus a
good selection of wines and Alsatian
alcools blancs (fruit liquor). They work
wonders with centuries-old recipes —
as well as up-to-the-minute dishes.

A. BEAUVILLIERS △

52 rue Lamarck, 18ᵉ ☎42-54-54-42. *Map
3C9* ▥ 🍺 ➤ *Closed Sun, Mon lunch.
Métro: Lamarck-Caulaincourt.*
One has the sense, here, of being a
guest in a calm and beautiful 19thC
private house, and that is precisely the
effect that owner Edouard Carlier has
striven to create. The restaurant is filled
with lovely things: antique silver,
porcelain, flowers, and Carlier's own
superb collection of prints. The house
itself stands on the hillside of Montmartre and has a delightful terrace. The
food, served either indoors or on the
terrace, matches the surroundings —
Carlier aims for top quality, and always
seems to achieve it.

BISTRO DE LA GARE – I

30 rue St-Denis, 1ᵉʳ ☎40-26-82-80. *Map
9H9* ▥ *Last orders 1am. Métro:
Châtelet-Les-Halles.*

BISTRO DE LA GARE – II

59 blvd. du Montparnasse, 6ᵉ
☎45-48-38-01. *Map 13K6* ▥ *Last orders
1am. Métro: Montparnasse-Bienvenüe.*

BISTRO DE LA GARE – III
73 av. des Champs-Élysées, 8ᵉ
☎43-59-67-83. *Map 6F4* ▢ *Last orders 1am. Métro: George-V.*

BISTRO DE LA GARE – IV
38 blvd. des Italiens, 9ᵉ ☎48-24-49-61. *Map 8F8* ▢ *Last orders 1am. Métro: Richelieu-Drouot.*

This group has proved to be among Paris' best stand-bys for people who want a reliable, quick meal. They provide — every day of the year till the early hours — limited but carefully balanced set menus at a reasonable price. The simplest *formule* (formula) menu — just main course and a salad — is ideal at lunchtime, while for a little more, you have a wide choice of starters and main dishes. There is also the option to eat *à volonté* (all you can eat for one price).

The Montparnasse branch boasts one of the finest Art Nouveau decors in Paris.

BISTROT DE LA NOUVELLE MAIRIE ▰
19 rue des Fossés-St-Jacques, 5ᵉ
☎43-26-80-18. *Map 14K9* ▢ *Last orders midnight. Closed Sat, Sun. Métro: Cardinal Lemoine, Luxembourg.*

A few minutes' walk from the Jardin du Luxembourg is this attractive prewar café. The small selection of good hot snacks and sandwiches is really only a pretext for cracking open a bottle from their succinct but excellent range of Beaujolais and Loire wines, or for trying the proprietor's superb old rum. To improve your knowledge while you drink, the walls are decorated with maps of the wine regions.

BISTROT DE PARIS
33 rue de Lille, 7ᵉ ☎42-61-16-83. *Map 7H7* ▢ *to* ▥ *Closed Sat lunch, Sun. Métro: Rue-du-Bac, Solférino.*

This fashionable gastronomic meeting place is the jewel in the crown of restaurant supremo Michel Oliver. Tables are packed, the conversation animated, the Art Nouveau decor ravishing, and the food first class. The bill undoubtedly reflects not only the food, but the famous faces to be found eating there.

BOULANGERIE ST-PHILIPPE ▰
73 av. Franklin-D-Roosevelt, 8ᵉ
☎43-59-78-76. *Map 6G5* ▢ *to* ▥
Closed for dinner and Sat. Métro: Franklin-D-Roosevelt, Champs Élysées Clemenceau.

Elbow your way through the crowds of gourmet shoppers and office workers buying snacks in this busy bakery, and you'll find a pleasant little lunch restaurant serving surprisingly sophisticated *plats du jour*. The butter and cream used in these dishes, and in the delicious desserts and pastries, comes from Echiré, which has an *appellation*, like a wine-producing area.

LA BOUTIQUE À SANDWICHS ▰ ✿
12 rue du Colisée, 8ᵉ ☎43-59-56-69. *Map 6F4* ▢ *to* ▥ ▤ ▰ *Last orders midnight. Closed Sun. Métro: Franklin-D-Roosevelt.*

There is hidden treasure behind the rather modest name and exterior. Two Alsatian brothers run the place with great dash, flair and friendliness. On the ground-floor is a sandwich "boutique," but an unusually good one, selling some 40 different varieties, all made to order. Upstairs is a cozy dining room where you can count on the kind of wholesome cooking for which Alsace is famous — the *pickelfleisch* (salt beef) and *raclette valaisanne* (fondu cheese with potatoes, pickles and charcuterie). Hearty portions at bargain prices. Located just off the Champs-Élysées and open late, this is a useful stand-by for movie-goers.

BRASSERIE FLO
7 cour des Petites-Écuries, 10ᵉ
☎47-70-13-59. *Map 4F10* ▥ ▨ ▣
Métro: Château-d'Eau.

One of Jean-Paul Bucher's six Paris restaurants (see also **La Coupole, Julien, Terminus Nord** and **Le Vaudeville**), Brasserie Flo reflects his Alsatian origins in its food and drink, and there is beer drawn from the barrel, a rarity in Paris. The turn-of-the-century decor, with its stained-glass panels, leather-covered bench seating and old brass luggage racks and hat-stands, is equally reminiscent of France's most Germanic province. Pianola music gives the right period feel. Stays open until 1.30am.

LE BRISTOL ♤

Hôtel Bristol, 112 rue du Faubourg-St-Honoré, 8ᵉ ☎42-66-91-45. Map **6**F5 ▥ ᴀᴇ ◉ 🔄 🚗 Métro: *Miromesnil, Champs-Élysées-Clemenceau.*

It's the decor and the clientele that are most distinctive and distinguished here (see also WHERE TO STAY). The dining room, gently lit from above and lined with *Régence* wood paneling, is one of the most elegant settings to be enjoyed in any luxury Parisian hotel. The cuisine is best described as discreetly *nouvelle.*

CHARDENOUX

1 rue Jules Vallès, 11ᵉ ☎43-71-49-52. Off map **16**J14 ▥ to ▥ Métro: Charonne.

Not far from the Bastille, this is an excellent and very popular old Parisian bistro. The impression of age given by the decor and setting is totally authentic and you can expect to get here a very good meal at a very moderate price.

CHARTIER 🍽 ♣

7 rue du Faubourg-Montmartre, 9ᵉ ☎47-70-86-29. Map **3**F9 ▭ Last orders 9.30pm. Métro: Rue-Montmartre.

When we first recommended Chartier, 10 years ago, we advised you to hurry to get a last glimpse of Paris' sole surviving mid-19thC *bouillon* decor (*bouillons* were popular restaurants, or soup kitchens) before it becomes transmogrified into a chic "eatery." The fashion for modernization has gone, and the management have held onto their most precious asset — an unspoiled historic decor.

The unassuming facade is easily missed; it's down an alleyway opposite the Cité Bergère just before the blvd. Montmartre. Prices don't seem to have risen much in the last 100 years either. No reservations. Arrive early. The Bohemian atmosphere, and not the food, is what it's all about. There is another branch, which is of equally good value (*103 rue de Richelieu, 2ᵉ* ☎42-96-68-23).

LE CHÂTELET GOURMAND ♣

13 rue des Lavandières-Ste-Opportune, 1ᵉʳ ☎40-26-45-00. Map **8**H9 ▥ ᴀᴇ ◉ Closed Sun. Métro: Châtelet.

An attractive but charmingly unpretentious restaurant, serving well-presented *nouvelle cuisine* in a part of town not over-endowed with comparable places to eat.

LE CHAT GRIPPÉ

87 rue d'Assas, 6ᵉ ☎43-54-70-00. Map **14**L8 ▥ ▤ 🚗 Closed Sat lunch, Mon. Métro: Port-Royal.

Le Chat Grippé is a small, elegant and well-regarded establishment in the hinterland of the Luxembourg Gardens, an area not over-endowed with restaurants. The proprietor provides a broad-based menu, geared to seasonal availability. Strong points in his repertoire include *foie gras au ratafia de champagne*, and some mouthwatering desserts such as *"pastis" quercynois avec sorbet à la pomme.*

LE CHERCHE MIDI

22 rue du Cherche Midi, 6ᵉ ☎45-48-27-44. Map **13**J7 ▥ to ▥ Last orders midnight. Métro: Sèvres-Babylone.

If you fancy a change to Italian cuisine, this friendly, informal restaurant could be a good choice, in an area that is less well provided for. It offers a small but consistently good-quality menu with a variety of fresh pastas, as well as such dishes as Parma ham, and *carpaccio* made with mushrooms, celery and parmesan.

CHEZ EDGARD

4 rue Marbeuf, 8ᵉ ☎47-20-51-15. Map **6**G4 ▥ ᴀᴇ ◉ 🔄 Last orders 12.30am. Closed Sun. Métro: Alma Marceau.

Perhaps the most startling thing about this excellent if rather noisy restaurant, which is located in the plush business quarter of avenue George-V, is its wide spectrum of prices. The food is not the bargain it once was, but you can still eat a 3-course meal there for an extremely reasonable price. The fare is simple but imaginative, with the accent mostly on seafood.

CHEZ FRED

190bis, blvd. Pereire, 17ᵉ ☎45-74-20-48.
▥ ▣ ▣ ▣ *Closed Sun. Métro: Ternes.*
A cozy bistro serving good, solid traditional Lyonnais dishes (*terrines, coq au vin* etc.) in an area where such places do not lie thick on the ground. Chez Fred is a great favorite with television and showbiz personalities.

CHEZ RIBE ♣

15 av. de Suffren, 7ᵉ ☎45-66-53-79. *Map 11I3* ▥ ▣ ▣ ▣ *Closed Sun. Métro: Bir-Hakeim.*
Bistro Parisian-style, offers 10 starters and 10 main course menu options on a very reasonaby priced fixed menu.

AU CLOCHER DU VILLAGE

8bis rue Verderet, 16ᵉ ☎42-88-35-87 ▥ *to* ▥ *Closed Sat, Sun, Aug. Métro: Église d'Auteuil.*
A picture-postcard place with the atmosphere of an old *auberge*, located in a charming little village square. Lace curtains, old posters on the walls, wine presses hanging from the ceiling, the place positively oozes charm. The food is excellent — well-prepared, classic French cuisine, leaving you glad to have had a taste of the "real France."

LA CLOSERIE DES LILAS

171 blvd. du Montparnasse, 6ᵉ
☎43-26-70-50. *Map 14L8.* ▥ ▣ ▣ ▣
Open until 2am. Métro: Port Royal.
La Closerie has always been, and is still, the haunt of literati, artists and plain hacks. Nowadays they tend to congregate in the bar and brasserie section, whose prices are lower than in the restaurant proper, where a pleasant terrace accommodates an altogether more *bourgeois* crowd, and the food is appropriately classical.

LA COUPOLE

102 blvd. du Montparnasse, 14ᵉ
☎43-20-14-20. *Map 13K7* ▥ ▣ ▣
Open 11am-2am. Métro: Vavin.
La Coupole is Paris' largest brasserie, and an institution, and its 600 seats continue to be sought-after, from pre-lunch to the early hours. It probably serves the most motley crowd of customers to be found in any Paris eating place — politicians and movie-producers to photographers and students — all, no doubt, appreciative of the excellent exposure afforded by La Coupole's open plan with its long, broad aisles. Intelligently refurbished and part of the **Flo** group, La Coupole offers good-quality fare. Go for the ambience, but do not expect a tranquil meal; this is food-consumption at its noisiest.

DARU

19 rue Daru, 8ᵉ ☎42-27-23-60. *Map 1E4* ▥ *to* ▥ *Closed Sun, Mon, Aug. Métro: Courcelles.*
White Russians, many of them taxi-drivers, used to recall the "good old days" over a glass of vodka and a *zakouski* in this grocery/snack bar opposite the Russian Orthodox Church. Although most of them have since departed this world, the Daru remains a repository of Russian tradition, boasting a score of Russian and Polish vodkas. There is also tasty food for every purse, from *tarama* and *bortsch* to smoked salmon and caviar.

DODIN BOUFFANT ♣

25 rue Frédéric-Sauton, 5ᵉ ☎43-25-25-14. *Map 14J9* ▥ ▣ ▣ *Closed Sun. Métro: Maubert-Mutualité.*
One of the finest restaurants in the capital — and certainly one of the cheapest for quality food. There are saltwater tanks in the cellar, where oysters, mussels, clams, and other shellfish co-exist peacefully before expiring at your command. A winter speciality is game, particularly hare. The restaurant offers wonderful fish combinations, a sumptuous and utterly fresh *plateau de fruits de mer,* and unusual meat dishes, everything market fresh.

L'ÉCAILLE DE PCB

5 rue Mabillon, 6ᵉ ☎43-26-73-70. *Map 14J8. Closed Sat lunch, Sun* ▥ ▣ ▣ *Métro: Mabillon.*
Excellent fish restaurant, close to the church of St-Sulpice. Very popular with publishing and literary types.

L'ÉCLUSE:

Branches at:
15 quai des Grands-Augustins, 6ᵉ
☎46-33-58-74. Map 8I9. Métro: St-Michel.
64 rue François-1ᵉʳ, 8ᵉ ☎47-20-77-09.
Map 6F4. Métro: George-V.
15 pl. de la Madeleine, 8ᵉ ☎42-65-34-69.
Map 7F6. Métro: Madeleine.
Rue Mondétour, 1ᵉʳ ☎47-03-30-73. Map
8H9. Métro: Châtelet-Les-Halles.
▥ at all branches. Last orders 1.30am.
Throughout this wine bar chain, the
good selection of vintage wines available at reasonable prices can be accompanied by excellent "super-snacks":
carpaccio, foie gras, smoked salmon,
saucisson sec, goat cheese, and a superbly rich and sticky chocolate cake that
connoisseurs travel far to sink their
teeth into.

LA FERMETTE MARBEUF 1900

5 rue Marbeuf, 8ᵉ ☎47-20-63-53 Map 6G4
▥▥ 🖦 AE ⬤ 🚘 Métro: Alma-Marceau.
One of perhaps three of the finest surviving Art Nouveau restaurants in Paris.
This busy and rather noisy eating place
offers high-quality food that is light and
refined, with good meat and fish specialities and plenty of seasonal changes.
It caters to a mixed bag of business and
media people. Very useful, as it remains
open all year round and serves till late.

AUX FINS GOURMETS

213 blvd. St-Germain, 7ᵉ ☎42-22-06-57.
Map 7I6 ▥▥ No cards. Closed Sun, Aug.
Rue-du-Bac.
A cheerful little bistro that prides itself
on being unmodernized — one of the
few remaining bastions of yellowing
lincrusta wallpaper and banquette seating, and where one feels totally at
home, sitting elbow-to-elbow with the
French, who are out in force at this
excellent outlet for the country cuisine
of the southwest. Huge helpings of cassoulet, filling desserts and a generous
cheeseboard made a warm impression,
as did the low final price.

GÉRARD BESSON ♣

5 rue du Coq-Héron, 1ᵉʳ ☎42-33-14-74.
Map 9G9 ▥▥ to ▥▥ 🎓 AE ⬤ Closed Sun.

Métro: Louvre-Palais-Royal.
The lunchtime menu served by Gérard
Besson, owner-chef of easily the best
restaurant in the Les Halles area, is such
good value it verges on the philan-
thropic. Besson, whose career took in a
period at **Jamin**, has a classical yet very
personal style that contrasts refresh-
ingly with the striving-after-effect of
which some nouvelle cuisine chefs are
guilty. He also lays down his own
wines, with a stock of some 45,000
bottles.

LE GRAND CAFÉ

4 blvd. des Capucines, 9ᵉ ☎47-42-75-77.
Map 8F8 ▥▥ AE ⬤ 🚘 Open 24hrs.
Métro: Quatre-Septembre.
This is the best of the handful of Paris
brasseries and serves full meals 24
hours a day. Its late-night clientele are
hungry local shift-and night-workers
(mainly journalists), topping up with
solid or liquid nourishment. By day, the
place is forever crowded with shoppers
from the nearby grands magasins, and
the turn-of-the-century decor is still
much appreciated.

LE GRAND VÉFOUR △

17 rue de Beaujolais, 1ᵉʳ ☎42-96-56-27.
Map 8G8 ▥▥ AE ⬤ Closed Sat lunch, Sun,
Aug. Métro: Bourse, Pyramides.
If you walk out of the Palais-Royal at its
N end, you will pass, under the arcade,
a dimly-lit restaurant that looks like a
rare fossil from another age. This is the
world-famous Le Grand Véfour, formerly home ground of much-traveled
author and cook Raymond Oliver, now
the property of M. Taittinger, of champagne fame. Its decor, which dates from
the Directoire, is one of the oldest ex-
tant restaurant interiors in Paris (it is
classified as a historical monument).
The excellent food, created by chef
Jean-Claude Lhonneur, pupil of the
great Robuchon, is classical, and has
won great acclaim in recent years.

LA HULOTTE ♣

29 rue Dauphine, 6ᵉ ☎46-33-75-92. Map
8I8 ▥▥ AE ⬤ 🚘 Closed Sun, Mon, Aug.
Métro: Odéon, Pont-Neuf.

This restaurant's snug little upstairs dining-room is a haven of reliability in the shark-infested waters of Latin Quarter catering. A basket of brown bread served, unusually for Paris, with a little dish of butter and a jug of good cheap wine will keep your hunger and thirst at bay while you wait for a very reasonable *filet d'agneau à l'estragon*. Follow that with one of their excellent desserts and you'll leave contented.

INSTITUT DU MONDE ARABE (Restaurant FAKHR EL DINE)

1 rue des Fossés-St-Bernard, 5ᵉ
☎46-33-47-70. Map **15**J10 ▥ to ▥ AE
⊡ Closed Sun eve, Mon. Métro: Cardinal Lemoine, Sully-Morland.

This widely acclaimed new building has attracted international attention. The s facade overlooking the visitor entrance is composed of geometric shapes that open and close according to the light. The 9th-floor restaurant, by contrast, is set within a sweeping terrace that views the river through walls of glass and metal. The view equals that at La Tour d'Argentl but at half the price. The food, mainly good Lebanese Arab specialities, should be taken as part of an overall experience.

JAMIN (Robuchon)

32 rue de Longchamp, 16ᵉ ☎47-27-12-27.
Map **5**G2 ▥ ▤ AE ⊡ Closed Sat, Sun, July. Métro: Trocadéro, Iéna.

Reservations weeks, perhaps even months, ahead at Jamin, the altar at which the great chef Joël Robuchon is worshiped, are quite normal. Awarded the Michelin 3-star rating and the Gault-Millau 19.5/20 commendation, the fame of this master chef is justified beyond measure. The illusion of simplicity in his cooking is deceptive. He is known as the master of detail, and the thoughtful and controlled accumulation of detail is what goes to create the subtlest of dishes. Nor does he produce just one or two chefs d'oeuvre a year — the list is almost endless. Go there — if you can afford either the wait or the final account. It is the gastronomic experience of a lifetime.

JULES VERNE

Tour Eiffel, 2ᵉ étage (2nd floor), 7ᵉ (access via s pillar) ☎45-55-61-44. Map **11**H3 ▥ to ▥ AE ⊡ ⬥ ✦ (private). Métro: Champ-de-Mars Tour Eiffel, Bir-Hakeim.

Built on a 500sq.m platform, between the great wheels and the pulleys of the tower's elevator mechanism, and 123m above the city, sits a restaurant that offers breathtaking views in every direction. Even the ceiling offers glimpses, through glass panels, of the metal structure up to the top of the tower, some 150m higher. Reserve — possibly weeks ahead; and, for the best of all views, ask for the intermediate room *(salle intermédiaire)* between the bar and the room facing the Palais de Chaillot. From here, the panorama takes in every conceivable sight. All that aside, the food, *nouvelle cuisine*, is good, too.

JULIEN

16 rue du Faubourg-St-Denis, 10ᵉ
☎47-70-12-06. Map **4**F10 ▥ AE ⊡ Last orders 1.30am. Métro: Strasbourg-St-Denis.

Jean-Paul Bucher, owner of six top Parisian eating places, has single-handedly done more than anyone to save authentic restaurant decors from the modernizer's axe. Although both **Brasserie Flo** and **Le Vaudeville** are splendid, the jewel in Bucher's crown must be Julien, which sports some of Paris' most fabulous Art Nouveau designs, including a number of murals by Alphonse Mucha — and is accordingly much favored by extrovert admen and showbiz people. The food is classical and straightforward, with a slight Alsatian bias.

LAPÉROUSE

51 quai des Grands-Augustins, 6ᵉ
☎43-26-68-04. Map **8**I9 ▥ AE ⊡ Closed Sun eve, Mon. Métro: St Michel.

The decor of this restaurant facing the Seine is that of a bourgeois interior of the 19thC, with its concealed doors, overladen woodwork and private rooms for four to eight diners, often frequented by politicians and writers. The cuisine is classic: *foie gras de canard, ris de veau à l'oseille, feuilleté aux poires*. A memorable place to dine.

LAURENT ⌂

41 av. Gabriel, 8ᵉ ☎*42-25-00-39. Map 6F5*
▥ 𝗔𝗘 💲 🚗 🍷 *Closed Sat, Sun. Métro:*
Champs Élysées Clemenceau.

Well-bred opulence is the keynote of this distinguished establishment, occupying a delectable pavilion in the parkland setting off av. des Champs-Élysées — all white and gold stucco on the outside, Second-Empire elegance inside, with a garden at the back where one can feast under the chestnut trees on a summer day. The menu is mostly *nouvelle cuisine,* with some traditional elements. Philippe Bourguignon, one of the top *sommeliers* in France, will offer discreet advice on choosing from the 600-strong wine list. Service is exceptionally good. In the evening, candlelight and a pianist add to the festive atmosphere. Prices are commensurately high, but in relative terms the value is good.

LIPP

151 blvd. St-Germain, 6ᵉ ☎*45-48-53-91*
(telephone reservations not accepted). Map
7I7 ▥ 🍴 𝗔𝗘 💲 🍷 *Open 8am (for*
breakfast) to 12.45am (main meals from
noon). Métro: St-Germain-des-Prés.

This delightfully intact turn-of-the-century brasserie attracts the capital's intellectual, political and showbiz élite in far greater swarms than any other Parisian restaurant, however chic. The previous owner, Roger Cazes, died in 1987, and the Lipp is now run by his niece, Mme Perrochon. She has followed the tradition of her uncle and is no doubt as careful as he was in seating clients. The unknowns usually get sent up to the first floor (where the occasional celebrity is to be spotted), but beware — it is perfectly possible to be turned away, even if the place is not full. Dogs are allowed — providing they have the right owners. Impeccable service by long-aproned and long-serving waiters, reliable *plats du jour,* and the herd instinct explain Lipp's phenomenal success.

LE LORD GOURMAND

9 rue Lord-Byron, 8ᵉ ☎*43-59-07-27. Map*

5F3 ▥ *to* ▥ 𝗔𝗘 *Last orders 2am.*
Métro: George-V.

This intimate, dressy restaurant offers some of the best food to be had in the vicinity of av. des Champs-Élysées. Owner-chef Roland Borne maintains a well-balanced menu, rich in creation. The fish dishes are recommended and the desserts are extremely good. One of the best places in the capital to go for a tête-à-tête celebration. But reserve in advance. Intimate means small, and the tables are sought after.

LE MAQUIS

69 rue Caulaincourt, 18ᵉ ☎*42-59-76-07.*
Map 3C8 ▥ *to* ▥ 🚗 *Closed Sun. Métro:*
Lamarck-Caulaincourt.

The streets bordering that center of kitsch art, place du Tertre are not a very good area for eating — some of the bad habits of picture-vendors seem to have rubbed off on restaurant owners. A 10-minute walk down the Butte, however, reveals this attractively decorated bistro, which offers an inexpensive set lunch and interesting *à la carte* food — unfussy, up-to-date, colorful and light.

LA MARCANDE

52 rue Miromesnil, 8ᵉ ☎*42-65-19-14. Map*
6E5 ▥ 𝗔𝗘 💲 🚗 *Closed Sat, Sun, three*
weeks in Aug. Métro: Miromesnil.

This elegantly appointed restaurant affords diners a view not only over a delightful courtyard garden, but also over part of the kitchens. Behind the glass partitions, a smart team of chefs prepares some of the most imaginative food to be had in this part of town, such as *papillote de Saint-Jacques au foie gras, galette de pigeonneau aux truffes* and *ragoût de champignons des bois.* The walls are hung with a changing exhibition of modern paintings.

MAXIM'S ⌂

3 rue Royale, 8ᵉ ☎*42-65-27-94. Map 7G6*
▥ 𝗔𝗘 💲 🍷 *Last orders 1am. Closed Sun*
in July, Aug only. Métro: Concorde,
Madeleine.

The reputation of this world-famous restaurant revived when it was taken over a few years ago, in the face of much skepticism, by fashion designer Pierre Cardin. In the event, those who said that a cobbler should stick to his last were proved wrong. Cardin has kept Maxim's essential character as a top-class restaurant (with top-class prices), and has maintained and renovated its marvelous Art Nouveau decor. The food is an artful combination of *nouvelle* and *classique*, with the simplest food being often the most exquisite. The *navarin d'agneau* is a delight, the duck with peaches most exciting. Reservations are essential.

LA MÉDITERRANÉE
2 pl. de l'Odéon, 6ᵉ ☎43-26-46-75. Map 14J8 ▥ ▥ ▥ ◛ 🚄 Closed Sat and Mon lunch, Sun. Métro: Odéon.
Fish dishes from the South of France are lavishly served at this venerable restaurant, which has carried a reputation since the heady days of the early 1960s when Jean Cocteau and Orson Welles were regulars. Menus and crockery all bear the Cocteau logo. All manner of crustaceans live in tanks, awaiting sacrifice. The front opens up to become a terrace in summer and overlooks a pleasant and none-too-busy square.

MIRAVILE
72 quai de l'Hôtel de Ville, 4ᵉ ☎42-74-72-22. Map 9I10 ▥ Closed Sat lunch, Sun. Métro: Pont-Marie.
This quayside restaurant, close to the Hôtel de Ville, has all the qualities you could wish for. Excellent classic cuisine, charmingly served. Prices are not cheap, but you can be assured of leaving with the feeling that the money was well spent.

MOROT-GAUDRY
8 rue de la Cavalerie, 15ᵉ ☎45-67-06-85. Map 11J3 ▥ 🚄 ◛ Closed Sat, Sun. Métro: La Motte-Piquet-Grenelle.
As majestically located as **La Tour d'Argent**, on the top floor of a ship-like 1920s building with a wonderful view of the nearby Eiffel Tower, this restaurant is much favored by bigwigs from UNESCO (also nearby). French food gurus can't seem to decide whether Jean-Pierre Morot-Gaudry's cuisine is *nouvelle* or not. No matter: his concoctions have the stamp of true originality (calf's liver with raspberries, crab *boudin*, red mullet with *chanterelles*). There is an excellent and reasonably priced set luncheon menu that is deservedly popular with businesspeople.

LE MUNICHE
22 rue Guillaume-Apollinaire, 6ᵉ ☎46-33-62-09. Map 7I7 ▥ ▥ ▥ Last orders 2am. Métro: St-Germain-des-Prés.
This bustling, noisy and cramped restaurant on two floors is the canteen of Left Bank literati — a truly Parisian sort of place, where seafood predominates and the only German note, apart from the name, is the sauerkraut. The Layrac brothers also run the neighboring **Le Petit Zinc**. Delightful Art Nouveau decor by Slavik; mirrors everywhere. Reservations essential for dinner.

AU PACTOLE
44 blvd. St-Germain, 5ᵉ ☎46-33-31-31. Map 15J10 ▥ to ▥ ◛ ▥ Closed Sat lunch, Sun. Métro: Maubert-Mutualité.
Lunch is the best time to eat here, because, with luck, the sun will be streaming through the windows of the attractive covered terrace. The decor has bright tones of orange and yellow.
Roland Magne is an inventive yet unfussy cook with a penchant for unusual combinations (kid with mint, lamb with violets). His set menu is a wonderful bargain.

LE PAVILLON MONTSOURIS ♣
20 rue Gazan, 14ᵉ ☎45-88-38-52 ▥ to ▥ ▥ ▥ ◛ 🚄 Métro: Cité-Universitaire.
This restaurant, decorated in Belle Époque style, is set in a peaceful pavilion in the Parc Montsouris. A shady veranda and a summer terrace facing banks of flowers in the park, or a winter log fire, provide pleasant settings for what is becoming recognized as masterful *nouvelle cuisine* with an extremely wide choice of dishes. Good value.

AU PETIT MONTMORENCY

5 rue Rabelais, 8ᵉ ☎*42-25-11-19. Map 6F5* ▥ ▦ *Closed Sat, Sun, Aug. Métro: Miromesnil, Franklin D. Roosevelt.*

Chef Daniel Bouché follows no school of cooking but his own. Discover this restaurant while you still can at such reasonable prices. A faithful and rather chic clientele comes back again and again for such inventive delights as rabbit with sea-urchins, beef cheek with calf's foot, or coffee-and-whiskey ice cream. The decor is pleasantly old-fashioned — plants everywhere, ancient kitchen utensils and engravings on the walls.

AU PETIT RICHE

25 rue Le Peletier, 9ᵉ ☎*47-70-68-68. Map 3F8* ▥ ▦ ▣ *Closed Sun. Métro: Richelieu-Drouot.*

A quite exceptional decor, which, with its decorated frosted windows, large mirrors and brass luggage-racks, is somewhat more Edwardian than Belle Époque. Still divided into a number of small dining rooms, this fine bistro accommodates the after-theater crowd at night. Good, solid *cuisine bourgeoise* without pretension is served here, and a commendable selection of Loire wines.

LE PETIT ZINC

11 rue St-Benoit, 6ᵉ ☎*46-33-51-66. Map 7I7* ▥ ▦ ▣ *Last orders 2am. Métro: St-Germain-des-Prés.*

Probably the best late-night restaurant in town; a good set-price menu and an interesting *carte* attracts a varied clientele. Mustachioed waiters in traditional long white aprons give warmly efficient service. Gorgeous Art Nouveau decor, full of scrolls and sinuous curves. Always busy — reservations are advised for dinner.

LA PETITE CHAISE

36 rue de Grenelle, 7ᵉ ☎*42-22-13-35. Map 7I7* ▥ ▬ ▦ *Métro: Rue-du-Bac.*

The patina of 300 years shines in this quaint old inn, especially in the dark and intimate bar. The decor within the dining room is more stark, perhaps a

little Puritan, but it has its appeal, particularly for American visitors who come back again and again. The fixed-menu-only policy pays dividends and gives plenty of choice. The cuisine is modest, and the prices too.

AU PIED DE COCHON

6 rue Coquillière, 1ᵉʳ ☎*42-36-11-75. Map 8G9* ▥ ▣ ▣ ▦ *Open 24hrs. Reservations only until 8.30pm. Then you make a line. Métro: Les Halles.*

This old landmark of Les Halles has, alas, succumbed to the winds of change, adopting a strange, gaudy Italian style in recent years. The restaurant no longer has the atmosphere of the old Les Halles for which it was once famed. Still open day in, day out. Au Pied de Cochon customers eat their way through a tonne of shellfish every day and 80,000 pigs' feet a year.

PHARAMOND

24 rue de la Grande-Truanderie, 1ᵉʳ ☎*42-33-06-72. Map 9H9* ▥ to ▥ ▣ ▣ ▬ *Closed Sun, Mon lunch. Métro: Les Halles.*

This gem of a restaurant is a listed building, with its Art Nouveau mirrors and *faïence* created for the 1900 World Fair. It is the last-remaining vestige of the heart of Les Halles market. Always famed for its succulent tripe, *andouillette* and pig's feet, it now features some more modern dishes too.

PIERRE VEDEL ♥

19 rue Duranton, 15ᵉ ☎*45-58-43-17* ▥ *Closed Sat, Sun, last 2wks July, week of Christmas and New Year. Métro: Boucicaut.*

Genuine Mediterranean restaurants do not lie thick on the ground in Paris, so all the more reason to be thankful for the existence of this welcoming bistro. Vedel himself, who comes from the fishing port of Sète, naturally feels most at home with seafood (excellent garlicky lobster soup, fillet of *rascasse* in saffron-flavored aspic), but he also has a talent for inventive vegetable dishes, for example, stuffed cabbage and a gamut of combined vegetable mousses. Extremely good value for such quality.

POLIDOR 🍴 ♧

41 rue Monsieur-le-Prince, 6ᵉ
☎43-26-95-34. No advance reservations.
Map **14**J8 ▢ Last orders 12.30am (Sun
10pm). Métro: Odéon.

Polidor gives away a 3-course set meal
for a fantastically low price. Little has
changed in this 150-year-old *bouillon*
since the days of Verlaine, Valéry and
Joyce: there are still lace curtains, numbered napkin lockers (some in use), a
spiral staircase, and even waitresses in
turn-of-the-century dress. Good *cuisine
bourgeoise, ragoûts, blanquettes*.

LE PRÉ CATELAN △

Route de Suresnes, Bois de Boulogne, 16ᵉ
☎45-24-55-58 ▥ AE ⊡ 🍴 ⌓ Closed
Sun eve, Mon, one week in Feb.

Many well-heeled Parisians who han-
ker after tiptop food in an accessible
pastoral setting make for this establishment in the Bois de Boulogne. A few
years ago, somewhere drab was converted into a palatial summerhouse.
Now, in winter you can dine in front of
logs blazing in the vast black marble
fireplace, or in summer in the orangery,
surrounded by the splendid gardens.

LE PROCOPE

13 rue de l'Ancienne-Comédie, 6ᵉ
☎43-26-99-20. Map **8**I8 ▢ to ▥ AE ⊡
Last orders 1am. Closed July. Métro: Odéon.

The oldest restaurant in Paris, Le Procope opened as a café in 1686. Previous
customers include La Fontaine, Voltaire, Benjamin Franklin, Jean-Jacques
Rousseau, Robespierre, Napoléon, Balzac, George Sand and Huysmans. Its
two floors have retained their warm,
original atmosphere. The fare is traditional *cuisine bourgeoise* with a good
selection of sea food. Live jazz groups
grace the lobby Wednesday to Saturday
from 11pm-1am.

RÉGENCE △

25 av. Montaigne, 8ᵉ ☎47-23-78-33. Map
6G4 ▥ ▤ AE ⊡ 🍴 ⌓ Métro:
Franklin-D-Roosevelt, Alma Marceau.

People come to the more expensive of
the two restaurants at the **Hôtel Plaza-
Athénée** (see WHERE TO STAY), to savor

the glittering company as much as the
food. In summer, the inner courtyard is
a marvelous, ivy-festooned haven of
coolness. The cuisine is a mixture of
classical and new styles, and the wine
list is superb.

ROBUCHON   See JAMIN.

LE SANCERROIS 🍴

12 rue du Champ-de-Mars, 7ᵉ
☎45-55-13-47. Map **12**I4 ▢ ⌓ Closed
Sat evening, Sun, Aug. Métro: École-Militaire.

People from the nearby TV studios appreciate the quiet atmosphere of this
friendly, unpretentious café-restaurant.
The food is Auvergnat, and the handful
of wines, mainly Loire and Beaujolais,
all impeccably chosen.

TAILLEVENT △

15 rue Lamennais, 8ᵉ ☎45-61-12-90. Map
6F4 ▥ ▤▤ ⌓ ▤ Closed Sat, Sun, Aug.
Métro: Charles-de-Gaulle-Étoile, George V.

Taillevent, named after one of the first
great French cooks who lived in the
14thC, who has made it one of the capital's top five restaurants. It is run by
Jean-Claude Vrinat, who follows new
cooking trends and is also always on the
look-out for excellent lesser-known
wines to fill out his vast list. He buys
some of his cheeses direct from the
farm. Taillevent is much frequented by
politicians and top businessmen. The
decor in this lovely mid-19thC mansion
is suitably discreet. Reserve weeks —
even months — ahead.

LA TAVERNE DU SERGENT
RECRUTEUR ♧

41 rue St Louis-en-l'Île, 4ᵉ ☎43-54-75-42.
Map **9**J10 ▢ ⌓ Open for dinner only.
Last orders midnight. Closed Sun. Métro:
Pont-Marie.

In the 18thC, when the French army was
short of men, it would employ a recruit-
ing sergeant, a sly character who would
ply his victims with food and drink until
they signed his enlistment papers without objection. This is just the sort of
place where you can imagine him at
work: leaded windows, stone-flagged
floor, heavy wooden beams and stone

arches. At this restaurant, you get similar lavish treatment but without the penalty; make sure that you have a big appetite. There is no *à la carte*, only a 4-course, fixed-price menu of remarkably good value.

LA TAVERNE DES TEMPLIERS
106 rue Vieille-du-Temple, 3
☎42-78-74-67. Map 10H11 ▢ ▢ ▢ ▢
Closed Sun. Métro: Filles-du-Calvaire.
Curiously, this part of the old and picturesque Marais quarter contains almost no restaurants of any quality. But here is the exception. The Taverne des Templiers occupies a building dating from 1229 and restored in 1500, not long after the Marais was drained by the Knights Templar. You can dine in a wonderfully atmospheric room, beneath a superb, beamed ceiling. French traditional cuisine is the staple, under the careful guidance of Pascale Etiemble.

LE TÉLÉGRAPHE
41 rue de Lille, 7 ☎40-15-06-65. Map
7H7 ▢ to ▢ ▢ ▢ ▢ *Last orders
midnight. Métro: Rue du Bac, Solférino.*
Only a stone's throw from the Musée d'Orsay, Le Télégraphe's astonishing popularity continues. Publishers, journalists and politicians foregather to talk shop, and in the evenings (when reservations are essential) fashionable young Parisians flock here.

The superb décor, by François-Joseph Graf, is the main reason, although he started with an enviable advantage: for this room, the astonishing refectory of a former dormitory for female Post Office workers, came equipped with arches, arcades, stained-glass windows and Art Nouveau woodwork. A pleasant veranda overlooks a small garden, and the food is light and *nouvelle.*

TERMINUS NORD
23 rue de Dunkerque, 10 ☎42-85-05-15.
Map 4D10 ▢ ▢ ▢ *Métro: Gare-du-Nord.*
Cafés and restaurants near stations tend to treat their irregular, hurried and captive clientele in less than gentlemanly fashion. A notable exception is the Terminus Nord, another restaurant in the

stable of Jean-Paul Bucher (see **Brasserie Flo**, **La Coupole**, **Julien** and **Le Vaudeville**). An ideal place at which to eat before taking a train from the station opposite, this brasserie offers food that is good enough to attract swarms of gourmets who have no intention of leaving town.

LA TERRASSE FLEURIE ♣
Hôtel Inter-Continental, 3 rue de Castiglione,
1 ☎44-77-11-11. Map 7G7 ▢ ▢ ▢
▢ ▢ *Métro: Tuileries.*
This all-year-round terrace restaurant is unusual for a luxury hotel (it's part of the **Hôtel Inter-Continental**: see WHERE TO STAY) in that it offers a set menu, which, in view of its copiousness and high quality, is a very good value indeed. The chef shows a refreshing interest in the kitchen garden, and his two *plats du jour*, themselves traditional rather than inventive, are imaginatively served.

THOUMIEUX
79 rue St-Dominique, 7 ☎47-05-49-75.
Map 12H5 ▢ *Métro: La Tour-Maubourg.*
This spacious, vaguely Art Deco brasserie, attached to a hotel of the same name and not far from the Tour Eiffel, has been in the same family for three generations, serving good traditional food from the southwest region: country *charcuteries,* an excellent *cassoulet, tête de veau vinaigrette,* and a very good fixed menu.

TOUTOUNE ♣
5 rue de Pontoise, 5 ☎43-26-56-81. Map
9J10 ▢ ▢ *Closed Sun, Mon lunch.*
Métro: Maubert-Mutualité.
Good food cuts across class divisions (in France at least), which probably explains Toutoune's wide spectrum of customers, from casually-dressed students to elderly *bourgeois* couples. The friendly atmosphere is effortlessly created by the blonde Toutoune herself, a former TV food presenter who has kept a strong following. The formula: a lavish 5-course set menu chalked up each day on a blackboard: a soup, a good choice of *entrées* and main dishes, two

cheeses in peak condition, and a battery of desserts. The *cuisine* is sophisticated provincial — like the best of grand-mother's recipes.

AU TROU GASCON
40 rue Taine, 12ᵉ ☎43-44-34-26 ⬜ to ⬜ ⬛ *Closed Sat, Sun. Métro: Daumesnil.*
The acclaimed chef Alain Dutournier, creator of this restaurant, has turned it over to his wife, who has continued in the same style. The restaurant offers a most unusual blend of new ideas and provincial (Gascon) tradition, and an equally rare selection of wines (some 450), ranging from prestigious Bordeaux to humble, little-known *crus*, all annotated in detail on the city's most compulsively readable wine list. Throw in the amazing collection of Armagnacs, and the restaurant's turn-of-the-century decor (a riot of mirrors and moldings), and you have the makings of a memorable meal.

LE VAUDEVILLE
29 rue Vivienne, 2ᵉ ☎40-20-04-62. Map **8F8** ⬜ to ⬜ ⬛ ⬛ ⬛ ⬛ *Last orders 2am. Métro: Bourse.*
Revived by Jean-Paul Bucher (see also **Brasserie Flo**, **La Coupole**, **Julien** and **Terminus Nord**), who reinstated the establishment's Egyptian-style walls and opaque fittings to their former glory, and put professionals in charge of the kitchens. It now offers very good classical cuisine at highly competitive prices — and, being open until 2am, it is a boon for people wanting a bite after a show.

AU VIEUX BERLIN
32 av. George-V, 8ᵉ ☎47-20-88-96. Map **6F4** ⬜ to ⬜ ⬛ ⬛ *Closed Sat, Sun. Métro: George-V.*

Movie and showbiz people (Serge Gainsbourg, Jacques Dutronc) appreciate the discretion and attentive service available at this accurate reproduction of a prewar Berlin eating house (complete with pianist and candles in the evening). The food, although mainly German (plenty of game in season, pumpkin soup with bacon, knuckle of pork with split peas), has an attractively light and — dare one say it? — French touch.

LE VIVAROIS △
192 av. Victor-Hugo, 16ᵉ ☎45-04-04-31 ⬜ ⬛ ⬛ ⬛ ⬛ *Closed Sat, Sun. Métro: Av. Henri Martin.*
This is the most unusual of the city of Paris' pantheon of first-class restaurants, frequented by well-heeled gourmands and run by a true eccentric, chef-patron Claude Peyrot, who likes nothing better than to discuss philosophy with his customers. Peyrot is no disciple of *nouvelle cuisine*, rather a past-master at dishes that defy categorization. His aim is not flashy inventiveness but utter perfection of both raw materials and the end-product. By reputation, he succeeds every time.

WILLI'S
13 rue des Petits-Champs, 1ᵉʳ ☎42-61-05-09. Map **8G8** ⬜ ⬛ *Open 11am-11pm. Closed Sun. Métro: Bourse, Palais-Royal*
Willi's (named after owner Mark Williamson) is a faithful copy of a typical London wine bar, except that the large number of wines (many available by the glass) and the quality of the food (Anglo-French) are much higher than you would normally expect in Britain. It is crowded with English expatriates and tweedy French Anglophiles.

Cafés

The café is one of the most civilized institutions ever invented. It is a living stage, a forum for debate, a club, a home away from home. Paris was among the earliest cities to establish a café society, and it remains one of the few where traditional café life still thrives; in fact the French capital without its cafés would be unthinkable. In them, revolutions have been plotted, poems written, philosophies born. As literary and artistic circles have migrated from one district to another, so different cafés have had their spells as fashionable meeting places. Some of the famous ones have disappeared, others have been ruined by modernization, but many are still virtually intact.

There are more than 10,000 cafés in Paris, catering, between them, to almost every need a Parisian might have. An often staggering range of **alcoholic, soft and hot drinks** is available; **solid fare** includes *croissants,* hard-boiled eggs and sandwiches, and sometimes hot snacks and even sit-down meals, especially at lunchtime. You can make local and sometimes long-distance **calls** *(appel inter)*, although both will cost much more than from a public phone booth. The main brands of French **cigarettes** can be found in most cafés, but *cafés-tabacs* (recognizable by their red lozenge sign) sell a wide range of cigarettes, cigars, pipe- and even chewing-tobacco, snuff, stamps, envelopes, postcards, pens, and state lottery tickets.

If the letters **PMU** are displayed outside, it means the *café-tabac* turns into a betting shop on certain days, and you can have a wager on the horses via the state *pari-mutuel* system. Other café **amusements** may include pinball machines (known as *flippers*), electronic games, jukeboxes, miniature soccer, American pool and French billiards. It is totally OK to use the lavatories in cafés — the standards vary but these days they are adequate. Leave say 2f in the dish that is usually positioned in the toilet lobby, or at the counter as you leave, if you are not using the café.

There are free attractions, too. You can read, write, work or just while away the time with or without friends for as long as you like (except in one or two cafés on blvd. St-Michel, where notices fiercely warn you that your order will be automatically renewed every hour!). Cafés with terraces are good vantage points for observing the passers-by on, say, the av. des Champs-Élysées or one of the busy boulevards. But expect to be asked to pay more here: you're paying also for the prime location.

If you simply want to rest your feet or appease the children, look for a side-street café, which will be quieter and cheaper, as well as providing friendlier and more personal service.

There is a **two-tiered pricing system** at most cafés, depending on whether you drink at the bar or occupy a table. Often, the price difference is quite steep, and you can pay up to 50 percent less if you choose not to sit on the terrace. Watch the price of certain drinks — non-French beer, bottled mineral water, Coca Cola, whiskey and vodka.

You may encounter several different types of café. **Buvettes**, which are getting rarer every day, are grocery stores or wine merchants with a counter (called a *zinc*) but usually no tables; here, and at the now almost extinct **bougnats** (tiny, Spartan cafés), you may glimpse a little of the authentic flavor of prewar Paris.

In a **café-tabac**, the prices may also be a little lower than in cafés and the atmosphere a little livelier. **Brasseries**, "**drugstores**" and "**pubs**" (the last two bear little relation to the American or British originals) are large and you can get hot meals throughout the day.

At the most elegant end of the spectrum, there are the **salons de thé**, which are sometimes incorporated into *pâtisseries* and do not serve alcoholic drinks. A genuine *salon de thé*, if you can afford it, is the best place for a good Continental breakfast.

Tipping in cafés is no longer a problem — the tip is clearly included on the bill.

There are far too many interesting cafés in this city to list exhaustively, but here, arranged according to area, are a few favorites.

LEFT BANK
Montparnasse (Maps **13** & **14**)
This is still the center of Bohemian life in Paris. Genuine artists, intellectuals, writers, movie people and hangers-on of every description gather in **La Coupole** (see WHERE TO EAT) or **Le Select Montparnasse** (*99 blvd. du Montparnasse*), which has hardly changed since it was frequented by Erik Satie, Francis Poulenc, Robert Desnos and Foujita. Across the way, **Le Dôme** (*108 blvd. du Montparnasse*) is still cashing in on its reputation as a favorite watering-hole of Modigliani, Stravinsky, Picasso and Hemingway. Unfortunately, its hybrid 1920s decoration has diminished its former charm. A further five minutes' walk along the boulevard is the still-lively **Closerie des Lilas** (described in WHERE TO EAT).

St-Germain-des-Prés (Maps **7** & **8**)
Two of the most famous of all cafés, **Les Deux Magots** (a *magot*, by the way, is a Chinese miniature figure and not what you might think) and **Le Flore** (*6 pl. St-Germain-des-Prés and 172 blvd. St-Germain respectively*), are to be found, side by side, right in the heart of this district. The list of their customers past and present reads like a roll call of French intellectual life over the last hundred years — Huysmans, Jarry, Barrès, Giraudoux, Sartre, de Beauvoir, Breton, Camus, and the Prévert brothers. The Existentialist movement was born in one or other of them, or both, as were many of Sartre's philosophical and literary works — he preferred to write at a café table rather than at a desk. Nowadays, however, times have changed, and only the wealthier literati can afford to hold court regularly at the two renowned cafés.

On the other side of the boulevard there is still plenty of action at **Lipp** (see WHERE TO EAT), where getting in is not as easy as you might expect. It can all depend on who you are — or what you seem. Today's intellectuals have retreated to the quieter waters of the English "pub" around the corner, **The Twickenham** (*70 rue des Sts-Pères*). Another "pub" in the area is the vast **Pub St-Germain** (*17 rue de l'Ancienne-Comédie*), which boasts an unrivaled range of draft and bottled beers, teas and whiskeys, and is open all day and all night. Two doors away is the famous **Le Procope**, the first-ever café in Paris and open since 1686. Although its prime function is now as a restaurant (see WHERE TO EAT), you can still drink coffee and tea there throughout the day.

The man considered to be the finest *pâtissier* in Paris, **Christian Constant** *(26 rue du Bac),* has a *salon de thé* in his shop. Try it.

St-Michel *(Map 14)*
The cafés on boulevard St-Michel itself are no longer as interesting as they used to be. Two of them have become fast food outlets, although several around place St-Michel are popular with the Latin Quarter crowd. There are also two afternoon-only *salons de thé* within easy reach: **La Bûcherie** *(41 rue de la Bûcherie)* and **The Tea Caddy** *(14 rue St-Julien-le-Pauvre),* where you could enjoy scones, muffins and cinnamon toast.

RIGHT BANK
Av. des Champs-Élysées *(Map 6)*
There are only two cafés of any real interest actually on av. des Champs-Élysées: **Fouquet's** *(#99)* and **L'Alsace** *(#39).* At the first, you can pay a lot just to sit on the terrace. No unaccompanied ladies are allowed at the bar within. L'Alsace is a brasserie that serves genuine Alsatian beer, wine and food 24 hours a day. The **Drugstore Publicis** near place Charles de Gaulle (just past the **Bureau de Tourisme**) is a bright and breezy source of quick food, or a place just to sit and chat.

Not far from the av. des Champs-Élysées there are some good establishments serving refreshments and snacks outside meal times. Try **Le Val d'Or**, the bar of **Au Vieux Berlin**, **L'Écluse** and **Boulangerie St-Philippe**. **La Boutique aux Sandwichs** offers excellent take-out snacks (see WHERE TO EAT for addresses).

Opéra/Boulevard Haussmann *(Maps 7 & 8)*
Once the hub of café society, this is now mainly a business and shopping quarter, and becomes quiet after the early evening. But with French office-workers being as demanding as they are, most cafés are reliable, particularly those that are tucked away down side streets.

One of the most celebrated establishments in Paris is, of course, the **Café de la Paix** *(12 blvd. des Capucines).* It emerged from meticulous restoration a few years ago with its deliciously ornate green and gold decor, designed by Charles Garnier, architect of the Opéra opposite, and with its clientele (wealthy tourists for the most part) unscathed. Some of the best coffee, homemade *croissants* and other pastries are to be found at the smart but stark *salon de thé* of **Fauchon** *(26 pl. de la Madeleine),* Paris' most famous food store. After a day's shopping in RUE DU FAUBOURG-ST-HONORÉ, treat yourself to tea at **Angélina** *(226 rue de Rivoli).* The *pâtisseries* are delectable concoctions of cream, chocolate and meringue.

A number of cafés serve good wines and snacks. Look out for **Au Rubis** *(10 rue du Marché St-Honoré),* **Ma Bourgogne** *(133 blvd. Haussmann),* frequented by French executives, and **Le St-Amour** *(4 rue de Rome),* a friendly and rollicking café usefully located near the big department stores on blvd. Haussmann. An excellent **Café Flo** (see **Brasserie Flo** in WHERE TO EAT) can be found on the top floor of **Printemps**

Haussmann, under the glass dome (see DEPARTMENT STORES in SHOPPING).
Les Halles *(Map 9)*
The transformation of this *quartier* is now well and truly complete. A mixture of new and refurbished buildings, it sports a reasonable number of places to sit, or to grab a quick bite. One of the most stylish terraces in town is at **Café Costes** *(rue des Innocents).* It's worth a detour, if only to admire the minimalist, modern decor created by superstar designer Philippe Starck. Opposite the excellent wine bar **La Cloche des Halles** *(28 rue Coquillière)* is a pleasant, traditional café with nothing extraordinary about it except its name, **La Promenade de Vénus** *(44 rue du Louvre).* This resulted in its being selected by André Breton as the meeting place for fellow Surrealists. Around the corner, the best-known restaurant in the area, **Au Pied de Cochon** (see WHERE TO EAT), uses its terrace as a café. The restaurant itself is open 24 hours a day every day of the year, but they serve coffee and snacks only in the afternoon.
Le Marais *(Maps 9 & 10)*
If you wander around this fascinating old quarter, which has retained an almost provincial calm, you're bound to find several small cafés, rich in character and filled with regulars. On the beautifully intact 17thC place des Vosges, there is the cozy and altogether trendier **Ma Bourgogne** *(#19),* which serves reasonably good wines. But for a really wide and reliable selection of vintages, try **La Tartine** *(24 rue de Rivoli)* on the southern edge of Le Marais; this bustling café has not changed much since Lenin and Trotsky drank there.
Montmartre/Pigalle *(Map 3)*
All self-respecting painters have long since fled place du Tertre in Montmartre, which is now crammed with terrible paintings of sad-eyed children and dogs. Pigalle seems to have become a sex-shop jungle.

In both areas, cafés have turned the exploitation of tourists into a fine art, but as soon as you move away from the bright lights you may find a genuine Montmartre café. One such establishment is the delightful **Aux Négociants** *(27 rue Lambert),* where excellent and inexpensive wines flow freely as regulars converse, conveniently gathered around the tiny, horseshoe-shaped bar.

> Cafés form one of the specialities of Paris, and some of them
> should be visited by the stranger who desires to see Parisian life
> in all its phases. An hour or two may be pleasantly spent
> in sitting at one of the small tables with which the pavements
> in front of the cafés on the Boulevards are covered
> on summer evenings, and watching the passing throng.
> Chairs placed in unpleasant proximity to the gutter should,
> of course, be avoided. Most of the Parisian men spend
> their evenings at cafés, where they partake of coffee, liqueurs
> and ices, meet their friends, read the newspapers,
> or play at cards or billiards . . .
> The best cafés may with propriety be visited by ladies . . . .
> (Karl Baedeker, *Paris,* 1882)

Entertainments

by Virginie Duverger

Paris after dark

Paris — in appearance anyway — is a mighty gay place at night. The sidewalks are crowded with the little tables of the coffee and liqueur drinkers. The music of a hundred orchestras bursts forth from the lighted windows. The air is soft with the fragrance of a June evening, tempered by the curling smoke of fifty thousand cigars. Through the noise and chatter of the crowd there sounds unending the wail of the motor horn.

Quiet, conservative people in Paris like to get to bed at three o'clock; after all, what is the use of keeping late hours and ruining one's health and complexion? If you make it a strict rule to be in bed by three, you feel all the better for it in the long run — health better, nerves steadier, eyes clearer, and you're able to get up early — at half-past eleven — and feel fine.

(Stephen Leacock, *Behind The Beyond,* 1918)

When in Paris, make the time to go out in the evening for more than just an eating-and-drinking experience. You will find a choice of entertainment of considerable quality in every field, and in many cases language is not a problem even if your grasp of French is minimal.

There are countless **theaters**, and the fact that new ones are opening is a sign of the popularity of theater as an art form — Parisians just love theater. Great creativity in this area is obvious from the number of theater schools producing exciting young performers.

Café-théâtres, mainly offering the alternative humor that is beyond the grasp of most foreign visitors, have demonstrably gone from strength to strength with the Parisian theatergoing population.

Movie-going has kept its popularity in France, and it is in Paris that there is the greatest number of movie theaters per head of population. There are more than 400 screens offering new, blockbuster movies, films shown in their original English versions, and revivals of golden oldies; there are panoramic screens even in smaller neighborhood cinemas, and the choice before you is enormous.

As for less cultural nightlife, "Gay Paree" still conjures up visions of can-can dancers, champagne, and a level of cosmopolitan sophistication unique to the French capital. Ever since the Belle Époque, the combination of Bohemian artists, international café society and madcap expatriates seems to have given Paris a slightly naughty but very glamorous after-dark reputation.

Although the favored form of nightlife among certain natives nowadays is eating out in preference to other forms of slumming, Paris is still very lively indeed by night. At the most expensive end of the scale, the spectacular **revues** with feathered and sequined scantily-clad beauties continue to flourish. The chief (and cheapest) visitor spectator-sport — **people-watching** — can be accomplished in many cafés, particularly on the Left Bank (see CAFÉS).

Parisians have always loved dancing, so **clubs and discos** are crowded and colorful. Like revues and cabarets, they tend to charge by the drink *(consommation)* rather than by the combination of admission fee plus drink. Prices can range from inexpensive at the more popular discos to vastly expensive at the most lavish nightclubs. Bar-hopping is not really a Parisian diversion, although many good **bars** welcome customers for the apéritif hour, or for a late-night drink. **Wine bars** are also very popular, especially with the under 35s.

Jazz clubs, with their echoes of the postwar era, have remained largely unchanged since the 1950s, and they consequently offer both nostalgia and entertainment. Paris has always been *the* center for jazz in Europe, and there are a number of excellent clubs hosting performers from all over the world.

RESERVATIONS

If visiting in summer, remember that many theaters and performance centers close for a month or more. Many theaters take reservations only a couple of weeks in advance, but **SOS Théâtres** *(☎ 42-25-67-07)* or **Chèque-Théâtre** *(☎ 42-46-72-40)* provide last-minute assistance.

If you would rather avoid using the telephone, you can go directly to the box office of the venue of your choice. These are generally open from 11am-6pm, but are often closed on Sundays.

There are several **ticket reservation agencies**.

- **FNAC** rue de Rennes, 6e, map **13**K6, or rue Pierre-Lescot, Forum des Halles, 1er, map 9H9. No telephone reservations.
- **Virgin Megastore** 52 avenue des Champs-Élysées (basement), 8e, map **6**F4 ☎40-74-06-48. Open daily 10am-midnight (Fri and Sat until 1am), Sun noon-midnight.
- If you decide to go out at the last minute, there are Kiosque-Théâtres ticket booths at place de la Madeleine (map **7**F6)or in the RER station at Châtelet-Les Halles *(map 8H9),* where tickets can be purchased for half price on the day of the performance.

PUBLICATIONS

Whatever your taste in entertainment, indispensable publications that cost next to nothing are *Pariscope* and *l'Officiel des Spectacles,* published every Wednesday. They give performance times, telephone numbers, and lots more suggestions.

Performing arts

OPERA, BALLET AND DANCE

The most opulent of the performing arts has a new setting in the OPÉRA BASTILLE, and the old and new opera houses have complementary programs, offered under the joint promotional title of **Opéra de Paris**. The old Opéra Garnier houses classical ballet and contemporary dance, while full-scale operatic productions now benefit from the advanced technical facilities at the Opéra Bastille. Both opera houses have the deepest stages in existence. See the entries on both in A TO Z OF PARIS SIGHTS.

- **Opéra Bastille**   120 rue de Lyon, 12e ☎40-73-13-00. Telephone reservations from 11am-5.45pm. Map **16**J12. Métro: Bastille. The new Opéra has the advantage of superior facilities, but lacks the splendor of the Opéra Garnier.
- **Opéra-Garnier**   Place de l'Opéra, 9e ☎47-42-53-71. Map **7**F7. Métro: Opéra. Magnificent opulent setting. Garnier has the largest *corps de ballet* in the world, under the direction of Patrick Dupond. International touring contemporary dance companies perform here regularly.
- **La Salle Favart** or **Opéra Comique**   5 rue Favart, 2e ☎42-60-04-99. Telephone reservations Mon-Fri 10am-6pm. Map **8**F8. Métro: Richelieu-Drouot. A superb 19thC setting for the music of that epoch. Since it reopened in 1990, the Salle Favart has offered a varied program, with 19thC French operas and operettas as well as the classic operatic repertoire.

THEATER

There are well over a hundred theaters in Paris, offering presentations of all kinds. If your French is excellent, the world is your oyster. You might take the opportunity to see a play from the classic repertoire, or else a more traditional *vaudeville* play that has a fine balance of humor, banter and wit.

Some commercial theaters offer the expected international spectacular hits, such as *Cats* or *Les Misérables,* and others stage concerts, ballet and even small-scale operatic productions.

Reservations can often be made only 2 weeks ahead, and there are often seats available on short notice.

Theaters offering plays, plus dance, music and operatic productions

- **Théâtre de l'Atelier**   1 place Charles-Dullin, 18e ☎46-06-49-24. Map **3**D9. Métro: Anvers. A lovely building, mounting big productions, including musical spectaculars.
- **Théâtre des Champs-Élysées**   15 avenue Montaigne, 8e ☎49-52-50-50. Map **6**G4. Métro: Franklin-D-Roosevelt. Remains faithful to its tradition of offering all types of music, symphony and chamber concerts, dance and opera.
- **Théâtre de Mogador**   25 rue Mogador, 9e ☎48-78-04-04. Map **2**E7. Superb classic productions such as *Cyrano de Bergerac.*

- **Théâtre Musical de Paris (Théâtre du Châtelet)** See page 236.
- **Théâtre National de Chaillot** 1 place du Trocadéro, 16ᵉ ☎47-27-81-15. Reservations Mon-Fri 11am-7pm, Sat 11am-5pm. Map **11**H2. Métro: Trocadéro. Large-scale new interpretations of classical works, from Molière to Shakespeare as well as modern pieces. Apéritif-concerts for jazz lovers. Restaurant looks out over the fountains of the Trocadéro and the Tour Eiffel.
- **Théâtre du Rond-Point** or **Théâtre Renaud-Barrault** 2bis avenue Franklin-D-Roosevelt, 8ᵉ ☎42-56-60-70. Reservations Tues-Sat 11am-6pm, Sun noon-5pm. Map **6**G5. Métro: Champs-Élysées-Clemenceau. Founded by the legendary couple of French theater, Jean-Louis Barrault and Madeleine Renaud; once a forerunner of powerful 20thC drama. A new departure is the presentation of performance arts of other cultures — for example, Japanese theater and Indian dance.

International spectaculars

International dance companies and singers with a worldwide reputation usually appear at the **Palais Omnisports de Paris-Bercy** *(8 blvd. de Bercy, 12ᵉ ☎44-68-44-68)* or the **Palais des Congrès** *(2 pl. de la Porte Maillot, 17ᵉ ☎40-68-22-22)*. Big touring productions such as *Cats* or *Les Misérables* appear at the **Palais des Congrès** or the **Palais des Sports** *(1 pl. de la Porte de Versailles, 15ᵉ ☎48-28-40-48)*.

Traditional plays

- **Les Bouffes du Nord** 209 rue du Faubourg-St-Denis, 10ᵉ ☎42-39-34-50. Map **4**D11. Métro: La Chapelle. Home to English director Peter Brook's French company, and a receiving house for international contemporary theater.
- **Les Bouffes Parisiens** 4 rue Monsigny, 2ᵉ ☎42-96-60-24. Reservations from 11am-7pm. Map **8**G8. Capacious (700 seats), famous and well-respected theater.
- **La Comédie Française** 2 rue de Richelieu, 1ᵉʳ ☎40-15-00-15. Map **8**H8. Métro: Palais-Royal Musée du Louvre. French classical dramatic repertoire of the 17thC was born during the reign of Louis XIV. Molière died on stage here, playing the role of *Le Malade Imaginaire.* The Comédie still presents the works of Molière, Racine, Corneille, Shakespeare etc., but also 19th and 20thC playwrights such as Hugo, Anouilh, Pirandello and Brecht. See also page 119.
- **Théâtre de La Bruyère** 5 rue de La Bruyère, 9ᵉ ☎48-74-76-99. Map **3**E8. Métro: St-Georges. Known for its well-chosen repertoire of comic plays. Always successful.
- **Théâtre Marigny** Carré Marigny, 8ᵉ ☎42-56-04-41. Map **6**G5. Métro: Champs-Élysées-Clemenceau. A large, very beautiful commercial theater with a preference for well-known French literary works .
- **Théâtre des Mathurins** 36 rue des Mathurins, 9ᵉ ☎42-65-90-90. Map **7**F7. Presents plays with a humorous leaning.
- **Théâtre National de la Colline** 15 rue Malte-Brun, 20ᵉ ☎43-66-43-60. Map **18**C5. Métro: Gambetta. Lively new theater, opened

in 1988, with a program entirely of 20thC plays, many of which are premieres of new works. Outstanding new steel-and-glass building of considerable architectural merit.

- **Théâtre National de l'Odéon** or **Théâtre de l'Europe**   1 place de l'Odéon, 6e ☎44-41-36-36. Tickets on sale half an hour before performance starts. Map **14**J8. Métro: Odéon. One of the high spots of contemporary writing.
- **Théâtre de la Renaissance**   20 boulevard St-Martin, 10e ☎42-08-78-50. Reservations 11.30am-6.30pm. Map **9**G10. Métro: Strasbourg St-Denis. This 700-seat theater is close by the Porte St-Martin, where several vaudeville theaters are clustered.

Comedy theater

- **Bobino**   20 rue de la Gaieté, 14e ☎43-27-75-75. Map **13**L6. Métro: Gaieté. Of the many theaters in this lively area, Bobino attracts the biggest comedy stars.
- **Théâtre du Gymnase**   38 boulevard de Bonne-Nouvelle, 10e ☎42-46-79-79. Map **3**F9. Métro: Bonne-Nouvelle. Atmospheric theater along the Grands Boulevards.
- **Théâtre du Palais-Royal**   38 rue de Montpensier, 1er ☎42-97-59-81. Reservations from 11am-7pm. Map **8**G8. Métro: Palais-Royal, Musée du Louvre. Farces, comedy plays and occasional comic one-man shows.

CAFÉ-THÉÂTRES

Alternative comedy follows the same pattern in Paris as anywhere else. The great comedians of tomorrow are cutting their teeth in the 100-seat *café-théâtres* of today.

One condition of entry — go only if your French is way above average. Tickets are generally bought on the night.

- **Blancs-Manteaux**   15 rue des Blancs-Manteaux, 4e ☎48-87-15-84. Map **9**H10. Métro: Hôtel-de-Ville, Rambuteau.
- **Café d'Edgar**   58 boulevard Edgar-Quinet, 14e ☎42-79- 97-97. Reservations 2.30-7.30pm. Map **13**L6. Métro: Edgar-Quinet.
- **Café de la Gare**   41 rue du Temple, 4e ☎42-78-52-51. Map **9**H10. Métro: Hôtel-de-Ville.
- **Petit Casino**   17 rue Chapon, 3e ☎42-78-36-50. Map **9**H10. Métro: Arts-et-Métiers. Dinner available here.
- **Point Virgule**   7 rue Ste-Croix-de-la-Bretonnerie, 4e ☎42-78-67-03. Map **9**I10. Métro: Hôtel-de-Ville.

CINEMA

Although cinema audiences may be declining slowly, the French still appreciate movies and retain their taste for both French and foreign films. Many prefer to see movies in their original version, with French subtitles, and these films bear the inscription **VO** *(version original)*.

Unless you particularly want to see the version that was dubbed in French, avoid movies that carry the inscription **VF** *(version française)*.

Smoking is now universally forbidden in French movie theaters.

For new French and foreign movies

The biggest and best cinemas are to be found in the Opéra quarter *(along boulevard des Italiens)*, in Montparnasse *(métro: Montparnasse)*, around the Odéon *(métro: Odéon)*, at the Forum des Halles *(RER Châtelet-Les Halles)* and, in particular, along the avenue des Champs-Élysées *(métro: Franklin-D-Roosevelt)*.

* Choose a **Gaumont**, **UGC** or **14 juillet** movie theater; there are numerous locations around Paris and they have the widest screens and the best sound equipment.
* **La Pagode**   57bis rue de Babylone, 7ᵉ ☎47-05-12-15. Map **12**J5. Métro: St-François-Xavier. In an impressive Chinese pavilion, this is unquestionably the most unusual and beautiful movie theater in Paris. Try the tea room, too.
* **Studio 28**   10 rue Tholozé, 18ᵉ ☎46-06-36-07. Map **3**C8. Métro: Blanche. Built in 1928, and today the only cinema on the *Butte*. Extraordinary chandeliers — a gift of Jean Cocteau in 1950.

Wide-screen cinemas showing new movies

* **Le Gaumont Grand Écran**   30 place d'Italie, 13ᵉ ☎45-80-77-00. Map **15**M10. Métro: Place d'Italie. Newly built, and opened in 1992, this movie theater boasts the widest screen in Paris (24m/78ft).
* **Le Gaumont Grand Écran Grenelle**   60 avenue de la Motte-Picquet, 15ᵉ ☎43-06- 50-50. Map **11**J3. Métro: La Motte-Picquet-Grenelle. One of the most elegant movie theaters.
* **Le Grand Rex**   1 boulevard Poissonnière, 2ᵉ ☎36-65-70-23. Map **3**F9. Métro: Bonne-Nouvelle. Giant theater (2,800 seats) for big, spectacular movies.
* **Le Max Linder Panorama**   24 boulevard Poissonnière, 2ᵉ ☎36-65-70-21. Map **3**F9. Métro: Rue Montmartre.

Panoramic screens showing documentary films

* **La Géode**   26 avenue Corentin-Cariou, 19ᵉ ☎40-05-80-00. Map **18**C5. Métro: Porte de la Villette. Enormous hemispheric screen in the grounds of the Cité des Sciences et de l'Industrie.
* **Le Dôme IMAX**   Parvis de La Défense, Colline de l'Automobile, La Défense ☎46-92-45-45. Map **17**C3. Métro: La Défense. Spectacular presentations in 180° vision.
* **Paristoric**   78bis boulevard des Batignolles, 7ᵉ ☎42-93-93-46. Map **2**D6. Métro: Rome, Villiers. Fascinating 45-minute program for visitors and Parisians alike, showing Paris, its history, its moods, its many facets. Multi-image projection, with simultaneous translation in 7 languages. See page 166.

Art cinemas showing festival programs and re-releases

* **Le Champo**   51 rue des Écoles, 5ᵉ ☎43-54-51-60. Map **14**J9. Métro: St-Michel, Cluny-La-Sorbonne. Catch some superb re-releases with students from the area.
* **La Cinémathèque Française**   Musée du Cinéma, Palais de Chaillot, avenue Albert-de-Mun, 16ᵉ ☎47-04-24-24. Map **11**H2. Métro:

Trocadéro. Closed Monday. See also A TO Z OF PARIS SIGHTS. This and **Salle Garance** are France's two national film theaters: sometimes obscure, always fascinating.

- **Le Mac-Mahon** 5 av. Mac-Mahon, 17e ☎43-29-79-89. Map **5**E3. Métro: Étoile. Lovely prewar movie theater with star-spangled ceiling. Shows the great American classic movies, in original version, of course.
- **La Salle Garance** Centre Georges Pompidou, rue Rambuteau, 4e ☎42-77-12-33. Map **9**H10. Métro: Rambuteau, Châtelet-Les Halles. See CINÉMATHEQUE FRANÇAISE on previous page.
- **Les 3 Luxembourg** 67 rue Monsieur-Le-Prince, 6e ☎46-33-97-77. Map **14**J8. Métro: Luxembourg, Odéon. They hold regular late-night showings.

CLASSICAL CONCERTS

The range of music is almost matched by the spread of its habitat. Conventional *salles* vie with theaters, museums, gardens, grand houses and, best of all, the old churches of Paris.

The churches, some of which have superb acoustics, regularly present concerts by chamber, baroque and symphony orchestras. The best known and most popular are: **La Sainte Chapelle** *(Île de la Cité)*, **La Madeleine**, **St-Germain-des-Prés**, the oldest church in Paris, and **St-Roch** *(near the Louvre)*.

The venue for true music-lovers is:

- **La Salle Pleyel** 252 rue du Faubourg-St-Honoré, 8e ☎45-61-06-30. Reservations 11am-6pm, closed Sun and hols. Map **5**E3. Métro: Ternes. Good acoustics and a comfortable atmosphere combine to make this the high-spot of the capital's music venues.

Other concert halls include:

- **Auditorium du Louvre** Musée du Louvre (below the pyramid), 1er ☎40-20-52-29. Reservations Mon-Fri 2-5.30pm for 8.30pm concerts. Map **8**H8. Métro: Palais-Royal Musée du Louvre. Concerts of traditional music take place in the evening *(8.30pm)*, but there are also Thursday lunchtime concerts *(12.30pm — no reservation necessary)* which combine nicely with a visit to the museum.
- **Maison de Radio-France** 116 avenue du Président-Kennedy, 16e ☎42-30-23-08. Map **17**D3. Métro: Ranelagh. The concert hall is situated right in the center of the recording studios at the MAISON DE LA RADIO and you can hear mainly traditional music and sometimes jazz. About twice a month, there are free concerts.
- **La Salle Gaveau** 45 rue de la Boétie, 8e ☎49-53-05-07. Map **6**F5. Métro: Miromesnil.
- **Théâtre des Champs-Élysées** See THEATER on page 232.
- **Théâtre Musical de Paris (Théâtre du Châtelet)** 1 place du Châtelet, 1er ☎40-28-28-40. Reservations 11am-7pm, closed Sun. Map **9**I9. Métro: Châtelet. This large venue presents contemporary music as well as chamber music, opera and musical comedies. Programming is done jointly with:

- **Auditorium du Châtelet**   105 rue Rambuteau, Level 2, Forum des Halles, 1er (enter through Porte St-Eustache) ☎40-28-28-40. Map **9**H9. Métro: Les Halles.

VARIETY AND POPULAR CONCERTS

As for variety and pop concerts, with both French and foreign performers, the biggest happen at the **Palais Omnisports de Paris-Bercy**, **Le Zénith** at La Villette or at **La Cigale** *(128 blvd. Rochechouart, 18e)*. That bastion of French variety, **L'Olympia**, has been threatening to close its doors.

JAZZ

Paris is *the* place for jazz. All the original big American jazz names play here, as well as some very talented members of the postwar generation of jazz musicians.

The "Musts"

- **Le Bilboquet**   13 rue St Benoît, 6e ☎45-48-81-84. Map **7**I7. Métro: St-Germain-des-Prés. A jazz hot-spot and an institution, first opened in 1947. You can eat here too.
- **Bar Lionel Hampton**   Hôtel Méridien, 81 boulevard Gouvion-St-Cyr, 17e ☎40-68-34-34. Map **5**D2. Métro: Porte-Maillot. Top New Orleans jazz and Blues musicians in a chic hotel setting. Sunday jazz-brunch too.
- **New Morning**   7-9 rue des Petites-Écuries, 10e ☎45-23-51-41. Map **4**F10. Métro: Château d'Eau. You go to this hangar-like venue principally for its 9.30pm concerts featuring all the top jazz names.
- **Le Petit Journal St-Michel**   71 boulevard St-Michel, 5e ☎43-26-28-59. Map **14**J9. Métro: Luxembourg. A very well respected jazz venue which has a distinctly relaxed atmosphere. They serve dinner here too.

The others

- **Le Cambridge**   17 avenue de Wagram, 17e ☎43-80-34-12. Map **5**E3. Métro: Charles-de-Gaulle-Étoile. Mainly traditional jazz; also has a restaurant.
- **Caveau de la Huchette**   5 rue de la Huchette, 5e ☎43-26-65-05. Map **14**J9. Métro: St-Michel. Very popular, with excellent live music. Parisians go there above all for the dancing.
- **Le Montgolfier**   Hôtel Sofitel, 8-12 rue Louis-Armand, 15e ☎40-60-33-73. Map **17**D3. Métro: Porte de Versailles. Traditional jazz on the 23rd floor of this modern hotel. Superb views, of course.
- **Les Trottoirs de Buenos-Aires**   37 rue des Lombards, 1er ☎40-26-28-58. Map **9**H9. Métro: Les Halles. Argentina comes to Paris, with tango rhythms, danced and sung, classical and modern.

Nightlife

BARS

Some of the most sophisticated bars are found in the smart hotels, where the atmosphere is truly international. Some suggestions: the **Plaza-Athénée**, the **Crillon**, the **Ritz**, the **George-V**, the **Raphael** and the **Bristol**. See WHERE TO STAY on pages 192-205 for details.

Prices are generally high, especially for aperitifs or champagne. There is no harm done in asking for something that is more Parisian and cheaper too, such as *kir* (white wine and blackcurrant *sirop*), a *pastis*, a beer or a nonalcoholic drink such as *citron pressé*.

Bars are almost always crowded before dinner, and then again very late, after everything else has closed. They tend to open around 5pm, and some stay open till dawn. Unlike many other cities, Paris has no legal closing hours.

Some suggested addresses:

- **Bar du Lenox**   9 rue de l'Université, 7e ☎42-96-10-95. Map **7**I7. Métro: Rue-du-Bac. 1930s decor; an agreeable setting for a quiet rendezvous.
- **La Closerie des Lilas**   171 boulevard du Montparnasse, 6e ☎43-26-70-50. Map **14**L8. Métro: Vavin. The haunt of Hemingway still attracts assorted artists and literati. Good brasserie. See RESTAURANTS A TO Z in WHERE TO EAT.
- **La Coupole**   102 boulevard du Montparnasse, 14e ☎43- 20-14-20. Map **13**K7. Métro: Vavin. Cultural landmark for generations of artists. See RESTAURANTS A TO Z.
- **L'Entre-pots**   14 rue de Charonne, 11e ☎48-06-57-04. Map **16**J13. Métro: Ledru-Rollin. Good for cocktails and snacks, and conveniently close to the OPÉRA BASTILLE.
- **Le Forum**   4 boulevard Malesherbes, 8e ☎42-65-37-86. Métro: Madeleine. Map **7**F6. Rather British in style, and very relaxed. 150 kinds of cocktail and 85 whiskeys.
- **Le Fouquet's**   99 avenue des Champs-Élysées, 8e ☎47-23-70-60. Map **6**F4. Métro: George-V. Old haunt of actors in the days of black-and-white movies. Mix of regulars and tourists, with a very occasional famous face. See also CAFÉS.
- **Le Hard Rock Café**   14 boulevard Montmartre, 9e ☎42-46-31-32. Map **8**F8. Métro: Richelieu-Drouot, Rue Montmartre.
- **Harry's New York Bar**   5 rue Daunou, 2e ☎42-61-71-14. Map **7**F7. Métro: Opéra. "Sank Roo Doe Noo": an all-American institution. Popular with Parisians too. Stocks 160 kinds of whiskey. Good piano bar in the basement. Closes only on Christmas Day.
- **Kitty O'Shea's**   10 rue des Capucines, 2e ☎40-15-08-08. Map **7**F7. Métro: Opéra. Parisian sister of Dublin's famous pub.
- **Mayflower**   49 rue Descartes, 5e ☎43-54-56-47. Map **14**K9. Métro: Cardinal-Lemoine. Irish bar with cocktails.
- **La Mousson**   9 rue de la Bastille, 4e ☎42-71-85-20. Map **10**I12. Métro: Bastille. Colonial ambience right in the center of the newly-popular Bastille *quartier*. Restaurant, too.

- **Pacific Palissades** 51 rue Quincampoix, 3ᵉ ☎42-74-01-17. Map **9**H10. Métro: Les Halles, Rambuteau. The same pianist and singer has entertained there for years, with great success.
- **La Palette** 43 rue de Seine, 6ᵉ ☎43-26-68-15. Map **8**I8. Métro: Mabillon. The eternal St-Germain-des-Prés day or night rendezvous for young and old students. It's always good to sit and sip a hot, spiced wine in this old-fashioned bistro-style bar.
- **Polly Magoo** 11 rue St-Jacques, 5ᵉ ☎46-33-33-64. Map **14**J9. Métro: St-Michel. Chess . . . and a true Bohemian atmosphere. Open until 4am.
- **Rosebud** 11bis rue Delambre, 14ᵉ ☎43-35-38-54. Map **13**L7. Métro: Vavin. Former rendezvous for the likes of Sartre and de Beauvoir: a classic Montparnasse meeting-place. Still holds good.
- **Le Sous Bock** 49 rue St-Honoré, 1ᵉʳ ☎40-26-46-61. Map **9**H9. Métro: Les Halles. Beer, beer and more beer. 400 different kinds, including raspberry beer in a champagne flute.
- **La Villa** 29 rue Jacob, 6ᵉ ☎43-26-60-00. Map **8**I8. Métro: St-Germain-des-Prés. Ultra-designer flair in this daringly modern hotel (see WHERE TO STAY). Split-level salons: cocktails, piano bar.

CABARETS AND REVUES

Revues and cabarets can have an international, American flavor or be typically French; you can find humorous drag stars or imitators of the singers of yesteryear.

At the best-known establishments, the prices are commensurately high, but you get a whole lot of spectacle for your money. In most places, two combinations are available: show and dinner or show and a half-bottle of champagne.

- **Crazy Horse Saloon** 12 avenue George-V, 8ᵉ ☎47-23-32-32. Map **6**F4. Métro: George-V. Strip show without the strip: dancers are already *déshabillée*. Artistic lighting and risqué costumes. Excellent entertainment with magicians too. But it's crowded, and very expensive.
- **Éléphant Bleu** 49 rue de Ponthieu, 8ᵉ ☎43-59-58-64. Map **6**F5. Métro: Franklin-D-Roosevelt. Glamorous Thai dancers and spectacle, with dinner.
- **Folies Bergères** 32 rue Richer, 9ᵉ ☎42-46-77-11. Map **3**E9. Métro: Cadet, Rue Montmartre. It was here that Maurice Chevalier and Mistinguett sang in the old days. The 1930s decor is magnificent, and the show is more traditional.
- **Au Lapin Agile** ♣ 22 rue des Saules, 18ᵉ ☎46-06-85-87. Map **3**C8. Métro: Lamarck-Caulaincourt. Old haunt of Renoir and Picasso, now devoted to tourists and offering song, humor and poetry. Good value for money.
- **Lido** 116bis avenue des Champs-Élysées, 8ᵉ ☎40-76-56-10. Map **5**F3. Métro: George-V. (Next door to the Normandie cinema.) Paris' most lavish revue, with 100 artistes — singers, dancers, skaters and even live animals on stage. Very expensive.
- **Michou** 80 rue des Martyrs, 18ᵉ ☎46-06-16-04. Map **3**D8. Métro:

Pigalle. Burlesque-style impressions of the great stars of stage and showbiz. Marvelous drag performances — very funny.

- **Moulin Rouge (Bal du Moulin Rouge)**   Place Blanche, 9ᵉ ☎46-06-00-19. Map **2**D7. Métro: Blanche. Immortalized by Toulouse-Lautrec, this was the birthplace of the can-can. The show is of the same quality as the **Lido**, but in a more Parisian style. Delightful ballroom decor with Chinese lanterns.
- **Paradis Latin**   28 rue du Cardinal-Lemoine, 5ᵉ ☎43-25-28-28. Map **15**K10. Métro: Cardinal-Lemoine. Wonderful theater, built by Eiffel and restored to glory in the 1980s. Proceedings are run by Sergio, a formidable and stylish old-time master of ceremonies. The most Parisian of all the shows.

CASINOS

Gaming is forbidden in Paris and gaming clubs are, as a consequence, exclusive and private. The nearest good casino is at **Enghien** *(☎34-12-90-00),* 16km (10 miles) NW of the city. It has a restaurant. The location is attractive, with its large lake.

DANCING

Paris has superb discotheques, but if you prefer something a little more conventional, a number of dance-halls and discotheques offer afternoon tea-dances *(thé-dancing),* as well as evening dances of the more traditional kind. This is not an expensive pastime.

- **Chez Félix**   23 rue Mouffetard, 5ᵉ ☎47-07-68-78. Map **15**K10. Métro: Monge. Samba all night. Brazilian orchestra. Show featuring singers and impressionists.
- **Club 79**   79 avenue des Champs-Élysées, 8ᵉ ☎47-23-68-75. Map **5**F3. Métro: George-V. Large basement dance-hall in chic location; daily tea-dances.
- **La Coupole**   102 boulevard du Montparnasse, 14ᵉ ☎43-20-14-20. Map **13**K7. Métro: Vavin. Dancing to old-fashioned tangos and waltzes; select clientele. See also BARS and WHERE TO EAT.
- **Madeleine Plaza**   8 boulevard de la Madeleine, 9ᵉ ☎42-66-60-68. Map **7**F7. Métro: Madeleine. Nostalgia sessions and daily tea-dances.
- **Retro République**   23 rue du Faubourg-du-Temple, 11ᵉ ☎42-08-54-06. Map **10**G12. Métro: République. Tea-dances throughout the week; Retro orchestra on weekends.

DISCOTHEQUES

The very word *discothèque* is, of course, French. Paris' discos tend to be wonderfully flashy affairs, with glittery decor and glittery people, throbbing lights and pulsating music. Fashions change, but there are some places, given below, that are at the fore from one generation to the next. See also PRIVATE CLUBS.

- **Les Bains**   7 rue du Bourg l'Abbé, 3ᵉ ☎48-87-01-80. Map **9**G10. Métro: Rambuteau, Etienne-Marcel. In an interestingly converted bathhouse, this has been the Number One spot in town for years.

- **Le Balajo**   9 rue de Lappe, 11e ☎47-00-07-87. Map **10**I12. Métro: Bastille. Old memories of postwar Paris, wholeheartedly adopted by the new generations. Authentic dancing Monday, Friday to Sunday 3-6.30pm. International variety shows at night.
- **La Main Jaune**   Place de la Porte-Champerret, 17e ☎47-63-26-47. Map **17**C3. Métro: Porte-de-Champerret. Roller disco on the edge of the autoroute.
- **Le Neil's**   27 avenue des Ternes, 17e ☎47-66-45-00. Map **5**E3. Métro: Ternes. A copy of Neil's in New York. Library-style decor, with books and wood-paneling. Good restaurant. If you want to dance, avoid Saturday nights. Neil's is a private club, so how you look is all-important.
- **Le Palace**   3bis Cité Bergère, 9e ☎42-46-10-87. Map **3**F9. Métro: Rue Montmartre. Parisian nightclub with wide age-appeal.
- **La Scala**   188bis rue de Rivoli, 1er ☎42-60-45-64. Map **8**H8. Métro: Palais-Royal Musée du Louvre. Spacious disco with all the latest electronic gadgetry and stunning lighting. Young atmosphere.
- **Le Slow Club**   130 rue de Rivoli, 1er ☎42-33-84-30. Map **8**H9. Métro: Châtelet. Way down in the cellars, the band strikes up and you can dance to jazz and rock in a great atmosphere.

PRIVATE CLUBS

In Paris, as elsewhere, a nightclub is normally "private," although there are varying degrees of privacy, particularly for visitors. However, if you are young, or pretty, or well-dressed (or ideally all three), the chances increase of being given entry. Hotel *concièrges* are often knowledgeable about what is "in" for foreign visitors.

- **Le Neil's**   27 avenue des Ternes, 17e ☎47-66-45-00. Map **5**E3. Métro: Ternes. See DISCOTHEQUES above. Neil's is not as frightfully exacting as some clubs, although how you look is still important.

The private clubs of Paris are ultra-famous and ultra-expensive. If you gain entry, you can expect to encounter screen stars, top models and leading journalists. For men, ties or bow ties are expected; women, however, can be as outrageous as they like.

If you must go, and want to spend 120f on a drink, ask about **Castel-Princesse**, **Olivia Valère** and, of course, **Régine's**. These are the big names on today's club scene, as they have been for years.

Paris is the throne of . . . sensuality and godless frivolity.
(King Ludwig II of Bavaria — lived 1845-86)

Shopping

A seductive city for shopping

Paris gave the world the boutique, the small speciality shop that still embodies the intimate character of Parisian shopping. Entire *quartiers* are blanketed with boutiques, the specialities of which range from antiques to zippers. There are some very good department stores, but it is the boutiques that exhibit the individuality, variety and flair that makes Paris Europe's most seductive city for shopping.

WHAT TO BUY
Fine tailoring, luxurious fabrics and the indefinable chic of Parisian clothing is epitomized by the *haute couture* and designer ready-to-wear. But Paris fashion is also translated into the reasonably-priced clothing that can be found in hundreds of small boutiques. Everything to do with fashion is a good buy, provided it is of French origin, mainly because you cannot get the same thing elsewhere at the same price. French perfume, cosmetics, home accessories and lingeries make Paris the woman's ultimate shop window, while men's and children's wear take a distinct second place.

Food and everything related to it — kitchen gadgets, cook-books, herbs, linens — are especially close to the French heart, with a huge variety available in even the smallest neighborhood shops.

WHERE TO GO
One of the most satisfying things about shopping in Paris is that just about everywhere you go, you will find plenty to tempt you. Shops in Paris are part of life. Because many people live in the tall apartment buildings that have shops on the ground floor, and work in offices contained in such buildings, there is less need to go on shopping expeditions. The shops are there to be enjoyed as part of the day-to-day routine.

There are quarters dedicated to the promotion of one type of thing, and taking a stroll in such places is one good way to soak in a particular atmosphere. The booksellers of the Left Bank are an obvious example, but if you are passing, peek at the antique stores around the Left-Bank **rue Bonaparte**, or browse in the windows of the stamp dealers around the auction house at Richelieu-Drouot off **boulevard Haussmann** in the 9ᵉ, or the glassware and crystal in **rue de Paradis** in the 10ᵉ·

Boulevard Haussmann contains those bastions of one-stop shopping the department stores *(les Grands Magasins)* Galeries LaFayette and Printemps. Also in the 8ᵉ and 9ᵉ *arrondissements*, the w end of the **Grands Boulevards** *(blvd. des Capucines and blvd. des Italiens),* leading toward the Opéra, contains probably the capital's most wide-ranging selection of fashion stores, including the very best in jewelers, shoe stores and perfumeries.

Much of the 8ᵉ is devoted to expensive fashion, primarily **avenue Montaigne**, **rue St-Honoré** and **avenue Victor-Hugo** . Rue du Faubourg-St-Honoré combines luxury shopping with smaller boutiques in a highly concentrated area. A window-shopper's trip to heaven is to be found around **rue Etienne Marcel** and the surrounding part of the 1ᵉʳ and 2ᵉ, although the prices tend toward the skies too.

The **avenue des Champs-Élysées** holds a little less allure for shoppers than it once did, as a number of downmarket stores have changed the mood. However, the city of Paris has taken steps to keep traders — and parked cars — off the sidewalks, and this fine avenue is undoubtedly on the up again.

Paris' best-kept secrets are contained in the *galeries* and *passages* — handsome, glass-roofed 19thC arcades that run in intricate warrens through the 1ᵉʳ, 8ᵉ and 9ᵉ. From the ultra-smart **Galerie Colbert** and **Galerie Vivienne**, near the Palais-Royal, to the eclectic **Passage Jouffroy** and **Passage des Panoramas** off blvd. Montmartre in the 9ᵉ, there is pleasure to be taken in their state of preservation, and a host of fascinating, specialist stores to be inspected. Pipes, walking canes, exotica from the Far East, antiquarian books are all there, as well as excellent and often inexpensive eating places.

Trendier and less expensive is the area that has blossomed around the old **Les Halles** *quartier.* The Forum des Halles, a vast, underground shopping mall, combines designer boutiques with colorful, avant-garde fashion, plus furniture, *batterie de cuisine* and interesting home accessories. Adjacent streets are jammed with a collection of original shops with offbeat merchandise, although quality and price are less likely to go hand in hand.

A little farther on, the **Marais quarter** has become very fashionable, but in a more elegant and discreet way. Designer clothing boutiques are to be found alongside art galleries, antique dealers and traditional craftsmen. This is also a splendid spot for a casual stroll, in an area of narrow streets bordered by magnificently restored 17th and 18thC mansions.

The area surrounding **place de la Bastille** remains in a state of flux despite the completion of the Opéra Bastille, although its new status is already reflected in the number of art galleries that have opened up. Still on the Right Bank, the bustling **rue de Passy**, in the smart 16ᵉ, is worth a look, as it offers a choice of both classic and up-to-the-minute ready-to-wear fashions at prices lower than you might expect.

On the **Left Bank**, the whole of the **St-Germain quarter** is fairly bursting with designer fashion boutiques for those who dress young. The quarter extends all along the **blvd. St-Germain** as far w as rue du Bac. There is also a very lively concentration of shops around the **Odéon** and in the little streets around **rue de Seine**.

USEFUL TO KNOW

- **OPENING HOURS**   Department stores remain open from 9.30am-6.30pm Monday to Saturday, and some are open until 8pm on Wednesday. Smaller boutiques generally open Monday to Saturday 10am-7pm, although they may close for an hour at lunch. Although neighborhood shops often observe the traditional Monday closing, shops in the center stay open. And, although August was once the universal vacation month, most of the larger shops now remain open throughout the summer.

- **TAX REFUNDS**   Foreign visitors should ask for the *détaxe,* a refund of the French excise tax (13 percent or 16 percent, depending on the item), if spending over a certain amount. If you are an EC resident, you need to spend 4,200 francs per *item,* but for non-EC residents (e.g., Americans) the terms are much more generous, with a spend of only 2,000 francs per *shop* needed in order to qualify. The tax is returnable once you have left the country with your purchases. Remember that you will need your passport for this type of purchase. (See CUSTOMS on page 39 for a reminder of the rules.)

- **"DUTY-FREE"**   Many shops advertise "duty-free" *(hors-taxes)* goods, meaning that tax is deducted from the price on the spot. Be wary of this, however, for the basic price may have been raised. It is often worth shopping around, particularly when buying perfumes and choosing designer accessories.

- **SALES**   Look out for the word *Soldes,* which means Sales. In the current, Europe-wide financial gloom, you may see this even more often than the normal January and June periods.

- **SHIPPING**   Many stores are pleased to arrange to ship certain items home, and will look after the paperwork for you. If you want to mail home smaller items, it is useful to know that you can buy strong boxes made of card at any post office.

- **CLOTHING SIZES** are infuriatingly different in the US/ UK/Europe. If in any doubt, turn to the useful **clothing sizes chart** near the end of the book.

- **VOCABULARY:** The means to communicate clearly is essential when you're shopping. Turn to WORDS AND PHRASES near the end of the book for a host of typical words, questions, responses and requests in French and English.

ABOUT THIS CHAPTER

In the 18 pages that follow, there is detailed shopping information covering the following subjects:

- CLOTHING AND ACCESSORIES (Women's clothing; Couturier boutiques; *Haute couture;* Men's clothing; Unisex and junior fashion; Children's clothing; Hats; Jewelry; Leather goods; Lingerie; Shoes; Bargains)

- ANTIQUES; COOKWARE; DEPARTMENT STORES; DRUGSTORES; FOOD AND DRINK; GIFTS; HOUSEHOLD ACCESSORIES; MARKETS; MUSEUM SHOPS; PERFUME AND COSMETICS; TEXTILES; TOYS.

CLOTHING AND ACCESSORIES

Women's clothing

Paris is renowned for its fashion stores, which are liberally scattered in every part of the city. A selection of recommended boutiques is listed here, but you will certainly make your own discoveries. Refer to page 63 for a breakdown of areas.

AGNES B
3 rue du Jour, 1ᵉʳ. Map 8G9. Métro: Les Halles.
Smart quilted coats, and sportswear in wild colors.

AZZEDINE ALAÏA
7 rue de Moussy, 4ᵉ. Map 9I10. Métro: Hôtel-de-Ville.
Glamorous designs, based around stretch fabrics and leathers, from a creator whose background is in *haute couture.*

ANASTASIA
18 rue de l'Ancienne-Comédie, 6ᵉ. Map 8I8. Métro: Odéon.
Capes, romantic country clothes with a Russian flair.

ARMANI
6 pl. Vendôme, 8ᵉ. Map 7G7. Métro: Opéra.
Soft, classical elegance, with a fitting price tag.

AUTOUR DU MONDE
12 rue des Francs-Bourgeois, 8ᵉ. Map 10I11. Métro: Saint-Paul.
Fashionable sportswear for the younger generation.

DOROTHÉE BIS
17 rue de Sèvres, 6ᵉ. Map 13J7. Métro: Sèvres-Babylone. 10 rue Tronchet, 9ᵉ. Map 7F7. Métro: Madeleine. Forum des Halles, 1ᵉʳ. Map 9H9. Métro: Châtelet-Les-Halles.
Young, inventive clothes in bright colors and avant-garde styles.

BOUTIQUE LACOSTE
372 rue St-Honoré, 8ᵉ. Map 7G6. Métro: Concorde.
The entire range of Lacoste clothes and luggage is available here, all emblazoned with that instantly recognizable crocodile.

CACHAREL
165 rue de Rennes, 6ᵉ. Map 13J7. Métro: St-Sulpice. 34 rue Tronchet, 9ᵉ. Map 7F7. Métro: Madeleine. 7 rue de Passy, 16ᵉ. Map 5H1. Métro: Passy.
Young, classical clothes that are never quite in or out of style.

CHANTAL THOMASS
5 rue du Vieux Colombier, 6ᵉ. Map 13J7. Métro: St-Sulpice.
Revival of very sexy and feminine styles for women of just about every generation. See also LINGERIE entry on page 252.

CHLOÉ
60 rue du Faubourg-St-Honoré, 1ᵉʳ. Map 7F6. Métro: Concorde.
Casual yet deluxe ready-to-wear.

CORINE COBSON
28 place du Marché St-Honoré, 1ᵉʳ. Map 7G7. Métro: Pyramides.
Bubbly fashion knitwear.

COMME DES GARÇONS
40 rue Étienne Marcel, 2ᵉ. Map 9G9. Métro: Étienne Marcel.
This is still Japan's most strikingly original fashion house, with beautifully-made clothes.

COULOUNTJIOS ✿
2 rue Pasquier, 8ᵉ. Map 7F6. Métro: Madeleine.
Exciting furs with attractive hand-painted linings.

INÈS DE LA FRESSANGE
81 rue des Sts-Pères, 6ᵉ. Map 7I7. Métro: St-Germain-des-Prés.
Real Parisian chic — a complete range of clothing and accessories with the aristocratic designer touch.

JEAN PAUL GAULTIER
6 rue Vivienne, 2e. Map 8F8. Métro: Bourse.
Provocative and up-to-the-minute.

ROMÉO GIGLI
46 rue de Sévigné, 3e. Map 10I11. Métro: St-Paul.
Flowing lines and fine fabrics make the creations of this Italian designer into real works of art. High prices.

IRIÉ
8 rue du Pré-aux-Clercs, 7e. Map 7I7. Métro: St-Germain-des-Prés.
Flowing materials and printed silks, Japanese-style.

KENZO
3 pl. des Victoires, 2e. Map 8G8. Métro: Bourse.
Still considered to be one of Paris's most innovative designers, Kenzo originates offbeat styles that are often later adopted by other couturiers.

LAÏMOUN ✿
2 rue de Tournon, 6e. Map 14J8. Métro: Odéon.
Everything here is designed in Lebanon and is finely crafted from beautiful, hand-woven fabrics. Casually elegant day wear, sumptuous caftan-style gowns and an extensive range of unusual accessories.

LOLITA LEMPICKA
3bis rue des Rosiers, 4e. Map 10I11. Métro: St-Paul.
Feminine and romantic styles, mainly in pastel colours.

ISSEY MIYAKÉ
3 pl. des Vosges, 4e. Map 10I11. Métro: St-Paul.
Sculptural creations that cleverly use fabrics with Japanese-paper-style folds.

THIERRY MUGLER
10 pl. des Victoires, 2e. Map 8G8. Métro: Bourse.
Tough chic.

MAUD PERL
47 quai des Grands Augustins, 6e. Map 8I8.
Métro: Odéon, St Michel.
If you are saving your money for a Paris creation that is both elegant and versatile, this is it. Designed by Maud Perl, all the clothes are fashioned from hand-dyed silk in every texture and color you can imagine.

Every item is a well-made classic, suitable for almost any occasion.

CLAUDIE PIERLOT
23 rue du Vieux Colombier, 6e. Map 13J7. Métro: St-Sulpice.
Simple and easy-to-wear fashions, but with subtle touches that add that extra something.

GEORGES RECH ✿
54 rue Bonaparte, 6e. Map 13J7. Métro: St-Germain-des-Prés. 23 av. Victor-Hugo, 16e. Map 5F2. Métro: Charles-de-Gaulle-Étoile.
Smart, wearable clothes co-ordinated into chic, elegant ensembles.

SONIA RYKIEL
4 and 6 rue de Grenelle, 6e. Map 13J7. Métro: St-Sulpice. Also at 70 rue du Faubourg-St-Honoré, 8e. Map 7G6. Métro: Concorde.
Sleek, unlined knits and accessories, plus glamorous evening wear. Original and amusing.

VENTILO
25 rue du Louvre, 2e. Map 9G9. Métro: Sentier.
Handsome dresses and separates in unusual fabrics.

GIANI VERSACE
67 rue des Sts-Pères, 6e. Map 7I7. Métro: Sèvres-Babylone.
Highly tailored ready-to-wear outfits, with a characteristically strong Left Bank accent.

VICTOIRE
12 pl. des Victoires, 1er. Map 8G8. Métro: Bourse.
Top designers, very chic, with relaxed sales personnel. Also sell co-ordinated accessories; a real favorite with fashion editors.

YOGHI YAMAMOTO
25 rue du Louvre, 1er. Map 9G9. Métro: Étienne-Marcel.
Japanese minimalism in a collection of lovely, discreet styles. The quality is superb.

Couturier boutiques

Designers' clothing, ready-to-wear and at much lower prices than the *haute couture*, is still expensive but stunning, with high-quality styling and fabrics, and an excellent standard of workmanship. Today, couturier designs are aimed at every generation.

PIERRE BALMAIN
44 rue François-1er, 8e. Map 6G4. Métro: Franklin-D-Roosevelt.
Attractively simple and always a safe investment.

PIERRE CARDIN
27 av. Victor-Hugo, 16e. Map 5F2. Métro: Charles-de-Gaulle-Étoile.
Eccentric women's fashions; men's clothing as well.

CHANEL
31 rue Cambon, 1er. Map 7G7. Métro: Concorde.
Inimitable little suits, handbags and jewelry.

COURRÈGES
40 rue François 1er, 8e. Map 6G4. Métro: Franklin-D-Roosevelt.
Futuristic-fashions-become-classics.

CHRISTIAN DIOR
26-32 av. Montaigne, 8e. Map 6G4. Métro: Alma-Marceau.
Discreet daytime dresses, glamorous evening wear; sportswear in the boutique **Tricots**.

LOUIS FÉRAUD
2 pl. de la Porte Maillot, 17e. Map 5E1. Métro: Porte-Maillot. 88 rue du Faubourg-St-Honoré, 1er. Map 6F5. Métro: Champs-Élysées-Clemenceau.
Noted for a good selection of long gowns and glittering evening wear, Féraud is still a favorite of showbiz clients.

GIVENCHY
3 av. George-V, 8e. Map 6G4. Métro: Alma-Marceau. 66 av. Victor-Hugo, 8e. Map

5F2. Métro: Victor-Hugo.
Wide selection of classic styles.

CHRISTIAN LACROIX
73 rue du Faubourg-St-Honoré, 8e. Map 7F6. Métro: Concorde.
A whole universe of creativity, from the man who brought new life to *haute couture* in the 1980s. Beautiful accessories and jewelry, too.

LANVIN
22 rue du Faubourg-St-Honoré, 1er. Map 7G6. Métro: Concorde.
Attractive cocktail wear and evening dresses.

TED LAPIDUS
35 rue François-1er, 8e. Map 6G4. Métro: Franklin-D-Roosevelt.
Good casualwear, especially coats, and lovely fabrics. Classic and fanciful designs in a variety of colors. Several other branches.

GUY LAROCHE ♣
29 av. Montaigne, 8e. Map 6G4. Métro: Alma-Marceau.
The least expensive designers' ready-to-wear; nothing is too way out, but everything is very wearable if you like a "good," timeless look. Four other boutiques.

HANAE MORI
62 rue du Faubourg-St-Honoré, 8e. Map 7F6. Métro: Concorde.
Sumptuous silks, interpreted through a Japanese-inspired design.

NINA RICCI
39 av. Montaigne, 8e, Map 6G4. Métro:

Franklin-D-Roosevelt.
Safe fashions in beautiful fabrics. Irresistible evening accessories.

ST-LAURENT RIVE GAUCHE
6 pl. St-Sulpice, 6ᵉ. Map 13J7. Métro: St-Sulpice.
Still supreme after all these 30 years. Elegant and classic, with dash and versatility. Collectible fashions that can be built on each season.
There are four other branches.

JEAN-LOUIS SCHERRER
5 avenue Montaigne, 8ᵉ. Map 6G4. Métro: Franklin-D-Roosevelt.
The place to go for suits with an impeccable fit.

Haute couture

Opulent, made-to-measure clothing is the speciality that made the Paris fashion industry the best and most famous in the world. Each couturier has a distinct style, which can be seen during the fashion shows, normally in January (for summer) and July (for winter clothing) when the new collections are modeled for prospective clients. The collections from fall 1993 onward will be shown in the new PALAIS DE LA MODE.

Tickets for these fashion shows can be obtained through hotel *concièrges,* or directly from the couture houses, and for this purpose, telephone numbers are given below. *Concièrges* can also arrange a private video presentation of any of the main current collections.

- **Pierre Balmain**   44 rue François-1ᵉʳ, 8ᵉ ☎47-20-35-34. Map 6G4. Métro: Franklin-D-Roosevelt
- **Pierre Cardin**   27 avenue Victor Hugo, 16ᵉ ☎45-01-69-53. Map 5F2. Métro: Charles-de-Gaulle-Étoile
- **Chanel**   31 rue Cambon, 1ᵉʳ ☎42-61-54-55. Map 7G7. Métro: Concorde
- **Christian Dior**   30 avenue Montaigne, 8ᵉ ☎47-23-54-55. Map 6G4. Métro: Alma-Marceau
- **Louis Féraud**   88 rue du Faubourg-St-Honoré, 8ᵉ ☎42-65-27-29. Map 6F5. Métro: Champs-Élysées-Clemenceau
- **Christian Lacroix**   73 rue du Faubourg-St-Honoré, 8ᵉ ☎42-65-79-08. Map 7F6. Métro: Concorde
- **Ted Lapidus**   35 rue François-1ᵉʳ, 8ᵉ ☎47-20-56-14. Map 6G4. Métro: Franklin-D-Roosevelt
- **Guy Laroche**   29 avenue Montaigne, 8ᵉ ☎47-23-78-72. Map 6G4. Métro: Alma-Marceau
- **Hanae Mori**   17 avenue Montaigne, 8ᵉ ☎47-23-52-03. Map 6G4. Métro: Alma-Marceau
- **Nina Ricci**   39 avenue Montaigne, 8ᵉ ☎47-23-78-88. Map 6G4. Métro: Franklin-D-Roosevelt
- **Yves St-Laurent**   5 avenue Marceau, 16ᵉ ☎47-23-72-71. Map 5G3. Métro: Alma-Marceau
- **Jean-Louis Scherrer**   51 avenue Montaigne, 8ᵉ ☎43-59-55-39. Map 6G4. Métro: Alma-Marceau
- **Torrente**   9 rue du Faubourg-St-Honoré, 1ᵉʳ ☎42-66-14-14. Map 7G6. Métro: Concorde
- **Emmanuel Ungaro**   2 avenue Montaigne, 8ᵉ ☎47-23-61-94. Map 6G4. Métro: Alma-Marceau

Men's clothing

French styling combines English conservatism with Italian flair. Many couturiers design men's lines (for addresses see women's COUTURIER BOUTIQUES). But with a few exceptions, France is not the place to go for memorable men's clothing.

AGNÈS B. HOMMES
22 rue St-Sulpice, 6ᵉ. Map 14J8. Métro: St-Sulpice.
Male version of the famous women's and children's label. Inimitable styles that flatter many forms.

ARNYS
14 rue de Sèvres, 7ᵉ. Map 13J6. Métro: Sèvres-Babylone.
Impeccably elegant outfits of the best quality.

CERRUTI 1881
27 rue Royale, 8ᵉ. Map 7G6. Métro: Madeleine.
Traditional top-quality Italian suits.

CHARVET
28 pl. Vendôme, 1ᵉʳ. Map 7G7. Métro: Opéra.
Highly celebrated gentlemen's tailor offering a range of cravats and kerchiefs as well as suits and shirts.

EQUIPEMENT
46 rue Étienne Marcel, 2ᵉ. Map 8G9. Métro: Étienne-Marcel.
Shirts in cotton or in silk, in just about every color.

FAÇONNABLE
25 rue Royale, 8ᵉ. Map 7G6. Métro: Madeleine.
Well-cut sportswear outfits, shown in an excellent wide range of materials and colors.

ISLAND
3 rue Montmartre, 1ᵉʳ. Map 9H9. Métro: Les Halles.
Elegant sportswear — jackets, shirts, sweaters and accessories, to make a style statement or blend with your own.

MARCEL LASSANCE
17 rue du Vieux Colombier, 6ᵉ. Map 13J7. Métro: St-Sulpice.
Wide choice of tasteful styles at reasonable prices.

RALPH LAUREN
3 pl. de la Madeleine, 8ᵉ. Map 7F6. Métro: Madeleine.
Clothing from the basic to the sophisticated, tastefully presented.

THIERRY MUGLER
49 av. Montaigne, 8ᵉ. Map 6G4. Métro: Alma-Marceau.
The height of fashion, stated simply and without superfluous details.

GIANNI VERSACE
67bis rue des Sts Pères, 6ᵉ. Map 9I7. Métro: Sèvres-Babylone, St-Germain-des-Prés.
Refined Italian style.

Unisex and junior fashion

AUTOUR DU MONDE
12 rue des Francs-Bourgeois, 3ᵉ. Map 10I11. Métro: St Paul.
Casual clothes with a decidedly African flavor.

BENETTON
59 rue du Commerce, 15ᵉ. Map 11K3. Métro: Av. Émile Zola.
Benetton is . . . Benetton.

CASTELBAJAC
5 rue des Petits-Champs, 1ᵉʳ. Map 8G8. Métro: Palais-Royal Musée du Louvre.
Comfortable clothes, presented with flair. For young adults too.

CHEVIGNON
5 pl. des Victoires, 2ᵉ. Map 8G8. Métro: Palais-Royal Musée du Louvre.
Recognizably *Chevignon*; not cheap.

CHIPIE
49 rue Bonaparte, 6ᵉ. Map 7I7. Métro: St-Germain-des-Prés.
Good, casual styles. Not cheap either.

LE GARAGE
23 rue des Francs-Bourgeois, 4ᵉ. Map 10I11. Métro: St-Paul.

MARITHÉ ET FRANÇOIS GIRBAUD
38 rue Étienne Marcel, 1ᵉʳ. Map 9G9. Métro: Étienne-Marcel.

KENZO
3 pl. des Victoires, 2ᵉ. Map 8G8. Métro: Palais-Royal Musée du Louvre.
Lastingly popular for his own blend of fabrics. Readily distinguishable from the rest.

LACOSTE
2 rue de Sèvres, 6ᵉ. Map 13J7. Métro: Sèvres-Babylone.
Classic sportswear, all bearing the famous crocodile.

Children's clothing

Paris is renowned for its stylish and chic children's clothes. Exquisite layettes and hand-embroidered gowns can still be found in Paris, but children's fashions are extremely expensive. Many designers (Dior, Hechter and others) make a children's line if you want to buy something really special.

The best selection is to be found in the department stores on the Grands Boulevards, where price is acceptable and quality is just right for most children's brief needs.

AGNÈS B (ENFANTS)
2 rue du Jour, 1ᵉʳ. Map 9G9. Métro: Étienne-Marcel.
Another branch of the popular Agnès B. — this time for children.

ARTISANAT MONASTIQUE
68bis av. Denfert-Rochereau, 14ᵉ. Map 13M7. Métro: Denfert-Rochereau.

BABY DIOR
28 av. Montaigne, 8ᵉ. Map 6G4. Métro: Franklin-D-Roosevelt.
Luxurious and pricey christening outfits, as well as a range of baby clothes.

BONPOINT
67 rue de l'Université, 7ᵉ. Map 7H6. Métro: Solférino.
Classic children's wear with a demure, traditional feel.

CACHAREL
34 rue Tronchet, 9ᵉ. Map 7F7. Métro: Madeleine.

JACADI
60 blvd. de Courcelles, 17ᵉ. Map 1D4. Métro: Monceau.
Competitively priced, smart outfits with the accent on fashion.

Hats

JEAN BARTHET
13 rue Tronchet, 8ᵉ. Map 7F7. Métro: Madeleine.
The best known and most talented milliner in the capital, and supplier of headwear to the international jet-set. Custom-made and off-the-shelf lines are both available.

GÉLOT CHEZ LANVIN
15 rue du Faubourg-St-Honoré, 8ᵉ. Map

6E4. Métro: St-Philippe-du-Roule.
Headwear for male heads. Gélot's superb panamas for men are widely sought after.

MARIE MERCIÉ
23 rue St-Sulpice, 6ᵉ. Map 14J8. Métro: St-Sulpice.
A designers' designer, whose creations are hailed for their wit, sensitivity and chic.

PHILIPPE MODEL
33 pl. du Marché St-Honoré, 8ᵉ. Map 7G7.
Métro: Pyramides.
Switched-on headwear fashions, plus a range of complementary accessories and shoes.

MOTSCH
42 av. Georges-V, 8ᵉ. Map 6F4. Métro: Georges-V.
This 100-year-old establishment offers a large choice of caps, trilbies and other sporting hats, all made-to-measure.

Jewelry

In Paris, even jewelry is subdivided into *haute joaillerie* and ready-to-wear. Both are extremely stylish; a wide and interesting range is offered and, compared with the rest of the world, most items are competitively priced.

The *"hautes"* are mostly clustered together around pl. Vendôme.

- **Boucheron**   26 pl. Vendôme, 1ᵉʳ. Map 7G7. Métro: Opéra, Concorde
- **Cartier**   13 rue de la Paix, 1ᵉʳ. Map 7F7. Métro: Opéra
- **Jean Dinh Van**   7 rue de la Paix, 2ᵉ. Map 7F7. Métro: Opéra
- **Ilias Lalaounis**   364 rue St-Honoré, 1ᵉʳ. Map 7G7. Métro: Opéra, Madeleine
- **Mauboussin**   20 pl. Vendôme, 1ᵉʳ. Map 7G7. Métro: Opéra, Tuileries.
- **Van Cleef et Arpels**   22 pl. Vendôme, 1ᵉʳ. Map 7G7. Métro: Opéra, Pyramides
- **Zolotas**   370 rue St-Honoré, 1ᵉʳ. Map 7G7. Métro: Madeleine, Concorde

Jewelry boutiques

Stylish and up-to-the-minute jewelry is becoming increasingly easy to find in Paris nowadays.

As well as the addresses given below, take a look in the suggested MUSEUM SHOPS (detailed on page 261) for lovely, contemporary work, especially in silver.

- **Agatha**   97 rue de Rennes, 6ᵉ. Map 13J7. Métro: Rennes
- **Eugit Amor**   11 rue des Francs-Bourgeois, 4ᵉ. Map 10I11. Métro: St-Paul
- **Isabel Canovas**   16 avenue Montaigne, 8ᵉ. Map 6G4. Métro: Alma-Marceau
- **Fabrice**   54 rue Bonaparte, 6ᵉ. Map 8I8. Métro: St-Germain-des-Prés
- **Mademoiselle Zaza**   29 boulevard Raspail, 7ᵉ. Map 13J7. Métro: Sèvres-Babylone
- **Pulcinella**   10 rue Vignon, 9ᵉ. Map 7F7. Métro: Opéra, Madeleine
- **Reminiscence**   22 rue du Four, 6ᵉ. Map 13J7. Métro: St-Germain-des-Prés, St-Sulpice
- **Utility-Bibi**   27 rue du Four, 6ᵉ. Map 13J7. Métro: St-Germain-des-Prés, St-Sulpice

Leather goods

*   **La Bagagerie** ♣   41 rue du Four, 6ᵉ. Map **14**J8. Métro: St-Germain-des-Prés. 12 rue Tronchet, 8ᵉ. Map **7**F7. Métro: Madeleine. 74 rue de Passy, 16ᵉ. Métro: Muette
*   **Hermès**   24 rue du Faubourg-St-Honoré, 1ᵉʳ. Map **7**F6. Métro: Madeleine
*   **Hervé Chapelier**   13 rue Gustave Courbet, 16ᵉ. Métro: Trocadéro
*   **Lancel**   43 rue de Rennes, 6ᵉ. Map **13**J7. Métro: St-Germain-des-Prés; another branch at: 4 rond-point des Champs-Élysées, 8ᵉ. Map **6**G5. Métro: Franklin-D-Roosevelt
*   **Lindblad**   1 pl. Alphonse Deville, 6ᵉ. Map **13**J7. Métro: Sèvres-Babylone
*   **Prada**   5 rue de Grenelle, 6ᵉ. Map **7**I7. Métro: St-Germain-des-Près
*   **Upla**   17 rue des Halles, 6ᵉ. Map **9**H9. Métro: Châtelet
*   **Louis Vuitton**   79 avenue Montaigne, 8ᵉ. Map **6**G4. Métro: Franklin-D-Roosevelt

Lingerie

To the French, beautiful underwear is considered nearly as important as outerwear. Even men's underwear is sexy. Prices are generally quite high, but the goods are worth the expense. Lingerie stores often sell bathing suits.

*   **Erès**   2 rue Tronchet, 8ᵉ. Map **7**F7. Métro: Madeleine
*   **Les Nuits d'Élodie**   1bis avenue Mac-Mahon, 17ᵉ. Map **5**E3. Métro: Charles-de-Gaulle-Étoile
*   **Capucine Puérari**   55bis rue des Sts-Pères, 6ᵉ. Map **7**I7. Métro: St-Germain-des-Prés
*   **Sabbia Rosa**   71 rue des Sts-Pères, 7ᵉ. Map **7**I7. Métro: Sèvres-Babylone
*   **Chantal Thomass**   11 rue Madame, 6ᵉ. Map **13**J7. Métro: St-Sulpice; also at 1 rue Vivienne, 1ᵉʳ. Map **8**G8. Métro: Bourse

Shoes

Most shoe stores carry goods for men and women, and many stock handbags and luggage. The well-known labels are expensive, but Paris is still a wonderful place to buy shoes, with plenty of choice of both French- and Italian-made styles.

*   **Accessoire**   6 rue du Cherche Midi, 6ᵉ. Map **13**J7. Métro: St-Sulpice
*   **Bally**   11 boulevard de la Madeleine, 1ᵉʳ. Map **7**F7. Métro: Madeleine; also at: 35 boulevard des Capucines, 9ᵉ. Map **7**F7. Métro: Opéra; 20 other branches
*   **Carel**   4 rue Tronchet, 8ᵉ. Map **7**F7. Métro: Madeleine. Various other branches
*   **Céline**   58 rue de Rennes, 6ᵉ. Map **13**J7. Métro: St-Germain-des-Prés; also at 24 rue François-1ᵉʳ, 8ᵉ. Map **6**G4. Métro:

Franklin-D-Roosevelt; and at: 3 avenue Victor-Hugo, 16e. Map **5**F2. Métro: Charles-de-Gaulle-Étoile

- **Robert Clergerie**   5 rue du Cherche Midi, 6e. Map **13**J7. Métro: St Sulpice
- **Maud Frizon**   7 rue de Grenelle, 6e. Map **13**J7. Métro: Sèvres-Babylone; 83 rue des Sts-Pères, 6e. Map **7**I7. Métro: St-Germain-des-Prés
- **Charles Jourdan**   12 rue du Faubourg-St-Honoré, 8e. Map **7**G6. Métro: Concorde; also at 5 boulevard de la Madeleine, 1er. Map **7**F7. Métro: Madeleine; and at 86 avenue des Champs-Élysées, 8e. Map **6**F4. Métro: Franklin-D-Roosevelt
- **Stephane Kélian**   62 rue des Sts-Pères, 6e. Map **7**I7. Métro: St-Germain-des-Prés; also at: Forum des Halles, 1er. Map **8**H4. Métro: Châtelet-Les-Halles; and 6 pl. des Victoires, 1er. Map **8**G8. Métro: Palais-Royal Musée du Louvre
- **Tokio Kumagai**   52 rue Croix-des-Petits-Champs, 1er. Map **8**G8. Métro: Palais-Royal Musée du Louvre
- **Mancini**   72 avenue Victor-Hugo, 16e. Map **5**F2. Métro: Victor-Hugo. Ready-made + made-to-measure shoes (allow at least 2 weeks)
- **Laurent Mercadal**   3 pl. des Victoires, 1er. Map **9**G8. Métro: Palais-Royal Musée du Louvre
- **Andrea Pfister**   4 rue Cambon, 1er. Map **7**G7. Métro: Concorde; 56 rue du Four, 6e. Map **14**J8. Métro: Mabillon
- **St-Laurent**   See COUTURIER BOUTIQUES
- **Pucci Verdi**   68 rue des Sts-Pères, 6e. Map **7**I7. Métro: St-Sulpice, St-Germain-des-Prés

Bargains

Couturiers and ready-to-wear designers often sell last season's styles at half-price. They may appear without the original labels *(dégriffé)*.

Rue St-Placide, 6e *(Métro: Sèvres-Babylone)* and rue d'Alésia, 14e *(Métro: Alésia)* are lined with discount stores for men, women and children.

ANNA LOEWE
*35 av. Matignon, 8e. Map **6**F5. Métro: Miromesnil, Franklin D. Roosevelt.*
Prestige labels and *haute couture* at a quarter of the normal price.

AZZEDINE ALAÏA ♣
*18 rue de la Verrerie, 4e. Map **9**I10. Métro: Hôtel de Ville.*
Last year's collection at half price.

BAB'S ♣
*89bis av. des Ternes, 17e. Map **5**D2. Métro: Porte-Maillot. 29 av. Marceau, 16e. Map **5**G3. Métro: Alma-Marceau.*

Designer-wear by Nina Ricci, Guy Laroche and others. Gorgeous silk blouses.

BIDERMANN ♣
*114 rue de Turenne, 3e. Map **10**H11. Métro: Filles-du-Calvaire.*
Suits for men by St-Laurent and others.

DOROTHÉE BIS STOCK ♣
76 rue d'Alésia, 14e. Métro: Alésia.
Clothing and accessories from designer J. Jacobson. The Doroténis sportswear label can be picked up in the boutique next door.

MENDÈS YVES SAINT-LAURENT
65 rue Montmartre, 1er. Map 8F9. Métro: Rue Montmartre.
Half-price sale of suits, dresses and other end-of-range clothing from the YSL Rive Gauche collections.

LE MOUTON À 5 PATTES ✿
8-10 and 48 rue St-Placide, 6e. Map 13J6&7. Métro: St-Placide.
All sorts of bargains for men, women, girls and younger children, are to be found in this shop, which sells everything from last year's shoes and boots to imperceptibly flawed suits and dresses.

LA SOLDERIE
85 rue la Boétie, 8e. Map 6F4. Métro: St-Augustin.
Goods by high-class couturiers, such as St-Laurent and Chanel, at cut prices.

ANTIQUES
Whether you're a browser or intent on purchasing, there are three main areas to concentrate on.
* The **Louvre des Antiquaires** 2 pl. du Palais-Royal, 1er. Map **8**H8. Métro: Palais-Royal. Around 250 dealers all in one location.
* **Village Suisse** 56 avenue de la Motte-Picquet (at av. de Suffren), 7e. Map **11**J3. Métro: La Motte-Picquet-Grenelle. Over 100 shops.
* Out on the streets this time, to the **St-Germain** quarter, where you will find a number of small antique stores offering all kinds of memorabilia at all kinds of prices. Check out the **rue Bonaparte**, **rue Jacob** and **quai Malaquais** axis.
* See also MARKETS (page 260) for addresses of flea markets.

COOKWARE
Paris is a cook's heaven. No other city can compete with the array of food-related objects, often cheaper than and sometimes simply unobtainable elsewhere. Department stores all have large cookware departments, but it is more fun to go directly to the major specialists. Be prepared to pay cash, and ask for shipping and *détaxe* information.

DEHILLERIN ✿
18 rue Coquillière, 1er. Map 8G9. Métro: Étienne-Marcel.
Perhaps the best restaurant supply house in the world, but also sells happily on a smaller scale. Outstanding buys in copper, carbon steel knives, casseroles. Free catalog in English. Excellent shipping service.

KITCHEN BAZAAR
11 av. du Maine, 15e. Map 13K6. Métro: Gare-Montparnasse.
Everything you could want in the way of modern and decorative kitchen equipment and accessories, from an electric carving knife to a traditional French-style dishwashing mitten.

MORA
13 rue Montmartre, 1er. Map 8G9. Métro: Étienne-Marcel, Les Halles.
Smaller selection is offered than at the Dehillerin supply house, but this is still a shop for true professionals. You may find the cool, even casual service difficult to take, but be persistent.

A. SIMON
36 rue Étienne-Marcel, 2e. Map 8G9. Métro: Étienne-Marcel, Les Halles.
Divided into two shops: one with metalware, knives and electrical appliances, the other devoted to pottery, glassware and a reasonable selection of porcelain. Colorful displays and helpful staff make shopping here a pleasure.

DEPARTMENT STORES

Paris has a number of excellent department stores *(grands magasins)* where you can spend the day doing some one-stop shopping. Many offer special discounts for tourists, and have staff geared to handling export documentation.

BAZAR DE L'HÔTEL DE VILLE ♣
55 rue de la Verrerie, 4ᵉ. Map 9I10. Métro: Hôtel-de-Ville.
Excellent sporting goods, garden tools, books, records, and a dazzling array of hardware.

BON MARCHÉ
38 rue de Sèvres, 7ᵉ. Map 13J6. Métro: Sèvres-Babylone.
A true department store comprising fresh foods along with clothing, home furnishings and a wide selection of linens.

FNAC ♣
Forum des Halles, 1ᵉʳ; map 9H9; métro: Châtelet-Les-Halles; also at 136 rue de Rennes, 14ᵉ; map 13K6; métro: Montparnasse-Bienvenüe. 26 av. de Wagram, 8ᵉ; map 5E3; métro: Ternes.
This shop sells discount records, books, small appliances, sports goods and photo equipment. The Forum shop specializes in records, audiovisual supplies, photo goods and sports goods; Montparnasse concentrates on video and books; and av. Wagram stocks the largest selection of audiovisual goods to be found in Paris.

GALERIES LAFAYETTE
40 blvd. Haussmann, 9ᵉ. Map 7F7. Métro: Chaussée-d'Antin-Lafayette, Auber; Maine-Montparnasse Centre, 14ᵉ. Map 13K6. Métro: Montparnasse-Bienvenüe.
A serious attempt to update its fashion image has succeeded in turning both branches of this store into trendy fashion spots, with vast home furnishings departments and a wide selection

of porcelain, glassware and cookware. A variety of good, slick ideas, and an abundance of color. Fashion shows are held weekly *(information and reservations from hotel concierges or ☎ 48-74-02-30)*. Generous visitor discounts are available from time to time. Call at the ground floor Welcome Desk to see what's on offer.

LE PRINTEMPS
64 blvd. Haussmann, 9ᵉ. Map 7F7. Métro: Havre-Caumartin, Auber.
Elegant, with deluxe ready-to-wear on the *Rue de la Mode*, and a magnificent stained-glass cupola that is a historical monument. Wide range of lingerie, gourmet boutiques, and a top-floor restaurant, the **Brasserie Flo** (see RESTAURANTS), renowned for its Art Nouveau decor. Weekly fashion shows.

SAMARITAINE ♣
Pont Neuf, 1ᵉʳ. Map 8H9. Métro: Pont-Neuf.
An old-fashioned shop noted for its uniforms (chefs' clothes and bartenders' outfits), sports goods and household items. The 10th story of Magasin 2 provides an unparalleled panoramic view over the city. Have coffee and gaze.

AUX TROIS QUARTIERS
17 blvd. de la Madeleine, 8ᵉ. Map 7F7. Métro: Madeleine.
This traditional store was lavishly renovated several years ago, and now aims at the deluxe market. As well as designer labels such as Kenzo, Dorothée Bis, Kélian etc, they have a wide selection of gifts, accessories and linens. Worldwide shipping service.

DRUGSTORES

These have nothing to do with American-style drugstores, although they all have pharmacies. The **Drugstores Publicis** are mini-shopping centers, meeting places and classy emergency shops, which often in-

clude movie theaters and restaurants among their distractions. Open daily 9am-2am, they have counters devoted to books, perfume, food, gifts, toys and tobacco. Excellent selection of newspapers and periodicals in foreign languages. There are branches at:
- 149 boulevard St-Germain 6e, map 7I7. Métro: St-Germain-des-Prés
- 133 avenue des Champs-Élysées 8e, map 5F3. Métro: George-V
- 1 avenue Matignon 8e, map 6F5. Métro: Franklin-D-Roosevelt

FOOD AND DRINK
Every neighborhood has *charcuteries*, selling pork products, prepared foods and a bit of everything, and its *fromageries, caves* and *pâtisseries*. The area around place de la Madeleine is particularly exciting.

ANDROUËT
41 rue d'Amsterdam, 8e. Map 2E7. Métro: St-Lazare.
Owned by Pierre Androuet, this shop is a temple to cheese. Special boxes for traveling.

BARTHÉLÉMY
51 rue de Grenelle, 7e. Map 7I6. Métro: Rue-du-Bac.
Tiny shop outlet for this famed specialist in mature cheeses who is appointed supplier to the Élysée palace.

BATTENDIER
8 rue Coquillière, 1er. Map 8G9. Métro: Étienne-Marcel.
A chic *charcuterie* known for its sausages, ham and pâtés.

BERTILLON
31 rue St-Louis-en-l'Île, 4e. Map 9J10. Métro: Pont-Marie.
Superb ice cream and sorbets, made from the freshest fruits, which change with the seasons.

CAVES DE LA MADELEINE
Passage Berryer, 24 rue Boissy d'Anglas, 8e. Map 7G6. Métro: Madeleine.
This shop is nestled in a delightful mews and run by Englishman Steven Spurrier. A wide selection of wines and liquor. Gift-wrapping and a delivery service.

DALLOYAU
99-101 rue du Faubourg-St-Honoré, 8e. Map 7F6. Métro: Madeleine.
Caterer of high repute for chocolates, *pâtés* and other delicacies.

FAUCHON
28 pl. de la Madeleine, 8e. Map 7F6. Métro: Madeleine.
One of the world's most celebrated food stores, with three large boutiques, including one with a restaurant, Fauchon carries more than 20,000 products. Also a mini-Fauchon, open until 10pm. Wonderful gift service; will ship anywhere.

LA FERME ST-HUBERT
21 rue Vignon, 8e. Map 7F7. Métro: Madeleine.
Superb cheeses; helpful service.

FOIE GRAS LUXE
26 rue Montmartre, 1er. Map 8F9. Métro: Rue Montmartre.
Foie gras and smoked salmon at wholesale prices.

FOUQUET
32 rue François 1er, 8e. Map 6G4. Métro: Franklin-D-Roosevelt.
A wide range of coffees, condiments and other quality products.

GANACHAUD
150 rue de Ménilmontant, 20e. Métro: Couronnes.
Indisputably the best bread in Paris mixed by the best baker in France. Specializes in *flûtes* (thin *baguette*) but they also sell a good range of cakes and *petits fours*.

HÉDIARD
21 pl. de la Madeleine, 8ᵉ. Map 7F6. Métro: Madeleine.
A smaller Fauchon, with exotic products and spices, rare fruits and an outstanding wine selection. Five Paris branches.

JADIS ET GOURMANDE
27 rue Boissy d'Anglas, 8ᵉ. Map 7G6. Métro: Concorde.
Chocolates that are every bit as good to look at as they are to eat.

LABEYRIE
6 rue Montmartre, 2ᵉ. Map 8G9. Métro: Étienne-Marcel.
Foie gras, truffles, *confits* of duck and goose, and all the wonderful foods of the Landes region.

LEGRAND ♣
1 rue de la Banque, 2ᵉ. Map 8G8. Métro: Bourse.
They sell reasonably priced wines and alcohol, and some interesting culinary products.

LENÔTRE
44 rue d'Auteuil, 16ᵉ. Métro: Michelange-Auteuil.
Now a famous chef, Lenôtre was first a caterer and then became a really outstanding *pâtissier*. Excellent chocolates, ice cream and prepared food.

MAISON DU MIEL
24 rue Vignon, 8ᵉ. Map 7F7. Métro: Madeleine.
Fragrant and flavorsome honeys from every French province.

MAISON DE LA TRUFFE
19 pl. de la Madeleine, 8ᵉ. Map 7F6. Métro: Madeleine.
Truffles, of course, and an astounding selection of *charcuterie*.

MARIAGES FRÈRES
30 rue du Bourg-Tibourg, 4ᵉ. Map 9I10. Métro: Hôtel-de-Ville.
The only tea stockist that can compete with the London outlets. 400 varieties, originating from 30 countries, plus a range of their own blends, books and fantastic teapots.

ALBERT MENÈS
41 blvd. Malesherbes, 8ᵉ. Map 7F6. Métro: St-Augustin.
This delicatessen offers excellent preserves, condiments and candies.

LE PETIT BACCHUS
13, rue du Cherche Midi, 6ᵉ. Map 13J7. Métro: St-Sulpice.
150 different wines, selected by Steven Spurrier.

PÉTROSSIAN
18 blvd. de La Tour-Maubourg, 7ᵉ. Map 12H5. Métro: Latour-Maubourg.
The finest caviars, smoked fish . . . and Russian vodka.

PIÈTREMENT
58 rue Jean-Jacques Rousseau, 1ᵉʳ. Map 9G9. Métro: Les Halles.
Foie gras, truffles, dried mushrooms.

POILÂNE
8 rue du Cherche Midi, 6ᵉ; map 13J7; métro: St-Sulpice; also at: 49 blvd. de Grenelle, 16ᵉ; map 11I2; métro: Bir-Hakeim; and at Forum des Halles, 1ᵉʳ; map 9H9; métro: Châtelet-Les Halles.
Baked in wood-fueled ovens and containing no preservatives, Lionel Poilâne's crusty loaves are the best in Paris.

SOLEIL DE PROVENCE
6 rue du Cherche Midi, 6ᵉ. Map 13J7. Métro: St-Sulpice.
Sunny merchandise, indeed: fruity olive oil, honeys and olive oil soap.

Food markets

Every neighborhood has its street market selling mainly food. Straw baskets and kitchen gadgets can also be good buys.

In addition there are several streets known for outdoor food stores, primarily **rue Mouffetard** *(5ᵉ, map 15K10, Métro: Censier-Daubenton)* and **rue Cler** *(7ᵉ, map 12 I4, Métro: École-Militaire).*

The following are some of the better, more central markets: **avenue President-Wilson** *(16ᵉ, map 5 G3, Métro: Alma-Marceau);* **avenue de Saxe** *(7ᵉ, map 12 J4, Métro: Ségur);* **boulevard de Grenelle** *(15ᵉ, map 11 J3, Métro: La Motte-Picquet-Grenelle);* **Cité Berryer** *(26 rue Royale, 8ᵉ, map 7 G6, Métro: Madeleine, Concorde).*

GIFTS

AU CHAT DORMANT
13 rue du Cherche Midi, 6ᵉ. Map 13 J7. Métro: St-Placide.
A cats-only boutique, selling everything feline, from pillows to postcards. A collector's dream.

AXIS
18 rue Guénégaud, 6ᵉ. Map 8 I8. Métro: Odéon.
Traditional and futuristic gadgetry.

BEAUTÉ DIVINE
40 rue St-Sulpice, 6ᵉ. Map 14 J8. Métro: St-Sulpice.
Old-fashioned beauty accessories. Ask for their gift-wrap service, to have your goods wrapped in their fragrant *tricolore* silk paper.

CASA LOPEZ
32-36 galerie Vivienne, 2ᵉ. Map 8 G8. Métro: Bourse.
Flowers, floral wreaths and baskets of fruit — a large selection of *petit-point* canvases ready to embroider.

CHRISTIAN TORTU
13 rue St-Florentin, 6ᵉ. Map 7 G6. Métro: Concorde.
Vendors of sublime floral bouquets that blend together aromatic plants, garden flowers and unusual vegetable forms.

JARDINS IMAGINAIRES
9bis rue d'Assas, 6ᵉ. Map 13 J7. Métro: Sèvres-Babylone.
Anything to do with the garden, plus paintings, vases, potpourri.

JULES DES PRÉS
19 rue du Cherche Midi, 6ᵉ. Map 13 J7. Métro: Sèvres-Babylone.
Decorative creations entirely to do with

plants, plus an excellent choice of spices and individual *pot pourri.*

LESCÈNE-DURA
63 rue de la Verrerie, 4ᵉ. Map 9 I10. Métro: Hôtel-de-Ville.
Equipped to satisfy the needs of the most accomplished cellarman; fancy barrels, bistro glasses, corks, thermometers, wine-growers' charts etc . . . plus 60 different kinds of corkscrew.

GENEVIÈVE LETHU
Forum des Halles (level 2), 1ᵉʳ. Map 9 H9. Métro: Châtelet-les Halles.
Everything for house and kitchen.

LES LUNES NOIRES
Louvre des Antiquaires, 2 pl. du Palais Royal, 1ᵉʳ. Map 8 H8. Métro: Palais-Royal Musée du Louvre.
A large choice of collectible fans from the 17th-20thC.

MOKUBA
18 rue Montmartre, 1ᵉʳ. Map 9 G9. Métro: Les Halles.
A modern temple dedicated to ribbons, in every conceivable width, material and color.

FLORENT MONESTIER
47bis av. Bosquet, 7ᵉ. Map 12 I4. Métro: École-Militaire.
A wide range of designer gadgets at a wider range of prices.

NOUEZ-MOI
27 rue des Sablons, 16ᵉ. Off map 5 G1. Métro: Trocadéro.
A jolly miscellany whose shelves are crowded with tableware, frames and boxes, plus a section devoted entirely to party goods.

PAPIER PLUS
9 rue du Pont Louis Philippe, 4ᵉ. Map 9I10. Métro: Pont-Marie.
Writing paper by the sheet, notebooks, photograph albums, all in a delightful range of subtle colors.

SOULEÏADO
78 rue de Seine, 6ᵉ. Map 14J8. Métro: Odéon.
Household linens and other objects, and shirts made with beautiful Provençal fabrics.

STERN
47 passage des Panoramas, blvd. Montmartre, 9ᵉ. Map 8F9. Métro: Rue-Montmartre.
One-time supplier to Napoleon III and the European nobility, the house of Stern has kept up its tradition of hand-engraving. Go there for visiting cards, letterheads and *ex libris* labels.

TERRITOIRE
30 rue Boissy d'Anglas, 8ᵉ. Map 7F6. Métro: Madeleine.
Stocks change according to the seasons, so look for ideas for the home and the garden. The children's department sports a wonderful collection of old, refurbished toys.

H G THOMAS
36 blvd. St-Germain, 5ᵉ. Map 15J10. Métro: Maubert Mutualité.
Every kind of gift for men.

VIRUS
32 rue du Bourg-Tibourg, 4ᵉ. Map 9I10. Métro: Hôtel-de-Ville.
A tiny shop selling nothing but kites, in every style and color, from the childish to the sophisticated.

HOUSEHOLD ACCESSORIES, CHINA, GLASS AND SILVER

AU BAIN MARIE
12 rue Boissy d'Anglas 8ᵉ. Map 7G6. Métro: Concorde.
Charming, old-fashioned objects and linens.

BACCARAT
30bis rue de Paradis, 10ᵉ. Map 4E10. Métro: Château-d'Eau.
World-renowned crystal, beautiful gifts. Also a fascinating museum of the history of crystal.

CHRISTOFLE
12 rue Royale, 8ᵉ. Map 7G6. Métro: Madeleine.
Magnificent silver flatware in modern and retro patterns.

DAUM
4 rue de la Paix, 2ᵉ. Map 7G7. Métro: Opéra.
Creations in colored glass, by contemporary artists.

DINERS EN VILLE
27 rue de Varenne, 7ᵉ. Map 7I5. Métro: Varenne.
Porcelain, glassware and silver — everything for the gourmet table — attractively displayed, with a mixture of famous brands and individual makers.

GIEN
39 Rue des Petits-Champs, 1ᵉʳ. Map 8G8. Métro: Bourse.
A stockist of traditional French crockery that also sells creations by contemporary craftsmen.

LALIQUE
11 rue Royale, 8ᵉ. Map 7G6. Métro: Madeleine.
Collection of crystal, particularly frosted Art Nouveau and Deco patterns.

LIMOGES-UNIC ♣
12 and 58 rue de Paradis, 10ᵉ. Map 4E10. Métro: Château-d'Eau.
Outlet for France's famed porcelain, at bargain prices.

PETER
191 rue du Faubourg-St-Honoré, 8ᵉ. Map 6E4. Métro: Ternes.
Exclusive table settings. Specialist for 200 years.

PUIFORCAT
2 av. Matignon, 8ᵉ. Map 6F5. Métro: Franklin-D-Roosevelt.
World-famous silversmith noted for well-designed silver and silver plate.

QUARTZ
12 rue des Quatres-Vents, 6ᵉ. Map 14J8. Métro: Odéon.

Contemporary glassware of the very highest quality.

XANADOU
10 rue St-Sulpice, 6ᵉ. Map 14J8. Métro: Odéon.
A selection of household items — teapots, glasses, ashtrays etc. — designed, curiously, by famous 20thC architects.

MARKETS

Each weekend Paris blossoms with flea markets on the periphery, selling antiques of varying quality, old clothes, books, and just plain junk. Open Saturday, Sunday and sometimes Monday, they invite bargaining.

Most vendors will not accept charge or credit cards, but many will gladly ship their merchandise worldwide.

The most famous flea market is the MARCHÉ AUX PUCES at St-Ouen, where major antique dealers can be found alongside more humble dealers in second-hand items and bric-à-brac stalls. If you are interested in a serious shopping visit, buy a copy of the official guide, which lists stallholders according to type. It is published in English and Japanese, as well as French (☎ 40-12-93-21 to obtain a copy).

But Paris can offer other open-air shopping experiences too, notably its riverside booksellers *(bouquinistes)* on the Left Bank. Some markets are for spending money in; others offer superb photographic opportunities, or are worth visiting simply for the sights and sounds.

See page 257, and TEXTILES on page 262.

Animals

- **Quai du Louvre** and **quai de la Mégisserie**   1ᵉʳ. Map 8H8 and I9. Métro: Palais-Royal Musée du Louvre, Pont-Neuf.

Birds

- **Pl. Louis-Lépine**   4ᵉ. Map 8I9. Métro: Cité. Sunday only.

Booksellers *(bouquinistes)*

- **Quais des Grands-Augustins**, **Conti** and **Malaquais**   6ᵉ. Map 8I8. Métro: St-Michel
- **Quai du Louvre** and **quai de la Mégisserie**   1ᵉʳ. Map 8H8 and I9. Métro: Palais-Royal Musée du Louvre, Pont-Neuf
- **Quai Voltaire**   6ᵉ. Map 7H7. Métro: Musée d'Orsay

Flea markets

- **Marché d'Aligre**   pl. d'Aligre, 12ᵉ. Map 16J13. Métro: Ledru-Rollin. Open daily. A small and rather expensive market.
- **Puces de Didot**   avenue Georges Lafenêstre, 14ᵉ. Métro: Porte-de-Vanves.
- **Puces de St-Ouen**   18ᵉ. Métro: Porte de Clignancourt.

- **Puces de Vanves** 14e. Métro: Porte de Vanves. Better bargains to be found here. Open Saturday, Sunday, Monday, but primarily Saturday morning for bric-a-brac.

Flowers
- **Place Louis-Lépine** quai de la Corse, 4e. Map **8I9**. Métro: Cité.
- **Place de la Madeleine** 1er. Map **7F6**. Métro: Madeleine.
- **Place des Ternes** 8e. Map **5E3**. Métro: Ternes.

Stamps and postcards
- **Avenue Gabriel** 1er. Map **6F5**. Métro: Franklin-D-Roosevelt. Open Thursday, Saturday, Sunday from 10am.

MUSEUM SHOPS
Some very attractive designer goods can be found in some of the larger museums and galleries, and they offer an interesting range of contemporary artefacts and reproduction goods, as well as a good choice of books, cards etc.

Each has merchandise specifically geared toward the likely interests of its own visitors. Such shops are generally inside the museum or gallery doors but before you reach the ticket desk, so casual visits are possible without visiting the exhibit. Seriously worth a detour.

The best of the museum shops are to be found at:

CENTRE GEORGES POMPIDOU	MUSÉE D'ART MODERNE DE
MUSÉE DU LOUVRE	LA VILLE DE PARIS
MUSÉE D'ORSAY	MUSÉE DES ARTS DÉCORATIFS

PERFUME AND COSMETICS
Many shops offer "duty-free" perfumes, meaning that the price is lowered by the excise tax; others just offer discounts. Comparison-shopping is useful, since the best prices are at the duty-free airport shop, although the selection there is certainly more limited.

Dozens of shops surround the Opéra, all selling the major brands of cosmetics and perfumes. The following indicates where the slightly more unusual shops are to be found.
- **L'Artisan Parfumeur** 84bis rue de Grenelle, 6e. Map **7I6**. Métro: Rue-du-Bac. Charming, unusual scents such as grapefruit and cinnamon, lovely potpourris and gifts for men and women.
- **Caron** 34 avenue Montaigne, 8e. Map **6G4**. Métro: Franklin-D-Roosevelt.
- **Dans un Jardin** 71 rue la Boétie, 8e. Map **6F5**. Métro: St-Philippe-du-Roule. Custom-made perfumes and unusual gifts.
- **Diptyque** 34 boulevard St-Germain, 5e. Map **15J10**. Métro: Maubert-Mutualité
- **Annick Goutal** 14 rue de Castiglione, 1er. Map **7G7**. Métro: Tuileries
- **Guerlain** 68 avenue des Champs-Élysées, 8e. Map **5F3**. Métro:

George-V; also at: 2 pl. Vendôme, 1er. Map **7**G7. Métro: Tuileries; and at: 29 rue de Sèvres, 6e. Map **13**J7. Métro: Sèvres-Babylone.

* **Séphora**   Forum des Halles (level 1), 1er. Map **9**H9. Métro: Les Halles
* **Sur la Place**   12 pl. St-Sulpice, 6e. Map **13**J7. Métro: St-Sulpice. Old-fashioned bath jellies, Breton algae, natural beauty products.
* **Michel Swiss ♣**   16 rue de la Paix, 1er. Map **7**F7. Métro: Opéra.

TEXTILES

The backbone of the fashion industry, French textiles are sumptuous, beautifully designed and often very reasonably priced.

* **Alexandra**   95 rue du Faubourg-St-Honoré, 8e. Map **7**G6. Métro: Concorde.
* **Bouchara ♣**   54 boulevard Haussmann, 9e. Map **7**F7. Métro: Havre-Caumartin. Five other branches also.
* **Marché St-Pierre** (open-air)   pl. St-Pierre, 18e. Map **3**D9. Métro: Anvers.
* **Max**   70 avenue des Champs-Élysées, 8e. Map **6**F4. Métro: George-V.
* **Rodin**   36 avenue des Champs-Élysées, 8e. Map **6**F4. Métro: Franklin-D-Roosevelt.

TOYS

French toys can be sophisticated, well designed and expensive. Internationally-known toys, like Lego, cost considerably more than at home.

ALI-BABA
*29 av. de Tourville, 7e. Map **12**I4. Métro: École Militaire.*
A huge choice of toys for all ages. They specialize in lead soldiers.

LE CIEL EST À TOUT LE MONDE
*10 rue Gay-Lussac, 5e. Map **14**K8. Métro: Luxembourg.*
Everything that can fly: saucers, airplanes, kites.

FARANDOLE
*48 av. Victor-Hugo, 16e. Map **5**F2. Métro: Victor-Hugo.*
Two floors of scientific and classic toys, and they also have some rather astonishing gasoline-engine cars for older children.

JOUETS ET COMPAGNIE
*1} blvd. de Sébastopol, 1er. Map **9**H9. Métro: Châtelet.*

The nearest thing to a hypermarket, where you can find almost everything — and pay less for it.

AU NAIN BLEU
*406 rue St-Honoré, 8e. Map **7**G7. Métro: Madeleine.*
Famous outlet for high-quality toys.

SI TU VEUX
*68 galerie Vivienne, 2e. Map **8**G8. Métro: Bourse.*
Traditional toys and games, some of them ultra-sophisticated. Miniature furniture, jointed wooden puppets and animals, and a most appealing section devoted to parties and fancy dress.

LE TRAIN BLEU
*55 rue St-Placide, 6e. Map **13**K7. Métro: St-Placide.*
Specialist in trains and other remote-controlled toys.

Recreation

Paris for children

Paris is a city of adult pleasures, where the world of childhood innocence is a restricted domain — and perhaps all the more cherished on that account. The needs of children are catered to in many imaginative ways, and Paris can be a rich and exciting place for the young. But it can also be frustrating, especially for parents of active youngsters.

The perfect illustration is the Parisian park. Although the city has a large amount of green space per inhabitant, much of it is in the form of small, well-tailored public gardens bristling with signs telling visitors to keep off the grass. There is inevitably a children's play area, with sandpit, climbing frames, slides and swings all of the highest quality, but this is not always a substitute for an open space where children can kick a ball or roll on the grass.

On the positive side, the larger parks offer more exciting distractions such as pony and donkey rides and miniature farms, and there are many fun places for young visitors: zoos, museums, theaters and circuses.

Having children with you in Paris means careful planning if they are to get the best out of their stay. A good way to find out about children's events is to consult the section *Pour les jeunes* in the weekly guides *l'Officiel des Spectacles* and *Pariscope*.

For **toys** and **clothes**, see previous chapter on SHOPPING.

PARKS AND ZOOS

Top of the list is the **Jardin d'Acclimatation** *(open daily 10am-6pm* ⌧ ✏⃠*)*, which is a veritable children's paradise on the edge of the BOIS DE BOULOGNE. It offers enough distractions to please the most demanding youngster, including a puppet show, distorting mirrors, an archery range, miniature golf, a dolphinarium and a small zoo. Kids will enjoy riding to it, on a miniature train from Porte-Maillot *(afternoons in July, August)*. The rest of the Bois is not really ideal for children, but there is a boating lake.

The BOIS DE VINCENNES also has boating lakes, and the best **zoo** in Paris, which has lots of wild animals *(open daily 9am-6.30pm* ⌧*)*. Its **Parc Floral** *(open daily 9.30am-8pm* ⌧*)* has an excellent range of play facilities and a delightful butterfly farm.

Within the city itself, the zoo in the JARDIN DES PLANTES boasts a fantastic collection of snakes and crawlies instead of the usual elephants and giraffes *(open daily until 6pm* ⌧*)*. It has a good *crêperie*, too.

Other parks to take children to are:

- The **BUTTES-CHAUMONT**: dramatic scenery, grass you can walk on, roller-skating, and donkey rides. Although a little off the beaten track, this park is worth a detour. Perched on a hillside, it has an artificial mountain and lake, a waterfall cave and a mini ferryboat.
- The **CHAMP-DE-MARS**: a playground for roller-skating and skate-boarding. There are also pony rides and puppet shows, and a lovely old-fashioned merry-go-round. This is worth a detour if you have just been to the nearby TOUR EIFFEL.
- The excellent **LUXEMBOURG** gardens: ideally located for a respite from your visit to the LATIN QUARTER. It has donkey rides, a pond for toy boats, sailboats to rent, old-fashioned swings, and a large marionette theater. A special grassed area reserved for parents and children under 6. A spacious park, but very crowded on sunny weekends.
- The **PALAIS DE CHAILLOT** gardens: on the E side there's an underground aquarium and small playground.
- The **PARC DE MONCEAU**: an elegant 18thC landscaped park. Under its gigantic plane trees can be found a tremendous playground and merry-go-round, plus a lake populated by eager ducks.
- The **PARC DE MONTSOURIS**: another elegant park, to the S of the city. This one has a puppet theater as well as the usual range of play equipment and some rather challenging climbing frames. Remember to take bread for the waiting ducks.
- There's the highly imaginative **Jardin d'Enfants aux Halles**, with tunnels and mountains as well as slides, in the area in front of the church of St-Eustache near the FORUM DES HALLES. *(One-hour sessions for 7-11s, on the hour. Closed Mon; also closed Fri and Sun morning* ☎ *Reserve on site.)* Staff speak English.
- Also in the center of Paris, the **TUILERIES** gardens, where there are small play areas, donkey rides, puppet shows and a lovely model boat pond. In summer, a full-sized fairground moves in.
- Whether or not you plan to go into the **Cité des Sciences** (see below), the **PARC DE LA VILLETTE** is a pleasant place to go, and has a good playground outside the main entrance.

VISITOR ATTRACTIONS, MUSEUMS AND WORKSHOPS

The main museums that give special emphasis to children and offer supervised activities are the **Musée en Herbe** in the **Jardin d'Acclimatation** of the BOIS DE BOULOGNE, the **Musée des Enfants** (part of the ART MODERNE DE LA VILLE DE PARIS museum at the PALAIS DE TOKYO), the ARTS DÉCORATIFS museum and the POMPIDOU CENTER.

The Pompidou Center has the advantage of combining plenty to interest adults, and sights and sounds that are much more geared toward play. Inside this building — which is worth a look in its own right for its resemblance to an oversized child's toy — can be found a *vidéothèque* and a free children's workshop. Just outside the center, in the pedestrianized place Kandinsky, is a decorative (i.e., not for wading in) pool that contains a number of larger-than-life, brightly-colored sculptures. This is a good place for a 10-minute spot of rest and relaxation.

But for sheer old-fashioned fun, there is no place to beat the MUSÉE GRÉVIN. Its very convincing waxworks (everyone from Napoléon and Alfred Hitchcock to Laurel and Hardy and Michael Jackson) will fascinate older children. There's also a 1900s "spectacle of illusion" and a conjuring show in the theater, all within a glorious building. Very good value for money. An entertaining little store just outside in the passage Jouffroy offers all kinds of masks and tricks that make a fun souvenir.

For serious-minded teenagers, there's a smaller but equally fascinating branch of the GRÉVIN at the FORUM DES HALLES, which concentrates on scenes from *Belle Époque* Paris. Older teenagers and more tolerant parents might visit LES MARTYRS DE PARIS (a new wax museum offering slightly tacky chills of every indescribable kind — go only if possessed of a strong stomach or the ability to laugh nervously at the misfortunes of another age) and the ROCK'N'ROLL HALL OF FAME (McCartney, Presley, Hendrix *et al*), both in the Forum des Halles.

Other museums that are geared toward children:

- The ARTS ET TRADITIONS POPULAIRES museum, which shows everyday French objects, including toys, from past centuries.
- The PALAIS DE LA DÉCOUVERTE, a science museum with a planetarium.
- The **Musée de l'Armée** (Army Museum) at LES INVALIDES.
- The MUSÉE DES TECHNIQUES (technical museum), with its push-button working models of machines.
- The MUSÉE DE LA MARINE, with its attractions for 8-11s.
- Best of all, for those with even the slightest leanings toward the sciences, is a day at PARC DE LA VILLETTE, where the **Cité des Sciences et de l'Industrie** is based. Don't be put off by the rather dry-sounding name: there's an **Inventorium** (a discovery-through-play environment), a **planetarium**, and **Explora**, which offers hands-on experience of all kinds of things, including computers, and there's the **Géode**, a panoramic cinema experience that takes place within a space-age dome.

THEATERS, MOVIES, CIRCUSES AND OTHER EVENTS

Apart from the puppet shows in the parks, there are many theaters that stage special performances for children. A list of these, along with other children's events such as children's movies and circuses, can be found in the *Pour les jeunes* section of *l'Officiel des Spectacles.*

There's more than a good chance of catching a favorite movie while in Paris, as there are more than 200 movie theaters, many screening English-language movies in their original version (advertised as V.O. — *version originale).*

"EXPERIENCES" AND THRILLS

Most older children enjoy climbing up to the high **vantage points** (the most popular are: TOUR EIFFEL, TOUR MONTPARNASSE, ARC DE TRIOMPHE, NOTRE-DAME, SACRÉ-COEUR, PANTHÉON and ARCHE DE LA DÉFENSE — but see VIEWPOINTS on page 101 for the full list) or, by contrast, plunging underground into the ÉGOUTS (sewers) or the CATACOMBS — but the latter, with its thousands of skulls, is not for the young or squeamish.

EuroDisney

The experience to cap it all, if time allows, is of course EURODISNEY (full details in EXCURSIONS). The RER takes you all the way there in 30 minutes, and you can bombard your senses with a visit to the Magic Kingdom in Europe. If you have never been to a Disneyland before, don't miss it. If you have, you'll know what to expect. The Paris one is still at the early-development stage, and it is perfectly possible to "do" the whole thing properly in two, maybe three, days.

The cost of admission is not cheap, but it is not expensive either, if you know how to get the most out of your trip. Ideally, you should stay overnight at one of the hotels, get up and get through those gates very early and plan to stay until 11pm (in summer). Many of the rides, for which 40-minute lines are the norm, are much easier to get onto if you go early or stay late.

The spectacular Disney parade brings the streets almost to a standstill each afternoon, as a hundred costumed characters pass down Main Street USA on carnival floats like you've never seen before. Even though the floats tower way above the heads of the crowds, you might still find a little pocket periscope useful!

The lavish daily firework display and seemingly endless (half an hour with a child on your shoulders . . .) but quite magical Electric Parade make nightfall worth the wait, and to glide through the tunnels of the Pirates of the Caribbean or to climb the Swiss Family Robinson's tree home after dark is quite thrilling. If you are visiting outside the summer season, check ahead what time the park will close and whether or not there are parades or fireworks that day.

Two hints on time- and money-saving.

- Try to buy your admission ticket ahead, either from your hotel or from the Office du Tourisme. That way, you go straight in when you arrive, avoiding any lines. 2- or 3-day tickets are cheaper.
- Eat cheap and eat quick. There's some very good food to be eaten, but you can lose anything up to two hours if you wish to eat a full meal. The many kinds of fast food are quite tasty and filling. Children's portions are reasonably priced. Drinks are expensive.

MAMMALS, BIRDS, FISH . . . .

- The PARC OCÉANIQUE JACQUES COUSTEAU, also conveniently in the Forum des Halles, will thrill most children, and everything there is bilingual. On arrival, a ride on a train shoots you up into space, then plunges you down to the depths of the sea. There are plenty of hands-on experiences — and nowhere else in Paris can you step inside a whale.
- At the MUSÉE NATIONAL DES ARTS AFRICAINS ET OCÉANIENS at the BOIS DE VINCENNES, there's a splendid aquarium and some crocodiles too.
- There's a city farm, **Ferme Georges Ville** at Bois de Vincennes *(Route du Pesage, 12ᵉ, open Sat, Sun, bols, Mar-Oct 10am-7pm, Nov-Feb 10am-5pm)*.
- The Sunday **bird market** on the ÎLE DE LA CITÉ is always crowded with visitors.

TRANSPORT

- **River trips** are also popular with the young (see USEFUL ADDRESSES on page 52), although the canal trip organizers will often not accept young children, lest they disrupt the tranquillity of the other passengers.
- The CENTRE INTERNATIONAL DE L'AUTOMOBILE, in Pantin to the E of Paris, is well worth a trip for any child old enough to handle a simulator.
- A little way to the N of Paris is the MUSÉE DE L'AIR ET DE L'ESPACE at Le Bourget airport.
- If you go to MONTMARTRE you can take the kids up to the summit on the **funicular railway** or the little **tourist train** that trundles you up the narrow streets to the Sacré-Coeur.

SPECIAL EVENTS AND SPORTS

Some **annual events** will bring a lot of excitement for kids — for example the Fête du Pont-Neuf, Marais Festival and Feux de St-Jean (see EVENTS IN THE PARIS CALENDAR on page 56 for a fuller list).

For information about **sports**, including roller-skating and cycling, see ACTIVITIES AND SPORTS, particularly for details of the superb **Aquaboulevard** leisure center *(4 rue Louis-Armand, 15ᵉ, map 17D3)*, where you might easily spend a whole day.

BABYSITTING

Babysitters of various nationalities can be hired from **Allô, Maman Poule** *(47-48-01-01)* or **Kid Services** *(47-66-00-52)*. Rates will vary according to your location and on the time of day, but count on between 35-55f per hour.

Activities and sports

In a city as devoted to urban pleasures as Paris, it is perhaps surprising to find that there is a rich choice of sports both for those who want to take part and for those who prefer to watch. Within the city boundaries, where space is scarce, it is easier to pursue indoor than outdoor sports, but on the periphery, many open-air sports are available.

Sport in Paris can be an expensive business, but need not necessarily be so. Many facilities, often in the form of multipurpose leisure complexes, are provided by the City of Paris, and these can be used by the public at relatively low cost.

For details on all aspects of sporting activity for visitors, including information on major spectator events, contact **Allô Sports** (☎ *42-76-54-54 Mon-Fri daytime only)*. Some sporting facilities are also listed in the weekly magazines *L'Officiel des Spectacles* and *Pariscope* and in the monthly English magazine *Passion*. The best way to keep abreast of events is to read the daily sports newspaper *L'Équipe*.

Conveniently, the 16ᵉ contains the major tennis and soccer/rugby stadiums, **Roland-Garros** *(2 av. Gordon Bennett, 16ᵉ map 17D3 ☎ 47-*

43-48-00 and **Parc des Princes** *(24 rue du Cdt. Guilbaud, 16ᵉ ☎42-88-02-76),* as well as **Longchamp** and **Auteuil** racecourses, both located in the Bois de Boulogne.

The main arena for spectator sport is the **Palais Omnisports de Paris-Bercy** *(2, blvd. de Bercy, 12ᵉ, map 16L13* ☎ *43-42-01-23)* near the Gare de Lyon, where you can see anything from basketball and judo to motorcycle racing and show jumping.

As a starting point, the following section is an A-Z guide to the main sports, games and other leisure activities in and around Paris.

ATHLETICS See TRACK AND FIELD.

BALLOONING

Montgolfier first flew his balloon over Paris in the 18thC. Nowadays, for a 3-hour round-trip in a balloon, contact **Espace Plus** *(14 rue de Sèvres, 92100 Boulogne-Billancourt* ☎*46-05-91-25; trips all year round, weather permitting),* or **France Montgolfières** *(76 rue Balard, 15ᵉ* ☎*40-60-11-23).*

It's hardly cheap, at about 1,300f per person (children under 12 at reduced price) for the flight (including champagne on landing . . .), but the experience will prove unforgettable. For meteorological reasons, flights take place either early in the morning or late in the afternoon. Advance reservations are essential: allow one week.

BOATING

Pleasure boats *(barques)* can be rented at the following parks. Turn to PARKS AND OPEN SPACES on pages 91-9 for fuller details.
Bois de Boulogne   Métro: Porte-Dauphine. Map **17**C3.
Bois de Vincennes   Métro: Château-de-Vincennes. Map **18**D5.
Parc des Buttes-Chaumont   Métro: Buttes-Chaumont. Map **18**C5.

BOULES

This game, and its close relative, *pétanque,* are national obsessions in France. Walk into almost any park in Paris on a Saturday or Sunday afternoon, and you will find a series of amateur matches in progress on any convenient patch of earth or gravel.

BOWLING

The largest alley is the **Bowling de Paris** *(Jardin d'Acclimatation, Bois de Boulogne* ☎*40-67-94-00, map 17C3)* and the **Bowling du Montparnasse** *(27 rue du Cdt.-Mouchotte, 15ᵉ* ☎*43-21-61-32).*

Other "bowlings" are advertised in the weekly listings magazines *L'Officiel des Spectacles* and *Pariscope.*

BRIDGE

There are several good bridge clubs in Paris where you can also play backgammon and gin rummy. Try **Bridge Club de Paris** *(68 blvd. de Courcelles, 17ᵉ* ☎*47-63-68-31, map 1D4)* or **Bridge Club Étoile** *(99 rue de la Pompe, 16ᵉ* ☎*45-53-54-40, map 5F1).*

CYCLING

Cycle-racing is a French passion, culminating in the annual Tour de France, which finishes in Paris in July. If you would like to cycle when you're in Paris, the best way is to make use of the *Train plus vélo* scheme offered by the French National Railways (SNCF). This scheme gives you a day's excursion (or longer), with bicycle rental thrown in.

Information on renting bicycles in Paris and the Île de France is given in GETTING AROUND on page 45.

Remember the possible dangers of cycling in Paris traffic. Outlying places such as the Bois de Boulogne are pleasant and more free of traffic.

For general inquiries get in touch with the **Fédération Française du Cyclisme** *(5 rue de Rome, Bâtiment Jean Monnet, 93561 Rosny-sous-Bois Cedex* ☎ *49-35-69-00).*

DANCE

Whether your bent is toward classical ballet, flamenco, rock or folk, there is likely to be a dance center somewhere in Paris to suit you. Ask at the **Fédération Française de la Danse** *(12 rue St-Germain-l'Auxerrois, 75001 Paris* ☎ *42-36-12-61, map 8 I9).*

FISHING

Twenty different types of fish can be caught nowadays in Paris waters. An annual permit costs about 350f (depending on what type of club you are affiliated to) from **Fédération des Associations de Pêche et de Pisciculture de Paris et la Petite Couronne** *(83 rue Léon Frot, 11ᵉ* ☎ *43-48-36-34),* who will give information on the many lakes, canals and quays.

FOOTBALL (SOCCER)

The main Paris stadium is the **Parc des Princes** *(Porte de St-Cloud, 16ᵉ, map 17 D3)* near the s end of the Bois de Boulogne, where such events as the French Cup Final (either May or June) take place. See EVENTS IN THE PARIS CALENDAR on page 57.

For more details contact the **Fédération Française de Football** *(60bis av. d'Iéna, 75016 Paris* ☎ *44-31-73-00)* or the **Ligue Parisienne de Football** *(5 pl. de Valois, 75001 Paris* ☎ *42-61-56-47).*

GARDENS

There are floral gardens in the BOIS DE VINCENNES *(Parc Floral, map 18 D5)* and the BOIS DE BOULOGNE *(La Bagatelle, map 17 C3-D3),* which also has the **Jardins des Serres d'Auteuil** *(métro: Porte d'Auteuil, map 17 D3, open daily* ☒*),* where all the city administration's flowers are grown. There is also a greenhouse with exotic and tropical plants, as well as a palm house.

Also worth a journey is the peaceful **Jardin des Plantes** *(map 15 K11, closed Tues* ☒*)* and, farther afield, the **Albert Kahn Gardens**, on the banks of the Seine in Boulogne-Billancourt *(métro: Boulogne-Pont de St-Cloud, closed Mon* ☒*)* and the **Roseraie** (rose garden) **du Val de Marne** *(rue Albert-Vatel, 94 L'Häy-les-Roses, open daily* ☒ *).*

GOLF

Most of the best golf courses belong to clubs, which will admit players on payment of a green fee and where you can also rent clubs and other golfing equipment. Public golf courses also welcome visitors.

For further details about golfing facilities contact the **Fédération Française de Golf** (*69 av. Victor-Hugo, 75016 Paris* ☎ *43-02-13-55*). See also MINI-GOLF on the following page.

GYMNASTICS

There are plenty of gymnasiums in Paris. A list is available from **Allô Sports** (☎ *42-76-54-54*) or the **Fédération Française d'Éducation Physique et de Gymnastique Volontaire** (*41-43 rue de Reuilly, 75012 Paris* ☎ *43-41-86-10*).

HEALTH CLUBS

Although there are many health clubs in Paris, most are open to members only. Many larger hotels now have saunas and other fitness facilities for residents. For exercise classes, including aerobics and "dancersize," go to **Espace Vit'Halles** (*48 rue Rambuteau, 4ᵉ* ☎ *42-77-21-71, map 9H10*). For the whole lot, and much more, try the **Aquaboulevard de Paris** leisure center (see next page).

HELICOPTER RIDES

Pleasure trips in a helicopter are run by a number of companies operating from the **Héliport de Paris** in the 15ᵉ *(map 17D3)*. Try **Hélifrance** (*45-54-95-11*) or **Hélicap** (*45-57-75-51*).

HORSE-RACING

The principal racecourses *(hippodromes)* are at **Longchamp** (*Bois de Boulogne, map 17D3*) and **St-Cloud** (*12km/8 miles W of Paris*) for flat-racing, and **Auteuil** (*Bois de Boulogne, métro: Porte d'Auteuil, map 17D3; Mon, Thurs*) for steeple-chasing.

Other courses in or comfortably near Paris are to be found at **Chantilly** *(Fri, Sun, Tues)*, **Evry** *(Wed, Sat)*, **Enghien**, **Maisons-Laffitte** and **Vincennes** *(Fri and Tues eve)*.

See EVENTS IN THE PARIS CALENDAR on pages 56-8 for the most important of the annual meetings.

ICE-SKATING

There are several ice-rinks in Paris where skates can be rented. One is the **Patinoire des Buttes-Chaumont** (*30 rue Edouard Pailleron, 19ᵉ* ☎ *42-08-72-26, map 18C5*). For a list of other rinks and for more specific information, try the **Fédération Française des Sports de Glace** (*42 rue du Louvre, 75001 Paris* ☎ *40-26-51-38*).

KARTING

Go-Karting seems very French (remember the debate in *Un Homme et Une Femme?* — *"Au golf? Non, au karting!"*). The **Kart Buffo** racetrack is 35km (22 miles) SE of Paris (*at Les Étards on RN 19* ☎ *64-07-62-97*).

LANGUAGE COURSES

Courses can be reserved before you leave home. Your French Consulate will have general information as well as details of how to apply.

Courses for all ages and all levels are organized by **Alliance Française** *(101 blvd. Raspail, 75006 Paris ☎ 45-44-38-28)* and **Eurocentre de Paris** *(13 pge. Dauphine, 75006 Paris ☎ 43-25-81-40).*

LEISURE CENTERS

For a leisure center to end all leisure centers, make a day at **Aqua-boulevard de Paris** *(4 rue Louis-Armand, 15ᵉ ☎ 40-60-10-00, map 17D3; métro: Balard).* Here you will find an aquatic park with wave machine, water cannon, giant slides and special water games for children, as well as aerobics, bowling, billiards, golf, gymnasium, health club and massage, solarium, squash, tennis and yoga. You can even play Scrabble, chess or bridge, watch horse-racing — or just eat and drink.

LE MANS

One of the world's great auto-racing circuits is at **Le Mans**, about 184km (115 miles) sw of Paris, where the 24-hour road race takes place every year in mid-June.

For information contact the **Fédération Française de Sport Automobile** *(136 rue de Longchamp, 75016 Paris ☎ 47-27-97-39).*

MINI-GOLF

There's an 18-hole miniature golf where you can play in the wee hours, at **Châlet du Lac** at Bois de Vincennes *(Métro: Saint-Mandé-Tourelles ☎ 43-28-09-89, open Fri, Sat from 10pm till dawn; Sun 2.30-7.30pm).*

PARACHUTING

If you want to risk life and limb while you're abroad, parachuting is one exhilarating possibility. Contact the school for parachuting at the **Centre de Parachutisme Sportif de Paris Île de France** to the SE of Paris *(L'Aérodrome, 77320 La Ferté-Gaucher ☎ 64-04-01-73, open Fri, Sat, Sun and holidays).*

RIDING

There are many riding stables in the Paris region, although they tend to be in the outlying areas, such as the Bois de Boulogne and the Bois de Vincennes.

ROLLER-SKATING

There are a number of outdoor roller-skating and skate-boarding pistes such as the big concourse at the **Palais de Chaillot**.

Or try a roller-skating discotheque such as **La Main Jaune** *(pl. de la Porte-de-Champerret, 17ᵉ ☎ 47-63-26-47, map 17C3; métro: Porte-de-Champerret),* where you can rent skates. Telephone to check which evenings; it's open to children during the day.

RUGBY

For rugby union contact the **Fédération Française de Rugby** *(7 cité d'Antin, 75009 Paris* ☎ *48-74-84-75)*. Big rugby (and soccer) games happen at **Parc des Princes** *(Métro: Porte de St-Cloud, map 17D3)*.

SQUASH

Although squash is increasingly popular in France, there are still relatively few courts in the center of Paris, and they usually require membership. There are excellent courts at **Le Squash Front de Seine** *(21 rue Gaston-de-Caillavet, 15ᵉ* ☎ *45-75-35-37, map 11J1)*. Expect to pay a small monthly membership fee.

SWIMMING

There are many municipal pools, details of which can be obtained from **Allô Sports** *(* ☎ *42-76-54-54)*, by looking in the telephone directory under *Piscines*, or from a leaflet obtainable at the Office du Tourisme. The excellent leisure center **Aquaboulevard** offers much more than just swimming (see LEISURE CENTERS on the previous page), and the FORUM DES HALLES has a first-class pool.

TENNIS

Municipal courts (for example in the Luxembourg gardens) and many private ones are available. Information from **Allô Sports** *(* ☎ *42-76-54-54)*. The **Stade Français** club *(Porte de St-Cloud, 2 rue du Cdt.-Guilbaud, 16* ☎ *46-51-66-53, map 17D3)* is open to visitors.

TRACK AND FIELD

There are numerous centers in Paris for track and field. Contact the **Ligue de l'Île de France de l'Athlétisme** *(39 rue de Palestro, 75002 Paris* ☎ *42-33-23-50)*.

WALKING AND RAMBLING

Historical and cultural guided walks around Paris take place all year round. See *Randonnées Pédestres* in *L'Officiel des Spectacles*, or *Pariscope*. For general information, contact the **Fédération Française de Randonnées Pédestres** *(8 av. Marceau 75008* ☎ *47-23-62-32)*.

An annual event for people, including foreign visitors, who know Paris quite well, is the **Transparisienne**. This is a cross between a treasure hunt and an orienteering expedition, with a route book to follow and questions to answer (available in English), along a choice of themes such as "Nature" or "Beaux-Arts." This popular event is attended by thousands of people and is likely to be over-subscribed. Reserve ahead (☎) by contacting the **Office du Tourisme** *(* ☎ *47-23-61-72)*.

The date for 1993 is May 8. The date for 1994 is not yet fixed.

ZOOS

Zoos can be found at BOIS DE VINCENNES, BOIS DE BOULOGNE (**Jardin d'Acclimatation**) and the JARDIN DES PLANTES. See PARIS FOR CHILDREN on page 263 for locations, and see ZOOS in the INDEX.

Excursions

Environs of Paris

Paris has always been the center of power, politics and the arts in France, and over the centuries, great châteaux have grown up within easy striking distance of the city. Several important cathedral towns are also close at hand, as well as pretty villages and many magnificent forests, a famous feature of the Île de France. All these sights make easy one-day excursions from Paris by car or by public transport.

Five of the best-known sightseeing towns near Paris — **Chartres**, **Fontainebleau**, **Reims**, **Rouen** and **Versailles** — are described in full. At the end of this section, there is a comprehensive guide to **EuroDisney**, the first European outpost of the magic kingdom. The chapter begins with short descriptions of some of the most interesting smaller places within easy reach of the capital.

* See map of Northern France on page 274, Paris Environs maps **17** & **18**, and map of Versailles on page 288.

Short trips

Barbizon
58km (35 miles) SE of Paris **i** 41, rue Grande ☎60-66-41-87. **By train**: from Gare de Lyon; **by car**: on A6 or N7.

This small village, close to Fontainebleau, is famed for its artistic associations in the 19thC, when several Romantic painters settled there. They included Rousseau and Millet, whose studios are open to the public. The *auberge* where they gathered, Pierre Ganne's, is being totally refurbished, to house the **Musée Municipal de l'École de Barbizon**, which now occupies Rousseau's former studio (☎60-66-22-38, *open Apr-Sept 10am-12.30pm, 2-6pm; Oct-Mar 10am-12.30pm, 2-5pm; closed Tues*). **Millet's studio** (☎60-66-21-55, *open 9.30am-12.30pm, 2-5.30pm*), is now a private gallery.

Work on the new museum is scheduled for completion in spring 1994. In tandem with the restoration, the museum's collection has been enriched by the recent acquisition of some 360 works.

Beauvais
76km (45 miles) N of Paris. **By train**: from Gare du Nord; **by car**: on N1.

Although the center of Beauvais was destroyed in a 1940 air raid, the Gothic cathedral miraculously survived. Also of interest is the **Galerie**

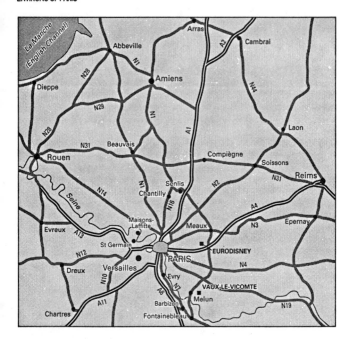

Nationale de la Tapisserie et d'Art Textile (*rue Saint-Pierre* ☎ *44-05-14-28, open Apr-Sept 9.30am-noon, 2.30-5pm, Oct-Mar 10am-noon, 2.30-5pm; closed Mon*), with a collection of State-owned tapestries dating from the 15thC to the present day.

The remarkable group of buildings, once the episcopal palace and now the **Musée départemental de l'Oise** (☎ *44-84-37-37, open 10am-noon, 2-6pm, closed Tues and some public holidays*), houses paintings ranging from those of Renaissance master Antoine Caron to the 19thC French School, as well as local pottery and carvings in stone and wood.

Blérancourt

110km (70 miles) N of Paris. **By car:** *on A1.*

Not far from Blérancourt, in a railway carriage parked in the woods (see COMPIÈGNE), the Armistice was signed that ended World War I. Since 1931, the local château has housed the **Musée National de la Coopération Franco-Américaine** (☎ *23-39-60-16, open mid-Apr to mid-Oct 10am-12.30pm, 2-5pm; mid-Oct to mid-Apr 2-5pm, open to groups mornings by appointment*), commemorating US aid to France between 1914 and 1945. It highlights the activities of Anne Morgan, the American heiress who in 1917 turned the building into the hub of an operation to deliver medical and social services to a French population traumatized by war.

The scope of the museum covers more than the two world wars; it deals with the entire history of cooperation between the two nations, beginning with the role the French played in the American Revolution. The new **Florence Gould pavilion**, opened in 1989, displays a remarkable collection of 19th and 20thC paintings and sculpture by American artists in France and French artists in America.

The grounds retain their 17thC elegance. An arboretum and two gardens of American plants (one flowers in spring, the other in the fall) are more recent additions.

Chantilly
50km (30 miles) N of Paris. **By train:** *from Gare du Nord;* **by car:** *on N16.*
Chantilly is famed for its cream (now parodied in spray-cans everywhere), its hand-worked lace, and its racecourse, but most of all for its elegant château, which houses two museums.

The **Musée Condé** (☎ *44-57-08-00, open Nov-Feb 10.30am-5pm; Mar-Oct 10am-6pm; closed Tues*) comprises a group of 16th-17thC buildings bequeathed with their contents by the Duke of Aumale to the French Institute. Rare books, paintings of the French, Italian, Flemish, Dutch and British schools, fine tapestries and furniture, form one of the most outstanding private collections ever assembled. The grounds, laid out by Le Nôtre, are magnificent.

The **Musée du Cheval** (☎ *44-57-13-13, open 10.30am-6pm; closed Tues*) occupies the great stables of the château, considered by many to be the finest in the world.

Compiègne
82km (50 miles) NE of Paris. **By train:** *from Gare du Nord;* **by car:** *on A1.*
The impressive palace here was a favorite royal hunting residence, and is surrounded by the majestic Compiègne Forest, where in 1918 and 1940 two very different armistices were signed (see BLÉRANCOURT).

Constructed during the reigns of Louis XV and Louis XVI, the château (☎ *44-40-02-02, open 9.30-12am, 1.30-5pm; closed Tues*) contains three museums: the **historic apartments**, with original furniture dating from the days of Louis XVI, Napoleon I and Napoleon III; the **Second Empire Museum**, with various *objets* and furniture associated with Napoleon III and his court; and the **Vehicle and Tourism Museum**, covering road transport from the 18thC to the automobile.

Giverny
87km (54 miles) NW of Paris, 4km (2 miles) SE of Vernon. **By train:** *from Gare St-Lazare to Vernon, then short taxi-ride.* **By car:** *on A13, to Vernon exit (D181), then D5.*
The idyllic home and studios of the leader of the Impressionist movement, Claude Monet, is the scene of many touristic pilgrimages. The interior of the house, where Monet lived from 1883 to 1926, has been restored in its original vibrant colors. A selection of Monet's prized Japanese prints is displayed on the walls. The vast studio in which Monet worked on the vast canvases of his *Water-lilies* is a few steps from the house.

The gardens, laid out by Monet as "a picture painted with nature's own materials," were considered by contemporaries to be one of his finest masterpieces, and formed the subject of many of his best-known works.

They have been restored to an exact replica of their former glory.

The **water garden**, with its Japanese bridge overhung with weeping willows and wistaria, surrounded by azaleas, glitters once again with the jewel colors that inspired the *Water-lilies* series.

The gardens are open all year round, but the house is closed from November to March (☎ *32-51-28-21*).

Malmaison
*6km (4 miles) w of Paris, map **17**C2.* **By Métro/RER:** *to Rueil-Malmaison;* **by car:** *N13 via La Défense.*

The châteaux of Malmaison and **Bois-Préau** together house a national museum devoted to the history of Napoleon I and the Empress Joséphine before 1804 and to the Emperor himself in the period after Waterloo. Interesting things to see at Malmaison include Napoleon's library, and Josephine's bedroom and clothes. The museum at Bois-Préau covers Napoleon's second and permanent exile, at St Helena in the South Atlantic, and the Napoleonic legend. *(Château de Malmaison, 1, av. du Château, 92500 Rueil-Malmaison ☎47-49-20-07. Open 10am-12.30pm, 1.30-5.30pm; Oct-Mar closes 5pm. Closed Tues. Château de Bois-Préau open 10.30am-1pm, 2-6pm; Oct-Mar closes 5pm. Closed Tues.)*

St-Germain-en-Laye
*21km (12 miles) w of Paris, map **17**C2.* **By Métro/RER:** *to St-Germain-en-Laye;* **by car:** *on N13.*

A smart suburb of Paris, with interesting old streets and a château, which houses the **Musée des Antiquités Nationales** *(place du Château ☎34-51-53-65* 🔲 *for under-18s* 🔳 *discount for under-25s and over-60s* ♿ *open 9am-5.15pm; closed Tues)*. Created by Napoleon III in 1862, its collection traces the epic history of Man, spanning the millions of years from his origins to the Middle Ages. The original exhibits have been greatly enriched by the archeological discoveries of the 19th and 20thC, so that the museum's Prehistory collection can claim to be the richest of its kind in the world.

A reconstitution of the Lascaux Caves, the oldest representation of a human face — a 22,000-year-old Venus — and the tomb of a Celtic prince are just some of the high points of the collection.

The château itself was once a royal residence; various French kings spent time here, and Louis XIV, the Sun King, was born here.

St-Germain-en-Laye also has **The Prieuré County Museum** *(2 bis, rue Maurice-Denis ☎39-73-77-87* 🔲 *children* 🔳 *discounts for students, elderly people, groups)*. The museum is devoted to Symbolist art, particularly that of the Nabi group (admirers of Gauguin) and Maurice Denis (1870-1943), the painter who lived and worked in the converted priory. Denis' **studio**, where he painted his vast frescoes for the Théâtre des Champs-Élysées, and the **chapel** in the grounds, which he restored, are other points of interest.

The museum is designed to give the visitor an excellent grasp of the development of Symbolism through the period from 1880-1945. Works by painters such as Gauguin, Bonnard, Vuillard and Maurice Denis are among the many on display.

The winding paths and solitary corners of the gardens, which today provide a soothing retreat, were the perfect backdrop for the artist's contemplative and mystical inclinations.

Senlis
51km (30 miles) NE of Paris. **By train:** *from Gare du Nord;* **by car:** *on A1.*
This well-preserved old town, the cradle of French royalty, has narrow streets, a royal castle, a 12thC cathedral and museums stocked with enough artistic and historical interest to make a visit worthwhile.

The **Musée de la Vénerie** *(Château Royal* ☎ *44-53-00-80* **𝒦** *compulsory 10am, 11am, 2pm, 3pm, 4pm and 5pm, except on Tues and Wed mornings),* housed in the magnificent royal palace and the Priory of St-Maurice, contains relics and art works, including a number of important paintings, engravings and sculpture, all devoted to the subject of hunting.

Bordering the former earldom of the Valois, the **Abbaye et Domaine de Chaalis** *(Fontaine-Chaalis* ☎ *44-54-00-01; museum open Mar-Nov Mon, Wed, Sat 1.30-6pm; Sun, holidays 10am-midday, 1.30-6pm; grounds open 10am-6pm throughout the year, closed Tues; rose garden open May-Nov)* is a magnificent estate containing a partially ruined Cistercian abbey that houses Rousseau's *Desert* and *Sea of Sand,* as well as a number of objects associated with Rousseau's last hours. The collection also includes paintings and sculpture of the Middle Ages and the centuries preceding the French Revolution. In summer and fall, visitors can see the magnificent **rose garden**.

Vaux-le-Vicomte
60km (35 miles) SE of Paris. **By train:** *from Gare de Lyon;* **by car:** *on N5.*
The harmony of this fabulous château — still privately owned — shows the influence of 17thC French art. Designed by the artists Le Vau, Le Brun and Le Nôtre between 1656 and 1661, it was an inspiration for the most famous château of them all, VERSAILLES.

Strolling around the château's interior is fascinating, in particular by candlelight (see below). But the truly stunning aspect of this gem of a château, less well known (and so less crowded) than those of Fontainebleau or Versailles, is the gardens. The sober frontage is inadequate preparation for the vast, baroque magnificence of the rear gardens, with its statues, topiary and pools. *(Château, gardens and carriage museum open Nov 11am-5pm; Jan-Mar 11am-5pm; Apr-Oct 10am-6pm; closed Dec; candlelight visits Sat eve May-Oct 8.30-11pm).*

Cathedrals and châteaux

CHARTRES

*88km (55 miles) sw of Paris. Population: 41,250. **By train**: from Gare Montparnasse; **by car**: N10 or A11; **by bus**: tours from Cityrama, 4 pl. des Pyramides, 1ᵉʳ ☎42-60-30-14 and Paris-Vision, 214 rue de Rivoli, 1ᵉʳ ☎42-60-31-25 i pl. de la Cathédrale ☎37-21-50-00.*

"Chartres is the very mind of the Middle Ages in visible form," said Émile Male, speaking of Chartres' celebrated cathedral, which occupies a privileged place in the pantheon of the world's great "bibles in stone." The cathedral's architecture, stained glass and sculpture, and the way in which it has withstood the vicissitudes of history, make it an unparalleled masterpiece. But magnificent as it is, the cathedral is not the only reason for a visit to Chartres. The old district along the banks of the River Eure is beautiful and unspoiled. Here you can wander past old stone bridges, half-timbered houses and gardens reflected in the water, with the cathedral visible at every turn above the jumble of rooftops.

Chartres Cathedral

✗ (compulsory in crypt). Cathedral open daily Apr-Sept 7am-7.30pm, Oct-Mar 7.30am-7pm. Opening hours of crypt, tower and treasury can vary according to season.

No one who has seen the cathedral of Notre-Dame at Chartres will ever forget the experience, for it is a building of potent beauty, a representation of the New Jerusalem on earth, as well as a shrine to the Virgin Mary. The building as it now stands was erected on the site of an earlier church. This burned down in 1194, leaving only the crypt with its precious relic, the **Sancta Camisia** (now in the treasury), said to be the garment which the Virgin was wearing when she gave birth to Jesus.

The fire and the survival of the relic were taken to be a sign from the Virgin that she wanted a more impressive shrine. Accordingly, enormous donations poured in from all over Christendom, and a huge army of craftsmen set to work, completing the basic structure of the cathedral in the extraordinarily short span of about 25 years. This rapidity explains the unique unity of the building as an architectural and esthetic whole.

The cathedral overflows with visual riches, but one of its most famous features is the abundant **stained glass** (★), which includes three breathtaking rose windows. The imagery of the stained glass, its graceful tracery depicting legends of saints, could by itself occupy many hours of study. Another attraction is the curious **maze** set into the floor of the nave near the w door, to which many people attribute an esoteric significance. The rich sculpture around the **portals** should also not be missed, nor the intricately worked **screen** separating the choir from the ambulatory.

If you have time, climb up to the roof (◀≶) via a stairway on the N side, for a dizzying view to the N and w through the flying buttresses. It is worth taking one of the excellent English lecture-tours of the cathedral.

Other buildings worth visiting include the churches of **St-Pierre, St-André, St-Martin-au-Val** and **St-Aignan** and the Bishops' Palace, now the **Musée des Beaux-Arts** (🖼 *open 10am-noon, 2-6pm; closed Tues)*, which contains many fine works of art from medieval ivories to 18thC paintings.

If your visit to the cathedral fires your curiosity about **stained glass**, a visit to the **Centre International du Vitrail** (near the cathedral) will be of interest.

🛏   **Le Grand Monarque** *(22 pl. des Épars, 28000 Chartres* ☎*37-21-00-72* ▥*)*, grand and sedate; **Hôtel de la Poste** *(3 rue du Général Koenig* ☎*37-21-04-27* ▣*)*.

🍽   **Le Buisson Ardent** *(10 rue au Lait* ☎*37-34-04-66* ▣ *to* ▥*)*, delicious and interesting food in an old Chartres house; reserve ahead for the restaurant of **Le Grand Monarque** *(see hotel address above* ☎*37-21-00-72*▥*)*, which serves exceptionally good *nouvelle cuisine*.

🍽   **Le Dix de Pythagore** *(2, rue de la Porte Cendreuse* ☎*37-36-02-38* ▥*)*, and **Haute-Couture** *(45, rues des Changes* ☎*37-21-99-36* ▥*)* serve good food at prices to suit less lavish pockets.

🍵   **Le Moulin** *(21 rue de la Tannerie)*, by the river; **Salon de Thé Bergamote** *(opposite N door of cathedral)*.

FONTAINEBLEAU ★

65km (40 miles) SE of Paris. Population: 19,500. By train: from Gare de Lyon to Fontainebleau station, then bus to the palace; by car: on A6 or N7; by bus: tours with Cityrama, 4 pl. des Pyramides, 1ᵉʳ ☎*42-60-30-14 or Paris-Vision, 214 rue de Rivoli, 1ᵉʳ* ☎*42-60-31-25* **i** *31 pl. Napoléon Bonaparte* ☎*64-22-25-68.*

Ideally your visit to Fontainebleau should be a two-day affair, one to visit the **palace and town**, another to explore the **forest**. This great expanse of woodland is a remarkable natural phenomenon. Over the millennia, a strange alchemy of glacial action and erosion has produced a surreal terrain of hills, ravines and extraordinary rock formations. Giant boulders with organic-looking contours lie everywhere, some resembling stranded whales, others sculptures by Henry Moore. Little wonder that the forest has been used as a setting for more than 100 movies, in which it has served to represent, among other things, the terrain of the Holy Land, the Wild West and the Switzerland of William Tell.

A visit to Fontainebleau can easily be combined with a short trip to nearby BARBIZON (see page 273).

The palace of Fontainebleau

☎*64-22-27-40* 🖼 ✗ *Open Mon, Wed-Sun 9.30am-12.30pm, 2-5pm. Closed Tues.*

As a former royal residence, the palace of Fontainebleau is just as interesting as Versailles and possesses a much more subtle beauty; even the name has a magical quality, deriving from a fountain in the grounds of the palace, *fontaine belle eau* (fountain of beautiful water). The town also has its charm, a place of well-heeled grace and elegance, with leafy avenues and large, quietly prosperous houses. All around it lies the lovely Fontainebleau forest.

If you have time to spare before visiting the palace, take a walk (allow 45 to 50 minutes) through the thickly wooded park, and approach the palace through the **formal garden** with its carp pond, its great parterres designed by Le Nôtre in 1664, and its curious statues, which include a pair of sphinxes.

A royal residence from the 12thC, Fontainebleau saw the birth of two French Kings, Philippe The Fair (le Bel) and Louis XIII. But the palace is linked particularly with the colorful François I (1494-1547), rake, military adventurer, friend of Leonardo da Vinci and one of the greatest royal patrons of the arts in French history. In 1528 he knocked down most of the existing medieval edifice and began to build a new château according to the Renaissance principles that had influenced him during his Italian campaigns. All over the building, carved in stonework and paneling, you will see the fire-breathing salamander that was his emblem. Henry II, Catherine de Medicis and Henry IV added to the palace.

Most of the French sovereigns lived for a time at Fontainebleau, and the palace has witnessed a rich pageant of history: Louis XIV's decision to revoke the Edict of Nantes was made there; Pope Pius VII lived as a virtual prisoner in the palace from June 1812-January 1814; Napoleon I made it his favorite residence after the TUILERIES, and it was here that he came when he abdicated in 1814, before departing for St Helena.

Fontainebleau has been described as a "rendezvous of châteaux," for it is really a sprawling conglomeration of buildings of different periods, built around five courtyards. Before entering, take a walk around the palace. On the N side is the charming **Garden of Diana**, with its fountain decorated with a statue of the goddess. Traveling counter-clockwise, pass into the White Horse Courtyard, or **Courtyard of Farewells**, which was the scene of Napoleon's farewell to his guard. Note the graceful double-horseshoe staircase with its hermetic caduceuses carved in the stonework of the balustrade.

To the right of the stairway is an arch leading into the **Fountain Courtyard** looking onto the carp pond. On the right, the two stone statues of fierce-looking Fô dogs guard the entrance to the Empress Eugénie's Chinese salons.

Through another archway to the W is the **gilded door** that is one of the most famous features of the palace. This huge gateway, with its three superimposed loggias, was the first structure to be completed when rebuilding began in 1528.

From here, the way leads NE along the facade of the ballroom. Turn left to stand between the **Oval Courtyard** to the SW, with its domed gateway, and the **Courtyard of the Kitchens** to the NE. The gateway to the latter is decorated by two huge **Hermes heads** in stone.

Arguably the most remarkable room in the palace is the **François I Gallery** (★), which was decorated in the years 1534-37 by a team of Italian artists and craftsmen. The walls are adorned with 14 frescoes surrounded by rich decorative stucco work and illustrating events or allegorical subjects connected with the reign of François I. One shows an elephant decorated with the fleur-de-lys — an allegory of the king's wisdom; another, symbolizing the unity of the state, depicts François I presenting a pomegranate, symbol of concord, to representatives of different classes.

Another splendid Renaissance-style room is the vast **ballroom**, which was designed by Philibert Delorme under Henry II. It has deep, arched bays, frescoes of mythological scenes, and a coffered ceiling, the design of which is reflected in the woodwork of the floor.

The rooms known as the **apartments of the King and Queen** are a rich confection of different periods, much of the decoration being in the overblown 19thC style of King Louis-Philippe.

Equally ornate is the series of **Napoleonic rooms**, including the Emperor's Throne Room, bedroom and council chamber. The Napoleonic bee emblem of industry and discipline figures prominently in the decoration.

Those interested in Napoleon and in militaria should visit the **Musée Napoléonien d'Art et d'Histoire Militaires** *(88 rue St-Honoré; open Tues-Sat 2-5pm)*, which has a splendid collection of military paraphernalia.

☞ **Aigle Noir** 🏨 *(27 pl. Napoléon-Bonaparte, 77300 Fontainebleau* ☎*64-22-32-65* 🏨*); **Napoléon** *(9 rue Grande, 77300 Fontainebleau* ☎*64-22-20-39* 🏨*).*

🍽 **Aigle Noir** *(*🏨 *to* 🏨 *see hotel address above);* **François I** *(3 rue Royale* ☎*64-22-24-68* 🏨 *to* 🏨*).*

REIMS

143km (89 miles) NE *of Paris. Population: 183,500.* **By train:** *from Gare de l'Est;* **by car:** *on A4;* **by bus:** *tours with Cityrama, 4 pl. des Pyramides, 1ᵉʳ* ☎*42-60-30-14 and Paris-Vision, 214 rue de Rivoli, 1ᵉʳ* ☎*42-60-31-25* **i** *2 rue Guillaume de Machault* ☎*26-47-25-69.*

Reims is famous for two main reasons: its **Gothic cathedral** and the fact that it is the **capital of the Champagne Country** and the place where many of the big producers have their cellars. On a day excursion from Paris, try to arrive early, as the town has much to offer. Avoid going on Monday or Tuesday, when the most interesting museums are closed.

Despite the heavy damage suffered in World War I, Reims has remained a gracious place, with quietly elegant streets, solid houses, wide boulevards, fashionable shops and a lively air. Particularly fine is the 18thC **place Royale**, which was built with Classical simplicity as one unit.

Reims was an important city in Roman times, and some fine monuments of that era remain; the most striking is the **Mars Gate** near the station. This three-arched edifice is thought to have been the largest of its kind in the Roman Empire. The mythological themes carved on it include the story of Romulus and Remus, and local etymology has it that the latter was the founder of the city — hence the name. The Roman forum also survives, in the center of the **place du Forum**, and includes among other things an imposing vaulted colonnade, which has been beautifully restored.

Notre-Dame Cathedral ★ *(open 8am-7pm, high sections closed in winter)*, begun in 1211, is one of the chain of great Gothic churches that includes CHARTRES, Amiens and NOTRE-DAME DE PARIS. Its special importance lies in the fact that all but three kings of France were crowned there. It was one of Joan of Arc's triumphs to take the Dauphin to Reims in 1429, escorting him with an army of 12,000 men through English-held territory, for his coronation as Charles VII.

The cathedral is not as overwhelming as that at Chartres, but it has a graceful splendor. The **w facade**, with its three portals and its sculpture, has eroded over the centuries, but some fine statues still survive, notably the angel to the right of the center door, whose face bears a curiously mischievous smile.

Inside, the cathedral has the typical majesty and grace of its era, with the characteristic soaring **ribbed ceiling**. The large **rose window** at the w end retains its original 13thC stained glass; most of the original glass was destroyed in World War I, but some of the modern glass is of a very high standard, most notably the three **windows by Chagall** at the E end, and the intriguing windows in the s transept depicting aspects of the Champagne industry.

The **Palais du Tau** *(☎ 26-47-74-39 ▧ open daily 10am-noon, 2-6pm)* to the right of the cathedral, is a museum containing the cathedral treasury. It was once a royal residence, and dates from the 12thC. It was damaged in World War I and has been extensively restored. Other churches include the 11thC **Basilica of St-Remi** and the small 20thC **Chapelle Foujita**, in rue du Champ-de-Mars, which was designed and decorated by the Japanese artist Léonard Foujita, who lived in France.

A delightful museum is the **Hôtel Le Vergeur** *(36 pl. du Forum ☎ 26-47-20-75 ▧ open Tues-Sun 2-6pm)*, in a lovely rambling house, parts of which date from the 13thC. The museum was formerly the residence of the art collector and traveler Hugues Krafft, and the contents range from antique furniture and works of art to a priceless collection of original Dürer engravings of the *Apocalypse* and the *Passion of Christ*. The museum also illustrates the history of Reims, and the garden contains a fascinating collection of old facades and doorways.

There are other interesting museums too. The **Musée des Beaux-Arts** *(8 rue Chanzy ☎ 26-47-28-44 ▧ open daily 10am-noon, 2-6pm; closed Tues and hols)* is a museum of fine arts with a collection of sculpture, furniture, *objets d'art* and French paintings from the 15th-20thC. It contains works by many great French painters, from Poussin to Delacroix, from Monet to Gauguin. Special collections include a series of 25 religious canvases painted between 1460 and 1520, and 28 Corot landscapes.

The **Ancien Collège des Jésuites** *(1 pl. Museux ▧ ✗ open Mon, Wed, Thurs, Fri 10am-noon, 2-6pm)* is a 17thC building with some magnificent rooms, a fine art and furniture collection, and a planetarium *(▧ ✗ on weekend afternoons only)*.

Champagne cellars and vineyards

"It's only Champagne if it comes from Champagne," goes the saying, and a visit to the Reims area without sampling its legendary sparkling product would seem almost sacrilegious. If your interest extends beyond the passing *flute,* a prime focus of your stay here must be a visit to the cellars of one or more of the champagne producers dotted around the town.

The flourishing of the world's most famous wine in this area is due to the chalky sub-soil covered with clay, the cool climate, and the perfectionism of the Champagne producers. The secret of the much-emulated *méthode* is a second fermentation in the bottle, caused by yeasts reacting slowly on sugar. This natural phenomenon produces fine bubbles and a light, persistent *mousse* (froth), both of which are characteristics of Champagne.

At the premises of **Piper-Heidsieck**, for example, you descend 18m (54ft) below ground and then proceed, in wagons pulled by an electric car, through catacombs flanked by stacks of bottles. An audiovisual program on champagne production is shown.

The easiest way to visit the cellars and vineyards of Reims and also of **Épernay**, 24km (15 miles) to the s, is to take a day trip by bus from Paris. These are offered by Cityrama, Paris-Vision and other tour operators. If you have your own car, a brochure, obtainable from the Reims Tourist Office, gives enough details to enable you to choose a route.

The following champagne cellars in Reims and Épernay welcome visitors and many give tours in English. Always call ahead for days and hours of opening as these will vary according to season, and some cellars prefer to make appointments.

Reims

- **Champagne Abel Lepitre**, blvd. du Val de Zesle ☎26-85-05-77
- **Champagne Veuve Clicquot-Ponsardin**, 1 pl. des Droits-de-l'Homme ☎26-40-25-42
- **Champagne Heidsieck & Co Monopole**, 83 rue Coquebert ☎26-07-39-34
- **Champagne Henriot**, 4 blvd. Henri Vasnier ☎26-82-63-22
- **Champagne Krug**, 5 rue Coquebert ☎26-88-24-24
- **Champagne Lanson**, 12 blvd. Lundy ☎26-78-50-50
- **Champagne G.H. Mumm**, 34 rue du Champ-de-Mars ☎26-49-59-70
- **Champagne Piper-Heidsieck**, 51 blvd. Henri-Vasnier ☎26-84-43-00
- **Champagne Pommery**, 5 pl. Général-Gouraud ☎26-61-62-55
- **Champagne Ruinart**, 4 rue des Crayères ☎26-85-40-29
- **Champagne Taittinger**, 9 pl. St-Nicaise ☎26-85-45-35

Épernay

- **De Castellane**, 57 rue du Verdun ☎26-55-15-33
- **Mercier**, 73 av. Champagne ☎26-54-75-26
- **Moët & Chandon**, 20 av. Champagne ☎26-54-71-11
- **Perriet-Jouët**, 26 av. Champagne ☎26-55-20-53
- **Pol Roger**, 1 rue Henri-Lelarge ☎26-55-41-95
- **De Zenoge**, 30 av. de Champagne ☎26-55-01-01

☞ **Altea Champagne** *(31 bd. P-Doumer, 51100 Reims* ☎ *26-88-53-54* ▥▯ *),* a stylish modern hotel with above-average service; **La Paix** *(9 rue Buirette, 51100 Reims* ☎ *26-40-04-08* ▥▯ *),* quiet, comfortable and modern, with a good restaurant; **Boyer "Les Crayères"** *(64 bd. Vasnier* ☎ *26-82-80-80* ▥▯ *),* an elegant hotel with a delightful garden and one of the best-regarded restaurants in France, offering superb *nouvelle cuisine.*

⇌ **L'Assiette Champenoise** *(40, av. P. Vaillant-Couturier, 51430 Tinqueux* ☎ *26-04-15-56* ▥▯ *);* **Le Chardonnay** *(184 av. d'Épernay* ☎ *26-06-08-60* ▥▯ *to* ▥▯ *);* **Les Ombrages** *(*▯▯ *to* ▥▯ *see hotel Altea Champagne above);* **Les Reflets bleus** *(12, rue Gabriel Voisin* ☎ *26-82-59-79* ▥▯ *).*

ROUEN

124km (87 miles) NW *of Paris. Population (Greater Rouen): 400,000.* **By train:** *from Gare St-Lazare;* **by car:** *on the A13* ℹ *25 pl. de la Cathédrale, 76008 Rouen* ☎ *35-71-41-77. Avoid visiting on Tues, as many museums are closed.*
For centuries the capital of the powerful duchy of the Seine, capital of Normandy for many centuries and now capital of the province of Upper Normandy, Rouen is an active sea- and river-port as well as one of France's greatest trade and industrial centers. This city of 100 spires has always been an important strategic prize and has suffered regular sieges and ransacking, culminating in severe damage from heavy bombardment from both sides in World War II.

Despite this, it has retained an intimate domestic atmosphere, some superb church and secular architecture, fine museums, and a bustling social and shopping center. It is an ideal city for walking and much of the ancient center has been pedestrianized.

A WALK AROUND ROUEN

The following route *(allow at least two hours)* takes in most of the main sights. Some, which appear below in SMALL CAPITALS, are described more fully on the following page.

Begin at the place de la Cathédrale, a short walk from the railway station or parking lots. The **Office de Tourisme** is to be found in a beautiful Renaissance building *(#25)* with cherubs above the door. This was built in the 16thC as the Bureau des Finances or tax collector's office. It is, of course, essential to visit the **CATHEDRAL**, which dominates its surroundings and demonstrates the development of various periods of Gothic style spanning the 12th-16thC.

After this, you should leave by the w door, and follow rue St-Romain, along the N side. This is the antique dealers' quarter of Rouen. The timber-framed houses, dating from the 14th-19thC, are typical of the region, where stone was scarce and oak forests plentiful. The overhanging buildings date from before 1525 when local law forbade the style in order to prevent streets from becoming too dark. On the right, look at the **Vieille Maison** of 1466 and the restored **Archbishop's Palace** (14th-16thC). There is a plaque recording that Joan of Arc was condemned here in 1431 and then officially rehabilitated 25 years later.

Across the rue de la République is the ornate church of **Saint-Maclou**

(**III**). Built in 1552, it shows the limits attained by the Flamboyant Gothic style, and its carved doorways and five-gabled portal are famous examples of their kind. Behind the church is the **Aître Saint-Maclou**, a curious early 16thC timber building that was once used as a bonehouse and has the remains of dance of death sculptures still curiously visible. The building now houses the Academy of Fine Arts.

Pass along rue Martainville and the pretty rue Damiette, which is still reminiscent of ancient times. From place du Lieutenant Aubert, you can catch a glimpse of the sculpted facade of the **Hôtel d'Etancourt**, a superb 16th-17thC mansion in rue d'Amiens. The next street to the right, rue Eau de Robec, is named after the brook in which newly-dyed cloth was washed. Look up to see the open attics in which the cloth was dried.

The nearby enormous abbey church **l'Abbatiale St-Ouen** *(open mid-Mar to end Oct 10am-12.30pm, 2-6pm, closed Tues; Nov to mid-Mar 10am-12.30pm, 2-4.30pm, closed Mon, Tues, Thurs, Fri; closed mid-Dec to mid-Jan)* was once a powerful Benedictine monastery. It is worth a visit for the soaring lines that make it a fine specimen of Gothic architecture, and for the beauty of the diffused light through its stained glass.

Leave the abbey gardens by the restored 18thC **Hôtel de Ville** and across place du Général-de-Gaulle to reach the shaded **place du Rougemare**, where there are pleasant cafés. Rue du Cordier leads from the square to rue du Donjon, where the **Tour Jeanne d'Arc** *(✪ open 10am-noon, 2-5pm or 5.30pm; closed Tues and holidays)* is to be found. This *donjon*, with its pepperpot roof, is all that remains of Philip Augustus' castle built in 1204. In it is the somber, bare room where Joan of Arc was brought before her accusers and threatened with torture.

Turn back along rue du Donjon, then right into rue Jaques Villon at the end of which, on the left, is the old church of St-Laurent, which houses an important collection of wrought-iron work in the MUSÉE LE SECQ-DES-TOURNELLES. The MUSÉE DES BEAUX-ARTS is on the opposite side of the street. This substantial provincial collection includes works by Delacroix, Monet and Sisley. After this, take a right into rue Thiers, then left to rue Jeanne d'Arc until you reach the rue du Gros Horloge, which leads, on the right, to the **place du vieux Marché**. This square, where Joan of Arc was burned at the stake, bears a concrete-and-metal cross in tribute to the soldier maid. The MUSÉE JEANNE D'ARC, also in the square in a 15thC crypt, unfolds her tragic story in a series of waxwork tableaux.

Here, at the heart of the ancient city, is a striking and joyous combination of the old and the new — a forerunner of architect I.M. Pei's achievement with the LOUVRE pyramid. The tall, black-and-white timbered houses overlook a light and airy modern church (1979), the **Église Sainte Jeanne d'Arc**, whose sweeping roofs stretch toward the sky in an evocation of the flames of the stake. The church retains the 16thC stained glass windows salvaged from another church after the 1944 bombardment.

Returning from the square, take the rue du Gros Horloge, a busy and characterful street with a number of 14th and 15thC half-timbered houses. The street is spanned by the **GROS HORLOGE** within which is the **BELFRY MUSEUM**. Then continue along the street as far as the rue du Bec which leads to the delightful **Palais de Justice**. The only remaining part of this 16thC Norman parliament building is the central block.

From here, by turning right along rue aux Juifs and then right again into rue des Carmes, it is easy to get your bearings to return to the place de la Cathédrale where the walk began.

🏃 Walking tours of the city are offered throughout the year *(in French, morn, aft and eve July-mid-Sept, Sat, Sun and hols for rest of year; in English daily every aft mid-July to mid-Aug* ☎ *details from Office de Tourisme).*

Rouen Cathedral (Notre-Dame) 🏛 ★

Cathedral open Mon 9am-noon, 2-7pm, Tues-Sat 7.30am-noon, 2-7pm, Sun 7.30am-6pm. Closed hols. Crypt and Lady Chapel ☎ 🏃 *(compulsory) 2nd half of April, July-Aug, 1st week Sept, at 10am, 11am, 2.15pm, 3pm, 4pm, 5pm, except closed Sun morning and public hols; (no tours May and June, 2nd week Sept to mid-April).*

Rouen's cathedral soars above the city in extravagant confidence. The main w facade climbs from the solid base of the St-Romain Tower on the N side and the two outer portals, sole remnants of the cathedral that burned down in 1201, to a dramatic skyline, the late 15thC work of Guillaume Pontis. It reaches its climax in the **Tour de Beurre** (Butter Tower) on the s side, which was paid for by indulgences granted to allow citizens to eat butter during Lent. The ornate decoration, always in comfortable proportion, is typical of the Flamboyant Gothic style.

The cathedral's interior is more austere but just as harmonious, and the highlights, the **11thC crypt** and the **Lady Chapel**, with its 14thC windows and Renaissance tombs of the two cardinals of Amboise, are worth the obligatory guided tour.

The cathedral is now regularly illuminated *(every Sat and Sun, Easter, holidays, July and Aug, 2wks at Christmas/New Year)* and it is worth making the trip back into town to see this spectacular silhouette if you are staying overnight.

Gros Horloge and Musée du Beffroi (Belfry Museum) 🔆

Rue du Gros-Horloge. Renovations during 1993. Normal hours of opening when back in operation: open from Palm Sunday (1wk before Easter) to end Sept; closed Tues, Wed morn, hols ☎ *(joint admission with Musée des Beaux-Arts).*

The enormous and colourful Renaissance clock straddles the street named after it, adorning a gatehouse completed in 1527, inside which is the belfry museum where you can examine the workings of the clock, made in the late 14thC, as well as two 13thC bells. The highlight is the view of the city and Seine valley, making the long climb up the spiral staircase worthwhile.

Musée des Beaux-Arts

Square Verdrel ☎ *35-71-28-40. Open 10am-noon, 2-6pm. Closed Tues, Wed morning and hols* ☎ *Ticket also gives admission to Musée du Beffroi.*

This rich collection forms one of France's most important regional museums, and contains masterpieces by Delacroix, Ingres and Gerard David, whose *Virgin and Saints* is a work of great calmness and sensitivity. Other notable artists whose works are displayed are Jouvenet,

Monet and Sisley, and there are single works by Velázquez and Clouet. There are paintings of the Italian, Flemish and Dutch Schools and French Masters of the 17th, 18th and 19thC, with a focus on Géricault and the Impressionists.

Musée de Céramique

Hôtel de Hocqueville, 1 rue Faucon ☎ *35-07-31-74. Opening details as Musée des Beaux-Arts* 🔲 ✗ *Sat afternoon July-Aug.*

A newly restored 17thC mansion is now host to this collection of ceramics of various origins. Emphasis is on the *Vieux Rouen* style of local earthenware.

Musée Jeanne d'Arc

Place du Vieux Marché ☎ *35-88-02-70. Open daily May to mid-Sept 9.30am-6.30pm; mid-Sept to end Apr 10am-noon, 2-6.30pm, closed Mon* 🔲

Life-sized wax figures recreate the tragic story of Jeanne d'Arc, in a museum in a 15thC crypt that is also filled with models and reproductions of historic documents.

Musée le Secq-des-Tournelles ☆

Rue Jacques Villon, in the old church of St-Laurent 🔲 *Opening details as Musée des Beaux-Arts* ✗ *Sat afts July-Aug.*

This unusual museum houses a collection of all sorts of wrought ironwork, displayed to perfection in an old church. The arches are hung with *auberge* and tradesmen's signs, and the alcoves and galleries are full of tools, jewelry and locks.

🛏 The **Hôtel de la Cathédrale** *(12 rue St-Romain, 76000 Rouen* ☎ *35-71-57-95* 🔲*)* is a hotel of the traditional kind; **Altea Champ-de-Mars** *(av. Aristide Briand, 76000 Rouen* ☎ *35-52-42-32* 🔲*)* has every facility.

🍽 **Les Nympheas** *(7 rue de la Pie* ☎ *35-89-26-69* 🔲 *to* 🔲 *closed Sun evening)* in the old market area, has traditonal Norman decor and a garden where you can have aperitifs or coffee; **Au Bois Chenu** *(23 pl. de la Pucelle* ☎ *35-71-19-54* 🔲*)* is tiny and offers good value; **La Couronne** *(31 pl. du Vieux-Marché* ☎ *35-71-40-90* 🔲*)*, reputedly the oldest *auberge* in France, specializes in classic French cuisine.

VERSAILLES ☆

*24km (15 miles) sw of Paris. Located on map **17**D2; town center and château map on following page. Population: 97,150. By train/RER: from Gare St-Lazare or Gare Montparnasse/RER line C; by car: on N10; by bus: tours with Cityrama, 4 pl. des Pyramides, 1ᵉʳ* ☎ *42-60-30-14 and Paris-Vision, 214 rue de Rivoli, 1ᵉʳ* ☎ *42-60-31-25* ℹ *7 rue des Réservoirs* ☎ *39-50-36-22.*

The name of Versailles is so closely linked with the palace that the town itself tends to be neglected by tourists. It is worth knowing, however, that Versailles is one of the earliest examples of what we now call town planning. It was built by royal command in the 17thC following a carefully designed layout. Its regular, grid-like pattern of streets and squares (exemplified in the elegant **place Hoche**) inspired the designers of such cities as St Petersburg, Karlsruhe and Washington, DC. Today it preserves a wealth of domestic architecture dating from the time of Louis XV and XVI. Two churches worth visiting are

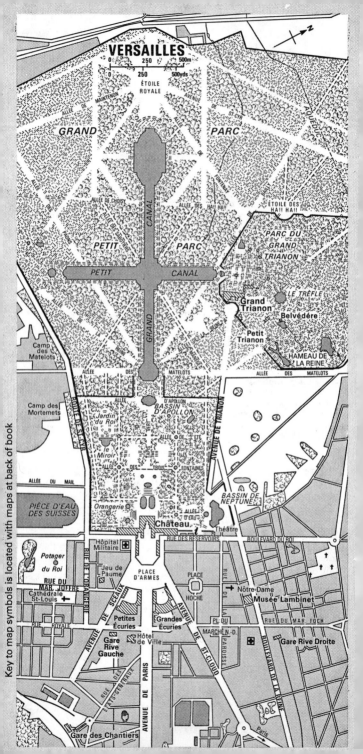

Notre-Dame, built by J.H. Mansart in the 1680s, and **St-Louis**, built by Mansart de Sagonne in the mid-18thC.

Musée Lambinet

54 bd. de la Reine ☎ *39-50-30-32* 🖾 ✗ *Open Tues-Sun 2-6pm. Closed Mon, public holidays.*

This museum fulfills two objectives: to give an insight into 18thC life, and to cover the history of the town of Versailles. One room is dedicated to Charlotte Corday, and others to 19th and 20thC paintings by artists such as Corot and Boilly.

Le Château de Versailles

State apartments open Tues-Sun 9.45am-5pm; Grand Trianon (separate 🖾*) open 9.45am-noon, 2-5pm; Petit Trianon (separate* 🖾 *or cheaper if combined with Grand Trianon) open 2-5pm; gardens open daily dawn to dusk. Palace closed Mon, public holidays.*

For information on opening times, programs, group visits ☎ *30-84-74-00* 🖾 *but various discounts for children, students and over-60s, depending on day of week and type of entry (e.g., if not taking guided tour, under-18s always* 🔟*; over-18 and under-26, or over-60, reduced rate Tues-Sat; everyone, reduced rate on Sun)* �︎ 💻 ♿ ✄

✗ *Compulsory in some parts of building; tours available in English. For guided tours, go to entrance 1; for nonguided tours, go to entrance 2. Audio-guides available.*

The palace of Versailles is perhaps the greatest monument to absolute monarchy ever built. It is overwhelming, fascinating, unforgettable, but to many people not exactly beautiful. Louis XIV, the Sun King, who built it, was extremely vain, and his palace is an expression of egomania in stone, plaster and gold leaf.

The site was first occupied by a hunting lodge and then by a small brick-and-stone château, built by Louis XIII and enlarged by his son Louis XIV, the work continuing from 1661 for about 50 years. The architects were first Le Vau, then Jules Hardouin-Mansart. The decoration was supervised by Le Brun, and the gardens were planned by Le Nôtre, creator of the TUILERIES gardens. At the height of the building work, 36,000 men and 6,000 horses were employed.

In 1682 Louis decided to make Versailles the court residence and seat of government, and it retained this function until the Revolution. Thus Versailles was the capital of France for more than 100 years. It was the scene of a glittering court, which in its heyday included a thousand nobles, who lived in the palace along with a vast retinue of servants.

Approaching the palace from the station and avenue de Paris, the **stables** *(Grandes* and *Petites Écuries)* are to the right and left of the vast **place d'Armes** in front of the palace. Passing through the great wrought-iron gates, the visitor enters the enormous courtyard, with its equestrian statue of Louis XIV, erected by King Louis-Philippe, in the middle. Enter by the doorway on the right of the courtyard, and follow the stairway to the upper chapel vestibule, from where the **chapel** can be seen. Dedicated to St-Louis (King Louis IX of France), it is a frothy confection in white and gold, with a sumptuously painted ceiling.

From here you pass into the series of **State apartments** leading into the astonishing **Hall of Mirrors**, where the 17 windows that overlook the gardens are matched on the opposite wall by a row of arches filled with reflecting glass.

Beside the Hall of Mirrors are the sumptuous **King's apartments**, with the bed where each morning and night the monarch's *levée* and *couchée* took place in front of the assembled courtiers. Louis XIV died of gangrene on this bed on September 1, 1715.

At the opposite end of the Hall of Mirrors are the **Queen's apartments**, followed by the **Coronation Room** and then the s wing. Its first floor is taken up almost entirely by the **Hall of Battles**, built by Louis-Philippe, which contains 33 paintings of war scenes. Also on the first floor are several rooms, including the **private apartments of the King and Queen**.

The **Royal Opera**, which occupies the end of the N wing, can also be visited only on a guided tour. Its interior is entirely of wood, ornately carved and painted in gold, blue and pink.

The gardens
▣ *Open daily, dawn-dusk. Picnics not allowed.*

To understand Versailles fully, it is necessary to appreciate that the whole complex, palace and gardens, is a kind of symbolic Utopia in which one theme is constantly emphasized: that of a solar deity around which everything revolves, just as the state revolves around the king.

This comes across particularly clearly in the **gardens**, which were laid out by Le Nôtre in a series of highly formal terraces adorned with *parterres,* statues, vases and fountains. Nature is subdued, as a demonstration of the power of the Sun King, who is represented here as Apollo.

Bear this in mind as you approach the main focus of the garden, the **fountain of Apollo**, down a long avenue flanked by statues and with a carpet of lawn stretching away into the distance. The figure of Apollo in his chariot emerges out of the water, just as in legend the sun rose out of the sea at daybreak. You can also witness the amazing spectacle of the **illuminated fountains**, by night, and the **Grandes Eaux Musicales** by day, generally Sundays only, from May to September (☎ *39-50-36-22 — the Office de Tourisme — for exact details of times and tickets).* The **Grande Fête de Nuit**, a firework spectacular on the Bassin de Neptune, takes place for a few nights only in July and September.

Beyond the fountain of Apollo stretches the **Grand Canal**, on which there once sailed a flotilla of small-scale ships and gondolas. Today you can rent a boat to row on the canal, in more modest style. The waterway forms a cross, the northern arm of which leads to the **Grand Trianon** and **Petit Trianon**. These are well worth a visit, the former with its pink marble colonnade and lavish interior, the latter more elegant and restrained, with its exquisite theater in which Marie-Antoinette used to act.

Close by is the **Hameau de la Reine** (Queen's hamlet), a collection of mock-rustic buildings where the same queen used to play at leading the simple life.

Recognizing that some of these points of interest are 15-20 minutes' walk from the château, the management has introduced glass-sided trains (☎ ☎ 39-50-55-12 *for information and reservations),* which offer a running commentary in several languages, and interludes of classical music. These either make a driving circuit, slowing down but not stopping, or allow passengers to descend and be collected again $1\frac{1}{2}$ hours later.

🐾 **St-Louis** *(28 Rue St-Louis, 78000 Versailles* ☎ *39-50-23-55* ▯ *to* ▯ ▱ *).*

🚆 **Le Champfagou** *(3 Rue des Deux-Portes* ☎ *39-50-64-04* ▯ *to* ▯), set in a pedestrianized street and serving the recipes of yesteryear; **La Flotille** *(Parc du Château* ☎ *39-51-41-58* ▯*),* a delightful little restaurant near the E end of the canal, in the palace gardens.

EURODISNEY

Boîte Postale 100, 77777 Marne-La-Vallée CEDEX 4 ☒ *One payment gives free admission to everything within the park except certain named events and sideshows* 🚆 🖥 ♿ ✳ 🚗 ⒶⒺ *Open summer 9am-midnight; winter 10am-6pm. Times may vary, and will change for school vacations (e.g., 9am-9pm), public holidays, etc. Times and dates of parades and firework displays will also vary according to season. Check with Paris Bureau de Tourisme.*

Why bring the Magic Kingdom east? That most American of institutions launched itself upon Europe in spring 1992, fulfilling the wish made by Walt Disney himself some 30 years earlier.

And why Paris? Geographical commonsense dictated it must be so. Some 132 millions of affluent Europeans live within a day's journey, and that is some catchment area. Add to that the millions of visitors lured to Paris from all over the world, and it soon becomes clear why this site was the obvious choice.

Marne La Vallée, 32km (20 miles) E of Paris, off the A4 to Strasbourg, is one of five new towns created in the Île-de-France region in the 1960s and '70s. It had already become a township of some substance before EuroDisney's decision to move in next door. Even the high-speed train, the TGV, will stop there from 1994.

The Kingdom provides some local employment, of course, but the majority of the staff (known as the "cast") are foreigners — from the United Kingdom, Belgium, the Netherlands, Germany, Spain, Italy and so on — useful for their linguistic skills, their youth and enthusiasm and their liking for dressing up in fancy costumes.

The ultimate success of EuroDisney should never be in any doubt. For those who argue that it is an alien civilization dropped onto the cultured French, comes the valid counter-argument that Cinderella and Sleeping Beauty are French stories, Peter Pan is English, Pinocchio Italian, Snow White German; and Discoveryland carries tributes to Jules Verne and to Leonardo da Vinci.

That mouse, surprisingly to a first-time visitor, is not the dominant feature of the park, even though much of the merchandizing is geared toward Mickey and his chums, and every fourth child or so is wearing a pair of black ears.

GETTING THERE

By train: RER trains (line A4) stop at Marne La Vallée/Chessy, outside the main gates. From June 1994, this same station will be served by the TGV *(train grande vitesse)*, providing fast links to Strasbourg, Brussels and, eventually, London. **By car**: Route A4 due E of Paris (the road to Reims), leaving at the exit marked "Parc EuroDisneyland." There is day-visitor parking for 11,500 cars and the charge is not expensive. A moving walkway will sweep you from the parking lot along toward the main gates, if your two legs need to conserve their energy for a little exercise later in the day. **By air**: to Roissy/Charles-De-Gaulle or Orly airports, then by direct airport VEA Shuttle Bus; the journey time is about 45 minutes from either airport.

ADVANCE PLANNING

To get the most out of your visit, it helps to know what to expect.

- Ideally, you will stay in one of the **on-site hotels**. That way, you can be up and out first thing in the morning, taking full advantage of your day-long admission ticket, and going on some of the rides without having to line up for too long.
- If you are not staying locally, **purchase your tickets in advance**. Lining up for an attraction is one thing, but lining up, for maybe an hour, just to buy an admission ticket is a terrible waste of time.
- **Plan to stay** all day and all evening. It's the only way really to get the most from your ticket.
- You should also expect to **stand in line**. It's not so bad, as the lines really do move, and you shuffle past a whole lot of visual stimuli and not too many blank walls. Nevertheless, do think up how you might pass the time if you have kids to entertain.

ARRIVING AT THE GATES

For the uninitiated, this may seem a little like knocking on heaven's door. You descend through a fragrant and pretty, formal garden where little fountains play. Beyond this, a vast and palatial building, in shades of pink with red turrets, spreads out across the panorama, cleverly concealing any glimpse of the kingdom within. This is the Disneyland Hotel — the first ever Disneyland hotel to offer a panoramic view of the theme park from its rooms. Pass below the hotel: non-ticketholders to the left; if you have your charge-card-shaped ID/ticket, sail straight on through.

ENTRANCE TO THE MAGIC KINGDOM — MAIN STREET, USA

You're in the main square. Straight ahead is **Main Street, USA**. Before you stretches a whole, long street of stores large and small, restaurants, canteens and ice-cream parlors, hotels, all in glorious turn-of-the-century American style. The "cast" are to be seen, sporting their fine period costume. Many ways to spend money here — but unless you can't wait for your mouse ears, save the stores for later, when you need a rest.

Make one very important stop-off. At **City Hall**, the first large building on the left of Main Street USA, is the visitor information center. Here you can pick up a free copy of a detailed **site guide and map**, which is exactly what you will need to find your way around.

FOUR "LANDS"

The real fantasy starts at the far end of Main Street, USA. Sleeping Beauty's castle looms up ahead — instantly recognizable as the standard Disneyland image, yet this castle has been subtly amended from its American prototypes and derives from a famous and beautiful medieval French illuminated book *Les Très Riches Heures du Duc de Berry.*

Within, is a whole gallery full of stained-glass windows telling the story of Sleeping Beauty, and in a dripping cavern below lies a sleeping dragon who wakes from time to time to unleash a fierce warning.

Fantasyland . . . Adventureland . . . Discoveryland . . . Frontierland . . . .
Whichever way you turn lies hours of fascination.

In **Fantasyland** you can ride high in the air with Dumbo, whirl around on a dizzy ride in the Mad Hatter's teacups, take flight over the rooftops of London with Peter Pan, be whisked through a retelling of the story of Pinocchio, get lost in Alice's mysterious maze, ride a marvelous merry-go-round, travel through the Black Forest to see the adventures of Snow White and her seven dwarfs, and join hundreds of singing and dancing children on a voyage round the world. Although still fun for older children and adults, this really is the end of the park to take your children if they are under six.

Adventureland is a trip to the Caribbean. In Adventure Isle, you can spend hours exploring pirate ships and secret caves and crossing high-up rope-and-barrel bridges; climb the winding stairways through the tree house built by the Swiss Family Robinson; or glide silently in a boat on a thrilling underground ride as the Pirates of the Caribbean battle and plunder. Take this trip, if you can, on a warm summer's evening, and climb the tall tree house against the setting sun with the warm breeze in your hair.

Discoveryland is where fantasy and science collide. An amazing sky ride — the Orbitron — dominates the scene; on it, you can pilot your own spaceship, flying in competition with other weird machines prototyped by Leonardo da Vinci. The Star Tours ride takes you on a simulated flight through a movie created for Disney by George Lucas, while Michael Jackson stars as Captain EO in a stunning 3-D musical motion picture. Anyone more than one meter (39 inches) high can have a go at driving their own car on the Autopia racing circuit: it's quite safe. Videopolis is a music and video center primarily for teenagers; it has a performance space where live shows happen. Probably most breathtaking of all is the Visionarium, a 360° motion picture journey through time and space in which Jules Verne travels in company with the Timekeeper, an animatronic robot who runs the whole proceedings live on stage.

Frontierland holds the biggest thrills. There's the much-publicized Phantom Manor, with all its ghostly inhabitants; encircling Thunder Mountain, there's a giant lake where you can travel in an Indian canoe, explore the rustic waterways on a keelboat, or set out in style on a full-size

Mississippi-style paddle steamer. The Big Thunder Mountain Railroad ride, in the carriage of a runaway train as it gains frightening speed through tunnels and gullies, is the one to wait for. It's thrilling.

AND THAT'S NOT ALL . . . .

Pick up the EuroDisneyland railroad from Main Street, for a scenic ride around the park, which includes a trip through an improbably mini-ature diorama of the Grand Canyon.

The parades are worth taking time out to see, although if you have already seen one, then it's a good time to get onto some of the rides without waiting too long. Each afternoon, a massive parade gets under way and thousands of people stop to wave at the larger-than-life colorful characters as they roll past. At night, a firework display precedes another parade, this time all-electric, each float lit with thousands of tiny lights.

Beyond the main entrance, opposite the RER station, is **Festival Disney**, an entertainment center with a quirky modern design by Cali-fornia architect Frank Gehry. This is a separate attraction (☎) contain-ing discos, stores, food of all kinds, and the spectacular Buffalo Bill's Wild West Show, presented by American Express. Performed twice-nightly, it is based on the show toured by Buffalo Bill Cody 100 years ago, in the US and in Europe. A truly Texan spectacular, with sharpshooting, Indian stunts, live buffalo, a generous feast and a lot of audience participation. Not cheap, but very good value.

WHERE TO STAY

Why not go the whole way and stay in one of the resort hotels? All are very close, and the farther ones are linked to the park by a never-en-ding stream of complimentary buses. Each hotel is designed around a different, quintessentially American theme. From the luxury of the **Dis-neyland Hotel** to the ruggedness of the **Hotel Cheyenne**, to the pioneering log cabins of **Camp Davy Crockett**, staying at EuroDisney makes very good sense. **Reservation inquiries**: in the UK ☎(071) 753 2900; from other countries call Paris ☎(33) 1 49-41-49-10.

Words and phrases

A guide to French

This glossary covers the basic language needs of the traveler: for pronunciation, essential vocabulary and simple conversation, finding accommodation, visiting the bank, shopping, using public transport or a car. Finally, there are phrases connected with food — eating, choosing, ordering — and a detailed 7-page menu guide.

PRONUNCIATION
It is plainly impossible to give a summary of the subtlety and richness of the French language, but there are some general tips about pronunciation that it will be helpful to remember once you have decided to communicate with the French in their own language.

French tends to be pronounced in individual syllables rather than in rhythmic feet. For example, the word *institution* has four stresses in French but only two in English. In French the voice usually rises at the ends of words and sentences, whereas it drops in British (although not always in American) English. French vowels and consonants are shorter, softer and generally more rounded than their English counterparts.

The French language is full of characteristic sounds — the r, the u, the eau sound and the nasal sounds (e.g., an, en, ien, in, ain, on, un). These are not as difficult as they may seem: the key is to have confidence.

The best way is to speak English while mimicking a strong French accent. The poet Verlaine used this method with his English pupils.

REFERENCE WORDS

Monday	*lundi*	Friday	*vendredi*
Tuesday	*mardi*	Saturday	*samedi*
Wednesday	*mercredi*	Sunday	*dimanche*
Thursday	*jeudi*	Public holiday	*jour férié* (m)

January	*janvier*	July	*juillet*
February	*février*	August	*août*
March	*mars*	September	*septembre*
April	*avril*	October	*octobre*
May	*mai*	November	*novembre*
June	*juin*	December	*décembre*

0	*zéro*	11	*onze*	22	*vingt-deux*
1	*un*	12	*douze*	30	*trente*
2	*deux*	13	*treize*	40	*quarante*
3	*trois*	14	*quatorze*	50	*cinquante*
4	*quatre*	15	*quinze*	60	*soixante*
5	*cinq*	16	*seize*	70	*soixante-dix*
6	*six*	17	*dix-sept*	80	*quatre-vingts*
7	*sept*	18	*dix-huit*	90	*quatre-vingt-dix*
8	*huit*	19	*dix-neuf*	100	*cent*
9	*neuf*	20	*vingt*	500	*cinq cent*
10	*dix*	21	*vingt-et-un*	1,000	*mille*

1993/94/95 *mil neuf cent quatre-vingt-treize/quatorze/quinze*

First	*premier, -ière*	Quarter-past . . .	. . . *et quart*
Second	*second, -e*	Half past . . .	. . . *et demie*
Third	*troisième*	Quarter to . . .	. . . *moins le quart*
Fourth	*quatrième*	Quarter to six	*six heures moins*
. . . o'clock	. . . *heures*	le quart	

Mr	*monsieur/M.*	Ladies	*dames*
Mrs	*madame/Mme.*	Men	*hommes*
Miss	*mademoiselle/Mlle.*	Gentlemen	*messieurs*

BASIC COMMUNICATION

Yes	*oui* (*si*, for emphatic contradiction)	Here/there	*ici/là*
No	*non*	Over there	*là-bas*
Please	*s'il vous plaît*	Big	*grand, -e*
Thank you	*merci*	Small	*petit, -e*
I'm very sorry	*je suis désolé/pardon, excusez-moi*	Hot/cold	*chaud, -e/froid, -e*
Excuse me	*pardon/excusez-moi*	Good	*bon, bonne*
Not at all/you're welcome	*de rien*	Bad	*mauvais, -e*
Hello	*bonjour, salut* (familiar), *allô* (on telephone)	Well	*bien*
		Badly	*mal*
		With	*avec*
		And	*et*
Good morning/afternoon *bonjour*		But	*mais*
Good evening	*bonsoir*	Very	*très*
Good night	*bonsoir/bonne nuit*	All	*tout, -e*
Goodbye	*au revoir*	Open	*ouvert, -e*
Morning	*matin* (m)	Closed	*fermé, -e*
Afternoon	*après-midi* (m/f)	Left	*gauche*
Evening	*soir* (m)	Right	*droite*
Night	*nuit* (f)	Straight ahead	*tout droit*
Yesterday	*hier*	Near	*près/proche*
Today	*aujourd'hui*	Far	*loin*
Tomorrow	*demain*	Up/down	*en haut/en bas*
Next week	*la semaine prochaine*	Early/late	*tôt/tard*
Last week	*la semaine dernière*	Quickly	*vite*
. . . days ago	*il y a . . . jours*	Pleased to meet you. *Enchanté.*	
Month	*mois* (m)	Agreed.	*D'accord.*
Year	*an* (m) / *année* (f)	How are you?	*Comment ça va?*
		(Formal: *comment allez vous?*)	

296

Very well, thank you. *Très bien, merci.*
Do you speak English? *Parlez-vous anglais?*
I don't understand. *Je ne comprends pas.*
I don't know. *Je ne sais pas.*
Please explain. *Pourriez-vous me l'expliquer?*
Please speak more slowly. *Parlez plus lentement, s'il vous plaît.*
My name is . . . *Je m'appelle . . .*
I am American/English/Japanese *Je suis americain,-e,/anglais,-e/ japonais, -e.*
Where is/are? *Où est/ sont . . . ?*
Is there a . . . ? *Y a-t-il un . . . ?*
What? *Comment?*
How much? *Combien?*

How much does it cost? *Ça coute combien?*
That's too much. *C'est trop.*
Expensive *cher/chère*
Cheap *pas cher/bon marché*
Free *gratuit*
Paying *payant*
I would like . . . *Je voudrais . . .*
Do you have . . ? *Avez-vous . . ?*
You're right/wrong. *Vous avez raison/tort.*
You've made a mistake. *Vous vous trompez.*
Just a minute. *Attendez une minute.* (On telephone: *ne quittez pas!*)
That's fine/OK. *Ça va/OK/ça y est/d'accord.*
What time is it? *Quelle heure est-il?*
I don't feel well. *Je ne me sens pas bien/j'ai mal.*

ACCOMMODATION

Making a reservation by letter

Dear Sir or Madam, *Monsieur, Madame,*
I would like to reserve one double room *Je voudrais réserver une chambre pour deux personnes* (with bathroom), *(avec salle de bain),* one twin-bedded room *une chambre avec deux lits* and one single room (with shower) *et une chambre pour une personne (avec douche)* for 7 nights from 12th August. *pour 7 nuits à partir du 12 août.*

We would like bed and breakfast/half board/full board, *Nous désirons le petit déjeuner/la demi-pension/pension,* and would prefer a quiet room *et préférerions une chambre tranquille* overlooking the courtyard. *qui donne sur la cour.*

Please send me details of your terms with the confirmation. *Je vous serais obligé de m'envoyer vos conditions et tarifs avec la confirmation.*
Yours sincerely,
Veuillez agréer l'expression de mes sentiments distingués.

Arriving at the hotel
Do you have a room?
Avez-vous une chambre?
I have a reservation. My name is . . .
J'ai une réservation. Je m'appelle . . .
A quiet room with bath/shower/toilet/wash basin
Une chambre tranquille avec bain/douche/toilette/lavabo
. . . overlooking the park/street/back.
. . . qui donne sur le parc/la rue/la cour.

Does the price include breakfast/service/tax?
Ce prix comprend-il le petit déjeuner/le service/les taxes?
This room is too large/small/cold/hot/noisy.
Cette chambre est trop grande/petite/froide/chaude/bruyante.
That's too expensive. Have you anything cheaper?
C'est trop cher. Avez-vous quelquechose de moins cher?
Where can I park my car?
Où puis-je garer ma voiture?
Is it safe to leave the car on the street?
Est-ce qu'on peut laisser la voiture dans la rue?

Floor/story *étage* (m)	Porter *portier/concierge* (m)
Dining room/restaurant *salle à*	*porteur (station)*
manger (f)/*restaurant* (m)	Manager *directeur* (m)
Lounge *salon* (m)	Maid *femme de chambre* (f)

Do you have a room? *Avez-vous une chambre?*
What time is breakfast? *À quelle heure est le petit déjeuner?*
Can I drink the tap water? *L'eau du robinet est-elle potable?*
What time does the hotel close? *À quelle heure ferme l'hôtel?*
Will I need a key? *Aurai-je besoin d'une clé?*
Is there a night porter? *Y a-t-il un portier de nuit?*
I am leaving tomorrow morning. *Je partirai demain matin.*
Please give me at call at . . . *Voulez-vous m'appeler à . . .*
Come in! *Entrez!*

SHOPPING

Where is the nearest/a good . . . ?
Où est le . . . le plus proche?/Où y a-t-il un bon . . . ?
Can you help me/show me . . . ?
Pouvez-vous m'aider/voulez-vous me montrer . . . ?
I'm just looking.
Je regarde.
Do you accept charge/credit cards/travelers' checks?
Est-ce que vous acceptez les cartes de crédit/chèques de voyage?
Can you deliver it to . . . ?
Pouvez-vous me le livrer à . . . ?
I'll take it/I'll leave it.
Je le prends/je ne le prends pas.
Can I have it tax-free for export?
Puis-je l'avoir hors taxe pour exportation?
This is faulty. Can I have a replacement/refund?
Celui-ci ne marche pas. Voulez-vous me l'échanger?
I don't want to spend more than . . .
Je ne veux pas mettre plus de . . .
I'll give . . . for it.
Je vous donne . . .

Shops

Antique store   *antiquaire* (m/f)
Art gallery   *galerie d'art* (f)
Bakery   *boulangerie* (f)
Bank   *banque* (f)
Beauty parlor   *salon de beauté* (m)
Bookstore   *librairie* (f)
Butcher   *boucherie* (f)
Horse butcher   *boucherie chevaline* (f)
Pork butcher   *charcuterie* (f)
Tripe butcher   *triperie* (f)
Cake shop   *pâtisserie* (f)
Chocolate shop   *confiserie* (f)
Clothes store   *magasin de vêtements/de mode* (m)
Dairy   *crèmerie* (f)
Delicatessen   *épicerie fine* (f)/ charcuterie (f)
Department store   *grand magasin* (m)
Fishmonger   *marchand de poisson/poissonnier* (m)
Florist   *fleuriste* (m/f)
Greengrocer   *marchand de légumes* (m)
Grocer   *épicier* (m)
Haberdasher   *mercier* (m)

Hairdresser   *coiffeur* (m)
Hardware store   *droguerie* (f)
Jeweler   *bijouterie/ joaillerie* (f)
Market   *marché* (m)
Newsdealer/newsagent   *marchand de journaux* (m)
Optician   *opticien* (m/f)
Perfumery   *parfumerie* (f)
Pharmacy/chemist   *pharmacie* (f)/ *drugstore* (m)
Photographic store   *magasin de photographie* (m)
Post office   *bureau de poste* (m)
Shoe store   *magasin de chaussures* (m)
Souvenir store   *magasin de cadeaux/souvenirs* (m)
Stationer   *papeterie* (f)
Supermarket   *supermarché* (m)
Tailor   *tailleur* (m)
Tobacconist   *bureau de tabac* (m)
Tourist office   *syndicat d'initiative* (m)/*bureau/office de tourisme* (m)
Toy store   *magasin de jouets* (m)
Travel agent   *agence de voyage* (f)

At the bank

I would like to change some dollars/pounds/travelers' checks.
Je voudrais changer des dollars/livres/chèques de voyage.
What is the exchange rate?
Quel est le cours du change?
Can you cash a personal check?
Pouvez-vous encaisser un chèque?

Can I obtain cash with this charge/credit card?
Puis-je obtenir de l'argent avec cette carte de crédit?
Do you need to see my passport?
Voulez-vous voir mon passeport?

In town

Banlieue   suburb
Bois   wood
Boulevard   avenue
Caisse   cash desk
Défense d'entrer   no entry
Défense de fumer   no smoking
Entrée   entrance
Escalier   stair
Étage   floor
Gare   station
Guichet des billets   ticket office

Hôtel de ville   town hall
Pont   bridge
Porte   city gate
Pousser   push
Quai   platform/quay
Rue   street
Sortie   exit
Sortie de secours   emergency exit
Tirer   pull
Voie   track (at railway station)

From the pharmacy

Antiseptic cream   *crème antiseptique* (f)
Aspirin   *aspirine* (f)
Bandages   *pansements* (m) *bandes* (f)
Cotton (wool)   *coton hydrophile*
Diarrhea/upset stomach pills   *comprimés* (m) *pour la diarrhée/ l'estomac dérangé*
Indigestion tablets   *comprimés pour l'indigestion*)
Laxative   *laxatif* (m)
Sanitary napkins   *serviettes hygiéniques* (f)

Shampoo   *shampooing* (m)
Shaving cream   *crème à raser* (f)
Soap   *savon* (m)
Sticking plaster/Band-Aid   *sparadrap* (m)
String   *ficelle* (f)
Suntan cream/oil   *crème solaire* (f)/*huile bronzante* (f)
Tampons   *tampons* (m)
Tissues   *mouchoirs epapier* (m)
Toothbrush   *brosse à dents* (f)
Toothpaste   (*pâte*) *dentifrice* (f)
Travel sickness pills   *comprimés pour les maladies de transport*

Clothing

Bra   *soutien-gorge* (m)
Coat   *manteau* (m)
Dress   *robe* (f)
Jacket   *veste/jaquette* (f)
Pants   *slip* (m)
Pullover   *pull* (m)
Shirt   *chemise* (f)

Shoes   *chaussures* (f)
Skirt   *jupe* (f)
Socks   *chaussettes* (f)
Stockings/tights   *bas/collants* (m)
Sunglasses   *lunettes de soleil* (f)
Swimsuit   *maillot de bain* (m)
Trousers   *pantalon* (m)

Miscellaneous

Film   *film* (m)/*pellicule* (f)
Letter   *lettre* (f)
Money order   *mandat* (m)

Postcard   *carte postale* (f)
Stamp   *timbre* (m)
Telegram   *télégramme* (m)

DRIVING

Service station   *station-service* (f)
Fill it up.   *Le plein, s'il vous plaît.*
Give me . . . francs worth.   *Donnez m'en pour . . . francs.*
I would like . . . liters of gas/petrol.   *Je voudrais . . . litres d'essence.*
Can you check the working condition of . . . ?   *Voulez-vous vérifier l'état de marche de . . . ?*
There is something wrong with the . . .   *Il y a quelque chose qui ne va pas dans le . . .*

Battery	*batterie* (f)	Oil	*huile* (f)
Brakes	*freins* (m)	Tires	*pneus* (m)
Exhaust	*échappement* (m)	Water	*eau* (f)
Lights	*phares* (m)	Windshield	*pare-brise* (m)

My car won't start.   *Ma voiture ne veut pas démarrer.*
My car has broken down/had a flat tire.   *Je suis tombé en panne/J'ai eu une crevaison.*
The engine is overheating.   *Le moteur chauffe.*
How long will it take to repair?   *Il faudra combien de temps pour la réparer?*

Car rental

Is full insurance included?   *Est-ce que l'assurance tous-risques est comprise?*
Is it insured for another driver?   *Est-elle assurée pour un autre conducteur?*
Unlimited mileage   *kilométrage illimité*
Deposit   *caution* (f)
By what time must I return it?   *À quelle heure devrais-je la ramener?*
Can I return it to another depot?   *Puis-je la ramener à une autre agence?*
Is the gas tank full?   *Est-ce que le réservoir est plein?*

Road signs

Aire (de repos)   stopping place/layby
Autres directions   other directions
Camion   truck
Centre ville   town center
Chaussée deformée   irregular surface
Essence (sans plomb)   (lead-free) gasoline
Garage   garage/multistory car park
Ne pas se garer devant la porte   keep exit clear
Parking interdit   no parking
Parking ouvert   parking lot
Passage à niveau   level crossing
Passage protégé   priority for vehicles on main road

Péage   toll point
Piétons   pedestrians
Priorité à droite   priority for vehicles coming from the right
Ralentir   slow down
Rappel   remember that a previous sign still applies
Route barrée   road blocked
Sens obligatoire   through traffic
Sortie   exit
Sortie de secours   emergency exit
Stationnement interdit   no parking
Stationnement toléré   literally, parking tolerated
Toutes directions   all directions
Verglas   (black) ice on road
Vitesse   speed
Voie sans issue   no through road

Other means of transport

Aircraft   *avion* (m)
Airport   *aéroport* (m)
Bus   *autobus* (m)
Bus stop   *arrêt d'autobus* (m)
Coach   *car* (m)
Couchette/sleeper   *wagon-lit* (m)
Ferry/boat   *ferry/bateau/bac* (m)
Ferry port   *port du ferry/bateau/bac* (m)

Hovercraft   *hovercraft/aéroglisseur* (m)
Station   *gare* (m)
Train   *train* (m)
Ticket   *billet* (m)
Ticket office   *guichet* (m)
One-way/single   *billet simple*
Round-trip/return   *billet aller-retour*
Half fare   *demi-tarif*

When is the next . . for . . ?   *À quelle heure est le prochain . . pour . . . ?*
What time does it arrive?   *À quelle heure arrive-t-il?*
What time does the last . . . for . . . leave?   *À quelle heure part le dernier . . . pour . . . ?*
Which platform/quay/gate?   *Quel quai/port?*
Is this the . . . for . . . ?   *Est-ce que c'est bien le . . . pour . . . ?*
Is it direct? Where does it stop?   *C'est direct? Où est-ce qu'il s'arrête?*
Do I need to change anywhere?   *Est-ce que je dois changer?*
Please tell me where to get off?   *Pourrez-vous me dire ou descendre?*
Is there a buffet car?   *Y a-t-il un wagon-restaurant?*

Food and drink

Have you a table for . . . ?   *Avez-vous une table pour . . . ?*
I want to reserve a table.   *Je voudrais réserver une table.*
A quiet table.   *Une table bien tranquille.*
A table near the window.   *Une table près de la fenêtre.*
Could we have another table?   *Est-ce que nous pourrions avoir une autre table?*
Set menu   *Menu prix-fixe*
I did not order this   *Je n'ai pas commandé cela*
Bring me another . . .   *Apportez-moi encore un . . .*
The bill please   *L'addition, s'il vous plaît*
Is service included?   *Le service est compris?*

Some essential words

Breakfast   *petit déjeuner* (m)
Lunch   *déjeuner* (m)
Dinner   *dîner* (m)
Hot   *chaud*
Cold   *froid*
Glass   *verre* (m)
Bottle   *bouteille* (f)
Half-bottle   *demi-bouteille*
Beer/lager   *bière* (f)/ *lager* (m)
Draft beer   *bière (à la) pression*
Orangeade/lemonade   *sirop d'orange/de citron* (m)
Mineral water   *eau minérale* (f)
Fizzy/carbonated water   *eau gazeuse* (f)
Still water   *eau non-gazeuse*
Sparkling   *pétillant*
Nonsparkling   *plat*
Fruit juice   *jus de fruit* (m)
Red wine   *vin rouge* (m)
White/rosé   *vin blanc/ rosé*
Vintage   *année* (f)

Dry   *sec*
Sweet   *doux* (of wine)
    sucré (of food)
Plain   *nature*
Salt   *sel* (m)
Pepper   *poivre* (m)
Mustard   *moutarde* (f)
Oil   *huile* (m)
Vinegar   *vinaigre* (m)
Bread   *pain* (m)
Butter   *beurre* (m)
Cheese   *fromage* (m)
Milk   *lait* (m)
Coffee   *café* (m)
Tea   *thé* (m)
Decaffeinated   *décaféiné*
Herbal tea   *infusion* (f)
Chocolate   *chocolat* (m)
Sugar   *sucre* (m)
Steak   *bifteck* (m)
    well done   *bien cuit*
    medium   *cuit à point*
    rare   *saignant*
    very rare   *bleu*
vegetarian   *végétarien*

MENU GUIDE

à l'Alsacienne   food cooked Alsace-style is served with *choucroute,* ham and frankfurter-style sausages
à l'Anglaise   cooked in the English way — boiled or with boiled vegetables
à l'Armoricaine   fish, especially lobster, cooked Breton-style with white wine, brandy, tomatoes,
onions and herbs
à l'Arlésienne   fish or meat cooked Arles-style, with tomatoes, onions, olives
Agneau   lamb
Agneau de pré salé   young lamb grazed in fields bordering the sea
Aiglefin   haddock
Aigre-doux   sweet and sour
Aiguillettes   thin slices

Ail   garlic
Ailerons   chicken wings
Aïoli   garlic mayonnaise
Allumettes   puff pastry strips garnished or filled
Alouette   lark
Alouette sans tête   thin slices of beef or veal around a savory illing
Amandes   almonds
Ananas   pineapple
Anchoïade   anchovy paste, usually served on crispy bread
Anchois   anchovies
Andouilles   cooked pork sausage with strips of chitterling
Andouillette   chitterling sausage
Anguille   eel
Arachides   peanuts
Artichaut   artichoke
Asperges   asparagus
Assiette anglaise   mixture of cold meats
Assiette assortie   mixture of cold hors d'oeuvres
Avocat   avocado
Baguette   long bread loaf
Banane   banana
Barbue   brill
Barquette   pastry boat
Basilic   basil
Baudroie   anglerfish, monkfish
Bavarois   cream and custard dessert, often with fruit
Béarnaise   sauce made mayonnaise-style, with tarragon
Bécasse   woodcock; roast with truffles *(à la Diane);* on fried bread with *foie gras (à la riche)*
Béchamel   white sauce flavored with onion or bay leaf
Beignet   sweet or savory fritter
Belle-Hélène   sauce (for pear) with ice cream and chocolate
Belons   flat-shelled oysters
Bergère, à la   chicken or meat cooked shepherd-style, with mushrooms, ham, onions and sliced potatoes
Betterave   beetroot
Beurre   butter
Bifteck   beefsteak
Bignorneaux   winkles

Bisque   thick creamy soup usually of shellfish made with white wine, cream and potatoes
Blanchailles   whitebait
Blanquette   white meat cooked in a white sauce eg *blanquette de veau*
Blé   corn, wheat
Blé noir   buckwheat
Boeuf   beef
Bombe   elaborate dessert with ice cream
Bonne femme   poached in white wine with mushrooms
Bordelaise, à la   cooked Bordeaux-style, in a red wine sauce with shallots, tarragon and bone marrow
Bouchée   tiny vol-au-vent
Boudin (noir ou blanc)   (black or white) sausage pudding
Bouillabaisse   Mediterranean fish soup with fresh fish and saffron
Bouillon   stock or broth
Bourgeoise, à la   braised meat or chicken with bacon, onions and carrots
Bourride   Provençal soup of mixed fish with *aïoli*
Branche, à la   whole — as in vegetables like broccoli, spinach
Brandade de morue   purée of salt cod, milk and garlic
Bretonne, à la   cooked Breton-style in onion sauce with haricots
Brioche   soft bread
Broche, à la   spit-roasted
Brochet   pike
Brochette   meat or fish on a skewer
Brouillé   scrambled
oeufs brouillés   scrambled eggs
Brûlé   flamed
Cabillaud   fresh cod
Cachir   Kosher
Caille   quail
Cake   British-style fruit cake
Calamar   squid
Canard or *caneton*   duck
Carbonnade   braised or grilled meat
Carpaccio   thin slices of marinated raw beef
Carré (d'agneau)   loin (of lamb)

Carrelet   plaice
Carottes Vichy   carrots glazed with sugar and butter
Casse-croûte   snack
Cassis   blackcurrant
Cassoulet   casserole from Languedoc with beans, preserved goose and pork
Cèpes   wild, dark brown mushrooms
Cerise   cherry
Cervelles   brains
Champignon   mushroom
Chantilly   whipped cream with sugar
Chapon   capon
Chasseur   cooked hunter-style, with wine, mushrooms and shallots
Châtaigne   chestnut
Cheval   horse
Chèvre or *Chevreau*   goat
Chevrette   shrimp
Chevreuil   venison
Chicorée or *frisée*   curly endive/chicory
Chou   light puff pastry/cabbage
Chou-fleur   cauliflower
Choucroute   pickled white cabbage/sauerkraut
Choux de Bruxelles   Brussels sprouts
Citron   lemon
Citron vert   lime
Citrouille   pumpkin
Civet de lièvre   jugged hare
Clafoutis   baked batter pudding with cherries
Cochon de lait   sucking pig
Coeur   heart
Colin   hake
Concombre   cucumber
Confit   meat covered in its own fat, cooked and preserved
Confit d'oie   preserved goose
Confiture   jam
Contre-filet   sirloin steak
Coquillages   shellfish
Coquilles St-Jacques   scallops, usually cooked in wine
Corbeille de fruits   fruit basket
Cornichon   gherkin
Côte, côtelette   chop, cutlet

Coulis   thick purée, served as a sauce
Coupe   ice cream dessert
Court-bouillon   stock made with herbs, vegetables and white wine
Couscous   North African dish of cooked, rolled grains of semolina steamed over a stew of lamb, chicken and vegetables
Crabe   crab
Crème   cream
Crêpe   thin pancake
Cresson   watercress
Crevettes grises   shrimps
Crevettes roses   prawns
Croque-monsieur   toasted cheese-and-ham sandwich
Croquette   rissole
Croustade   small bread or pastry mould with savory filling
Croustille   snack of fried potato slices
Croûte, en   cooked in a pastry case
Cru   raw
Crudités, assiette de   selection of raw, sliced vegetables
Crustacé   shellfish
Cuisine du marché   dishes based on seasonal ingredients
Cuisine du terroir   local dishes
Cuisses (de grenouilles)   (frogs') legs
Cuit   cooked
Culotte de boeuf   rump of beef
Darne   thick slice, usually of fish
Daube   meat slowly braised in a rich wine stock
Dauphinoise, à la   (potatoes) sliced and baked in milk
Daurade   sea bream
Dijonnais   meat or poultry cooked with mustard sauce
Dinde   turkey
Dorade   sea bream
Échalote   shallot
Écrevisses   freshwater crayfish
Émincé   thinly sliced
Endive   chicory
Entrecôte   rib steak
Entremets   sweets
Épaule (d'agneau)   shoulder (of lamb)
Éperlans   smelts

Épices   spices
Épinards   spinach
Escabèche   various fish, fried, marinated and served cold
Escalope à la Viennoise   veal dipped in egg and breadcrumbs then sautéed
Escargots (à la Bourguignonne)   snails stuffed with garlic butter and parsley
Espadon   swordfish
Estouffade   a stew marinated and fried, then slowly braised
Estragon   tarragon
Faisan   pheasant
Farci   stuffed
Faséole   kidney bean
Faux-filet   sirloin steak
Fenouil   fennel
Feuilleté   light flaky pastry
Figue   fig
Filet Américain   raw minced steak
Filet mignon   small fillet steak
Flageolets   small French beans
Flambé   flamed in spirit, especially brandy
Flétan   halibut
Florentine   food, often lightly poached eggs, cooked with spinach
Foie   liver
Foie gras (d'oie)   (goose) liver
(au) Four   cooked in the oven
Fourré   stuffed
Frais, fraîche   fresh
Fraises   strawberries
Framboises   raspberries
Frappé   served on crushed ice
Fricadelle   kind of meat ball
Fricassée   chopped white meat, ie veal or chicken, cooked in thick white sauce
Frisée   curly endive or chicory
Frit   fried
Frites   chips/French fries
Fritots   fritters
Fromage   cheese
Fromage de porc   brawn
Fruits de mer   seafood
Fumé   smoked
Galantine   cooked meat, fish or vegetables served cold in a jelly

Galette   a pancake made with buckwheat flour
Gambas   large prawns
Garbure   very thick soup
Garni   garnished
Gâteau   cake
Gaufre   wafer biscuit or waffle
Gelée, en   in aspic
Gibier   game
Gigot (d'agneau)   leg (of lamb)
Gingembre   ginger
Glace   ice cream
Glacé   iced, frozen, glazed
Goujons   small strips of fish, coated in breadcrumbs and deep-fried
Gratin, au   dish with a crust of browned breadcrumbs mixed with cheese
Grenouilles   frogs
Grillé   grilled
Grive   thrush
Groseille   redcurrant
Groseille à maquereau   gooseberry
Hachis parmentier   minced lamb, topped with mashed potato
Hachis   minced
Harengs   herrings
Haricot   stew with vegetables/ beans
Haricots verts   green beans
Hollandaise   sauce made with butter, wine and lemon juice, thickened with egg yolks
Homard   lobster
Homard à l'Armoricaine   lobster served with a sauce of brandy, white wine, onions, tomatoes and herbs
Homard thermidor   sautéed lobster cooked in a creamy white wine sauce
Huile (d'olive)   (olive) oil
Huîtres   oysters
Ile flottante   favorite French dessert; an island of egg white poached in custard
Jambon d'Ardennes   salty, smoked ham from the Belgian Ardennes
Jambon, jambonneau   ham
Julienne   thin vegetable strips poached in butter

Jus juice, gravy
Lait milk
Laitue lettuce
Langouste spiny lobster or crayfish
Langoustine Dublin bay prawn
Langue (de boeuf) (ox) tongue
Lapin rabbit
Légumes vegetables
Lièvre hare
Limande dab (fish)
Limon lime
Lotte de mer anglerfish, monkfish
Loup de mer sea bass
Lyonnaise, à la potatoes or liver, Lyons-style, cooked with onions
Magret (de canard) breast (of duck) served pink and rare
Maïs sweetcorn
Mange-tout crisp, small pea pods, eaten whole
Maquereaux mackerel
Marcassin young wild boar
Marrons chestnuts
Matelote freshwater fish stew
Méchoui barbecued lamb, North African-style, often with cumin
Médaillon small round fillet steak
Menthe mint
Merlan whiting
Meunière, à la flour-coated and grilled or fried with butter, lemon juice and parsley
Miel honey
Mignonette small round fillet of lamb
Mille-feuille flaky pastry slices sandwiched with jam and cream
Mode, à la marinated meat usually beef, braised in wine and vegetables
Morilles edible dark-brown fungi
Mornay with a cheese sauce
Morue dried/salted cod
Moules mussels
Moules parquées raw mussels
Moules marinière mussels cooked with white wine and shallots
Moutarde mustard
Mouton mutton
Mûre mulberry
Mûre de ronce blackberry

Museau de porc pig's snout
Myrtille bilberry
Navarin stew of lamb and young root vegetables
Navet turnip
Niçoise, à la Nice-style, with tomatoes, garlic, anchovies and olives
Noix nuts, usually walnuts
Noix de veau a small round cut of veal
Nouilles noodles
Oeuf/s egg/s
Oeuf brouillé scrambled egg
Oeuf à la coque soft-boiled egg in its shell
Oeuf en cocotte egg cooked in a small ramekin
Oeuf dur hard-boiled egg
Oeuf frit or *à la poêle* fried egg
Oeuf mollet soft-boiled, shelled egg
Oeuf poché poached egg
Oie goose
Oignons onions
Oiseaux sans tête see *Alouette*
Oseille sorrel
Oursins sea urchins
Paillettes d'oignons frits fried, crisp onion rings
Pain bread
Palourdes clams/cockles
Pamplemousse grapefruit
(en) Papillote cooked in oiled or buttered paper
Parmentier a dish containing potatoes
Pâte pasta or pastry
Pâte d'amandes marzipan
Pâte brisée shortcrust pastry
Pâte à chou choux pastry
Pâte feuilleté flaky/puff pastry
Pâte frollée almond-flavored pastry
Pâte sablée rich shortcrust with sugar
Pâté de campagne coarse pâté
Pâté de foie gras goose-liver *pâté*, sometimes with truffles
Pâté maison smooth *pâté*, usually chicken or pig's liver
Paupiette thin slices of meat or fish rolled up and filled

Pêche Melba   peach on ice cream with raspberry purée
Pêche   peach
Perdrix   partridge
Persil   parsley
Petit salé   salted pork
Petits fours   tiny cakes and sweets
Petits pois   peas
Pieds de porc   pigs' feet
Pigeonneau   young pigeon
Pignons   pine nuts
Piments doux/forts   sweet/Chili peppers
Pintade   guinea fowl
Pissaladière   bread dough or pizza covered with tomatoes
Pissenlits   dandelion leaves, used in salads
Pistou   vegetable soup with a paste of garlic, basil and oil
Plat du jour   dish of the day
Poché   poached
Pochouse   fish stew
Poire   pear
Poireaux   leeks
Poires Belle-Hélène   cooked pears with ice cream and hot chocolate sauce
Poisson   fish
Poitrine de porc   belly of pork
Pomme   apple
Pomme de terre   potato
Porc   pork
Pot-au-feu   beef stew
Potage Crécy   carrot soup
Potage   soup
Potage parmentier   a potato-based soup, often with leeks
Poularde   capon
Poulet   young spring chicken
Poulet Marengo   chicken with garlic, mushrooms and tomatoes
Poulpe   octopus
Poussin   very small baby chicken
Praliné(e)   caramelized
Primeurs   young vegetables or wines
Provençale, à la   cooked the traditional Provençal way with oil, tomatoes, peppers, garlic, anchovies
Prune   plum
Pruneau   prune

Quenelle   boat-shaped mousse of puréed fish or white meat poached in liquid
Queue de boeuf   oxtail
Quiche   egg- and milk-based open pie
Radis   radishes
Ragoût   a stew prepared peasant-style
Raie   skate
Raifort   horseradish
Raisin sec   raisin
Raisins   grapes
Ratatouille   Provençal dish of eggplants, peppers, tomatoes, zucchini and garlic, cooked in olive oil
à la Reine   with chicken
Rémoulade   mayonnaise seasoned with mustard and herbs, capers or gherkins
Rillettes   potted minced or cubed pork, slow-cooked then shredded
Rillons   crisp pieces of pork or goose, browned and preserved in fat
Ris (de veau)   (calf's) sweetbreads
Riz   rice
Rognons   kidneys
Romarin   rosemary
Rosbif   roast beef
Rôti   roast
Rouget   red mullet
Rouille   garlic and chili sauce usually served with fish soups
Safran   saffron
Saint Pierre   John Dory
Salade Niçoise   salad including tomatoes, beans, potatoes, black olives and tuna
Salé   salted
Sanglier   wild boar
Saucisses   fresh wet sausage
Saucisson   dry sausage (salami-type)
Sauge   sage
Saumon, darne de   salmon steak
Saumon (fumé)   (smoked) salmon
Saumon   salmon
Saumon blanc   hake
Selle (d'agneau)   saddle (of lamb)

Selon grosseur   priced according to size, for example with lobster
Sole meunière   sole fried with lemon
Sole bonne femme   sole poached in white wine with mushrooms
Soubise   onion cream sauce
Soupe de poissons   fish soup
Steak tartare   raw minced steak
Sucre   sugar
Suprême de volaille   chicken breast and wing fillet
Tapenade   purée of black olives and olive oil
Terrine   coarse form of potted meat or *pâté*
Tête (de veau)   (calf's) head
Thon   tuna fish
Thym   thyme
Timbale   dome-shaped mold or the pie cooked within it
Tournedos Rossini   steak with truffles, *foie gras* and Madeira sauce
Tournedos   small beef fillet
Tourte   covered tart
Tranche   slice/rasher

Tripe, oeufs à la   chopped hard-boiled eggs with onions
Tripes à la mode de Caen   tripe stewed with onions and herbs in cider
Truffes   truffles
Truite saumonée/de mer   salmon trout
Truite   trout
Vapeur, à la   steamed
Veau, blanquette de   breast of veal cooked in a white sauce
Veau   veal
Venaison   venison
Viande   meat
Vichyssoise   smooth and creamy leek and potato soup
Vinaigrette   oil-and-vinegar dressing
Vol-au-vent   puff pastry case filled with meat or fish
Volaille   poultry
Waldorf   salad of apple, walnut and celeriac
Washington   chicken served American-style with sweetcorn
Williams   type of pear
Yaourt   yogurt

Index

- **Bold** page numbers indicate main entries.
- *Italic* page numbers indicate illustrations and maps.
- See also LIST OF STREET NAMES on page 323.

Abadie, 174
Abbatiale St-Ouen, Rouen, 285
Abelard and Héloise, 70, 96
Abstract Expressionism, 169
Académie des Beaux-Arts, 147
Académie Francaise, 33, 140
Accidents, automobile, 54
Activities and sports, **267-72**
Adam Mickiewicz Museum, 70
Addresses and telephone numbers, **51-3**
African and Oceanic Arts, Museum of, 99, **106**, 266
Air et de l'Espace, Musée de l', **103**, 267
Air and Space Museum, **103**, 267
Airlines/air travel:
   addresses, 52
   domestic, 45
   helicopters, 46, **270**
   to and from Paris, 39-40
Albert Kahn Gardens, 269
Alcohol, duty-free allowances, 39
Alembert, Jean Le Rond d', 34
Alexander III, Czar, 170
Ambulances, 54
American Center, 13, 32, 32, 66, 123
American Express:
   bus tours, 51
   credit cards, 38
   currency exchange, 46
   General Delivery, 41
   MoneyGram®, 38
Travel Service, 46, 51
   travelers checks, 38
Amicus, Edmondo de, 81
Ancien Collège des Jésuites, Reims, 282
André, Edouard, 143
Animal markets, 260
Anne of Austria, 188
Anne of Brittany, 17
Antiques, **254**
Antiquités Nationales, Musée des, St-Germain-en-Laye, 276
Antoine, Jacques Denis, 149
Apollinaire, Guillaume, 34, 79, 90
Apollo of Piombino, 131
Aquariums:
   Musée National des Arts Africains et Océaniens, 106
   Parc Océanique Jacques Cousteau, **121-2**
ARC (Animation, Recherche, Confrontation), 106
Arc de Triomphe, 29, 59, 67, **103-4**, *103*, 114, 115, 120, 135, 265
Arc de Triomphe du Carrousel, 88, 97, **104**, 132, 135
Arcades, **165-6**
Architecture, **26-32**
Archives Nationales, 73, **104-5**
Arènes de Lutèce, 26, 71, **91**, 105
Argonaut, 190
Armée, Musée de l', 59, **140-1**, 265
Arménien, Musée, **105-6**, 123, 147
Army Museum, 59, **140-1**, 265
Arrondissements (districts), **62-3**
Arsenal, Pavillon de l', **166**
Arsenal Basin, 109
Art Juif, Musée d', 78
Art Moderne, Musée National d', **169**
Art Moderne de la Ville de Paris, Musée d', **106**, 162, 264
Art Nouveau, **29-30**, 107, 127, 158, 159
Arts, **33-5**
Arts Africains et Océaniens, Musée National des, 99, **106**, 266
Arts Asiatiques Guimet, Musée National d', **106-7**, 114, 131
Arts de la Mode et du Textile, Musée des, **107**
Arts Décoratifs, Musée des, **107**, 157, 264
Arts et Traditions Populaires, Musée des, 93, **108**, 147, 265
Assemblée Nationale, 86, **108**, 120
Athletics, 272
Auctions, Hôtel des Ventes, **138**
Aulenti, Gae, 31, 157
Aumale, Duke of, 275
Auteuil racecourse, **93**, 112, 268, 270
Auto racing, 271
Automobile, Centre International de l', **108-9**, 267

Babysitting, **267**
Baccarat, Musée, 165
Baedeker, Karl, 229
Bagatelle, 91-2
Baïf, Jean Antoine de, 33
Ballet, **232**
Ballooning, **268**
Baltard, Victor, **20**, 125, 175-6, 179
Balzac, Honoré de, 14, **20**, 34, 84, 89, 90, 96, 115, 140, 161
  Maison de, **109**
Bande Noire painters, 158
Banks, 46
  French words and phrases, 299
Barbizon, **273**, 279
Barbizon school, 158
Baroque architecture, **28**
Barrault, Jean-Louis, **20**, 233
Barrès, Maurice, 227
Bars, 231, **238-9**
Bartholdi, Frédéric Auguste, **20**
Bastien-Lepage, Jules, 158
Bastille, Place de la, **109-10**, 173
Bastille quarter, 63
Bateau-Lavoir, 34, 76
Baudelaire, Charles, 34, 70, 80, 88, 122, 201
Beach, Sylvia, 72
Beaubourg *see* Pompidou Center
Beaumarchais, 75
Beauvais, **273-4**
  tapestries, 126
Beauvoir, Simone de, 35, 80, 90, 227, 239
Beaux-Arts de la Ville de Paris, Musée des, **167**
Beaux-Arts, École nationale supérieure des, **110-11**
Beaux-Arts, Musée des, Chartres, 279
Beaux-Arts, Musée des, Reims, 282
Beaux-Arts, Musée des, Rouen, 285, **286-7**
Beffroi, Musée du, Rouen, **286**
Belfry Museum, Rouen, **285-6**
Belgrand, Eugène, 123
Belle Époque, 34, 170, 230
Belleville, 63
Bennett, Arnold, 175
Bercy, 63, **66**
  Entrepôts de, **123-4**

Bérégovoy, Pierre, 20
Berlioz, Hector, 34, 142, 179
Bernard, Émile, 159
Bernhardt, Sarah, 34
Bernini, Giovanni Lorenzo, 181
Berthelot, Comte, 164
Bertolucci, Bernardo, 157
Besnard, Albert, 158
Bibliothèque Forney, 74, 138
Bibliothèque Nationale, 82, **111**
Bibliothèque Publique d'Information, **169**
Bicycling, 45, **269**
Biographies, **20-5**
Bird markets, 69, 260, 266
Biron, Hôtel, 29, **173**, *173*
Biron, Marshal, 173
Blanche, 158
Blérancourt, **274-5**
Boats:
  boating, **268**
  canal trips, 94
  river trips, 45-6, 52
Bocuse, Paul, 206
Boffrand, Germain, 29
Boilly, Louis-Léopold, 289
Bois de Boulogne *see* Boulogne, Bois de
Bois de Vincennes *see* Vincennes, Bois de
Bois-Préau, 276
Boldini, Giovanni, 158
Bonnard, Pierre, 159, 167, 276
Bookbinding, School of, 113
Books:
  bouquinistes, 71, 88, 260
  guidebooks, **36**
  English bookstores, 50
Botanical Gardens, **143-4**
Botticelli, Sandro, 143
Bouchardon, Edmé, 172
Boucher, François, 33, 105, 118, 143
Boucicault *Book of Hours*, 143
Bougnats, 227
Boules, **268**
Boul'Mich (Blvd. St-Michel), 71, 145, 181, 228
Boulogne, Bois de, 57, 62, 90, **91-3**, 108, 112, 115, 147, 160, 263, 264, 269
  boating, 268
  bowling, 268
  gardens, 269
  map, *92*

Bouquinistes, 71, 88, 260
Bourbon, Duchess of, 108
Bourdelle, Antoine, 112, 135
  Musée Antoine Bourdelle, 80, **112**
Bourguereau, 158
Bourse des Valeurs, **112**
Bourse du Commerce, 68, **112-13**, 125, 136, 166
Boutiques, 242, **247-8**
Bowling, **268**
Brancusi, Constantin, **20-1**, 80, 169, 170
Braque, Georges, **21**, 34, 76, 106, 169
Brasseries, 207, 227
Breton, André, 34, 69, 227, 229
Breughel, Pieter, 116
Bridge clubs, **268**
Bridges *see* Pont
Brosse, Salomon de, 94
Bruant, Aristide, 77
Bruant, Libéral, **21**, 140, 184
Budé, Guillaume, 118-19
Buffalo Bill Cody, 293
Bullant, 113
Bulwer-Lytton, Edward, 84
Buren, 162
Burne-Jones, Edward, 158
Buses:
  from airports to city, 41
  in Paris, 43
  to and from Paris, 40
Butte *see* Montmartre
Buttes Chaumont, Parc des, **93**, 113, 264, 268
Buvettes, 226

Cabarets, **239-40**
Caesar, Julius, 15
Café-théâtres, 230, **234**
Cafés, 90, 208, **226-9**, 231
  bougnats, 227
  brasseries, 207, 227
  buvettes, 226
  Champs-Élysées, 226, 228
  drugstores, 208, 227
  Les Halles, 229
  history, 34
  Left Bank, 227-8
  Le Marais, 229
  Montmartre/Pigalle, 77, 229
  Montparnasse, 79, 89, 227
  Opéra/Blvd. Haussmann, 228-9

prices, 226
pubs, 227
Right Bank, 228-9
salons de thé, 208, 227
St-Germain-des-Prés, 84,
227-8
St-Michel, 228
tarteries, 208
-tabacs, 227
tipping, 227
Calder, Alexander, 67, 188
Calendar of events, **56-8**
Camondo, Count Moïse de,
113
Camondo, Musée Nissim
de, 107, **113**
Camus, Albert, 35, 90, 227
Canal St-Martin, **93-4**, 113
Canals, 52, 113, 267
Carême, Marie Antoine, 206
Carmontel, 95
Carnavalet, Musée *see*
Grand Carnavalet
Caron, Antoine, 273-4
Carrousel du Louvre, 88
Cars:
accidents, 54
auto-racing, 271
breakdowns, 55
Centre International de
l'Automobile, **108-9**, 267
La Cité de l'Automobile,
135
documents required, 37
driving in Paris, 43-4
French words and
phrases, **300-1**
parking, 44
renting, 44, 301
speed limits, 44
*Carte Musées et
Monuments*, 102
Cartes de séjour, 37
Casimir, John, King of
Poland, 181
Casinos, **240**
Catacombes, 80, **113-14**,
265
Cathedrals:
Notre-Dame, Chartres,
27, **278-9**
Notre-Dame de Paris, 11,
27, *27*, 59, 87, 88, 118,
127, 139, **151-4**, *151*,
176, 181, 265
Reims, 282
Rouen, 284, **286**
Sacré-Coeur, 29, 60,
174-5, *174*, 265
St-Denis, **177-8**
Cellini, Benvenuto, 132

Cemeteries:
Catacombes, **113-14**
Cimetière de Montmartre,
78
Cimetière de
Montparnasse, 80, 88
Cimetière St-Vincent, 77,
78
Père Lachaise, 63, **96**,
166
Centre de Création
Industrielle, **169**
Centre International de
l'Automobile, 267
Centre International de
Paris, **160**
Centre National d'Art et de
Culture Georges-
Pompidou *see* Pompidou
Center
Céramique, Musée de,
Rouen, **287**
Cerceau, Androuet du, 170
Cercle National des Armées
de Terre, de Mer et de
l'Air, 30
Cernuschi, Musée, 113,
114
Cézanne, Paul, 156, 158,
167, 168
Chaalis, Abbaye et Domaine
de, 277
Chagall, Marc, **21**, 79,
155, 282
Chaillot, Palais de *see*
Palais de Chaillot
Challe, 182
Champ-de-Mars, 59, 63,
94, 114, 123, 160, 264
Champagne, 281, **282-3**
Champollion, 132
Champs-Élysées, Avenue
des, 59, 63, 97, 104,
114-15, 120, 124, 134,
167
cafés, 226, 228
hotels, 193
Channel, ferries and
hovercraft, 40
Chantilly, **275**
racecourse, 270
Chapelle Expiatoire, 68, 82,
115
Chapelle Foujita, Reims, 282
Charge cards, 38
Charles, Prince of Wales, 31
Charles IV the Fair, 16
Charles V, King, 16, 98,
128, 161, 180
Charles VI the Well-Beloved,
16

Charles VII, King, 16-17,
282
Charles VIII, King, 17
Charles IX, King, 17
Charles X, King, 18-19,
91-2, 97, 110, 159-60
Charles-De-Gaulle, Place,
103, **115**
Chartres, **278-9**
Chasse et de la Nature,
Musée de la, 73, **116**
Château de la Bagatelle, 92
Château de Versailles,
289-91
Château de Vincennes, 57,
98, 263, 266, 272
Chemetov, Paul, 124, 125
Chemists, late-night, 54
Cheret, Jules, 136
Cheval, Musée de, Chantilly,
275
Chevalier, Maurice, **21**, 239
Childebert I, King, 180
Childeric, 15
Children, **263-7**
babysitting, **267**
Centre International de
l'Automobile, 108-9
clothes stores, **250**
EuroDisney, **291-4**
Jardin d'Acclimatation,
263, 264
Jardin d'Enfants aux
Halles, 125
Musée des Enfants, **106**,
264
Musée en Herbe, 93, 264
museums and
workshops, **264-5**
Parc de la Villette, 190
parks and zoos, **263-4**
Pompidou Center, 170
toy stores, **262**
China stores, **259-60**
Chirac, Jacques, 12, 20,
31, 115
Chopin, Frédéric, 70, 78,
96, 189
Churches, 52-3
listed, 100
*see also individual
churches*
Cimetière de Montmartre,
78
Cimetière de
Montparnasse, 80, 88
Cimetière St-Vincent, 77, 78
Cinemas, 230, **234-6**
for children, **265**
Cinémathèque Française,
116, 160, 235-6

Musée du Cinéma Henri-Langlois, **116**, 150, 160
  Salle Garance, Pompidou Center, 170, 236
  Vidéothèque de Paris, 125
Circuses, **265**
Cité de l'Automobile, 135
Cité de la Musique, 190
Cité des Sciences et de l'Industrie, 13, 93-4, 189, **190**, *190*, 264, 265
Cité du Vin et de l'Alimentaire, 66, **123-4**
Cité Universitaire, 95, 116-17
City of Science and Industry *see* Cité des Sciences et de l'Industrie
Classicism, architecture, **28**
Clemenceau, Georges, **21**, 117
  Musée, **117**
Climate, 40
La Closerie des Lilas, 79, 89, 227, 238
Clothing, 40, 242
  bargains, **253-4**
  French words and phrases, 300
  Musée de la Mode et du Costume, **147-8**
  Palais de la Mode, 161
  shops, **245-50**
  sizes, 244
Clouet, 287
Clovis, King, 15
Cluny, Thermes de, 26, *26*, **117-18**, 152
  plan, *117*
Cocteau, Jean, **21**, 35, 79, 235
Cognacq, Ernest, 118
Cognacq-Jay, Musée, 75, **118**
Coins, Musée de la Monnaie, **149**
Colbert, Jean-Baptiste, **21**, 129, 146
Colette, **21**, 35, 96, 145
Collège de France, 71, **118-19**
Colonne de Juillet, 109-10, *110*
Comédie Française, 33, 82, 84, 90, **119**, 233
Comedy theater, **234**
Commodities Exchange, **112-13**
Commune, 19, 97, 138, 145, 152, 156, 161, 162, 176

Compiègne, **275**
Concerts, **236**
La Conciergerie, 59, 63, 69, **119-20**, 161, 177
Concorde, Place de la, 29, 60, 86, 88, 96-7, 104, 114, 115, **120-1**, 135, 172
Condé, Musée, Chantilly, 275
Conservatoire des Arts et Métiers, 185
Conservatoire National de Musique, 190
Constantine the Great, 15
Consulate style, architecture, **29**
Consulates, 53
Conti, Princesse de, 149
Cookware, **254**
Coopération Franco-Américaine, Musée National de la, Blérancourt, 274-5
Le Corbusier, 30, 95, 117, 121
  Fondation Le Corbusier, **121**
Corday, Charlotte, 171, 289
Cormon, 158
Corneille, 33, 84, 119, 182
Corot, Jean-Baptiste-Camille, **21**, 133, 159, 167, 282, 289
Cortot, 103
Cosmetics, **261-2**
Cotte, Robert de, 140, 142, 182
Cottet, Charles, 158
La Coupole, brasserie, 79, 89, 227, 238
Courbet, Gustave, **21**, 34, 158, 167
Cousteau, Jacques-Yves, 122
  Parc Océanique, 87, **121-2**, 125, 266
Cousteau, Jean-Michel, 121
Coustou, Guillaume, 120
Couturier boutiques, **247-8**
Coysevox, Antoine, 120, 126
Cranach, Lucas, 116
Credit cards, 38
Cresson, Édith, 20
Crillon, Hôtel de, 120, 196
Cristalleries, Musée des, 149, 165
Crowley, Aleister, 79
Crown Jewels, 132
Crypte Archéologique, Notre-Dame, 59, 69, **122**, **154**

Cubism, 106, 168, 169
Cuisine bourgeoise, 210
Curie, Marie, 70
Currency, 38
Currency exchange, 46
Customs and etiquette, 49
Customs and excise, 38-9
Cycling, 45, **269**

Dadaism, 169
Dagobert, 177
Dalí, Salvador, 34, **122**, 169
  Espace Salvador Dalí, 78, **122**
Dancing, **240**, **269**
Danton, Georges Jacques, 18, 119, 171
Daumier, Honoré, 34, 158
David, Gérard, 286-7
David, Jacques Louis, 133
Decorative Arts, Museum of, **107**
La Défense, 13, 32, 62, **66-7**, 104, 115, 120, 132, 134
Deffand, Madame de, 34
Degas, Edgar, **21**, 34, 158
De Gaulle, Charles, 19-20, **21**, 25, 115, 141, 157
Delacroix, Eugène, **21**, 34, 74, 95, 108, **122**, 132, 133, 158, 159, 167, 183-4, 189, 282, 285, 286
  Musée National Eugène Delacroix, 85, **122**
Delorme, Philibert, **21**, 113, 281
Denis, Maurice, 276
Denis, St, 15, 76, 153, **177**
Denon, 188
Dental emergencies, 54
Department stores, 242, 243, 244, **255**
Derain, André, **21**, 106, 156
Desnos, Robert, 227
Détaxe, 39, 244
Deux Guerres Mondiales, Musée des, **141**
Les Deux Magots café, 84, 90, 227
Dialing codes, 47, 48
Dickens, Charles, 102, **172**
Diderot, Denis, 34, 182
Disabled travelers, 49-50
Discotheques, 231, **240-1**
Discovery, Palace of *see* Palais de la Découverte
Disney, Walt, 291

Districts, listed, 100
Doctors, 38
Documents required, **37**
Le Dôme, café, 79, 89
Dôme church, 28, *28*, 59,
  140, **142**, 185
Donatello, 143
Doueb, Raphaël, 149
Douglas, William and
  James, 181
Dreyfus, Alfred, **21**
Driver's licenses, 37
Drugs, laws, 49
Drugstores, 208, **255-6**,
  227
Duban, 158
Dufau, Pierre, 199
Dufy, Raoul, **22**, 106, 158
Duhamel, Jacques, 157
Dumaine, Alexandre, 206
Dumas, Alexandre, 89
Dürer, Albrecht, 282
Duty-free allowances, 38-9
Duty-free goods, 244

École des Beaux-Arts, 33,
  82-3
École du Breuil, 98
École Militaire, 29, 94, **123**
Église Sainte Jeanne d'Arc,
  Rouen, 285
Égouts, **123**, 265
Eiffel, Gustave, **22**, 158,
  186
Eiffel Tower *see* Tour Eiffel
Eleanor of Aquitaine, 16
Electric current, 49
Élysée Palace, **161**, 196
Embassies, 53
Emergency information,
  54-5
Emerson, Ralph Waldo, 68
Empire style, architecture,
  29
Enfants, Musée d', **106**, 264
Enghien:
  casino, 240
  racecourse, 270
Ennery, Adolphe d', 106,
  123
  Musée National d', 106,
    123, 147
Entrepôts de Bercy, 66,
  123-4
Épernay, **283**
Epstein, Sir Jacob, **22**, 96
Ernst, Max, 34, 169
Escoffier, Auguste, 206
Espace Montmartre, 78
Espace Salvador Dalí, 78,
  122

Etex, 103
Ethnic cookery, 207, 210
Étoile, Place de l', **115**,
  132
Eudes, King, 16
Eugénie, Empress, 155,
  280
Eure, river, 278
Eurocards, 38, 46
EuroDisney, **266**, **291-4**
Eustache, St, 179
Evreux, Comte d', 161
Evry, racecourse, 270
Excursions, **273-94**
Existentialism, 84, 90, 227

Famous homes, listed, 100
Fantin-Latour, Henri, **22**
Fashion, 242, 243, **245-50**
  bargains, 244, **253-4**
  boutiques, 242, **247-8**
  couturier boutiques,
    247-8
  haute couture, **248**
  men's, **249-50**
  Musée de la Mode et du
    Costume, **147-8**
  Palais de la Mode, 161
  shoes, **252-3**
  shows, 56, 57, 161
Fast food, 208
Faubourg-St-Germain, 181
Faubourg-St-Honoré, Rue
  du, 63, 80, 115, **124**
Fauves, 106, 169
Ferme Georges Ville, 266
Ferries, Channel, 40
Festival Disney, 32, 293
Films *see* Cinema
Finance, Ministry of, 66,
  124
Fire services, 54
Fishing, **269**
Fitzgerald, F. Scott, 34, 89
Flamboyant Gothic,
  architecture, **27**
Flandrin, Hippolyte, 181
Flaubert, Gustave, 89, 95
Flea markets, 62, **146**,
  260-1
Le Flore, café, 84
Flower markets, 69, 261
Foch, Maréchal, 142
Folies Bergère, 196, 239
Fondation Le Corbusier, 147
Fontaine des Innocents, 28,
  68-9, 87, 125
Fontaine des
  Quatre-Saisons, 83, **172**
Fontainebleau, 28, 157,
  279-81

Food and drink:
  bars, 231, **238-9**
  brasseries, 207, 227
  cafés, 208, **226-9**
  Champagne, 281, **282-3**
  cooking styles, 206-7,
    209-10
  drugstores, 208, 227
  fast food, **207-8**
  French words and
    phrases, **302-8**
  in hotels, 192
  markets, **257-8**
  nouvelle cuisine, 206, 209
  salons de thé, 208
  shops, 242, **256-7**
  tarteries, 208
  wines, **209-11**
  see also Restaurants
Football (soccer), **269**
Forney Library, 27, 74, 138
Forum des Halles, 30, 35,
  59, 68, 87, 112, **124-5**,
  136, 166, 179, 243,
  264, 265, 266
Fouché, Joseph, 18
Foujita, Tsuguhara
  (Léonard), **22**, 282, 227
Fountains, 120
  Fontaine des Innocents,
    28, 68-9, 87, 125
  Fontaine des Quatre-
    Saisons, 83, **172**
  Medici, 94-5
  Molière, 82
Four Seasons Fountain,
  83, **172**
Fragonard, Jean-Honoré,
  33, 118, 143
France, Anatole, 84
Franck, César, 80
Franco-Prussian war, **174**
François I, King, 17, 28,
  33, 118, 128, 132-3,
  280-1
  mausoleum, 177
François II, King, 17
Freemasonry Museum, **134**
French language, words
  and phrases, **295-308**
French Revolution, **18**, 31,
  127, 151-2, 162, 176,
  177, 179, 181, 186
Funicular railways,
  Montmartre, 78, 267

Gabriel the Elder, 123, 173
Gainsborough, Thomas,
  118, 133
Gainsbourg, Serge, 80
Galeries, 165, 243

Galleries, listed, 101
Galliéra, Duchesse de, 148
Gambetta, Léon Michel, **22**
Gambling, 240
Ganne, Pierre, 273
Garbo, Greta, 116
Gardens *see* Parks and gardens
Gare Montparnasse, 79
Garibaldi, Giuseppe, 134
Garnier, Charles, **22**, 29, *29*, 155, 158, 197, 198, 228
Gaudin, Henri, 174
Gauguin, Paul, **22**, 158, 159, 276, 282
Gehry, Frank, 32, *32*, 66, 293
General delivery, 41
Geneviève, Ste, 15, **22**, 163, 178
La Géode, 94, 190, *190*, 235
Geoffrin, Madame, 34
Georges-Michel, 79
Gérard, François, 127
Géricault, Théodore, **22**, 287
Germanus, St, 180
Gide, André, 35
Gift stores, **258-9**
Ginsberg, Allen, 90
Giraudoux, Jean, 227
Giscard d'Estaing, Valéry, 20, **22**
Giverny, **275-6**
Glass, stained, 278, 279
Glass:
  Glassware Museum, 165
  shops, **259-60**
  see also Stained glass
Gluck, Christoph Willibald von, 33
Gobelins, Manufacture Nationale des, 113, **125-6**, 143
Godefroy, 104
Golf, **270, 271**
Goncourt brothers, 186, 189
Gondouin, 188
Gothic architecture, **26-7**
Goujon, Jean, **22**
Goya, Francisco José de, 133
Graf, François-Joseph, 213
Grand Carnavalet, Musée Historique de la Ville de Paris, 28, *28*, 59, 73, 75, 109, **126-7**, 141
Grand Écran Gaumont, 13, 235

Le Grand Louvre, 13, 14, 28, *31*, 32, 60, 66, 67, 82-3, 87, 88, 96, 97, 104, 120, **127-34**, 135, 157, 172, 179, 187
  Colonnade Galleries, 29, 132
  Cour Carrée, 28, 128
  Cour Napoléon, 128, 129
  Crypt of St-Louis, 131
  Galerie d'Apollon, 132
  Hall Napoléon, 129
  Marsan pavilion, 107
  plan, *130*
  Salle des Caryatides, 131
Grand Orient de France, Musée du, **134**
Grand Palais, Galeries Nationales du, 29, 88, **134**, 160, 167, 170
Grand Trianon, Versailles, 290
Grande Arche de la Défense, 13, 32, 67, 104, 120, **134-5**, *135*, 265
Grande cuisine, 206, 209
Grands Boulevards, 60, 63, **67-8**, 115, **134**, 156, 164, 171
Grandval, Gérard, 161
El Greco, 133
Greuze, Jean-Baptiste, 143
Grévin, Alfred, 135
Grévin, Musée, 60-1, 87, 125, **135-6**, 149, 166, 171, 196, 265
Gris, Juan, 34
Gros Horloge, Rouen, **285-6**
Guérard, Michel, 206
Guides, 51-2
Guimard, Hector, **22**, 29-30, 158, 159
Guimet, Émile, 106
Guimet, Musée *see* Arts Asiatiques, Musée National des
Gymnastics, **270**

Les Halles, 63, **68-9**, 124, **136**, 166, 168, 179
  cafés, 229
  Fontaine des Innocents, 28
  Jardin d'Enfants, 264
  shops, 243
Hardouin-Mansart, Jules, **22**, 28, 140, 142, 182, 188, 289
Harry's New York Bar, 82, 238

Hat shops, **250-1**
Haussmann, Georges Eugène, 19, **22**, 80, 86, 93, 115, 158, 165, 175
Haussmann, Raoul, 169
Haute couture, **248**
Haute cuisine, 206, 209
Hawthorne, Nathaniel, 128
Hazlitt, William, 11
Health clubs, **270**
Hébert, Ernest, 137
  Musée National Ernest Hébert, **136-7**
Helicopters, 46, **270**
Help lines, 54
Hemingway, Ernest, 34, 72, 79, 89, 191, 227
Henner, Jean-Jacques, 137
  Musée National Jean-Jacques Henner, **137**
Henri I, King, 16
Henry II, King, 17, 280, 281
  mausoleum, 177
Henry II, King of England, 16
Henry III, King, 17
Henry IV, King, 17, 119, 170, 181, 190-1, 280
Henry V, King of England, 16, 98
Henry VI, King of England, 17
Henri de Navarre, 180
Hera of Samos, 131
Herbe, Musée en, 93, 264
Hippodrome de Vincennes, 98-9
Histoire Contemporaine, Musée de l', **141**
Histoire de France, Musée de l', 73, **104-5**
Histoire Naturelle, Muséum National d', **143-4**
Historial de Montmartre, 78
Historic buildings, listed, 100
Historique de la Ville de Paris, Musée *see* Grand Carnavalet
History, **15-20**
Hitch-hiking, 49
Hitler, Adolf, 142
Hoggart, Simon, 25
Holidays, public, 46
Holographie, Musée de l', 125
Homer, Winslow, 158
Homme, Musée de l', **137**, 160
Hôpital Salpêtrière, **184**

Horses:
  racing, 93, 112, 268, **270**
  riding, **271**
Horta, Victor, 30
Hospitals, 38, 54
Hostels, 205
Hôtel des Ambassadeurs de Hollande, 75
Hôtel des Archevêques de Sens, 27, *27*, 74, **137-8**
Hôtel Biron, 29, 84, **173**, *173*
Hôtel Bristol, 124
Hôtel Carnavalet, 28, *28*, 73, 126
Hôtel de Chatillon, 75
Hôtel de Cluny, 27, 117
Hôtel de Courteilles, 83
Hôtel de Crillon, 86, 120
Hôtel-Dieu, 69
Hôtel Donon, 118
Hôtel Drouot-Montaigne, 138
Hôtel Drouot-Richelieu, 138
Hôtel du Grand-Veneur, 73
Hôtel de Guénégaud des Brosses, 73, **116**
Hôtel des Invalides, 83
Hôtel Lambert, 70
Hôtel de Lamoignon, 75
Hôtel de Lassay, 108
Hôtel de Lausun, 70
Hôtel Le Peletier de Saint-Fargeau, 73, 126, 127
Hôtel Le Vergeur, Reims, 282
Hôtel Libéral-Bruand, 73
Hôtel de la Marine, 120
Hôtel de Matignon, 83, 203
Hôtel de Montrésor, 73
Hôtel de Polastron-Polignac, 75
Hôtel de Rohan, 73, **105**, 137
Hôtel Salé, 73
Hôtel de Salm, 145
Hôtel de Sens, 27, *27*, 74, **137-8**
Hôtel de Soubise, 29, 73, **105**, 138
Hôtel de Sully, 75
Hôtel des Ventes, **138**
Hôtel de Ville, 12, 30, 74, 76, 87, **138-9**, 146, 173
Hotels, **192-205**
  bars, 238
  breakfasts, 192
  charge/credit cards, 193

Chartres, 279
  choosing, 192, 193
  Fontainebleau, 281
  French words and phrases, **297-8**
  listed by *arrondissement*, 194
  meals, 192
  prices, 193, 194
  Reims, 284
  reservations, 192, 297
  Rouen, 287
  tipping, 192
  Versailles, 291
Household accessories, shopping, **259-60**
Hovercraft, 40
Hubert, St, 179
Huet, Christophe, 105
Hugo, Victor, **22-3**, 34, 78, 90, 112, 123, **139**, 151, 191, 233
  Maison de, **139**
  tomb of, 163
Hugues Capet, 16
Hunting and Nature, Museum of, **116**
Huysmans, J.K., 88, 90, 150, 186, 227

IAMAT (International Association for Medical Assistance to Travelers), 38
Ice-skating, **270**
Identity cards, 37
Île de la Cité, 11, 15, 59, 62, 63, **69-70**, 71, 87, 88, 119, 127, 139, 152, 161, 170, 176, 266
Île St-Louis, 62, 63, 69, **70-1**, 139, 184
Impressionists, 34, 144, 147, 156, 157, 158, 159, 287
Industrial Design Center, **169**
Ingres, Jean-Auguste-Dominique, **23**, 158, 159, 286
Institut Catholique de Paris, 181
Institut de France, **139-40**, 143
Institut de Recherches Contemporaines Acoustiques Musicales, **169**
Institut du Monde Arabe, 32, **148**
  restaurant, 219

Insurance:
  car, 37
  medical, 37-8
  travel, 37-8
International Conference Center, 13
International green card, **37**
Interpreters, 51-2
Invalides, Hôtel National des, 59, 63, 123, **140-2**, 170, 173, 184, 265
Ivry, Constant d', 145

Jacob, Max, 34, 79
Jacob (cabinet-maker), 113
Jacquemart, Nélie, 143
Jacquemart-André, Musée, **143**
James, Henry, 11, 155
Jardin d'Acclimatation, 92-3, 112, 263, 264, 272
Jardin d'Enfants aux Halles, 125, 264
Jardin des Plantes, **143-4**, 184, 263, 269, 272
Jardin des Serres d'Auteuil, 93, 269
Jardins du Carrousel, 13, 32, 161
Jardins du Luxembourg see Luxembourg
Jardins des Tuileries see Tuileries, Jardins des
Jarry, Alfred, 227
Jay, Louise, 118
Jazz clubs, 231, **237**
Jean I, King, 16
Jean II, King, 16
Jeanne d'Arc, Musée, Rouen, 285, **287**
"Jesuit" style, architecture, 28
Jeu de Paume, Musée du, 97, 120, **144**, 156, 157
Jewelry stores, **251**
Jewish art, 78
Jewish quarter, 75
Joan of Arc, 16-17, 105, 175, 282, 284, 285
  Museum, Rouen, 285, **287**
Joséphine, Empress, 136, 276
Jouvenet, Jean, 286
Joyce, James, 34, 72
Julian the Apostate, 15
July column, 109, *110*

Kafka, Franz, 157
Kandinsky, Wassily, 169

Kardec, Allan, 96
Karting, **270**
Kerouac, Jack, 90
Klimt, Gustav, 158
Knights Templar, 73
Krafft, Hugues, 282

La Fosse, Charles de, 142
La Tour, Georges de, 133
Lac Daumesnil, 99
Lac Inférieur, 93
Lac des Minimes, 98
Lady with the Unicorn, 118
Lafayette, Marquis de, **23**, 33, 134
La Fontaine, Jean de, 113
Lalique, René, 159
Laloux, Victor, 156
Lambert, Madame de, 34
Lambinet, Musée, Versailles, 289
Lang, Fritz, 116
Lang, Jack, 35
Language courses, **271**
Lapin Agile, 77
Late-night pharmacies, 54
Latin Quarter, 59, 62, 63, **71-2**, 87, 117, 118, 145, 171, 182, 184-5, 228, 264
map, *72*
Lavatories, public, 48, 226
Law, John, 182
Law Courts, **161**
Laws and regulations, 49
Le Breton, Gilles, 28
Le Brun, Charles, **23**, 132, 277, 289
Le Gallienne, Richard, 121, 170
Le Lorrain, Robert, **23**, 105
Le Mans, auto-racing, **271**
Le Nôtre, André, **23**, 96-7, 115, 182, 275, 277, 280, 289, 290
Le Peletier, Michel, 127
Le Vau, Louis, **23**, 70, 140, 184, 277, 289
Leacock, Stephen, 230
Leather goods stores, **252**
Leclerc, General, 79
Left Bank (*Rive Gauche*), 62, 139
cafés, 227-8
literary walk through, **88-90**
nightlife, 231
shops, 242, 243
see also Latin Quarter; Montparnasse; St-Germain
Lefuel, 158

Léger, Fernand, 169
Légion d'Honneur, Musée National de la, 85, **145**
Leisure centers, **271**
Lemercier, Jacques, 28, 128, 182, 185
Lemoyne, 105
Lenin, Vladimir Ilyich, 79, 229
Lenoir, 177
Leonardo da Vinci, **17**, **133**, 280
Lepère, 188
Lescot, Pierre, 28, 128
LHeureux, 66
Libraries, 53
Assemblée Nationale, 108
Bibliothèque Forney, 27, 74, 138
Bibliothèque Nationale, 82, **111**
Bibliothèque Publique d'Information, **169**
La Sorbonne, 185
Musée des Arts Décoratifs, 107
Ste-Geneviève, 71
TGB-Bibliothèque de France, 13, 32, 66, 111
Lingerie stores, **252**
Lipp, Brasserie, 84, 220, 227
Liszt, Franz, 189
Local publications, 50, 231
Longchamp racecourse, 93, 112, 268, 270
Lost property, 55
passports, 55
travelers checks, 38, 55
Louis IX, King (St-Louis), 16, 70, 175, 176, 177, 185, 290
Louis VI the Fat, 16
Louis VII, King, 16, 177
Louis VIII, King, 16
Louis X the Quarrelsome, 16
Louis XI, King, 17
Louis XII, King, 17, 112-13
Louis XIII, King, 17, 128, 153, 181, 280, 289
Louis XIV, King, 17-18, 33, 67, 82-3, 98, 105, 108, 119, 126, 128, 132, 140, 141, 142, 153, 161, 170, 171, 179, 182, 184, 188, 276, 280
at Versailles, 289-90
Louis XV, King, 18, 33, 98, 119, 120, 149, 163
Louis XVI, King, 18, 33, 82, 97, 115, 120, 136, 147, 180

Louis XVIII, King, 18, 82, 115
Louis-Philippe, King, 19, 97, 110, 120, 281, 289, 290
Louvois, 141
Louvre, Musée du *see* Le Grand Louvre
Ludwig II of Bavaria, 241
Lully, Jean-Baptiste, 33
Luxembourg, Jardins du, 71, 89, **94-5**, 149, 264
Luxembourg, Palais de, **94**, 183
Lycée Henri IV, **71**

Mackintosh, Charles Rennie, 159
La Madeleine, 29, 67, 80, 82, 86, 120, 134, **145-6**, 156
Magritte, René, 34
Maine-Montparnasse shopping center, 187
Maison de la Villette, 190
Maison de Radio France, 96, **172**, 236
Maison Renan-Scheffer, 189
Maison de la Villette, 190
Maisons-Laffitte, racecourse, 270
Male, Émile, 278
Malmaison, **276**
Malraux, André, **23**, 73
Manet, Edouard, **23**, 158, 159, 167
Mankind, Museum of, **137**
Mansart, François, **23**, 28, 73, 116, 126
Mansart, Jules Hardouin *see* Hardouin-Mansart, Jules
Mansart Gallery, 111
Maps:
Bois de Boulogne, *92*
Bois de Vincennes, *99*
excursions, *274*
Latin quarter, *72*
Le Marais, *74*
Montmartre, *77*
Northern France, *274*
Opéra quarter, *81*
orientation, *64-5*
St-Germain quarter, *83*
Versailles, *288*
walks, *87*, *89*
Le Marais, 59, 63, **73-6**, 116, 124, 126, 137, 146, 173, 185, 191
cafés, 229
hotels, 193

map, 74
restaurants, 207
shops, 243
Marat, Jean Paul, 18, 136,
162, 171
Marcel, Étienne, 16, 138
Marché aux Puces, **146**,
260
Marguerite de Valois, 180
Marie-Antoinette, 18, 82,
115, 119-20, 136, 290
Marine, Musée de la, **146**,
160, 265
Markets, **260-1**
animal, 260
birds, 69, 260, 266
books, 260
flea, 62, **146**, 260-1
flower, 69, 261
food, **257-8**
stamps and postcards, 261
Marly horses (statues), 120
Marmottan, Jules, 147
Marmottan, Musée, **147**,
156
Marmottan, Paul, 147
Marochetti, Carlo, 145
Les Martyrs de Paris, 125,
147, 265
Masson, André, 34
Matisse, Henri, **23**, 106,
156, 158, 168, 169
Maugham, Somerset, 79
Maupassant, Guy de, 80,
88, 140
Mazarin, Cardinal, **23**, 111,
140
Mazarin Gallery, 111
Medical emergencies, 54
Medical insurance, 37-8
Medici fountain, 94-5
Medicis, Catherine de, 17,
97, 113, 159, 180, 280
Medicis, Marie de, 17, 94
Mémorial de la Déportation,
69
Ménilmontant, 63
Men's clothing, **249-50**
Menus, **208-9**
French words and
phrases, **302-8**
Mesmer, F.A., 189
Métro, 12, 29, 42, 47
map, *see* end of book
Michelangelo, 132
Mickiewicz, Adam, 70
Mignand, 188
Miller, Henry, 34, 56, 72,
89, 143
Millet, Jean François, 158,
159, 273

Mini-golf, **271**
Mint (Musée de la Monnaie),
85, **149**
Miró, Joan, 67, 169
Mistinguett, 198, 239
Mitterrand, François, 13,
20, **23**, 128, 136
Mode et du Costume,
Musée de la, **147-8**
Modern Art of the City of
Paris, Museum of, **106**
Modigliani, Amedeo, 79,
96, 106, 227
Mohammed Ali, 120
Molière, 33, 82, 84, 90,
96, 119, 140, 179, 233
Molière fountain, 82
Mona Lisa, 33, 133
Monceau, Parc de, 63, **95**,
114, 148, 264
Monde Arabe, Musée de
l'Institut du, 32, **148**
restaurant, 219
Le Monde de l'Art, **148-9**,
165
Monet, Claude, **23**, 34,
147, 156, 159, 167,
282, 285, 287
Giverny, **275-6**
Money, 38
Monnaie, Musée de la, 85,
149
Montagne Ste-Geneviève
see Latin Quarter
Montesquieu, 33
Montmartre, 11, 34, 60,
62, 63, **76-8**, 93, 149,
150, 177, 189
cafés, 229
Cimetière de, 78
funicular railway, 78, 267
map, 77
Musée de, 77
Sacré-Coeur, 29, 60,
174-5, 265, 267
Montparnasse, 12, 34, 62,
63, **78-80**, 112, 149,
187
cafés, 227
Cimetière de, 80, 88
hotels, 193
Montparnasse Tower *see*
Tour Montparnasse
Montreuil, Pierre de, 16,
23, 27
Montsouris, Parc de, **95**,
264
Monuments, listed, 100
Monuments Français,
Musée National des,
150, 160

Moore, George Augustus,
95
Moore, Henry, 188
Moreau, Gustave, **23**, 34,
150, 158
Musée Gustave Moreau,
150
Moreau, Mathurin, 176
Morgan, Anne, 274
Morris, William, 158, 159
Morrison, Jim, 96
Motor racing, 271
Mouffetard, Rue, **150-1**
Moulin, Jean, 164
Moulin-Rouge, 76, 78, 240
Movie theaters *see* Cinemas
Moyen Âge, Musée National
du, 71, **117-18**, 152
plan, 117
Mucha, Alphonse, 30, 127
Munch, Edvard, 137, 158
Murger, Henri, 34, 89
Murillo, Bartolomé Esteban,
133, 143
Museums *(Musées)*:
for children, **264-5**
listed, 101
opening hours, 102
shops, **261**
Music:
concerts, **236**
discos, **241**
jazz, **237**
opera, **232**
Musique, Cité de la, 190
Musset, Alfred de, 96

Nabis, 276
Nanterre, 67
Nantes, Edict of, 105
Nanteuil, Robert, **23**
Napoleon I, Emperor, 18,
103, 105, 123, 127,
128, 136, 140, 141,
143, 145, 146, 161,
182, 183, 185, 188-9,
280, 281
Malmaison, 276
tomb, **142**, 185
Napoleon II, King of Rome,
142
Napoleon III, Emperor, 19,
62, 68, 80, 98, 114,
115, 128, 144, 155,
161, 275, 276
Napoléonien d'Art et
d'Histoire Militaire,
Musée, Fontainebleau,
281
National Archives, 73,
104-5

National Assembly, 86, **108**, 120
Natoire, Charles, 105
Natural History Museum, **143-4**
Neoclassicism, **29**, 158
Neo-Impressionists, 158
Nerval, Gérard de, 191
New Paris, listed, 101
  architecture, 31
Nightclubs, 231, **241**
Nightlife, **230-41**
Nissim de Camondo, Musée, 107, **113**
Notre-Dame, Rouen, **286**
Notre-Dame, Versailles, 289
Notre-Dame cathedral, Chartres, 27, **278-9**
Notre-Dame cathedral, Reims, 282
Notre-Dame de Paris, 11, 27, 27, 59, 63, 69, 70, 87, 88, 118, 127, 139, **151-4**, 151, 176, 181, 265
  Crypte Archéologique, **154**
  plan, 153
Notre-Dame-des-Blancs-Manteaux, 75
Nouvel, Jean, 32, 148
Nouvelle cuisine, 206, 209

Obelisk of Luxor, 120
Observatoire de Paris, **154**
Offenbach, Jacques, 34, 155
Open Air Sculpture Museum, **184**
Opening hours, shops, 46-7
Opera, **232**
Opéra Bastille, 13, 32, 35, 63, 66, 110, 110, **154-5**, 156, 232, 243
Opéra de Paris, 155
Opéra Garnier, **29**, 29, 35, 60, 80, 81, 86, 154, **155-6**, 158, 159, 232
Opéra Quarter, 63, **80-2**, **156**, 159
  cafés, 228-9
  map, 81
Orangerie, Musée de l', 97, 120, 144, **156**
Ordre de la Libération, Musée de l', **141**
Orientation map, 64-5
Orléans, Duke of, 95
Orléans family, 162
Orly airport, 40, 41
Orsay, Musée d', 35, 60, 85, 144, 147, **156-9**
Ott, Carlos, 32, 154

Palace of Discovery see Palais de la Découverte
Palaces:
  Fontainebleau, **279-81**
  Louvre, **127-34**
  Versailles, **287-91**
Palais Bourbon, Assemblée Nationale, 108
Palais de Chaillot, 30, 30, 63, 88, 116, 137, 150, **159-60**, 264
Palais des Congrès, 30, **160**
Palais de la Découverte, 134, **160**, 265
Palais de l'Élysée, **161**
Palais Galliéra, 148
Palais de Justice de Paris, 59, 63, 69, 119, **161**, 176
Palais de Luxembourg, **94**, 183
Palais de la Mode, 13, 32, 88, 104, 107, **161-2**
Palais Omnisports de Paris-Bercy, 66, 123, 233, 268
Palais-Royal, 60, 82, 119, **162**, 165, 182
Palais des Sports, 233
Palais du Tau, Reims, 282
Palais de Tokyo, 30, 106, 157, **162-3**, 264
Panthéon, 29, 71, 139, **163-4**, 163, 178, 265
Parachuting, **271**
Paradis, Rue de, **164-5**, 171
Parc Océanique Jacques Cousteau, 87, **121-2**, 125, 266
Parc Zoologique de Paris, 99
Paris school, 106
Paris Symphony Orchestra, 160
Paristoric, 60, **165**, 235
Parking, 44
Parks and gardens, **90-99**, **269**
  Albert Kahn Gardens, 269
  Arènes de Lutèce, **91**
  Bagatelle, 91-2
  Barye sq., 70
  Blérancourt, 275
  Bois de Boulogne, 57, 62, 90, **91-3**, 108, 112, 115, 147, 160, 263, 264, 268, 269
  Bois de Vincennes, 57, 62, 90, **97-8**, 263, 266, 268, 269, 272

Buttes Chaumont, **93**, 113, 264, 268
Carrousel du Louvre, 88
Chaalis, 277
Champ-de-Mars, **94**, 114, 160, 264
for children, **263-4**
Fontainebleau, 280
Forum des Halles, 125
Georges-Cain sq., 75
Giverny, 276
Jardin d'Acclimatation, 92-3, 112, 263, 264, 272
Jardin d'Enfants aux Halles, 264
Jardin des Plantes, **143-4**, 184, 263, 269, 272
Jardin des Serres d'Auteuil, 93, 269
Jardins du Luxembourg, 71, 89, **94-5**, 149, 264
Louvois sq., 82
Monceau, 63, **95**, 114, 148, 264
Montsouris, **95**, 264
Musée de la Sculpture de Plein Air de la Ville de Paris, 184
Musée Rodin, 173
Observatoire de Paris, 154
Palais de Chaillot, 264
Palais de l'Élysée, 161
Palais Galliéra, 148
Parc de Bercy, 66
Parc de la Turlure, 78
Parc floral, Vincennes 98
Place des Vosges, 191
Pré Catalan, 92, 112
Roserai du Val de Marne, 269
Shakespeare Garden, 92, 112
Tuileries, 60, 88, **96-7**, 104, 107, 120, 128, 144, 156, 162, 172, 182, 187, 264, 289
Vaux-le-Vicomte, 277
Versailles, **290-1**
La Villette, 13, **97**, **189-90**, 264, 265
Pascal, Blaise, 33, 178, 187
Pascin, 106
Passages, **165-6**, 243
Passports, 37
  lost, 55
Pasteur, Louis, 166
  Musée Pasteur, **166**
Paul, Elliot, 61

Pavillon de l'Arsenal, **166**
Pavillon des Arts, 125
Pavillons de Bercy, 66, 123-4
Pei, I.M., 13, 31-2, 128, 285
Pepin the Short, 15
Père Lachaise, Cimetière du, 63, **96**, 166
Performing arts, **232-7**
Perfume:
　duty-free allowances, 39
　shops, **261-2**
Périphérique (beltway), 12, 62
Perrault, Claude, 128
Perrault, Dominique, 32, 111
Pétanque, 268
Petit Luxembourg, 94
Petit Palais, Musée du, 29, 88, 134, **167**, 170
Petit Trianon, Versailles, 290
Pharmacies:
　French words and phrases, 300
　late-night, 54
Philippe I, King, 16
Philippe II, Regent, 162
Philippe III, King, 16
Philippe IV le Bel, King, 16, 119, 280
Philippe V the Tall, 16
Philippe VI, King, 16
Philippe the Bold, 177
Philippe Auguste, King, 16, 98, 128, 285
Philippe Égalité, 162
Phonecards, 47
Piaf, Édith, **24**, 35, 96, 136
　Musée, **167**
Piano, Renzo, 31, 168
Pic, André, 206
Picasso, Pablo, **24**, 34, 76, 106, 150, 156, **167-8**, 169, 188, 227, 239
　Musée Picasso, 73, **167-8**
Piccoli, Michel, 163
Pierre, J.B., 182
Pigalle, 76
　cafés, 229
Pigalle, Jean-Baptiste, **24**, 179, 183
Pilon, Germain, **24**, 132
Pissarro, Camille, 34, 167, 201
Pius VII, Pope, 280
Planetariums:
　Cité des Sciences et de

l'Industrie, 190, 265
　Palais de la Découverte, 160, 265
　Reims, 282
Plans-Reliefs, Musée des, **141**
Pléiade, 33
Point, Fernand, 206
Poitiers, Diane de, 143
Police, 54
Police Museum, **171**
Pompadour, Madame de, **24**, 33, 34, 161, 179
Pompidou, Georges, 12, 20, **24**, 168, 187
Pompidou Center, 31, 35, 59, 68, 75, 76, 87, 124, 136, **168-70**, *168*, 264
Pont Alexandre III, 29, 88, 134, **170**
Pont des Arts, 83
Pont-Aven school, 158, 159
Pont-Neuf, 59, 69, 96, **170**
Pont-Royal, 82
Pontis, Guillaume, 286
Popular Arts and Traditions, Museum of, 93, **108**, 147, 265
Porte Dorée, Fontainebleau, 28
Porte St-Denis, 67, 149, **171**
Porte St-Martin, 67, 149, **171**
Post-Impressionists, 158
Post offices, 41, 47, 51
Postal codes, 62
Postal services, 47
Postcards, markets, 261
Poste, Musée de la, 80, **171**
Poste restante, 41
Poster Museum, **171-2**
Poulenc, Francis, 227
Pound, Ezra, 72
Poussin, Nicolas, **24**, 129, 133, 282
Pradier, Jean Jacques, **24**
Pré Catelan, 92, 112
Préfecture de Police, Musée des Collections Historiques de la, **171**
Prévert brothers, 227
Prieuré County Museum, 276
Le Procope, 84, 90, 228
Pronunciation, **295**
Proust, Marcel, **24**, 34, 140
Public holidays, 46
Public Information Library, **169**

Public lavatories, 48, 226
Public transport, 42
Publications, local, 50, 231
Publicité, Musée de la, 107, **171-2**
Pubs, 227
Puvis de Chavannes, Pierre, **24**, 158, 164

Quartier *Latin see* Latin Quarter
Quartiers (quarters), **62-3**, **66-85**
Quatre-Saisons, Fontaine des, 83, **172**
Quays, 70-1
Queneau, Raymond, 90

Rabelais, François, 33, 129
Racecourses, 93, 112, 268, **270**
Racine, Jean, 33, 84, 90, 119, 178
Radio-France, Maison de, 96, **172**, 236
Railways, 45
　from airports to city, **41**
　funicular, 78, 267
　Métro, 12, 29, 42, **47**
　to Paris, 40
　RER, 42-3
　terminal stations, **45**
　tickets, 45
　train plus vélo scheme, 269
Rambling, 272
Rameau, Jean-Philippe, 33
Rampin Horseman, 131
Raphael, 133
Realism, 158
Récamier, Madame, 127
Redon, Odilon, 158, 167
Regional cookery, 206, **210**, 211
Reims, **281-4**
Relief Maps and Plans, Museum of, **141**
Rembrandt, 118, 133, 143
Renaissance, **28**, 33
Renan, Ernest, 189
Renoir, Auguste, 34, 136, 156, 158, 159, 168, 197, 239
Renting:
　bicycles, 45
　cars, 44, 301
RER (Réseau Express Régional), 42-3
Rest rooms, public, **48**, 226

Restaurants, **206-225**
　Chartres, 279
　choosing, **207**
　cooking styles, 206-7,
　　210-11
　Fontainebleau, 281
　foreign, 207
　listed by *arrondissement*,
　　212-13
　menus, **208-9, 302-8**
　nouvelle cuisine, 206, 209
　Reims, 284
　Rouen, 287
　Versailles, 291
　wines, **209-11**
Restoration architecture, **29**
Revues, 231, **239-40**
Reynolds, Sir Joshua, 118,
　133, 143
Rhys, Jean, 76
Richelieu, Cardinal de, 17,
　24, 33, 162, 179, 185,
　191
Riding, **271**
Riesener, Jean Paul, 113
Right Bank *(Rive Droite)*,
　62, 139
　cafés, 228-9
　shops, 243
Rilke, Rainer Maria, 79
Rive Droite see Right Bank
Rive Gauche see Left Bank
River trips, 45-6, 52, 267
Rivoli, Rue de, 68, 80, 87,
　97, 136, 156, **172-3**,
　187
Robert the·Pious, 16
Robespierre, Maximilien de,
　18, **24**, 119-20
Robuchon, Joël, 206, 219
Rocard, Michel, 20
Rock 'n' Roll Hall of Fame,
　125, **173**, 265
Rococo architecture, **28-9**
Rodin, Auguste, **24**, 89,
　112, 139, 145, 158,
　173-4
　Musée Rodin, 29, 59, 84,
　85, **173-4**, *173*
Rogers, Richard, 31, 168
Roissy/Charles-De-Gaulle
　airport, 40, 41
Roller-skating, **271**
Roman architecture, **26**,
　91, 117-18, 281
Romanesque architecture,
　26
Romanticism, 158
Roosevelt, Franklin D., 134
Roseraie du Val de Marne,
　269

Rossetti, Dante Gabriel, 158
Rossini, Gioacchino, 96
La Rotonde, café, 79, 89
Rotonde Colbert, 111
Rouen, 27, **284-7**
Rousseau, Henri "Le
　Douanier," **24**, 79, 158,
　159, 168
Rousseau, Jean-Jacques, 33
　tomb of, 164
Rousseau, Theodore, 273,
　277
Royal Academy of Painting
　and Sculpture, 118
Rubens, Peter Paul, 116,
　179
Rude, François, **25**, 103,
　145
Rudkin, Mark, 162
Rugby, **272**
Ruggieri, Cosimo, 113
Rush hours, 47
Sacré-Coeur, Basilique du,
　29, 60, 63, 76, 77, 93,
　174-5, *174*, 265, 267
Sagonne, Mansart de, 289
St-Aignan, Chartres, 278
St-André, Chartres, 278
St-Augustin, 67, 68, **175-6**
Sainte-Chapelle, 27, 59,
　63, 69, 161, **176-7**,
　176, 178
Sainte-Chapelle, Vincennes,
　98
St-Cloud racecourse, 270
St-Denis, Basilique, 26, *26*,
　27, 62, 82, **177-8**
St-Denys-du-Sacrement, 74
St-Étienne-du-Mont, 28, 71,
　178-9, *178*
St-Eustache, 125, 166, **179**
Ste-Geneviève library, 71
St-Germain, Blvd., 145
St-Germain l'Auxerrois, 26,
　27, **179-80**
St-Germain quarter, 35, 60,
　63, **82-5**, 90, 180, 181
　cafés, 227-8
　hotels, 193
　map, *83*
　shops, 243
St-Germain-des-Prés
　church, 26, 60, 84, 86,
　180-1, 181
St-Germain-des-Prés
　district, 82, 181
St-Germain-en-Laye, **276-7**
St-Gervais-St-Protais, 74
St-Jacques-la-Boucherie,
　187
St-Joseph-des-Carmes, **181**

St-Julien-le-Pauvre, 71, 72,
　181
St-Louis, Versailles, 289
St-Louis-des-Invalides, **142**
St-Louis-en-l'Île, 70
St-Maclou, Rouen, 27,
　284-5
St-Martin-au-Val, Chartres,
　278
St-Martin-des-Champs, 185
St-Médard, 151
St-Merri, 76
St-Michel, Blvd. (Boul'Mich),
　71, 145, 181, 228
St-Nicolas-des-Champs, 73,
　181-2
St-Nicolas-du-Chardonnet,
　71
St-Paul-St-Louis, 28, 74-5,
　173
St-Pierre, Chartres, 278
St-Pierre de Montmartre,
　26, 77
St-Remi, Reims, 282
St-Roch, 82, **182**
Saint-Saëns, Camille, 80
St-Séverin, 27, 71, 72,
　181, **182-3**
St-Sulpice, 84, **183-4**
St-Thomas d'Aquin, 84
Salazar, Tristan de,
　Archbishop of Sens, 138
Salle Favart, 82, 232
Salle Garance, Pompidou
　Center, 170, 236
Salons, 33, 34, 158
Salons de thé, 208, 227
Salpêtrière, Hôpital, **184**
Sand, George, 89, 90, 95,
　189
Sanisettes (public rest
　rooms), 48
Sartre, Jean-Paul, **25**, 35,
　80, 84, 90, 227, 239
Satie, Erik, 79, 227
Saunier, 113
Sauvage, Henri, 127
Savonnerie, 126, 143
Scheffer, Ary, 189
Schmidt (carpenter), 85
School of Fine Arts,
　110-11
School of Tropical
　Agronomy, 98
Science and technology
　sights, listed, 100
Sciences et de l'Industrie,
　Cité des, 189, **190**, *190*,
　264, 265
Sculpture de Plein Air,
　Musée de la, **184**

Second Empire Museum, Compiègne, 275
Second Empire style, architecture, **29**
Secq-des-Tournelles, Musée, Rouen, 285, **287**
Seine, river, 11, 12, 45-6, 52, 59, 62, 69, 70-1, **88**, **96**, 113, 139, 140, 160, 170, 184, 187
Le Select, café, 79, 89
Senderens, Alain, 206
Senlis, **277**
Sérusier, Paul, 159
Servandoni, Giovanni, 183
Seurat, Georges, **25**, 158
Sévigné, Madame de, 33, 126, 191
Sewers, **123**, 265
Shakespeare and Co., bookstore, 90
Shakespeare Garden, 92, 112
Shoe stores, **252-3**
Shopping, **242-62**
 antiques, **254**
 bargains, **253-4**
 bookstores, 50
 bouquinistes, 71, 88
 boutiques, 242, **247-8**
 cookware, **254**
 department stores, 242, 243, 244, **255**
 drugstores, **255-6**
 fashion, 242, 243, **245-50**
 food and drink, 242, **256-8**
 French words and phrases, **298-9**
 gifts, **258-9**
 hats, **250-1**
 household accessories, **259-60**
 jewelry, **251**
 leather goods, **252**
 lingerie, **252**
 markets, **260-1**
 museum shops, **261**
 opening hours, 46-7, 244
 passages, **165-6**
 perfume and cosmetics, **261-2**
 shoes, **252-3**
 textiles, **262**
 toys, **262**
Silver, **259-60**
Simenon, Georges, 35
Sisley, Alfred, 167, 285, 287
Skating, **270**, **271**
Smoking laws, 49, 234

Soccer, **269**
Sommer, François, 116
Sorbon, Robert de, 184-5
La Sorbonne, 71, 119, 145, **184-5**
Sorbonne church, 28
Sorolla, 158
Soubise, Prince and Princesse de, 105
Soufflot, Jacques-Germain, **25**, 164
Soutine, Chaim, 106, 156
Speed limits, 44
Sports, **267-72**
Spreckelsen, J.O. von, **32**, 134-5, *135*
Squash, **272**
Staël, Mme de, 145
Stained glass:
 Chartres, 278, 279
 Moyen Âge, Musée National du, 118
 Sainte-Chapelle, 176
 St-Étienne-du-Mont, 179
 St-Séverin, 183
Stamp markets, 261
Starck, Philippe, 69, 229
Statue of Liberty, 172
Stein, Gertrude, 34, 89
Steinlen, Théophile Alexandre, 78
Stendhal, 89, 95
Sterne, Laurence, 170
Stinco, Antoine, 144
Stock Exchange, **112**
Stravinsky, Igor, 79, 227
Suger, Abbot, 27, *177*
Sulpicius, St, 183
Surrealism, 34, 169, 229
Swimming, **272**
Symbolists, 34, 150, 158, 159, 276
Synagogues, 53, 75

Tapestries, Gobelins, 113, **125-6**, 143
Tapisserie et d'Art Textile, Galerie Nationale de la, Beauvais, 273-4
Tarteries, 208
Taxes:
 détaxe, 244
 Value-Added Tax, 39
Taxis, 41, 43
 tipping, 43, 49
Techniques, Musée National des, 73, **185**, 265
Télécartes (phonecards), 47
Telegrams, 48
Telephone services, 47-8
 tourist information, 51

Temple, Quartier du, 73
Temple des Billettes, 27, **75**
Temple Bouddhique, 99
Tennis, **272**
Textiles, stores, **262**
TGB-Bibliothèque de France, 13, 32, 66, 111
Thackeray, William, 110
Thé-dancing, 240
Theaters, 230, 231, **232-4**
 for children, **265**
 Théâtre National de Chaillot, 160, 233
 Théâtre Paris-Villette, 190
Theimer, Yvan, 94
Thermal Baths, 26, *26*
Thermes de Cluny, 26, *26*, 71, **117-18**, 152
 plan, *117*
Thermes de Lutèce, **117-18**
Thomas, Gabriel, 135
Tickets:
 bus and Métro, 42, 43
 museums, 102
 theater, 231
 train, 45
Tiepolo, Giovanni Battista, 118, 143
Time zones, 46
Tipping, 43, 49, 192, 227
Titian, 133, 143
Tobacco, duty-free allowances, 39
Tolbiac, 32, 63, 66, 111
Tomb of the Unknown Soldier, 104
Toulouse-Lautrec, Henri de, **25**, 76, 78, 136, 158, 240
Tour Eiffel, 11, 29, 59, 63, 88, 94, 114, 123, 135, 137, 158, 160, 168, **186-7**, *186*, 264, 265
Tour Jeanne d'Arc, Rouen, 285
Tour Montparnasse, 12, 30, 79, 135, **187**, 265
Tour operators, 51
Tour St-Jacques, 27, 76, 87, **123-4**, **187**
Tourist information, **37-55**
 addresses and telephone numbers, **51-3**
 calendar of events, **56-8**
 emergencies, **54-5**
 hotel reservations, 192
 local publications, 50
 Office du Tourisme, 51
 on-the-spot, **46-50**
Tourist offices, 41

Town Hall, **138-9**
Toyshops, **262**
Track and field, **272**
Trains see Railways
Transparisienne, 272
Transports Urbains, Musée des, 187
Travel:
  air, 39-40, 45
  bicycling, 45
  buses, 40, **43**
  cars, 43-4
  ferries and hovercraft, 40
  French words and phrases, **301**
  from airports to city, 41
  helicopters, 46, **270**
  insurance, 37-8
  Métro, 12, 29, 42, 47
  railways, 42-3, 45
  river trips, 45-6, 52, 267
  rush hours, 47
  taxis, 41, 43
  trains, 40
  walking, 44
Travelers checks, 38
  lost, 38, 55
Trotsky, Leon, 79, 229
Tuileries, Jardin des, 60, 88, **96-7**, 104, 107, 120, 128, 144, 156, 172, 182, 187, 264, 289
Turner, J.M.W., 150, 201
Twain, Mark, 91

Uccello, Paolo, 143
UNESCO, **188**
University of Paris, 185
Urban Transport Museum, 187
Utrillo, Maurice, **25**, 34, 77, 78, 145
Val-de-Grâce, 28, **188**
Valentino, Rudolph, 116
Value Added Tax, 39
Van Dongen, Kees, 34, 79, 158
Van Gogh, Vincent, **25**, 78, 158, 159
Van Loo, 105
Vantage points, 265
Vaux-le-Vicomte, **277**
Vehicle and Tourism

Museum, Compiègne, 275
Velázquez, Diego de Silva y, 133, 287
Velde, Henri van de, 158
Vendôme, Place, 80, 82, **188-9**
Vénerie, Musée de la, Senlis, 277
Venus de Milo, 131
Verlaine, Paul, 84, 89, 90, 95, 295
Vernet, 146
Veronese, 133
Versailles, 28, 29, 157, 182, 277, **287-91**
  gardens, **290-1**
  map, 288
  palace, **289-91**
  town, **287-9**
Vespasiennes, 48
Vidéothèque de Paris, 125
Vie Romantique, Musée de la, **189**
Viewpoints, listed, 101
Village St-Paul, 74
La Villette, Parc de, 13, **97**, **189-90**, 264, 265
Villiers de l'Isle Adam, Comte de, 34, 89
Villon, François, 33
Vincennes, Bois de, 62, 90, **97-9**
  boating, 268
  gardens, 269
  map, 99
  racecourse, 270
Vincennes, Château de, 57, **98**, 263, 266, 272
Vineyards, 77
Viollet-le-Duc, Eugène-Emmanuel, **25**, 152, 153, 158
Visconti, 142
Voltaire, 33, 84, 105, 172
  tomb of, 164
Vosges, Place des, 75, **191**
Vuillard, Edouard, 276
Walking in Paris, 44, **86-90**, 272
  maps, 87, 89
Walter-Guillaume collection, 156
Watteau, Jean-Antoine, **25**, 33, 118, 133, 143

Waxworks:
  Les Martyrs de Paris, **147**, 265
  Musée Grévin, 60-1, 87, 125, **135-6**, 149, 166, 171, 265
  Rock 'n' Roll Hall of Fame, **173**
Weather, 40
Welles, Orson, 157
Whistler, J.A.M., 79
Whitman, George, 72
Wilde, Oscar, 90, 96, 198, 201
Wines, **209-11**
  Champagne, 281, **282-3**
  Cité du Vin et d'Alimentaire, **123-4**
  food and, **211**
  wine bars, 208, 231
Winged Victory of Samothrace, 131
Women's clothing, **245-8**
Words and phrases, **295-308**
  emergencies, 55
Workshops, for children, **264-5**
World Wars, Museum of, **141**
Wright, Frank Lloyd, 158, 159

Youth organizations, 53, 205

Zadkine, Ossip, 184, 191
  Musée Zadkine, **191**
Le Zénith, 190
Zip codes, 47
Zola, Émile, **25**, 34, 68, 136, 140
  tomb of, 164
Zoos, **272**
  Jardin d'Acclimation, 263, 272
  Jardin des Plantes, 143, 263
  Parc Zoologique de Paris, 99
  Vincennes, 263, 272
Zouave (statue), 96

List of street names

Map numbers are printed in **bold type**.

It has not been possible to label every street drawn on the maps, although all major streets and most smaller ones have been named. However, even those streets that have not been labeled have been given map references in this list, to serve as an approximate location that will nearly always be enough to get you there.

The **numbering of houses** in Paris is not always easy to fathom, and the following may be useful:

For streets, boulevards and avenues that run more or less parallel to the Seine, the house numbers follow the river's pattern, rising with the flow (the river flows from the east to the west of Paris). **Even** numbers *(pair)* are on the right and **odd** numbers *(impair)* are on the left.

On streets that run perpendicular to the Seine, the numbers begin at the river; with your back to the river, **even** is on the right and **odd** on the left.

There is often a large distance between numbers on opposite sides of the street. Wherever new buildings were infilled, no new numbers were available, and the words *bis* (meaning twice) and *ter* (meaning thrice) appear.

Aguesseau, rue d', **7F6**
Albert-de-Mun, av., **11H2**
Alésia, rue d', **13M5-N6**
Aléxandre III, pont, **6G5-H5**
Alger, rue d', **7G7**
Aligre, pl. d', **16J13**
Alma, pont de l', **6G4-H4**
Alphonse Deville, pl., **13J7**
Alphonse-Laveran, pl., **14L8**
Amsterdam, rue d', **2E7-D7**
Anatole-France, quai, **7H6-7**
Ancienne-Comédie, rue de l', **8I8**
André Malraux, pl., **8H8**
Anjou, quai d', **10J11**
Antin, cité d', **8F8**
Antoine-Bourdelle, rue, **13K6**
Arago, blvd., **13M7-15M10**
Archevêché, pont de l', **9J10**
Archives, rue des, **9I10-10H11**
Arcole, pont d', **9I10**
Arrivée, rue de l', **13K6**
Arsénal, rue de l', **15J11-16J12**
Arts, pont des, **8I8-H8**
Assas, rue d', **13J7-L8**
Athènes, rue d', **2E7**
Auber, rue, **7F7**
Aubriot, rue, **9H10**
Auguste-Vacquerie, rue, **5F3**

Babylone, rue de, **12J5-13J7**
Bac, rue du, **7J6-H7**
Banque, rue de la, **8G8**
Barbet-de-Jouy, rue, **12I6**

Barres, rue des, **9I10**
Barye, sq., **10J11**
Bastille, blvd. de la, **10K12-J12**
Bastille, pl. de la, **16J12**
Batignolles, blvd. des, **1D5-2D7**
Bayard, rue, **6G4**
Beaubourg, plateau, **9H10**
Beaubourg, rue, **9H10-G10**
Beaujolais, pge. de, **8G8**
Beaujolais, rue de, **8G8**
Beaumarchais, blvd., **10H12-I12**
Beauregard, rue, **9F9-10**
Beaux-Arts, rue des, **8I8**
Bellechasse, rue de, **7I6-H6**
Belzunce, rue de, **4E10**
Bercy, blvd. de, **16L13-14**
Bercy, quai de, **16L13-M14**
Bergère, Cité, **3F9**
Berri, rue de, **6F4-E4**
Berryer, cité, **7G6**
Béthune, quai de, **9J10-10J11**
Bichat, rue, **4F11-12**
Birague, rue de, **10I11**
Blanche, pl., **2D7**
Blanche, rue, **2D7-E7**
Blancs-Manteaux, rue des, **9H10-10I11**
Boétie, rue de la, **6F4-7E6**
Boissy d'Anglas, rue, **7G6-F6**
Bonaparte, rue, **13J7-8I8**
Bonne-Nouvelle, blvd. de, **3F9-4F10**
Bosquet, av., **12H4-I4**
Boul'Mich see St-Michel, blvd.

Bourdonnais, port de la, **11H3**
Bourdonnais, rue des, **8H8**
Bourg-l'Abbé, pge. du, **9G10**
Bourg-l'Abbé, rue du, **9G10**
Bourg-Tibourg, rue, **9I10**
Bourgogne, rue de, **7H6**
Bourse, pl. de la, **8F8**
Branly, quai, **11I2**
Bûcherie, rue de la, **14J9**
Buci, rue de, **8I8**

Cadet, rue, **3F9-E9**
Caire, pge. du, **9G10**
Cambon, rue, **7G7-F7**
Canettes, rue des, **14J8**
Capucines, blvd. des, **7F7-8F8**
Cardinal-Lemoine, rue du, **15K9-J10**
Carmes, rue des, **9J9**
Carnot, av., **5E2-3**
Carrée, cour, **8H8**
Carrousel, pl. du, **7H7**
Carrousel, pont du, **7H7**
Cassette, rue, **13J7-K7**
Castiglione, rue de, **7G7**
Caulaincourt, rue, **2D7-3C9**
Cavalerie, rue de la, **11J3**
Cdt. René-Mouchotte, rue du, **13L6**
Célestins, quai des, **10J11**
Chaligny, rue, **16K14**
Champ-de-Mars, rue du, **12I4**
Champs-Élysées, av. des, **5F3-7G6**
Chanoinesse, rue, **9I10**
Chapon, rue, **9G10-H10**

Chaptal, rue, **3**D7-8
Charenton, rue de, **16**J12-K14
Charles-de-Gaulle, pl., **5**F3
Charles-Dullin, pl., **3**D9
Charonne, rue de, **16**J12-I14
Chat-qui-Pêche, rue du, **9**I9
Châteaubriand, rue de, **5**F3-6F4
Châtelet, pl. du, **9**I9
Chemin-Vert, rue du, **10**I12
Cherche Midi, rue du, **13**K6-J7
Chevalier-de-la-Barre, rue du, **3**C9
Choiseul, pge., **8**F8
Choiseul, rue de, **8**F8
Christine, rue, **8**I8
Ciseaux, rue des, **14**I8
Clément, rue, **14**J8
Cler, rue, **12**H4-I4
Cléry, pge. de, **9**F10
Clichy, blvd. de, **2**D7-3D8
Colbert, gal., **8**G8
Colisée, rue du, **6**F4-5
Colombe, rue de la, **9**I10
Commerce, rue du, **11**K3-J3
Commerce-St-André, cour du, **14**I8-9
Concorde, pl. de la, **7**G6
Concorde, pont de la, **7**H6
Conférence, port de la, **6**G4
Constantine, rue, **12**H5
Conti, quai de, **8**I8
Contrescarpe, pl. de la, **14**K9
Copernic, rue, **5**F2
Coq-Héron, rue du, **9**G9
Coquillière, rue, **8**G8-9
Cortot, rue, **3**C8
Courcelles, blvd. de, **5**E3-6D5
Croix-des-Petits-Champs, rue, **8**H8-G8
Crozatier, rue, **16**J13-K13
Cygne, rue du, **8**H9

Daguerre, rue, **13**M6-7
Daru, rue, **1**E4
Daumesnil, av., **16**J12-K14
Daunou, rue, **7**F7
Dauphine, pge., **8**I9
Dauphine, pl., **9**I9
Dauphine, rue, **8**I8
Delambre, rue, **13**L7
Denain, blvd. de, **4**E10
Denfert-Rochereau, pl., **13**M7
Descartes, rue, **14**K9
Deux Pavillons, pge. des, **8**G8

Docteur-Roux, rue du, **12**L5
Double, pont au, **9**J9
Dragon, rue du, **7**J7-I7
Drouot, rue, **3**F8-E8
Dunkerque, rue de, **3**D9-4E10
Duperré, rue, **3**D8
Dupont, cité, **9**G9
Dussoubs, rue, **9**G9-10

Eblé, rue, **12**J5
Écoles, rue des, **14**J9-15J10
Écouffes, rue des, **10**I11
Edgar-Quinet, blvd., **13**L6-7
Edmond-Valentin, rue, **6**H4
Elzévir, rue, **10**I11-H11
Émile-Goudeau, pl., **3**C8
Éperon, rue de l', **14**J8-I8
Ermitage, rue de l', **9**H9
Étienne-Marcel, rue, **9**G9-H10
Étoile, rue de l', **5**E3
Étoile see Charles-de-Gaulle, pl.

Fabert, rue, **12**H5
Faubourg-du-Temple, rue du, **10**G11-F13
Faubourg-Montmartre, rue du, **3**E8-F9
Faubourg-St-Denis, rue du, **4**F10-D11
Faubourg-St-Honoré, rue du, **5**E3-7G7
Fauconnier, rue du, **10**I11
Favart, rue, **8**F8
Fer-à-Moulin, rue du, **15**L10
Ferronnerie, rue de la, **8**H9
Figuier, rue du, **10**I11
Filles-du-Calvaire, blvd. des, **10**H12
Filles-du-Calvaire, rue des, **10**H11-12
Fleurs, quai aux, **9**I10
Fleurus, rue de, **13**K7
Foch, av., **5**F1-3
Folie Méricourt, rue de la, **10**G12-H13
Fontaine, rue, **3**D8
Fontenoy, pl. de, **12**J4
Fossés-St-Bernard, rue des, **15**K10-J10
Fossés-St-Jacques, rue des, **14**K9
Four, rue du, **13**J7-**14**J8
François-1er, rue, **6**F4-G5
Francs-Bourgeois, rue des, **9**H10-**10**I12
Franklin, rue, **11**H2

Franklin-D-Roosevelt, av., **6**F5-G5
Frédéric-Lemaître, sq., **10**G12
Frédéric-Sauton, rue, **14**J9
Friedland, av. de, **5**F3-6E4
Furstemberg, pl. de, **8**I8
Furstemberg, rue de, **8**I8

Gabriel, av., **6**F5-7G6
Gaîté, rue de la, **13**L6
Gaston-de-Cavaillet, rue, **11**J1
Gay-Lussac, rue, **14**K8-L9
Général-Camou, rue du, **5**H3
Général-Eisenhower, av. du, **6**G5
George-V, av., **6**F4-G4
Georges-Cain, sq., **10**H11
Gît-le-Coeur, rue, **14**I9
Gobelins, av. des, **15**L10-M10
Gouvion-St-Cyr, blvd., **5**E1-D2
Gozlin, rue, **14**I8
Grand-Cerf, pge. du, **9**G9-10
Grande-Armée, av. de la, **5**E2
Grande-Truanderie, rue de la, **9**H9-10
Grands-Augustins, quai des, **8**I8-9
Grégoire-de-Tours, rue, **14**J8-I8
Grenelle, blvd. de, **11**I2-J3
Grenelle, quai de, **11**J1-I2
Grenelle, rue de, **12**I4-7J7
Grenier-St-Lazare, rue du, **9**H10
Grève, pl. de see Hôtel de Ville, **9**I10
Guénégaud, rue, **8**I8
Guillaume-Apollinaire, rue, **7**I7
Guillemites, rue des, **9**I10

Halévy, rue, **7**F7
Haussmann, blvd., **6**E4-8F8
Hoche, av., **5**E3-6E4
Hôpital, blvd. de l', **15**M10-K11
Horloge, quai de l', **9**I9
Hôtel-de-Ville, pl. de l', **9**I10
Hôtel-de-Ville, quai de l', **9**I10
Huchette, rue de la, **14**J9
Hulot, pge. de, **8**G8

Iéna, av. d', **5**H2-G3
Iéna, pl. d', **5**G3
Iéna, pont d', **11**H2

Île-de-France, sq. de l', **9J10**
Innocents, rue des, **9H9**
Innocents, sq. des, **9H9**
Italie, pl. d', **15M10-N10**
Italiens, blvd. des, **8F8**

Jacob, rue, **7I7-8I8**
Jacques Rousseau, rue, **10I11**
Jardins-St-Paul, rue des, **10I11**
Jarente, rue de, **10I11**
Jean-de-Beauvais, rue, **14J9**
Jean-du-Bellay, rue, **9I10**
Jean-Jacques Rousseau, rue, **9G9**
Jean-Mermoz, rue, **6F5**
Jean-Rey, rue, **11I2**
Jeûneurs, rue des, **8F9-G9**
Joffre, pl., **12J4**
Jolivet, rue, **13L6**
Joseph-de-Maistre, rue, **2B7-3C8**
Jouffroy, pge., **8F9**
Jour, rue du, **9H9-G9**

Kléber, av., **5G2-F2**

La Bruyère, rue, **2D7-3E8**
La Rochefoucauld, rue de, **3E8-D8**
La Tour-Maubourg, blvd. de, **12I5-6H5**
Lamarck, rue, **2B7-3C9**
Lambert, rue, **3C9**
Lamennais, rue, **6F4**
Lappe, rue de, **10I12-J13**
Laugier, rue, **5D3**
Lavandières-Ste-Opportune, rue des, **8H9**
Lemoine, pge., **9G10**
Léonard-de-Vinci, rue, **5F2**
Lille, rue de, **7H6-I7**
Linné, rue, **15K10**
Lombards, rue des, **9H9-10**
Longchamp, rue de, **5G1-3**
Lord-Byron, rue, **5F3-6F4**
Louis XVI, sq., **7F6**
Louis-Lépine, pl., **9I9**
Louvois, sq., **8G8**
Louvre, pl. du, **8H8**
Louvre, quai du, **8H8**
Louvre, rue du, **9H8-G9**
Lyon, rue de, **16J12-K12**

Mac-Mahon, av., **5E3**
Madame, rue, **13K7-J7**
Madeleine, blvd. de la, **7F7**
Madeleine, pl. de la, **7F6**
Madrid, rue de, **2E6**
Maine, av. du, **13K6-N7**

Maître-Albert, rue, **15J10**
Malaquais, quai, **8I8**
Malesherbes, blvd., **7F6**
Marbeuf, rue, **6G4-F4**
Marceau, av., **5F3-G3**
Marcellin-Berthelot, pl., **14J9**
Marché-St-Honoré, pl. du, **7G7**
Marché-St-Honoré, rue du, **7G7**
Mare, rue de la, **3E8**
Marigny, carré, **6G5**
Martyrs, rue des, **3E8-D8**
Mathurins, rue des, **7F6-7**
Matignon, av., **6F5**
Mazarine, rue, **8I8**
Mégisserie, quai de la, **9I9**
Miromesnil, rue, **6D5-F5**
Mogador, rue, **2E7-F7**
Molière, rue, **8G9**
Monceau, rue de, **1E4-D5**
Mondétour, rue, **8H9**
Monge, rue, **15J9-L10**
Monsieur-le-Prince, rue, **14J8**
Monsigny, rue, **8G8-F8**
Mont-Thabor, rue du, **7G7**
Montagne Ste-Geneviève, rue de la, **9K9-J9**
Montaigne, av., **6G4**
Montalembert, rue, **7I7**
Montebello, quai, **8J9**
Montmartre, blvd., **8F8-9**
Montmartre, rue, **8F9-G9**
Montmorency, rue de, **9H10**
Montorgueil, rue, **9G9**
Montparnasse, blvd. du, **13K6-14L8**
Montparnasse, rue, **13K7**
Montpensier, rue de, **8G8**
Motte-Picquet, av. de la, **11J3-12I5**
Mouffetard, rue, **15K9-L10**
Moussy, rue de, **9I10**

Napoléon, cour, **8H8**
Navarre, rue de, **15K10**
New York, av. de, **11H2-G3**
Nollet, rue, **2C6**
Notre-Dame-des-Champs, rue, **13K7-14L8**

Oberkampf, rue, **10H12-G13**
Observatoire, av. de l', **14L8-K8**
Odéon, carrefour de l', **14J8**
Odéon, pl. de l', **14J8**
Odéon, rue de l', **14J8**
Opéra, av. de l', **7F7-8G8**

Opéra, pl. de l', **7F7**
Orfèvres, quai des, **8I6**
Orléans, quai d', **9J10**
Orsay, quai d', **6H4-7H6**

Paix, rue de la, **7G7-F7**
Palais, blvd. du, **9I9**
Palais-Royal, pl. du, **8H8**
Palestro, rue de, **9G10**
Panoramas, pge. des, **8F9**
Panthéon, pl. du, **14K9**
Paradis, rue de, **3E9-4E10**
Parc-Royal, rue du, **10H11**
Parcheminerie, rue de la, **9J9**
Parvis-Notre-Dame, pl. du, **9I9**
Pasquier, rue, **7F6**
Passy, rue de, **5H1**
Patriarches, pge. des, **15L10**
Paul-Chatrousse, rue, **14J8**
Paul-Painlevé, pl., **9J9**
Pavée, rue, **10I11**
Payenne, rue, **10I11**
Peletier, rue Le, **3F8-E8**
Penthièvre, rue de, **6F5-6**
Pereire, blvd., **1C3-5**
Pergolèse, rue, **5E2**
Perle, rue de la, **10H11**
Petites-Écuries, cour des, **4F10**
Petites-Écuries, rue des, **3F9-4F10**
Petits-Champs, rue des, **8G8**
Pierre 1er-de-Serbie, av., **5G3**
Pierre-Charron, rue, **6G4-F4**
Pierre-Demours, rue, **5D2-3**
Pierre-Lescot, rue, **9H9**
Pigalle, pl., **3D8**
Plâtre, rue du, **9H10**
Poissonnière, blvd., **8F9**
Poissonnière, rue, **8F9**
Pompe, rue de la, **5F1**
Ponceau, pge., **9G10**
Pont Louis-Philippe, rue du, **9I10**
Pont-Neuf, **8I8-I9**
Pont-Royal, **7H7**
Ponthieu, rue de, **6F4-5**
Pontoise, rue de, **9J10**
Porte-Maillot, pl. de la, **5E1**
Postes, pge. des, **15L10**
Potier, pge. de, **8G8**
Poulbot, rue, **3C8**
Pré-aux-Clercs, rue du, **7I7**
Président-Kennedy, av. du, **11I1-2**

Président-Wilson, av. du, **5**H2-G3
Prêtres St-Séverin, rue des, **9**J9
Princesse, rue, **14**J8
Printemps, rue du, **2**C5
Puits-de-l'Ermite, pl. du, **15**L10
Pyramides, pl. des, **7**G7
Pyrénées, rue des, **7**G7

Quatre-Septembre, rue du, **8**F8-G8
Quatre-Vents, rue des, **14**J8
Quincampoix, rue, **9**H10

Rabelais, rue, **6**F5
Rambuteau, rue, **9**H9-10
Raspail, blvd., **13**
Raynouard, rue, **11**I1
Reine, cours la, **6**G5-6
Reine-de-Hongrie, pge. de la, **9**G9-H9
Renard, rue du, **9**I9-H10
René Viviani, sq., **9**J9
Rennes, rue de, **13**K6-I7
République, pl. de la, **10**G11
Résistance, pl. de la, **6**H4
Richelieu, pge. de, **8**G8
Richelieu, rue de, **8**G8-F8
Richer, rue, **3**F9
Rivoli, rue de, **7**G6-10**I**11
Rochechouart, blvd., **3**D8-9
Rochefoucauld, rue de La, **3**E8-D8
Rome, rue de, **7**E6-F7
Rosiers, rue des, **10**I11
Royale, rue, **7**G6
Rude, rue, **5**E2

Sablons, rue des, **5**G1
Sabot, rue du, **5**E3
St-André-des-Arts, pl., **8**I8-9
St-André-des-Arts, rue, **9**I9
St-Antoine, rue, **10**I11-12
St-Augustin, rue, **8**G8
St-Benoît, rue, **7**I7
St-Bernard, quai, **15**J11-K11
St-Denis, blvd., **4**F10
St-Denis, rue, **9**H9-F10
St-Dominique, rue, **12**H5-7H6
St-Eustache, imp., **9**H9
St-Florentin, rue, **7**G6
St-Germain, blvd., **7**G6-15J10
St-Germain-des-Prés, pl., **8**I8

St-Germain-l'Auxerrois, rue, **8**H9-I9
St-Honoré, rue, **7**G6-8H9
St-Hyacinthe, rue, **7**G7
St-Jacques, rue, **14**L8-J9
St-Jacques, sq., **14**M8
St-Julien-le-Pauvre, rue, **14**J9
St-Louis, pont, **9**J10
St-Louis-en-l'Île, rue, **9**J10-10**J**11
St-Marc, rue, **8**F8-9
St-Martin, blvd., **9**G10-10**G**11
St-Martin, rue, **9**I9-G10
St-Merri, rue, **9**H10
St-Michel, blvd. (Boul'Mich), **14**L8-I9
St-Michel, pl., **8**I9
St-Philippe-du-Roule, rue, **6**F4
St-Pierre, pl., **3**D9
St-Placide, rue, **13**J6-K7
St-Roch, rue, **7**G7
St-Simon, rue de, **7**I6
St-Sulpice, pl., **13**J7-14J8
St-Sulpice, rue, **14**J8
St-Vincent, rue, **3**C8-9
Ste-Anne, rue, **8**G8
Ste-Croix-de-la-Bretonnerie, rue, **9**H10-I10
Ste-Foy, pge., **9**G10
Ste-Geneviève, pl., **14**K9
Ste-Opportune, pl., **9**H9
Ste-Opportune, rue, **9**H9
Sts-Pères, rue des, **7**J7-I7
Saules, rue des, **3**C8-B8
Savoie, rue de, **8**I8-9
Saxe, av. de, **12**J4-K5
Scribe, rue, **7**F7
Sébastopol, blvd. de, **9**H9-F10
Seine, rue de, **8**I8-14J8
Servandoni, rue, **14**J8
Sévigné, rue de, **10**I11
Sèvres, rue de, **12**K5-13J7
Singes, pge. des, **9**I10
Solidarité, rue de la, **14**J9
Sorbonne, rue de la, **14**J9
Soufflot, rue, **14**K8-9
Sourdière, rue de la, **7**G7
Strasbourg, blvd. de, **4**F10
Suffren, av. de, **11**I2-12K5
Suffren, port de, **11**I2-H2
Suger, rue, **14**J8-I9
Sully, pont de, **10**J11

Temple, rue du, **9**I10-10G11

Temple, sq. du, **10**G11
Ternes, av. des, **5**D2-E3
Ternes, pl. des, **5**E3
Tertre, pl. du, **3**C8
Thorigny, rue de, **10**H11
Tilsitt, rue de, **5**E3
Tiquetonne, rue, **9**G9
Tour-Maubourg, blvd. de la, **12**I5-H5
Tournelle, pont de la, **9**J10
Tournelle, quai de la, **15**J10
Tournon, rue de, **14**J8
Tourville, av. de, **12**I4-5
Trinité, pge. de la, **9**G10
Trocadéro, pl. du, **11**H2
Tronchet, rue, **7**F7
Turbigo, rue de, **9**G9
Turenne, rue de, **10**I11-G11

Université, rue de l', **7**H6-I7

Valois, pl. de, **8**H8
Valois, rue de, **8**H8-G8
Vaneau, rue, **13**I6-J6
Varenne, rue de, **7**I5-7
Vaugirard, blvd. de, **13**L5-6
Vaugirard, rue de, **12**L4-14J9
Velasquez, av., **1**D5
Vendôme, pl., **7**G7
Vercingétorix, rue, **13**L6
Verdeau, pge., **8**F9
Verrerie, rue de la, **9**I10
Vert-Galant, sq. du, **8**I8
Viarmes, rue des, **9**H9
Victoire, cour de la, **12**I5
Victoire, rue de la, **2**E7-3E8
Victoires, pl. des, **8**G8
Victor-Hugo, av., **5**F1-3
Victoria, av., **9**I9-10
Vide-Gousset, rue, **8**G9
Vieille-du-Temple, rue, **9**I10-10H11
Vieux-Colombier, rue du, **13**J7
Vignon, rue, **7**F7
Villiers, av. de, **1**D3-5
29-Juillet (vingt-neuf), rue du, **7**G7
Vivienne, galerie, **8**G8
Vivienne, rue, **8**G8-F8
Volta, rue, **9**G10-10G11
Voltaire, quai, **7**H7
Vosges, pl. des, **10**I11-12

Wagram, av. de, **5**E3-D3
Washington, rue, **6**F4-E4
Winston-Churchill, av., **6**G5

KEY TO MAP PAGES

1-16 PARIS CITY GUIDE
17-18 PARIS ENVIRONS
PARIS MÉTRO / RER

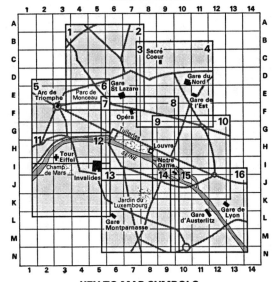

KEY TO MAP SYMBOLS

City Maps

- ▨ Place of Interest or Important Building
- ▨ Built-up Area
- ▨ Park
- ⊤ ⊤ Cemetery
- ✝ Church
- ☾ Mosque
- ✡ Synagogue
- ⊞ Hospital
- ⓘ Information Office
- ⊠ Post Office
- ⊙ Police Station
- ⊷ Garage / Parking Lot
- Ⓜ Métro / RER Station
- → One-way Street
- ⊨ Stepped Street
- ╫ No Entry
- ▶9 Adjoining Page No.

Area Maps

- ▪ Other Place of Interest
- ▨ Built-up Area
- ▨ Wood or Park
- ⊤ ⊤ Cemetery
- =O= Autoroute (with access point)
- == Autoroute under construction
- ▬ Main Road / Four-lane Highway
- ▬ Other Main Road
- ▬ Secondary Road
- ▭ Railway
- ⊶ RER (with station)
- ✈ Airport

```
0   100  200  300  400  500m
0   100  200  300  400  500yds
```

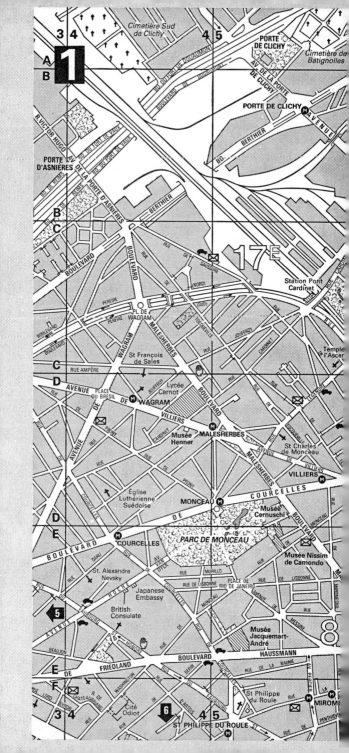

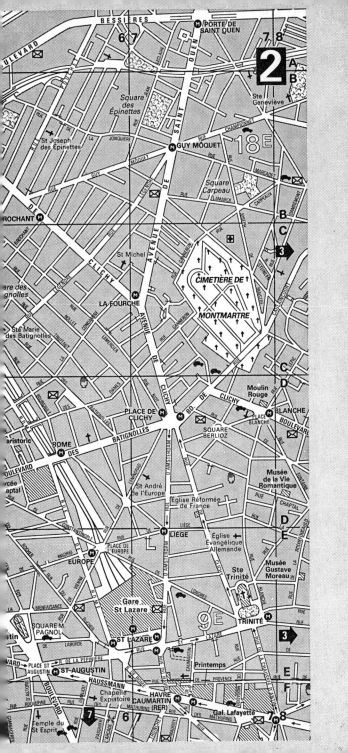

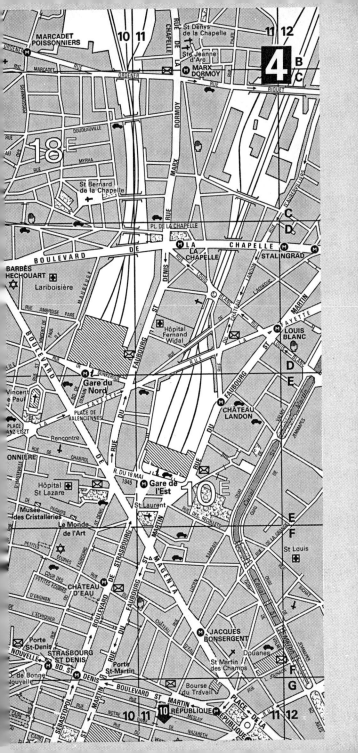

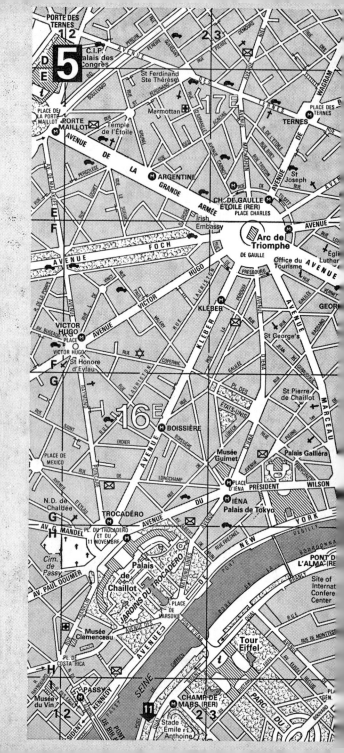

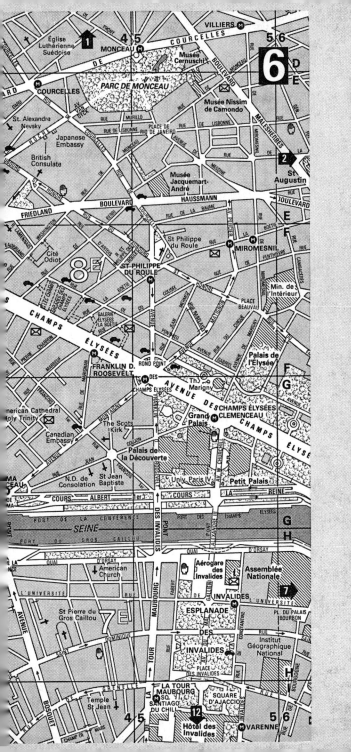

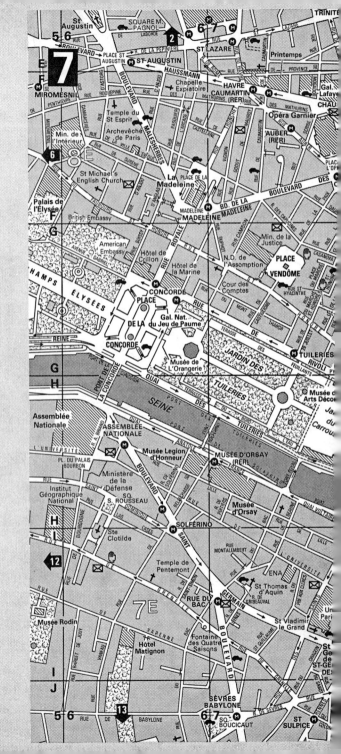

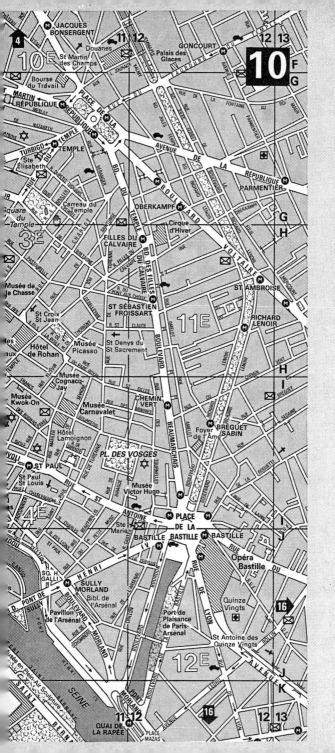

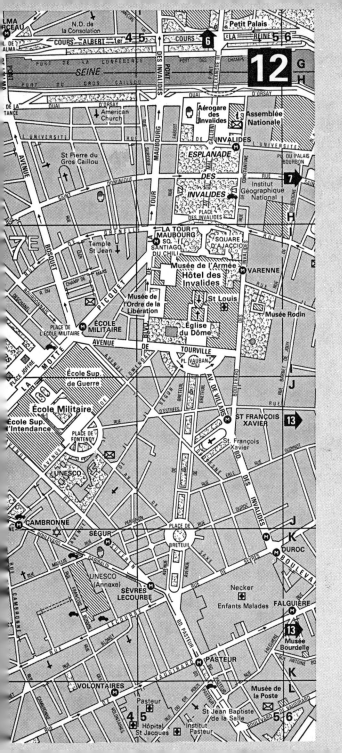

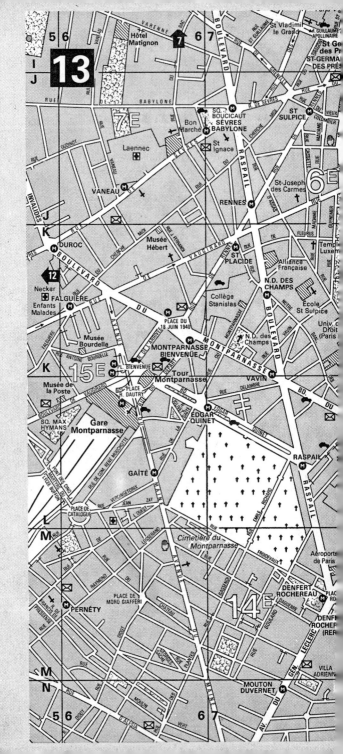

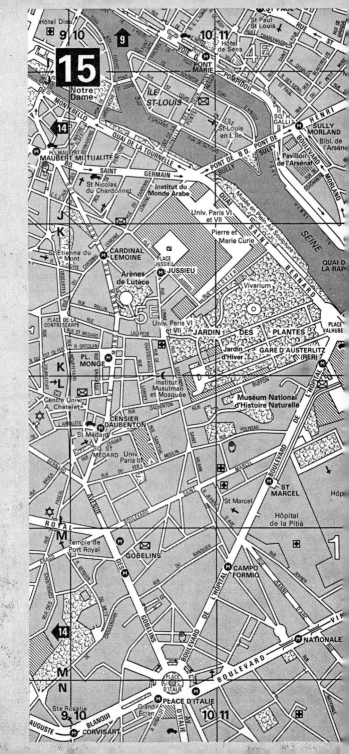

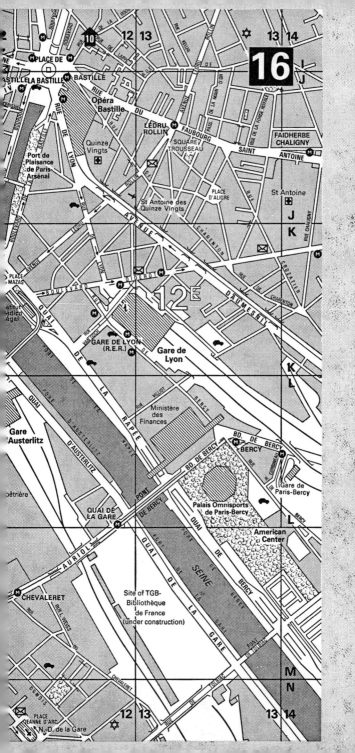

PARIS métro/RER

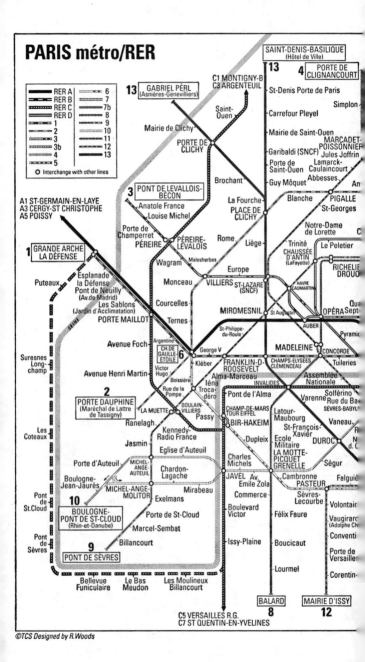

©TCS Designed by R.Woods

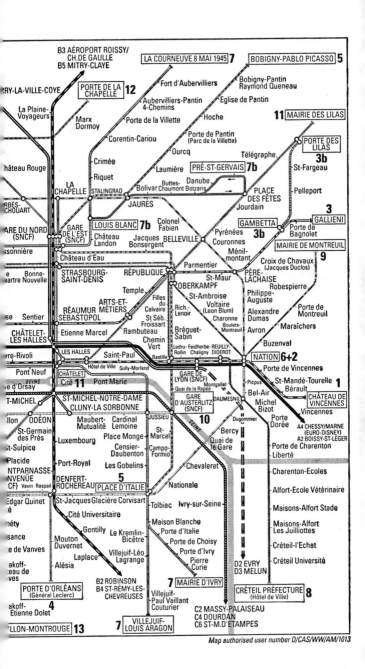

B3 AÉROPORT ROISSY/
CH.DE GAULLE
B5 MITRY-CLAYE

LA COURNEUVE 8 MAI 1945 **7**

BOBIGNY-PABLO PICASSO **5**

RY-LA-VILLE-COYE

PORTE DE LA CHAPELLE **12**

Fort d'Aubervilliers

Bobigny-Pantin
Raymond Queneau

La Plaine-
Voyageurs

Aubervilliers-Pantin
4-Chemins

Eglise de Pantin

11 MAIRIE DES LILAS

Marx
Dormoy

Porte de la Villette

Hoche

hâteau Rouge

Corentin-Cariou

Porte de Pantin
(Parc de la Villette)

PORTE DES LILAS **3b**

Crimée

Ourcq

Télégraphe

St-Fargeau

LA
CHAPELLE STALINGRAD

Riquet

Laumière

PRÉ-ST-GERVAIS **7b**

RBÉS-
CHOUART

Bolivar

Buttes-
Chaumont Botzaris

Danube

Pelleport

JAURÈS

PLACE
DES FÊTES

GARE DU NORD
(SNCF)

GARE
DE L'EST
(SNCF)

LOUIS BLANC **7b**

Colonel
Fabien

Jourdain

3

GAMBETTA

GALLIENI

ssonnière

Château
Landon

Jacques
Bonsergent

BELLEVILLE

Pyrénées

3b

Porte de
Bagnolet

Château d'Eau

Couronnes

MAIRIE DE MONTREUIL **9**

e Bonne-
artre Nouvelle

STRASBOURG-
SAINT-DENIS

RÉPUBLIQUE

Parmentier

Ménil-
montant

Croix de Chavaux
(Jacques Duclos)

St-Maur

PÈRE-
LACHAISE

Temple

OBERKAMPF

St-Ambroise

Robespierre

ARTS-ET-
RÉAUMUR
SÉBASTOPOL

Filles
du
Calvaire

Rich.
Lenoir

Voltaire
(Leon Blum)

Philippe-
Auguste

se Sentier

St Séb.
Froissart

Charonne

Alexandre
Dumas

Porte de
Montreuil

CHÂTELET-
LES HALLES

Etienne Marcel

Rambuteau

Bréguet-
Sabin

Boulets-
Montreuil

Avron

Maraîchers

Chemin
Vert

Ledru- Faidherbe- REUILLY-
Rollin Chaligny DIDEROT

Buzenval

re-Rivoli

LES HALLES

Saint-Paul

Bastille

NATION **6+2**

Pont Neuf

CHÂTELET

Hôtel de Ville

Sully-Morland

Porte de Vincennes

e d'Orsay

Cité **11**

Pont Marie

GARE
DE LYON (SNCF)

Picpus

St-Mandé-Tourelle **1**

Quai de la Rapée

Montgallet

Bel-Air

Bérault

T-MICHEL

ST-MICHEL-NOTRE-DAME
CLUNY-LA SORBONNE

GARE
D'AUSTERLITZ
(SNCF)

DAUMESNIL

Michel
Bizot

CHÂTEAU DE
VINCENNES

llon ODÉON

Maubert-
Mutualité

Cardinal
Lemoine

JUSSIEU

10

Dugommier

Porte
Dorée

Vincennes

St-Germain
des Prés

Luxembourg

Place Monge

St-
Marcel

Bercy

A4 CHESSY/MARNE
(EURO-DISNEY)
A2 BOISSY-ST-LÉGER

t-Sulpice

Censier-
Daubenton

Campo-
Formio

Quai de
la Gare

Porte de Charenton
Liberté

Placide

Port-Royal

Les Gobelins

Chevaleret

Charenton-Ecoles

NTPARNASSE
NVENUE
CF) Vavin Raspail

DENFERT-
ROCHEREAU

PLACE D'ITALIE

Nationale

Alfort-Ecole Vétérinaire

Edgar Quinet
é

St-Jacques Glacière Corvisart

Tolbiac

Ivry-sur-Seine

Maisons-Alfort Stade

Cité Universitaire

5

néty

Gentilly

Maison Blanche

Maisons-Alfort
Les Juilliottes

sance

Mouton
Duvernet

Le Kremlin-
Bicêtre

Porte d'Italie

Créteil-l'Echat

e de Vanves

Laplace

Villejuif-Léo
Lagrange

Porte de Choisy

Créteil Université

akoff-
eau de
ves

Alésia

Pierre
Curie

D2 EVRY
D3 MELUN

PORTE D'ORLÉANS
(Général Leclerc)

4

B2 ROBINSON
B4 ST-RÉMY-LES-
CHEVREUSES

Villejuif-
Paul Vaillant
Couturier

MAIRIE D'IVRY **7**

CRÉTEIL PRÉFECTURE
(Hôtel de Ville) **8**

akoff-
Etienne Dolet

VILLEJUIF-
LOUIS ARAGON **7**

C2 MASSY-PALAISEAU
C4 DOURDAN
C6 ST-M.D'ÉTAMPES

LLON-MONTROUGE **13**

Map authorised user number D/CAS/WW/AM/1013

CONVERSION FORMULAE

To convert	Multiply by
Inches to Centimeters	2.540
Centimeters to Inches	0.39370
Feet to Meters	0.3048
Meters to feet	3.2808
Yards to Meters	0.9144
Meters to Yards	1.09361
Miles to Kilometers	1.60934
Kilometers to Miles	0.621371
Sq Meters to Sq Feet	10.7638
Sq Feet to Sq Meters	0.092903
Sq Yards to Sq Meters	0.83612
Sq Meters to Sq Yards	1.19599
Sq Miles to Sq Kilometers	2.5899
Sq Kilometers to Sq Miles	0.386103
Acres to Hectares	0.40468
Hectares to Acres	2.47105
Gallons to Liters	4.545
Liters to Gallons	0.22
Ounces to Grams	28.3495
Grams to Ounces	0.03528
Pounds to Grams	453.592
Grams to Pounds	0.00220
Pounds to Kilograms	0.4536
Kilograms to Pounds	2.2046
Tons (UK) to Kilograms	1016.05
Kilograms to Tons (UK)	0.0009842
Tons (US) to Kilograms	746.483
Kilograms to Tons (US)	0.0013396

Quick conversions

Kilometers to Miles	Divide by 8, multiply by 5
Miles to Kilometers	Divide by 5, multiply by 8
1 meter =	Approximately 3 feet 3 inches
2 centimeters =	Approximately 1 inch
1 pound (weight) =	475 grams (nearly $\frac{1}{2}$ kilogram)
Celsius to Fahrenheit	Divide by 5, multiply by 9, add 32
Fahrenheit to Celsius	Subtract 32, divide by 9, multiply by 5

Clothing sizes chart

LADIES
Suits and dresses

Australia	8	10	12	14	16	18	
France	34	36	38	40	42	44	
Germany	32	34	36	38	40	42	
Italy	38	40	42	44	46		
Japan	7	9	11	13			
UK	6	8	10	12	14	16	18
USA	4	6	8	10	12	14	16

Shoes

USA	6	$6\frac{1}{2}$	7	$7\frac{1}{2}$	8	$8\frac{1}{2}$
UK	$4\frac{1}{2}$	5	$5\frac{1}{2}$	6	$6\frac{1}{2}$	7
Europe	38	38	39	39	40	41

MEN
Shirts

USA, UK Europe, Japan	14	$14\frac{1}{2}$	15	$15\frac{1}{2}$	16	$16\frac{1}{2}$	17
Australia	36	37	38	39.5	41	42	43

Sweaters/T-shirts

Australia, USA, Germany	S		M		L		XL
UK	34		36-38		40		42-44
Italy	44		46-48		50		52
France	1		2-3		4		5
Japan			S-M		L		XL

Suits/Coats

UK, USA Australia, Italy,	36	38	40	42	44
France, Germany	46	48	50	52	54
Japan	S	M	L	XL	

Shoes

UK	7	$7\frac{1}{2}$	$8\frac{1}{2}$	$9\frac{1}{2}$	$10\frac{1}{2}$	11
USA	8	$8\frac{1}{2}$	$9\frac{1}{2}$	$10\frac{1}{2}$	$11\frac{1}{2}$	12
Europe	41	42	43	44	45	46

CHILDREN
Clothing
UK

Height (ins)	43	48	55	60	62	
Age	4-5	6-7	9-10	11	12	13

USA

Age	4	6	8	10	12	14

Europe

Height (cms)	125	135	150	155	160	165
Age	7	9	12	13	14	15

What the papers said:

• "The expertly edited American Express series has the knack of pinpointing precisely the details you need to know, and doing it concisely and intelligently." (*The Washington Post*)

• "*(Venice)* ... the best guide book I have ever used." (*The Standard* — London)

• "Amid the welter of guides to individual countries, American Express stands out...." (*Time*)

• "Possibly the best ... guides on the market, they come close to the oft-claimed 'all you need to know' comprehensiveness, with much original experience, research and opinions." (*Sunday Telegraph* — London)

• "The most useful general guide was *American Express New York* by Herbert Bailey Livesey. It also has the best street and subway maps." (*Daily Telegraph* — London)

• "...in the flood of travel guides, the *American Express* guides come closest to the needs of traveling managers with little time." (*Die Zeit* — Germany)

What the experts said:

• "We only used one guide book, Sheila Hale's *Amex Venice,* for which she and the editors deserve a Nobel Prize." (Eric Newby, London)

• "Congratulations to you and your staff for putting out the best guide book of *any* size *(Barcelona & Madrid)*. I'm recommending it to everyone." (Barnaby Conrad, Santa Barbara, California)

• "If you're only buying one guide book, we recommend American Express...." (*Which?* — Britain's leading consumer magazine)

American Express Travel Guides

spanning the globe....

EUROPE

Amsterdam, Rotterdam
  & The Hague
Athens and the
  Classical Sites *‡
Barcelona, Madrid &
  Seville #
Berlin, Potsdam &
  Dresden * (‡ as Berlin)
Brussels
Dublin
Florence and Tuscany
London
Moscow & St Petersburg *
Paris
Prague #
Provence and the
  Côte d'Azur *
Rome
Venice #
Vienna & Budapest

NORTH AMERICA

Boston and New
  England *
Los Angeles & San
  Diego
Mexico #
New York
San Francisco and
  the Wine Regions
Toronto, Montréal and
  Québec City #
Washington, DC

THE PACIFIC

Cities of
  Australia
Hong Kong
  & Taiwan
Singapore &
  Bangkok *‡
Tokyo

---

*   Paperbacks in preparation   #   Paperbacks appearing August 1993
‡   Currently available as hardback pocket guides

Clarity and quality of information, combined with outstanding maps — the ultimate in travelers' guides